# Law and Language

**The International Library of Essays in Law and Legal Theory**
*Series Editor: Tom D. Campbell*

*Schools*

**Natural Law, Vols I & II** *John Finnis*
**Justice** *Thomas Morawetz*
**Law and Economics, Vols I & II** *Jules Coleman and Jeffrey Lange*
**Critical Legal Studies** *James Boyle*
**Marxian Legal Theory** *Csaba Varga*
**Legal Reasoning, Vols I & II** *Aulis Aarnio and Neil MacCormick*
**Legal Positivism** *Mario Jori*
**American Legal Theory** *Robert Summers*
**Law and Language** *Fred Schauer*
**Sociological Theories of Law** *Kahei Rokumoto*
**Rights** *Carlos Nino*
**Law and Psychology** *Martin Levine*
**Feminist Legal Theory, Vols I & II** *Frances Olsen*
**Law and Society** *Werner Krawietz*
**Contemporary Criminological Theory** *Francis Cullen and Velmer Burton*

*Areas*

**Criminal Law** *Thomas Morawetz*
**Tort Law** *Ernest Weinrib*
**Contract Law, Vols I & II** *Larry Alexander*
**Anti-Discrimination Law** *Christopher McCrudden*
**Consumer Law** *Iain Ramsay*
**International Law** *Martti Koskenniemi*
**Property Law, Vols I & II** *Elizabeth Mensch and Alan Freeman*
**Constitutional Law** *Mark Tushnet*
**Procedure** *Denis Galligan*
**Evidence and Proof** *William Twining and Alex Stein*
**Company Law** *Sally Wheeler*
**Privacy, Vols I & II** *Raymond Wacks*
**Administrative Law** *Denis Galligan*
**Child Law** *Harry Krause*
**Family Law, Vols I & II** *Harry Krause*
**Welfare Law** *Peter Robson*
**Medicine and the Law** *Bernard Dickens*
**Commercial Law** *Ross Cranston*
**Environmental Law** *Michael Blumm*
**Conflict of Laws** *Richard Fentiman*
**Law and Religion** *Wojciech Sadurski*
**Human Rights Law** *Philip Alston*
**European Community Law, Vols I & II** *Francis Snyder*
**Tax Law, Vols I & II** *Patricia White*
**Media Law** *Eric Barendt*

*Legal Cultures*

**Comparative Legal Cultures** *Csaba Varga*
**Law and Anthropology** *Peter Sack*
**Hindu Law and Legal Theory** *Ved Nanda*
**Islamic Law and Legal Theory** *Ian Edge*
**Chinese Law and Legal Theory** *Michael Palmer*
**Socialist Law** *W. Butler*
**Japanese Law and Legal Theory** *Koichiro Fujikura*
**Law and Development** *Anthony Carty*
**Jewish Law and Legal Theory** *Martin Golding*
**Legal Education** *Martin Levine*
**Civil Law** *Ralf Rogowski*

*Future Volumes*

Labour Law, African Law and Legal Theory, Postmodernism and Law, Law and History, Law and Ethics and Cumulative index.

# Law and Language

*Edited by*

Frederick Schauer

*Frank Stanton Professor of the First Amendment*
*John F. Kennedy School of Government*
*Harvard University*

NEW YORK UNIVERSITY PRESS
REFERENCE COLLECTION

First published in the U.S.A. in 1993 by
NEW YORK UNIVERSITY PRESS
Washington Square
New York NY 10003

**Library of Congress Cataloging-in-Publication Data**
Law and language / edited by Frederick Schauer.
p. cm. — (The International library of essays in law and legal theory. Schools ; 10)
"New York University Press reference collection."
Includes bibliographical references.
ISBN 0-8147-7952-2 (cloth)
1. Law—Language. 2. Law—United States—Language. I. Schauer, Frederick F. II. Series.
K213.L395 1992
340'.014—dc20 92-33362
CIP

# Contents

## PART III CONTEMPORARY DEBATES ABOUT INDETERMINACY



## PART IV A PANOPLY OF PERSPECTIVES

# Acknowledgements

The editor and publishers wish to thank the following for permission to use copyright material.

The Aristotelian Society for the essay: Jonathan Cohen (1955), 'Theory and Definition in Jurisprudence', *Proceedings of the Aristotelian Society (Supplement)*, **29**, pp. 213–38. Reprinted by courtesy of the Editor of the Aristotelian Society: © (1955).

Blackwell Publishers for the essay: David Lyons (1986), 'Constitutional Interpretation and Original Meaning', *Social Philosophy and Policy*, **4**, pp. 75–101.

Boston University Law Review for the essay: Margaret Jane Radin (1989), 'Reconsidering the Rule of Law', *Boston University Law Review*, **69**, pp. 781–819.

David O. Brink (1989), 'Semantics and Legal Interpretation (Further Thoughts)', *Canadian Journal of Law and Jurisprudence*, **2**, pp. 181–91. Copyright © David O. Brink.

Cleveland State Law Review for the essay: Mary Jane Morrison (1989), 'Excursions into the Nature of Legal Language', *Cleveland State Law Review*, **37**, pp. 271–336.

Deborah Charles Publications for the essay: Robert W. Benson (1989), 'The Semiotics of International Law: Interpretation of the ABM Treaty', *International Journal for the Semiotics of Law*, **2**, pp. 257–76.

Harvard Journal on Legislation for the essay: Allan C. Hutchinson and Derek Morgan (1984), 'The Semiology of Statutes', *Harvard Journal on Legislation*, **21**, pp. 583–95. Permission granted by the Harvard Journal on Legislation. Copyright © 1984 by the President and Fellows of Harvard College.

Harvard Law Review for essays: Oliver Wendell Homes (1989), 'The Theory of Legal Interpretation, *Harvard Law Review*, **12**, pp. 417–20; and Max Radin (1930), 'Statutory Interpretation', *Harvard Law Review*, **43**, pp. 863–85. Copyright © by the Harvard Law Review Association.

The Modern Law Review and Peter Rush for the essay: Peter Rush (1990), Semiotics in the Trial of Jurisprudence', *Modern Law Review*, **53**, pp. 121–9. Copyright © The Modern Law Review and Peter Rush.

Dennis M. Patterson (1989), 'Realist Semantics and Legal Theory', *Canadian Journal of Law and Jurisprudence*, **2**, pp. 175–9 and (1989), 'What was Realism?: A Reply to David Brink', *Canadian Journal of Law and Jurisprudence*, **2**, pp. 193–5. Copyright © Dennis M. Patterson.

Frederick Schauer (1990), 'Rules and the Rule–Following Argument', *Canadian Journal of Law and Jurisprudence*, **3**, pp. 187–92. Copyright © Frederick Schauer.

Sweet & Maxwell Limited for the essay: Glanville L. Williams (1946), 'Language and the Law', (in five parts), *Law Quarterly Review*, **61**, pp. 71–86, 179–95, 293–303, 384–406, **62**, pp. 387–406.

Texas Law Review for essays: Gerald Graff (1982), '"Keep off the Grass", "Drop Dead", and Other Indeterminacies: A Response to Sanford Levinson', *Texas Law Review*, **60**, pp. 405–13. Published originally in **60** Texas Law Review 405–13 (1982). Copyright © 1982 by the Texas Law Review Association. Reprinted by permission; and Sanford Levinson (1982), 'Law as Literature', *Texas Law Review*, **60**, pp. 373–403. Published originally in **60** Texas Law Review 373–403 (1982). Copyright © 1982 by the Texas Law Review Association. Reprinted by permission.

University of California, Los Angeles Law Review and Fred B. Rothman & Co for the essay: Frederick Schauer (1982), 'An Essay on Constitutional Language', *UCLA Law Review*, **29**, pp. 797–832. Originally published in **29** UCLA L. Rev. 797, Copyright © 1982, The Regents of the University of California. All Rights Reserved.

The Yale Law Journal and Fred B. Rothman & Co. for essays: J.M. Balkin (1987), 'Deconstructive Practice and Legal Theory', *The Yale Law Journal*, **96**, pp. 743–86. Reprinted by permission of The Yale Law Journal Company and Fred B. Rothman & Company from The Yale Law Journal, Vol. **96**, pp. 743–786; Frederick Schauer (1988), 'Formalism', *The Yale Law Journal*, **97**, pp. 509–48. Reprinted by permission of The Yale Law Journal Company and Fred B. Rothman & Company from The Yale Law Journal, Vol. **97**, pp. 509–548; and Martin Shapiro (1981), 'On the Regrettable Decline of Law French: Or Shapiro Jettet le Brickbat', *The Yale Law Journal*, **90**, pp. 1198–1204. Reprinted by permission of The Yale Law Journal Company and Fred B. Rothman & Company from The Yale Law Journal, Vol. **90**, pp. 1198–1204.

Every effort has been made to trace all the copyright holders, but if any have been inadvertently overlooked the publishers will be pleased to make the necessary arrangement at the first opportunity.

# Series Preface

The International Library of Law and Legal Theory is designed to provide important research materials in an accessible form. Each volume contains essays of central theoretical importance in its subject area. The series as a whole makes available an extensive range of valuable material which will be of considerable interest to those involved in the research, teaching and study of law.

The series has been divided into three sections. The Schools section is intended to represent the main distinctive approaches and topics of special concern to groups of scholars. The Areas section takes in the main branches of law with an emphasis on essays which present analytical and theoretical insights of broad application. The section on Legal Cultures makes available the distinctive legal theories of different legal traditions and takes up topics of general comparative and developmental concern.

I have been delighted and impressed by the way in which the editors of the individual volumes have set about the difficult task of selecting, ordering and presenting essays from the immense quantity of academic legal writing published in journals throughout the world. Editors were asked to pick out those essays from law, philosophy and social science journals which they consider to be fundamental for the understanding of law, as seen from the perspective of a particular approach or sphere of legal interest. This is not an easy task and many difficult decisions have had to be made in order to ensure that a representative sample of the best journal essays available takes account of the scope of each topic or school.

I should like to express my thanks to all the volume editors for their willing participation and scholarly judgement. The interest and enthusiasm which the project has generated is well illustrated by the fact that an original projection of 12 volumes drawn up in 1989 has now become a list of some 60 volumes. I must also acknowledge the vision, persistence and constant cheerfulness of John Irwin and the marvellous work done by Mrs Margaret O'Reilly and Mrs Sonia Bridgman.

TOM D. CAMPBELL
Series Editor
*The Faculty of Law*
*The Australian National University*

# Introduction

Like most other human institutions, law is both a product of and dependent on language. In that respect the relation between law and language is important, but much the same could be said of politics, medicine, international trade, journalism, architecture, etiquette, manufacturing, finance, sports and innumerable other activities whose operation without language would be dramatically different. Yet the relationship between law and language seems in some ways special. To say why that is so, however, or even to maintain that it is so at all, is itself to take a position on one or another contested position of legal theory. In explaining why thinking about language is important to thinking about law, therefore, I will not be describing the common ground shared by all of the essays that follow this introduction. Instead I will be situating the relationship between law and language in a particular view of law and in a particular view of language, either or both of which are explicitly or implicitly challenged in much of what others have said (in essays in this volume or elsewhere) about this same large and slippery topic.

## I

Language is many things, but one of them is that it is general, having rules (or, some would say, practices or, others would say, conventions) that are neither speaker- nor situation-specific. Indeed, that is just what makes for rules (or practices or conventions). Thus, nouns other than proper names do or at least can refer to many things or events, and the compositional nature of language, pursuant to which a speaker of a language can understand a sentence he or she has never heard before, is facilitated (or defined) by the way in which rules of grammar and structure are similarly applicable wholesale rather than being made up anew instance-by-instance.

In much the same way, law as an institution differs from other forms of social interaction largely because of its generality. When John Austin in *The Province of Jurisprudence Determined* distinguished laws from commands according to the generality of the former and the particularity of the latter, he identified something widely held to be at the heart of understanding the operation of law and legal systems. Although special legislation is not unknown to the law, and although numerous jurisdictional rules often empower judges and other decision-makers to make largely particularistic determinations, law in one way or another commonly extends over time, over persons and over events.

Numerous devices of the law reflect this generality. More often and more strongly than other forms of decision-making, law commonly takes the constraints of precedent seriously, requiring that prior decisions be followed just because they are prior. More frequently than most other decision-making institutions, the decision-making institutions of the law ordinarily provide written reasons for their decisions, preserving those reasons in elaborately indexed series of books so that they will be available (by way of guidance or constraint) to future decision-makers. And with especial frequency law employs statutes, regulations, codes an other instruments by which those in power attempt to order or control large numbers of futu actions and events.

Were law not so much about obeisance to the past and control of the future, were it focuse more on now, and were it not so commonly spatially-general rather than situation-specifi the relationship between law and language would be important, but less specially so. B because law so often is the instrument of temporal and spatial generality, it has a speci use for language shorn of many of the normal conversational and contextual embellishmen ordinarily discussed under the heading of pragmatics. Language is part and parcel of mo interpersonal transactions, but removing language from an interpersonal context puts particul weight on language in its own right, on what is called in the speech-act tradition 'utteranc meaning' rather than speaker's meaning. In all of the variations just mentioned, decisio makers attempt to project decisions made here and now into a larger and less-known futur they do this by relying on the generality of language – on the ability of what they say no to be understood by unknown others in the future, and on the ability to say things now th will apply to a large and open-ended number of situations. Because legal decision-make can do this only insofar as language allows them to do, language plays a central role in th operation of law that is different from, even if not necessarily greater than, the role it play in facilitating many other forms of human interaction.

## II

The weight that the language of the law is expected to bear is compounded by the fact th people commonly expect the legal system to serve a major role in the resolution of dispute whether between individuals or between citizen and state. Although the inevitable or intention indeterminacies of language may at times generate disputes where none would otherwise exis more commonly the substance of the dispute is at least logically antecedent to the languag of the law. When that is the case, the disputants will home in on actual or potential weaknesse in the pertinent language, disproportionately focusing the attention of the legal system an its participants on the epiphenomenal failings of language rather than on its typical an consequently invisible successes.

Thus it may be that, although language is important to law, it is especially important t lawyers and judges – the actors whose professions are so often focused on linguisti breakdown. Just as many aspects of language may be more important to those who analys works of literature than to those who simply read them, so too may many aspects of languag be more important to the lawyers and judges who concentrate on disputes than to th enforcement officials and citizens who see law in its more common guise of less controversia social ordering. Just as we normally reserve the word 'interpretation' for those application of language that present some sort of problem, so too might those whose job it is to so out (or to prevent) these problematic applications have a need to focus on language in particularly self-conscious way.

Lawyers and judges might therefore be seen as the pathologists and the surgeons of th legal system, professionally preoccupied with disease rather than health, or at least (so a not to press the comparison too far) as those whose job description focuses on cases in whic egal norms do or might operate unusually, whether for good or for ill. If this is so, then t might explain why lawyers and judges are so preoccupied with linguistic breakdown and not with linguistic success, for theirs is a job in which the breakdowns come to their attention while the successes do not.

## III

When seen this way, the fact that so much of the focus on linguistic indeterminacy in the law has been of American origin is no longer surprising. Largely because courts and litigation are so comparatively pervasive in the United States, with a higher percentage of disputes resulting in litigation and a higher percentage of policy made by the courts, American legal theory has been overwhelmingly focused on courts and judges in a way that seems bizarre to legal theorists from other countries. Other explanations are possible as well, one of which is surely that most American legal theorists are professionally more tied to the practice of training practising lawyers than is the case in many other countries. But whatever the reason, there seems little doubt that much of American legal theory, of which the work of Ronald Dworkin (when compared to that of non-Amerian legal philosophers) is the best contemporary example, takes place figuratively within the courtroom.

With the courtroom and especially the appellate courtroom as its philosophical locus, it should not be surprising that American legal theory has been much more concerned with the indeterminacy than with the determinacy of language. No one, except perhaps for rhetorical effect, claims that language is completely determinate, for it is now a commonplace not only that the rules of language are contingent and thus, however slowly, in a state of constant flux, but also that vagueness, ambiguity and metaphor are central and ineradicable features of linguistic communication. And conversely, no one, except for rhetorical effect, claims that language is completely indeterminate, for no one seriously denies the ability of language to serve passably as the vehicle for a wide range of communicative activities. Despite this common ground, however, there are clearly disagreements, and much of the history of the jurisprudential focus on language (a history which is, for the reasons just mentioned, disproportionately American) has been a history on the one hand of claims that language is less determinate than commonly supposed and on the other of counter-claims defending the ability of language to do more of what is expected of it than its critics allow.

Claims about the indeterminacy of law are not new. They were central to Bentham's attack on the common law and have been a large part of the successively influential movements of the *Freirechtschule*, American Legal Realism and Critical Legal Studies, along with many others of less prominence. But a claim about legal indeterminacy need not entail a claim about linguistic indeterminacy. Were some legal system to contain a rule requiring what another rule prohibited, the indeterminacy flowing from the deontic conflict would have nothing to do with any indeterminacy of the language of the relevant rules. And where rules leave unregulated areas of conduct which may still give rise to disputes, legal indeterminacy may again arise other than on the back of linguistic indeterminacy.

Still, many of the claims of legal indeterminacy have been premised on claims about linguistic indeterminacy. Least controversial are the claims that law, again particularly American law, often uses terms that are plainly open-ended, failing to indicate in themselves one and only one result in any particular case. To the extent that statutes, regulations, constitutional provisions and common law judicial opinions employ language such as 'unreasonable searches and seizures', 'due process of law', 'equal protection of the law', 'contracts, combinations or conspiracies in restraint of trade' and 'device or artifice to defraud', they are often intentionally indeterminate, using language like this as a vehicle for empowering courts in the future to work out the details as they are faced with concrete cases. There is also little controversy about the extent to which users of language may frequently fall victim to unintentional vagueness or ambiguity, to this extent unwittingly creating indeterminacies which they would have preferred to avoid.

The range of theoretical controversy may be even narrower, for few would now deny the indeterminacy side of H.L.A. Hart's repeated claim that language and the rules based on it contain both a core of settled meaning and a penumbra of uncertainty. The disputes are over whether the core is as comparatively large as Hart and others maintain, whether the core is as settled as is supposed, and whether the notion of core (or plain or literal) meaning is coherent at all. Those holding the last mentioned position argue that a wide range of varying contextual factors across a linguistic community are necessary to give even a minimal meaning to any item of language.

I cannot within this brief Introduction attempt to resolve any of these disputes, but I do believe it important to remain continuously alert to the phenomenon that Karl Llewellyn first identified and what modern law and economics refers to as the 'selection effect'. Because there is ordinarily little incentive to dispute the indisputable, whether in the courtroom or elsewhere, those cases that do finish up in court represent a skewed sample of legal events, selected largely on the basis of their disputability. Thus litigated cases, and especially appellate cases, will be those existing in the penumbra; it is consequently mistaken to generalize too much about the indeterminacy of legal language in general from a sample of cases selected precisely for their indeterminacy.

## IV

If one of the issues in the debate about the indeterminacy of law concerns the determinacy of language itself, it becomes clear that, like most other 'law and...' topics, an inquiry into law and language is fruitfully interdisciplinary. But whereas there is little doubt about the companion discipline called upon when the topic is 'legal history', 'law and literature', 'law and economics' or 'law and sociology', there is no one discipline with an exclusive claim over inquiries into the nature and operation of language. The philosophy of language, linguistics, semiotics, rhetoric, literary studies and communications theory, among others, all have something to teach us about language; what we learn from each may fruitfully be applied to thinking about law. Not surprisingly, therefore, the subject of law and language is not one but many subjects, varying with the disciplinary focus of the attention on language that is thought to illuminate our understanding of the operation of law.

The discipline selected as the window through which to view legal language may determine which aspect of law is the focus of attention. And even from a common disciplinary perspective, the features of law illuminated by attention to language may vary considerably. Thus, for example, disputes about the extent to which legal decision-making differs from other forms of decision-making, and related disputes about the extent to which law is methodologically or sociologically autonomous, are ones that can (but need not) focus on the language of the law. This is because the more the language of the law is in some way different, the more plausible it is to claim that law itself is in some way different.

The example of the distinctiveness (or not) of legal language points to a deeper divide about what we are doing when we look at law through the window of language. In the heyday of ordinary language philosophy, it was maintained with some vehemence that one could learn a great deal about any phenomenon by attending to the distinctions embedded in the language used to talk about that phenomenon. Language operates here as a microscope (or telescope, if you will), enabling us to see things that would otherwise escape our notice. Thus, Hart's ordinary language analysis of 'obligation' in *The Concept of Law* is not an inquiry into legal language, but rather the use of a close analysis of the language we use to talk *about* the law as a way of seeing something of importance about the law itself.

This kind of focus is different from a focus on the language that law (or any other institution) uses as one of its own mechanisms. Just as the subject of the philosophy of language differs from the method of ordinary language analysis, so too does attending to the language of the law differ from looking at law by closely examining the language we use to talk about it. At the risk of unwarranted definitional imperialism, it might be safe to say that the subject of law and language is larger than the subject of the language of the law; within the latter, however, there is no reason to claim that one perspective on the language of the law has any pride of place over any other, at least definitionally.

## V

All of this explains why there is perhaps less coherence among the selections in this volume than there is among the selections in other volumes in this series. Those who write about law and language do not all train their attention on the same problem, do not all employ the same methods or perspectives, and thus are often not even involved in the same debate.

Moreover, the admirable goal of this series, designed to make available otherwise less retrievable materials, has generated the constraint of omitting works otherwise available in collected essays, whether by one author or many. As a result, essays that some might think central to the subject, such as Hart's 'Definition and Theory in Jurisprudence' or the Hart/Fuller debate in the *Harvard Law Review*, are not found here; this only means they are readily available elsewhere. Much the same can be said about most of the work in law and semiotics, almost all of which appears in a series of annual volumes edited by Roberta Kevelson and published by the Plenum Press. Moreover, some authors who seem to have been neglected, such as Ronald Dworkin, Stanley Fish and James Boyd White, are missing only because almost all of their work is published in book form, with few of their major essays and articles not already collected in their own volumes. Others are omitted only for reasons of length, the sole explanation for the exclusion of, for example, Michael Moore's (1981) 'The Semantics of Judging' (*Southern California Law Review*, **54**, 151–294) and his (1985) 'A Natural Law Theory of Interpretation' (*Southern California Law Review*, **58**, 277–398), as well as Heidi Hurd's (1990) 'Sovereignty in Silence' (*Yale Law Journal*, **99**, 945–1028). Finally, much that might not implausibly be found in this volume is found instead in other volumes in the series; the reader interested in the broad topic of law and language will find much of interest in the volumes on American Legal Theory, Critical Legal Studies, Feminist Legal Theory, Legal Reasoning, and Law and Literature.

When the constraints of length and non-appearance in other collections are added to the intrinsic messiness of the subject itself, what emerges is likely to appear as largely *bricolage*. I have tried to remedy this somewhat by stressing articles that both describe the existing literature in their fields and take a particular position, and also by including a number of responses and review essays which give insights into the positions responded to and the books reviewed, as well as the views of the responders and reviewers. But if what remains is still to some excessively disconnected, I do not take this to be a bad thing. For the non-specialist this approach may provide a wider survey of conceivable approaches than would otherwise have been possible; for the specialist, the diversity of treatment can indicate new areas of exploration outside the cabined debates in which most specialists find themselves. Because both law and language are so pervasive, a volume on law and language that appeared as coherent and unidisciplinary would be one that sacrificed breadth of interest and insight to the goals of a highly focused inquiry. That sacrifice is often one worth making, but in light both of the objectives of this series and of the nature of this subject, it does not seem to be a sacrifice worth making here.

# Part I
# Language and the Autonomy of Law

# [1]

## EXCURSIONS INTO THE NATURE OF LEGAL LANGUAGE

MARY JANE MORRISON*



Holmes's favorite topic of the language of the law[1] has been moving from the back burner to the front burner during the last few years. There are arguments between interpretivists and noninterpretivists about how to treat the language of the Constitution[2] and there are symposia on "law and literature."[3] There also are nascent discussions of whether the language of the law is a technical language. One scholar has described the law as being "a language activity," saying what legal scholars have uniquely to contribute is "our special familiarity with the legal language."[4] He then found himself accused of having joined the "*law as* language movement," which "is aimed principally at reasserting the autonomy of law — at returning law to lawyers by claiming that law is a specialized language that only lawyers can speak."[5]

---

* Professor of Law, Hamline University. B.A., University of Florida 1965; A.M., University of Illinois 1971; J.D., College of William and Mary 1981; Ph.D., University of Illinois 1981. I have been indebted for many years to Fred Schauer for long hours of conversation about this topic and for his comments on an earlier draft of this article. All the mistakes, of course, are mine.

[1] O.W. HOLMES, *The Path of the Law*, in COLLECTED LEGAL PAPERS 167 (1920); *see also The Theory of Legal Interpretation*, in *id.* at 203.

[2] The dispute is over the extent to which the text of the Constitution is open or closed. *See* Schauer, *An Essay on Constitutional Language*, 29 UCLA L. REV. 797, n.1 (1982) (citing works of Ely, Brest, Grey, Linde, Monaghan, Perry, and Richards) [hereinafter Schauer, *Essay*]. *See also* Morris, *Interpretive and Noninterpretive Constitutional Theory*, 94 ETHICS 501 (1984).

[3] *See, e.g., Symposium: Law and Literature*, 60 TEX. L. REV. 373 (1982); *Symposium: Legal Scholarship: Its Nature and Purposes*, 90 YALE L.J. 955 (1981); *Symposium: Law and Literature*, 32 BUFFALO L. REV. 603 (1979).

[4] Stone, *From a Language Perspective*, 90 YALE L.J. 1149 (1981).

[5] Shapiro, *On the Regrettable Decline of Law French: Or Shapiro Jettet Le Brickbat*, 90 YALE L.J. 1198, 1200 (1981) (emphasis in original) (commenting on Stone, *supra* note 4). One of Professor Shapiro's primary concerns is that Professor Stone's thesis will encourage persons of less able minds than Professor Stone's to conclude that legal language belongs only to those trained in the law and will return us to "the jurisprudence of concepts." *Id.* at 1200.

The tone of that criticism suggests that no one can say, in one and the same breath, that the language of the law is a technical language accessible to all speakers of English, lawyers and laymen alike. Yet, another scholar has asked for an inquiry into the ways ordinary English and the language "in legal culture" are related to one another and the ways the language of the "law must simultaneously function for professionals [who work] within the legal system and for citizens [who]" live within it.[6] He notes that "legal language, as a technical language, often operates in a context that makes legal terms have meanings different from those they bear"[7] in nonlegal contexts of use; but, he says, "the law speaks largely if not exclusively in English,"[8] and "legal English must remain attached to ordinary English"[9] because the former is "parasitic" on the latter.

In this article, I explore some of the truths on each side of the issue of whether the language of the law is a technical language and whether lawyers speak in a technical language when they speak with each other about the law. I try to make sense of saying "lawyers make technical uses of language" without falling into the dangerously false thesis of "only lawyers know what the law is because only they speak the language of the law." For theorists who would like to say the language of the law is technical, I develop several definitions that allow for such claims. But I also set out the consequences and limitations of those claims.

In Part I of this article, I examine the due process limitations on the thesis that the law is in a technical language and I draw distinctions between speaking carefully and speaking technically. The points I draw in the latter section are independent of any view we might decide to take about technical languages and about whether the language of the law is technical, but they will aid us in avoiding a too-provincial view of the language of the law. In Part II, I set out the technical language views of H.L.A. Hart and Charles Caton. By taking back-bearings on the views of Hart and Caton, I then develop a third view of technical terms. With that view in hand, I investigate the language of the law in Part III. I conclude that although Hart's and Caton's views will allow us to say the language of the law is technical, its technicality is not interesting or illuminating under these views and is in danger of being an "experts only" language. Under my view we may not say the language of the law is technical, although some of the most interesting terms are ones surrounded by theory and although lawyers may speak technically by making technical uses of ordinary English. I also explain, however, how a word that is central to a prescriptive institution sometimes may require

---

[6] Schauer, *Precedent*, 39 STAN. L. REV. 571, 586 n.35 (1987) [hereinafter Schauer, *Precedent*]. Literally, he notes a dearth of inquiry into the ways "in which *law* must simultaneously function for professionals within the legal system and for citizens *outside* it . . . ." (emphasis added), but I take this to be a two-fold slip of the pen.

[7] *Id.* (citing Schauer, *Speech and "Speech" – Obscenity and "Obscenity": An Exercise in the Interpretation of Constitutional Language*, 67 GEO. L.J. 899 (1979)).

[8] *Id.* at 586.

[9] *Id.* at 586 n.35 (citing C. CATON, PHILOSOPHY AND ORDINARY LANGUAGE vii-viii (C. Caton ed. 1963)).

interpretation that runs slightly ahead of settled ordinary use, and I use as an example "speech" of the first amendment. In contrast to this phenomenon is the more usual legal phenomenon of terms that have exactly the same meaning in legal use as they have in ordinary use. My example here is "promise," and I relate the theory surrounding "speech" to the one ordinary language itself provides for "promise."

Much of what I will say is obvious; with luck, it also will be, as the curse goes, interesting. With great good fortune, it will strike a responsive chord with persons who have wondered about what "thinking like a lawyer" means[10] and who have been concerned by some of the subterranean undercurrents in recent attacks on the jury system.[11] I will also, however, be speaking of the meanings of words in ways that, in one sense, sometimes may appear to cut against the "meaning is use" grain of contemporary philosophy.[12] Under some formulations of that received view, I ought not to be speaking of the meanings of words themselves, but of speakers' uses of words in sentences,[13] or in speech acts,[14] or of speakers' uses of strings of words to be taken by someone to mean something,[15] and so on. In short-circuiting to speak of the meanings of words, I sometimes may be short-changing some of the richness of our linguistic practices. Even more problematic, however, is my use of "language of": I use the phrase in a very loose way only moderately abstracted from an identification with the linguistic practices of enthusiasts in or participants of a

---

[10] Each fall, as deans welcome first-year students, the phrase "thinking like a lawyer" wafts from the windows of law schools across the land. Both Professors Stone and Shapiro view this incantation of "thinking like a lawyer" as an "institutional conceit." Stone, *supra* note 4, at 1150; Shapiro, *supra* note 5, at 1199-1200, 1204.

*But see* Levinson, *Taking Law Seriously: Reflections on "Thinking Like a Lawyer"*, 30 STAN. L. REV. 1071 (1978) (review of R. DWORKIN, TAKING RIGHTS SERIOUSLY (1977)). He says that, instead of dismissing notions of thinking like a lawyer as "ritual cant," it should be recognized "as central to the ideology of legal education." *Id.* The phrase implies at least "(1) that there is a particular way lawyers think; and (2) that this particular way is also a desirable way .... Both of these propositions are debatable." *Id.* For example, not all law professors, who teach budding lawyers to think, themselves think alike, and similarly for judges, who write the cases these students study. *Id.* at 1071-73. More importantly, "'thinking like a lawyer' and 'thinking like a morally acute individual' can cut in radically different directions." *Id.* at 1104. Conversely, he argues, in agreement with Professor Dworkin, "all citizens in a constitutional democracy have the capacity, and indeed the right, to engage in legal analysis." *Id.* at 1101 (footnote omitted).

[11] *See, e.g.*, B. ACKERMAN, RECONSTRUCTING AMERICAN LAW (1984) (arguing for lawyers to redeem the promise of the New Deal in part by putting law into the hands of experts at agencies). *But see* Schauer, *The Role of the People in First Amendment Theory*, 74 CALIF. L. REV. 761 (1986) (analyzing the current view of the relationship between jury power and free speech).

[12] In another sense, I clearly will not; for nothing I say here fairly could be taken to be a form of essentialism. That is, I clearly am talking about meanings of words, not "*the*" meaning and, indeed, not the meaning.

[13] *See, e.g.*, Alston, *The Quest for Meaning*, 72 MIND 79 (1963).

[14] *See, e.g.*, J. SEARLE, SPEECH ACTS (1969).

[15] *See, e.g.*, Grice, *Meaning*, 66 PHIL. REV. 377 (1957).

subject, discipline, or activity. What I say, therefore, is more nearly like an impressionist's charcoal of a landscape than it is a color photograph or a cartographer's topological map, and I do not wish anyone to be misled by my unqualified assertional tone. My tone is sometimes misleading in that I do not finish with any line of argument until I have uncovered and developed all lines of argument, and each point is subject to critical recapitulation and reformulation.

## I. Local and Global Features of the Language of the Law

### *A. The Problem: Anti-Reductionism and Reductionism*

The bald contention that legal language is a language that only lawyers can speak is one of several forms of an anti-reductionist thesis. This view is that legal language differs from English, cannot be reduced to English — or, at least, cannot be reduced to ordinary English. But the expression of that view tends to crop up in the contexts of some other point, so that determining whether a theorist intends to advance an anti-reductionist view is difficult.

For example, someone may say innocently that "it is a commonplace that that which gives the language of the law its distinctive flavor is something other than the King's or the commoner's English."[16] To say that the "great mass of the language used by lawyers is ordinary English"[17] still is innocent because it does not itself indicate a position with respect to the rest of the language lawyers use. It does not even necessarily draw a distinction of ordinariness for the "great mass" and nonordinariness for the rest; for someone may make, as shall I, the great-mass-ordinariness point to clear-away noncontroversial areas of the language of the law in order to facilitate analysis of the rest. With saying "[o]nly the lawyer can exploit the capabilities of the language of the law, he alone even recognize[s] some of its limitations,"[18] however, the innocence begins to fade; and it pales entirely in the rhetorical excess of a statement that "the language of the law depends for survival upon those it unites in priesthood — the lawyers."[19] For here we arrive at the bud of a claim that there is something lawyers know about the language of the law and do with it that nonlawyers do not do exactly because nonlawyers are nonlawyers. Even then, determining whether the theorist intends to convey an anti-reductionist message is difficult.[20]

---

[16] D. Mellinkoff, The Language of the Law 10 (1963).

[17] *Id.* at 9.

[18] *Id.* at 454.

[19] *Id.* at 453.

[20] The last of Professor Mellinkoff's remarks quoted in the text, for example, itself is in the context of his saying, "Law language is no longer — as lawyers once wanted it — bottled in bond, that their discipline might not be made common among the vulgar." *Id.* at 453.

On the other side of the coin, what are we to think when someone compares learning the language of the law to learning a foreign language and says that "it is useful to treat common-law mens rea terms, and indeed much of the language of the law, as words that must be translated into ordinary language before one can learn what they mean and how to use them"?[21] That sort of statement certainly is not anti-reductionist, but just how innocent is it? It suggests that the legal language can be reduced to English, but only in translation, and that in turn is to deny that the language of the law is already part of English. It also does not tell us whether the result of the translation leaves any cognitive dissonance between the original law and the English translation. Are there any shades of the Innuit's distinctions among snows left over, any niches in the German's *gemutliche Ecke* left unilluminated, and so on? That is, are there any translation failures, and do lawyers come to see things differently than nonlawyers? If not, why? Nor does the view suggest how a translation failure is possible, given that men and women make the law. More pointedly, if law students need to carry around a translation manual until they have learned the foreign words of the language of the law, are all the commentators who argue that Shakespeare may have been a lawyer themselves lawyers, and did all his playgoers go to law school, or did they sit mutely in the audience not understanding some of the words and phrases of his plays?[22]

A dispute about the nature of legal language is not unique to jurisprudence. Philosophers and mathematicians long have argued about whether mathematical propositions are reducible to empirical generalizations (for example, "2 + 2 = 4" to propositions about counting objects) or to symbol-manipulation rules ("2 + 2 = 4" to propositions about the conventional uses educated people make of certain symbols) or are not reducible at all because they are *sui generis*, in a language unique unto itself and cut off from other languages. One philosopher, who characterized the former two views as "radical" and the latter view as "conservative," argued that the conservative view that mathematical propositions are *sui generis* is "perfectly correct, but rather unsatisfactory and unilluminating, whereas opinions of the 'radical' type are untrue, but interesting and illuminating."[23] The theory I ultimately will be presenting is of the radical kind. My thesis is that statements of our law and the central, substantive legal words, rather than being *sui generis*, are ordinary English, albeit perhaps not always in the ordinary language sense in which J.L. Austin and others may speak of ordinary language.[24] This thesis thus

[21] P. LOW, J. JEFFERIES, JR., & R. BONNIE, CRIMINAL LAW: CASES AND MATERIALS 198 (2d ed. 1986).

[22] To be sure, the commentators argue not only on the basis of Shakespeare's adept usages of legal terms and legal maxims, but also his apparently autobiographical remarks — such as "I am a wise fellow, and one that knows the law" from *Much Ado About Nothing*, act iv, scene 2 — to fill some otherwise unaccounted years in his life. *See* W. KNIGHT, SHAKESPEARE'S HIDDEN LIFE: SHAKESPEARE AT THE LAW 1585-95 (1973); W. RUSHTON, SHAKESPEARE'S LEGAL MAXIMS 9, 60-61 (1907; 1973); F. HEARD, SHAKESPEARE AS A LAWYER 7, 10-11, 13 (1883; 1977).

[23] Gasking, *Mathematics and the World* (1940), reprinted in LOGIC AND LANGUAGE (First and Second Series) 204 (A. Flew ed. (1965)).

[24] *See, e.g.*, J. AUSTIN, HOW TO DO THINGS WITH WORDS (1962).

is more radical than even the radical thesis that legal language can be reduced to English, because the thesis is that the law already is in English, and my view, therefore, runs even greater risk of being "untrue."

Examples of views that take a fully conscious position on the nature of legal language are hard to find, and this is no less true of anti-reductionism (or reductionism or translationism). With two notable exceptions, few scholars have paid attention to the nature of legal language.[25] One of the notable exceptions is legal theorist H.L.A. Hart; and the other is philosopher Charles Caton, who practices analytic philosophy within the ordinary language tradition. Caton's view is that the language of the law is a technical language that, like all technical languages, is an "adjunct" of or "parasitic" on ordinary languages such as ordinary English or ordinary French.[26] Caton's view is not anti-reductionist although the reasons it is not are complex. Hart's view, however, is anti-reductionist. That Hart is an anti-reductionist comes as no surprise to students of his works in one sense, for he rejected the view that legal concepts and rules can be reduced to moral and political concepts and rules.[27] Yet Hart is an anti-reductionist about the language of the law although he also practices analytical jurisprudence within a tradition of ordinary language philosophy.[28]

This disagreement between two scholars who practice within the same tradition alone is enough to make the thesis that the language of the law may not be reduced to English worth investigating. There is another reason that is even more compelling, however, and it is that the anti-reductionist thesis is false.

### *B. The Due Process Limits for Anti-Reductionism*

One of the basic propositions of Anglo-American law is that each individual will be accorded due process of law, or due process under the law. As part of that enforming proposition, we presume each person knows the law. This, of course, is a myth, if we take "each person knows the law" to mean each person does know the law. That is, it is empirically false. When we say the law presumes each person knows the law, we do not even mean each person is able to know the law, with or without the

[25] There are exceptions, all of which build within and on the tradition begun by J. AUSTIN, *supra* note 24, in which Austin gives an extensive examination of "promise" and promising. *See, e.g.*, Hancher, *Speech Acts and the Law* in LANGUAGE USE AND THE USES OF LANGUAGE 245 (R. Shuy & A. Shnukal eds. 1980); Samek, *Performative Utterances and the Concept of Contract*, 43 AUSTRALASIAN J. PHIL. 196 (1965); Comment, *The Language of Offer and Acceptance: Speech Acts and the Question of Intent*, 74 CALIF. L. REV. 189 (1986).

[26] C. CATON, PHILOSOPHY AND ORDINARY LANGUAGE v, viii (C. Caton ed. 1963). *See also* section II B, *infra*, for full discussion of his views. The description of the relationship of technical language to ordinary language as "parasitic" comes from Schauer, *Precedent*, *supra* note 6, at 586 n.35.

[27] *See generally* H.L.A. HART, THE CONCEPT OF LAW (1961). *See also* N. MACCORMICK, H.L.A. HART 20-28 (1981).

[28] N. MACCORMICK, *supra* note 27, at 12-19.

weasel "*ceteris paribus*." We may try to say that what we mean is something more nearly like the proposition that there are no surprises in the law, that the law fits within standards of behavior and general moral precepts members of society recognize; but that will not do either. We must give up the empiricist and dispositional claims for the presumption.[29]

When we say the law presumes — that is, we presume — each person knows the law, we are setting the limits of the law and setting a prescriptive standard for the law to meet for both law-making and law-enforcing. We are constructing a myth[30] not in the sense of falsity, but in the sense of a story that is part of the fabric of our lives and of our society and that we are to give solid reality, although there never will be a universal empirical truth in "each person knows the law." And we have made a good start, after centuries of different practice, in giving it reality by establishing legal aid societies, by understanding the Constitution to require that poor persons accused of crime have a lawyer, and so on. We have more solid reality than these recent developments on which to rely, however; and that reality is solid because the myth is a truth. It is the truth that the law is ours, not lawyers', and is in our tongue, not in argot. We mark this truth in due process clauses although the truth hinges into a deeper sense of due process than merely those clauses. And we enforce due process requirements that the law be in our language and be ours. If only lawyers could "speak the law," then only lawyers could be prosecuted for crimes or held in contempt or sued in tort or held to administrative regulations.

In criminal law, our legal system imposes due process limitations against the law's not being comprehensible to ordinary persons. No one may be convicted of a crime absent fair notice that the act is punishable. The Supreme Court, under the "principle of criminal law" that only statutory offenses are punishable, has established that there are no federal

[29] This presumption is one of the many presumptions or constituting-propositions through which the law increasingly has become "objectivized" over the centuries but particularly since around the time of the industrial revolution, although forms of this particular presumption have a more ancient history in criminal law. All of these objectivizations of the law probably are related to controlling juries, to dealing with an increasingly complex and large society, and to the rise of the middle class, who came to court in ever increasing numbers as the ranks of lawyers also swelled. Consider, as just one example, the objectivizational shift in English law that came with Hadley v. Baxendale, 9 Exch. 341, 156 Eng. Rep. 145 (1854) (limiting contract damages to those that are foreseeable because they naturally or usually arise from breaches of this type of contract and those that are foreseeable because, although they are unusual, they were within the contemplation of the parties at the contracting) compared to Black v. Baxendale, 1 Exch. 410 (1847) (allowing the jury to award "reasonable" contract damages); and think of the ways that *Hadley* has been further objectivized today.

[30] This myth, then, is part of our narrative and sets a range of meaning for legal discourse. *See generally* Cover, *Nomos and Narrative*, 97 HARV. L. REV. 4 (1983); White, *Law as Language: Reading Law and Reading Literature*, 60 TEX. L. REV. 415 (1982).

common law crimes.[31] Most states agree.[32] Even those states that purport to recognize common law crimes mean only that crimes existing at common law continue to exist without specific individual positive enactment.[33] They do not mean that courts may create brand new felonies out of whole cloth;[34] and, were a court to claim the power to do so, it would run afoul of the constitutional requirement of due process.[35]

The due process requirement for criminal law is thus two-fold at one level. There must be notice that the act is prohibited and is punishable, for which shared notions of blameworthiness are not sufficient.[36] At another level, due process requires that the people be the source of the criminal law. The former requirement entails the language of the criminal law be in a language that is comprehensible to the people to whom it applies, and the latter requirement ensures the satisfaction of the former.

The fair notice due process criminal cases are replete with arguments about whether the criminal statute is in words and phrases that long

---

[31] United States v. Eaton, 144 U.S. 677, 687-88 (1892); United States v. Coolidge, 14 U.S. (1 Wheat.) 415 (1816); United States v. Hudson & Goodwin, 11 U.S. (7 Cranch) 32, 34 (1812). As will become clear in this section, I am in fundamental and abiding disagreement with statements such as: "As an original proposition, United States v. Hudson and Goodwin was probably wrong. . . . But the proposition is too well settled now for argument." W. LaFave & A. Scott, Jr., Criminal Law § 9, at 60 n.17 (1972) (citing 1923 and 1933 law review articles and notes).

[32] *See, e.g.*, Ala. Code § 13A-1-4 (1982); State v. Bowling, 5 Ariz. App. 436, 427 P.2d 920 (1967); Ga. Code Ann. § 26-201 (1988); Ill. Rev. Stat. ch. 38, para. 1-3 (1961); State v. Campbell, 217 Iowa 848, 251 N.W. 717 (1933); Kan. Stat. Ann. § 21-3102 (1984 Supp.); State v. Heymann, 256 La. 18, 235 So. 2d 78 (1970); Minn. Stat. Ann. § 609.015 (West 1987); Mitchell v. State, 42 Ohio St. 383 (1884); 18 Pa. Cons. Stat. Ann. § 107 (Purdon 1973); Lund v. Commonwealth, 217 Va. 688, 232 S.E.2d 745 (1977); Wis. Stat. Ann. § 939.01 (West 1988). *See also* Model Penal Code § 1.05(1) (1962).

[33] *See, e.g.*, State v. Egan, 287 So. 2d 1 (Fla. 1973); Pope v. State, 38 Md. App. 520, 382 A.2d 880 (1978); Commonwealth v. Chapman, 54 Mass. 68 (1847); N.M. Stat. Ann. § 30-1-3 (1984). *See also* United States v. Davis, 167 F.2d 228 (D.C. Cir.), *cert. denied*, 334 U.S. 849 (1948).

[34] Authorities continue to insist that:

> in the absence of statute [depriving courts of the power to create new crimes, a] majority of jurisdictions still recognize the power of courts to create common law crimes . . . [although] [t]he trend today is in the direction of abolishing such crimes, so that conduct not forbidden and punished by a statute is not a crime.

W. LaFave & A. Scott, *supra* note 31, § 9, at 57. *See also* R. Perkins & R. Boyce, Criminal Law § 2, at 37-38 (3d ed. 1982).

[35] U.S. Const. amend. V, amend. XIV § 1. Arguments to the contrary are based on cases decrepit with age. *See, e.g.*, the dates of the cases cited in W. LaFave & A. Scott, *supra* note 31, at 66 nn.66-67. Moreover, the arguments ignore that ours is a legislative age and that our view of constitutional due process has broadened and deepened in the last 200 years.

[36] There must be a statute that declares the prohibition, in terms that meet conditions I will discuss in the text following this note, and that sets the penalty. *See, e.g.*, United States v. Evans, 333 U.S. 483 (1948) (federal statute prohibited concealing an alien, but did not create a crime because the penalty prescribed was too vague); Commonwealth v. Cunningham, 365 Pa. 68, 73 A.2d 705 (1950) (statute prohibited driving overweight trucks, defined "overweight" four ways but set penalty for only one; the other three are not crimes). *But see* State v. Bishop, 228 N.C. 371, 45 S.E.2d 858 (1947) (treating statutorily prohibited conduct for which there was no statutory penalty as a misdemeanor).

have been in use among speakers of English, or whether an ordinary-English speaker would understand the words in the statute to have the particular meaning in question. Consider *Rose v. Locke*,[37] in which the Supreme Court upheld a conviction for cunnilingus under a "crime against nature" statute on grounds that due process requires only that "the law give sufficient warning that men may conduct themselves so as to avoid that which is forbidden."[38] That requirement was met in *Rose*, the Court said, because "crime against nature" "has been in use among English-speaking people for many centuries," with a meaning anyone could determine, in a state in which the highest state court nearly twenty years earlier had rejected a contention that "crime against nature" did not include fellatio.[39] Now, *Rose* is perhaps the most difficult case on many levels for a claim that criminal statutes are valid under the due process clause only if the meaning is within the common understanding of the words of the statute. Critics could charge, of course, that the *Rose* Court twisted the history of the common law because centuries ago "crime against nature" covered only bestiality and sodomy, with the latter taken in its narrowest sense of penis-anus sexual acts between human beings, i.e., buggery.[40]

The relevance of the earlier state case then was two-fold: First, it took the broader view of "sodomy" as including penis-mouth sexual acts, thereby breaking the connection of "crimes against nature" to its most conservatively narrow possible historical meaning by saying an anus is not necessary to a sodomous act, i.e., that it includes fellatio. This in turn made possible and foreseeable the further interpretation of "sodomy" as including sexual acts in which a penis is not involved, i.e., that it includes cunnilingus; and the defendant therefore had notice that satisfies due process. Second, the earlier case was relevant because the defendant was giving a narrow linguistic attack on the interpretation of the statute as applying to him on the basis of citations to common law cases and commentary. To the latter, the Court's due process reply essentially is, "Cite cases to us, and we'll cite cases right back to you." That is, a defendant cannot have things both ways in a due process argument about the meaning of a statute. He or she cannot pick and choose among meanings when all of them are available meanings under common usage and decided cases or are natural rationalizations and implications of common usage or decided cases.

That point in turn takes us back to the first reason the earlier case was relevant on the issue of due process notice. There always are natural extensions of one case to the next by way of "theory-construction" that rests in the nature of language itself, and perhaps particularly in the English language, and that is compounded in the nature of judicial review on the basis of precedent. Language is elastic, i.e., open textured, and this especially is true of English in part because English often has more than one word for a thing. With "sodomy," for example, the English word

[37] 423 U.S. 48 (1975).
[38] *Id.* at 50.
[39] *Id.* at 50, 52.
[40] *See* R. PERKINS & R. BOYCE, *supra* note 34, at 465-69.

was and is both the generic word and the particular-act word. Even when words start out their lives as particular-instance words, they can become generic over time through the common use of the words by speakers' not marking distinctions because these distinctions do not matter to the speakers most of the time. In the absence of a court's clearly limiting a particular-instance word to its particular-instance meaning, a word that hovers on the edge of being a generic word may in the next case be applied on the generic basis rather than on the particular-instance basis.[41] This is especially likely to happen to men who enter next-door neighbors' apartments by pretext and wield butcher knives to force sexual relations with their unwilling neighbors, even if the acts are cunnilingus and the state's cases heretofore have dealt with sodomy and fellatio in the narrowest sense and have held both of the latter to be covered by the meaning of "crime against nature" but never have rejected coverage of cunnilingus.[42]

The interesting due process question thus is not the one in *Rose* itself, but in the earlier state case or, rather, the first case to have departed from the narrowest meaning of "sodomy" and hence of "crime against nature." Assuming arguendo that when sodomy became an English crime after the demise of ecclesiastic courts,[43] the extant sodomy convictions were for only penis-anus sexual acts between human beings, was the first person convicted under a sodomy statute or crime-against-nature statute for having engaged in fellatio afforded due process?[44] There would be legitimate grounds for arguing for the court to take a narrow view. If a court were to refuse the prosecution on grounds of denial of due process, the court would slow the elastic development of the word "sodomy" or phrase "crime against nature" for a time, perhaps forever. In that event, forces in society, were the need sufficient, would find a way around by stretching some other word or by changing the statute.

Whether this conservatism was a necessity in the first nonnarrow sodomy prosecution is none too certain, however. After all, the ecclesiastic wrong could be equally and legitimately viewed as any nonprocreative sexual act, not merely penis-anus sodomy. If, then, a defendant were to object to being prosecuted under the crime-against-nature statute on the ground that his sexual act did not involve sodomy in its narrowest sense, but involved fellatio, a court could reject that argument and, if the ecclesiastic understanding were within the collective recent memory of the populace, probably would reject it.

The brutal fact of the matter is that crime-against-nature statutes had and have been vehicles for prosecuting homosexuals. In one sense, then,

---

41 *See generally* Schauer, *Precedent*, *supra* note 6. *See also* Morrison, *Choice of Law for Unlawful Searches*, 41 OKLA. L. REV. 579 (1988).

42 *See, e.g.*, Rose v. Locke, 423 U.S. 48, 48-49 (1975).

43 R. PERKINS & R. BOYCE, *supra* note 34, at 466.

44 Nothing turns, here, on my using fellatio as the first case; it equally could have been cunnilingus. I am assuming, however, that the statutory terms are "sodomy" (or "sodomy and bestiality") or "crime against nature" and not "buggery and bestiality."

the defendant's argument basically would be an appeal to the court to limit "crime against nature" or "sodomy" to homosexual acts. As an argument about the public's common understanding of "crime against nature" or "perverse sexual act" or "sodomy," this argument would be well-taken in the sense that this limited-to-homosexuals meaning probably once was and still might be the common understanding. Cast in this light, however, the common-understanding argument is hoist by its own petard equally with an argument that cites some but not all cases and law that are arguably and equally on point. Ecclesiastic courts, not constrained by notions of either due process or equal justice for all, can get away with viewing "crime against nature" as applying only to homosexual acts on grounds that homosexuality is an abomination in the eyes of God. When the people's courts take over interpretation of "crime against nature," however, the court cannot interpret general words of a statute to save them from a common-understanding due process challenge by imposing a narrowing construction that makes the clause violate basic notions of equal protection of the laws. (Or so any reasonable person would have believed until *Bowers v. Hardwick*,[45] which may be every bit as dreadful a decision as the one that took a Civil War to overturn.)[46]

Other fair notice due process cases provide easier lessons than the message in *Rose* because their lessons are more on the surface of the decisions. Thus, in *McBoyle v. United States*,[47] Justice Holmes noted that although a criminal is unlikely to consider "the text of the law before he murders or steals, it is reasonable that a fair warning should be given to the world in language that the common world will understand, of what the law intends to do if a certain line is passed."[48] A criminal statute that defines "motor vehicle" as "an automobile . . . truck . . . wagon, motorcycle, or any other self-propelled vehicle not designed for running on rails" does not cover an aircraft, although an aircraft is self-propelled, is a vehicle,

---

[45] 478 U.S. 186 (1986). *Hardwick*, of course, was a due process case of a different sort, namely privacy due process. But a full understanding of that kind of privacy links privacy to the source-of-the-law point I made earlier in the text about due process because, on one view, at that level the question is whether, in agreeing to be governed under law, the minority agreed that the majority may outlaw the minority's morally respectable views by taking a narrower view on moral grounds. *See, e.g.*, Tribe, *Structural Due Process*, 10 HARV. C.R.-C.L. L. REV. 269 (1975) (interventions of courts during periods of moral flux allows new consensus to form); Tribe, *Foreword: Toward a Model of Roles in Due Process of Life and Law*, 87 HARV. L. REV. 1, 32 (1973) ("some types of choices ought to be remanded, on principle, to private decision-makers unchecked by substantive governmental control"). For a slightly different account of privacy due process, see Morrison, *Constitutional Reasoning for Rights*, 54 MO. L. REV. 29 (1989).

[46] *Hardwick* merely shows what we have known all along. First, we cannot limit our notions of due process or justice to what any court is willing to dispense because courts do not have a monopoly on perceptions of justice. They are not constituted of Plato's philosopher kings. Moreover, the justice they are to dispense is ours, not theirs, where "our justice" paradoxically is both majoritarian and nonmajoritarian. Finally, persecuted minorities in the long run are better off having their persecution out of the closet so that we all may do battle with devils in daylight rather than box at shadows who hide in the darkness of night.

[47] 283 U.S. 25 (1931) (Holmes, J.).

[48] *Id.* at 27.

and is not designed to run on rails.[49] "[I]n everyday speech, 'vehicle' calls up the popular picture of a thing moving on land," and the "theme" of the statutory definition here was of "a vehicle that runs, not something, not commonly called a vehicle, that flies."[50]

Although the individual words must be comprehensible to the persons to whom they apply, these words do not always have to be comprehensible to all English speakers. There is no due process impropriety in using "trade" words in a statute that applies only to persons who know the meanings of those words. New York meat dealers, for example, are not deprived of proper notice by a statute that prohibits them from falsely representing nonkosher meat as kosher when the dealers sell both kinds of meat. Similarly, sheepherders have proper notice when a statute prohibits them from grazing sheep on a "cattle range" in an area in which there are both sheep ranchers and cattle ranchers.[51] Further, a law is not unconstitutionally vague simply because it throws upon people the risk of "estimating rightly . . . some matter of degree."[52] Yet when the law fails to indicate what normative standard people must meet, the law fails to give due process notice even if the statute consists of simple words even children know, such as a prohibition against "annoying" others on a sidewalk.[53]

Thus criminal statutes must give fair warning to all those to whom the statutes apply. The more universal the class, the more nonspecialized the language of the statute must be. But the statute cannot be so inexact and general that each person must guess as to its meaning because each of us legitimately could construe the words in significantly different normative ways.

This due process standard also is the theme of the criminal and civil contempt due process cases. No defendant can be held in contempt of an order stated in terms that are not comprehensible to her. Enjoined de-

---

[49] *Id.* at 26.

[50] *Id.*

[51] Hygrade Provision Co. v. Sherman, 266 U.S. 497, 498-502 (1925) (Sutherland, J.). Omaechevarria v. Idaho, 246 U.S. 343, 345 n.3, 348 (1918) (Brandeis, J.). *See also* Connally v. General Construction Co., 269 U.S. 385, 391-92 (1926) (Sutherland, J.). *Cf.* Lanzetta v. New Jersey, 306 U.S. 451, 452-55, 458 (1939) (Butler, J.) ("gangster" and "gang" had no common law meanings and have varied dictionary and scholarly meanings). Notice, then, that a criminal statute written in technical legal terms would be enforceable under *Hygrade* against all and only lawyers or persons who happened to know these technical legal terms. To a certain extent the same would be true, then, for civil actions and for administrative regulations, hence the statement in the text at the beginning of this section. *See also* text following note 58, *infra*.

[52] Nash v. United States, 229 U.S. 373, 377 (1913) (Holmes, J.) ("undue restraint of trade" in Sherman Act). *Cf.* International Harvester Co. v. Kentucky, 234 U.S. 216, 219, 221-23 (1914) (Holmes, J.) ("real market value" for manufacturers in a market already disrupted by lawful combinations of farmers).

[53] Coates v. City of Cincinnati, 402 U.S. 611, 611 n.1, 614 (1971) ("men of common intelligence must necessarily guess at its meaning"); *cf.* Colten v. Kentucky, 407 U.S. 104, 108-11 (1972) (similar sidewalk statute upheld when it had been construed by state courts as not prohibiting the lawful exercise of constitutional rights).

fendants, as Justice Holmes has said, "ought to be informed as accurately as the case permits what they are forbidden to do."[54] The "paramount interests of liberty and due process make it indispensable for the chancellor . . . to speak clearly, explicitly, and specifically . . . ."[55] This is because of the risks of both civil and criminal contempt proceedings, namely that the contemnor may be sent to jail or be fined. Federal orders, for example, must set forth the reasons for issuance, be specific in terms, and describe the act to be enjoined in reasonable detail in the order itself, rather than by cross reference to, or incorporation of, some other document.[56] The standard of comprehensibility and completeness is not whether the judge who wrote the order understands it, nor whether lawyers would understand it. The proto-typical ordinary person for these contempt cases is a person who is not trained in the law:

> [T]he language of the injunction should in all cases be so clear and explicit that an unlearned man can understand its meaning, without the necessity of employing counsel to advise him what he has a right to do to save him from subjecting himself to punishment for a breach of injunction.[57]

The same general theme runs through our civil common law, but here the connection between the law and its language is less obvious and the connection between the ordinary person and her knowledge of the law is more obvious. Because of this difference in obviousness with respect to our common law of torts, contracts, restitution, and so on, we might be inclined to say there essentially is no due process bar to having these areas of the law "conducted" in some other language that one learns only by going to law school. For, aside from a pro se limitation, which requires only that anyone be *allowed* to represent herself in court,[58] we might believe we could say that ultimately the only limitation on private law

---

[54] Swift & Co. v. United States, 196 U.S. 375, 401 (1905) (Holmes, J.).

[55] H.K. Porter Co. v. National Friction Products, 568 F.2d 24, 27 (7th Cir. 1977).

[56] FED. R. CIV. P. 65(d). State procedural rules are similar.

[57] Laurie v. Laurie, 9 Paige ch. 234 (1841) (Walworth, C.) (ex parte order in a separation suit, enjoining the husband from "annoying, following," etc., his wife or children; modified after he was charged with contempt for sending her an annoying letter).

[58] Adult natural persons have a common law right to appear personally or by counsel. Osborn v. United States Bank, 22 U.S. 738, 828 (1824) (Marshall, C.J.); Hightower v. Hawthorn, 12 F. Cas. 142 (Super. Ct. Ark. 1826) (No. 6,478b). This right is an alternative one. Talbot v. Talbot's Representatives, 25 Ky. (2 J.J. Marsh.) 3, 4 (1829). It is distinct from the privilege of practicing law, *i.e.*, from the privilege of appearing on behalf of others, which privilege is limited by statute to active members of the bar. Gray v. Justice's Court of Williams Judicial Township, 18 Cal. App. 2d 420, 63 P.2d 1160 (1937). The right to proceed *pro se* or *in propria persona* partly is a consequence of the liability to be sued, Werckman v. Werckman, 4 Civ. Proc. Rep. 146, 147 (N.Y. Sup. Ct. 1883); and, in criminal cases, is a right guaranteed by the sixth amendment, Faretta v. California, 422 U.S. 806, 819, 821-36, 834-35 n.46 (1975). The *pro se* right often today is codified. *See, e.g.*, 28 U.S.C. § 1654 (1976); N.Y. CIV. PRAC. L. & R § 321(a) (McKinney Supp. 1983).

is that the *principles* of the law be in, so to speak, "English concepts." That is, someone could believe that, theoretically, the statements of the rules of law in civil statutes and in civil cases could be in any language whatever, including a language that all and only lawyers speak when they are speaking qua lawyers, as long as the rules thusly stated contained no surprises in terms of normative standards for tortfeasors, tort plaintiffs, contracting parties, etc., once these people come to court.[59]

This view, however, is founded on two mistakes. First, if the pro se limitation has any real meaning as a limitation on the law, the person who must be allowed to represent herself must not be met with an inexorable "catch 22" when she exercises her right. That is, she must not be told that she may represent herself without a lawyer, only to find that she herself must be a lawyer to represent herself. Second, and vastly more important, there is no such thing as an "English concept" that cannot be embodied in the English language. Were we to say that the only ultimate limitation on private law is that the principles of that law must comport with our shared understandings of proper conduct, and thus with our "shared concepts," so that ordinary persons not trained in the law are not met with surprise when they come to court, we would be advancing a thesis that contravenes what gives the law both its origin and its continuing-existence legitimacy, namely ourselves. Of course, the civil common law is grounded in the fabric of our daily lives — shared values, problems, distinctions, and solutions. But that truth cannot be turned upon its head to justify using some language other than the language of our daily lives for the language of the law.

The only reasons to try to use some language in the law other than the ordinary language of the people are to generate income for lawyers or to enhance the mystery of the law, much as Latin came to enhance the mystery of the Trinity. To say the language of the law is one only lawyers can understand because it is a technical language is to cloak ourselves in the modern mystique of the sciences, much as we once may have cloaked ourselves in each of the twin images of Stendal's *The Red and the Black* by our descriptions of ourselves as "champions of justice."

Thus our shift from French Law was, in a sense, one of our greatest democratic revolutions because it made statements of the law accessible to us, even if we are not lawyers. That revolution further is built into our legal system through the right to trial by jury made up of ordinary men and women.[60] Each accused and each defendant is entitled to be held

---

[59] But the political clout of Parti Quebecois is *not* the explanation for the facts that French and English are the official languages of Canada; that statutes, records, and journals of Canada's Parliament are required to be in both French and English; and that either French or English may be used in courts established by Parliament. Canada, Constitution Act, *Canadian Charter of Rights and Freedom*, § 16-20 (1982).

[60] U.S. CONST. amend. VI (all criminal trials), amend. VII (federal trials at law). State constitutions have similar guarantees. *See, e.g.*, VA. CONST. art I, § 8 (criminal trials), § 11 (civil trials).

responsible in accordance with the law;[61] and, unless the men and women who decide the pivotal issues in criminal and civil cases have been instructed in terms that are comprehensible to them, we cannot be certain the jurors have decided in accordance with the law. Instructions are to guide the jurors in their decisionmaking, and instructions that require a law degree to understand simply fail to guide laypersons.[62] Jury instructions necessarily are supposed to be in English, not in some language only lawyers understand, and are not to be replete with legal jargon or "legal niceties."

Our legal system simply does not operate under an assumption that each person has a lawyer on retainer to translate the law into English.[63] Rather, we can engage in and live the myth that each person knows the law because it is in English, whether statute or common law rule.

For the judiciary, then, to say to the sovereign that only judges know what the law is, is one thing. When Coke addressed the King, the issue

---

[61] Screws v. United States, 325 U.S. 91, 106-07, 113 (1945) (question of intent not submitted to jury with proper instructions; noted *sua sponte* and new trial ordered because error was fundamental: "Even those guilty of the most heinous offenses are entitled to a fair trial"); Sheppard Fed. Credit Union v. Palmer, 408 F.2d 1369 (5th Cir. 1969); O'Brien v. Willys Motors, Inc., 385 F.2d 163 (6th Cir. 1967) (error in placing burden).

[62] Jury instructions "couched in such lawyerly cant as 'prima facie case' and 'shifting the burden of proof,' would only . . . confuse [ ] the jury" and are properly refused by the court. Hagelthorn v. Kennecott Corp., 710 F.2d 76, 85 (2nd Cir. 1983). An instruction ought to be tailored to the jurors' common sense and give them adequate guidance. *Id.* at 85-86. *See also* Rangel v. Badolato, 133 Cal. App. 2d 254, 284 P.2d 138 (1955); Wekman v. Howard Zink Corp., 97 Cal. App. 2d 418, 428-31, 218 P.2d 43 (1950) (concurring opinion).

[63] For arguments based on the fact that, for example, even nonlawyer Presidents are sworn to uphold the law and must then have a duty and ability to interpret the law, see P. BREST, PROCESS OF CONSTITUTIONAL DECISIONMAKING 15-44 (1975); Brest, *The Conscientious Legislator's Guide to Constitutional Interpretation*, 27 STAN. L. REV. 585 (1975). On the right and duty of citizens to interpret the Constitution, see Levinson, *supra* note 10, at 1074 n.12, 1101-04. The role the people play as the source of law *may* be uniquely American on the northern part of this continent in the most ultimate form of that role. We long have thought of ourselves as being the source of our Constitution and the powers of our government. U.S. CONST. preamble ("We the People . . . do ordain and establish this Constitution . . . ."); McCulloch v. Maryland, 17 U.S. (4 Wheat.) 316 (1819) (Marshall, C.J.) (the people, not the states, adopted the Constitution and created the federal government). *See also* U.S. CONST. art. V (allowing for amendment to the Constitution by constitutional conventions). Compare Canada, Constitution Act 1982, Part V (allowing for amendments only by resolutions of the Senate and House of Commons and of two-thirds of the provincial legislatures having at least fifty percent of the population, etc. and providing certain matters — e.g. the French/English requirement and composition of Supreme Court of Canada — may be amended only by unanimous agreement of Senate, House of Commons, and all provincial legislatures).

was an institutional conflict, a dispute about balance of power.[64] For the judiciary to say this to a man in the docket or to a woman sued in tort is quite another. When a court officer told Penn that Penn could not understand the common law because he had not spent a lifetime studying law,[65] the heart of the court's message was an "expert's only" message, a message that only lawyers know the law and only lawyers speak the law. Coke may have intended that same message; but if he did, he was no less misguided and false-speaking than was the court officer who addressed Penn. For the law is ours, yours, theirs and mine, whatever our station in life and whatever our training. This principle has been a formal part of our Anglo-American legal tradition since at least 1215 A.D., when our noble ancestors met King John under the trees at Runnymede, and was renewed in 1791, when the fifth, sixth, and seventh amendments became part of our Constitution and renewed again with the passage of the fourteenth amendment.

The bald contention that only lawyers speak the law, or that the law is in a language only lawyers can speak, is false — patently, historically, legally, and dangerously false. There is no question of whether legal language can be reduced to English because the law already is in English.

Is there, then, *no* truth in some form of the "expert's only" thesis? The answer is, there is some truth. There is something distinctive about how lawyers speak, although this feature is not distinctive to only legal language; and there is something distinctive about the meanings of some

---

[64] It was a dispute about whether common law courts were interfering with ecclesiastic courts. James inclined to side with the archbishop and claimed the right to decide to which court cases should go.

> Then (this is Coke's account) the king said that he thought the law was founded upon reason, and that he and others had reason as well as the judges. To which it was answered by me that true it was that God had allowed His Majesty excellent science and great endowments of nature; but His Majesty was not learned in the law of his realm of England and causes which concern the life or inheritance or goods or fortunes of his subjects; they are not to be decided by natural reason, but by the artificial reason and judgment of law, which law is an art which requires long study and experience before that a man can attain to the cognizance of it; and that the law was the golden met-wand and measure to try the causes of the subjects, and which protected His Majesty in safety and peace. With which the king was greatly offended, and said that then he should be under the law, which was treason to affirm, as he said. To which I said that Bracton saith *quod Rex non debet esse sub homine set sub deo et lege.*

F. MAITLAND, THE CONSTITUTIONAL HISTORY OF ENGLAND 268-69 (1913) (citing Coke, *Reports*, XII, 65).

[65] William Penn and William Mead were indicted for causing a tumultuous assembly. Penn demanded to know upon what ground they were indicted and the Recorder, a court official, replied "Upon the common-law."

> *Penn.* Where is that common-law?
>
> *Rec.* You must not think that I am able to run up so many years, and over so many adjudged cases, which we call common-law, to answer your curiosity.
>
> *Penn.* . . . if it be common, it should not be so hard to produce.
>
> * * *
>
> *Rec.* You are an impertinent fellow, will you teach the court what law is? It is Lex non scripta, that which many have studied 30 or 40 years to know, and would you have me to tell you in a moment?

Trial of Penn, 6 HOW. ST. TRIALS 951, 958-59 (1670) (report written by Penn and Mead).

"legal" words although this distinctive feature falls short of turning the language of the law into a technical language that only lawyers speak and falls short of being unique to legal language.

### *C. Speaking Carefully and Speaking Technically*

Lawyers who speak carefully draw distinctions between "verdict" and "judgment," "accused" and "defendant," "plaintiff" and "libelant," "summons" and "subpoena in chancery." In this, lawyers do not essentially differ from painters who distinguish between "China black" and "lampblack," or from stockmen who chuckle at hearing a steer called a "cow," or from kennelwomen who do not use the word "dog" to describe a puppy even if the puppy is a male. In each of these latter cases the speakers mark a preference for one of several ordinary English meanings of a word. Independent of whether "accused" and "defendant" are ordinary English words or are technical legal words of a different order, lawyers also are marking a preference among ranges of meanings when they call persons sued civilly "defendants" but persons sued criminally "accuseds."

This preference-among-meanings phenomenon is a function of a more narrowly focused interest than usually shows up in ordinary conversation, and it sometimes inhibits ordinary conversation. Speaking with a colorist, whether a painter or a paint seller, about color, for example, can be a painful experience because the colorist can divide and redivide blues from blues and reds from reds, with words for each. Not everyone knows the variety of words for individual colors, and some people simply cannot *visually* distinguish between certain shades of red-orange and red. Constant reminders from a colorist to a neophyte that the name of this blue is "Persian turquoise" but the name of that one is "American turquoise," especially when a number of other words for other shades of blue have cropped up in the conversation, eventually leads one of the conversationalists to pique or to despair. This especially is true when the neophyte merely wanted to buy some paint for the den — she is not always interested in noticing nice distinctions between very near shades of turquoise, let alone between the words for these shades. (Even colorists speaking among themselves find using "this" and "that," together with numbered paint chips, easier and more accurate than using names for the colors.)

Conversations between lawyers and laypersons are subject to the same difficulties, for the same reasons, as those between the colorist and the neophyte. In neither kind of conversation need anyone be speaking a technical language and in each, usually, the conversationalists strike some balance about how fine-tuned they will make their use of "plaintiff" or "turquoise," and so on. The question here may be only how much or how little jargon or "trade talk" the conversationalists can endure. The potential jargon level of the average lawyer's conversations qua lawyer, however, is not what makes talking to lawyers painful for ordinary desultory conversationalists.

The painfulness of talking with lawyers rests on something else. Even lawyers who considerately eschew legal terms in speaking with laypersons make those persons uneasy because (good) lawyers speak carefully, listen well, and ask questions. Careful speakers say what they mean and mean what they say. They are aware of their speech and of the speech of others. They know, for example, the difference between what a person knows and what she merely believes, and they recognize when a person implies knowledge in her speech and how to probe linguistically to determine whether she intends to claim knowledge or merely is being careless or colloquial in her speech in expressing belief. Careful speakers similarly hear the difference between "Only rollerskaters may use these lanes" and "Rollerskaters may use only these lanes," and they are apt to query the speaker to discover whether the speaker means what she says and says what she means — or, indeed what she means if she says, "Rollerskaters may only use these lanes."

The painfulness of talking to lawyers rests on their being careful speakers in this say-mean/mean-say sense and on their being apt and able to be careful speakers at all times in all conversations with all persons about all subjects. This is not something unique to lawyers. Any moderately educated speaker of ordinary English (or German or Swahili) can be a say-mean/mean-say careful speaker. Nor are only lawyers systematically trained to be such careful speakers or regularly and pervasively inclined to be such careful speakers. Philosophers, perhaps particularly those who work in the contemporary analytic tradition, similarly are systematically trained to be, and are inclined pervasively to be, careful say-mean/mean-say speakers. There are, of course, a great many more lawyers than there are philosophers in our society, and few philosophically trained people become lawyers. Perhaps this accounts for our particularly noticing lawyers' speech abilities and proclivities. If we are to make any headway in analyzing the "language of the law," however, we need to remember not to take a provincial view of the (good) lawyer's mastery of the tools readily at hand to any thoughtful and careful person through careful uses of an ordinary language. Some bricklayers are more careful speakers of English than are some lawyers, who consequently are poor lawyers.

Sometimes, bricklayers, lawyers, and the rest of us make technical uses of language. Our speaking technically in this sense makes us particular instances of careful speakers. A technical use of language is the issue central to, for example, *Frigaliment Importing Co. v. B.N.S. International Sales Corp.*[66] An American firm had ordered chickens from a Swiss firm. Although the communications between the firms were in German, there was no dispute about whether the key word "*Hunner*" translated to "chicken." The only dispute was about whether in the context of these communications, "chicken" meant only young chickens suitable for broiling or frying or also included older chickens suitable only for stewing. Certainly, the ordinary English word "chicken" (like the ordinary German word "*Hunner*") has a generic meaning that includes all the meanings the two parties in *Frigaliment* ascribed to the word. Among the ordinary

[66] 190 F. Supp. 116 (S.D.N.Y. 1960).

English meanings of "chicken" are the broad generic meaning "a domestic fowl" and the narrower particular-instance meaning "a domestic fowl of less than one year old." Only the latter chickens are suitable for broiling or frying.

The problem in *Frigaliment* thus was whether, among these many ordinary language meanings, the trade usage was sufficiently standard to distinguish broilers and fryers from stewers, i.e., to distinguish young chickens from old chickens. If it was, then "chicken" was a term for which there was a technical *use* among persons in the poultry trade. But "chicken" would not itself be a technical *term*[67] even among members of the poultry trade. In the trade "chicken" would be an ordinary English word with an ordinary English meaning but with a technical *use*, i.e., with a settled convention for its use by poultry people in that they had a settled preference for one among many ordinary English meanings of the word. Two physicists may engage in an argument over unified field theory, on the other hand, using the technical language of physics as well as making technical uses of language. One of the interesting features of such a discussion among physicists, speaking as physicists, is that their interesting technical terms are theoretical terms, i.e., are from the general and special theories of relativity, the theory of gravitational fields, and so on as I shall explain later. Yet the *most* interesting feature of physicists' talk as physicists is that, as I also explain later, overwhelmingly, what they say is in ordinary English or ordinary French, etc.[68]

Sometimes, perhaps not very often, a word starts out life as a technical word, itself suggested through associations with ordinary words; but speakers get careless in using the word until it no longer is a technical word. That is, in speakers' failing to make technical distinctions in speaking, the word loses its usefulness as a technical word, thereby losing its status. This appears to have happened to "neurosis." Freud and others took to using "neurosis" because of its associations (in German, French, and English by way of Greek) with "nerve" and "nervous." They used it to describe a particular psychological condition. Trouble for the technicality of the word came, however, when ordinary language speakers went around calling every minor eccentricity or emotional problem a "neurosis" and referring to other people as "neurotic" without paying attention to distinctions theoretical and clinical psychiatrists and psychologists would make. Worse yet, psychiatrists and psychologists began using the word in contexts that did not fit the original context in which the pioneers in the field introduced the term. A few years ago, professional associations of psychiatry and psychology abandoned "neurosis" as being no longer

---

[67] Whether "chicken" is a technical term in the poultry trade, or merely is an ordinary English word with a technical use in the poultry trade, turns on whether the term has one or more relational properties I describe in the next section. I am content here simply to say flatly that "chicken" has a technical use, but is not a technical term in the poultry trade, and make the case during the rest of the article.

[68] C. CATON, *supra* note 26, at vii-viii. The anchor for all my views is his point in the text to which this note attaches.

technically useful.[69] Today it is a word of ordinary English for which there are no technical uses, and it also no longer is a technical term.

Learning to make technical uses of words — whether the words are of an ordinary language or of a technical language — is crucial to learning to speak as do members of the trade, players of the game, professionals in the field, or masters of the discipline. And making technical uses of words needs to be distinguished from speaking carefully in some of the say-mean/mean-say senses. There is, for example, no "technical use" of "only," but a speaker who says what she means and means what she says does not throw that word just anywhere into a sentence. Similarly, I do not say I will call a friend if I intend to write; and I do not say I will write a letter if I intend to write a note; nor do I ask to borrow a little sugar and then take a pound. Yet, if I do say and then do these things, we are entitled to say that, technically, I did not mean what I said or say what I meant. That is, sometimes "technical" and, especially, "technically" mean the same as "exact" or "exactly"; and the contextual standards for exactness sometimes vary with the circumstances. If I have no intention or ability to repay, I may ask to "borrow" a stamp from a friend, because our social and linguistic conventions allow this, but I better ask to "have" a stamp of a stranger.

When lawyers correct the speech of their nonlawyer friends by saying, "You mean 'manslaughter,' not 'murder' " or correct the speech of law students by saying, "You mean 'justifiable homicide,' not 'excusable homicide,' " the lawyers are not necessarily using technical terms or teaching others to use technical terms. They are, however, trying to teach word usages that go with distinctions in meaning, and sometimes the distinctions are technical in the sense that they involve niceties of use. To most of us, a dog is a dog; to a kennelwoman, a dog is an adult male of that species. Similarly, lawyers distinguish between "contracts supported by consideration" and "contracts supported by a consideration-substitute." Making technical uses of these legal phrases, however, need be nothing more technical than the kennelwoman's "dog."

## II. Three Views of Technical Language

### A. Hart's Thesis

In his Oxford Inaugural Lecture of 1953,[70] H.L.A. Hart argues that legal theorists have gone awry because they have neglected four distinctive characteristics of legal language and have been misled by the apparent similarity of "What is a corporation" to "What is a dog."[71] They

---

[69] *See, e.g.*, Diagnostic & Statistical Manual of Mental disorders 9 (1980) (DSM-III) ("At the present time . . . there is no consensus . . . as to how to define 'neurosis.' ").

[70] Hart, *Definition and Theory in Jurisprudence*, 70 Law Q. Rev. 37 (1954) [hereinafter Hart, *Definition*].

[71] *Id.* at 39-41.

therefore have failed to see that legal language is *sui generis*, is unique unto itself.

When someone asks, "What is a dog?" we can answer by pointing to a dog or by giving a verbal definition by noting its genus and its differentiating features.[72] But these modes of definition are inappropriate to the crucial words of legal language, Hart argues, because there are no ordinary factual counterparts to these words.[73] That is, questions about the meanings of legal words cannot be answered in the ways that we can answer questions about the meanings of ordinary English words because, although we can point to a dog, we cannot point to a right or a duty or a corporation; therefore, we cannot *define* the *words* "right," "duty," or "corporation."[74] Rather, he says we must "elucidate" the sentences "She has a right to be paid by him" or "He has a duty to pay her" or "Smith & Co., Ltd. has a contract with you."[75] These elucidations will show that "the use of these sentences silently assumes . . . the existence of a legal system . . . [b]ut . . . do[es] not *state* that it exists."[76] Legal language thus presupposes, but does not assert, the existence of a legal system, a system of rules of law; and this presupposition is one of "four distinctive features"[77] or "distinctive characteristics of legal language."[78] The second distinctive feature is related to the first and concerns the use of legal terms. Those uses presuppose the related rules of law that give the words contextual meaning, and the statements we make using those legal terms are conclusions of law we derive from applying the presupposed rules of law to the unstated but presupposed facts.[79] To explain to Jones the meaning of "Smith & Co., Ltd. owes $10 to White," we have to introduce Jones to the English law of limited companies.[80]

Hart does not term these "elucidations" "contextual definitions," but the notion aptly captures his central thesis that the legal terms have meaning only in the context of the existence of a legal system and only through particular rules of law. Putting his thesis in terms of "contextual definitions" also allows us to fit Hart's work into the tradition of Jeremy Bentham, Bertrand Russell, and P.F. Strawson in such a way that we can see exactly what, and how much, is at stake in his treatment of legal language as being *sui generis*.

In 1905 Russell argued that we cannot define "the present King of France" in terms of some object of denotation because there is no present King of France, yet "The present King of France is bald" is not meaningless.[81] Russell secured meaning for "the present King of France" by

[72] *Id.* at 46.

[73] *Id.* at 38, 42, 45-47.

[74] *Id.*

[75] *Id.* at 47-49.

[76] *Id.* at 42 (emphasis in original).

[77] *Id.* at 42.

[78] *Id.* at 41, 45.

[79] *Id.* at 42-43.

[80] *Id.* at 50, 52-53. Hart imagines Jones is a "lawyer innocent of theories of corporate personality because he was educated in a legal Arcadia where rights and duties were ascribed only to individuals and all legal theory is banned." *Id.* at 50.

[81] Russell, *On Denoting* (1905), in B. RUSSELL, LOGIC AND KNOWLEDGE 39 (R. Marsh ed. 1956).

laying down the meaning of "The present King of France is bald" as a whole, i.e., by specifying the conditions under which the proposition is true or false. Those conditions are that (1) there is at least one present King of France, (2) there is at most one present King of France, and (3) there is nothing that is presently King of France and not bald. Because (1) is false, the whole proposition is false and, having a truth value, is not meaningless. Russell also applied this mode of definition — or analysis — to "King" and "France" until these, too, disappear and what is left are words and phrases that denote things in the world or that are such logical particles as "and." The "things" turn out to be sense data, whose names are "this" and "that," although Russell is willing to allow "this table" to denote this table as long as we understand that the table is a fiction, i.e., a constructed entity.[82]

Hart rejects the fictional approach to the issue of what corresponds to "company" or "right," and he rejects the idea that "company" can be defined mediately through existing things.[83] He therefore gives an account of the meaning of "company" more closely aligned with Strawson's 1950 account of "The present King of France is bald." Strawson suggested that Russell had confused referring to an entity with asserting the existence of an entity. According to Strawson, a speaker who says, "The present King of France is bald" refers to the present King of France and presupposes there is such an entity; i.e., the speaker assumes, but does not assert or state, that there is a present King of France. Because this presupposition is false, the purported reference fails; the statement the speaker makes, therefore, is neither true nor false, although Strawson says the sentence the speaker uses to make this statement is meaningful.[84] The similarity between Hart's "elucidations" to Strawson's notion of presuppositions then is apparent in the way Hart sets out the elucidation of "a legal right."[85]

The Russell-Strawson enterprise is a *meaning* enterprise and one that struggles with epistemological and metaphysical questions. Hart's strug-

---

[82] *See generally* B. RUSSELL, OUR KNOWLEDGE OF THE EXTERNAL WORLD (1960); B. RUSSELL, THE PROBLEMS OF PHILOSOPHY (1968).

[83] Hart, *Definition*, *supra* note 70, at 39, 45, 57-58. His primary target is Bentham, however, not Russell.

[84] *See generally* Strawson, *On Referring*, 59 MIND 320 (1950), *reprinted in* C. CATON, *supra* note 26, at 162.

[85] Hart, *Definition*, *supra* note 70, at 50, 52-53.

> I would, therefore, tender the following as an elucidation of the expression "a legal right": (1) A statement of the form "X has a right" is true if the following conditions are satisfied:
>
> (a) There is in existence a legal system.
>
> (b) Under a rule or rules of the system some other person Y is, in the events which have happened, obliged to do or abstain from some action.
>
> (c) This obligation is made by law dependent on the choice either of X or some other person authorized to act on his behalf so that either Y is bound to do or abstain from some action only if X (or some authorized person) so chooses or alternatively only until X (or such person) chooses otherwise.
>
> (2) A statement of the form "X has a right" is used to draw a conclusion of law in a particular case which falls under such rules.

gle is with the nature of the law, but it also is a *meaning* enterprise. Having identified two kinds of presuppositional relations for legal statements, he then sets out the other two distinguishing features of legal language. Hart's third distinguishing general characteristic of legal language is that sentences of legal language differ in meaning, import or effect (or all three) depending upon who utters them, where, and when.[86] For example, a judge's saying from the bench, "Smith has a right to be paid $10 by White" has the effect of making White legally liable to Smith. But when a bus driver or a judge who is not on the bench utters the same sentence, there is no legal effect at all although the bus driver and the nonsitting judge are expressing conclusions of law.[87] Actually, Hart's view is even more complicated than this; for, said by a judge in a case, "Smith has a right" is not meaningless, although it is neither true nor false, because it is "official, authoritative and . . . final." What the judge says may be "wrong," but if so its wrongness does not lie in falsity and does not arise in the same sort of way that the wrongness of "This ball is red" arises when said of a blue ball. Moreover, whereas any of us may correct the person who says "This ball is red" of a blue ball, none of us may correct the judge who says wrongly "Smith has a right." There is no remedy when the umpire wrongly calls a player out.[88]

What accounts for part of the complexity of Hart's view here is a subrosa speech act analysis, and particularly a performative-verb analysis of the sort for which J.L. Austin is famous.[89] Hart's view also appears to be an early version of Paul Grice's extreme view that a difference in speech acts of the order of the difference between the umpire's saying "You're out!" and a Red Sox fan's saying "You're out!" is sufficient to yield a difference in meaning in the two cases.[90] This view in *Definitions* is intermediate between the view Hart developed in his 1948 essay[91] and in his 1968 book,[92] where he repudiated a totally ascriptional view of legal language, and I therefore will omit further reference to this aspect of Hart's view.

The fourth characteristic of legal language rests on a distinctive feature of a universal function of any rules, which function is to apply to more than one fact. Rules are general. Empirical rules are generalizations across different facts; for example, the rule of the effects of gravity on unsupported bodies is a generalization across the facts of falling leaves, falling feathers, and falling stones.[93] Hence, a rule conversely can apply

---

[86] *Id.* at 43-44.

[87] *Id.*

[88] *Id.*

[89] See § II. B., *infra.*

[90] See generally Grice, *supra* note 15.

[91] Hart, *The Ascription of Responsibility and Rights*, *reprinted in* A. FLEW, LOGIC AND LANGUAGE 151 (First and Second Series) (A. Flew ed. 1965).

[92] H.L.A. HART, PUNISHMENT AND RESPONSIBILITY (1968).

[93] The popular version of the generality of laws of science is that they are inductions from facts or data; in truth, they usually are deductions from theories which explain the data, although the data may "prompt" the theories. Experiments of the last two years may eventually show to everyone's satisfaction that there is a fifth force in nature that can affect the rate of fall of objects of different composition.

to different facts to yield the same conclusion, for example, that different objects, irrespective of their weights, each will take so many seconds to fall so many feet in a vacuum. Similarly, the same legal rule may make Smith liable in negligence for leaving roller skates on the path and Jones liable in negligence for leaving tennis balls on the sidewalk.[94] For rules of law, however, Hart claims that the variation among fact patterns is an essential element in the application of legal rules[95] because the same pattern of facts can be unified under different rules to yield the same *or* different legal conclusions.[96]

Hart begins by noting that any rule may "attach identical consequences to . . . very different facts."[97] The same consequence flows in baseball after the batter has three strikes or fails to reach first base before the ball gets there, etc. (Hart's example is in terms of cricket.) In each case the batter is out, and "no one of these different ways of being out is more essentially what the word means than the others, and . . . there need be nothing common to all these ways of being out than their falling under the same rule . . . ."[98] But one of "the essential elements of the language of legal corporations" shows that separate rules of law may apply to the facts to yield conclusions about separate individual rights and duties of "the lives of the men that overlap but do not coincide," thus treating the men as "a collection of individuals . . . but their actions may fall under rules of a different kind . . . [so that] we may speak in appropriately unified ways . . . using a terminology . . . of corporate law which will show that it is *this* sort of rule we are applying to the facts."[99]

This phenomenon of multiplicity-of-applicable-rules, he says, is apt to lead us to look for a way to give unity to the facts and thus lead us to look for a continuing, identifiable, definable thing to anchor the various facts.[100] For example, if Smith and Jones break White's finger, we can subsume this fact under a rule of law that makes Smith and Jones individually liable to White — or jointly and individually liable. But we also could subsume the same action of breaking White's finger under a different rule of law that makes Smith & Co., Ltd. liable to White. The possibility of these two different subsumptions — one to natural persons and one to a corporation — may lead us to look for a way of distinguishing them by saying that the facts differ and that in the latter case there is a "fact" that Smith & Co., Ltd. broke White's finger, as if there were something to correspond to "Smith & Co., Ltd." of the same sort, and in the same way as, Smith corresponds to "Smith." We are prompted to this view, Hart contends, because of the similarity of "Smith & Co., Ltd. is liable to White" to "Smith is liable to White."

Because there is nothing corresponding to "Smith & Co., Ltd." and because "Smith & Co., Ltd." has meaning only insofar as the law of

---

[94] Hart, *Definition*, *supra* note 70, at 44. The particular extrapolations and examples I give here are mine, not Hart's.

[95] *Id.* at 45.

[96] *See id.* at 44-45.

[97] *Id.* at 44.

[98] *Id.*

[99] *Id.* at 45.

[100] *Id.* at 45.

English limited companies gives it meaning, Hart says, we must account for the similarity between "Smith is liable to White" and "Smith & Co., Ltd. is liable to White" by saying that different rules apply to the same facts, instead of saying the facts differ. To account for the similarity between the two liability judgments by saying the facts differ is to make the conceptual mistake of treating Smith & Co., Ltd. as if it would be a something-in-the-world even if there were no English law of limited companies.

The gist of Hart's view then is the following. Legal language is distinctive because it presupposes the existence of a legal system and presupposes particular rules of law, against the background of which legal language obtains its meaningfulness and particular meaning, and because of the distinctive feature of rules of law as rules. There are such things as dogs apart from law, apart from society, and apart from all language (including English). "A rose by any other name would smell as sweet." The word "dog" is part of ordinary English, and its meaning can be given verbally by naming the genus and differentiating features or by pointing to one and saying, "That is a dog." In contrast, because there is nothing to which we can point and say, "That is a company," there are no such things as companies apart from the law. The word "company" is a legal word (a law word) whose meaning is given only by and accessible only through the law. In using "company" we "speak the law" and know what we are saying only insofar as we know the law of companies.

There are a number of points on which to criticize what Hart says. Whether Hart seriously intends to say that only legal rules have the multiplicity-of-applicable-rules feature, i.e., that different rules can apply to the same facts, is not entirely clear. He *says* it is one of "four distinctive features" of legal language.[101] But, of course, this phenomenon is *not* distinctive. Two different laws of physics can apply to the same facts and each yield true conclusions. For example, the different rules of Newtonian mechanics and Einsteinian physics can apply to the same facts to yield, within certain limits, the same conclusions or to yield, within other limits, different conclusions (although certainly, at some point, the Newtonian rule will "break down.") We simply cannot explain the differences between Newtonian results and Einsteinian results by saying the facts differ in the two cases; what differ are the rules, not the facts.

This is not to deny, of course, that in some areas of physics we do distinguish by saying the facts differ — or, better, by saying the views of the facts differ, for we do not have theory-independent ways of assessing what "the facts" are. For example, under certain measurement-rules light exhibits particle behavior, but under other rules it exhibits wave behavior, yet we cannot say that light *is* made of particles (or is waves) independent of the particle-measuring rules, etc. And under some rules, light is "wavical," i.e., these rules are neutral as to what light "is" on the particle-wave continuum. Similarly, we have a Euclidean theory of space,

[101] *Id.* at 42, 45.

which fits Newtonian physics, and a Riemannian theory of space, which fits the general theory of relativity; but we have considerable difficulty in "deciding" whether parallel lines converge in "real space."

Thus, there is a level of Hart's discussion of legal rules that is exactly correct. Different rules of law can apply to the same facts, and we err if we try to distinguish the rules by distinguishing the facts. But this feature of legal rules is not distinctive of legal rules. It is not unique to them. Nor is this the only one of the four distinctive features he identifies for legal language that fails to be distinctive in any fundamental sense. As to his point about the presupposition of legal statements, we could point out that any use of language, short of "The universe exists," presupposes, but does not assert or state, that a universe exists. Similarly, any use of language presupposes there is a point to using language. Speech, after all, is other-regarding. Why stop, then, with the presupposition that a legal system exists? Why not add as a presupposition that the universe exists or that there are other persons in the world? Even supposing Hart could give sound reasons for limiting the most general presupposition of legal language to the presuppositions that a legal system exists, wherein lies the distinctiveness of legal language if biological language or baseball language, for example, presupposes a taxonomic system exists or that baseball exists? What is special about legal language, if the same kind of point can be made about moral language, or political language, or scientific language, or metaphysical language, or even, *mirabile dictu*, ordinary language?

What is important in Hart's view, is that he is attempting to tell us how we can use the word "company" or the word "right" without there being any *thing* that corresponds to these terms. But this project itself puts him in deeper trouble. His answer is that the meanings of these words are given by the system of the rules of law, that this system carves out a category of "objects," albeit not in any ordinary sense of "object," for there is not now and never will be anything to which we can *point*. Rather, the rules of law about limited companies or the rules of law about rights not only give the meanings of these words, but also denominate — constitute — what counts as a company or a right. They lay down the criteria for something's counting as a company by laying down, in a sense, the proper modes of speaking; in so laying down the criteria, they effectuate a categorization. Further, he says, when we use these legal words whose meanings are constituted under rules of law in connection with other words that do have corresponding objects (either directly or mediately), the other words shift in meaning and become legal words, too. Thus, the word " 'will' shifts its meaning when we use it of a company . . . ."[102] We then do not mean the same things by these words when we say "Lee Iacocca wills himself to greatness" and "The Chrysler Corporation wills itself to greatness," or when we say "Iacocca can pay a bill" and "The Chrysler Corporation can pay a bill." On Hart's view, therefore, all of legal language ultimately would be *sui generis* because even such

[102] *Id.* at 59.

apparently ordinary English words as "can" take on a special legal meaning when we use them with words such as "company" that have meaning only in and through rules of law.

Indeed, he does qualify his view here, by saying that these words — e.g., "will" and "can" — retain their ordinary connections to the facts, but also then carry the legal connections: "[A]ny ordinary words or phrases when conjoined with the names of corporations take on a special legal use, for the words are correlated with the facts, *not solely by the rules of ordinary English* but also by the rules of *English law* . . . ."; but he really cannot carry this qualification out fully as is evident in the full context of this quote.[103]

Hart need not have gone to these extremes with respect to the meanings of ordinary language words. What he needs is a method of anchoring statements involving certain fundamental legal terms to the world, by securing meanings for these terms without invention, because these terms are not meaningless yet, on his view, do not directly or mediately correspond to entities in the world. Having secured meanings for these fundamental legal terms, he need not have secured *legal* meanings for terms of ordinary language, which already have meanings. He need not have given "can" or "will" legal meaning,[104] any more than he would need to give "red" or "round," "dollars" or "English pounds" legal meaning. Further, if he insists on making "will" or "can" into a legal word when used in connection with "company," he cannot explain why he does not similarly need to give a legal meaning for "and" or "&" when used in "Smith & Co., Ltd." Hart's legal language ends up being completely a language unto itself, and that is a mistake. What stood in need of elucidation was not everything, but only that which played a central role in legal talk but for which there was not something to which we could point and say "That is a so-and-so."

Charles Caton fares better than Hart in defining technical languages, among which he also numbers the language of the law. In particular, his views expressly reject the possibility that technical language users use "and" or "hardly" any differently than ordinary language users do.

---

[103] *Id.* at 58 (emphasis added).

> It was once said that a corporation has no real will but a fictitious will imputed by law, and that since such a will so imputed could effect only lawful ends, we cannot, if we are logically consistent, say that it could commit a crime, or even perhaps a tort. Of course this use of the fiction theory does conjure up an allegorical picture. . . . But the picture is more misleading than even an allegory should be, because it conceals the fact that the word "will" shifts its meaning when we use it of a company: the sense in which a company has a will is not that it wants to do legal or illegal actions but that certain expressions used to describe voluntary actions of individuals may be used of it under conditions prescribed by legal rules. And from the bare fact that the law does prescribe such conditions for a wide range of expressions (which is all that imputing a will to a company can mean) it cannot be deduced that these conditions do not include the commission of a criminal or tortious act. *Analogy* with a living person *and shift of meaning are therefore of the essence of* the mode of *legal statement* which refers to corporate bodies. But these are just what they are. Analogy is not identity . . . and shift in meaning is not fiction . . . .

*Id.* at 58-59 (emphasis added).

[104] Hart, *Definition*, *supra* note 70, at 56-58 ("can"), 58-59 ("will").

### B. Caton's view

Almost twenty-five years ago, Charles Caton wrote a five-page sketch of technical language,[105] and no one appears to have done more or better in the intervening years. The point Caton emphasizes is that "technical language is always an adjunct of ordinary language," whether ordinary English, ordinary French, or ordinary Swahili.[106] Technical languages have the same syntax as ordinary language, and speech acts performable in ordinary discourse are performable in technical contexts; for example, "requests, assertions, questions, explanations of what one was referring to, etc."[107] Further, clarifications are made in the same ways in technical languages as they are in ordinary languages, and "the presuppositions, implications, suggestions, etc. of technical language seem to be of the same sorts and achieved by the same means as in ordinary language . . . ."[108] The substantial part of these latter similarities is that words and phrases such as "the," "a," "is," "all," "two," "at least," "and," "or," "if . . . then," "hardly," "very," and so on, "occur in technical contexts in the same senses [as] in everyday contexts."[109]

There may be a very few speech acts, he says, that are performable in technical languages that are not ordinary speech acts, "perhaps, things like deposing, sentencing a prisoner, and saying 'J'adoube.' "[110] But a technical language may be "defined only by reference to some particular discipline or occupation or activity among the practitioners of which it is current . . . [and] consists largely, if not entirely, of vocabulary items . . . ."[111] He then describes these vocabulary items and gives an example for each type, "i.e., words and phrases not part of the related ordinary language at all (e.g., 'meson') or not having in ordinary language the senses given them in the discipline in question (e.g., 'ring' in algebra)."[112]

We learn technical languages "against the background of ordinary language" because the technical languages are adjuncts to the ordinary language.[113] Some technical languages we learn as we grow up, and others we learn by study, because we come to know, develop interest in, and do things "that not everyone or even most people do . . . and thus [acquire]

---

[105] C. CATON, *supra* note 26, at v., vi-xi.

[106] *Id.* at viii.

[107] *Id.*

[108] *Id.* To say that the syntax of technical and ordinary languages is the same and that the inferences, suggestions, etc. of the former are of the same sorts and by the same means as the latter is not necessarily to deny that there may be some transformational differences. For example, "red roses" and "roses that are red" in English are transformational equivalents but "punitive damages" and "damages that are punitive" are not fully transformational equivalents in legal language in every context of use. Morrison, *Getting A Rule Right and Writing a Wrong Rule: The IRS Demands a Return on all Punitive Damages*, 17 CONN. L. REV. 39, 41-42 (1984).

[109] C. CATON, *supra* note 26, at vii (examples from original).

[110] *Id.*

[111] *Id.* at vii. I will refer to this as "the practitioners' definition."

[112] *Id.*

[113] *Id.*

the technical language that accompanies knowing, learning about, and doing these things."[114] Allowing for differences in intelligence and interest, however, technical languages are "as available . . . as ordinary language."[115]

Caton's comments and examples make plain that he counts the languages of physics, mathematics, farming, chess, and the law as among technical languages; and three of the several examples he gives of technical terms are "meson" from physics, "ring" from algebra, and "J'adoube" of chess.[116]

As is true of dispositional definitions, defining technical languages by cross-reference to how members of a discipline, occupation, or activity talk with one another raises some questions. Certainly, if someone who speaks a technical language uses that language in speaking with someone who does not know the language, the conversation may never get off the ground. The other may not understand at all or may misunderstand and so on. But there are other problems. What shall we say, for example, about the phenomenon of a nonparticipant's correctly using a technical term, or a participant's using an expression from the technical language in a conversation with someone who does not know the technical language but who does *not* misunderstand?

For example, I am neither in the position to dub knights nor do I have any interest in or know how to play chess; but I can and do say "J'adoube" in speaking to a colleague as I adjust his or her hood just before the graduation procession. Moreover, as a matter of my own linguistic history, I am none too sure I knew "J'adoube" had royal or chess uses until well after I had taken to using it. Someone may have told me about the chess use, but the first time I remember hearing the expression was one day in Paris as a Frenchman removed a leaf from my hair as we stood on the corner while he gave me a miniature French lesson in "right," "left," and

---

[114] *Id.* at ix. Caton clearly is right about this. For example, in these days of mass media, everyone has an opportunity to learn bits of biology and its language simply by reading the newspaper. An Associated Press wire service story in 1984 taught a biology lesson (that the snail darter is a member of the perch family), a linguistic lesson (that *Percina tanasis* is "snail darter" "in English"), gave legal information (that the snail darter had been moved from the endangered species list to the threatened species list), recounted an item of history (that construction of a dam had been halted for two years because it threatened the existence of the tiny fish) and, in the headline, made a biological pun on a legal matter: "Snail darter taken off special perch." St. Paul Pioneer Press/Dispatch, Saturday, July 7, 1984, 10A col. 1. Consider also, then, the phenomena of Lewis Thomas and Stephen Jay Gould, who are prize winning, best selling writers. L. THOMAS, THE LIVES OF A CELL (1974); S.J. GOULD, THE PANDA'S THUMB (1980). Only adults with mental blinders today can keep from learning some of the facts and theories of the vast and exploding horizons of knowledge in the sciences and the arts. And only they can avoid having some familiarity with a variety of the languages of these areas of expertise. On the other hand, only those persons who have studied these areas of expertise have become fully conversant in the related languages. These are the sorts of points Caton has in mind.

[115] C. CATON, *supra* note 26, at viii.

[116] Caton may have intended "J'adoube" in its knight-dubbing ceremonial use, but the rest of his discussions suggest he had the chess use in mind.

"two blocks" so that I could find my way to a museum. I could not speak or read French at the time, and he did not speak English. Did I learn French, or did I learn a technical expression of the language of chess that he borrowed for the nonchess occasion? Now that I know there is a chess use, do I borrow the technical term, or am I speaking French as I adjust a colleague's hood? If we both played chess, would that affect the nature of the expression when I use it as I adjust the hood?

Similarly, what shall we say of the following conversation between the politically conservative horseman-farmer father of a college student and the student's friend. Father: "Jim tells me you two are learning about rings and fields and learning right ideals." Jim's friend: "Well, our rings and fields are hardly the kind you could keep a horse in, sir, and we're learning about left ideals and two-sided ideals, too." In Jim's previous conversation with his father, he may have made puns on "ring," "field," and "ideal" by playing off the algebraic words; and the father now is doing that, too. Or Jim may have misdirected his father by playing off those algebraic words — he is supposed to be studying agriculture and staying away from those pinko-liberals in the math department, and now his friend has given the game away. Or possibly the father, having caught only the surface of Jim's explanation of his abstract algebra course, is making puns by playing off the ordinary English words "field" and "ideal." Is, then, his pun on "ring" a horseman's pun or an English speaker's pun? That is, which of the three — ordinary English, farmer/horseman's language, or algebraist's language — is his "ring" from and against which one does it play?

Consider some of the immense varieties of ways — noun, verb, etc., and idiom — any of us may use "ring": We say that we wear wedding rings, kiss bishops' rings, wear button earrings, remove napkin rings, count rings of trees, bemoan rings around our eyes, beware rings around the moon, open ring binders, make rings around others, sit in groups in rings, hear the ring at the door or the ringing telephone, hear a speech that does not ring true or that rings a bell or that rings with emotion; curtains ring up at theaters and down on life, we have ringing headaches and our ears ring, and we ring in the new year while shots ring out in the dark. After all this, is the farmer/horseman's "ring" or the circus performer's or dressage learner's "ringmaster" a technical word of the language of farmers or horsemen or of circuses or dressage?

Of course, these uses of "ring" and "ringmaster" do not fit either of the two descriptions Caton gives of the "vocabulary items" that make up a technical language. These are words that have a use in ordinary language, unlike the physicists's "meson"; and they are not words "not having in ordinary language the senses given them in the discipline in question." But then neither does "J'adoube" fit Caton's descriptions as far as I can see. The question then is, what wears the skirt in this description of technical languages — the definition that can be given "only by reference to some particular discipline or occupation or activity," or the two descriptions of technical terms?

If the participants' definition of technical languages is the controlling factor, then the horseman's "ring" is a technical term. That goes too far.

It allows any term that practitioners of any art use with some regularity among themselves to be a technical term. What, then, makes the mathematician's "ring" a technical term must be inextricably tied up with not only the "participants'" factor but also with its having one of the two characteristics Caton describes for technical terms. Caton suggests that what makes "ring" technical in algebra is that its ordinary use does not have the senses it has in mathematics. That *looks* right:

> Definition: A *ring* (R, *,") is a nonempty set R, together with two binary operations (compositions) * and ", such that *R* is a commutative group with respect to * and a semi-group with respect to ", and such that the right and left distributive laws of " over * hold . . . [where * is addition and " is multiplication].[117]

But, of course, it is not quite right. After all, mathematicians did not name these things "rings" for no reason, otherwise they might just as well have called them "shelves," "sofas," or "exxadexxes." Noticing this is the converse of noticing that the physicist's "meson" or "quark" is "not part of . . . ordinary" English. That is, even if we agree the mathematician's "ring" has a sense that is not part of the everyday sense of "ring" that does not mean the mathematician's "ring" is *as arbitrary* as the physicist's "quark."

There are two advantages of Caton's view over Hart's, however. First, Caton does not have to provide a technical-meaning explanation for each word physicists, farmers, and chess players use in speaking among themselves about, respectively, matters of physics, farming, or chess. This is because Caton's technical language is an adjunct of — parasitic on — ordinary language, and most of the words technical language users will use in everything they say is in ordinary English or ordinary French and so on, even when they speak the technical language of physics, farming, or chess. Hart's deepest trouble is that, under his view, technical terms affect the meaning of each other word used in connection with the technical word, and that is too large a project for his view to handle. Far from being parasitic on ordinary language, Hart's technical language is cut off from ordinary English at each turn. Whatever is intuitively correct about Hart's view with respect to how difficult technical language sentences are to comprehend for those who do not know the discipline, occupation, or activity and consequently do not know the associated language, he goes too far in spreading that comprehension-difficulty to each element of the whole sentence.

The second advantage of Caton's view over Hart's is that the former's definitions and descriptions allow us to say the languages of physics and of mathematics are technical languages, where that means again that

---

[117] W. BARNES, INTRODUCTION TO ABSTRACT ALGEBRA 77 (1963). For an a, b, and c members of *R*, then
(b * c) " a = (b " a) * (c " a), and
a " (b * c) = (a " b) * (a " c).
*Id.*

the users thereof mostly use ordinary language words but also use technical terms of one of the two types Caton describes. One of our basic intuitions about technical languages is that, however we characterize them, the languages of mathematics and of the physical sciences are technical languages. As to the languages of farming or the law or chess, we may have no intuitions; at least, we may have different views among ourselves about the technicality of these languages.

Under Hart's view, however, although the languages of the law and of chess or of baseball are technical languages, the languages of mathematics and of the physical sciences essentially are not. This is because of the way Hart's rose-is-a-rose-is-a-rose principle works in conjunction with the heart of his anti-reductionist, technical language view, namely constitutive meanings. What makes his "corporation" a technical word is that it has meaning only in and through the rules of law, which lay down the conditions under which a corporation exists and under which we correctly may use "corporation." The word "dog," on the other hand, is not such a constitutive noun; this word has meaning we can determine by pointing to a dog or by naming its genus and differentiating features. Moreover, irrespective of what we *say*, dogs exist and are what they are; but corporations and knights of chess exist only because and as we say they do. This is Hart's rose-principle. That very principle then prevents almost all of the interesting words of physics from being technical words. We can point to some of them, although we need special equipment sometimes to do so; more importantly, the other interesting words are for things that exist even if we do not, but are at least as hard to point to as corporations. For example, gravity exists and is what it is independent of us every bit as much as is true of a dog; and the same is true of the fundamental constituents of matter, which physicists call "quarks." Indeed, the only words of the languages of science that are technical in Hart's constitutive sense are the procedural words, i.e., the words for doing things in a physics or chemistry laboratory and so on.

This looks like a mistake. Whatever a technical language is, we are sure the languages of physics, chemistry, biology, etc., are such languages; and we are sure their technicality does not rest on words as marginally related to physics, etc., as procedural (i.e., doing) words are. If this is the price of explaining the technicality of the language of the law, it is too high a price because it is too deeply counter-intuitive.

In the next two sections I will be developing a third view of technical languages. That theory importantly is related to both Caton's view and Hart's view. My view rests on Caton's insight that technicality rests on a few words technical language users use while they concurrently are using words of ordinary language in the same ways any of us uses these ordinary language words. It also expands upon the definitions of these few, special words, the characterizations of which Caton began with his two descriptions of technical terms, i.e., the ones of which "meson" of physics and "ring" of algebra are examples.

I also draw on two of Hart's insights. We may give very adequate explanations of the technicality of procedural terms using his constitutive approach; and that approach will strike most people as being intellectually more satisfying for the procedural terms of the language of the law than is Caton's, although I will construct an explanation under my version of Caton's view that some of us will find sufficiently decent. The second of Hart's insights is the one we obtain by looking at his constitutive approach at an angle or without our analytic glasses, so to speak. The word "quark," for example, is a word that gets its meaning only against and through particular theories of physics. Only with reference to those theories can we use the physicist's word, and this view vaguely echoes Hart's constitutive view of the meaning of "corporation."

Once I have set out these points in detail, I will turn to the nonprocedural terms of the language of the law and investigate whether it is a technical language in the sense I have developed.

### *C. Familiar Terms and Theoretical Terms*

What makes the physicist's language a technical language? The short answer is, she speaks a technical language of physics insofar as when she is speaking as a physicist, she uses words or terms that are not familiar to those of us who have an excellent grasp of English but do not know physics. As answers go, however, this one is not yet helpful, and I need to flesh it out.

Familiar words are part of the ordinary English language, and a word is familiar when speakers of English from all stations of life use the word in much the same ways specialists do. That is, when the specialist's meaning, even if it deviates slightly from our own, is available to us because we speak English already, then the word is familiar and is not a technical term. A physicist, for example, might say a table is not solid and might confuse us for a moment because we both know a 65 lb. rock is resting on top of it. But the physicist just means the table is made up of matter that is "scattered" — "That is," she says, "the thing has holes in it." We understand that use of "not solid"; we use the phrase the same way when describing slices of Swiss cheese. Of course, *we* also talk of tables as being solid and thus talk about the phenomenon of a table's being able to bear some object without collapsing or having the object fall through the table. This may lead us to doubt the physicist's "factual" claim, until we understand she is not talking about that phenomenon in using "solid" as she does. The physicist's "solid" is just as much a part of our English language as is our "solid," although there is a difference between her use and our everyday uses. That difference is a difference of deployment or emphasis. She emphasizes the existences of spaces that we ignore or do not notice and thus counts fewer things as being solid than do we. But she does this only while she is "speaking physics"; when she buys furniture, she ignores those very same spaces. And the word "solid" is not a technical word at all, even when a physicist uses it with an emphasis that differs from ours. Words with deployment or emphasis differences are like the technical-use words that are fixed to one-among-many meanings, such as the poultry tradist's "chicken." The physicist's "not solid," then, applied to a sturdy wooden table would be a technical use of the ordinary English word "solid." The technical use is in English, however, just as the poultry tradist's technical use of "chicken" is, although this happens to be true of "solid" for a different reason than for "chicken": In English we use "solid" with different deployments; it is only superficially a one-placed predicate, and that is at bottom what accounts for our using "solid" of different things not all of which are solid in the same way. That is, our English "solid" always is comparative or always has deployment-differences built into or undergirding it. When an astrophysicist uses "solid fuel," for example, there is no special emphasis-difference from our use of "solid table" and "solid block of Swiss cheese." No wonder "solid" is not a technical term in physics. It is "in" physics, if at all, only to the extent that ordinary English words are part of the linguistic scene in physics, and its deployment-difference potentials already are built in from ordinary English.

Similarly, the word "cell" is English, is part of our ordinary language, and is a familiar word although the architect uses it to speak of part of a vaulted ceiling; the beekeeper, of a honey comb; the biologist, of a living organism; the botanist, of an anther; the chemist, of a battery; the entomologist, of an insect's wing; the policeman, of a jail; the mathematician, of a table; the monk, of a monastery; the politician, of a party; etc. The architect and the mechanic use the chemist's "cell" to talk about why the architect's car did not start this morning; the prisoner, the lawyer, and the journalist use the policeman's "cell" to talk about where the prisoner will spend the night; and we all use the biologist's "cell" to talk about the basic structural unit of plant and animal life. Further, the monk's use of "cell" may create an ambiguity. He may be speaking about a small room in his monastery, or he may be speaking of his monastery's relation to his religious house, which is not a building. In either case, the ambiguity is in English not in some technical language. One who is not an ecclesiastic can create the same ambiguity in the course of writing a romance novel. In short, the word "cell" is not a technical term even when it occurs in a technical language such as the language of biology.

In this, the biologist's "cell" significantly differs from the physicist's "quark." For, although the former's "cell" means "basic structural unit of plant and animal life" and the latter's "quark" means "fundamental constituent of matter," "cell" already is part of English whereas "quark" is not, and may never become, part of English. One, but not the sole, reason for this difference is that we can see the biologist's cells (sometimes even without the aid of a microscope), but we cannot see the physicist's quarks. Another, more important reason for this difference is that all of the varieties of meanings or uses of "cell" are undergirded by our familiar concepts of bounded spaces, whereas the meaning or use of "quark" is undergirded by sophisticated concepts of contemporary theoretical physics, a point to which I shall return. "Cell" is ordinary English, but "quark" is a technical term and, moreover, is a theoretical term. With the exception of the occasional reference to one sentence in James Joyce's *Finne-*

*gans Wake*,[118] speakers of English who use the word "quark"[119] today use a theoretical and technical term of physics.[120] Their sentences are meaningful because the words, in this order, are; and "quark" is meaningful because certain theories of physics give it meaning. The speakers may fully know the meaning of the sentences in which they and others use "quark"; if so, they know contemporary theoretical physics fully. On the other hand, the speakers may have some lesser grasp of physics and a consequently less full understanding of the meaning of "quark." In any event, speakers either attempt to use the physicist's meaning or else do not use the physicist's word, even if they utter or write a sound or symbol that appears to be the same as the physicist's "quark." *Only* with reference to the theory of physics can we test the proper use of the technical predicate ". . . is a quark."

Just because the individual words in a sentence are familiar, however, does not mean that there is not a technical language related in some way to that sentence. Thus, compare "This is a catenary curve" with "y = k cos h (x/k)" — the former is in ordinary English, but the latter is in the language of mathematics, which contains some English words such as "equals" although its symbol often is "=" and although it never occurs in the past tense, etc. The mathematician and the telephone linecrew both use "catenary" to describe the curve of the telephone line between two poles, and they utter English sentences in so doing, for example, "This catenary curve is too deep; we'd better raise the ends of the line or put the poles further apart." If there are a canary and a cat around, they may make a joke, and so on. Yet when the mathematician writes "y = k cos h (x/k)" on the blackboard or utters it in teaching, she writes or utters a sentence of mathematics, not of English. You and I will understand what she writes or says when we learn some mathematics (and vice versa). We cannot survive here on even an excellent command of English.

Further, when next she writes, "$x^2a^2$ - $y^2b^2$ = 1" on the board, she has stated another sentence of mathematics, namely of geometry. Suppose she then says, "This equation written on the board describes a hyperbola, which is a set of points in a plane whose distances to two fixed points in the plane have a constant difference. That is," she says, "a hyperbola is a curve consisting of two distinct and similar branches, formed by the intersection of a plane with a right circular cone when the plane makes a greater angle with the base than does the generator of a cone." Although each of her words, including "hyperbola," is an ordinary English word —

---

[118] J. JOYCE, FINNEGANS WAKE 383 (1939) ("Three Quarks for Muster Mark!").

[119] Compare the "non-English, non-German" "quark" of physics with the German word that sounds like "quark" and is the name of a food.

[120] Or perhaps the word is just a theoretical term. In any event, such things as answers to questions about the word do not count because then the word is being mentioned to talk about the word, not being used to talk about the fundamental constituent of matter. (For example: "The way to spell 'quark' . . . "; "The word he missed on the test was 'quark' "; "What does 'quark' mean?") Similarly, nonsense and misspeakings/mistypings do not count. (For example: "Bring me a quark of stars" or "Bring me a quark of milk.")

i.e., is a familiar word — and although the grammatical form of what she says is that of English grammar, if this is English, most of us would prefer to "speak Mathematics," i.e., $x^2a^2 - y^2b^2 = 1$, especially if we recognize a hyperbola when we see one.

The language of mathematics is a technical language, and it supremely embodies one of the hallmarks of technical languages: One of the primary utility features of a technical language is that it enables those of us who speak it to say more in a more comprehensible, thorough, and exact way, using less time and fewer words than would using ordinary English or German or Swahili. The mathematician's "$x^2a^2 - y^2b^2 = 1$" is not *simply* shorter. It is more easily comprehensible, to those who know mathematics, than is the English equivalent. Conversely we have the ability to restate a mathematical sentence in English; but, although we can make such restatements, they are not worth the effort in the long run, except for teaching purposes and even then only in small doses, because the restatements are too dense for comprehension. We can make the restatements because we used English in learning the technical language. Think of our old high school geometry textbook. Except for the diagrams and the "proofs," virtually every sentence in each paragraph was in ordinary, everyday, garden variety English. Think, too, of how many such sentences there were and how, now that you and I know plane geometry, we would not need for the textbook to contain anything more than the axioms and theorems. Why, then, did we once have to read all those English sentences and paragraphs? The answer is, they helped us pick up the notions of geometry and the language of geometry. They also are the sentences we would use to teach someone else that language; and for that purpose, for example, we might now ourselves use forty or so, patiently uttered, English sentences initially for the theorem about the hypotenuse.

Except for these teaching purposes, there is little point, however, in attempting to "analyze" the technical language of mathematics back into English because the restated sentences either will be too dense for easy comprehension (the definition of hyperbola) or the restatements will require an entire book for even the simplest set of technical language sentences to be comprehensible to the ordinary English speaker (the axioms and theorems of plane geometry), and the very complex sentences will take volumes (for example, topology). Of course, there are such books or volumes of books if we think, for example, of each book on topology as "including" the first grader's arithmetic book, etc., the ninth grader's algebra book, the tenth grader's geometry book, and so on.

Further, just as the language of mathematics is a technical language, so too is the language of physics; indeed, there is a substantial sense in which mathematics *is* the language of physics.[121] Yet, here, there is an

[121] Similarly with respect to musical notation, the notation may be the — or a substantial part of a — language of music. People who can read the notation can read a symphony the way you and I can read a poem. Composers quote one another, and they write what other readers of the notation recognize as something like a question-and-answer sequence in the unresolved chord and its consequent passage (which may not be immediate). They call Mahler's 6th symphony, for example, "tragic" because it ends in a minor key and an "unrelieved mood." On

odd phenomenon; for a physicist can explain to us one of physics' most theoretical notions, that of a quark, in one book of modest length written in English.[122] After reading such a book we come closer to being able to understand the physicist who speaks of quarks (even if we skipped past the occasional mathematical sentence) than we (if we are not learned in mathematics) ever will come to understanding the mathematician's solution to the four-color problem, which is the problem of proving that four colors are adequate to the task of coloring a map without having distinguishable areas become indistinguishable because they are of the same color. If we are cartographers or painters in the style of Mondrian (but without his black division lines), we will be happy to know *that* we safely can use four colors rather than five, but we would have to be mathematicians to understand *why* this is true. The difference between the four-color problem and the quark, in part, is that the heart of the four-color problem is one of proof, hence of mathematics and of a sophisticated sort,[123] whereas the quark is part of a general theory of the universe and, in a way, there is more "room" for us to have a modest explanation of that theory couched in a language that vastly, overwhelmingly is ordinary English. For all that, "quark" is a technical term of the technical language of physics, and the substantial aspect of its technicality rests in its being given meaning in a theory.

Perhaps most terms central to theories are technical terms, but not all of them are. For example, "cell" is part of the theory (or theories) of biology, but it is not a technical term. We do not have to learn the biologist's theories to learn the meaning of "cell" even as the biologist uses it. Her theory is that a cell is the basic structure of plant and animal life, but she can teach us to use "cell" of the same thing she does by pointing them out to us under a microscope. Her pointing method of teaching works here because we already know about using "cell" of jails, of batteries, and of the Communist party.[124] We may make sense of saying "cell" is a theoretical term in biology; however, it is not a technical term.

---

the other hand, although readers of music can "hear" what they read, good cooks can "taste" a recipe they read. And on this unresolved chord, let me just say that I have not come close to giving an adequate description of language or of technical language in this article. Some of the things an adequate description would have to take into account are what to say about bridge codes and musical notation and perhaps even about the pictorial messages of art. Here, too, there seems to be something very close to theoretical terms, and that may indicate there is a technical language of art.

[122] H. FRITZSCH, QUARKS (Eng. trans. 1983). Actually, he wrote in German.

[123] Indeed, the proof in this particular case has raised substantial metatheoretic questions because of its style — it essentially is a computer print-out of all possible variations and permutations. Thus, this proof is something like a truth table and does not comport with traditional notions of mathematical proof.

[124] Philosphers have queried whether we can teach the meanings of words by pointing: (To *what* do we point? The shape? color? texture? use?) These philosophers, however, are talking about a different level of instruction via pointing as being problematic; my biologist will round out her pointing by saying things such as "Do you see these walls or wall-like membranes?" and will be talking to someone who already speaks English.

Not only are not all of the central terms in the sciences not technical terms, although they need to be connected to theory in that science to be central terms, but also not all theoretical terms are in the sciences. Further, some words appear to present difficulties for "translation" into everyday English that are of a different order than the "mathematical restatements" problem and for an entirely different reason. Think, for example, of how we learn religious language. I say "I made this chair"; you say "God made this rainbow." We learn your use after we learn mine, and the "standardness" of my use creates some puzzles about your use. For example, if we both understand God to be outside of time, yet agree this rainbow is in the here and now, and if you really mean to be speaking of this rainbow itself (rather than of its archetype, so to speak), then there is a puzzle about how something that is outside of time can act in time. We might develop a complex theory to explain or solve the puzzle. When we do we will create a language of theology.[125]

Similarly, if I say, "Pharaoh spoke to Moses," you can ask, "In what language did Pharaoh speak?" and I can answer (falsely) "In English" or (truly) "In some form of ancient Egyptian." But if you say "God spoke to Moses," there is no clearly true answer to my question, "In what language did God speak?" Indeed, the question is "wrongheaded" and shows that I have not fully understood the effect that the word "God" has on the remainder of the words in "God spoke to Moses." We could say you are using "spoke" metaphorically or anthropomorphically; but if we mean to be fully fair, we would say you are speaking the language of religion, i.e., are making a religious use of the ordinary English word "spoke." That may appear to be equivalent in effect to saying that "translating" the "religious" sentence "God spoke to Moses" into English ultimately is impossible because the word "God" always carries religious-language ties, even for nonbelievers. That appears to be a mistake, however, as I shall explain below.

This sort of phenomenon is one that lies within ordinary English. When we begin a story by saying, "Once upon a time . . ." all of us know that we cannot treat what follows as having a truth value, but we also know there are canonical restrictions on what we may say. A child does not speak nonsense if she says, "Daddy, the little girl with the three bears was Goldilocks, not Cinderella; you've mixed up the stories." Similarly, some things "fit" Hamlet and others do not: that he might have worn earrings fits, that he might have wanted to have become an Australian sheepherder does not.

Do words in the language of the law work the way "God" and "once upon a time" do? Hart essentially says "corporation" does.[126] That is what he means when he says "will," "can," etc. suffer a "shift in meaning" when we use them in conjunction with "corporation." Hence, when a caterer says, "The Chrysler Corporation ordered three vegetarian dinners for the

[125] I will distinguish this from the language of religion.

[126] See § II. A., *supra*.

banquet, so reduce the steak dinners by three," all of a sudden each word after "corporation" has shifted in meaning. As I explained earlier, this is a mistake. Someone might think to avoid the mistake by saying that, just as "God" "blocks" certain questions about how God spoke, the word "corporation" at least "blocks" a sentence such as "The Chrysler Corporation had three vegetarian dinners last night" and explain that a corporation's being a person is a legal construct, a legal fiction; hence corporations do not eat, do not swallow, do not die, and so on.

I have news. Out in the hinterland, away from lawyers and law schools, corporations swallow each other up, sometimes eating them alive, only to find they have swallowed undigestible poison pills, which sometimes kill them off, and they are then dead and buried. This is the way we talk. Do not say, "Ah, that's metaphorical." It is not, although sometimes it may be idiomatic. If you and I are lucky, our quarrels will be dead and buried, and we may merge our lives into one by marrying.

Consider again, then, "God spoke to Moses." In what sense is this sentence not in English? In what sense is it part of a technical language? Of course it is English, ordinary English, as is the rest of the Bible (or the Koran or Mao's Little Red Book, and so on). There is no "translation failure" in getting "God spoke to Moses" "into" English; it is English. That of course does not mean its meaning should be crystal clear and without mystery; nor does it mean *theologians* do not speak technically among themselves when they are talking about religious matters. Nor does it mean we do not need to surround "God made this rainbow" with theories. Nor, most emphatically, does it mean we cannot fall into disagreement about the meaning of "God" or of "God made this rainbow."[127] When we do give theories we will construct theoretical terms that we will use with some precision. The language of religion itself, however, is ordinary English or ordinary Hebrew or ordinary Greek, and so on.

Armed with these insights and clarifications, I am now ready to describe technical languages in greater detail and to begin the analysis of the language of the law. The shortest gloss of my view is that the language of the law is like the language of religion and unlike the language of physics.

### *D. Critical Recapitulation and a Third View*

Hart's constitutive approach, taken as a mode of defining technical languages, is too counter-intuitive because it is not sufficiently expansive. The languages of the law and of baseball turn out to be technical under that approach; but, under the principle of a rose-is-a-rose-is-a-rose, the languages of mathematics, physics, and the other sciences are not technical languages, except insofar as these latter languages involve procedural terms for doing the sciences. That does not fit the way we talk at

[127] If our disagreements are sufficiently great and strongly held, we may fall into different religious practices.

all. That is, the languages we pre-analytically are most sure are technical languages are those of physics, chemistry, astronomy, and so on.

Hart's view does suggest, however, albeit obliquely, what makes scientific procedural terms technical, namely that they lay down what counts as, for example, and to speak very loosely, an experiment. Scientists use "experiment" in a much more confined way than ordinary language users do, and their rules for conducting experiments — requiring verifiability through independent confirmation and repetition, and so on — specify the meaning of "experiment" for science or for their particular sciences. Further, the laws of gravity, red shifts, etc. exist even if we do not (the rose-principle), but experiments do not exist unless we do exist and do lay down the procedures for conducting them. Scientists' procedural terms thus are constitutive terms in Hart's sense and, therefore, are technical terms in his sense.[128] Of course, scientists cannot lay down just any old rules for conducting experiments and still produce the scientific *truths* we know, whereas we may lay down whatever rules for baseball we like and have baseball or some other game.

On this range, law's procedural terms are in between those of science and of baseball. Scientist's procedural terms are dictated by something into having particular contours. That something may be the nature of our minds or the limits of our understanding, or it may be the nature of natural laws or of mathematico-scientific truth. We cannot come to, cannot find and know we have found, mathematical or scientific truth by talking among ourselves and laying down the laws. Rather, these truths are independent of us in some fundamental sense that even the Copenhagen school of quantum physics would recognize; and to ensure that we have arrived at them, we must conduct proofs or experiments that meet certain conditions. The procedural terms of any game, however, may be anything we like, e.g., how many referees or umpires, where they stand, who has what jurisdiction, etc. Which procedures we lay down affect "what game" we play, just as what other rules we lay down affects what the game is. Because there is no thing any game is independent of what we say the game is, however, nothing constrains us in laying down the terms unless we want to construct *the* baseball game, *the* chess game, and so on. Even here, we know we can change the rules and still have the game; we can move the pitcher's mound up and out, change the ball, change the third-base line, and so on.

For the procedural terms of the law there appear to be some constraints, given that substantive laws are what they are. Having created substantive law that recognizes a right to exclude others from real property to

[128] I am explaining here how we may adapt Hart's technical language view so as to make some terms of the sciences be technical terms, namely by focusing on his constitutive-definition view. I ultimately am dissatisfied with his view, because it still is too under-and-over-inclusive, and I prefer to describe physicists' and psychologists' uses of "experiment" as technical uses of the ordinary English word "experiment." My preference here stems in part from the view of technical terms I develop later in this section, however; and I here am trying to make plain how and how far Hart's view can take us. I set out Hart's view in § II. A. and the notion of making technical uses of language in § I. C.

which someone holds title, for example, we need a mode of protecting that right and, therefore, need something like an ejectment action, which is nothing more than one procedure among many possible procedures for protecting the right. The right also is a qualified right, and we therefore also need ways to cut it off through, for example, statutes of limitations and so on. We did not have to have the substantive rules we do have; had we not created them, we would be a different sort of society and a different people. But that is a phenomenon like the one with games. There still would be a game if we created game rules and called it "baseball" even if it were not baseball as we now know it, and vice versa if we called it something else, etc. For the law, as long as we hold a particular theory of rights and recognize certain rights, we have to have modes of protecting those rights, i.e., procedures of a certain sort. Within the sort we still have choices, however, in a more ample sense than physicists have. We may not be able to choose to protect life and property rights by hue-and-cry methods today (because our views have changed), but we may choose between having certain rules of evidence and other rules of evidence and still stay within the parameters set by the rights we recognize in crime victims and the ones we recognize in crime defendants. This is even more clearly true in, for example, tort. We need not have a trial tort system. Rather, we could redress all tortious wrongs through government largess or insurance. The latter two procedures change some of our substantive views, but not much more than changing the third-base line changes baseball.

Hart's constitutive view thus allows us to be clear about how the procedural words of the law may be described as technical. We cannot get more for the law than that out of his view, however, and the languages of mathematics and the sciences are not technical, except for their procedural, i.e., doing, words. We need to look further for a theory for the language of the law.

Caton's mode of defining technical languages — by cross-reference to participants in a discipline, occupation, or activity and to words that do not have an ordinary language meaning (use) at all or have a different one than the ordinary ones — however, either has something missing or is too broad. His examples of technical languages include the languages of chess, as would Hart's, and, unlike Hart's, Caton's approach captures as technical the languages of mathematics and physics.[129] This list better fits our intuitions in including the latter as technical languages, and their terms initially appear to fit the two types of technical terms he identifies. But the terms of chess are not so obviously of either type.[130] Moreover, Caton includes the language of farming as a technical language; and, although our intuitions about whether the language of farming is a technical language give out at this point (as they always do in middle cases), we find we are in some trouble if we say the dressage "ring" or the farmer's "field" is a technical term in either of his two senses.[131] Too much becomes

[129] See § II. B., *supra*.
[130] See § II. B., *supra*.
[131] Only the second sense is even a possibility of course.

technical, and part of the problem here stems from his having defined technical languages by cross-reference to participants of a "discipline or occupation or activity."

We know what prompts him to use this cross-reference; we all have had the experience of hearing a conversation among enthusiasts of something about which we know little and having that conversation go around us or over our heads. Moreover, Caton's enterprise-point is to de-mystify technical languages by getting us to see that we ourselves know a lot of technical languages: ways of talking about activities, for example, that not everyone knows because they know little or nothing about those activities. He would not be concerned, then, that "too much" becomes technical *because* being technical merely is a part-relational property between words and certain people, not something about the words themselves. The other part-relational property is between the way these certain people use those words and the way the rest of us use those words.

Here he identifies two they-we configurations: First, they use a word that we do not use at all; for example, physicists use "quark," but we do not use "quark" *unless* we are "speaking physics." That is, "quark" has no ordinary English uses; it is, so to speak, an arbitrary word from the view of ordinary English and, as I have explained earlier,[132] is a theoretical word, i.e., is the word for a theoretical entity. (This, of course, does not mean such entities are not "real" entities. Rather, it means they are known through theory.) The same is true of "quasar;" the Motorola television people are not using an astrophysicist's word, although the TV people wish subliminally to make that connection. The second they-we configuration Caton identifies is the one in which they use a word that we also use, but the way they use it is not the way we use it in ordinary language. Their use, then, is cut off from ours. Here he gives the example of algebra's "ring."

Yet algebra's "ring" does not seem to be an example of a word "not having in ordinary language the senses given them in the discipline in question" because the substantial sense of algebra's "ring" is one our "ring" has in ordinary language. The ordinary "ring" perhaps does not have *all* the senses algebra's "ring" has (and vice versa);[133] but they share a fundamental sense although this may not be obvious. The algebraist's "ring" started out its life in mathematics in connection with solving problems of transformations of vector space by transforming the problems into linear equations instead of continuing with the Cartesian method of representing numbers geometrically and carrying out operations geometrically or instead of using matrix rectangular arrays of numbers, and so on. Once von Neumann introduced rings of operators, algebra became the tool for quantum physics and is continuous with geometry in a sense Descartes might recognize. In short and more clearly, mathematicians

---

[132] See § II. C., *supra*.

[133] Caton's text is not clear as to whether this is his point or whether he means to say our sense and the mathematician's sense are wholly different although we each use words that *look* the same.

used and still use "ring" instead of "sofa" or "shelf" because the geometric curve for the set of integers is a 360 degree curve, which in plane geometry is like the age-rings of a tree if we allow for geometry's curve's not having any width. Hence, the mathematician's "ring" in substantial part is one of the senses of our "ring." This is something like the poultry tradist's "chicken" vis-a-vis our "chicken,"[134] although there is an important difference I shall explain in a moment.

Nor is this story of the mathematicians' "ring" unique; the relation of their "group" to our "group" is even plainer. They use "group" for the set of natural numbers taken together with an associative binary operation, such that the result of applying the operation to an element of the set with the unity element is the first element and to an element of the set and its inverse element of the set is the unity element.[135] Put this way, we might easily miss that they use "group" in a sense that is fundamental to the way we use it. To use "group" of something in English there must be an associative relation of *some* sort for the members of the group — group of people, group of people in the room, group of shouting people in the room, group of shouting people in the room having their picture taken, and so on.[136] This does *not* mean the mathematician's "group" is not a technical term; it most emphatically is. They use that word in sentences that Horatio would never dream of using and would not grasp without learning mathematics. But their use is connected at this level with the way we use it. (The same is true, of course, with their uses of "associative relation" and ours.) When they get to the "outer perimeters" of their uses of "group," their uses may well be cut off from ours in the sense that only by understanding mathematics could we trace back from these outer-

---

[134] See § I. C., *supra.*

[135] That is, a group is the set of natural numbers together with a binary operation (one that operates on two numbers at a time) that is associative (i.e., the equation reads with any pairings), such that the result of an operation on any element in the set with the unity element *e* in the set is the original element [as in 6 x 1 = 6 or -6 x 1 = -6] and such that the result of operating any element in the set by its inverse element in the set is equal to the unity element *e* [as in 6 x 1/6 = 1 or -6 x 1/-6 = 1]. That is, for natural numbers a, b, c, . . . and binary operation O/, with unity element e and an inverse element a-1 for each element *a*, a group G is defined as follows:

G = {a, b, c, . . . ] with (a, b) O/ = a * b such that

(1) $a * (b * c) = (a * b) * c$

(2) $a * e = a$

(3) $a * a\text{-}1 = e$

*See, e.g.*, W. BARNES, *supra* note 117, at 17. Of course, this definition not only defines this group; here it specifies the operation in such a way as to specify multiplication as the meaning of " * ". What this group G *is*, is a set of numbers that group together under multiplication in a certain (here, the usual) way. More importantly, any set of anything that functions *this* way under any operation is a group, and this is the reason abstract algebra is valuable to physics.

[136] I find using "group" easier than using "ring" and herewith switch to it. I will use it to draw some distinctions Caton did not draw and, more importantly, to rectify what I have suggested are defects in his view. He, of course, may be more nearly right than I; and those who prefer his definitions to mine may be able to construct a sense for "technical language of the law" more nearly to their liking than mine may be for them.

perimeter uses to the algebraic "group" I have just described and make a connection between our "group" and theirs. When their uses are that far out, are cut off, the term is technical in the sense of "not having in ordinary language the senses given them in the discipline in question" because the word will have picked up new, nonordinary meanings and attenuated further its ordinary-language connection on its outward journey.

In the meantime, however, we have three types of technical terms: (1) terms that never have had ordinary uses because they are not from ordinary language at all and instead are from theories (physics' "quark"); (2) terms that once were connected to ordinary words at least marginally by using one among many of the meanings of the ordinary word but today function in theories that undergird the other uses (algebra's "group" today in its most extreme uses); and (3) terms that have uses in the discipline that are fixed to one among the many uses of the ordinary word, i.e., that are fixed on one out of the many meanings of the ordinary language word (algebra's "group" at its lowest level). Now the question is whether, for example, the poultry tradist's "chicken" is such a technical word. It is fixed on one among many of the meanings of the ordinary word "chicken." If this word is a technical word, then all of the language of the law is open to being technical.

Some theorists appear to be willing to allow that definition (3) of technical terms is sufficiently complete,[137] and I myself have taken that view once;[138] but I no longer am convinced it is not subject to an infelicity of the "too much becomes technical" sort, as well as other sorts of problems.[139] When I keep the mathematician's abstract algebra uses of "group" in view and close my eyes for the moment to the ways in which that term can move from a category (3) technical term to a category (2) technical term, one of the things that strikes me about all three categories of technical terms is that they are associated with theories of mathematics, physics, chemistry, and so on. Not all the theoretical terms of these disciplines fall into one of these three categories, of course, because not all of their theoretical terms are technical;[140] but, apart from their procedural "doing" terms, their technical terms are theoretical, too. The poultry tradist's use of "chicken," on the other hand, is so ordinary, so intuitively nontechnical, that we should be reluctant to include it in a group with the mathematician's "group" even of type (3). One way of separating "group" from "chicken" along principled lines, then, is to require that a category (3) technical term also be a theoretical term. Unless it functions as part of a theory, as algebra is a theory about numbers as well as of other things, or unless a theory undergirds the fixing on one-among-many meanings, the term is not category (3) technical.

---

[137] *See, e.g.*, Schauer, *Precedent*, *supra* note 6, at 586 n.35.

[138] *See* Schauer, *Essay*, *supra* note 2, at 804 n.26 (citing Morrison, *Technical Language (and the Law)*, 10 Colonial Law. 18 (1980) (out of print)).

[139] See text following note 116, *supra*, discussing "J'adoube."

[140] See discussion of the biologist's "cell": nontechnical but theoretical term in § II. C., *supra*.

Yet someone may say this will not separate "group" and "chicken" because the poultry tradist does have a "theory" undergirding the meaning-fixation, namely that young birds are better for broiling and frying than old birds, which are suitable only for stewing. The answer to that point is that this is too loose a use of "theory;" for there is only fact or explanation here, not theory at all in any sense in which we regularly use the word "theory." Theories do explain; moreover, they explain facts (or, rather, truths and laws), but they also embody laws or themselves are laws or make recourse to law. Of course, this reply appears to depend on making a fixed-meaning use of "theory;" for some people do say, "I have a theory about why she always comes late to class; she does not have a watch." That is an explanation of one fact through another fact by way of an unstated premise about a causal connection, and even that unstated premise does not leave the factual realm. But, this overlooks the distinction we mark in English by the difference between "theory" and "explanation." What we should say about this so-called "theory" that she is late because she has no watch is that the speaker ought to have said, "I have an explanation for her lateness."[141]

Similarly, the objection that the poultry tradist's "chicken" is undergirded by theory ineluctably overlooks that the very fact upon which the argument trades itself is bound up in the meaning of the poultry tradist's "chicken." Words have networks of meaning, and some aspects of these networks are facts.[142] Of the two sense of "chicken," generic and young-versus-old, the latter has "meaning facts" that are not *simply* temporal. That is, "(young) chicken" is not simply equivalent to " 'chicken' (generic) plus 'less than a year old.'" Rather, we also use "chicken" for ordering a broiler or fryer from the butcher. One of the facts about young chickens is that these are the uses to which we regularly put them. To pretend that the meaning of "young chicken" or of "chicken" does not "network" into that regular-purpose fact is to ignore how we use "chicken." If mean-

[141] That is, a careful speaker would not have used "theory" at all. If that is correct, then my point that "theory" cannot occur only with facts stands, and I have not used a technical term in using "theory" as I do. In that event, I do not need the second, controversial argument in the text. I give both arguments because I have discovered, first, that some people believe an ordinary-language argument/philosophy is "stuck" with how *everyone* talks, including the dim-witted; second, that my uses of English sometimes deviate from those of my learned colleagues who, for example, believe they can promise me that they will publish an unsolicited-yet-to-be-written article in the Harvard Law Review (evidently by writing an article so brilliant that it overbears the independent judgment of the Review's editors); and third, that lawyers never are content with just one argument to establish a point unless it is writ in an official report they have read and can cross-check now. I make no apology for drawing the theory/explanation distinction — it is a distinction that is there in ordinary English to use when we need it as I do now. I return to this last point in §§ III. B. and III. C., *infra*.

[142] *See generally* Morrison, *From Logical Atoms to Language Networks: An Examination of Part Russell's Philosophy of Logical Atomism* (Ph.D. dissertation, University of Illinois, Urbana) (1981). I argued there, for example, that someone who does not know unicorns are mythical creatures does not understand how the rest of us use "unicorn," i.e. does not know our meaning of "unicorn." This, obviously, is a controversial view, for it ultimately *really* threatens the analytic-synthetic distinction.

ing is use, then we cannot ignore what I shall call here the network meaning-fact; and that in turn means the argument that the poultry tradist's use of "chicken" is undergirded by theory is mistaken. The mistake is in using "theory" for an explanation that never leaves the realm of facts; i.e., the mistake is in thinking the fact of broiler/fryer regular-purpose for a young chicken is news of anything *more* than the definition, the meaning of, "chicken" for poultry tradists and for ourselves when we want to buy a broiler or fryer.

Hence, the poultry tradist's "chicken" is not a technical term under category (3) because it is not a theoretical term. When the poultry tradist uses "chicken" for broilers and fryers, however, the poultry tradist does put the ordinary language word "chicken" to a technical use, in the "settled preference for one among many meanings" sense I explored earlier.[143] If the trades people maintain this use by insisting upon exactness among themselves, the word will continue to have a useful life as a word put to a technical use.[144] Its technicality, however, should not lead anyone into thinking that nonparticipants are or can be cut-off from the meaning of the word even in the poultry tradist's mouth. That cannot happen because, even when put to technical use, the word *as so used* is an ordinary language word.

This final point allows us to recast the one with which I began this section, namely the nature of procedural (i.e., "doing") terms. We do not have to be content with using Hart's constitutive approach as an explanation for the technicality of these words, yet we will be able to leave the words in the control of the participant-users of the words, i.e., the chemist for laboratory procedure words, the lawyer for law's procedure words. We may say that, just as the poultry tradist makes a technical use of "chicken," so too the lawyer makes a technical use of "collateral

[143] See § I. C., *supra*.

[144] As I noted earlier, see § I. C., *supra*, words can move off the technical-term list; they also may move off a technical-use list. They do when the word no longer is useful as a technical word because ordinary people have adopted the word as their own, taking all or some of its technical meaning as the primary meaning for everyday purposes. This has happened to "neurosis," and someone may wonder why it has not happened to, for example, "electron." There are at least four reasons. First, "electron" in the mouths of physicists is protected by a very solid theory, whereas the theory surrounding "neurosis" not only was not universally accepted but also was not itself solid. Part of the trouble with Freudian theory is that it has an answer for each question. That is, it is not open to falsification, but the hallmark of science is exactly that its truths are falsifiable, although that strikes oddly on the ear to hear. *See generally* K. POPPER, THE OPEN SOCIETY AND ITS ENEMIES (5th ed. 1966). Second, when we use words such as "electronic ignition" we are coming linguistically from "electricity" at a time when no one knew about the flow of electrons; hence, physicists can treat our uses of "electro[ ]" as not threatening their uses. Third, "electron" is the word for something we know exists. And, fourth, all of us know this much science today: that "electron" is a scientific term for a particular part of an atom. In sum, just because "everyone" is a "participant" in some sense for the use of a word does not mean democracy rules and ordinary people get to dictate the meaning of the term. Rather, we can use the physicist's "electron" but it belongs to the physicist, who controls it through well developed theories of physics. Or, we can use our own "electro[ ]," but then we are not "speaking physics."

estoppel" or "interpleader" or "quiet title," as well as of "abatement" or "trespass" or "nuisance."

Consider "trespass," "nuisance," and "abatement." Most of us learned those words when we were very young children when, for example, our parents taught us the Lord's Prayer ("And forgive those who trespass against us"), told us to stop pestering them with questions when they were trying to do something else ("Stop making a nuisance of yourself"), or shouted to us to cut out the noise ("Abate that racket!"). Lawyers have more refined or more exact uses of "trespass," "nuisance," and "abatement," but the core of their meaning is available to all speakers of ordinary English. They make a technical use of an ordinary English word by taking care in their deployment to pick up some, but not all, the ordinary meanings.

With words of procedure, lawyers have a more open hand because ordinary language users do not have occasion to use the procedural words of the law unless they come to court. When they then return to "civilian" life and use those words, they tend to be less exact than lawyers are and their expansions now work to put the lawyer's use in a technical light.

This will strike some people as highly counter-intuitive. For them I offer as two cases-in-point the words "appeal" and "guilty." How often have all of us heard nonlawyer friends speak of a tort defendant's having been found guilty? With "appeal" the looseness with which nonlawyers talk is even more apparent. They talk about appealing to the Supreme Court when there is no federal question, or to the state supreme court when the trial is not over, and so on. They use "appeal" without distinguishing, for example, between a writ of certiorari and an appeal-of-right. There is nothing improper about that; "appeal" is to "appeal" and "certiorari" as "chicken" is to "chicken" and "young chicken" or as "umpire" is to "umpire" and "referee."

Even if procedural terms of any discipline, occupation, or activity constitute a fourth category of technical terms, that does not leave the law with much on which to hang a technical-language hat. We can use Hart's constitutive view to justify saying the procedural terms of the language of the law are technical, but we cannot extend that view to more of legal language without admitting the view is inadequate because the central terms of the languages of the physical sciences and mathematics are not technical under that view. Alternatively, we can say the procedural terms of the law are ordinary language terms put to technical uses and mean by this nothing more mysterious than that there are niceties of use for "appeal" in talking about the law that lawyers need to and do mark in their careful speech. Others safely can use "appeal" in a more-or-less way until they need to participate closely with the law. Then they, too, will need to be more exact, i.e., will need better to mark those nice distinctions and to put "appeal" to technical use, which they can learn to do without having to learn anything about, for example, justiciability.

This also is true of many "substantive" terms, such as "trespass," "nuisance," or "abatement." One of the crucial terms of contract law, on the other hand, does not have even the technical-use technicality in the language of the law. For "promise" is an ordinary English word bench and bar use *exactly* as do ordinary-English speakers. This may strike some lawyers as news, and they consequently may doubt my claim. I, therefore, sketch why "promise" is a "fully ordinary word used fully ordinarily" in the law in the next part of this article. I will also examine the nature of law's use of "speech" in first amendment cases. This word appears to be not only put to a technical use in either the different-deployment sense or the fixed-on-one-among-many-meanings sense, but also to be a term that is part of a theory. I attempt to explain, however, that this appearance is deceptive in that even those uses of words that do not qualify as "speech" under the first amendment also are not speech in ordinary English. Upon completing these further analyses I give of "promise" and "speech," I will rest my case on the nature of legal language. I then will conclude this article with some general comments about how lawyers may talk to other lawyers.

## III. The Language of the Law

### A. Due Process Revisited

Under the views of Hart and Caton, the language of the law is a technical language. Without regard to any of the problems I have uncovered for their views — and I have found a number of significant ones — this gives reason to believe the language of the law is technical in a sense more interesting than that the procedural terms are technical. In particular, under each view, the technicality they identify is of the "experts only" sort I railed against at the beginning of this article. Hart and Caton get to this "experts only" point by significantly different routes, but they fundamentally agree that to understand how lawyers talk to each other, including how judges talk to lawyers and vice versa, the rest of us have to go to law school in some sense or other. That is, we have to learn the law, just as we have to learn (some) chess or (some) physics if we are to "speak (some) chess" or "speak (some) physics."[145]

In the last section I conceded that the procedural terms of the language of the law may be technical terms in Hart's constitutive sense or in Caton's participants' sense. I opted, however, in favor of saying these terms are

[145] I may have taken some liberties with Caton's view; his five pages is not sufficient for me to tell whether my analytic extrapolations of his views fail to do him justice. The problem, again, fundamentally, is the problem of knowing whether the two kinds of technical terms he describes form the boundary on the participants' definition and, if so, what we are to say about some of the examples he gives of technical languages that do not fit within that boundary. In any event, the "go to law school" sense for him clearly need not be strong. Rather, he would say each of us absorbs this much law as part of being on the scene while we grow up and as we participate in society as adults. In the long run, he and I do not disagree about that ultimate point, but our explanations of the phenomenon differ. That is, he appears to believe we cannot but help learning this much of the technical language of the law, while I am arguing we cannot help but understand the law because it is in ordinary English and cannot help but learn the law because we read widely and because the law stems from ourselves, including the ways we talk.

ordinary language terms put to technical use either in the form of different deployment or in the form of one-among-many meanings. Under my view, "appeal" or "interpleader" is no more a technical term than is the poultry tradists' "chicken." I further argued the same is true of such more substantive terms as "trespass," "nuisance," and "abatement;" and the meanings with which the law uses these terms consequently are vastly more available to any ordinary speaker of ordinary English than are terms such as physics' "quark" or algebra's "ring" because the legal terms entirely are in ordinary English.

But, of course, saying this much does not test all of legal language. If I looked further I might find "real" technical legal terms. Moreover, my argument depends upon saying that a term is not a technical term if it is only a technical-use term in the different-deployment or one-among-many senses; and *ipse dixit* never is a substitute for analytic truth.

Why not say that technical-use terms are technical terms? My answer for the language of the law is that due process constrains us because technical terms can become cut off from ordinary language, hence from ordinary speakers of ordinary language, but due process requires that the law be available to each of us without the intercessional aid of someone who is trained in the law.

This due process consideration is of no concern for poultry tradists because they have their own natural constraint against having their technical-use terms become cut off from ordinary language and ordinary folk. There are so many overlapping participants' groups — from supplier to farmer to retailer to customer — that needs of commerce themselves constrain against towers of Babel. The same commercial constraints exist in commercial law. The courts and the lawyers are not the only participants' groupings. If anything, the shoe is on the other foot here. Business men and women and corporations and their consumer customers outnumber and "out vote" lawyers of bench and bar concerning the discourse. The commercial groups further are in competition, hence their groups subdivide; and they sometimes are in one subgroup (buyers), sometimes in the other (sellers). This atmosphere prevents any one subgroup from capturing the word and removing it from its one-among-many connections to the ordinary language word or from making the "different deployment" into a different word. Further, because the practitioners' groups in business must deal with consumer-customers or deal with groups that do so deal, and because each business man and woman and each corporate employee ultimately also is a consumer customer, the consumer customers are the engine that drives the machine of language. They are the ordinary language users, who may individually know some of these technical uses and who may concertedly adopt a technical use as their standard use, and so on; but they also are the group with whom the other participants' groups must remain in linguistic contact on pain of losing the customers.[146] These groups, and primarily the consuming public, dictate the

[146] This, of course, raises flip-side problems for business in the area of intellectual property. The business must take care to make sure that its trade name or trade mark does not become the generic term for the thing — e.g., "Kleenex" for facial tissues, "Coke" for colas; and some companies have lost this battle by failing to provide ordinary English alternatives for their trade name or mark, e.g., "aspirin."

terms of the law for lawyers. Indeed, they do more. They dictate the law itself.[147] The immediate consequence is that, for example, "promise" is not a technical term of the law. Rather, it is an ordinary language term the meaning of which is determined by extra-law forces in society, particularly in commercial society. The same is true of "reasonable" in tort. Here there are insurance companies on both sides; and there is the consuming public, which individually may end up on either side of a tort dispute. As the public's notions of what is reasonable change, the legal meaning of "reasonable" changes.

Not all of the law operates under these constraining conditions, however; and in some areas, there is danger that one participants' group will move the technical-use word, which had been connected to the ordinary word by the different-deployment relation or the one-among-many-meanings relation, to something that is more remote, the way the mathematician's "ring" is more remote, or to something that completely is cut off, as (but not the way) the physicist's "quark" is cut off from ordinary English. There is no danger when mathematicians and physicists use those kinds of technical terms for at least two reasons; seeing why will give us insight to remaining areas of legal language.

First, and most basically, the way mathematicians and physicists talk among themselves has no bearing on the lives of the public except insofar as we bear the financial and moral costs of their work and thus need to know what they are doing. Yet that is not much of a constraint. They may talk scientific Yiddish in the back of their laboratories as long as they talk English out front when they come to us with funding requests. This would be like saying lawyers may talk Law French or LawSpeak in court as long as they speak English in their offices to clients. But there is an obvious difference, which destroys the analogy of the language of the law to those of physics and mathematics. In court, the very same sort of people sit in the jury box as sit on the client's side of the office desk. And there is more. The whole point of "lawyers' law" is to lay down standards that apprise the persons subject to those standards of what the standards are. This particularly is true in criminal law for obvious practical reasons even if we had no due process clause. But, due process does require the law to stay in linguistic contact with ordinary language speakers. Further, the people are the source of the law; that is not true of physics or mathematics. The law better not be in Law French or LawSpeak then.

Second, mathematicians' and physicists' technical terms are parts of theories, well-articulated theories, and the most general and most central of the technical terms may be "unpacked and repackaged" for the general (and often inexact) consumption of nonmathematicians and nonphysicists. Using the technical terms allows mathematicians and physicists to speak in more precise, more comprehensible (for them) ways using fewer

[147] There is a fundamental sense in which Judge (formerly professor) Posner has the role of courts backwards when he says that their role in contracts cases, for example, is to normalize terms. R. POSNER, ECONOMIC ANALYSIS OF LAW (2d ed. 1977).

words and taking less time. Most importantly, they also have independent constraints on their theories through the requirements of proof and experiment, of coherence and completeness. That their technical words are cut off from ours, then, presents no issue of moment to society.

May the law similarly develop technical terms that are cut off from ordinary language, by being very remote or by being completely arbitrary or may it have technical terms that only obliquely connect to our uses, as long as the law surrounds the term with theory? And does the law do this? The answer is, the law may not and does not, although there are terms in the law that are surrounded by theory. Being a theoretical term in the law is not like being one of Hart's constitutive terms, however; rather, the theory for the term comes from ordinary language itself and *sometimes* from a prescriptive view of society, the general contours of which we ourselves have laid down. This is the topic of the next sections.

### *B. Ordinary Language as a Source of Theory: "Promise"*

There are distinctions within ordinary language that govern the proper use of the word "promise." These distinctions also are the ones lawyers and the law mark with "promise" — all legal promises are ordinary promises. Yet "promise" functions in some unusual ways in ordinary English compared to the noun "table" or to the verb "walk," and there is a mode of describing these unusual features of "promise" that will give us a notion of how ordinary English itself embodies distinctions that appear to be theory-laden distinctions when these same points arise in connection with the law's use of "speech" in first amendment cases. When the Supreme Court and commentators try to explain, for example, why burning a draft card to protest the war in Viet Nam is not speech but wearing an armband is, they find themselves making recourse to a notion about "symbolic speech."[148] That smacks immediately of theory-construction; and this impression deepens when we notice that the law draws distinctions between obscene speech and merely-dirty speech by saying the former is not speech at all, and so on. My aim in this section and the next one is to make plain that the theory at stake in the so-called "symbolic speech" cases is not the Court's theory but that of ordinary English itself. The Court, however, sometimes finds itself on the cutting-edge of societal problems and thus at a point that is slightly ahead of ordinary English and ordinary people. The Court cannot wait for our language to catch up and solve the problem; it must decide the case. In resolving the issue before it, the Court then points the way for future development of ordinary English; and, if the Court is successful, the way the Court uses "speech" never is cut-off from ordinary English because ordinary members of our society internalize the Court's cutting-edge use. Further, the Court's resolution turns on the Court's role as prescriptive interpreter of the first amendment, and the role we have set for the Court then is to tell us where we are going as it interprets "speech" under first-amendment guarantees.

[148] See § III. C., *supra*.

But this is the end of the story, and I need to begin at the beginning. That is the point at which a court plays a descriptive-institutional role and where ordinary English and the ordinary practices our linguistic distinctions mark reign by being fully adequate to the questions before a court by already embodying the distinctions for resolving the dispute.[149]

More than a generation ago, J.L. Austin described the ways in which "promise" in some of its uses differs from all of our uses of "walk."[150] When we use the verb "promise" in the nonhabitual, noncontinuous, first-person singular, present tense, to say "I promise that p" or "I hereby promise that p"[151] is to promise that p, where p is a proposition or nominalized sentence although there are constraints on the propositional content of p, as we shall see. To say "I walk to the store" is not thereby to walk, but to describe truly or falsely; "I did promise" is not to promise, but to report; and "I see that you are happy" is not to see, and so on. To say "I promise to pay" is to promise to pay. Nor is "promise" the only verb with this feature in this use. Other such verbs include "bet," "swear," "name," "demand," "order," "declare" (as to customs officials). Austin calls the verbs that have this feature "performative verbs" and their featured uses "performative verb speech acts." He also identifies two kinds of conditions that surround these verbs; if the conditions are not met, the speech act is "unhappy" or it "misfires." The reason for using "is unhappy" or "misfires" is that performative verb speech acts are neither true nor false. This is an important feature of their nature as a distinct class of uses of language.

For example, a sergeant usually has authority to order troops to fire during battle. She does this by saying "Fire!" or "I order you to fire." Consider the situations in which she says "I order you to fire!" to a civilian or to troops who have no firearms. We say there is no order in the former situation, even if she believed the civilian to be a trooper; her speech act "misfires." There is an order to the troopers, as long as she does not know the troopers have no firearms, but the order is "unhappy," i.e., we would say it is an ineffective order, which differs from being ineffective *as* an order. All of these distinctions flow straight out of the way we would talk about the situations and are undergirded by our shared understandings. Societal issues loom large on certain situations, of course, and may exceed our shared understandings. If the sergeant orders troops to fire upon women and babies, for example, we may fall into disagreement among ourselves as to whether there is an order.[152]

We mark similar sorts of distinctions with regard to "I promise." More-

---

[149] I am talking of a particular kind of problem here, not all legal issues.

[150] J. AUSTIN, *supra* note 24. *See also* Austin, *Other Minds*, PROC. ARISTOTELIAN SOC., Supp. Vol. (1964), reprinted in J. AUSTIN, PHILOSOPHICAL PAPERS (1961).

[151] The word "hereby" functions as a double-check for a performative use of a verb.

[152] This was especially pressing in Vietnam. The sticking point is over whether and when reasonable troops may view people who are not clad in conventional mufti as likely to be carrying concealed explosives. That we do not have a settled description on the misfire-unhappy spectrum for this sort of case is the result of and a sign of our not having settled yet the political and moral issues.

over, those distinctions control our uses of "She promised" and related words in ways that exactly comport with how lawyers talk about promises, and the following is a partial ordinary-language map of contract law: We do not say there was a promise unless we can drive a temporal wedge between apparently promising words and keeping the promise; lawyers say this by saying there is no promise in a present barter-and-exchange.[153] In order to speak of express or implied promises such as express or implied warranties, lawyers and the rest of us adhere to this temporal-wedge rule by expanding the time-frame.[154] Similarly, ordinary English users mark the distinction between failing to keep a promise out of negligence or deliberate choice, on the one hand, and failing to keep it for unavoidable reasons, on the other hand, by saying an apology is due for the former but only an explanation is due for the latter. We also say explanations are due if there is a misunderstanding and, if the misunderstanding is legitimate, the explanation functions to excuse failing to keep the promise; if not, we say there is an apology due. We describe someone who promises without intending to keep her word as having given an insincere promise but, because there is a promise, we can demand an apology when she fails to keep the promise.

Further there are uses of "I promise" that we, as speakers of ordinary English, say are not promises at all. One is the use of apparently promising words in circumstances when there cannot be a promise because the speaker cannot be giving her word. For example, to say "I promise to buy you a new collar" to a dog or "I promise to pay Sally" to the air is not to promise because the speaker cannot intend her words to be taken by another to be the giving of an assurance that she will do as she says. These may be resolutions, but they are not promises. The same is true when one says "I promise" to oneself. We also all know that when someone accepts a dinner invitation by saying, "I promise to come," there is no promise. We do not surround social situations with the seriousness necessary for us to say there is a giving of an assurance here, hence we do not take the words to be promising words even if she uses "promise." (Repeatedly saying "I'll be there" in response to requests for assurance, however, is promising in ordinary English, even if she never uses the word "promise.")

There are many other similar ways in which we assess words among ourselves without the help of lawyers as being or as not being promising words. If I say, "I promise to steal from you" we all say this is no promise because I cannot promise to do something we both know is bad for you; we say the same if I say, "I promise *not* to steal from you" because we expect no less. Further, we say someone misuses "promise" in saying she promises to do something she and we know she cannot do or cannot bring

---

[153] *See, e.g.*, A. CORBIN, CORBIN ON CONTRACTS § 4 (1952).

[154] This may (often does) come as news that smacks of legal truth or legal rule to law students; but they simply somehow have been left out of the shared conventional understandings of the rest of us about how to talk, perhaps because of their inexperienced youth or because they are reading the wrong things in high school and college.

about on her own; all she can promise here is to try her best. We also do not treat promising words on the stage as part of a play as a promise, and so on.

Another use of "I promise" in which ordinary-English speakers would say there is no promise arises when the "promised" act is so venal that society expands its understanding that I cannot promise you I will do something we both know is harmful to you to include a regard for third parties. Hence, we refuse to describe "I promise to murder Smith" as a promise. Courts may express this point by saying there is an unenforceable promise because the subject matter of the promise is an illegal act, but courts would be better off talking like the rest of us do and saying there is no promise at all. There are after all some promises that are unenforceable about which no one has the slightest hesitation in saying there is a promise — for example, where I promised but unforseen circumstances prevent me from keeping the promise, or in the law when a statute of limitations has run (the ordinary language equivalent here is "You're too late; too much time has passed and I reasonably thought you were not going to ask me to keep that promise"). These situations differ substantially from "I promise to murder Smith."

I now come to the situation that appears to refute my claim that all legal promises are ordinary language promises. There are cases in which the law recognizes promises-by-behavior. Upon explaining how even these cases fit our ordinary language uses of "promise," I will have completed dressing the stage to turn to "speech" in the first amendment.

The hard case is exemplified in *Allied Steel & Conveyors, Inc. v. Ford Motor Co.*[155] In 1955 Ford contracted with Allied to purchase some machinery for Ford's employees to install at one of Ford's plants. In 1956 Ford submitted another contract proposal to Allied to purchase more of such machinery, but with the change that Allied's employees would install this machinery. Under the first contract, Allied did not indemnify Ford for acts of negligence by Ford's employees; but under the second proposed contract, a broad indemnity clause would have made Allied indemnify Ford for acts of negligence by Allied's employees and by Ford's employees arising in connection with Allied's installation of the machinery. At least two months before Allied signed this second contract, Allied began the installation called for in the second contract. During that installation, and before the signing of that contract, some of Ford's employees negligently injured one of Allied's employees. The Allied employee sued Ford and won.

Ford, in the course of this suit, sought to bring Allied in as a third-party defendant, on the grounds of the broad indemnity clause of the second contract. Allied resisted, arguing that there had been no such contract at the time of the injury to the Allied employee, and that in any event both Ford and Allied had intended to void the broad indemnity clause before Allied signed the contract, thus leaving only the indemnity clause of the first contract to indemnify acts of negligence by Allied's employees.

[155] 277 F.2d 907 (6th Cir. 1960).

The court found for Ford on the grounds that Allied's beginning the performance called for under the second contract operated as an acceptance of Ford's offer to contract and operated as a promise to complete the performance on those terms. That is, the court found that Allied's beginning of performance was a ratification of the second contract every bit as effective as Allied's signature would have been, and that therefore, Allied was bound to all the terms of the second contract, including the broad indemnity clause. To the argument that Ford was not similarly bound, absent Allied's signature, the court said that Ford indeed also was bound through its acquiescence in Allied's beginning of performance. Thus, Ford would have been estopped from claiming there had been no contract absent Allied's signature because Ford has acquiesced in Allied's performance. What happens, then, is that behavior — actually performing on Allied's side, acquiescing in that performance on Ford's side — results in a contract and promises to complete performance on either side (finish the installation, pay for the work, respectively).

Now, it appears highly counter-intuitive to say that there is any behavior, however finely tuned, that could amount to a promise to indemnify someone's employees for accidents on the job. If anything ever appeared to need language of the promising sort, this does. Moreover, how could any behavior be so unambiguous as to be a promise to indemnify for negligence of employees of both companies, but not be behavior that promises to indemnify for only one company's employees? It cannot. No nonverbal behavior can speak as clearly as words, except when the behavior arises against a certain kind of background. That background is one of shared conventions. The conventions can be widespread throughout the country, or in the community, or between Ford and Allied.

What happens in *Allied* is that the behavior occurs against the background of an unsigned contract in which a promise is specified. Were Allied to do exactly what it did without this background, the court could never have found the particular indemnity promise. There might have been some way of making Allied indemnify Ford in that event, but this could not have been on the basis of Allied's behavior as amounting to this particular promise of indemnity. There would have been no such promise. As it is, the contractual background makes Allied a promisor by behavior. Because of this background, Allied's behavior is "promising speech." (This last gloss wants explaining of course.)

Still, the question is not so much whether we can make sense of the court's reasoning in deciding that there was a promise in Allied's behavior, but whether there are any ordinary life examples in which behavior is of this promising sort. The truly clear cases, however, are also cases that have been in court, such as Allied's promise. The reason for that is that only in such cases is there a possibility of finding an agreed conventional procedure that turns behavior into such finely tuned promises. Or, at least, these are the only ones of which we are likely publicly to hear. But family members and close friends often over the years manage to work out such procedures among themselves; hence, such cases as *Allied* do not embody counter-examples to my claim that all promises the law recognizes as promises are ones ordinary speakers of ordinary English will say are promises.

Moreover, I can offer analysis that bolsters this analysis. Usually when we engage in a performative verb speech act we do something more than utter words. At christenings, we sprinkle babies and smash champagne bottles on ships' hulls. When we bet, we put money down or throw a chip into the pot. When we order someone to do something or order food at a restaurant, we often point to something.[156] When we swear to something, whether officially or unofficially, we usually hold up a hand, fingers and thumb straight and together, and palm facing out.[157] These nonoral, nonwritten elements of the performative verb speech act are not always essential to the act; but, as Austin says, sometimes the act seems somehow incomplete without them.[158]

Just as some performative verb speech acts can be effectuated without any nonoral or nonwritten act elements, yet sometimes seem to need those latter elements, so too sometimes these latter elements can be complete replacements for the oral or written elements. For example, usually when we bet we say we are betting and put money down at the same time. Yet we may call or write our bookies and say we bet $50 on Stowaway to win. If our credit is good with the bookie, the oral or written speech alone is sufficient to perform the act.[159] Conversely, we may bet $5 on red 21 at the gaming table by putting money down in a certain place at a certain time. In order for words alone to accomplish the act of which the verb is the name, there has to be a lot of stage setting or shared conventions of a very particular sort. Our most general shared conventions, which give words meaning, will not be sufficient here. This context operates to make performative uses of the verb effective for the act, and they are determinative of whether there is such an act. Saying "I bet $5 I can beat you to the corner" while showing a $5 bill is not effective to bet if I am speaking to a dog, any more than placing $5 on the dresser at night results in a bet, because that is not how we bet. Within these convention-contexts, the word-elements of the act can drop out entirely for some, but not all, of the performative verbs. The more highly parti-

[156] Did you think you were merely "holding your place" in the unfamiliar menu text?

[157] Notice that this is exactly opposite to how we reach a hand out to an dog or a strange or injured animal; here, showing a palm (especially with stiff fingers held together) leads to bites because showing palms in this fashion to animals universally is a threatening gesture, particularly if we are reaching straight-on for the animal's head.

[158] J. AUSTIN, *supra* note 24, at 37. He is speaking particularly of christenings. To this point, my account of these speech acts essentially is his. From here on, he probably would not agree with what I say because my view is highly controversial or, as some people would have it, wrong. I do, however, borrow his notion of "accepted conventional procedures" but expand upon it greatly.

[159] There are consequences to this act, of course. If Stowaway does not win, I must pay my bookie $50. If Stowaway does win, my bookie must pay me. This is just like a judge's saying, "I sentence you to 20 years." There are cuffs to be snapped, cells to be locked, entries in records to be made as consequences of the judge's speech act. But none is requisite to performing the speech act itself. If, on the other hand, our credit with the bookie is not good, a telephone call alone will not result in a bet.

cularized the potentially performative speech act, the greater the need not only for words but for particular words, usually for performative uses of the verb for which the verb is the name. At the other end of the spectrum, the more general the act the less the need for any words at all because the potential speech act verb is so nonspecific that our shared conventions can become clearly what is determinative of the accomplishment of the act.

For example, to propose that the city council adopt this budget, instead of merely considering or studying it, I need to say somewhere and somehow that this is the proposal. One of the least ambiguous ways to do that is for me to say "I propose the council adopt this budget." To christen, I need to say "I christen" or "I name;" nothing else will do except some locution that includes some form of the words "christen" or "name" or, at least, some *words* (such as "Henceforth you shall be known as 'Mary' "). Yet we may question with a rising inflection on our words or command with a very emphatic tone on our words without saying "I question" or "I order," and we may question or deny or assent without words from ourselves at all: raise an eyebrow, shake our heads, nod our heads. The reason these body languages are effective as complete replacements for oral or written words is that our shared conventions so make them.

Where along the spectrum a potentially performative speech act falls — from no words at all to words-plus-particular-nonword-behavior to only-these-particular-words-are-sufficient — depends on our shared conventions. If we were Moslems, a husband could divorce a wife by saying "I repudiate you" three times. If we were a dueling society, one person could challenge another to a duel by slapping the other in a highly ceremonial way without words at all. Or we might make saying "I insult you" or "I slap you on the face," without accompanying gestures such as spitting or making hand contact, performatively operative. This would be to substitute one ceremony for another. Again, then, what makes Allied's beginning the installation of the equipment at Ford's plant a promise to indemnify Ford for acts of negligence by either Allied's or Ford's employees is that there was a highly particularized and specific background between them that functioned locally the way our standard conventional procedures function nationally. This very same ordinary-language basis marks the distinction between the Court's two most famous "symbolic speech" cases, as well as some related cases.

### C. When Ordinary-Language Theory Gives Out: "Speech"

When Mary Beth Tinker wore a black armband to school one day to protest the Vietnam war, the school sent her home as punishment; and the Court held that this violated her first amendment rights.[160] But when David Paul O'Brien burned his draft card to protest the Viet Nam war and was convicted for violating a federal statute, the Court held that this did not violate his first amendment rights.[161] There are a lot of ways to

[160] Tinker v. Des Moines Indep. Community School Dist., 393 U.S. 503 (1969).
[161] United States v. O'Brien, 391 U.S. 367 (1968).

distinguish the two cases, of course. We could note, for example, that his case came to the Court earlier than hers or we could note the gender difference, and we then could go on to draw political or social inferences. The true differences between the cases, however, is that her act was a speech act within the meaning of associated ordinary language words ("speech," "speak," "say"), whereas his was not. That is, we would say she said something by wearing the armband, but we would not say he said something by burning his draft card.

In our society, we recognize wearing a black armband just above the left elbow as signalling grief. It says, "Someone I know has died." It is akin to the German's hand signal that says someone "has a bird in his head" (meaning he is crazy) or the Italian's hand signal that says a husband has been cuckolded, or our most prosaic flipping-the-bird signal. This last signal, raised in the faces of the local draft board or to an army recruiting team during the 1960's says, exactly as plainly as does Paul Robert Cohen's lettered jacket,[162] what many people thought about the draft or about the war. It, however, usually is more purely emotive and less clearly truth-functional than are the German's and Italian's signals. The German says this person is crazy, and the Italian says the husband is cuckolded; but our finger signal does not truth-functionally say the draft is fucked. What the German and Italian say may be true or may be false; not so, usually, with our sign. (Cohen's jacket, however, did convey a truth-functional message, and I return to that point later.)

We understand the black armband wearing to say "I am mourning," "Someone I cared for has died," and so forth, and these are truth-functional statements, even if there are also emotive overtones. By donning the armband in the turbulent years of the Viet Nam war, in a community in which people have discussed this very act as a method of protesting the war, Tinker makes a more particularized statement than we normally do in wearing black armbands. The context in which she acts disambiguates her statement, crystallizes it, until what she does is *this* speech. But the general conventional background about wearing armbands already makes wearing one *some* speech.

Compare this to O'Brien's act. We have no convention for making the burning of a piece of paper a speech act of any sort, except for such *legal* conventions as revoking a will by intentional burning.[163] Ordinary language speakers would therefore say he did not say anything by burning his card. There was a lot of talk among the group in whose midst he burned the card, of course; and that talk was like the talk Tinker and her community engaged in before the armband wearing. In both groups, they all said they were doing these acts in order to protest the war and

---

[162] Cohen v. California, 403 U.S. 15 (1971). ("Fuck the Draft" on back of his jacket, which he wore to the courthouse to protest the war; convicting him of "willfully disturb[ing] the peace . . . by . . . offensive conduct" violates his first amendment rights).

[163] This is only a legal convention, not a "community convention" at all, in the same sense that "legal convention" merely is legal short-talk for distinguishing between intentional and accidental destructions of a copy of a will.

the draft. In Tinker's case that conversation turned her speech into particular speech, but our shared conventions already underlay the existence of some speech in armband wearing.

In O'Brien's case, the very same kind of conversation could work to disambiguate his card burning to particular war/draft protest speech if and only if our shared conventions already made intentional burnings of papers some speech. We have no such convention in our community, and a sub-group of the community (the rally group) cannot create such an understanding instanter that binds the rest of *us*. Compare, then, the sub-group of Allied and Ford and their special, shared understanding.[164] We as a society have no quarrel with sub-groups of whatever size working out shared understandings and conventions that bind only *them*.[165]

In the absence of a shared conventional procedure for making burning his draft card into some speech, O'Brien alternately needed a shared conventional understanding about the meaning of the draft card. He did not have that from us either. Had he, however, altered or burned an American flag (*cf.* perhaps a Soviet flag, a Girl Scout flag), his intentional burning or other manipulation of the flag would be speech because of our shared understanding about the meaning of this flag.[166]

With Cohen's jacket, of course, there was no similar problem at all on either side because his jacket had words we all give meaning through our shared understanding. He did not put "X rotsexl Ts" on the back of his jacket and then claim these symbols expressed his protest against the war and the draft. Had he so done and claimed, we would say he had said

---

[164] See § III. B., *supra*.

[165] Actually, of course, one of our conventions also functions in the background of Allied and Ford's understanding. Our view is that if you act to do part of what you and I have talked about as a "package deal" you imply you accept the entire deal because I did not agree to give you the right unilaterally to break the package up and take only those parts you want. This may sound like "Law," but it is not. The next time a friend suggests that she will do x if you will do y and z, try making a moral collection on x by doing only y in a circumstance in which there was no reason for you to do y unless you were intending to be taken to trigger her doing of x. But, as she said, her trigger-point is y and z, not y alone.

[166] *See, e.g.*, Spence v. Washington, 418 U.S. 405 (1974) (conviction for affixing peace symbol to American flag violates first amendment); Stromberg v. California, 283 U.S. 359 (1931) (statute prohibiting displaying any flag in "opposition to organized government" is unconstitutional; flag flown here was a red flag). The Court's statement in *Spence*, 418 U.S. at 409, that "governments constitutionally may forbid anyone from mishandling in any manner a flag that is *public* property" (emphasis added) is not contrary. The Court's speculations in *Spence*, 418 U.S. at 412-15, on governments' interests in preserving a national symbol by prohibiting destruction or mutilation of an individual's *own* American flag, however, indicates the Court might have a difficult time deciding the question of validity; but the Court has no doubt that such burning or mutilation itself is speech. In *Stromberg*, of course, the statute itself announced the community understanding. In Street v. New York, 394 U.S. 576 (1969), the Court overturned a conviction under a statute that prohibited mutilation or destruction of a flag or "cast[ing] contempt . . . by words" on grounds that the last clause was unconstitutional, without deciding whether the defendant's burning of the flag would be punishable, because the officer's testimony that he heard the defendant's words ("We don't need no damn flag") was enough for the Court to presume the defendant was arrested and convicted for his words alone.

nothing at all, let alone anything of that kind. When he puts "Fuck the Draft" on the back of his jacket, we know this is English. Our conventions make it speech. When he says, during the turbulent years of the war in Vietnam, he is wearing that sentence to protest the war and the draft, to say *that* he protests the war and the draft, we do not respond by saying "No, you said nothing at all." Rather our shared understandings are exactly that these words in this order form an English-language sentence and that we sometimes use "fuck" to express displeasure, to say that we are displeased, but put in scurrilous terminology. In Cohen's case, wearing the sentence said more; he, like Tinker said, "The war is wrong" or "We should get out of Vietnam" and so on. This is truth-functional propositional political and moral expression, not merely emotive discourse, arising in the political upheaval of the 1960's.

In short, then, the way ordinary language users talk in ordinary language about these incidents undergirds and justifies and dictates, with one exception, the Court's decisions in these cases. The exception is the so-called "symbolic speech" doctrine, which is no doctrine at all for two reasons: All speech is symbolic, i.e., is by way of symbols of one sort or another — usually by words, but sometimes by words and other signs, and sometimes by nonword acts alone (e.g., nodding heads). Moreover, all speech involves conduct or action of one sort or another — it always involves at a minimum either vocal-cord/tongue-mouth movements or finger-writing or finger-signing movements or handing written materials to someone, and so on; or else the speech requires a shared understanding that particular movements of the body (nod head) or manipulation of symbols, about which society already has a shared understanding of the meaning of the symbol (the American flag), are modes of expressing our propositional thoughts. Similarly, marching in a group of demonstrators is ordinary-language speech in at least the sense that ordinary speakers will say the marchers are saying something by marching. Sleeping in a park is not, and the difference is exactly one of shared notions about how to express propositional attitudes without using words, i.e., what we would say about these two positionings of our bodies.[167]

The "symbolic speech" doctrine is deep-seated philosophical nonsense from the vantage of the nature of ordinary language's "speech" itself. But neither that nor any of the other points I have sketched means the Court needs to engage in either philosophy of language or linguistics. Indeed, to believe I have suggested or implied such a view here is entirely to miss my point. The Court arrived at the proper results in each of these cases

[167] Clark v. Community for Creative Non-Violence, 468 U.S. 288 (1984) (federal ban on camping in park does not violate first amendment), thus reaches the right result but could have used an easier ground of no-speech. One reason the Court did not is that it is fond of the "symbolic speech" doctrine, and scholars have not done their jobs in disabusing the Court and each other of this doctrine. Another reason the Court did not use a no-speech approach was that the Court knew how to apply the rest of the tests of *O'Brien*, 391 U.S. 367, to reach the same no-infirmity result. The interesting questions for scholars, then, are whether the *O'Brien* protection analyses ever can lead to a result of constitutional-infirmity when there is no speech and whether the Court should avoid the no-speech analyses.

and gave reasons that were all-but-exactly the right ones to give, not because the Court is accomplished in philosophy or political theory or socio-psycho linguistics, but because the Court is made up of men and women who speak ordinary English, which already embodies these very distinctions on the basis of our shared understandings and vice versa.

Relatedly, every now and then I meet someone who insists that "the freedom of speech" is a technical language phrase because "speech" is a technical term under the Court's interpretation in that the Court applies the first amendment to nonoral, i.e., written, uses of language. These people imagine that the ordinary language meaning of "speech" is limited to oral communications from the stump, so to speak, and they point to "Did you read the President's speech" as being elliptical for "Did you read the text of the President's speech." We indeed do have both locutions, and the former may well be the elliptical form of the latter; but that does not prove their point. Nor does the pattern of the following exchange: I ask, "Did you speak to her?" You answer, "No, but I left her a note." The reason examples such as these (and they can be multiplied) do not establish that the Court's use of "speech" is a technical term in covering nonoral linguistic behavior is exactly the same sort of reason the Court's use of "speech" covers certain nonword behaviors that say something. This reason is that ordinary English speakers use the words "say," "speak" and "speech" both broadly and narrowly, i.e., both as generic words and as particular-instance words, just as we similarly use "chicken" as a generic word and as a particular-instance word.[168]

Nor is the Court's use deviant in the other direction, although this is decidedly harder to see, in failing to count certain speech acts as speech for first amendment purposes. Perjury, for example, and solicitation for sex are not first amendment speech. Solicitation for votes is, but not because of the speech act. Speech acts of the performative verb sort — "I promise," "I christen," etc. — are not first amendment speech because they are not speech but acts in the sense that the way to do these acts is to use words. Just as the only way to shoot someone is to shoot him or her, the only way to perjure is to lie under oath; the performative verb here is "I swear" and the oath is "to tell the truth, the whole truth, and nothing but the truth." We give that oath in circumstances in which *all* we can do is speak out loud or hold our tongues. We are not even able to use head nods or head shakes, because our questioner will say, "Answer the question, please, out loud so that the court reporter and the jury may hear it." This is not speech, but an act done through words.[169]

I have no doubt, of course, that if a court were required to rule on a first amendment freedom of speech challenge to a perjury prosecution, the court would reject the first amendment challenge by saying that provision of the Constitution protects truth; that falsity receives protec-

---

[168] See § I. C., *supra*.

[169] This is far from being Emerson's speech/conduct distinction, both in basis and in method, although it goes to one of his purposes, viz., to make plain that the first amendment is not about what glue carpenters use to join surfaces or about carpenters using glue to join surfaces.

tion only insofar as that is necessary in order to give breathing room for truthful speech and to avoid a chilling effect on truthful speech; and that the deliberate, knowing, injurious making of false statements under oath is not protected under "the freedom of speech."[170] But just as beating someone over the head with a hammer is not speech, we sometimes use certain words in certain ways to *do*, instead of using words to describe, ask, or say. I probably more safely would put my claim about performative verb speech acts by saying that, because in ordinary English they are different from other speech acts, i.e., are a special case differing from our other uses of words, they equally may be treated as a special case under "speech" in the first amendment.

But consider when we say, "She said she promised that p" instead of "She promised that p." We use the latter more naturally to report her speech act, and we reserve the former for occasions when we wish to cast doubt on her sincerity or to clarify what her words were without departing from indirect-quotation usages. I ask, "What did she do while I was away?" when I have no hint of her acts. If she said "I promise I will pay you" to Peter, you will report by saying "She promised to pay Peter;" but if she said "The governor may run a favorite-son campaign," you will report by saying "She said the governor will run a favorite-son campaign." In the latter case, you also may say, "She didn't do anything; she just talked about the governor's running a favorite-son campaign." But in the former case, no one would say, "She didn't do anything; she just promised Peter she would pay him."[171]

Of course, perhaps my discussion from my perjury point to here is wrong. My ear for ordinary English already may have been bent by the law's view; that performative verbs for committing perjury, for ordering, promising, betting, etc. do not raise a first amendment speech issue on their own and that, if there is one, it arises from the nominalized sentence or propositional content embedded behind the performative verb.[172] If that is true, then scholars who say the Court's use of "speech" in first amendment analysis picks up some, but not all, of what the ordinary English

---

[170] What the court *should* say, of course, is that perjury is not speech, rather than that it is not protected speech.

[171] I am contrasting two of her speech acts and the two reporting locutions; note, then, the similarity between "She promised to pay Peter" and "She kicked the dog."

[172] To carry out the details of my claim about performative uses of performative verbs I would need to do some trimming on the membership of that category. Austin, for example, once identified "I assert that p" and "I state that p" as performative verb speech acts, yet they obviously differ significantly from "I promise that p." They are, to speak loosely, more like "I say that p." That is, they may be put in front of virtually anything we utter or write. They also raise some of the same problems that the predicates ". . . is true" and ". . . is false" raise. *See, e.g.*, Tarski, *The Semantic Conception of Truth and the Foundations of Semantics*, 4 J. PHIL. & PHENOMENOLOGICAL RES. 341 (1944), *reprinted in* READINGS IN PHILOSOPHICAL ANALYSIS (H. Feigl & W. Sellars eds. 1949) at 52 (". . . is true" as a metalinguistic predicate of sentences); Strawson, *Truth*, 9 ANALYSIS (1949), *reprinted in* E. NAGEL & R. BRANDT, MEANING AND KNOWLEDGE 160 (1965) (performative theory of ". . . is true").

word "speech" covers are right,[173] although for different reasons than they may believe. In any event, it allows me to enter, by the backdoor, the other point I wish to make about the Court's use of "speech." Sometimes ordinary language, taken in the broad sense of how we talk about things, gives out as a source of information about what we think about them or what they are. When the Court faces a first amendment issue under "the freedom of speech" in these circumstances, the Court is at the cutting-edge of our language and of our societal beliefs.

Here the Court must rely on and must construct a theory in interpreting "the freedom of speech" and must treat the first amendment as one of our prescriptive institutions that is to function as one of the foundations of our free society. The Court uses a number of different theories, drawing strands from each: Mill's marketplace of ideas,[174] Meiklejohn's informed electorate,[175] Rawl's veil-of-ignorance contract,[176] Scanlon's personal autonomy,[177] Schauer's governmental ineptness,[178] and so on. When the Court is successful in fulfilling its role as prescriptive interpreter, society will follow to where the Court is leading by internalizing the values the Court identifies under the first amendment and the uses to which the

---

Further refinements would be necessary to deal with "I solicit," as in "I solicit you for sex" and "I solicit your vote." Austin's double-checking "hereby" does not sound right to my ear with "solicit," and I cannot "hear" speakers using "I solicit your vote for candidate Smith" — rather, here I hear "I am soliciting votes for candidate Smith; may we count on yours?" That is, "I solicit" from non-Smith persons sounds to my ear like canvassing voters and as not being noncontinuous. But Smith may stand on the stump and *may* say, "I solicit your votes in next Tuesday's election." Or so Sandy Levinson recently suggested to me in conversation. I never have heard that use of "solicit" from a politician; what I have heard them say using "solicit" is, "I am here to solicit your votes" or "I am soliciting votes," etc. Similarly, what I hear people saying is, "I would like to solicit a favor from you," not "I hereby solicit a favor from you." Relatedly, a prostitute's solicitation and solicitation of a prostitute "sounds" to me in someone's saying "I am soliciting you for sex," and not in "I hereby solicit you for sex," assuming "solicit" "sounds" in either locution. (That is, both of these locutions strike my ear as nonnatural.) As far as I can hear, "solicit" does not as a matter of fact function performatively the way "promise," "christen," "order," etc. do. That is, it could have, but it does not: We do not use it performatively.

In short, if Sandy Levinson is correct in claiming "solicit" does have a performative use of the sort that "promise" does, at least one of the performative verb speech acts, which are "doings" via words and not speech in ordinary English according to my view, is speech under the first amendment, albeit perhaps not always protected. In that event, the Court's use of "speech" captures some, but not all, of ordinary language "speech" in another sense than the one I discuss for "obscenity" in the text following this note, for I will have taken too seriously the title of Austin's book: "How to do things with words."

[173] *See, e.g.*, Schauer, *Speech and "Speech" — Obscenity and "Obscenity": An Exercise in the Interpretation of Constitutional Language*, 67 GEO. L.J. 899 (1979).

[174] J. MILL, ON LIBERTY (D. Spitz ed. 1975).

[175] A. MEIKLEJOHN, FREE SPEECH AND ITS RELATION TO SELF-GOVERNMENT (1948), *reprinted in* part I of his POLITICAL FREEDOM: THE CONSTITUTIONAL POWERS OF THE PEOPLE (1979).

[176] J. RAWLS, A THEORY OF JUSTICE (1971).

[177] Scanlon, *A Theory of Freedom of Expression*, 1 PHIL. & PUB. AFFAIRS 204 (1972).

[178] F. SCHAUER, FREE SPEECH: A PHILOSOPHICAL ENQUIRY (1982).

Court puts "speech." We have authorized the Court to do this by adopting the first amendment and creating the Court; and as we internalize the Court's uses of "speech," we will change our own ordinary uses of "speech." As long as that happens, we never can be cut off from the language of the first amendment because we will have the Court's opinion and its statement of theory for "stretching" "speech" to bide us over until we can internalize the cutting-edge use. Having to give an explanation that will hold up in the light of day in turn constrains the Court from jumping too far ahead of the rest of us.

The Court is at a cutting-edge point on "obscenity," for example. Obscene books and obscene nonmime plays involve words. Obscene movies often do involve words, but obviously need not, any more than artist's drawings need to involve words. The Court says obscenity is not first amendment speech,[179] and that looks counter-intuitive. That is, it looks contrary to the ordinary language word "speech" insofar as the Court is saying, for example, a book does not qualify under "speech" of the first amendment. To say this of artist's drawings is not similarly counter-intuitive, and it is even less counter-intuitive to deny speech status to sexual acts performed at high noon in Times Square. In saying obscenity is not speech under "the freedom of speech" and including books and nonmime plays and talking pictures along with artist's drawings when these all have certain characteristics in common with sexual acts in Times Square, the Court is building a theoretical stretch into "speech" for "the freedom of speech" and shaping the ordinary language words "obscenity" and "obscene." These theoretical stretches are difficult ones because sexual acts between human beings are not themselves obscene, and this means describing what the "certain characteristics in common" are is difficult.

A society that does not have a written first amendment stated in terms of "the freedom of speech" does not have to resolve the exact contours of meaning for "obscene" or "obscenity" with special reference to "speech." Our society does, however; and some of the difficulties of resolution are compounded by mass marketing of talking pictures. Over time, the Court's resolutions will affect the ways all of us talk about obscenity and speech and will affect our views of a just and free society. Contracts courts describe where we already are, but free-speech courts sometimes tell us where we are going. The former move with us and the way we talk in ordinary ways, but we sometimes move with the latter and learn to talk in new ordinary ways.

### *D. Speaking Entre Nous: Lawyers and Law Professors*

None of my arguments tell us how lawyers talk with each other about the law when clients are not around, nor how they may need to talk in

---

[179] Miller v. California, 413 U.S. 15 (1973); Roth v. United States, 354 U.S. 476 (1957).

that circumstance. If technical languages are useful in the sciences to enable clearer and faster communication from scientist to scientist and technical uses are similarly useful for trades people, lawyers have no less need for clarity and for efficiently quick modes of communicating with one another.

Lawyers certainly may and do make different-deployment and one-among-many-meanings technical uses of ordinary English. This kind of short or exact speaking goes with the territory of any fairly regular, fairly compartmented discipline, occupation, or activity. This, of course, does not get lawyers into speaking a technical language because these terms are ordinary English put to technical uses. The question is whether among themselves lawyers use technical terms in some more interesting sense. Do lawyers, speaking among themselves, have terms that are completely cut off from English and that obtain their meaning from theory; or terms that have meanings only part of which are marginally related to same-sounding, same-looking ordinary English words and that are central terms in a theory; or terms that are fixed to one among many ordinary language meanings but also are theoretical terms? Due process constrains the language of the law and constrains the language of lawyers in court, but due process does not constrain the language of lawyers among themselves away from clients and juries. Do they then have a technical language?

No. They do have jargon and argot. Some of these modes of short-talking are specific to a particular law firm or to divisions in the firm to the point that they almost are not even remotely English, but some kind of code. When lawyers go outside those groups and forget to switch out of code or short-talk, they sound inarticulate to the rest of us or, worse, incomprehensible. Usually someone in the group asks these lawyers to repeat themselves; and, as the joke's mark hits home, the smart ones then switch into English, and the others repeat themselves. Sometimes, of course, lawyers refuse to use ordinary English in order to impress or intimidate. That often backfires. Aside from whether some lawyers are making the rest of the profession look bad by being inarticulate or intimidating, I see no reason to worry about their jargon or argot or codes.

There is reason, however, to be concerned about some occasions of using ordinary English words with a technical use. Lawyers do not run into trouble talking among themselves using "consideration," for example; nor do they run into trouble using it with clients or before juries as long as they remember somewhere along the line to say that what they are talking about is bargained exchange. Even if they do not remember, probably nothing untoward happens because most ordinary-English speakers are familiar with this technical use of "consideration." But lawyers sometimes do worse than this. Not long ago, in a state that shall go unnamed, a jury-instruction-guidelines panel considered writing an instruction for the jury to answer "Is there consideration for the contract," as part of determining contract-formation issues. What, exactly, would a jury do with an instruction of this sort stated in *just* these words? The panel seems to me to have confused a legal-conclusion label that summarizes certain findings of facts with a factual finding, and I suspect the culprit here is that not enough of lawyers' audiences make lawyers speak plainly and drop road signs for their technical uses, until lawyers forget their technical use is technical.

Ordinary people who do not speak up and force candor from lawyers are at their mercy. With courts the matter is a bit otherwise because there are scholars who make their livings out of analyzing courts' opinions and assessing what the courts said or should have said. And, of course, these same scholars do the same to the analyses of other scholars. If lawyers make their livings on words, legal scholars make their livings on other people's words.

Scholars have a role to play, however, that is as important as the roles of lawyers for clients and judges for parties. For in critically analyzing and theorizing about the law, decided and yet-to-come, scholars help courts bridge the gap when settled conventions and ordinary language give out. Not only are judges not philosopher kings, they also are not psychologists, sociologists, engineers, linguists and so on. Even if they had the inclination, they do not have the luxury of time for the reflective study and thought that goes into theory-construction. When judges construct theories, then, they do not do so out of the air, but out of articles and books, as well as out of what they already know because they have grown up in our society. If scholars fail to do the spade work in preparation for the difficult issues courts will face or if they fail to be intellectually honest, the law may end up taking a blind turn. That may be more dangerous to freedom than a technical language of the law that only lawyers can speak.

# [2]

# On The Regrettable Decline of Law French: Or Shapiro Jettet Le Brickbat

**Martin Shapiro**†

Whenever a distinguished scholar prescribes a new scholarly endeavor, we must imagine it as practiced not by him alone but by the academic multitudes and thus in its most vulgarized form. What follows is unashamedly worst-case analysis, but—present precincts excepted of course—the worst case is often enough the real case. It may be particularly unfair to subject Professor Stone's paper to this sort of analysis, in part because his own past work is in such excellent contrast to the tendencies I am about to denounce and in part because he himself sees the dangers and repeatedly warns against them. Against such considerations, however, must be counterbalanced the finding of so many of the participants in this symposium that, no matter what the signals offered by the intellectual leadership, the bulk of legal scholarship continues to focus on routine doctrinal analysis. Perhaps a handful of particularly subtle minds will be able to practice the sensitivity to language for which Professor Stone calls without falling into arid self-contemplation, but I am more concerned with the place his paper will take in the overall movement of academic legal writing.

Professor Stone's call for "law *as* a language" may well be the first trumpet call of an essentially reactionary movement in legal scholarship, a retreat into the bowels of law from the various *law and* movements. Lawyers see the stream of law and sociology, law and politics, law and economics, law and psychology as fragmenting their scholarly core and corps. They do not want to bother mastering one *and* after another. They may not see great payoffs in the past *ands*. Here they are wrong, but the payoffs often have not been as great as the pioneering zealots have promised. In some instances, such as law and politics, the internalization of the *and* has been so great that the legal scholars have almost forgotten that it was an alien force they were absorbing.[1]

† Professor of Law, University of California at Berkeley.

1. *Compare* Deutsch, *Neutrality, Legitimacy, and the Supreme Court: Some Intersections between Law and Political Science*, 20 STAN. L. REV. 169 (1968) (treating political

Comment on Stone

The great monument to this resistance to *law and* is the continuity of structure and staffing of the American law school. Of course, the *avant garde* of the academy make a great to-do about the scatter of curriculum innovations and the dusting of social science faculty members. The contrast with medical schools, however, remains striking. Medical schools require their students to enter with extensive undergraduate preparation in the sciences on which medicine depends and, in spite of the ideological inroads of the 70s, cram two more years of science into them before doing much about medicine itself. The law schools still require nothing of their entrants and still teach them nothing but law, albeit law with an occasional incursion of something else.

Over and above the context of fatigue and *stasis* in which it is offered, the prescription of law as language may turn out to be reactionary in a far more fundamental sense. It has always been easier to deal with law as a closed system of concepts than as a real world set of behaviors. All the *law and* movements seek to treat law as a combination of the two. The *law as* language movement on the other hand is to be seen as a means of abstracting from the world as it exists. It is an assertion that the proper study of legal scholars is that most internal part of the law itself, the language of the law, a language seen as separate and peculiar, and one in which the scholar's task is to polish up the concepts and vocabulary until the language seems beautiful *to the native speakers.*

The *laws as* language approach may mask its retreat to formalism by appearing itself to be the latest of the *law and* movements, law and language, and thus also to be looking outward as well as inward. The turn toward language, however, moves law to precisely that area where the most subtle and slippery relation exists between conceptualization and the study of behavior. For the study of language can either be the study of language behavior—how specified speaker X communicates with specified listener Y—or it can be the study of how "we" speak. Once real speech of real speakers to real listeners is transformed into abstracted speech of universal speakers to universal audiences, the study of language turns into the clarification of words and concepts in the abstract or in prototypic contexts. Once law and lan-

science as subject independent of law) *with* J. ELY, DEMOCRACY AND DISTRUST (1980) (analyzing judicial review from perspective combining law and political science), Schuck, *The Graying of Civil Rights Law: The Age Discrimination Act of 1975*, 89 YALE L.J. 27 (1979) (examining nondiscrimination statute from same perspective), Stewart, *The Reformation of American Administrative Law*, 88 HARV. L. REV. 1667 (1975) (analyzing administrative law developments from same perspective).

guage begins to deal with what "we lawyers" say, it will easily slip down the slope into treating law as an independent, closed conceptual system. Law as language is aimed principally at reasserting the autonomy of law—at returning law to lawyers by claiming that law is a specialized language that only lawyers can speak. It is indicative that Stone turns to musical notation and mathematics, esoteric languages that allow their masters to claim that others cannot understand, let alone contribute to, their disciplines.

The suspicion that Stone is in reactionary retreat rather than advancing in new directions is heightened by the tone of Section VI.[2] Law is to examine its own navel carefully to see how its use of words varies—but only a bit and only subtly—from common English. In the process it will achieve waivering conclusions comparable to those in ethics and aesthetics. Law, aesthetics, and ethics are to exploit "the mutuality of our ignorance" to search out common "fundamental principles." Is this more than a prologue to yet another round in the endless search for the holy grail of neutral principles or reasoned elaboration or the law working itself clear? In lesser hands than Stone's, won't all this be a return to the jurisprudence of concepts? Will legal aesthetics be any different from the old German "legal science" except for allowing the ideological preferences behind the wordplay to show more clearly?

Is Professor Stone's paper a retreat to formalism followed by the promise that formalism can be just as good a tool for a new social democratic ideology as it was for the old liberal democratic ideology? I believe that there is a way of turning the law as language movement in a better direction. As I have just suggested, to begin with the question "what do we lawyers mean when we say 'the average reasonable man'?" is to court disaster: a barren exercise in analytic philosophy, Perelmanian rhetoric, or 1940s semantics that will lead only to the insight that lawyers don't talk exactly as other people and on the other hand they don't talk so differently either. If we begin instead by asking why a lawyer occupying a specific position (plaintiff's tort lawyer, trial judge, insurance company claims adjuster) uses the term "average reasonable man" when speaking to a specific audience (individual lay client, opposing counsel, judge, corporate client's in-house counsel, jury) in a particular setting (office conversation, appellate brief, letter stating claim, letter threatening suit, law review article), then law-as-language studies may help us to gain new

2. Stone, *From a Language Perspective*, 90 YALE L.J. 1149, 1168-73 (1981).

Comment on Stone

insights about the real world and insights that allow us to describe the real world more precisely. I believe that it is far more possible to describe the real world precisely than to describe legal language precisely, if we mean by legal language some general linguistic system. It is far easier to describe legal language in a new but vague way, however, than it is to describe the real world precisely. That is the pitfall in the Stone approach: its most probable consequence is the easy way out—more law jaw-jaw—rather than the harder but more useful way out—specific description of actual language behavior.

In short, I believe that law should not now make a last start down the high road of modern linguistic philosophy—which is probably not going anywhere anyway—but ought to start down the low road of pragmatics or semiotics or communications theory, or whatever you want to call the study of language in specific context. This context has (1) a specific pre-existing situation, (2) a specific sender, (3) a specific transmission medium, (4) a specific receiver, (5) a specific change in the pre-existing situation subsequent to the transmission. The low road would quickly lead us to (1) a new perspective, (2) a new body of data, and (3) new analytical tools.

(1) We have both deliberately and unconsciously treated law talk as the talk of judges to other judges and to lawyers contemplating future litigation (case method, *stare decisis*). But the two principal talks of lawyers are lawyer to client (counseling) and lawyer to lawyer (negotiating). We have assumed without empirical investigation that these two talks are so heavily determined by judge to judge and judge to lawyer talk that we may study the case law tail rather than the counseling and negotiating dog. What if we began our study of law with the proposition that law is not what judges say in the reports but what lawyers say—to one another and to clients—in their offices?

(2) What if our data were not the reports but office files?

(3) What if our tool was the historical reconstruction of the flow of talk rather than Lexis?

Such an approach would give us a more accurate description of law as it is. Would it do more: would it give us a tool for making law "better" in some sense? Yes, because it would allow us to spot failures of communications and so lead to the improvement of communications technique. More important, it would allow us to see where legal conflict or misunderstanding was a result of inadequate communication and where it was a result of differing purposes in different categories of senders and receivers.

My disagreements with (or perhaps only differences of emphasis from) Stone can be seen in the following diagramatic pastiche which, for the sake of completeness, also charts a middle road about which I know too little to comment. The difficulty with talking about law *as* language or even law *and* language is that it lumps together all the various paths so roughly sketched here. I accuse Professor Stone first of trying to reestablish the autonomy of legal discourse—law *as* its own language rather than law *and* everybody's language—and second of taking the high road on my sketch map while I take the low.

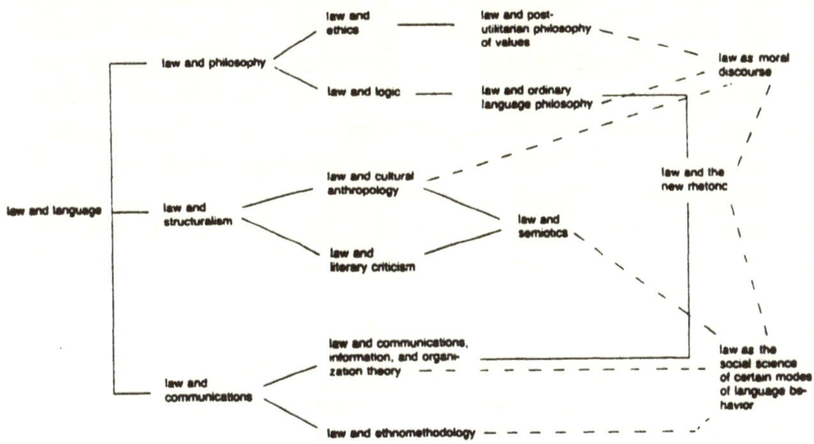


There are hints that Stone might be willing to head down the communications theory and ethno-methodology paths. His concentric circle image[3] appears to me ambivalent, on the one hand implicating practical and specific language behavior in the realm of legal scholarship, on the other reserving the central place of honor for abstract law-language analysis. If, however, he is in fact urging law and philosophy, then, as he himself repeatedly suggests, he is choosing an uncertain way. Ordinary language philosophy is already chasing its own tail. As to the new ethics, the lawyer's wish is father to the belief that it will get very far. The building of a post-consequentialist ethics is still at a rudimentary and confused stage,[4] and, as a number of the contributors to this symposium argue, such an ethics will prob-

3. *See id.* at 1173-79.

4. *See* Barry, *And Who Is my Neighbor?* 88 YALE L.J. 629, 630-34 (1979) (reviewing C. FRIED, RIGHT AND WRONG (1977)) (paradigm of moral philosophy to succeed consequentialism not yet fully formed).

Comment on Stone

ably be unable to provide a fully satisfactory moral justification for the liberal democratic state of which our law is a part.

I believe that Stone's preferred path actually lies along the lines to moral discourse and that he is really part of the new jurisprudence of values that we have already seen taking shape in legal and political theory,[5] in constitutional law,[6] and in the attacks on law and economics.[7]

This new jurisprudence of values has been generated in part by developments in philosophy but in far greater part by the renewed self-confidence of lawyers. Chastised by the New Deal and its realist fellow travelers, lawyers and judges had subsided into subordination to the demos. Revived by their singular success at exploiting the political structures of the 1950s, 60s, and 70s, and having become leaders of an elite, antidemocratic intellectual stratum bent on forcing equality and other virtues down the throats of the booboisie, lawyers and judges now commission the academy to tell us that they can correct the faults of a decadent polyarchy. At their most modest, the new scholars tell us that lawyers and judges should engage in representation reinforcing. At their most bumptious, they tell us that if only lawyers are left free to talk to one another—that is, to litigate—then their language, properly honed of the professionals, by the professionals, and for the professionals, will produce more correct ethical judgments than the rest of us can produce by our Doolittlian jabber.[8]

Professor Stone's paper is, in its own terms, a call for a more sensitive, self-conscious, and objective examination of legal language than has generally occurred in the advocacy-based scholarship that has been assailed by a number of contributors to this symposium. I believe, however, that the law as language approach that he chooses will, quite contrary to his own intentions, simply contribute to the hubris of the jurisprudence-of-values movement in particular and of academic lawyers in general. For in spite of the assorted pessimisms

5. *See, e.g.*, R. DWORKIN, TAKING RIGHTS SERIOUSLY (1977); C. FRIED, RIGHT AND WRONG (1977); M. WALZER, JUST AND UNJUST WARS (1977).

6. *See, e.g.*, B. ACKERMAN, SOCIAL JUSTICE AND THE LIBERAL STATE (1980); Fiss, *The Supreme Court, 1978 Term—Foreword: The Forms of Justice*, 93 HARV. L. REV. 1 (1979); Tribe, *The Puzzling Persistence of Process-Based Constitutional Theories*, 89 YALE L.J. 1063 (1980).

7. *See, e.g.*, Fletcher, *Fairness and Utility in Tort Theory*, 85 HARV. L. REV. 537 (1972).

8. It is because they are feeling their own oats, but have become accustomed to the various *law and* movements, that academic lawyers wish to impute a similar renewed self-confidence to moral philosophers who will be towed along as footnotes to the lawyers' self-assertions of moral grandeur.

The Yale Law Journal Vol. 90: 1198, 1981

and self-doubts expressed in this symposium by Professors Brest[9] and Tushnet,[10] law and philosophy will be the high road to assertions of the moral and intellectual, and thus political, superiority of lawyers.

I must conclude that some twenty years hence when the *Yale Law Journal* again has the temerity to hold a conference on legal scholarship, we shall have the new Cokes speaking, as Stone already does, of the artificial reason of the law, and that at the third such conference we shall be more than ready for the new Benthams.

9. *See* Brest, *The Fundamental Rights Controversy: The Essential Contradictions of Normative Constitutional Scholarship*, 90 YALE L.J. 1063, 1106-09 (1981).

10. *See* Tushnet, *Legal Scholarship: Its Causes and Cure*, 90 YALE L.J. 1205, 1223 (1981).

# [3]

# SYMPOSIUM: THEORY AND DEFINITION IN JURISPRUDENCE.

MR. JONATHAN COHEN AND PROFESSOR H. L. A. HART.

## I.

*By* JONATHAN COHEN.

I WISH to contest the challenging thesis about jurisprudence which Professor Hart so lucidly expounded in his Inaugural Lecture.[1]

Hart was concerned there with " those questions of analytical jurisprudence which are usually characterised as requests for definitions " (p. 3): What is a right? What is a duty? What is possession? What is a corporation? Of course, such interrogative sentences are sometimes used instead to demand " the cause or the purpose or the justification or the origin of a legal or political institution ". And these questions legitimately give rise to what Hart calls " theories ", which assert or deny " the claims of organised groups to recognition by the State " (p. 7) or propound sociological or psychological generalisations about the judicial process. But all too often, according to Hart, the two kinds of enquiry—the search for definitions and the search for some sort of theory—have become entangled to the detriment of the former. Theory has grown up " on the back of definition " and distorted it. In confirmation of this thesis Hart argues that juristic theories which purport to answer questions like " What is a right ? " or " What is a corporation? " fall " disquietingly often into a familiar triad " (p. 6). " Theories of one type tell us that a word stands for some unexpected variant of the familiar—a complex fact where we expect something unified and simple,

---

[1] *Definition and Theory in Jurisprudence* (1953), reprinted in *The Law Quarterly Review*, January 1954

a future fact where we expect something present, a psychological fact where we expect something external ". Thus the American Realists tell us that a right is a term by which we describe the prophecies we make of the probable behaviour of courts or officials, and others have argued that the name of a corporate body is " really just a collective name or abbreviation for some complex but still plain facts about ordinary persons ". Theorists of a second type, like Hägerström and Olivecrona, say that words like these stand " for what is in some sense a fiction ". And " theories of a third (now unfashionable) type ", like Gierke's theory of group personality, tell us that such a word " stands for something different from other things just in that we cannot touch it, hear it, see it, feel it ".

As against such " vast and irreconcilable " bodies of doctrine Hart argues that we surely can " elucidate the meaning of words which every developed legal system handles smoothly and alike " without assuming any " incubus of theory" (p. 6). Of course, many jurists, *e.g.*, Bentham (p. 8) and Maitland (p. 18 f.), have had occasional insights into the way in which legal terms function. But according to Hart analytical jurisprudence can and should now benefit from the fact that in modern linguistic philosophy " the general features have emerged of that whole style of human thought and discourse which is concerned with rules and their application to conduct " (p. 28). We can now see that the traditional method of definition by genus and difference is quite inappropriate to words like " right " and " corporation ". That method aims at the classification of entities, and thus it seeks for what a word " taken alone describes, for what *it* stands, for what *it* means " (p. 18). If the method is applied to the definition of fundamental legal terms it inevitably abstracts them from the complete sentences in which alone their full function can be seen, and provokes unnecessary philosophical puzzlement about what kinds of entity—" complex, recondite or fictitious " (p. 23)—are really named by these terms. The function of such terms can instead be illuminated by an analogy with the rules of games " which at many vital points have the same puzzling logical structure as rules of law " (p. 9). It will then be evident that the expression " a legal right " may be elucidated as follows:—" (1) A statement of the form ' *X* has a right ' is true if the following conditions are satisfied: (*a*) There is in existence a legal system. (*b*) Under a rule or rules of the system some other person *Y* is, in the events which have happened, obliged to do or abstain from some action. (*c*) This obligation is made by law dependent on the choice either of *X* or some other person authorised to act on his behalf so that either *Y* is bound to do or abstain from some action only if *X* (or some authorised person) so chooses or alternatively only until *X* (or such person) chooses otherwise. (2) A statement of the form ' *X* has a right ' is used to draw a conclusion of law in a particular case which falls under such rules " (p. 16 f.). Analogously, " if we put aside the question ' What is a corporation? ' and ask instead ' Under what types of conditions does the law ascribe liabilities to corporations? ', this is likely to clarify the actual working of a legal system and bring out the precise issues at stake when judges, who are supposed not to legislate, make some new extension to corporate bodies of rules worked out for individuals " (p. 24).

A great insight of Wittgenstein's—that a philosopher can benefit from asking how words are used rather than what they mean—has thus been applied by Hart to a field in which its cathartic influence was much needed. I do not dispute the value of this insight or of applying it in analytical jurisprudence, nor do I wish to defend any juristic theory's dependence on inappropriate methods of definition. With one important proviso (which I shall elaborate shortly) I agree with Hart's thesis that unnecessary puzzlement and confusion may be avoided if one does not try to elucidate fundamental legal terms entirely in abstraction from the verbal contexts in which they normally function. But I do not agree that one can thus screen off juristic definition as a relatively uncontroversial topic, from the heated atmosphere of juristic theory. I shall argue that any adequate elucidation of legal terms like " right " or

" corporation " is inevitably bound up—implicitly or explicitly, systematically or piecemeal—with what Hart would call " theory ", and that this connection need not involve any linguistic muddle.

My argument will hang largely on exploring why and in what sense it is true to say, as is not uncommonly suggested, that much correct judicial decision consists, not in subsuming cases under rules, but in bringing rules over cases, not in invoking *the* obviously relevant rule, but in selecting or enunciating, and then applying, a possibly relevant one. In the philosophy of law, as often elsewhere, it seems that " How is it used? " is not quite what we must ask, in order to reformulate the question " What does it mean? " We may be misled not merely by the transitiveness of the verb in the latter sentence, but also by its indicative mood. For where several conflicting patterns of use are in vogue, as there often are when puzzlement arises, a request for definition is, if it cannot be satisfactorily answered by lexicographers' tabulations of all uses, a cry for help. It seeks the reasoned recommendation of one selected use-pattern. If a jurist avoids treating requests for the definition of legal terms like " right " and " incorporation " as enquiries how these words *should* be used, he shows that for the moment he does not want to try and help those puzzled about the conflicting uses of such words in cases where the relevant law itself is, or has been, unclear. Perhaps he believes that puzzlement about the correct judicial decision in these cases is in the main independent of worry about definitions. But it is the abnormal situation as well as, if not more than, the normal one which tests the adequacy of theories claiming to express the general truth conditions of statements like Hart's " *X* has a right ". There would be considerably less controversy about " seeing " if drunkards never claimed to " see " pink rats. And I shall try to show that many definitional theories in jurisprudence can usefully be regarded as attempts to provide for word-usage in abnormal situations as well as in normal ones, rather than as misunderstandings about the function of legal nouns.

## II.

I said that I wished to make a proviso about agreeing with Hart on the utility, for some purposes, of not abstracting legal nouns from their sentential contexts. For I want to emphasise that there are two importantly different kinds of reason for this utility, corresponding to a difference in type among the fundamental legal concepts to which Hart applies his thesis.

(1) If concepts of legal right and duty created the same sort of puzzlement as concepts of possession and corporation, one would certainly expect that theories of the three kinds which Hart thinks disquietingly frequent would always be built around the offer of analogous definitions for both sets of concepts. Positivist definitions of " legal right " for, instance, would be accompanied by positivist definitions of " corporation ", and fiction theories of corporations would be bound up with fiction theories of rights. But in fact, of course, this is not so. By no means all these jurists approach their task with a single-minded metaphysical preconception about the correct analysis of all legal nouns. Admittedly, for Bentham legal rights were just as much fictions as were pledges of prosecution or bills in equity, even though the former were much more useful than the latter.[2] But Savigny held a fiction theory of corporations, and believed legal duties to be valid for a people just so far as they embodied its spirit.[3] Gierke, on the other hand, believed all corporations to have spirits of their own,while he adhered to the positivist theory that the validity of a legal duty depends on its imposition by the state.[4] Nor were these differences in either case the result of careless or

[2] *Bentham's Theory of Fictions*, ed. C. K. Ogden (1932), pp. 118, 142 and 146. Ogden has suggested (p. xi) a special origin for Bentham's excessive pre-occupation with fictions.

[3] *System des heutigen römischen Rechts* (1840), bk. ii, para. 60, and *Vom Beruf unserer Zeit für Gesetzgebung und Rechtswissenschaft* (1840), p. 43.

[4] Cf. *Political Theories of the Middle Ages*, ed. Maitland (1900), pp. xxvi, 98, et al., and *Natural Law and the Theory of Society*, ed. Barker (1934), vol. i, p. 226,

inconsistent thinking. Savigny held that corporations could only have a fictitious personality because the legal rules embodying a nation's spirit were primarily concerned to regulate the liberties of its individual members. And Gierke believed that corporations had a life of their own whether or not this achieved statutory recognition.

(2) It happens that under most, if not all, contemporary legal systems there are rights and duties of corporations and of possession. But that is a historical fact, not a logico-linguistic feature of rules. It is quite conceivable, though very unlikely, that no system of rules should ever deal with corporations or with possession. But under any system of rules for human conduct either duties or rights must arise, since all these rules must either enjoin or permit some course of action and the function of phrases including " has a right " and " has a duty " that is common to all such contexts is to convey permissions and injunctions, respectively. The use of a verb-plus-noun phrase " *X* has a duty (right) to do act *A* ' is—in its weakest sense—merely an idiomatic substitute for using an auxiliary verb as in " *X* ought to (may) do act *A* ". Moreover, there is an obvious and much-discussed[5] analogy between these so-called " deontic " modalities and the logical ones, though the analogy is sometimes blurred by ethical theories of non-waivable rights,[6] say, or by juristic distinctions, like Hohfeld's between rights, privileges, powers and immunities respectively.[7] According to the former of these two views one has a moral duty to insist on the satisfaction of any claim that it is morally permissible to make. According to the latter, acts legally permitted to any one person are divided into four main groups roughly corresponding to whether some other person has a duty not to interfere with the act, has no right to interfere with it, has a duty created for him by it, or has no power to interfere, respectively. But according to

[5] E.g., G. H. von Wright, *An Essay in Modal Logic* (1951), and A. N. Prior, " The Ethical Copula " in *Australasian Journal of Philosophy*, xxix (1951), p. 137 ff.

[6] E.g., W. G. Maclagan, " Self and Others: A Defence of Altruism " in *Philosophical Quarterly*, iv. (1954), pp. 124-5.

[7] *Fundamental Legal Conceptions*, ed. W. W. Cook (1934), p. 36 ff.

both these theories the phrase " . . . has a right . . . " is just as much confined to being a modal auxiliary as it would be if its proper sense were the much weaker one (=". . . may . . . " *simpliciter*) in which I am at present using it.

(3) Thus, in order to elucidate the concepts of duty and right relative to a system of legal rules, one must initially notice the way in which the words " duty " and " right " function in a complete sentence, as Hart claims. For these words function as modal auxiliaries to some crucial verb-phrase in the sentence which describes an act in law, like " to register a birth " or " to inherit an estate ", respectively. Uttered in isolation " I have a legal duty " and " I have a legal right " are not so much expressions of a legal concept as empty matrices for the application of one. But we have not got the same reason or the same necessity to study complete sentences when investigating the function of words like " corporation " or " possession ". For these words are themselves used to formulate legal concepts. They are not mere auxiliaries. It may, but need not, be true that their definitions must be contextual. In some and perhaps all legal systems " corporation " and " possession " may not be definable by the qualification of more general terms, in the way that Austin, for instance, defines *mora* in Roman law as the non-performance of an obligation.[8] One may have to say " A corporation may be said to exist under one or other of the following conditions and subject to the following exceptions . . . ", and then refer to registration as a limited liability company, incorporation by royal charter, and so on. But the reference is then to specific legal facts and not, as with " A right may be said to exist, under the following conditions . . . " to the logico-linguistic pattern of enunciating and applying rules.

(4) As a logical consequence of this, it makes sense to ask a Scots advocate or a professor of Scots law " Under

[8] *Lectures on Jurisprudence* (1869), p. 490. Choice between these two kinds of definition is sometimes influenced by the extent to which it is desired to restrict the judgment of courts applying the law in question: cf. the U.N. International Law Commission's remarks on the definition of aggression, discussed by J. Stone, *Legal Controls of International Conflict* (1954), p.334.

what conditions and with what exceptions is possession of a house, or the existence of a corporation, a legal fact in Scotland?" But it would either be a misdirected question or an incomplete one to ask such a person "Under what conditions is having a duty, or a right, a legal fact?" If one wanted to put a complete question to him one would have to specify some particular kind of duty or right, like the duty to register a company or the right to take possession of a house. On the other hand, the question "Under what conditions is having a duty, or right, a legal fact?" would not be either misdirected or incomplete if asked of a legal philosopher. For it would be one way of asking what differentiates statements of legal rights and duties from statements of moral, religious and other sorts of right or duty.

(5) Accordingly, we need at least to distinguish between two different kinds of juristic definition, which I shall call "general" and "particular", respectively.[9] Requests for the latter arise from someone's wondering how some particular technical term like "possession" is properly used within some particular legal system, the English one, say, or the French one. This sort of enquiry is commonest among students and practising lawyers and stimulates the writing of legal text-books, like Salmond's on tort, or Jean Ray's *Essai* and *Index*,[10] respectively. But requests for general juristic definitions arise when people are puzzled about, or interested in, concepts which seem to belong peculiarly and necessarily to all developed legal systems. And it is this kind of request that men like Austin and Kelsen have (most of the time) thought themselves to be meeting, though by their answers they have no doubt influenced the way in which text-book writers formulate particular definitions. Perhaps Salmond's views on tort,

[9] Cf. Austin's distinction between "general" and "particular" jurisprudence: ib. pp. 32–33 and 1107.

[10] *Essai sur la Structure Logique du Code Civil Français* (1926), and *Index du Code Civil Français* (1926).

for instance, were affected by a measure of legal positivism.[11]

(6) But it would be an over-simplification to suggest that distinguishing between framework concepts, like right and duty, and material ones, like possession and corporation, is always the same as distinguishing between the topics of general and particular definition, respectively, however much these two distinctions do tend often to coincide. Kelsen, for instance, had general views on the concept of corporation as well as on that of right.[12] Hence one needs to be especially wary of ambiguity in interrogative sentences like " What is a corporation ? " which can be used equally well to ask for a general or a particular definition.

## III.

Hart does not explicitly distinguish between general and particular juristic definitions. But in effect he treats " What is a legal right ? " as seeking one of the former (p. 16), and " What is a corporation ? " as seeking one of the latter (p. 24), while he regards both as questions of " analytical jurisprudence " (p. 3). Yet his strictures against binding up theory with definition cannot apply in quite the same way to both kinds of definition. For though a text book writer may implicitly or explicitly invoke juristic theories he would be giving his readers more than they want from him if he developed these theories as elaborately as a philosopher of law might do. Analogously, one does not normally go to a manual of genetics for a philosophy of science. Moreover, if definitional theories are a muddle when applied to English law, say, the same theories are equally a muddle in all legal systems. For the misunderstanding they all have in common, according to Hart, is not a mistake about the details of any particular legal system, though such a mistake may illustrate it, but

[11] E.g., in his reluctance to criticise decisions: cf. W. T. S. Stallybrass's preface to the 9th edition.

[12] *General Theory of Law and State* (1946), p. 96 ff.

about the logico-linguistic function of legal terms in any language. And certainly Hart's "familiar triad" of theories, which talk about complex, recondite or fictitious entities, respectively, have no regard for national frontiers. Accordingly, an attack on definitional theories in jurisprudence must be basically and directly concerned with general definitions, and only derivatively or illustratively with particular definitions.

I shall therefore concentrate on trying to show in what way Hart's own example of a theory-free general definition —his elucidation of "a legal right"—is incomplete and can usefully be supplemented by what he calls "theory". For I think it needs two distinguishable supplements. One of these should help solve the puzzles of practising lawyers in cases where the relevance of this or that legal rule is unclear. The other should satisfy the more academic requirements of jurists for a general criterion of when a rule is a legal rule. And I think that a supplement which is adequate to the latter requirement should show why the former kind of supplement is also required and why it is more likely to be controversial. It should elucidate, in effect, the apparent paradox that to call someone's right "a legal right" is to imply that relatively non-legal considerations of some sort may enter into the correct premisses for determining this right in the given situation. Of course, many juristic theories, perhaps most, try to provide a single criterion of both legalness and legality. Vyshinsky's theory amounts to this when he regards law, roughly, as the will of a dominant economic class elevated into a statute.[13] One might think it less controversial to say, perhaps, that systems of legal rules are those which law-courts explore for the decision of their cases, just as mathematical systems could be defined as the systems which mathematicians explore for the solution of their problems. But by both definitions, crude as they are, one would be begging a very controversial question. By the former one would be implying that law-courts always find the law and never

[13] *The Law of the Soviet State.* (1948), p. 13.

make any of it—what Roscoe Pound called the " phonograph " theory of the judicial function[14]—just as by the latter one would be endorsing a logicist and discountenancing an intuitionist philosophy of mathematics. And my first aim is not to answer the general juristic question " Under what conditions are legal statements true? " but to determine the field of this question without begging it in any way at the same time. I do not even wish to suggest that social or political philosophy is, or should be taken to be concerned with law in quite the same sense of that term as most jurists seem to be.[15]

Hart's elucidation of " a legal right " is incomplete in one respect, then, because it elucidates " right " (to some extent) but not " legal ". Rights or duties arise under all systems of rules. There is certainly nothing strained or even metaphorical in speaking of the duties of a cricket umpire or the right of an arts student at St. Andrews to take the general class in mathematics instead of that in philosophy. It is not sufficient therefore for a juristic definition of legal right to note the similarities between rules of law and other rules like those of games. One must also notice the crucial differences.

1. For all legal rules there must be a practical, institutional possibility of arguing how they apply to particular disputes. Law without reasoned legal controversy would be as mutilated as mathematics without proofs or disproofs. If no reasoned interpretation of legal rules could ever be announced by courts or pleaded before them in regard to particular cases, it would be as if every facet of human activity were being ordered by purely administrative fiat. Whether or not these fiats followed any system of rules there would be no opportunity for learning directly of any relevant rules, nor for stating reasoned conclusions from them, nor therefore for discussing the validity or invalidity of such statements. In effect, there would then be no subject-

[14] *An Introduction to the Philosophy of Law* (1925), p. 233.
[15] Cf. L. J. Cohen, *Principles of World Citizenship* (1954), p. 37 ff.

matter for jurisprudence. A regime of law would be like one of those children's games called "forfeits" in which a temporary tyrant can order anyone to do anything without giving a reason and the only express rule is "Do what you're told to do". But the practical possibility of legal argument distinguishes life under law, even if it be oppressive law, from a game or despotism of this sort. Indeed, cricket itself would not suffer seriously if everyone tacitly agreed to regard as "not cricket" those occasional disputes which take place about an umpire's decision in especially complicated circumstances. Accordingly, if one is going to compare the function of a judge to that of a cricket umpire, as does Hart (p. 9), one needs to qualify this comparison by recognising that a cricket umpire functions more as an administrator than as a judge. Otherwise one would seem to be blurring in one important respect the useful distinction normally drawn between "judicial" and "administrative" activity.

2. All systems of legal rules impose sanctions, either for the punishment of crimes against them, or for compulsory settlement of civil suits brought under them or for both. I do not mean that rules not habitually enforced are not law. For that is a familiar positivist theory in jurisprudence and I am trying to remain uncommitted to any such theory at this stage. Nor do I mean that all sentence of law in codes, statutes or text-books always occur in pairs, one enunciating a rule of conduct and the other specifying how infringements of that rule are to be punished. For this would be an absurdly over-simplified account, neglecting the great mass of what Bentham called "expository" matter,[16] the preambles affixed to many codes and statutes, and so on. Nor do I mean that in all systems of legal rules an appropriately specific sanction is ordained for each kind of offence or recalcitrance. For in practice much is often left to courts' discretion. But no duty is ever called a "legal" duty if the rules which enjoin it do not also enjoin

[16] Cf. *Principles of Morals and Legislation*, ed. W. Harrison (1948), p. 433.

some form of sanction for its non-performance—directly for perfect duties, indirectly for imperfect ones. If a man says " I have a legal duty to do this but am not therefore liable to any legal penalty or likely to be defeated in any suit if I do not ", he would not normally be taken as claiming the existence of a legal duty without appointed sanction. Instead, those who assumed that he was not contradicting himself would probably understand that he was boasting of some merely *de facto*, not *de jure* impunity, which had arisen through judicial corruption, perhaps, or through a private and not legally binding agreement to submit relevant disputes to unofficial arbitration. In this regard, if one wanted to examine the extent of the analogy between rules of law and rules of games, one would have to distinguish between games like soccer, on the one hand, in which referees often impose penalties as a part of the game, and games like chess tournaments, on the other hand, in which the normal function of the adjudicator is merely to decide the probable outcome of an unfinished match according to the rules of legitimate play.

3. The legal rules to which any individual is subjected provide at least some grounds for judicial pronouncement on every facet of his activity, unless the local law of evidence justifies in certain circumstances a verdict of " not proven ". No court has yet pronounced the judgment of " non liquet " which a small minority of theorists have claimed to be possible under international law. And under municipal law a man can certainly do nothing which might not be germane to some conceivable action or prosecution and which the court thus concerned, after determining the facts, would be in principle unable to declare either lawful or unlawful. Of course, the legal system under which a man lives may be clearly divisible into sub-systems, each pertinent to a distinct sphere of social relationships. In the mandated territory of Palestine, for instance, property in land was dealt with by Ottoman law, most family relations were subject to religious law of one sort or another, and English common law was applied to torts and contracts. But however

complicated, or trivial, the problem may be in particular cases, it always at least makes good sense to ask what (substantive and adjective) rules of law the competent courts apply in passing on the legality or illegality of this or that piece of human behaviour, whereas it would be absurd to ask what rule of cricket governs the present baking of cakes next door or which St. Andrews ordinance affects the adjudication of yesterday's chess tournament. Obedience to law is not in principle a part-time activity, like playing a game, even though during most of their lives most people may be well-behaved or lucky enough to have no worries about the legality of their actions.

I think that these three criteria go about as far as any can go towards elucidating what kind of rules are to be reckoned as "legal" rules for the purposes of general jurisprudence without begging any questions about how to determine rights in doubtful cases. But the criteria may therefore still seem incomplete in certain respects. They would certainly not be directly useful to a student of, say, Scots law who wanted to know how to tell a rule of Scots law from other sorts of rule. I have said nothing about the so-called "sources" of law, for these vary from system to system and their details are controversial in some (*e.g.*, in international law). Nor do my three criteria provide a sufficient condition for describing any set of rules as "legal" rather than "moral". It would make good sense, I think, to talk about a system of moral rules, which covers every aspect of human life, ordains punishments, and is developed by some morally authoritative institution in an intricately argued body of casuistry, whether or not such a system actually exists. But it also makes good sense to talk, as modern moralists often do, about systems of moral rules which lack one or all of these three features. These features are not *necessary* for other kinds of rule in the way that they are for legal rules. And to define "legal" rules in such a way that they could never completely overlap in any community with "moral" rules would beg the question of legal truth to the prejudice of natural law theories and many others.

## IV.

I do not know whether Hart would call my first supplement to his general definition or elucidation of the phrase "legal right" a theory or not. But if he accepts this first supplement he must, I think, also accept the need for a further and more controversial kind of supplement, which he would certainly call a theory. If the field of legal rules were restricted in some definite way, as chess rules are confined to controlling the moves of no more than thirty-two pieces over no more than sixty-four squares, a legislator might be able to predict, and provide for, all the particular cases in which there was an apparent conflict of applicable rules. Legal argument would then always have as straightforward a logic as the legitimation of particular moves by the rules of chess. Indeed, in every country very many cases do in fact occur in which the question of law at issue can be as simply answered as that. If such cases are not greatly in the majority anywhere, it is a sign that the system of legal rules in use there is comparatively inefficient in that it creates more trouble for judges, advocates and text book writers than is necessary. But since (by definition) the field of legal rules is not restricted, and since all human legislators must, for familiar reasons, fall short of omniscience, judges and advocates are bound to be faced from time to time with *prima facie* gaps, vaguenesses, or antinomies in their law. Moreover, the problems thus created are far from being of purely theoretical interest. Because (by definition) all systems of legal rules impose sanctions for their non-observance, there will always be more than merely intellectual satisfactions at stake in controversy about the resolution of some apparent gap, vagueness or antinomy in the law. And that is why it may be legitimate to invoke moral and political considerations in the course of such a controversy. Correspondingly, no elucidation of "legal right" is complete unless it includes a theory that copes with these situations.

Perhaps it would be as well to illustrate the kind of situation I mean by examples from several different legal

Q 2

systems. For it is easy to be too influenced in our appraisal of definitional theories by the extent to which the linguistic conventions of our nation's lawyers have affected our conceptualisation of law in general.

For the greater part of a century the United States Supreme Court so interpreted the " Due Process " clauses of the Fifth and Fourteenth Amendments as to invalidate state or federal legislation for the control of economic relations. The fact that this way of interpreting those clauses was later abandoned (when F. D. Roosevelt's judicial appointments took effect) indicates that there is wide room for doubt about the content of certain rights under the U.S. constitution. It is hardly surprising to find, therefore, that politico-moral considerations have sometimes been invoked in determining them. At least one judge in the *Pollock* case, for instance, explicitly argued from the need to defend the capitalist economic system in its entirety.[17] But, of course, this need is nowhere stated in the constitution: as Justice O. W. Holmes once put it, the U.S. constitution did not enact Herbert Spencer's social statics. Again, the concept of reasonableness can, in certain circumstances, be as vague and controversial as that of due process. In 1925 the House of Lords held that a borough council's uniform minimum wage policy for employees of both sexes was unreasonable and therefore not authorised by the allegedly relevant statute. This policy was unreasonable, Lord Atkinson said, because guided " by some eccentric principles of socialist philanthropy, or by a feminist ambition ".[18] But by 1944 the courts were no longer warning local authorities against such guides where a uniform weekly war bonus was at issue.[19]

Politico-moral considerations abound in common law judgments not merely because some key concepts like those of reasonableness and public policy are inherently vague and open to controversial differences of interpretation, but

[17] 157 U.S. 429 quoted in W. Friedmann, *Legal Theory* (1949), p. 58.
[18] In *Roberts* v. *Hopwood*, A.C. 578, quoted ib., p. 242.
[19] 1 K.B. 644 quotedi b., p. 165.

also because there is so often need to use these vague and controversial concepts. In many cases they appear to determine the crucial issue whether judges develop the law in a new kind of case by extending the scope of a prevailing rule or by qualifying it. (The whole balance of English public life may be changed, for instance, by which line of development is pursued with regard to the rule that the Crown is not bound by statute except when its obligation is specifically mentioned or necessarily implied.) Indeed an English judge is once reported to have said that nine-tenths of the cases which had ever gone to judgment in the highest court in England might have been decided the other way without any violence to the principles of common law.[20] It is even argued by some experts that there is no infallible method for ascertaining what precisely was the *ratio decidendi* of any particular English judgment.[21] But perhaps the main reason why we need to mention politico-moral considerations, as well as subsumption under rules, in any definition of " legal right " that is intended to apply to common law is because consistency is not nearly as important to common law judges as it is to logicians and mathematicians. In 1947, Lord Macmillan said in the House of Lords: " Your Lordships' task in this house is to decide particular cases between litigants and your Lordships are not called upon to rationalise the law of England." Lord Macmillan went on to quote Justice O. W. Holmes' well-known dictum that the life of law has not been logic, but experience, and to assert that arguments based on legal consistency are apt to mislead. " For the common law is a practical code adapted to deal with the manifold diversities of human life ".[22]

Continental code systems presuppose a greater reverence for consistency. But there may still be controversies about the correct application of a code in unusual circumstances or about how to reconcile its provisions with those of a subsequent statute which purports to supplement it.

---

[20] S. E. Baldwin, *The American Judiciary* (1905), p. 54.
[21] Cf. J. Stone, *The Province and Function of Law* (1947), p. 186 ff.
[22] A.C. 156,171 (1947), quoted by Friedmann, *op. cit.*, p. 94.

# Part II
# Legal Language and Legal Interpretation

# [4]

71

## LANGUAGE AND THE LAW—I.

LANGUAGE is perhaps the greatest of all human inventions. Most people think of it merely as the chief means of communication, but it is much more than that: it is the chief medium of thought. Almost all thinking, above a very primitive level, is in words. A person congenitally deaf, who of course cannot think in vocables, can hardly think or reason at all (that is, by civilized standards), until he is taught or develops a gesture-language, or until he is taught to speak or read, after which he is able to think in manual or oral gestures or in symbolic pictures. Exactly how far there can be thought without words, or without symbols of some sort, is a controversy into which it is not necessary to enter. Köhler's apes apparently thought without words, and so, perhaps, does a chess player or architect. One writer (Rignano) has argued that all reasoning is a series of operations or experiments perfoimed merely in thought, that it does not require words, and that even insects, reptiles, and others are in some degree capable of it. However this may be, it can be confidently asserted that without words we are hardly capable of forming and manipulating general notions; and Rignano himself admitted as much.

For lawyers language has a special interest because it is the greatest instrument of social control. Lawyers are perhaps apt to regard law as the sole, or chief, means of social control, forgetting that the law is only a special department of language and that, whereas the application of law is limited, language is all-pervasive. From nursery days words like 'coward', 'decency', 'manners', 'fairness', help to stimulate conduct considered socially desirable and to repress conduct considered undesirable; in later life words like 'success', 'blackleg' and 'patriotic' perform the same function. The law, with its verbal apparatus of 'rights', 'duties', and 'wrongs', is merely a particular application of language as a means of social control. It has, of course, special features.

Coming down to the more narrowly professional point of view, words are of central importance for the lawyer because they are, in a very particular way, the tools of his trade. Words occupy the lawyer's attention in the drafting and interpretation of statutes, wills, contracts and other legal documents. Other specialists, such as engineers, surgeons, and painters, are also concerned in part with words (namely, the words in which they communicate their ideas to each other), but not to the extent that lawyers are.

Such is my excuse for writing a paper the object of which is twofold: to explain the modern theory of the function of language, and to show the importance of this theory for the lawyer and the student of jurisprudence. The study with which I shall be concerned is sometimes called the study of symbolism, or meaning; an alternative title is 'semantics'. Semantics studies the meaning of words—not, indeed, the meaning of this or that particular word, but the nature of meaning in general. It also considers the general conditions that must be satisfied before a word can have meaning; the influence of words upon thought; and the non-symbolic (emotive) function of words. The subject is not an entirely new one, for it has long been nourished in the womb of philosophy, the mother of the sciences. Its birth as a distinct science may be attributed to C. K. Ogden and I. A. Richards's work, *The Meaning of Meaning*, first published in 1923, now in its sixth edition, and already a classic.[1]

The opinion is steadily growing that semantics is an important prolegomenon to the study of philosophy and of the so-called 'inexact' sciences, such as psychology and the social sciences. In the past philosophers have tended to mistake the structure of discourse for the structure of the universe, and a training in semantics helps to prevent this error. In psychology and the social sciences it is coming to be recognized that one of the greatest difficulties is the difficulty of statement, and that many disputes are due to the imperfections of language. Lawyers, perhaps, are not in such need of having the imperfection of language impressed upon them; for every case on construction is an object-lesson in it. Still, even they are not immune from error, as I shall seek to show. Jurisprudence, too, is in my opinion badly in need of semantic analysis. It is ridden with disputes, and many of them turn out on examination to be disputes not as to matters of fact or of value-judgment but purely as to the use of words. A student of jurisprudence who comes to the subject armed with an understanding of what is a verbal dispute, will find that his knowledge enables him to pare off the unprofitable matter from his subject. It helps him, in Locke's words,

---

[1] BIBLIOGRAPHY. The following are the principal works on semantics in English, excluding periodical literature. The chief predecessors of Ogden and Richards were the philosopher Locke (Essay Concerning the Human Understanding, 1690, hereafter referred to by book, chapter, and, sometimes, section), and two opponents of traditional logic, Alfred Sidgwick (various works, particularly The Use of Words in Reasoning (London, 1901)) and F. G. S. Schiller (Formal Logic (London, 1912)). It was apparently a Frenchman, Bréal, who coined the word *sémantique*, and his work on the subject (1897) was translated into English in 1900 under the title 'Semantics'. This is, however, more a work on philology or comparative grammar than on symbolism as Ogden and Richards understand it.

Works subsequent to the first edition of Ogden and Richards are: Ralph M. Eaton, Symbolism and Truth (Cambridge, Mass. 1925); A. N. Whitehead, Symbolism, Its Meaning and Effect (Cambridge, 1928); B. B. Bogoslovsky, The Technique of Controversy (London, 1928); Gustaf Stern, Meaning and Change of Meaning (Göteborg, 1931); Susan Stebbings, Modern Introduction to Logic, 2nd ed. (London, 1933), Chapter 2; John Dewey, How We Think, new ed. (Boston, etc., 1933); G. H. Mead, Mind, Self and Society (Chicago, 1934); I. A. Richards, Interpretation in Teaching (London, 1938); C. W. Morris, Foundations of the Theory of Signs (International Encyclopaedia of Unified Science, Chicago, 1938); L. Bloomfield, Linguistic Aspects of Science (*ibid.*, Chicago, 1939). A popular exposition is Stuart Chase, The Tyranny of Words (London, 1938).

For the Logical Positivists see below § 9.

Among the many works on the psychological side are W. B. Pillsbury, Psychology of Reasoning (New York, 1910) and Psychology of Language (New York, 1928); Bertrand Russell, Analysis of Mind (London, 1921); Eugenio Rignano, Psychology of Reasoning (London, 1923); H. L. Hollingworth, Psychology of Thought (New York, 1926); J. F. Markey, The Symbolic Process (London, 1928); Frank Lorimer, The Growth of Reason (London, 1929).

The work of Ogden and Richards is certainly not unknown among academic lawyers, but so far it seems to have had little effect upon legal literature, at any rate on this side of the Atlantic. In America it has had a greater vogue; it was used by Jerome Frank in writing his Law and the Modern Mind (New York, 1930) (though I think he misapplied its doctrine, as I hope to show elsewhere), and more recently it has inspired an entertaining article by Professor Chafee in the Columbia Law Review: 'The Disorderly Conduct of Words', (1941), 41 Col. L. R. 381, reprinted (1942) 20 Canadian Bar Review 752. Chase, The Tyranny of Words (above), also has a chapter on the law.

to clear the ground a little, and to remove some of the rubbish that lies in the way of knowledge.

In the present paper I shall (1) state Ogden and Richards's doctrine as succinctly as possible, (2) supplement it by the work of others, in particular by the work of certain unorthodox logicians and of the philosophical school known as the Logical Positivists, and (3) intersperse the discussion with remarks on its relation to law and jurisprudence. These remarks are, I fear, on very diverse topics; for semantics touches law and jurisprudence at many points, and I am anxious to show the range of its importance even at the risk of making my paper seem disjointed and rambling.

## § 1. The Use of Words as Symbols.

The use of words as symbols is well explained by Ogden and Richards. These writers were not the first in the field, for they were anticipated in many important particulars by Locke. But it is to Ogden and Richards that we must look for a modern statement of the subject.

The core of their theory is as follows. In themselves words are nothing; or at least they are (as an old-time lawyer expressed it) 'no other than the verberation of the air'.[2] Their importance consists in the fact that they are a kind of symbol, which is itself a kind of sign. Sign is the genus, symbol the species, and word the sub-species. Let us consider first signs in general. Skating over the difficulties of definition, the nature of a sign can best be explained by an example. Suppose a person sees smoke coming from a chimney: he promptly thinks 'There is no smoke without fire', and so concludes that a fire is burning underneath. Here the smoke is a sign of the fire. The ability of any particular person to interpret a sign that comes into his consciousness—*i.e.*, to find meaning in it—depends upon his past experience, in this case his past experience that smoke is a consequence of fire.

Symbols are a special class of signs. There are other signs than symbols; thus smoke is a sign, but it is not a symbol. A symbol is a conventional sign; it is a sign that is consciously designed to stand for something.

Words are a special class of symbols. There are other symbols than words, such as a traffic sign, a wink, and a numeral. But words are much the most important kinds of signs used in ordinary thinking and communication.

A word or other symbol is generally used to refer to an object or situation in the real world. It is convenient to have a technical term for this object or situation, and Ogden and Richards coin the term 'referent' to indicate it.[3] Words and phrases, then, are symbols that stimulate mental references to referents. The referent is that which is signified. The relation between a symbol and its referent is always indirect; between them there always intervenes the thought of some person. If there were no minds there would be no symbols and so no words.

---

[2] *Per* Saunders, *arg.*, in *Partridge* v. *Strange* (1552/3), 1 Plowd. 83.

[3] Stebbings, Modern Introduction to Logic, 2nd ed., 13, n. 2, suggested that this term was unhappily chosen, because 'referent' was already in use among logicians as a technical term with another meaning. She accordingly suggested instead the term 'referend'. Ogden and Richards have not themselves adopted this suggestion, and it has not been adopted by other writers.

This theory sounds and is so beautifully simple that there is danger of its revolutionary implications being missed unless they are expressly pointed out. In the next section I shall consider some errors in the use of language, particularly in connection with law, in order to indicate how much we have to mend our ways if we adopt the gospel of semantics.

## § 2. SOME COMMON ERRORS.

There are some errors in relation to the function of words that are so frequently committed that we must suppose them to be natural ways of thinking. Two of them will now be considered. (*a*) One is the idea that words are somehow important of themselves, and irrespective of their symbolic function. (*b*) Another is the supposition that real distinctions exist where in fact the only distinction is between two forms of words. In law this takes the form of making legal results depend upon purely verbal distinctions.

(*a*) The tendency to attach importance to words as such assumes its extreme form in the age-old tendency to identify words with things, and to suppose that words are in some way parts of things or always imply things corresponding to them. Somewhat similar is the supposition that words have immediate power over things. Among primitive peoples these ideas result in many forms of word-magic and word-taboos. Names, for instance, are regarded as part of the personality. Hence, among some primitives, a new-born infant is not regarded as a complete child until he has got a name. The name given to him is that of some ancestor, and the name is regarded as the soul of the ancestor. If two persons are given the same name, they have a certain identity. Some other primitive peoples, however, taboo the name of a dead man and refrain from applying it to any person or property that bears it, evidently out of fear of death. Again, there is a widely held belief that by means of the name injury may be done to a man. One can harm an enemy by making an effigy of him, giving it his name, and performing operations upon it. The same result can be achieved by giving his name to an animal captured in the chase, and then proceeding to mutilate it. Even merely alluding to a name is the same thing as assaulting the person who bears it. The consequence is that people conceal their 'real' names and go about under an alias, which is regarded as not really belonging to the man. What is true of the names of human beings is equally true of the names of animals and things; one avoids speaking of snakes, leopards, etc., because to pronounce their names is to invoke the presence of the animals so named, and is fraught with grave danger.[4]

The superstitions so prevalent among the primitive peoples studied by anthropologists are also to be found, to some extent, in the earlier civilizations. Witness, for example, the elaborate curses pronounced by the priests in Deuteronomy upon anyone who should break the law.[5] A

[4] Lucien Lévy-Bruhl, How Natives Think (Les fonctions mentales dans les sociétiés inférieures) (London, 1926) 50–4, 346–7; same, The 'Soul' of the Primitive (London, 1928) 208–10; same, L'Expérience mystique et les symbols chez les primitifs (Paris, 1938) 236–8; J. G. Frazer, Golden Bough, abridged ed. (London, 1922), ch. 22; L. T. Hobhouse, Morals in Evolution (London, 1906) i 46; Enc. Brit. s.v. 'Magic'.

[5] Deut. xxvii 15–26; cp. Hobhouse, *op. cit.* ii 52.

clear illustration of the reification of words is the story of Isaac's blessing of his son.

> 'Jacob secures by fraud the blessing intended for Esau, and once given, the blessing cannot be withdrawn. It is quite comparable to a piece of goods made over once for all and not to be resumed. The most Esau can hope is that the store may not be exhausted—"Hast thou not reserved a blessing for me?" "Hast thou but one blessing, my father?" Yet if the blessing were the true expression of the father's loving gratitude won by good service, Jacob should rather have had a curse for his deceit'.[6]

I have thought it desirable to start with these ancient illustrations in order to win the reader's agreement before venturing on the more modern, and therefore more controversial, instances of word-superstition. Let me begin these more modern illustrations with the royal title. In 1521 the title of *Fidei Defensor* was conferred by Pope Leo X upon King Henry VIII. But when the quarrel with Rome was in full swing, Pope Leo's successor deprived Henry of the title. His Majesty retaliated by procuring the passing of an 'Act for the ratification of the King's Majesty's Stile', which insisted upon the Sovereign's right still to be described, both in Latin and in the vulgar tongue, as 'Defender of the Faith'. This last Act was 'repealed, made frustrate, void and of none effect' by a statute passed under Philip and Mary, but was restored under Elizabeth.[7] All this controversy centred on a mere empty form of words. Whether Henry was a Defender of the Faith depended upon what one meant by 'Faith'; the word had not the same meaning for Henry as for the Pope. If Henry was a Defender of the Faith, no amount of denial by the Pope could alter the fact, and if he was not, no Act of Parliament could make him one. But the parties to this dispute were not using words to convey meaning; they were using them as though they were of importance in themselves.

It may be thought that this childish concern over the royal title is a thing of the past. But look at the preamble to the Statute of Westminster, 1931. In this it is gravely recited that the assent of the Dominions shall be required not only to any alteration in the law touching the succession to the throne (which is a comparatively important matter), but also in any alteration in the law touching the royal style and titles (which is a mere empty form of words). It is not impossible that a constitutional crisis might occur through Great Britain taking it upon herself to change His Majesty's title without the assent of the Dominions.

If word-fetishism had stopped at this it would not have been a very momentous error, but it did not. Perhaps its worst effect in the law has been in connection with offences having a religious or supernatural basis. The imaginary offence of witchcraft, for instance, was at one

[6] Hobhouse, *op. cit.* ii 53; Gen. xxvii 36–8. See also Hobhouse, *op. cit.* ii 69–70 (Egyptian Book of the Dead), 102 (Laws of Manu).

[7] 1 & 2 Ph. & M. c. 8, s. 20; 1 Eliz. c. 1. I owe these details to Theobald Mathew's For Lawyers and Others, 201.

Even the names of private individuals have sometimes occupied the attention of the Legislature; cp. the Scots Act of 1600 stamping out the name 'Ruthven', and the Act compelling Irishmen to take English names: Linell, Law of Names (London, 1938) 46.

time a felony punishable with death[8]; and the belief in the existence of witchcraft was partly due to the belief that evil effects could be produced by words. The crime of blasphemy, too, was originally based on the same kind of logophobia as the primitive taboo; the god was supposed to be personally offended by the desecration of his name. Even in the reign of Henry VIII a boy was put to death by burning because of some idle words he had chanced to hear respecting the sacrament, which he ignorantly repeated.[9] Nowadays, however, the maintenance of the crime of blasphemy is to be justified on a more rational ground, namely, the emotive power of words. Blasphemers are now punished not because they desecrate sacred formulae or because they revile Christianity, but because they may cause respectable Christians to break the peace.[10] This emotive power of words will be considered later (§ 7).

The only surviving offence that is still, to my mind, based largely on word-fetichism is bigamy. Bigamy became a felony by an Act of 1608[11] (it is perhaps not without significance that this Act immediately precedes on the statute book James I's notorious Witchcraft Act). At first punishable with death, bigamy is now punishable with a maximum of seven years' penal servitude.[12] The reason for punishing bigamy is frankly stated by Kenny: it is 'the broad one of its involving an outrage upon public decency by the profanation of a solemn ceremony'.[13] Consider what this means. If *A* deserts his wife and lives with a mistress he commits no crime, either in deserting his wife or in committing adultery. But if he tries to make the position appear more regular by going through a form of marriage with his mistress, then, even though the marrriage is totally null and void (as it necessarily is), so that the whole ceremony is a mere empty form of words, and even though he never thereafter cohabits with the woman, he commits a felony. And this simply because he is 'profaning a solemn ceremony'. The ceremony may have taken place in a Registrar's office, but that makes no difference to its solemnity in the eye of the law.

Suppose we were to press for a reason why this profanation of a ceremony should thus entail a liability to seven years' penal servitude. Is it because the wrath of the Deity needs to be appeased in this manner? That may have been the idea underlying the Act of 1603[14]; but it can hardly justify the continuance of the offence in modern law.[15] For one

---

[8] See 1 Jac. 1, c. 12. Earlier statutes were 33 Hen. 8, c. 8, and 5 Eliz. c. 16.

[9] Pike, History of Crime in England (London, 1876), ii, 56 (quoted by Ogden and Richards).

[10] The change dates from *R.* v. *Ramsay and Foote* (1883) 15 Cox C. C. 231. See further Nokes, The Crime of Blasphemy (London, 1928).

[11] 1 Jac. 1, c. 11.

[12] Offences against the Person Act, 1861, s. 57.

[13] Outlines of Criminal Law, 15th ed. (Cambridge, 1936), 361.

[14] The preamble declares that bigamy involves 'the great Dishonour of God, and utter undoing of divers honest Men's Children, and others'. It may be suggested that the second reason is a make-weight; it is difficult to see how the mere celebration of a void ceremony can 'undo' children.

[15] I do not want to offend susceptibilities, but when the sanctions of the criminal law are used to inflict suffering upon those who offend against the religious beliefs of others, persons holding such beliefs must expect to find them made the subject of discussion. It is, therefore, fair to ask those who consider the law of bigamy to have a religious justification, how they reconcile this view with the recognition of divorce by the secular authorities. If a bigamous marriage be regarded as sinful, while a second

thing, it involves an Old Testament conception of the Deity; for another, we now think that an act should not be made a crime unless its commission involves harmful social consequences. What are the harmful social consequences of bigamy? The answer that would probably be given by one who supported the present law is that bigamy often involves the practising of a grievous deceit upon an innocent woman. This is true, but then the law is not confined to this case. It frequently happens that a male offender has told the woman before the ceremony that he is already married. A ceremony performed in such circumstances is no more than a pathetic attempt to give a veneer of respectability to what is in law an adulterous association. Yet not only does the man remain guilty of the felony of bigamy, but the woman becomes guilty of it as well, as a principal in the second degree. It is therefore clear that the crime does not consist in the deception of the other party to the bigamous marriage.

A second possible reason for punishing bigamy is that the offender by procuring a marriage certificate to which he is not entitled has in a way committed forgery. But forgery proper involves an intent to defraud or deceive,[16] whereas a person can be branded of the felony of bigamy although he honestly believed that his first marriage was at an end and thus that his second marriage was valid.[17] Even if the bigamy were intentionally committed, the precise nature of the intent to defraud or deceive needs to be considered. Where both parties to the bigamous marriage have the guilty intent, their object in going through the ceremony is generally to hold themselves out to the world as man and wife. This is certainly an intent to deceive the world at large; but is anyone necessarily the worse for it? (It must be remembered that I am putting aside as irrelevant the desertion of the lawful spouse, which, though often a cruel moral wrong, is not in itself a crime, and am considering only the deception of the world at large.) Many petty deceits are practised in life without any punishment being assigned for them; why do we single out this one for punishment? Also, it is to be noted that where the intent to deceive the public exists without the bigamous ceremony having been performed—where a man and woman living in adultery declare to their friends that they have been married—no crime is committed, unless of course property is obtained by the fraud. On the other hand if the bigamous ceremony is performed, even though only in private, without any use being made afterwards of the marriage certificate, the crime of bigamy is committed.

The only anti-social consequences that are necessarily involved in the mere celebration of a bigamous marriage are (1) the falsification of the State records, and (2) the waste of time of the Minister of Religion or

marriage after a secular divorce is not sinful, this must be because the State authorities have divine sanction to dissolve marriages. In other words, the enormous red-tape of our divorce law is part of the law of God. For my part I cannot see how an intelligent person can believe this. It was this absurdity that gave point to Maule J.'s famous satirical address to the poor prisoner convicted of bigamy: see R. Walton, Random Recollections of the Midland Circuit (1869) i 154–6; Heard, Oddities of the Law (London, 1921) 48; Foss, Lives of the Judges (London, 1864) ix 225. Cp. (1932) Law Notes 3, where Rowlatt J. is reported to have said that in many bigamy cases 'it was a pity that the law could not look another way'.

16 Cp. Forgery Act, 1913, s. 3 (2).

17 *R.* v. *Wheat and Stocks* [1921] 2 K. B. 119.

Registrar. But as to (2), though one must not minimize the dishonesty of making false statements in order to procure a bigamous ceremony, or the affront to the feelings of the celebrating officer, it hardly seems justifiable to protect these feelings by penal sanctions, at any rate by the sanction of imprisonment; and as to economic loss, if the parties have made the usual disbursements on marriage, it may be thought that the economic loss is theirs rather than the celebrating officer's or the State's. As to (1), the falsification of the State records, I personally cannot regard it as a very important matter [18]; certainly not one deserving more than a moderate fine.

To sum up, the crime of bigamy as it now stands (having regard to the severity with which it is or can be punished) does not make sense except on the supposition that the marriage ceremony is a magic form of words that has to be protected from profanation at almost any cost in human suffering.

I should perhaps add that in writing the above I am not unaware of the tremendous social importance of the marriage ceremony. It is this ceremony that, through the force of tradition, maintains the institution of monogamy and keeps families stable. Punishment is perhaps justifiable if it is necessary to preserve such an important institution; but we should first make quite sure that it is necessary, and that monogamy can be maintained in no other way. What I contend is that the sanction of nullity is enough to prevent bigamous marriages in most cases, and that the exceptional cases where bigamy is committed are not (quasi-rape apart) [19] harmful enough to deserve anything more than a moderate fine on summary conviction. Where the bigamous ceremony has been performed merely in order to gain 'respectability', the sanction of a fine plus the attendant publicity is obviously enough to neutralise the 'respectability' gained by the ceremony; and it should be enough to keep the offence within bounds.

(*b*) The second error in relation to the function of words is the supposition that real distinctions exist where in fact the only distinction is between two forms of words. Judges have said more than once that 'there is no magic in words [20] but unfortunately this is not the case. That there is legal magic in words was admitted by Chitty J. when he said that 'a difference in the mere form of words does in several cases make a difference in law'.[21] For instance, if *A* lends money to *B* on mortgage, and stipulates that the interest shall be 5 per cent., but if not paid promptly 6 per cent., the latter part of the provision is void as a

[18] Nor does the State itself seem to do so, for it allows a man to marry ten of his nieces, one after another, without making any provision for his punishment (if the nieces are over the age of consent). Such marriages are not bigamous because there is no initial valid marriage to found upon; yet the falsification of the State records is the same as in bigamy. This anomaly is inconsistent with any theory of bigamy whatever.

[19] Where the 'second wife' did not know the ceremony to be bigamous, the case is of course altogether more serious, for morally it may be tantamount to rape. But I think we should distinguish between (1) cases where both the man and his 'second wife' wish to be faithful to each other, and (2) cases where he deserts her. In (1) it should be borne in mind that any punishment imposed on the man is an aggravation of the suffering of his victim.

[20] *Per* Lord Kenyon C.J. in *R.* v. *Inhabitants of North Nibley* (1792) 5 T. R. 24; *per* Lord Romilly M.R. in *Lord* v. *Jeffkins* (1865) 35 Beav. 16; *per* Jessel M.R. in *Re Caplen's Estate, Bulbeck* v. *Silvester* (1876) 45 L. J. Ch. 280 at 281.

[21] *Dean* v. *Dean* [1891] 3 Ch. 150 at 155.

penalty. Thus *B* need pay only 5 per cent., even if he does not pay promptly. Yet if *A* had provided that interest should be 6 per cent., but if paid promptly 5 per cent., the whole would have been good.[22] Lord Hatherley, with that reluctance to condemn a rule outright that seems to be a characteristic of the legal mind, called this a 'fine distinction '[23]; whereas actually it is not a distinction at all, except in words and in legal results. For the objective situation that is contemplated, the referent of the two forms of words, is the same in each case: namely, the situation in which *B* has to pay 5 per cent. interest if paid promptly or 6 per cent. if not paid promptly. If this situation is one in which it is thought that *B* is unfairly penalized for delay in paying, a change in the word-symbols used to refer to the situation cannot make any difference to the fairness or unfairness of the situation.

Another case where the law has become lost in mere words is in the famous distinction between 'but if' and 'until'—a distinction that an Irish judge considered to be 'little short of disgraceful to our jurisprudence'.[24] If *A* gives property on trust for *B*, 'but if *B* marries then for *C*', the gift to *C* is struck out, because it tends to induce *B* to remain unmarried, and the procreation of legitimate children is regarded as a public interest. Thus on this form of words *B* will take absolutely. But if the words used were 'on trust for *B* until he marries and thenceforth for *C*', the gift over would be valid and *B* would lose the property if he were to marry.[25] The difference is supposed to be between a gift subject to a condition subsequent and a determinable limitation. Yet the intention in each case is that *B* shall enjoy the property until he marries and that thereafter *C* shall enjoy it. Thus the referent is again the same. If the referent is the same the meaning must be the same. And if it is against public policy to tolerate the situation when one form of words is used, it must necessarily be against public policy to tolerate the same situation when the other form of words is used. No amount of subtle distinguishing between the emotional *nuances* of the two forms of words can affect this proposition.

Again, a covenant in a deed to pay an annuity of £1,000 free of income tax is illegal (by the terms of the Income Tax Act); but a covenant to pay such a sum (not mentioned in figures) as, after deducting income tax, would leave £1,000, is perfectly good.[26] Here again the law is simply playing with words. One can put it more strongly and say that the cases allowing the second form of words are a repudiation of an express provision of an Act of Parliament, namely, the provision that 'every agreement for . . . annual payment in full without allowing any such deduction [of tax] shall be void'.

Another illustration: if *A* agrees to give the whole of his time to the

---

22 *Strode* v. *Parker* (1694) 2 Vern. 316. Cp. *Wrigley* v. *Gill* [1906] 1 Ch. 165.

23 *Wallingford* v. *Mutual Society* (1880) 5 App. Cas. 685 at 702.

24 *Per* Porter M.R., in *Re King's Trusts* (1892) 29 L. R. Ir. 401 at 410.

25 See Underhill, Trusts, 9th ed., 78–80; but see the cases collected in (1943) 59 L. Q. R. 353, n. 36. There are other legal distinctions between 'but if' and 'until', all equally verbal: see *Re Randell, Randell* v. *Dixon* (1888) 38 Ch. D. 213; *Re Bowen, Lloyd Phillips* v. *Davis* [1893] 2 Ch. 491; *Re Talbot, Jubb* v. *Sheard* [1933] Ch. 895 (all on the perpetuity rule); *Whigham* v. *I. R.* [1941] 2 K. B. 18 (Finance Act, 1922); (1943) 59 L. Q. R. 352–3 (repugnancy).

26 Income Tax Act, 1918, rule 23 (2) of General Rules of All Schedules; Konstam, Income Tax, 9th ed., 181; *per* Greene M.R. in *Re Horlick's Settlement Trusts, Colledge* v. *Horlick* [1938] 4 A. E. R. 602 at 606.

service of *B*, this necessarily means that he will not serve anybody else during the period of his employment with *B*. But if *A* breaks his contract and enters into the service of somebody else, no injunction will be granted against him to prevent him from doing so. If, however, *A* had expressly agreed *totidem verbis* not to serve anybody else, an injunction will be granted to prevent him from doing so.[27] The granting of the injunction depends not upon the actualities of the case nor upon the intention of the parties as shown by their words, but upon the particular words chosen to express that intention.[28]

While I think that the foregoing are verbal distinctions, it must be admitted that the judge's lot is not always a happy one when he is faced with some ingenious attempt to drive a coach and four through a statutory or common law rule. It may not be at all easy to decide in a particular case whether a suggested distinction is purely verbal or whether it has some basis in fact or in distinct legal result. Even if the distinction is not purely verbal, the judge still has to decide whether the transaction is so glaringly *in fraudem legis* that it must be upset. To take an illustration, consider the rule that a person intending to make a testamentary disposition can do so only by an instrument that complies with the Wills Act. Suppose that *A* orally or by an unattested writing declares himself a trustee of his chattels for himself for life with remainder to *B* absolutely, reserving a power of revocation by instrument under hand, etc. If cunningly worded this transaction might (unless defeated by the Courts) achieve all or almost all the results of a will; yet it is in the form appropriate to a transfer *inter vivos*. Would it be defeated as an infringement of the Wills Act? A Court before whom the question came would first have to decide what it meant by a 'testamentary disposition', and having settled that it would have to decide whether the impugned transaction bore the marks of one. There is always the danger, in the absence of very clear thinking, that a verbal distinction will emerge.[29]

Even when the law has not gone so badly astray as in some of the foregoing examples, it does not always escape the charge of verbalism. At common law it was not at all infrequent for certain technical expressions to be required for effecting certain results, particularly in conveyancing and pleading. An obvious illustration is the requirement of the words 'to *A* and his heirs' to pass a fee simple. Occasionally a case can be made out for technicalities of this sort, but usually they are no more than irksome absurdities.

The case is of course different with technical terms or formulae that

---

[27] *Mortimer* v. *Beckett* [1920] 1 Ch. 571.

[28] Other examples of verbal distinctions: (1) In the law of charitable trusts a gift 'to my country England' is a good charitable trust; a gift 'for patriotic purposes' is not: *Re Smith, Public Trustee* v. *Smith* [1932] 1 Ch. 153; *A.-G.* v. *National Provincial Bank* [1924] A. C. 262; but see Albery in (1940) 56 L. Q. R. 49. (2) In the law of restraint of trade a compound covenant worded as a single covenant if partly bad is wholly bad (*Attwood* v. *Lamont* [1920] 3 K. B. 571), but if worded as several covenants may be partly bad and partly good (*Putsman* v. *Taylor* [1927] 1 K. B. 637 741). And this on a matter of public policy! (3) It has been suggested that the Courts would draw verbal distinctions under s. 4 of the Statute of Frauds: see Lord Wright in (1939) 55 L. Q. R. 206. (4) A release of one joint debtor or tortfeasor discharges the other; but a covenant not to sue does not: *Hutton* v. *Eyre* (1815) 6 Taunt. 289. (5) A verbal distinction has been suggested as to options to purchase in a mortgage deed: (1944) 60 L. Q. R. 191.

[29] Cp. (1935) 13 Can. B. R. 324 ff.

bow to an indication of contrary intention; the attaching of a 'fixed' meaning to such terms or formulae, in the absence of contrary intent, may be quite rational. An illustration or two may, however, show the fineness of the line that separates verbality from reason. A person with no knowledge of the law would probably see no difference between a tenancy at £52 a year payable weekly and a tenancy at £1 per week; yet the period of notice required by law for the first is at least six months, while for the second it is only a week. In a way this is a verbal distinction, but in a way it is not, for these forms of words have become established for indicating the period of notice that is required. The rule is not like those criticized above, for whereas the latter allow the evasion of fixed rules of law by the mere turn of a phrase, the present rule results from a genuine attempt to ascertain the intention of the parties, where the intention is all that matters. A second illustration is the rule that if two articles are given as one gift, the donee cannot disclaim one and accept one; whereas he can if they are given as two gifts.[30] Here, again, the Court is doing its best to guess what the donor would probably have intended, although the *indicia* of intention on which it is obliged to proceed are very slight.

## § 3. The Process of Abstraction.

A famous medieval controversy that was largely concerned with the problem of meaning was the dispute over the reality of universals. This dispute split the scholastic world into two camps (with many divergent divisions within each camp), called the 'realists' and the 'nominalists' The question was raised by Plato, but the medieval dispute is generally regarded as starting from a question of Porphyry (died 304), who asked whether classes (called by logicians genera and species) exist outside the mind or only in the mind. The question can be stated in simple language as follows. Very early in our lives we begin to notice that individual things have common characteristics and consequently a common name. We notice, for instance, that different individual flowers resemble each other, and we learn to call them by the name 'rose'. Perhaps one of the characteristics of these particular roses is a certain colour, which we learn to call by the name 'red'. Similarly we learn that Tom, Dick and Harry are all 'man'. The question to be decided is whether there is any objective reality corresponding to our concepts of 'rose', 'redness', 'man' and so on. Are there such things in the universe as 'rose', 'redness' and 'man', or are there simply individuals, such as individual roses, individual red things, and individual Toms, Dicks, and Harrys? If the latter, what are we to make of our concepts of 'rose', 'redness', and 'man'? Are these words without meaning—*i.e.*, without referents? Or, if these words have referents, what are these referents if they have no objective reality?

In the Middle Ages those philosophers who (following Plato) argued for the 'reality' of the concepts of quality and relation (such concepts being called 'universals') came to be known as 'realists', their opponents as 'nominalists'; but as I have said there were many variations of opinion within each group. Broadly speaking, the argument

[30] *Re Joel, Rogerson* v. *Joel* [1943] Ch. 311.

of the realists was this, that as Socrates is (at one time) real, and as Socrates is a man, man is real; then as man is real, and man is a rational animal, rationality and animality are real. In the same way it could be asserted that redness, heaviness and justice were real. From this the conclusion was drawn that humanity, animality, rationality, heaviness and the like existed in the world independently of their concrete manifestations. Against this view the nominalists contended that the only reality consisted of individuals with certain attributes, and that there could be no heaviness apart from heavy things, no justice apart from just acts. Heaviness and justice were simply names given to certain qualities, and had no special non-empirical mode of real being.

Such was the famous controversy, and to us it may seem incredible that it attracted so much attention. Partly this was because it had theological implications. On the whole it was the doctrine of the nominalists that finally attracted the greatest support, largely through the writings of William of Ockham; but the controversy has not wholly died in philosophical circles even at the present day.

The view of the semanticist may perhaps be stated as follows. All universals are arrived at as a result of a process of abstraction. (The same is true of individuals, as will be shown in the next section.) Abstraction may be defined as the imaginative selection of some one characteristic of a complex situation so that it may be attended to in isolation.[31] We are all familiar with this process from childhood; it is bound up with our earliest efforts to learn our mother tongue. Imagine a baby in whose household there is a terrier called 'Caesar'. The baby will be taught to call this dog 'bow-wow', because 'bow-wow' is easier to say than 'Caesar'. If he sees another dog he will guess or be told that this other dog is to be called 'bow-wow' as well. At first this transference of the word from one individual to another may well be due merely to the infant's inability to discriminate differences: one dog will be the same to him as another.[32] Later, however, when he comes to distinguish between the two dogs, his continued use of the same name for both of them, and his extension of it to other dogs that he knows to be different again, will be the result of abstraction. Abstraction is, in short, the perception of similarity in spite of differences.

The importance of abstraction in our thinking cannot be stressed too much. 'Without abstraction there can be no recognition of similarity; without the recognition of similarity there can be no advance in knowledge.'[33] But the process has its dangers. The danger is particularly present when we objectify ('hypostatize') our abstractions. As a matter of linguistic convenience we are accustomed to hypostatize words expressing qualities or properties, thus speaking of (say) 'justice' or 'redness' as though these things were part of the stuff of nature. But

[31] Stebbings, *op. cit.* 7. Cp. Locke, *op. cit.* 2. 11. 9; 3. 3. 5, 6; Schiller, *op. cit.* 22–3; Ogden and Richards, *op. cit.* 212–4; Russell, *op. cit.* Ch. 11.

[32] Thus James Ward (Psychological Principles (Cambridge, 1918) 304) denied that the formation of concepts was the result of abstraction: 'the same name is applied to different things or events [not out of conscious disregard for their differences but] because only their more salient features are perceived at all'. This may be true, but it does not affect the proposition that when class-names are continued in use by a person who has come to perceive individual differences, their use is a case of abstraction.

[33] Stebbings, *op. cit.* 7.

semantically there is no difference between the adjectives 'just' and 'red' and the nouns 'justice' and 'redness'; the difference is only in grammatical form. Qualities like these are not to be found by themselves anywhere; they are simply 'phantoms due to the refractive power of the linguistic medium'.[34] In real life there are simply people or things or conduct or events to which the qualities in question are applicable.[35] To speak of redness apart from red things is like speaking of the grin without the Cheshire cat. It is the same with words expressing relation. When we appear to speak of relations we are merely using the words as tools, which does not involve actual referents corresponding to them. All such words, then, are merely symbolic accessories, apparent symbols, which, though indispensable as machinery, have often proved to be dangerous impediments to straight thinking.[36] As Ogden and Richards drily remark, the consequences of supposing that such words symbolize real entities eternally fixed in the order of nature 'are sometimes called Philosophy'.[37] Philosophers of the so-called 'realist' school, from Plato onwards, have mistaken for a fundamental characteristic of reality what is merely a characteristic of language. But it is not only the philsophers who have the unfortunate habit of hypostatizing abstractions. 'How popular and how influential is this practice may be shown by such a list of terms as the following: Virtue, Liberty, Democracy, Peace, Germany, Religion, Glory. All invaluable words, indispensable even, but able to confuse the clearest issues, unless controlled.'[38] Such words are to be fought and died for; yet we do not always have a clear realization of what we mean by them. If these words mean anything it can only be a meaning in relation to the actual lives of individuals. By themselves they are simply abstractions, and many of them are abstractions on the meaning of which there is little agreement. The way to control such words is in every case to discipline ourselves to find the lower-order referent in the world of real life—that is, to find the real object in which the quality is conceived as inhering. Unless the speaker and his listener can agree on some such concrete referent for the word in question, a proposition relating to that word cannot be intelligently discussed.

At this point I must again interrupt the exposition of semantics by

[34] Ogden and Richards, *op. cit.* 96.

[35] The view of a scientist on this matter is not without interest: 'The idealist philosopher Plato gave abstract nouns like "justice" an existence independent of the social circumstances of the people who describe a social action as just or unjust. Plato's curious views about such words were closely connected with his curious views about numbers. Both were wafted into his firmament of universals which the scholastic theologians believed to be as definite a place as hell itself. Modern science began when men like Roger Bacon and Francis Bacon rejected the world of "universals" and set about making words describe the solid earth of human experience'; Hogben, Mathematics for the Million (London, 1936) 78.

[36] Ogden and Richards, *op. cit.* 63–4, 93–101, 133–4, 188–9. My account of the authors' views is slightly simplified, for I have avoided reference to the 'levels of interpretation' and to the 'contraction' of symbols.

[37] Ogden and Richards, *op. cit.* 93. Cp. *ibid.* 29: 'The persistence of the primitive linguistic outlook not only throughout the whole religious world, but in the work of the profoundest thinkers, is . . . one of the most curious features of modern thought. The philosophy of the nineteenth century was dominated by an idealist tradition in which the elaboration of monstrous symbolic machinery (the Hegelian Dialectic provides a striking example) was substituted for direct research, and occupied the centre of attention'.

[38] *Ibid.* 133–4.

trying to show the bearing of this branch of it upon the law. Chiefly, I think, it is important in jurisprudence; but it is also of some value in the work of the Courts. The consequences of failing to reduce an abstract word to its lower-order referent can perhaps be illustrated from the law of charitable trusts, and in particular from the cases on trusts for the promotion of sport. In *Re Nottage* (1895) [39] a bequest to provide a cup 'to encourage the sport of yacht-racing' was held by the Court of Appeal to be not a charitable trust, Lindley L.J. saying that 'a gift for the encouragement of a mere sport' could not be charitable. Taken in itself this sentence may mean either of two things: (1) that no gift for the encouragement of sport is charitable, or (2) that no gift for the encouragement of sport 'as such' is charitable, but that a gift to encourage human beings to take part in sport is (or may be) charitable. If Lindley L.J. meant (2), the distinction is clearly verbal. The referent of 'sport' or 'yacht-racing' is not a metaphysical entity *sport* or *yacht-racing* in the abstract, but is a number of actual yacht races (or other sporting events) by human beings. Actually, however, it seems that Lindley L.J. meant (1); according to the tenour of the rest of his judgment, no trust for the promotion of healthy sport can be charitable. Lopes L.J. was more cautious, for in one part of his judgment he said merely that 'a gift, the object of which is the encouragement of a mere sport or game primarily calculated to amuse individuals apart from the community at large, cannot upon the authorities be held to be charitable, though such sport or game is to some extent beneficial to the public'. This seems to contemplate *some* sports the promotion of which would be a charitable object. But it is not a very satisfactory statement, for in drawing a distinction between individuals and the community it must not be forgotten that the community consists of individuals. The phrase 'a sport calculated to amuse individuals apart from the community at large' means 'a sport that amuses some people but not all'. Now of course no sport amuses all people. Perhaps what Lopes L.J. meant was that the individuals amused by yacht-racing constituted a minority of the community. If this was the *ratio decidendi*, it implies that a trust to encourage a popular sport would be charitable. But, again, I do not think the learned judge meant this, for he went on in the rest of his judgment to assert the contrary.

*Re Nottage* thus appears to rest chiefly on the Victorian principle that *mens sana* is more important than *corpus sanum*, and it cannot itself be cited as an instance of the error under consideration. However, the principle laid down is not satisfactory, and the wording of the judgments is sufficiently unclear to tempt a twentieth-century judge to verbal distinguishing. In *Re Gray* [1925][40] Romer J. held that a gift to provide sport for a regiment was good, the chief reason being that it was in the public interest that soldiers should be physically fit. The learned judge purported to distinguish *Re Nottage* on the ground that that was a gift for the encouragement of sport, whereas the present gift was for the benefit of a regiment. It follows from what has already been said that this was a misleading way of expressing the distinction. The true contrast is not between 'sport' and 'a regiment' but between 'those who

[39] *Re Nottage, Jones* v. *Palmer* [1895] 2 Ch. 649.
[40] *Re Gray, Todd* v. *Taylor* [1925] Ch. 34.

take part in yacht-racing' and 'the members of a regiment'. Apparently the distinction means that the health of those who take part in yacht-racing is unimportant to the community, while the health of the members of a regiment is important to the community. The unsatisfactory nature of this distinction will be appreciated as soon as it is realized that those who take part in yacht-racing themselves form a section of the community.

More recently, the question has twice been raised whether a trust for the promotion of foxhunting is charitable, the answer of the judges being that it is not.[41] In the second of the two cases Lawrence J. said: 'The main purpose of the appellant society's activities is to benefit foxhunting, not to benefit the community'. Here again a translation into the lower-order referent destroys the sharpness of the verbal distinction. There being no metaphysical entity *foxhunting* that is capable of being benefited, and the object of foxhunting not being to benefit foxes, it must surely be admitted that a so-called benefit to foxhunting is in fact a benefit to those human beings who take part in foxhunting. These persons constitute a section of the community. It is true that they do not constitute the whole of the community, but it is not necessary to a charitable trust that it should benefit everyone. One may add, if the fact is of any relevance, that foxhunting is no longer the pastime exclusively of the upper classes.

Turning to jurisprudence, the denial of the independent reality of universals is important chiefly because it necessitates a theory of law that will not assume law to be some entity mysteriously existing on its own account, independently of the external world and of the world of mind. Such a theory has been well stated by Professor Olivecrona in his book *Law as Fact*. He writes as follows:—

> 'We are dimly conscious of a permanent existence of the rules of law. We talk of them as if they were always there as real entities. But this is not exact. It is impossible to ascribe a permanent existence to a rule of law or to any other rule. A rule exists only as the content of a notion in a human being. No notion of this kind is permanently present in the mind of anyone. The imperative appears in the mind only intermittently. Of course the position is not changed by the fact that the imperative words are put down in writing. The written text—in itself only figures on paper—has the function of calling up certain notions in the mind of the reader. That is all.
>
> In reality, the law of a country consists of an immense mass of ideas concerning human behaviour, accumulated during centuries through the contributions of innumerable collaborators. . . . The ideas are again and again revived in human minds, accompanied by the imperative expression: "This line of conduct *shall* be taken" or something else to the same effect'.[42]

Some philosophers will not have this common-sense solution. They will go on endlessly trying to make some independent 'reality' out of the universals. Take, for instance, Dr. Joad's discussion of what is in effect the same problem, namely, the 'reality' of Shakespeare's play

[41] *Re Thompson, Public Trustee* v. *Lloyd* [1934] Ch. 342; *Peterborough Royal Foxhound Show Society* v. *I. R.* [1936] 2 K. B. 497.

[42] Law as Fact (Copenhagen and London, 1939) 47–8.

*Hamlet*. Joad argues that *Hamlet* is in some way a subsistent object with an independent being (he would, I suppose, argue the same for *law*), and he discusses and rejects a number of alternative opinions. One opinion that he rejects is that *Hamlet* consists of 'ideas in our own minds, and in the minds of all those who are performing, or seeing, or reading the play, or at any time have performed, or seen, or read it and remember what they learned, saw, or read'. This, it will be observed, is much the same opinion as Olivecrona holds concerning the concept *law*. Joad rejects it on the following grounds (he is considering in particular the meaning of the sentence '*Hamlet* is a great play').

> '(1) It seems most improbable that we are in fact referring to all these minds and experiences, most of which are unknown to us, when we make the statement "*Hamlet* is a great play". (2) If we were referring to them, we should, in so far as our own experience is concerned, be paying a totally undeserved compliment to ourselves. . . . (3) If all those who are seeing and reading, and have seen and read *Hamlet*, were abolished, it would, if this view were true, cease to be a great play. I doubt if anybody who has really admired *Hamlet* believes this. (4) When we make this assertion about *Hamlet*, it certainly seems as if we are purporting to speak and we certainly believe ourselves to be speaking not about our own or about anybody else's experiences, but about something which *is the cause of* these experiences. Now this something is not, at least *prima facie*, itself an experience'.[43]

All these difficulties seem to me to disappear if we say that '*Hamlet*' means either or both of two things—(*a*) a certain collection of symbols capable of evoking ideas and emotions, and (*b*) the ideas and emotions themselves. There seems to me to be no reason whatever to conclude, as Joad does, that *Hamlet* is 'a member of the class of subsistent objects which are neither mental nor material but are, nevertheless, constituent factors of the universe possessing being in their own right'. To answer Joad's particular arguments, as to his argument numbered (1), we are referring not to other people's ideas but to the symbols and their meaning for us; as to (2), we pay the compliment not to ourselves but to the man who had the genius to put the symbols together in that way; as to (3), it is true that *Hamlet* would cease to have meaning if all beings capable of understanding the languages in which it is now written ceased to exist—whether *Hamlet* would then itself cease to exist is a question not admitting of a simple answer in the affirmative or negative; it would exist only as a number of marks on paper; as to (4), we are in fact speaking in part of something that is the cause of our experiences, namely, the marks on paper, or the general effect produced on the stage.

By the same analysis, 'the law' is a collection of symbols capable of evoking ideas and emotions, together with the ideas and emotions so evoked. We need not dispute whether it is primarily symbol or primarily idea or primarily emotion; sometimes one, sometimes another aspect may be predominant, but usually all three are inseparably connected.

(*To be continued.*)

GLANVILLE WILLIAMS.

[43] C. E. M. Joad, Guide to Philosophy (London, 1941) 269.

## LANGUAGE AND THE LAW—II.

(*Continued from page 86.*)

### § 4. Ambiguity; Central and Peripheral Elements in Meaning.

THIS section will be concerned with two different types of obscurity of meaning. The words that are commonly recognized to be obscure in meaning and consequently to give rise to difficulty of interpretation are the ambiguous or equivocal ones, the words of multiple meaning. It is not so generally appreciated that even 'univocal' words prove without exception to be extremely fractious when one comes to apply them to the facts of experience. I shall first make a few remarks on ambiguous words, and then pass to the larger subject of fringe meaning.

(1) *Ambiguity*. It was said at the outset of this article that language is perhaps the greatest of man's inventions. But it is an invention that he is a poor hand at improving. Language shows a most remarkable maldistribution of words, a great unevenness of density; for some ideas are expressible in a dozen different words and others have to be lumped together under one. The result is much false reasoning. As C. S. Peirce put it, 'The woof and warp of all thought and research is symbols, and the life of thought and science is the life inherent in symbols; so that it is wrong to say that a good language is *important* to good thought, merely, for it is the essence of it'.[1] Philosophy stands out as the striking example of the flatulencies that may gather round the unacknowledged puns of language.[2] On the whole lawyers have appreciated the danger, and have been at pains to construct and preserve a moderately precise technical language. Oddly enough, it is least precise in its most fundamental parts. We use the word 'right' in some half-dozen different senses and often pass insensibly from one to the other, of course with disastrous results upon our reasoning. We use the phrases '*in rem*'—'*in personam*' in four different meanings. It was through confusing together two of them that Langdell and Maitland came to compose a famous fallacy, which has been exposed by Hohfeld.[3] 'Ownership' has two distinct senses, called by Salmond 'corporeal' and 'incorporeal'—*i.e.*, ownership of things and ownership of rights; and the word 'estate' should be similarly differentiated, for it bears a different meaning when we speak of an estate in land from its meaning when we speak of an estate in a right. This last ambiguity makes havoc of section 1 of the Law of Property Act, 1925. 'Property' has at least seven different meanings, 'acceptance' four, 'special damage' three, and 'specific', 'condition', 'warranty', and 'implied contract' at least two each. 'Chose in action' is a well-known chameleon expression. The division of animals into 'tame' and 'wild' (*mansuetae naturae* and *ferae naturae*) is in fact not one classification but two, one in the law of property and quite another in the law of tort.

1 C. S. Peirce, Collected Papers (Cambridge, Mass., 1932) ii, 129.
2 Some examples are given by Adrian Coates, A Basis of Opinion (London, 1938), 42–3.
3 Fundamental Legal Conceptions (New Haven and London, 1923), 69, 106–10.

Notwithstanding these defects in our vocabulary, we are at best timid in our measures of reform and frequently oppose even timid reforms. When Hohfeld wished to sort out four meanings of the word 'right' and to give them (together with their correlatives) distinguishing names, he felt obliged to defer to conservative feeling to the extent of using only words already current. In two instances the only words that he could find were words ('liability', 'immunity') that were already in use with quite different meanings. The unfortunate result was that, while freeing the word 'right' from equivocation, he created new equivocations for the two words so transferred. Notwithstanding this, Hohfeld deserves great praise for the way in which he accomplished his main task, the clarification of the word 'right'. Pollock's comment does him less than justice, and indeed, in my opinion, praises him for his only defect. 'I do not doubt', wrote Pollock, 'that the late Professor Hohfeld was a learned and ingenious man, and he seems to have had at least the merit of not inventing new words. But it is strange how many rational beings believe the ultimate truths of the universe to be reducible to patterns on a blackboard.'[4] One must not treat a remark in correspondence, as this one was, as a considered opinion; but I must say that I have not seen anything in Hohfeld's work to suggest that he regarded himself as doing more than improving our symbolism, which seems to me to be a worthy purpose in itself.

The ambiguity of words gives trouble to lawyers not only in manipulating their own technical language but also in the construction of non-legal language in documents. Many words change their meaning in the course of time: (1) some become restricted, (2) some widened, and (3) some transferred by metaphor, the original meaning either remaining or disappearing. To illustrate: (1) 'asylum', originally any refuge, now means in particular a refuge for those mentally diseased; but the old meaning has not quite disappeared.[5] 'Accident' etymologically means anything that happens, and this meaning is preserved in the remarkable judicial determination that murder is an 'accident' within the Workmen's Compensation Acts[6]; but generally the word means only damage not caused intentionally, or (even more narrowly) damage not caused by fault. (2) 'Committee' originally meant one individual to whom something was committed, the stress being on the last syllable. Both this meaning and this pronunciation have survived in some contexts, *e.g.*, in lunacy law; but generally nowadays a committee is not one person but a body of persons, and in this meaning the stress is shifted to the middle syllable.[7] 'Animal' has undergone both processes: originally any creature with breath, it became widened in scientific circles to include all non-vegetable forms of life, *e.g.*, fish, and also became narrowed in popular use to include only quadrupeds.[8] Another instance of divorce between popular and scientific meaning is in the word 'fish', where the popular meaning (any animal—in the scientific sense—living in water) is wider than the scientific meaning

4 Pollock-Holmes Letters (Cambridge, 1942), ii, 63.
5 *Dilworth* v. *Stamps Comr.* [1899] A. C. 99, at 107–8.
6 *Nisbet* v. *Rayne* [1910] 2 K. B. 689; *Trim School* v. *Kelly* [1914] A. C. 667.
7 O. E. D., s.v.; Burrows's Words and Phrases, s.v.
8 O. E. D., s.v.; Burrows's Words and Phrases, s.v.

(cold-blooded vertebrate with gills, etc.).[9] (3) 'Spirit' once meant breath, 'person' meant a mask, 'governor' meant the steersman of a ship; so frequent are these changes that language has been well called a dictionary of faded metaphors. When the native meaning of a word has quite disappeared, as in the last examples, it does not vex us; but often the meaning is in a transitional state and then it does. Thus words like 'asylum', 'committee' and 'animal', when they appear in legal instruments, are capable of giving great difficulty of construction, and have in fact done so. Occasionally judges seem to be unduly slow to abandon an older literary meaning in favour of a newer popular one. There are two reasons for this: the first, that judges are often men of letters, and are through their reading more familiar with the older meaning than the ordinary person; the second, less creditable, that they are influenced by the 'proper meaning' fallacy, which is to be discussed in § 6. In general it may be said that words ought not to be given an archaic meaning that the parties, situated as they were, would probably not have intended them to bear. One other general observation may be made before passing on: with modern works of reference, a draftsman usually has no excuse if he uses ambiguous words in an ambiguous context. If, for instance, the draftsman of a statute uses a word like 'accident' or 'animal' without defining it, it cannot be said that he is properly discharging the duty of his office.

(2) *Fringe meaning.* Some words, though not equivocal in the sense of having two or more distinct definitions, are yet obviously vague in their meaning, as for example 'about', 'near', 'more or less'. Such words, which ought generally to find no place in legal documents, give considerable trouble when they do occur.[10] What I am concerned to demonstrate in this section is that not merely some but all words are capable of occasioning difficulty in their application.[11] This is perhaps implicitly recognized in legal works on interpretation, but it is well to make it explicit. I shall consider in turn (*a*) words indicating qualities of continuous variation, (*b*) class-names, (*c*) names suggesting unity, (*d*) mathematical terms, and (*e*) words uncertain in their time-reference.

(*a*) Consider words for opposites like 'white' and 'black', 'night' and 'day', 'open' and 'shut', 'good' and 'bad'. At first sight opposites like these may seem to be mutually exclusive. 'A door', says the French proverb, 'must be either open or shut'. Similarly we may in our less lucid moments be tempted to think that it must always be night or day, and cannot be both at the same time. So obvious did this seem to the founders of logic that they erected it into one of the three 'laws of thought': a thing, they said, cannot be both *A* and not-*A*.

---

9 Cp. *Leavett* v. *Clark* [1915] 3 K. B. 9, where winkles were held to be 'fish'—adopting the popular meaning.

10 See Burrows's Words and Phrases, s.v.; 44 E. & E. Dig. 146–8. In the Labrador Boundary dispute (1927) the Privy Council had to determine how wide is a 'coast': 137 L. T. 187.

11 This topic is not discussed by Ogden and Richards. Non-legal writers on it are three heretical logicians: Sidgwick, *op. cit.*; Schiller, *op. cit.*; Bogoslovsky, *op. cit.* Cp. Locke, *op. cit.* 3, 5–6; Russell, *op. cit.* 197–8; Stebbing, *op. cit.* 62, and Cohen and Nagel, Introduction to Logic and Scientific Method (London, 1934), 118. Legal writers are chiefly Wurzel, 'Methods of Juridical Thinking', in Science of Legal Method (New York, 1921), basing himself upon Wundt's Logik; also Frank, *op. cit.*; Chase, *op. cit.*; Clarence Morris, How Lawyers Think (Cambridge, Mass. 1938), 78–9.

This theory, which once seemed patently true, is now held by a school of heterodox logicians to be just as patently false. A door can be, in a sense, both open and shut, or neither open nor shut; for it may be ajar. If 'white' be defined as the property of reflecting all light, and 'black' as the property of absorbing all light, then nothing is completely white and nothing is completely black, but every so-called 'black' thing has elements of 'whiteness', and every so-called 'white' thing has elements of 'blackness'. Whiteness and blackness are therefore matters of degree. In fact, all words of the type instanced are simply the first and last members of a continuous series, and the extremes may be purely notional, having no existence in the world of sense-experience.

The difficulty of fixing the frontiers of words in situations like these was well brought out in the sophism of the schoolmen concerning the 'heap'. The sophism consisted in propounding the question: Does one stone make a heap? If the person questioned answered in the negative, the questioner then asked: Do one hundred stones make a heap? If this received an affirmative answer, the questioner asked similar questions for two stones, ninety-nine stones, three stones, ninety-eight stones, and so on, until he pinned his victim down to some such apparently absurd proposition as that eight stones do not make a heap but that nine stones do. The same game was played by asking how many hairs make a beard, or how many sheep a flock. The only sensible way of meeting the difficulty is to say that there is an area of uncertainty between the number of units that certainly do and those that certainly do not make the aggregate in question.

When one comes to consider them, one finds that these words for qualities of continuous variation exist in the language in altogether unsuspected numbers: and the fact of variation is obscured by the sharpness of the words used to describe the extremes. 'Sane' and 'insane', 'drunk' and 'sober', 'democracy' and 'dictatorship' are sharply contrasted words; but no chasm sunders the two states in the world as we know it.

Some logicians have pointed out two fallacies to which these polarities may give rise.[12] The first, which is much the commoner of the two, has been called 'the fallacy of white or black'. It consists in supposing that every object must be white or black, without allowing for the possibility of its being something in between. As applied to the words 'white' and 'black' the fallacy is obvious; but as applied to such words as 'good' and 'bad', 'honest' and 'dishonest', 'intelligent' and 'unintelligent', it foments much needless controversy.

The second fallacy consists in arguing that black is white because there is a range of half-tones in between. For instance, if it is desired to prove that 5,000 stones do not make a heap, this can be proved by assuming that one stone does not make a heap, and that the addition of one stone, in itself, does not convert that which is not a heap into that which is a heap. This was the argument of the man who broke his camel's back by heaping straws upon it one at a time, thinking that a single straw could not break a camel's back. The fallacy is an ever-present danger in law and ethics, for it is often hard to see the objection

[12] R. H. Thouless, Straight and Crooked Thinking (London, 1930), chap. 9; cp. L. S. Stebbing, Thinking to Some Purpose (Harmondsworth, 1939), 142–5.

to an argument of the 'if this why not that?' type, which, if allowed to be pressed far enough, will make every exception swallow up the rule.

The difficulty of using such words as these does not press upon the ordinary man because it usually does not matter to him whether, for instance, he calls a number of stones a 'heap' or not. All that matters is that he should make his meaning clear enough for the purpose on hand. Suppose that a housewife is following a cookery book which tells her to add a pinch of mustard to a particular dish. She cannot tell how many grains make a pinch, but she can guess what is meant by a pinch and if she puts too much, or too little, her palate will in due course discover her error.

With law it is different, for in law we make sharp consequences hang upon these words of gradation. The question whether a man is left in freedom or detained in a mental institution depends on whether he is judicially classified as sane or insane,[13] as also does the question whether his dispositions of property are upheld or not.[14] Whether a man is punished or acquitted may turn simply and solely upon whether an attempt to commit a crime was sufficiently 'proximate', or upon whether a statement that he falsely swore was 'material' to a judicial proceeding; and in a murder case it may be literally a question of life or death whether the accused intended to hurt by means of an act 'intrinsically likely to kill'.[15] Well may a convict echo the words of the poet—

> 'Oh, the little more, and how much it is!
> And the little less, and what worlds away!'

In tort we have one rule for reservoirs, another for duck-ponds; and the Court somehow has to draw the line between the two. A libel is in 'permanent' form and a slander in 'transient' form; but permanency is a matter of degree. In the law of negligence and nuisance the defendant pays full damages or nothing according as the Court puts his conduct at the 'reasonable' or 'unreasonable' end of what is in fact a continuous gradation. So also with remoteness of damage. The law of vicarious liability abounds in such puzzles; thus (*a*) the employer of an independent contractor is not liable for him merely because he is employed to do an ordinarily hazardous act, but is liable for him if he is employed to do an extra-hazardous act[16]; (*b*) the distinction between a servant and an independent contractor rests on the infinitely variable matter of control; (*c*) the master of a servant who exceeds his authority is responsible for some excess, but not for excessive excess[17]; and (*d*) the master of a vanman who deviates from his route and negligently

---

13 See, *e.g.*, Lunacy Act, 1890, ss. 4, 28, and Sch. 2, Form 8.

14 'The difficulty to be grappled with arises from the circumstance that the question is almost always one of degree. There is no difficulty in the case of a raving madman or a drivelling idiot in saying that he is not a person capable of disposing of property. But between such an extreme case and that of a man of perfectly sound and vigorous understanding, there is every shade of intellect, every degree of mental capacity. There is no possibility of mistaking midnight for noon; but at what precise moment twilight becomes darkness is hard to determine': *per* Lord Cranworth L.C. in *Boyse* v. *Rossborough* (1857) 6 H. L. C. 2 at 45, quoted by Hannen J. in *Boughton* v. *Knight* (1873) L. R. 3 P. & D. 64 at 67.

15 The terminology is that of Kenny (Outlines of Criminal Law, 15th ed., 155); but the word 'intrinsically' seems to be meaningless in this context.

16 *Honeywill & Stein* v. *Larkin Bros.* [1934] 1 K. B. 191.

17 *Poland* v. *Parr* [1927] 1 K. B. 236 at 243.

injures a pedestrian is liable if the deviation is a slight one but not if the deviation is such that every yard he goes is a yard away from his employment and not to it [18]—no precise angle being laid down. A contract to be valid must be 'certain in its terms', and certainty of meaning is, as it is the object of these pages to show, a question of degree. The 'lodger' shades off into the 'lessee of a flat'; yet somehow the Courts must draw a line between them, because the relative law is different. In some parts of the law, such as copyright and charities, we must distinguish between a thing that concerns 'the public or a portion of the public' and a thing that concerns 'private individuals', this resulting in innumerable perplexities.

Judges refuse to be frightened by these difficulties. They are not intimidated from saying that the case is on one side or the other of the line merely because they discover that the line is difficult to draw. Thus in one of the cases working out the limits of the rule against remoteness, where a limitation was upheld as not infringing the rule, Lord Nottingham said: 'It hath been urged at the bar, where will you stop if you do not stop at *Child and Bayly's Case*? I answer, I will stop everywhere when any inconvenience appears, no where before'.[19] Blackburn J. observed of the rule in *Hadley* v. *Baxendale*: 'It is a vague rule, and as Bramwell B. said, it is something like having to draw a line between night and day; there is a great duration of twilight when it is neither night nor day; but on the question now before the Court, though you cannot draw the precise line, you can say on which side of the line the case is'.[20] 'Courts of Justice', said Chitty J., 'ought not to be puzzled by such old scholastic questions as to where a horse's tail begins and where it ceases. You are obliged to say, "This is a horse's tail", at some time.'[21] Similarly Lord Coleridge C.J.: 'The Attorney-General has asked where we are to draw the line. The answer is that it is not necessary to draw it at any precise point. It is enough for us to say that the present case is on the right side of any reasonable line that could be drawn'.[22] And Lindley M.R.: 'It is urged that it is difficult to draw the line. I admit that it is extremely difficult. . . . It is always a question of degree. It may be asked, What is the difference between one cart and two, and so on? You cannot draw the line in that way. Nothing is more common in life than to be unable to draw the line between two things. Who can draw the line between plants and animals? And yet, who has any difficulty in saying that an oak tree is a plant and not an animal?' [23]

So also, judges are not always deterred in framing new legal rules by

[18] Pollock, Torts, 14th ed., 70–1.

[19] *Duke of Norfolk's Case* (1681) 2 Swans. 454 at 468; 3 Chan. Cas. 14 at 36.

[20] *Hobbs* v. *L. & S. W. Ry.* (1875) L. R. 10 Q. B. 111 at 121. Cp. Scrutton L.J. in *The San Onofre* [1922] P. 243 at 253.

[21] *Lavery* v. *Pursell* (1888) 39 Ch. D. 508 at 517. See also Pollock C.B. in *White* v. *Bluett* (1853) 23 L. J. Ex. 36 at 37: 'By the argument a principle is pressed to an absurdity, as a bubble is blown until it bursts.'

[22] *Mayor of Southport* v. *Morriss* [1893] 1 Q. B. 359 at 361.

[23] *Att.-Gen.* v. *Brighton & Hove Co-operative Supply Assn.* [1900] 1 Ch. 276 at 282. Cp. *per* FitzGibbon L.J. in *Gregg* v. *Fraser* [1906] 1 Ir. R. 545 at 578–9: 'This is in each case a pure question on the construction of a written document, whether the case lies on the one side or on the other of a definite *line* in the mathematical sense—a line without breadth—every case must lie on one side of that line or on the other . . . and "line balls" are barred.'

the consideration that they may be hard to apply. In the words of Bowen L.J.: 'It is not a valid objection to a legal doctrine that it will not be always easy to know whether the doctrine is to be applied in a particular case. The law has to face such embarrassments'.[24] In the *Pollock-Holmes Letters* Holmes writes: 'People in the law as elsewhere hate to recognize that most questions—I think I might say all legal questions—are questions of degree. I have just sent back an opinion of one of our JJ. with a criticism of an argument in it of the "where are you going to draw the line" type—as if all decisions were not a series of points tending to fix a point in a line'.[25]

Despite these brave words, it is to the interest of legal certainty that, other things being equal, the rules of law should be as clear of application as possible. Some words have a wider fringe of uncertainty than others, and for legal purposes those with the narrowest fringe are generally the best. Rules relating to 'dangerous things', 'extra-hazardous acts', and 'excessive excess', are *prima facie* objectionable, because they require so many cases to be litigated. But the difficulty is to know whether other things *are* equal, *i.e.*, whether other needs are sufficiently strong to counterbalance the need for legal certainty. An illustration or two will show how the Courts have veered in this matter. In *Winterbottom* v. *Wright* (1842)[26] Alderson B. expressed himself thus: 'The only safe rule is to confine the right to recover to those who enter into the contract; if we go one step beyond that, there is no reason why we should not go fifty'. This was the kind of reasoning that Holmes disapproved, and in fact *Winterbottom* v. *Wright* was restrictively distinguished in *Donoghue* v. *Stevenson* (1932).[27] Similarly in *Colgate* v. *Bacheler* (1602)[28] it was held that all contracts in restraint of trade were void; 'for as well as he may restrain him for one time or one place, he may restrain him for longer times and more places, which is against the benefit of the commonwealth'. This rule also has been abandoned, and the Courts now essay the difficult task of drawing the line between reasonable and unreasonable restraint.[29] Thus an argument based on the difficulty of drawing a line is not a strong one; but, as already said, it is not altogether without force.

As an illustration of a legal distinction that is both misty and unnecessary, consider the distinction between contracts of sale of goods and contracts for work and materials. This distinction is made in popular speech but is not at all precise. One speaks, for instance, of 'buying' a bottle of medicine from a chemist but not of buying one from a doctor. One 'buys' a tailor-made suit but not false teeth. An amateur photographer who has his prints made by a chemist would not be very certain whether he was 'buying' the prints or not; and one who orders a dog kennel to be specially made would probably not speak of 'buying' it: he would speak of 'getting a man to make it'. In ordinary life these verbal distinctions do not matter; but lawyers, having created a needless legal distinction between contracts of sale and contracts for work

24 *Dashwood* v. *Magniac* [1891] 3 Ch. 306 at 364.
25 Pollock-Holmes Letters (Cambridge, 1942), ii, 28.
26 10 M. & W. 109 at 115.
27 [1932] A. C. 562 at 588–9, 610.
28 Cro. Eliz. 872, Owen 143.
29 Holdsworth, H. E. L. viii, 58 ff.

and materials, have found themselves bogged in the uncertain borderland between them.

It is next to be observed that the situation in which a judge refuses to draw a precise line and determines simply whether a particular case is on the one or the other side of it is not always satisfactory. It appears to be satisfactory only because the same judge is not presented with a series of cases identical in all their facts except the variable fact under consideration. Take, for instance, the present rule as to deviation by servants driving vehicles in the course of their employment. At first sight this rule, which leaves everything to the judge's discretion, appears less arbitrary than a rule laying down a definite test of the employer's liability, *e.g.*, by fixing a precise angle, say forty-five degrees, as the maximum angle of deviation consistent with the employer's liability, or else by fixing the maximum proportion (*e.g.*, 50 per cent.) that the extra distance occasioned by the deviation must bear to the distance authorized by the master. But suppose that, with the law as it is, the same judge has to decide a series of cases involving the same vanman's deviation from the same line of his employment, the angle or proportionate length of deviation becoming greater and greater in each case. It is clear that he would have to fix on some angle, or to draw some line on the map, as marking the watershed between what is a mere deviation and what is altogether outside the course of the employment. The line so chosen would be an arbitrary one. If the same judge had to decide many groups of such cases, he would probably fix upon some one angle or proportion which he would apply to all of them as a rough rule of thumb. Decisions given in pursuance of this rule of thumb would not be any more arbitrary than those now rendered without any rule at all; but the arbitrariness would be announced beforehand, which would facilitate the settling of cases without litigation.

There are many branches of the law where this process of settling a line has in fact taken place. Precise periods of time are commonly laid down in statutes. Instances are the statutory periods of limitation, which, though arbitrary, are preferable to a vague rule that laches defeats rights. At common law the definition of 'night-time' for the purpose of the law of burglary was whether there was sufficient sun-light to discern a man's face [30]: by statute this was changed to the fixed period 9 p.m.—6 a.m.[31]

Sometimes fixed times are even laid down in the common law. A good illustration is the age of majority. The age of twenty-one was originally fixed by custom as the age of majority of tenants by knight's service. Pollock and Maitland, basing themselves on Bracton, suggest that it was the age at which heavy armour could be borne.[32] Other classes had their own rules: thus the young burgess was of full age when he could count money and measure cloth.[33] How the rule for tenants by knight's service became generalized we do not know; it may well have been the work of the judges. However it arose, the rule is clearly more satisfactory than one which bids us inquire whether the particular

30 Hale's P. C. i, 550–1.

31 See now Larceny Act, 1916, s. 46. For another statutory definition see Night Poaching Act, 1828 (c. 69), s. 12.

32 P. & M., 2nd ed., ii, 438–9; Bracton, f. 86b.

33 P. & M. *loc cit.*

individual has attained the ability to look after his own affairs. Again, the judges have recognized or created earlier ages for particular purposes. Ideas as to the average age of puberty yielded the ages for consent to marriage—twelve for a female and fourteen for a male,[34] and also the minimum age at which a boy could be convicted of rape (fourteen).[35] Children under seven were given complete exemption from criminal responsibility and those under fourteen a qualified exemption.[36] The period of minority became incorporated in the rule against remoteness,[37] and more recently in the rule against perpetual duration.[38] When the Court of Chancery wished to give extended protection to infants in respect of their ratifying contracts obtained during infancy by undue influence, it named one year as the extended period. 'In the Court of Chancery', said Lord Cranworth, 'we are obliged to cut the knot as to the question of time, by naming some time.'[39] In the law of bills of exchange, definite times have been laid down as the limit of what is normally a reasonable time for the presentation of cheques[40] and the giving of notices of dishonour.[41] So, too, the Courts, following the practice of conveyancers, fixed sixty years as the period of title in general required to be shown under an open contract of sale[42]; later this period was successively reduced by statute to forty[43] and thirty[44] years. Another example of definite times being laid down by the judges is in the law of evidence. When the rule was first invented that ancient documents 'prove themselves', no fixed meaning was assigned to the word 'ancient'. 'But a more definite standard naturally became desirable. Since the lack of living witnesses to the document was the justifying fact, and since such witnesses might be assumed to have been at least of age at the time of execution, they would presumably have disappeared from the stage of life after the lapse of forty or at most fifty years. Accordingly the period of forty years came, by the 1700s, to be taken as the time when a document was treated as "ancient" under this rule. But the reckoning was too strict, because the witnesses were more likely to have been mature persons, and therefore at least thirty years of age; and another thirty years would suffice to bring them near the end of their span. Ever since the second half of the 1700s, therefore, the period of thirty years has sufficed to constitute an "ancient" document; except under special statutory rules.'[45] It may be added that although the period was originally fixed by reference to the likelihood of the attesting witnesses being dead, the

---

34 Co. Lit. 78b (following the canon law); see now Age of Marriage Act, 1929.

35 Hale, P. C. i, 630; Archbold, 31st ed., 12, 1021. At the other end of life, there is no fixed age at which a woman is taken to be past child-bearing: Wigmore, Evidence, 3rd ed., § 2528.

36 Hale, P. C. i, 25–8; see now Children and Young Persons Act, 1933, s. 50.

37 Holdsworth, H. E. L. vii, 226–7.

38 *Re Hooper* [1932] 1 Ch. 38; Nathan, Equity Through the Cases, pp. 163–5.

39 *Smith* v. *Kay* (1859) 7 H. L. C. 750 at 772.

40 Byles on Bills, 20th ed., 18–19.

41 *Ibid.* 261–3.

42 Williams, Vendor and Purchaser, 4th ed., 112–5.

43 Vendor and Purchaser Act, 1874, s. 1.

44 Law of Property Act, 1925, s. 44.

45 Wigmore, Evidence, 3rd ed., § 2138. The period is reduced to twenty years by the Evidence Act, 1938, s. 4.

Courts now hold that it applies even though the witnesses are alive and in Court.[46]

Occasionally times have been fixed by analogy to a statute; that was how the year 1189 came to be hit upon for the period of prescription and custom,[47] and the period of seven years' absence as the period for presumption of death.[48] The former is a good example of the harmful nature of the fiction that judges do not make the law. Had the origin of the rule been frankly recognized, the rule might have been kept up to date by adopting the analogy of later statutes of limitation fixing new periods. As it was, the limit of legal memory was regarded as irrevocably settled, and it has become steadily more ridiculous with the passage of years.

There are other ways in which the common law has tied itself down to more or less precise rules. There is the forty-five degrees rule as a rough test of infringement of ancient lights.[49] The Statute of Forcible Entry, 1381, forbids an entry 'with multitude of people', and Coke reports the opinion that a multitude consists of ten or more people—*multitudinem decem faciunt*; but he adds that he does not himself share this opinion, holding that the precise number is at the discretion of the judges.[50] Superficially this may sound the more reasonable view, but it is suggested that if in one case ten persons are held to constitute a crowd, there can be no reason why in another case it should be held that eleven persons do not constitute a crowd; and so for other figures. It will be recollected that in the similar offence of unlawful assembly, an assembly is defined as a meeting of three or more persons.[51] In my submission this fixing of precise times and amounts is in every way a desirable one, and should be extended.

Another method of meeting the difficulty caused by continuous variation in nature is to provide a continuous variation in legal results. This can be done in some cases by giving the judge a wide discretion as to damages or punishment. A good illustration is *Kiddell* v. *Burnard* (1842),[52] where it was argued that a horse was not unsound within the meaning of a warranty if the unsoundness were slight. Parke B. said: 'An argument has been adduced from the slightness of the disease and facility of cure; but if we once let in considerations of that kind, where are we to draw the line? A horse may have a cold, which may be cured in a day; or a fever, which may be cured in a week or month; and it would be difficult to say where to stop. Of course, if the disease be slight, the unsoundness is proportionably so, and so also

[46] Phipson, Evidence, 8th ed., 515.

[47] Holdsworth, H. E. L. iii, 166; vii, 343-5.

[48] Originally perhaps, the number seven was chosen as a magic number. As a rule of English law the rule first appears, in special applications, in James I's Bigamy Act, 1603, and in an Act of 1667 (19 Car. 2, c. 6). The general seven-year rule was first laid down, on the analogy of these two statutes, in *Doe d. George* v. *Jesson* (1805) 6 East 80. See Thayer, Preliminary Treatise on Evidence (London, 1898), 319-24.

Apart from absence there is no fixed period for the presumption of continuance of life; nor is there a fixed period for the presumption arising from the possession of goods 'recently' stolen.

[49] *Colls* v. *Home & Colonial Stores* [1904] A. C. 179 at 204, 210; *Davis* v. *Marrable* [1913] 2 Ch. 421 at 430.

[50] Co. Lit. 257a.

[51] Dicey, Law of the Constitution, 9th ed., 562-3, 8th ed., 501; *Field* v. *Receiver of Metropolitan Police* [1907] 2 K. B. 853 (riot).

[52] 9 M. & W. 668.

ought to be the damages'. Another illustration is the Admiralty rule, now to be applied by statute to non-maritime cases, allowing apportionment of damages in cases of contributory negligence. There is no necessity to adopt an 'all or nothing' rule as the common law does in these cases; the damages can be made to vary according to degrees of fault.

Where perfect elasticity of legal consequence is impossible, something can be done to mirror nature by multiplying categories. Thus the Mental Deficiency Act, 1927, subdivides the class of mental defectives into idiots, imbeciles, feeble-minded persons, and moral defectives. But there is still a great gulf fixed between this class as a whole and the class of so-called normal persons. One day we may recognize that the class of 'normal' persons itself needs subdivision, for it includes neurotics and others needing therapeutic treatment and special economic assistance.

(*b*) Hitherto in this section we have considered chiefly pairs of words that indicate the poles of a continuous variation. We are now to consider class-names, which we shall find show much the same characteristic.

Classes are sometimes divided into two sorts, natural (*e.g.*, lions), and artificial (*e.g.*, buildings). Taking artificial classes first, it is obvious that very great difficulty may be found in determining what falls within them. 'The imperfection of human language', said Byles, J., in *Stevens* v. *Gourley* (1859),[53] 'renders it not only difficult, but absolutely impossible, to define the word "building" with any approach to accuracy. One may say of this or that structure, this or that is not a building; but no general definition can be given; and our lexicographers do not attempt it.' Many other instances of the difficulty of putting metes and bounds to artificial classes will be found in the reports. For instance: is an album a 'book'?[54] Is a bicycle a 'carriage'?[55] Is a flag a 'document'?[56] Is a flying-boat a 'ship or vessel'?[57] Are household goods 'money'?[58] Is ice-cream 'meat'?[59] Is sandstone a 'mineral'?[60] And so on.

These difficulties in the case of artificial classes are familiar enough to lawyers; but it may come as a surprise to learn that much the same puzzles are found in dealing with the so-called 'natural' classes.

One aspect of the medieval 'realist' theory was the idea that 'natural' classes exist in nature, ready-made, with clear-cut edges. The world was full of lions and tigers, trees and apples, gold and silver, and all that man had to do was to learn their names. This is still the attitude of the child. Even when it came to be admitted that words were of human invention, it was still thought that the classes to which they applied existed in nature, fixed and immutable.

Modern scientists and some modern philosophers reject this view.

53 7 C. B. (N.S.) 99 at 112.
54 Burrows's Words and Phrases, s.v.—no.
55 *Ibid.* s.v.—yes.
56 Phipson, Evidence, 8th ed., 524—no.
57 *Polpen Shipping Co.* v. *Commercial Union Assurance Co.* [1943] K. B. 161—no.
58 *Perrin* v. *Morgan* [1943] A. C. 399—yes.
59 *Slater* v. *Evans* [1916] 2 K. B. 403—no.
60 *North British Ry.* v. *Budhill, etc. Co.* [1910] A. C. 116; cp. Lord Macmillan, Law and Other Things (Cambridge, 1937), 155–7.

Their arguments run along two main lines, which may be called the logical and the evolutionary.

(i) Class-names being the result of abstraction, agreement upon class-names requires agreement upon the qualities that are regarded as essential to the class. Suppose that all the individuals hitherto regarded as belonging to a class possess the qualities a, b, c and d. It may come to be thought that these qualities are essential to qualify for the class-name. But now suppose that a new individual is found possessing qualities a, b and c, but not d. The question may then arise whether the former definition is to be maintained, resulting in an exclusion of the new-found individual from the class; or whether it is to be modified, allowing of his inclusion. A vivid illustration is that of the black swans of Australia: so imbued were zoologists with the idea that whiteness was a property of swans, that when black swans were discovered in Australia it was at first determined to allot them not to the genus *Cygnus* but to the genus *Chenopis*. Even to-day ornithologists are undecided whether to class bearded tits as tits; they possess some, but not all, the characteristics common to the other birds called tits. The question is, of course, a verbal one; but that it can be raised at all shows the artificiality of class-distinctions.

(ii) Astronomers, geologists, biologists and physicists combine in their different ways to prove the truth of the Heraclitan idea that reality is in a flux. To go back to the beginning, the earth was once a flaming mass, and life started with elementary forms. The classes that now seem to be so fixed in nature can be traced in large measure to an undifferentiated origin; nor can we be confident that the process of change has stopped. This is particularly evident in biology.[61] Take as an illustration the class *man*, symbolized by the word 'man'. In most of its applications the meaning of this word is clear. But man has developed out of the lower animals, and there is no serious break between him and the amoeba. At what point in the line of Adam's ancestors shall we first refuse to apply the label 'man'? Clearly our limit must be an arbitrary one. We may even find difficulty in applying the word to present-day situations, if, for instance, we are asked to consider a foetus or a corpse.

The difficulty that thus confronts us with the word 'man' is also experienced with other class-names, and indeed with all general names. There are no words for a class, quality or relation the application of which to concrete instances is not capable of giving rise to difficulty. It is not that similarities and differences do not exist in nature; they abound in nature. The difficulty is in drawing firm lines around or between them.

It is true that the likelihood of trouble in the case of some classes is so small that it may be ignored; or, as Sidgwick put it, 'some classes are, for all practical purposes to-day, conspicuously definite and unlikely to need any change of definition to-morrow'.[62] But this is a matter of

[61] 'The concept of species has lost all the quality of immutability originally postulated by Linnaeus. As a result of Darwin's work, the idea of change has supplanted that of changelessness in regard to all biological groups': Huxley, Haddon and Carr-Saunders, We Europeans (Harmondsworth, 1939), 95.

[62] Sidgwick, *op. cit.* 155. A good illustration is the distinction between living and dead things. But even this distinction is not absolutely sharp: see Bogoslovsky, *op. cit.* 63–5.

probability, not of certainty; and with the advance of science the scientist has become more and more reluctant to dogmatize on class-boundaries.

In the case of both artificial and so-called natural classes there are certain special elements of difficulty. One difficulty, already noticed in the case of natural classes, is in deciding when a thing begins and ends as a member of a class—when the egg becomes a chick, when coal becomes cinder, and so on.[63] A second difficulty arises from 'impurity'; thus 'water' is rigidly defined by the chemist, but one can put a progression ranging (say) from sea-water to cabbages in which the extent of application of the word will not be at all clear. In regard to biological terms, nature is continually inventing hybrids to puzzle and confuse us in our nomenclature.[64] A third difficulty is that of saying whether a part of an individual thing is entitled to the class-name enjoyed by the thing as a whole: for instance, whether an anchor is part of a 'vessel', so as to make a collision with an anchor a collision with the vessel to which the anchor is attached.[65] A fourth, felt particularly in the law, is the difficulty of distinguishing between 'land' and 'chattels'. Take any heavy article (*e.g.*, a piece of trade machinery) and imagine it screwed down; is it still what it was before—'trade machinery'—or is it now 'land'? [66]

The upshot is that the words we use, though they have a central core of meaning that is relatively fixed, are of doubtful application to a considerable number of marginal cases. In general, we try in our language to sharpen our distinctions beyond what is warranted by the facts of the case. It is a necessary feature of language that we should have to make this effort, and thus it is inevitable that our linguistic distinctions should constantly break down.

Once again it must be remarked that the ordinary man is not usually troubled with these perplexities. It does not matter to a seaman whether an anchor is or is not called part of a 'vessel'. A chemist does not need to answer the question, yes or no, does a rolled-gold watch come within the description 'gold'? Biologists may find difficulty with their classifications, but nothing turns on the question whether they classify a creature under one heading or another; it is simply a question of verbal expediency. With the lawyer it is different. The lawyer, like the theologian, is faced with a number of texts that he regards as authoritative, and that are supposed to settle any question that can conceivably arise. Each text was at one time drawn up by someone who presumably meant something by it; but once the document has left its author's hands it is the document that matters, not any unexpressed meaning that still remains in the author's mind. For the lawyer the words of the document are authoritative as words, and there is generally no possibility of obtaining further information from the author, either because the author is dead, or because of rules of evidence precluding reference to him, or because a reference to the author would infringe

[63] Cp. *Thomas W. Ward, Ltd.* v. *Waugh* [1933] S. L. T. 619, where the question was whether a ship that was being broken up was still a 'vessel'.

[64] Cp. *Heath's Case* (1801) 2 East P. C. 609–10, where it was held that 'any red or fallow deer' included the cross breeds, such as a bastard menald, bred from a menald buck and a fallow doe. ('Fallow' = light brown; 'menald' = dappled chestnut.)

[65] *Re Margetts and Ocean Accident, etc., Corpn.* [1901] 2 K. B. 792—yes.

[66] *Re Yates, Batcheldor* v. *Yates* (1888) 38 Ch. D. 112 (held, land).

a rule requiring the document to be in a certain form. It is this inability to refer to the author, coupled with the inherent vagueness of language, that makes interpretation such a perennial source of legal difficulty.

Before leaving the subject of classes, a few remarks may be made on some rules of law that refer explicitly to classes or kinds. One such rule is to be found in the law of remoteness of damage, or at any rate was to be found there before the decision in *Re Polemis* (1921).[67] The general principle was that if the consequence was not foreseeable by the defendant in kind, he was not responsible for it either in contract or in tort; but 'when it is found that a man ought to have foreseen in a general way consequences of a certain kind, it will not avail him to say that he could not foresee the precise course or the full extent of the consequences, being of that kind, which in fact have happened'.[68] Upon this distinction a wag once inquired whether the difference beween a difference of kind and a difference of degree is itself a difference of kind or a difference of degree. The answer that will be gathered from the foregoing pages is that it is a difference of degree. A difference of kind is merely a violent difference of degree.[68a] The impossibility of drawing a sharp line between kind and degree is clearly evidenced by the cases. If I push a man down, I can foresee that he may be hurt but I cannot foresee that he will die; yet if in fact he suffers from an egg-shell skull, a fatty heart, or haemophilia, and so unexpectedly dies, it was clear even before *Re Polemis* that I am liable for this consequence.[69] Thus, to save the rule, death must be regarded as a consequence of the same kind as pain; though many might think it a consequence of an altogether different kind. Sometimes the kind-degree distinction seems to be applied not to the ultimate harm but to the way in which the harm is brought about. If my quiet horse strays on the highway and kicks a child, the consequence before *Re Polemis* was too remote,[70] apparently because it was unforeseeable in kind. But if the horse strays and, being frightened by a boy, takes to flight and injures a child in its headlong career, inflicting precisely the same injury as in the previous instance it inflicted when at a standstill, the consequence (given an initial breach of duty [71]) was probably not too remote.[72] The damage is the same; it is only the causal sequence that is supposed in the first case to be different in kind from what could have been foreseen. When distinctions like these are drawn it may not seem altogether a bad thing that in *Re Polemis* (1921) the Court of

[67] [1921] 3 K. B. 560.

[68] Pollock in (1922) 38 L. Q. R. 167; *Smith* v. *L. & S. W. Ry.* (1870) L. R. 6 C. P. 14, particularly *per* Blackburn J. at 22–3; Goodhart, 'The *Palsgraf Case*', Essays in Jurisprudence and the Common Law (Cambridge, 1937), 129.

[68a] 'I recently asked a well-known biologist if he could give me from the whole field of biology one clear example of a difference which scientists would unequivocally agree upon as a difference in kind, and another which they would agree upon as a difference in degree, so that there would be no longer any doubt about the precise meanings of the two words. He was unable to give the required examples. I have since put the query to a number of other scientists and psychologists with no better luck': R. A. Wilson. The Miraculous Birth of Language (London, 1941), 81.

[69] *Per* Kennedy J. in *Dulieu* v. *White* [1901] 2 K. B. 669 at 679.

[70] *Cox* v. *Burbidge* (1863) 13 C. B. (N.S.) 430; cp. Williams. Liability For Animals (Cambridge, 1939), 159 ff.

[71] Cp. *Deen* v. *Davies* [1935] 2 K. B. 282.

[72] Cp. *Patterson* v. *Fanning* (1901) 2 O. L. R. 462; Williams, *op. cit.* 170, 382.

Appeal purported to abandon the test of reasonable foresight as a rule for remoteness of damage. According to this decision, damage is not too remote merely because the defendant could not have foreseen it in kind. The new rule, however, has difficulties of its own, and it is still not at all certain how far it will be applied. *The Edison* (1933)[73] casts doubt on the extent even of the rule that damage is not too remote merely because unforeseeable in degree. In that case the plaintiffs recovered damages for the loss of use of their dredger during a normal period of replacement, but not for loss of use during the extended period of replacement necessitated by their own poverty. It might have been thought that this was a mere difference in the degree of damage, for which the defendants were liable. Contract cases are in an equally puzzling state; some of them seem to apply the rule that the defendant is liable for an unexpected difference of degree,[74] but most do not.[75] Some sort of reconciliation can perhaps be made by distinguishing between remoteness of damage and measure of damages; thus it may be said that *Re Polemis* regulates the question whether the defendant is liable for the loss of the ship, while *The Edison* regulates the amount of damages that he must pay in respect of the ship if he is held to be liable for its loss, *i.e.*, it regulates the way in which the physical loss is to be translated into terms of money. But this distinction is itself a very unclear one, for it varies according to the loss that is being attended to. If in *The Edison* we consider the loss of the ship, the question whether the plaintiffs can recover for their loss in respect of their dredging contract appears as a question of measure of damages for the loss of the ship. But if we consider directly the loss in respect of the dredging contract, and inquire whether the defendant is liable for it, we turn the question into one of remoteness of damage.

All things considered, it seems that the best we can hope for in this part of the law is a number of detailed rules regulating as precisely as possible the situations that occur in practice. It seems evident that the effort to bring all cases under a very few broad principles is doomed to failure, or at best can result in nothing but the palest of generalities.

Comparable to remoteness of damage in civil law is transferred malice in criminal law. The rule is that malice may be regarded as 'transferred' where the harm done is of the kind intended, though not otherwise. It is settled that for the purpose of this rule an injury to *A* is of the same kind as a similar injury to *B*,[76] but an injury to the person is not of the same kind as damage to property.[77] To give an illustration of the difficulties met with in working the rule, suppose that the prisoner has

---

[73] [1933] A. C. 449.

[74] *Phillips* v. *L. & S. W. Ry.* (1879) 4 Q. B. D. 406 (plaintiff compensated for loss of income on basis of actual income, although unusually large; but Cockburn C.J. seemed to indicate that the damages might be reduced if 'the attempt to award full compensation in damages might be attended with ruinous consequences to defendant'); *Great Lakes S.S. Co.* v. *Maple Leaf Milling Co.* (1924) 41 T. L. R. 21 at 23 ('If grounding takes place in breach of contract, the precise nature of the damage incurred by grounding is immaterial').

[75] *E.g.*, *Hobbs* v. *L. & S. W. Ry.* (1875) L. R. 10 Q. B. 111 (recovery for inconvenience of having to walk home in the rain, but not for catching cold in consequence—surely more a difference of degree than the difference between pain and death, which is settled to be one of degree); *The Arpad* [1934] P. 189.

[76] *R.* v. *Latimer* (1886) 17 Q. B. D. 359.

[77] *R.* v. *Pembliton* (1874) 2 C. C. R. 119; Kenny, Outlines of Criminal Law, 15th ed., 170, 189–90.

intentionally (*i.e.*, in technical language, maliciously) set fire to chattels in a house, the fire then unintentionally spreading to the house; is the prisoner's malice transferred to the house? On the rule above stated, the answer depends on whether damage to chattels is regarded as being of the same kind as damage to a house (both being species of the genus 'damage to property'), or whether it is of a different kind. The answer given by the judges is that it is of a different kind.[78] Clearly the answer might just as well have been the other way. Similar verbal jugglery is possible in working the *ejusdem generis* rule.[79]

Consider again, the law of *non est factum*. This operates as an exception to the salutary general principle that a person who signs a document without taking the trouble to read it is liable on it, and cannot plead that he mistook its contents; it also operates as an exception to the general rule of estoppel. The exception is that if the defendant thought that the document he signed belonged to an entirely different legal category from that to which it in fact belonged, he can plead *non est factum* and escape liability although he did not trouble to read the document and although he misled the plaintiff into supposing that he was agreeing.[80] The exception is nothing but an archaic and irrational survival; it is objectionable on the score of policy, and it is also open to practical objection as involving the Courts in the difficulty of distinguishing between a mistake of terms and a mistake of legal category. A good illustration of the difficulty is *Howatson* v. *Webb* (1908).[81] A solicitor asked his clerk to take a conveyance of certain property at E. as his nominee, and the clerk complied. Later the clerk was asked by the solicitor to execute certain deeds 'transferring the E. property'; this he did without reading them, supposing them to be conveyances on sale. One was actually a mortgage containing a covenant by the clerk to repay the principal money and interest. The Court of Appeal, affirming Warrington J., held that the clerk was liable on the covenant. In the view of Warrington J., which was approved by the Court of Appeal, the mistake was merely 'as to the contents of the deed, not as to the character or class of the deed'.[82] This seems to mean that a conveyance on sale and a mortgage belong to the same legal class, namely, 'conveyance'. But the Court might easily have taken the opposite view, that conveyance on sale and mortgage were different types of transaction, as indeed most lawyers would suppose them to be.

A case in which it was held that the document signed belonged to a different class from that supposed is *Foster* v. *Mackinnon* (1869).[83] The defendant was induced to endorse a bill of exchange on the assurance that it was a guarantee; it was held that he could plead *non est factum*

[78] *R.* v. *Child* (1871) 1 C. C. R. 307; *R.* v. *Nattrass* (1882) 15 Cox 73.

[79] Williams, 'The Origin and Logical Implications of the *Ejusdem Generis* Rule'. (1943) 7 The Conveyancer, 119.

[80] On the question whether negligence alters the case see Anson in (1912) 28 L. Q. R. 190 and Underhay in (1930) 8 Can. Bar Rev. 661.

Landon in (1935) 51 L. Q. R. 274 points out that the plea of *non est factum*, *eo nomine*, was confined to actions of covenant brought upon deeds, the analogous pleas for simple contracts in writing being *nil debet* and *non assumpsit*. But it is convenient to have the single name '*non est factum*' for all cases, and this extended use of the expression is allowed by modern usage.

[81] [1908] 1 Ch. 1 (C. A.), affg. [1907] 1 Ch. 537.

[82] [1907] 1 Ch. 537 at 549.

[83] L. R. 4 C. P. 711.

even against a holder in due course. This is puzzling, for in law the endorsement of a negotiable instrument *is* a guarantee, though one of a special kind. It is therefore difficult to see how the Court could hold, as it did, that the contract was 'of a nature altogether different from the contract pretended to be read from the paper'.[84]

*Howatson* v. *Webb* and *Foster* v. *Mackinnon* afford good illustrations of the emptiness of a rule referring to classes when the classes are not specified in detail. Both decisions were unpredictable by means of this rule, and they have done little to establish a basis of prediction for new situations.

(*To be continued.*)

[84] Cp. the criticism on this score in (1921) 37 L. Q. R. 514 and (1923) 39 L. Q. R. 131.

## LANGUAGE AND THE LAW—III.

(*Continued from* p. 195.)

An understanding of the artificial nature of classes should help English lawyers to avoid importing into their system the complexities of the Roman law of *specificatio*, which was largely a product of erroneous Greek philosophy. According to the Greeks, every tangible thing was supposed to be a combination of matter (substance) and form. The purely linguistic character of this distinction was not perceived, and, to make matters worse, the Greeks disputed as to the relative importance of the two supposed elements. Aristotle and the peripatetics thought that form was primary, while the stoics gave primacy to matter. These differences (in reality verbal, like the root distinction from which they sprang) were thought by Roman lawyers to have important legal consequences. Two schools of thought sprang up corresponding to the two schools of philosophy. The Proculians, following Aristotle, held that a person who gave a thing a new form thereby created a new thing and acquired a new property in it, even though he did not own it before the change. The Sabinians, following the peripatetics, denied this. The Proculian view, which was partially adopted by Justinian, gave rise to any amount of subtlety on the question what was a change of form—*i.e.*, of species.[85] In the majority of cases the rule meant that merely altering a thing in such a way as to alter its name conferred property.

So far there is no conclusive authority compelling English lawyers to tread the same path. Bracton, indeed, gives a partial statement of the Roman rule, but very briefly and without discussion.[86] In the Year Books the question is discussed not as a question of *specificatio*, the making of a new species of thing, but on the distinctively English basis that ownership is lost when the marks of ownership are lost, *i.e.*, when the chattel becomes unrecognizable as the same chattel. It was for this reason that, in a case of 1489/90, it was held that the making of leather into shoes did not change the ownership, and the owner of the leather was entitled to recapt[87] the shoes.[88] In a case of 1559, shortly after

[85] See generally Cornil, Droit Romain (Brussels, 1921), 201; Buckland, Text-Book of Roman Law, 2nd ed. (Cambridge, 1932), 215–8; same, Main Institutions of Roman Private Law (Cambridge, 1931), 136–8.

[86] F. 10a: '*Adquiritur etiam nobis per specificationem, ut si quis de aliena materia speciem fecerit aliquam, dominus erit speciei qui fecit*'; cp. Azo in Maitland's Bracton and Azo (S.S.), 122–4, and see *ibid.* xx. So also Bl. Comm. ii, 404.

[87] This useful word is not in the dictionaries. Future dictionary-makers should give the credit for its invention to Professor Hollond, who uses it in his lectures.

[88] Y. B. (1489/90) H. 5 H. 7. 15b. pl. 6. 'And as to the cases of grain taken and malt made from it, the party cannot take it, because the grain cannot be known. And so it is with pennies or groats, where one piece is made of them, it cannot be taken, because of the pennies one cannot be known from another. And so it is if a man takes one piece, and strikes pennies from it at the mint, the party cannot take the pennies, because the pennies cannot be known one from another. And so of all like cases. And also in the case of the building of a house, now the timber is altered, for now it is freehold, and for this reason he cannot take it. But in every case where the things themselves can be known, there the party can take them, notwithstanding that some chattel is joined or mixed with them. As if a man takes a piece of cloth and makes a cloak for himself, the party can take it back well enough, because it is the same thing and not at all altered. And so it is in the case put, if one cuts a tree and squares

the end of the Year-Book period, the rule is given in a slightly 'philosophical' form by saying that notice—*i.e.*, the means of recognition—is not lost so long as that which remains is 'the principal part of the substance—*major pars substantiae*'.[89] Here the philosophy seems to be rather that of the stoics than that of Aristotle; if pushed far enough it would result in a denial of any change of ownership in cases of *specificatio*. The actual decision in the last case was that where trees were wrongfully cut and turned into timber, the owner could recapt the timber—for this there was Year-Book authority; but the Court added, apparently *obiter*, that the owner could have exercised his right of recaption even if the trees had been cut into boards. The latter remark appears to be inconsistent with the recognition theory, for trees can hardly be recognized after they have been cut into boards.[90] It seems, therefore, that the case, while paying lip-service to the recognition theory, shows a tendency to abandon it in favour of a theory of continuance of 'substance'. Another mixture of medieval legal ideas with philosophical notions is to be seen in Doderidge J.'s *English Lawyer*, published posthumously in 1681.[91] Doderidge begins by stating the Year-Book doctrine. He says that if a man steals my barley and makes it into malt, I cannot recapt the malt because I cannot distinguish it as mine. Similarly if my ox is killed, I cannot take the flesh because I cannot distinguish it; but if the ox be found hanging in the skin, whereby the mark may appear, I may seize it. This is good medieval law, but immediately afterwards Doderidge, who had a reputation as a civilian, gives it a philosophical twist.

> 'Inasmuch as the forme giveth the essence, it was said of Ulpian the Romane Lawyer, out of the rules of Logicke, that *mutata forma prope interimitur substantia rei*[92]: for so in the former examples wee see, that if a man take my Barley and make Malt thereof, it cannot be seised by the former Owner; and yet neither matter, quantity nor outward forme is lost, but is become a thing of another nature and use, because the inward forme (to speak as Morall Philosophers) whereof dependeth the use, is changed; for Morall Philosophy doth not so curiously observe the naturall causes as Naturall Philosophy; but according to the information of manners'.[93]

it, the party can take it well enough, because the tree can be known well enough, notwithstanding. And so it is of iron, where a smith makes of it a bar, etc. And so it was held by the whole Court'. The same doctrine was stated in Y. B. (1520) M. 12 H. 8. 9b, pl. 2, where it was held that the killing of a hart did not change the property, and the owner was entitled to retake the corpse from the killer. 'Although it is dead and has lost its name (for *bos mortuus non est bos*), still it is the same thing as was taken out of my possession, and so it is lawful for me to retake it': *per* Eliot J. at f. 10b. 'But if it be roasted or baked, then I cannot take it, for I have lost the notice of it; as if one takes my silver cup or my gold chain and melts it, I cannot take it, for I cannot have notice of it': *per* Brudnel J. at f. 11a.

[89] *Anon.*, Moore (K. B.) 19, pl. 67.

[90] But it will be recalled that in the case of 1489/90 (last note but one) it was said that a tree can still be known although it is squared, and iron although it is made into a bar. I should say that as a proposition of fact this is false.

[91] Pp. 126–7, 132–3.

[92] Dig. 10. 4. 9. 3: *Mutata forma prope interemit substantiam rei*—not on *specificatio* and evidently quoted by Doderidge from memory.

[93] Doderidge goes on to give other analogous rules. (1) If the bailee of a whole piece of cloth cuts it up and offers it back in this condition, this is no lawful restitution. This seems to mean that detinue lies. (2) A bequest of wool is adeemed if after the

In Doderidge's statement of the law, then, we can detect two distinct strands: (1) the medieval English rule, originally perhaps a rule of evidence but become a rule of substantive law, that ownership is lost when the thing itself cannot be recognized, and (2) the Proculian rule, based on the philosophy of Aristotle, according to which a thing that has been so altered as to deserve a new name becomes a new thing capable of new ownership. In the background, not consciously avowed but perhaps helping to maintain these technical rules, there may possibly be (3) some very slight tinge of an idea of fairness or public policy, according to which a person who has worked upon another's chattel, at any rate if he has acted in good faith, ought to be recompensed. But it must be admitted that the rules as stated give hardly any effect to this idea.

What is the law to-day? It is submitted that rule (2) is the result of an erroneous philosophy. There is no sufficient authority for saying that it has ever been made part of English law: at most there is the bare statement of Bracton, obviously copying Roman sources, and Doderidge's self-contradictory exposition in a didactic work. Rule (1) was the law once, but it is submitted that it has become obsolete with the decay of the idea that ownership depends upon the marks of ownership.[94] Thus, at the present day, the mere fact that a chattel has been changed beyond recognition, or has been so changed as to entitle it to a new name, does not create any new ownership in it. Nevertheless, as Salmond pointed out, over and above the question of ownership there arises the question of restitution.[95] It is this question that gives scope for the working out of (3) the idea of fairness and public policy. If *B* wrongfully takes *A's* chattel and does work upon it, *A* cannot get an order for specific restitution save at the discretion of the Court, and the Court will probably give him it only on terms that he pays for *B's* work, at any rate if *B* has not acted dishonestly. If *A* sues for damages, his damages will be based on the value of the article at the time when *B* took it, not upon its value in its embellished state.[96] The only trouble arises over recaption, and it is submitted that on this the medieval authorities are unsatisfactory. Recaption ought not to be permitted in any case where the defendant or a person through whom he claims has increased the value of the thing.

Another rule that may let in the subtleties of *specificatio* is the rule that while the destruction of a thing grounds trover, damage to a thing does not. Salmond suggested that 'the test of destruction, as opposed to mere damage, is presumably the disappearance of the identity of the

date of the will the testator converts his wool into cloth. (3) A common of estovers for a dwelling-house is lost if the dwelling-house be destroyed, even though another be built at another place near, or in another form; *aliter* if another house be built upon the same foundation, and in the same form. (4) A man has a water-corn-mill with a right of watercourse over a neighbour's land. If he changes the corn-mill into a fulling-mill he still has the right of watercourse, 'for that it did not belong unto the Corne-mill, as specially unto a Corne-mill, but it did belong unto it generally as unto a mill going on or driven with water, and not otherwise'.

[94] It is, however, uncritically repeated in Williams on Personal Property, 18th ed., 26.

[95] Salmond, Torts, 10th ed., 316–7, § 82. 3.

[96] *Reid* v. *Fairbanks* (1853) 13 C. B. 692, approved by Bramwell B. in *Chinery* v. *Viall* (1860) 5 H. & N. 288 at 295; *Caxton Publishing Co.* v. *Sutherland Publishing Co.* [1939] A. C. 178 (where the plaintiffs recovered the value of the sheets which were their fictional property but not the value of the books into which they had been bound); Mayne, Damages, 10th ed., 378 ff.

article. Grapes are presumably destroyed when they are turned into wine, cotton when it is woven into cloth, corn when it is ground into flour '.[97] It is submitted that, on the contrary, the test of destruction is whether the defendant's act has made the thing practically worthless. To admit Salmond's suggestion would be to introduce into the law the subtleties of classification that Salmond himself expels from it in his discussion of *specificatio*.

A similar question arises in the law of carriage by sea. The rule is that the shipowner cannot claim freight if he does not deliver the goods contracted to be carried, but can claim it if he does deliver them, notwithstanding that they are in a damaged condition (in both cases he may, of course, be liable in damages). The question arises whether the shipowner can claim freight where the goods have, in the current phrase, 'lost their identity', as 'where a valuable picture has arrived as a piece of spoilt canvas, cloth in rags, or crockery in broken shreds, iron all, or almost all rust, rice fermented, or hides rotten'. The test suggested by Willes C.J. was 'to ascertain from the terms of the contract, construed by mercantile usage, if any, what was the thing for the carriage of which freight was to be paid, and by the aid of a jury to determine whether that thing, or any and how much of it, has substantially arrived'.[98] This test is open to objection as depending merely upon the verbal classifications of things; nor has it been uniformly acted upon by the Courts. Thus in *Garrett* v. *Melhuish* (1858),[99] bricks were shipped and were found on arrival to be reduced to dust, which was afterwards sold for a very small sum. Stuart V.-C. held that freight was payable. It is submitted that this decision is consistent with the proper rule, which is that freight is payable notwithstanding that the goods carried have become so changed that we apply a new name to them, and is not payable only if they have become substantially worthless. The only doubt as to *Garrett* v. *Melhuish* is whether on the facts of that case the goods had become substantially worthless; but the fact that they were saleable at all seems to indicate a negative answer. In *Duthie* v. *Hilton* (1868)[1] the cargo was cement which became hardened into solid masses by the action of water. It was held that no freight was payable, Keating and Brett JJ. saying that the goods had been destroyed and Montague Smith J. saying that they had 'ceased to exist as cement'. It is submitted that the proper reason for the decision was not that the goods no longer deserved the name 'cement' but that they were worthless. In the next case *Asfar* v. *Blundell* (1895)[2] the question arose in particularly neat form, there the cargo consisted of dates, which were sunk and later raised; it was then found that the dates were inedible but of considerable value for the purpose of distillation into spirit. The Court of Appeal unanimously held that no freight was payable. Lord Esher M.R. said: 'The first point taken on behalf of the defendants, the underwriters of the freight, is that there has been no total loss of the dates. . . . The ingenuity of the argument might commend itself to a body of chemists, but not to business men. . . . The test is whether, as a matter of business, the nature of the things has been

[97] Torts, 10th ed., 294, § 74. 11.
[98] *Dakin* v. *Oxley* (1864) 15 C. B. (N.S.) 646 at 667.
[99] 4 Jur. (N.S.) Part I, 943.
[1] 4 C. P. 138.
[2] [1896] 1 Q. B. 123.

altered. The nature of a thing is not necessarily altered because the thing itself has been damaged; wheat or rice may be damaged, but may still remain the things dealt with as wheat or rice in business. But if . . . the thing . . . is so changed in its nature by the perils of the sea as to become an unmerchantable thing, which no buyer would buy and no honest seller would sell, then there is a total loss'. This statement is open to severe objection. The words in the last sentence 'which no buyer would buy' must mean 'which no buyer would buy under the original name of the article unless the nature of the damage were stated by the seller at the outset'. The words cannot mean what they say without qualification, for the dates in the case at bar were actually sold for the not inconsiderable sum of £2,400; yet there was held to be a total loss. But if the words are given the meaning first suggested, they fail to point a contrast with the damaged wheat or rice: for no buyer would buy, and no honest seller would sell, damaged wheat or rice unless the nature of the damage were stated before the contract; yet a buyer might buy them, and an honest seller might sell them, if such damage were stated and the price reduced accordingly.

Thus while *Asfar* v. *Blundell* must be taken as introducing the linguistic test into the law of freight, it should be regarded as an unfortunate decision, and the hope may be expressed that it will one day be overruled by the supreme tribunal.[3]

These cases on liability for freight are really part of the law of failure of consideration. A somewhat similar question of failure of consideration arises in the law of sale of goods. To take the classic illustration of Lord Abinger,[4] if there is a contract to sell peas and the seller delivers a different thing, *e.g.*, beans, this is a non-performance of the contract. It is not a question of warranty, nor (it seems) is there any need to speak of an implied condition. The delivery of the beans is altogether beside the point, just as much as the delivery of an elephant; the fact is that the seller has not delivered peas. There is thus a failure of consideration for the buyer's promise to pay, or for his actual payment.[5] On the other hand if the seller delivers peas, though inferior to the ones that the buyer was entitled to expect under the contract, there is no failure of consideration (unless indeed the proper quality of the peas was a condition—not a mere warranty—in the contract, and unless the buyer validly rescinds for breach of the condition). It is fortunate that this distinction is, in view of the provisions of the Sale of Goods Act, of small practical importance,[6] for numberless cases can be put in which it becomes a very difficult one. On a contract to sell a Singer car with a sliding roof, is the delivery of a Singer car with a fixed roof the delivery of a different thing, and so a quantitative failure in performance, or is it a mere failure in the mode or quality of performance? Questions like these show that the distinction between quantity and quality, like the distinction between kind and degree, is one of degree. It is submitted

[3] Cp. the criticism on a rather different ground in Scrutton, Charterparties, 14th ed., 410 n. (*t*).

[4] *Chanter* v. *Hopkins* (1839) 4 M. & W. 399 at 404.

[5] J. L. Montrose in (1934) 5 C. L. J. 275; Williams in (1941) 57 L. Q. R. 494–6; Williams in McElroy, Impossibility of Performance (Cambridge, 1941), 117.

[6] The question arises chiefly where the contract excludes conditions implied by the Sale of Goods Act. It seems that the law of failure of consideration is not excluded by such a clause.

that the solution of the difficulty is different from that suggested for the law of freight: in sale of goods, the rule should be that any departure by the seller from the contract description is a quantitative failure of performance and therefore a failure of consideration. The reason for the difference of rule is that in the law of freight the goods are, to start with, agreed upon, and the law should not tangle itself in verbal questions of *continued* identity; in the law of sale of goods, where unascertained goods are sold by description, no specific goods are agreed upon and the question is not one of continued identity but whether the goods tendered conform to the description. Translated in this way, the question when a thing is a 'different thing' loses most of its terrors.

(*c*) Modern philosophy perceives that just as classes are artificial, so is singleness. There is no 'single' fact in nature otherwise than as we choose to consider it so. 'Singleness' is always singleness for the particular purpose that we have on hand. This subjectivity of singleness may be shown in three ways. In the first place, every fact that we choose to regard as a unity can also be regarded as itself made up of unities, or else as being part of a larger unity. Second, many such facts have uncertain boundaries, and we are not certain how much can be added to or subtracted from them without affecting their notional unity. Third, every empirical fact that we regard as a single fact is also, if regarded temporally, a changing process. To illustrate: Nelson was verbally an individual and was 'the same' individual from his birth to his death. But (1) this individual Nelson was a society of individual living cells; (2) Nelson lost an eye, and might have acquired a glass eye and false teeth, have lost his memory and become mad, without affecting his 'individuality'; (3) the Nelson of actual fact was, like everything else, a process: his origin was in two cells belonging to two other individuals; he became a baby, a youth, and a man; the physical constitution of his body changed several times—all without affecting the notional unity that we impute to him.[7]

It should not be necessary to add that the above argument is not a denial of the individuality of Nelson in the sense in which it may be said that Nelson was a different person from Napoleon. What is asserted is simply that individuality is always individuality for a purpose, individuality in a context. Like classification it results from abstraction, for it results from our perception of similarities or relationships between the parts composing the individual notwithstanding differences between those parts, and of similarities between the manifestations of the individual at two points of time notwithstanding differences between those manifestations.

Although things are constantly changing without this affecting our notion of their unity, and so without its affecting our names for them, a change may be so striking that we regard it as placing the thing in a different category, and as entitling it to a different name. We have already seen that this gives rise to the pseudo-philosophical problem of

[7] In the expression "Nansen skates", Nansen is a grammatical proper noun and may therefore be supposed to stand for a particular and not a universal. But, as Stout points out, it is really a universal. Nansen perceived must be Nansen eating or Nansen sleeping or Nansen skating. The individual Nansen is a universal, as a connecting link of his own manifold and varying states, relations, qualities, and activities. We cannot *see* the individual Nansen except through this universal': W. M. Urban, Language and Reality (London, 1939), 142.

continuation of identity, to the Roman law of *specificatio*, to a certain unfortunate suggestion as to the English law of trover, and to an actual decision in the law of carriage by sea. The problem arises in an even more nebulous form with regard to the continuation of identity of unincorporated associations, such as charities. Suppose that a charity to which property is left by will changes in constitution or situation either before the testator's death or afterwards; does the gift fail or not? The test suggested by Professor Keeton is whether the charity 'may be regarded as having so far survived the changes . . . as to be capable of being identified with the institution named and contemplated by the testator'.[8] This test appears, with respect, not to advance the solution of the problem, for the answer to it must be purely subjective. It would be better to say that the gift goes with the rest of the charity's property to the 'new' charity, provided that the 'new' charity has objects similar to those of the 'old' charity that it has replaced.

Realization of the notional character of unity helps one to understand the difficulty experienced by the Courts in applying rules that presuppose unity—for instance, in fixing the precise temporal limits of an 'operation', 'work',[9] or 'transaction'[10] or the precise spatial limits of a 'house'[11]; in deciding whether several purchases made at the same time are one contract or several contracts[12]; or whether a part of a written contract, in form one clause, is one promise or several promises[13]; or whether, when a contract is altered by a later agreement, the later agreement is a mere variation of the previous agreement or amounts to a rescission of the previous contract and a new contract substituted for it[14]; or whether an interruption in a contract is 'so long as to destroy the identity of the work or service, when resumed, with the work or service when interrupted',[15] or in deciding where the 'repair' of a building stops and 'renewal' or 'reconstruction' begins.[15a] Decisions on questions of this sort are often unpredictable, because the Court is not determining facts but is simply deciding upon the attitude that it wishes to adopt towards facts.

(*d*) It is sometimes thought that in mathematics, at least, one reaches a haven of security in the use of words. 'Except in mathematics', said Grove J., 'it is difficult to frame exhaustive definitions of words; they must be construed with reference to the subject-matter to which they are applied.'[16] Now it is true that the words used in mathematics are sharply defined; but this does not mean that they are easily applied

[8] Keeton, Trusts, 3rd ed., 150; *Re Watt, Hicks* v. *Hill*, [1932] 2 Ch. 243.

[9] *Kent County Council* v. *Folkestone Corpn.* [1905] 1 K. B. 620 at 629.

[10] Phipson, Evidence, 8th ed., 52, 55 (*res gesta*); Underhill, Trusts, 9th ed., art. 92.

[11] Burrows's Words and Phrases, s.v. See also *Re Nielson, Cumming* v. *Clyde* (1929) 73 S. J. 765 (bequest of 'my law library in my room in the Temple' where some volumes were not in the room at the time of death); Jarman, Wills, 7th ed., 1233–4.

[12] Benjamin, Sale, 7th ed., Bk. 1, Pt. II, ch. 3.

[13] *Putsman* v. *Taylor* [1927] 1 K. B. 637.

[14] The cases on the importance of this distinction are in some confusion, the latest being *Bessler, Waechter, Glover & Co.* v. *South Derwent Coal Co.* [1938] 1 K. B. 408; cp. Phipson, Evidence, 8th ed., 576.

[15] *Per* Lord Dunedin in *Metropolitan Water Board* v. *Dick, Kerr & Co.* [1918] A. C. 119 at 128.

[15a] 'A covenant to repair a house is not a covenant to give a different thing from that which the tenant took": *per* Lord Esher, M.R. in *Lister* v. *Lane* [1893] 2 Q. B. 212 at 217; Woodfall, Landlord and Tenant, 24th ed., 699–701.

[16] *Wakefield Local Board* v. *Lele* (1876) 1 Ex. D. 336 at 343.

to the world of experience, or that they are immune from the general necessity of being construed with reference to the subject-matter. In applying mathematical terms it is just as necessary to decide questions of degree as in applying other words. Euclidean geometry, for instance, starts from notions of points and lines which, having no size, are not objects of sense; thus the figures constructed from these notions are not objects of sense either. Even if we modify the definitions by allowing points to have magnitude and lines breadth, we are still faced with the difficulty that the figures of geometry, such as the circle, are supposed to conform perfectly to definition, while we do not find such perfect figures in nature. No straight line that science finds is straight, nor do perfectly parallel lines exist in fact; indeed, on one occasion the House of Lords allowed the sides of an object to pass as 'parallel' although they fell far short of the ideal expressed by the word.[17] The numerals seem to be clear because they are precisely defined in terms of each other; but apply them to facts and the clarity ends. A big pea and a little pea may be regarded either as two peas or as one and a half peas according to the purpose in hand. Again, few words would seem at first sight to be so precise as the words of measurement. Every precaution has been taken to fix the length of an Imperial yard by an Act of Parliament making reference to certain bars of gun-metal lodged at the Board of Trade and other places[18]; and other distances, such as miles, are precisely defined in terms of yards. It would be the merest pedantry to deny that, as units of measurement, yards and miles are very exact when we choose to use them exactly. But in ordinary speech we do not always use them exactly. 'A yard of cloth' is probably only an approximation to the legal yard; how close an approximation is a question of degree. Again, difficulty can arise in determining what it is that is to be measured. Sometimes we measure distances in a straight line, sometimes not. Thus, on a covenant not to carry on a trade within a mile of a specified place, litigation may arise on the question whether this means a mile 'as the crow flies' or a mile by the nearest practicable road.[19]

(*e*) The last type of uncertainty to be noticed is uncertainty in the time to which words are to be applied. Does the word 'convict' or 'felon'[20] include a person who was a convict or felon once but who has served his sentence? We have touched upon this difficulty in discussing class-names; but further illustrations may be given. Property lawyers are familiar with the difficulties of interpreting such phrases as 'die without issue', or 'leaving no issue', and with the complicated rules that have had to be developed on the question when a class 'closes'. In interpreting a statute it is frequently difficult to know whether the words are to be applied to a situation at the passing of the Act, or to a situation that arises afterwards.[21] Again, suppose that a compulsory-

[17] *Clark* v. *Adie* (No. 2) (1877) 2 App. Cas. 423.

[18] Weights and Measures Act, 1878 (c. 49).

[19] *Mouflet* v. *Cole* (1872) L. R. 8 Ex. 32 (held to mean the former). Cp. *Langley* v. *Wilson* [1943] 2 A. E. R. 213 ('radius'). So also the question has arisen whether 'five miles square' refers to geometrical symmetry or merely to area: *Robertson* v. *Day* (1881) 5 App. Cas. 63 (held the latter).

[20] *Leyman* v. *Latimer* (1878) 3 Ex. D. 352—no.

[21] *Brighton Parish Union* v. *Strand Union* [1891] 2 Q. B. 156; *White & Hales* v. *Islington Corpn.* [1909] 1 K. B. 133.

purchase statute requires the authority to resell any land 'not required for the purposes for which it was acquired'; does 'not required' mean 'not immediately required', or 'not required in the future'?[22] Illustrations of this sort could be multiplied.

It will be noticed that the difficulties discussed above under the heading of 'fringe meaning' are very different from the difficulties caused by words of multiple meaning. In the first place, the difficulties here discussed cannot be cured by definitions, unless of course, the definition makes express provision for the particular difficulty that has arisen. If, for instance, it is found difficult to determine whether some early ancestor of man, such as *Pithecanthropus erectus*, is to be called 'man', it does not help in the least to remember that 'man' is a rational animal. For the two elements in this definition have their own difficulties, rationality being a quality of continuous variation, and 'animal' being a class-name carrying the same type of difficulty as the word 'man'.

In the second place, such difficulties cannot be cured by the adoption of a technical language. A technical language is useful to prevent equivocation; but it cannot cause 'univocal' words to become clear of application to the facts of experience.[23]

It is hard to state a case without exaggerating it. When Shakespeare wrote: 'Words are grown so false I am loath to prove reason with them', he put the remark into the mouth of a clown. However imperfect our symbolism we must use words in reasoning, because in general we cannot reason otherwise. Also, words *in contexts* are usually clear enough for practical purposes. Were it otherwise, language would be useless.

One way in particular in which context helps to give meaning to a word is in indicating the word to which the word in question is being opposed. Failure to recognize that words change in meaning according to the word to which they are being opposed leads to much idle controversy. For instance, the word 'freedom' has no single meaning. Freedom versus imprisonment; freedom versus legal duty; freedom verus deprivation of the franchise; freedom versus imposition; freedom versus economic bondage; freedom versus determinism; freedom versus licence—all these are different meanings.[24] Political philosophers who dispute with one another upon 'the meaning' of liberty, or 'the nature' of liberty, are wasting their time, unless indeed they begin by agreeing upon the contrast under discussion. Other chameleon words are 'democracy', 'law', 'state', 'right', 'ownership', 'property',

[22] *Att.-Gen.* v. *Teddington U. C.* [1898] 1 Ch. 66.

[23] This appears to be ignored by Morris R. Cohen in (1916) 29 H. L. R. 634. He seems to argue that the adoption of a technical language would get rid of the difficulties in applying phrases like 'direct tax', 'interstate commerce', 'restraint of trade'. But the trouble does not arise from the fact that these words have a popular as well as a legal currency; it arises from the fact that they all have a wide penumbra of uncertainty. Merely changing the symbol would not eliminate this uncertainty. Cohen elsewhere admits that 'even in scientific language there is a fringe of uncertainty as to the limits of the denotation or application of names': Cohen and Nagel, *op. cit.* 118.

[24] Cp. Bogoslovsky, *op. cit.* 121. Bogoslovsky says that some of the above are different aspects of the single concept *liberty*, but it would seem better to say that there is not one concept but many.

'interest', 'possession', 'agency',[25] and so on. Numberless attempts have been made to squeeze these words into the four corners of a single definition, but such attempts are mistaken in so far as they assume that each word represents a single unvarying concept.

A good illustration of the necessity for attending to context is the phrase 'the common law'. In practice this phrase is used, like the word 'layman' or 'alien', in a negative or residuary sense, meaning that which is left after the subtraction of something else. Thus the phrase may mean, according to context, the law that is not local law, or the law that is not statute law, or the law that is not equity. In the second of these senses it may include equity, in the third it may include statutes. This is a statement of the way in which the phrase is actually used. Observe, however, the treatment of it in Salmond's *Jurisprudence*. Salmond supposes that the phrase 'the common law' must represent a single, invariable concept, and thus he defines it as the whole of the law of England except statute law, equity, and special law in its various forms. Salmond expressly refuses to admit that its meaning varies with the context. 'The term always, in its proper sense, excludes statute law, equity, and all the forms of special law; but sometimes the particular contrast intended to be expressed is that between common law and statute law: sometimes it is that between common law and equity; and sometimes it is that between common law and special law.'[26] It is significant that when, later in the book, Salmond has occasion to use the phrase 'the common law', he uses it in one of the senses that he condemns as 'improper', namely, as including equity and perhaps special law, and excluding only statutes.[27] Salmond is unable in his own writing to keep the concept to the singleness that he himself desires.

Should the reader think that this discussion of the phrase 'the common law' is of merely academic interest, let him look at section 62 (2) of the Sale of Goods Act, 1893, which saves 'the rules of the common law' relating to the sale of goods, except in so far as they are inconsistent with the express provisions of the Act. In view of this opposition between 'the common law' and the Act, it seems clear that the phrase 'the common law' is meant to include equity. But if Salmond's idea of the 'proper' meaning of 'the common law' were applied, it would not include equity.

* * * * * * * *

I have already pointed a number of legal morals in the course of this section, but some general conclusions of legal interest remain to be drawn.

(1) In the first place, the theory here advanced destroys completely and for ever the illusion that the law can be completely certain. Since the law has to be expressed in words, and words have a penumbra of uncertainty, marginal cases are bound to occur. Certainty in law is thus seen to be a matter of degree. (2) Correlatively, the theory destroys the illusion that the function of a judge is simply to administer the law.[28] If marginal cases must occur, the function of the judge in

[25] Cp. Morris, How Lawyers Think, 102–3.
[26] Jurisprudence, 7th ed., § 24.
[27] *Ibid.* § 46.
[28] The illusion has, of course, been destroyed many times, notably by Dickinson, 'The Law behind Law' (1929) 29 Col. L. Rev. 113, 285. But it has extraordinary

adjudicating upon them must be legislative. The distinction between the mechanical administration of fixed rules and free judicial discretion is thus a matter of degree, not the sharp distinction that it is sometimes assumed to be. This is not to say that judges have an unlimited legislative power. A judge has a discretion to include a flying-boat within a rule as to ships or vessels; he has no discretion to include a motor car within such a rule.

If it be recognized that a judge when operating within the fringes of meaning is not interpreting a pre-existing intent but is exercising a legislative power, the conclusion ought to be that less attention should be paid to dictionary meanings and more to legislative policy. A good example of the proper approach to interpretation is the recent case of *Watkinson* v. *Hollington* (1943), [29] where it was held that distress damage feasant is not 'distress' within the Courts (Emergency Powers) Act, 1939. Verbally, distress damage feasant is by its very name a form of distress; moreover at common law it is procedurally similar to distress for rent. Nevertheless (i) it is a comparatively unusual form of distress, so that probably it was not present in the mind of the draftsman of the Act of 1939; and (ii) to apply the Act to it would be absurd. On a proper understanding of the nature of meaning, the decision of the Court of Appeal excluding distress damage feasant from the operation of the Act was not more legislative than the decision of the Court below including it; but it was much more sensible.

§ 5. SUBSTANCE AND QUALITY.

As we have seen, the philosopher's belief that the universals have some mode of existence independent of their concrete manifestations is due to the false idea that reality follows grammatical form. There is another danger lurking in the grammatical construction of language. It is this grammatical construction that leads us to distinguish between substance and quality, a distinction corresponding to the subject and predicate of the sentence. We say that this individual table now before us is wooden, or is square, or is brown, as though in nature there were two things: the substance, and its quality. Philosophers have now come to realize that this distinction is simply a matter of linguistic convenience and does not exist in nature.

The chief importance of this conclusion for lawyers is in connection with the distinction made in the law of contract and elsewhere between mistake of identity and mistake of attribute ('attribute' being another name for 'quality'). To discuss fully the exact nature of this last distinction would make the present section inordinately long and would take us too far away from the main theme of the paper. It is therefore left for discussion elsewhere.[30]

GLANVILLE L. WILLIAMS.

(*To be continued.*)

vitality. One still sees discussions among international lawyers upon the respective merits of legal tribunals and tribunals deciding *ex aequo et bono*, without any express statement by either side that the distinction is one of degree.

[29] [1944] K. B. 16.

[30] Williams, 'Mistake as to Party in the Law of Contract' (1945) 23 Canadian Bar Review, 271 ff.

# LANGUAGE AND THE LAW—IV.

(*Continued from p.* 303.)

## § 6. Interpretation.

THIS is a convenient heading under which to gather some remarks on interpretation in general and certain matters connected therewith. These will concern (1) the 'proper' meaning of words, (2) definition, (3) intended, comprehended and ordinary meaning, (4) logical implication, (5) literal and ulterior meaning, and (6) the transition from implied terms to rules of law. Considerations of space forbid detailed discussion of the legal rules of interpretation.

### (1) The 'Proper' Meaning of Words.

There is a famous passage in *Alice Through the Looking-Glass* (Chapter VI), where, to Humpty Dumpty's claim to use words in unusual senses, Alice made what may seem to the ordinary person to be an unanswerable objection. 'The question is', said Alice, 'whether you *can* make words mean different things.' 'The question is', replied Humpty Dumpty, 'which is to be master—that's all.' Humpty Dumpty's theory was that supported by Locke, who laid it down that the significance of all words is perfectly arbitrary, and that every man has an inviolable liberty to make words stand for what ideas he pleases.[1] This admirable statement has fallen on many deaf ears, and Ogden and Richards have again to deplore 'the curious instinctive tendency to believe that a word has its own true or proper use'.[2] Scientifically speaking, words have no true or proper meaning, except in two senses. First, words have an ordinary—*i.e.*, commonly-accepted—meaning. The ordinary meaning need not be current among the community as a whole: it may be confined to a particular section of the community, such as educated persons, business men, scientists or lawyers. (For instance, a lawyer may say that the proper meaning of the word 'contract' does not include contract bridge, meaning that it does not include it in the technical language of the law.) Second, the particular person who uses a word may assign to it a special meaning; the 'proper' meaning of the word for his purpose is then this assigned meaning. Apart from such ordinary or assigned meanings words have no 'actual', 'correct', 'essential', 'grammatical', 'legitimate', 'literal', 'natural', 'necessary', 'rational', 'real', or 'reasonable' meaning (all of which adjectives are common in legal literature). Similarly, 'historical', 'etymological', 'wide', 'narrow', 'strict', 'metaphorical', 'technical' and 'legal' meanings are all varieties of ordinary or assigned

[1] Essay Concerning the Human Understanding 3. 3. 8. B. Russell (Analysis of Mind 189–90) denies that words are conventional, but all he means is that language is part of the environment in which we grow up: we do not deliberately adopt it. This is true, but not a contradiction of the proposition that there is no connection between words and referents save in the mind.

[2] The Meaning of Meaning 123; cp. *ibid.* 206–7.

meaning. Historical or etymological meaning is simply the ordinary meaning of the word, or of the parts from which it is compounded, at some period of the past. It is an unreliable guide to the present meaning of a word, because meanings change.[3] 'Technical' (including 'legal') meaning is that current among a special class of persons; 'legal' meaning may also indicate a determination on the part of lawyers to read words in a particular way although they know that the user did not intend them to bear that meaning. 'Strict', 'narrow', and 'wide' refer to the denotation of ambiguous words, again as a matter of use. 'Proper' as contrasted with 'metaphorical' means the original meaning of a word as opposed to its transferred meaning; the expressions are acceptable provided that it is remembered that metaphorical meaning may overshadow or even wholly oust 'proper' meaning and so become the chief or only meaning. For example, many words for non-empirical facts or for values began as words for empirical facts; and it would be pedantic to assert that the 'proper' meaning of all such words is an empirical one (*e.g.*, that 'right' and 'wrong' properly mean straight and twisted). As one writer puts it, 'if we started on the principle of restricting words to their so-called proper meaning, and pursued this theory to its logical conclusion, we should ultimately reduce language to the few inarticulate ejaculations from which it began'.[4]

If a writer uses the phrase 'proper meaning' otherwise than in the sense of ordinary or assigned meaning, past or present, he must be using the phrase not scientifically but emotively, to express what he considers *ought* to be the ordinary meaning. Thus if a lawyer writes: 'The proper meaning of "implied contract" is contract implied in fact, not quasi-contract', he does not express what is now the invariable usage of lawyers (for in fact their usage does not always conform to this), but simply states what in his view should be the usage. The writer thus dresses up an expression of emotion to make it look like a proposition of fact, for he avoids the use of the optative 'ought' and uses instead the apparently factual 'is'. We all use this device, and it is often successful in winning agreement; but it is also the source of much fruitless controversy. For the mode of statement often tempts others to dispute the suggested 'proper meaning' as though it were a matter of fact, instead of a mere matter of choice of words.

It may be added that we may sometimes stigmatize a phrase as 'improper' because it seems to indicate that the species denoted by it belongs to a genus to which the species is not in fact regarded as belonging. Thus the phrase 'involuntary bailee', though much used, is 'improper' in the sense that an involuntary bailee is not a bailee *simpliciter*. So, a void contract is not a species of contract, a warranty *ex post facto* is not a species of warranty, and a service tenancy (in one sense of that phrase) is not a species of tenancy. We can call such phrases 'improper' or 'misnomers' without implying that words have inherently-proper meanings.

3 This was recognized by Kindersley V.-C., when he said: 'It is not necessary to go into the derivation of the word, for that sort of reasoning would not assist in the administration of justice': *Barrett* v. *White* (1855) 24 L. J. Ch. 724 at 726. '[Nephew] is derived from the Latin *nepos*, signifying a grandchild, but it is clear that such an interpretation could not now be given to the word': *per* Lord Cranworth L.C. in *Crook* v. *Whitley* (1857) 7 De G. M. & G. 490 at 494–5.

4 George Willis, The Philosophy of Speech (London, 1919) 167.

The worst form of the proper-meaning error is the supposition that words have not merely proper meanings but single proper meanings. On this view, every ambiguous word necessarily has one of its meanings 'proper' and one 'improper', and the task of science is to find out which is which. It is submitted that an example of this error occurs in Sir John Salmond's discussion of ownership. Salmond points out, correctly, that we speak sometimes of owning a right and sometimes of owning a thing; these two senses of the term he distinguishes by the useful names 'incorporeal ownership' and 'corporeal ownership' respectively. He then proceeds: 'If we look, therefore, no deeper than the mere usages of speech, it would seem as if the subject-matter of ownership were sometimes a material object and at other times a right. This, of course, would be a logical absurdity. Ownership may conceivably be in all cases a relation to a material object; or it may in all cases be a relation to a right; but it cannot be sometimes the one and sometimes the other'.[5] The author evades the supposed difficulty by saying that incorporeal ownership is ownership in the proper sense and that corporeal ownership is only a figure of speech, a metonymy. The truth is, however, that the difficulty does not arise. The supposed difficulty appears to arise from an assumption that there is some single entity in the universe, *ownership*, which cannot be defined in contradictory ways. This is an error. 'Ownership' is a word symbolizing an idea, and this idea, the meaning of the word, may and does vary according to context. There is therefore no logical absurdity in defining the word 'ownership' in two different ways. It may be added that Salmond's mode of escaping from his self-made difficulty is particularly unfortunate because it seems to suggest that incorporeal ownership is the original idea and corporeal ownership an extension of it, whereas the reverse is the case.

Realization of the fact that words have no inherently-proper meanings has great importance for the student of jurisprudence, because it enables him to write off almost the whole of the vast and futile controversy concerning the proper meaning of the word 'law',[6] as well as many others of less magnitude. In the realm of constitutional law, not only students but law lords need to be headed off the verbal question whether Canada is properly called a federation.[7] In the law of wills, a rule that badly needs attention from the semantic point of view is the rule stated by Wigram in the following words: 'Where there is nothing in the context of a will from which it is apparent that a testator has used the words in which he has expressed himself in any other than their strict and primary sense, and where his words so interpreted are sensible with reference to extrinsic circumstances, . . . the words of the will shall be interpreted in their strict and primary sense, and in no other, although they may be capable of some popular or secondary interpretation, and although the most conclusive evidence of intention to use them in such

[5] Jurisprudence (7th ed.) 279, § 87.

[6] The controversy is discussed in an article to be published in the British Year Book of International Law for 1946.

[7] The hare was started by Viscount Haldane L.C. in *Att.-Gen. for Australia* v. *Colonial Sugar Refining Co.* [1914] A. C. 237 at 252–3, contrasting what he called the 'loose' sense of the word 'federal' with 'the natural and literal interpretation of the word'.

popular or secondary sense be tendered '.[8] It will be seen that this rule does not merely prefer the strict and primary meaning of the words to some special meaning adopted by the testator alone: it even prefers it to the 'popular' meaning of the words, which is another kind of ordinary meaning. Hence the rule amounts to a statement that one kind of ordinary meaning is automatically and as a rule of law to be preferred to another kind, without regard to the particular meaning that was probably intended by the testator, and this merely because the former kind is supposed to be the 'strict and primary' meaning. It is assumed that the two kinds of meaning can be separated clearly enough for the purpose of applying the rule. Enough has already been said to indicate that the distinction is not nearly so clear as the wording of the rule would seem to suggest; also, recent cases indicate that the authority of the rule is less secure than was formerly supposed.[9]

A somewhat surprising challenge to Humpty Dumpty's assertion of human mastery over words came recently from no less a judge than Lord Atkin. This was in *Liversidge* v. *Anderson* (1941),[10] where the question was whether the words 'If the Secretary of State has' in a statutory regulation could be read as meaning 'If the Secretary of State thinks he has'. Lord Atkin said: 'I know of only one authority which might justify the suggested method of construction'. He then quoted Humpty Dumpty as being this one authority, and added: 'After all this long discussion the question is whether the words "If a man has" can mean "If a man thinks he has". I am of opinion that they cannot, and that the case should be decided accordingly'. With all respect to Lord Atkin, this rejection of Humpty Dumpty's doctrine is not happily phrased. It is not true to say that the one phrase cannot mean the other. If, for instance, the regulation had expressly stated that the words 'If the Secretary of State has' as used in the regulation meant 'If the Secretary of State thinks he has', then the one phrase would mean what is ordinarily meant by the other. Again, if the regulation had used the phrase 'If the Secretary of State thinks he has' several times, and then, in the crucial clause, used the phrase, 'If the Secretary of State has', it might be clear from the general context that no change of meaning was intended. What Lord Atkin probably meant to convey was that the one phrase did not normally mean the same as the other, and that there was nothing in the regulation to lead to the conclusion that their meaning was intended to be the same. The majority law lords took the opposite view on the latter point.

The denial that words have a proper meaning, independently of ordinary, assigned and desired meaning, is liable to be misunderstood unless certain qualifications are expressly stated. It is not denied that a writer ought generally to take meanings as he finds them. An important function of language is to communicate thought, and it can serve this function only if there is a general measure of agreement upon the meanings of words. Humpty Dumpty laid himself open to the charge of vexatiously and quite unnecessarily changing in his own speech the ordinary meaning of words. Even where some change in established

[8] Wigram, Extrinsic Evidence in Aid of the Interpretation of Wills, Proposition II.
[9] See, *e.g.* *Perrin* v. *Morgan* [1943] A. C. 399.
[10] [1942] A. C. 206 at 245.

usage is called for, it is not desirable to give a word a new meaning so divorced from its traditional meaning as to make the new use of the word aesthetically offensive to many people. Still less is it justifiable to debase the language by turning words of precise meaning into mere synonyms for other words, as, for instance, in the schoolgirl's use of the word 'chronic'.

### (2) Definition.

The function of definition is to explain the meaning of words. We do not learn the meaning of all words by definitions, for definition presupposes the existence of an understood language. In childhood we learn the meaning of such words as 'red' by being shown the objects to which they are to be applied; and in fact the names of colours remain indefinable throughout life. Most words, however, admit of being replaced by groups of other words. This process is called definition. As Ogden and Richards put it, definition is the substitution for the symbol to be defined of a symbol or symbols that can be better understood. It involves the selection of known referents as starting-points, and the identification of the referent of the *definiendum* by its connection with these. For instance, a referent may be located by its similarity to another referent, by its relation in space or time to another referent, or by its being the cause or effect of another referent.[11]

This view of definition throws overboard the theory initiated by Aristotle and widely accepted after his day. The latter theory supposes that there is only one true definition of every unambiguous word, namely, *per genus et differentiam*.[12] The view now accepted is that words have no 'true' definition and that it is possible and permissible to define variously, one definition being proper for one purpose, another for another. Genera and species are no longer regarded as an objective and rigid ordering of nature; they are seen to be no more than subjective conveniences of classification. Being man-made they are mutable, and it is possible to regard the same thing as belonging to distinct genera. Thus 'man' may be defined not only as a rational animal (the classical definition) but as a rational biped. Or, altering the *differentia*, he may be defined as a talking animal, an acquisitive animal, an imaginative animal, an artistic animal, a moral animal, a laughing animal, a weeping animal, or a superstitious animal. None of these definitions explains perfectly all uses of the word 'man', for the word may be applied to a lunatic, a deaf mute, a pauper, a philistine, an egoist, a hypochondriac, and so on. Conversely, these definitions may to some extent fit some of the lower animals. This trouble with words has already been observed: there is always the possibility of dispute as to the limits of their application, and no definition can get rid of this possibility.

The above view as to definition also involves a rejection of Aristotle's doctrine of essences. Aristotle taught that essences are fixed in nature, and that a definition is a phrase signifying this essence. On this view

---

[11] Ogden and Richards, *op cit.* 110, 113 ff. (The authors give a special heading to 'legal relations' (p. 120), but the treatment is not helpful.) For a previous statement of a similar view see Locke, *op. cit.* 2. 3. 10.

[12] *I.e.* by stating the genus of which the word to be defined is the species, and then stating the difference between this species and others of the same genus. Thus 'man' is (genus) animal, (difference) rational: man is a rational animal.

it is possible to dispute about 'true' definitions as though they are matters of fact. We now know that 'essence' simply means 'important feature', and that what is important is a subjective or emotional matter. No definition ever states the sum total of the qualities that seem to go to the being of a thing; it always involves a selection from those qualities, and the exact selection made depends very much upon the purpose of the definition.

These considerations reinforce the conclusions previously advanced in the discussion of 'proper meaning'. Every definition of a word is a definition of (i) its ordinary meaning, or of (ii) its specially-assigned meaning, or of (iii) its desired meaning. The only scientific dispute over definitions is a dispute over (i). Obviously there is no point in disputing (ii), and a dispute over (iii) is, except to the extent that common premises are agreed, a conflict of value-judgments, not a scientific dispute. As to (i), it is frequently possible to settle the dispute by taking a number of admitted referents of the word and abstracting from them enough of their common features to explain the use of the word. It must, however, be remembered that the number of features abstracted must often be a matter of choice, that words may have two or more ordinary meanings, and that every word is of doubtful application in marginal cases. Those who dispute about definitions and forget these points are wasting their time.

It is next to be observed that many questions and disputes that seem to be concerned with the empirical world are in fact concerned only with definitions. For instance, every question in the form 'What is . . . ?', or 'What is the nature of . . . ?', or 'What is a . . . ?', or 'What is the nature of a . . . ?' (followed in each case by the name of a class, quality or relation) is a request for a definition of a word. It is not a request for information about the empirical world, except to the extent that such information may happen to be furnished in the course of the definition. Examples of such questions are: 'What is an atoll?' 'What is a unicorn?' 'What is cause?' 'What is the nature of law?' 'What is possession?'[13]

Similarly, every inquiry into 'the nature of' (or, 'the essential nature of', 'the fundamental nature of') a class, quality or relation is a search for a definition; and every dispute about 'the (essential, fundamental) nature of' a class, quality or relation is a dispute about a definition. It is not an inquiry into, or dispute about, facts, except to the extent that it concerns the ordinary or assigned meaning of words. If this were generally realized the world would be saved much pseudo-philosophy.[14]

The only exception to the foregoing propositions is where the word in

[13] It is true that the answer to the question 'What is an atoll?' does not merely supply a definition of the word 'atoll'; it also gives information about part of the earth's surface. The context in which the question is asked and answered implies an understanding that atolls exist—*i.e.* that the description of an atoll is true of part of reality. But the context in which the question 'What is a unicorn?' is asked and answered would not, usually, imply an understanding that unicorns exist, and if it did the understanding would be false. Comparing these two questions, it is evident that a question of this form is invariably a request for a definition but not invariably a request for information about the empirical world. It is the latter only if the word in question happens to symbolize an empirical fact.

[14] See, generally, Ayer, Language, Truth and Logic, 64–5; Richards, Interpretation in Teaching, 354–5.

question is independently defined, so that there is no dispute about its application. Thus an inquiry into the nature of atolls, if there is no dispute as to which territorial formations are denoted by this word, would be a scientific investigation, for there are data to be observed. But an inquiry into the nature of atolls, or of law, or of possession, if the word in question is not independently defined, is not a scientific or factual inquiry, except to the extent that it is an inquiry into verbal usages.

Lest all this be thought to be tilting at windmills, it may be well to consider in greater detail a specific example of confusion between definitions and non-verbal facts. Let us take the usual legal or jurisprudential discussion of ' the nature of ' possession. As already stated, this discussion is in reality a discussion of the definition of the word ' possession '. This, however, is not the way in which the participants usually regard it. They seem to think that in discussing ' the nature of ' possession they are discussing, at least in part, some non-verbal fact. This assumption underlies the division of possession into ' possession in fact ' and ' possession in law '. Although the meaning of ' possession in fact ' is variously interpreted, the usual assumption is that possession in fact is, as the name implies, possession that is somehow visible in the facts of the case. Let us consider how far this assumption is true. To start with, we may picture a situation that raises difficulties in applying the idea of possession. In describing this situation it will be necessary to use words, but the reader is asked to imagine the scene in a non-verbal way, in order to reproduce as nearly as possible the raw material with which we have to deal. *A* has a pocket-book containing his name and address and some banknotes. He unknowingly drops it on the street and walks on. Many people pass, and eventually *B* finds the pocket-book and forthwith decides to keep it for himself. *B* gives it to his son *C* to hold for him, but shortly afterwards *C* is pursued by bandits, who succeed in wresting the pocket-book from him. This is the factual situation, and we have to apportion the possession of the pocket-book between *A*, *B*, *C* and the bandits. In doing this, since we are speaking of possession in fact in the sense above described, we have to do without the various rules that have been developed on the subject by different legal systems. Probably it will become clear after a moment's thought that the difficulty in the way of determining who at any moment has possession of the pocket-book is not a difficulty in ascertaining facts, for the material facts are practically all given, but is a difficulty in knowing what is meant by the word ' possession '. ' Possession ' is an abstract word of somewhat vague meaning. A theory of ' possession in fact ' seems to be one of two things: either a statement of the way in which, in the view of the writer, the word ' possession ', or the phrase ' possession in fact ', ought to be used (which is not a statement of fact at all, but a value-judgment), or else a statement of the way in which the word ' possession ' is ordinarily used by non-lawyers (which is a statement of fact only in the sense that it is a statement of verbal usage). If the particular theory of possession in fact is intended as the latter, a statement of the layman's meaning of ' possession ', the writer ought, if he is honest, to recognize that his theory is incapable of solving any of the difficult problems that arise in law-suits, for the simple reason that the layman has no clear idea of what he means by ' possession '.

Consider, in the light of this analysis, Sir John Salmond's treatment of possession. His treatment is singled out for discussion because the well-deserved esteem of the work in which it appears has made it the usual student's introduction to the theory of possession. Salmond begins by distinguishing between possession in fact and possession in law, and supposes that possession in fact is 'the truth of things'; it is possession 'in truth and in fact'; it is 'fact' in contrast to 'law'.[15] Having rubbed this well into the reader, Salmond suddenly calls possession in fact a 'conception'. This it certainly is, and of course a conception is a fact, so that the learned author is perhaps safe from the charge of self-contradiction. But it may be doubted whether he is safe from the charge of having misled the unwary reader. For if possession in fact is a conception, and so a fact, possession in law is also a conception, and so also a fact. Thus the contrast of 'law' and 'fact' breaks down.

One way of restoring it would be to say that possession in fact is the conception found among laymen, while possession in law is the conception found among lawyers. If this is the meaning, one would expect a work on Jurisprudence to be concerned with possession in law, that is, with possession as a technical legal term. Yet Salmond professes to concern himself only with possession in fact. It may also be noted that his discussion of it is far richer and more precise than a layman's discussion of it would have been.

To add to the perplexity, Salmond expressly denies that there are 'two ideas of possession, a legal and a natural'. He admits that 'were this so, we could dispense altogether with the discussion of possession in fact'—because then it would be our duty as lawyers to pay attention to the legal meaning only. But in reality, he says, 'there is only one idea, to which the rules of law do more or less imperfectly conform. There is no conception which will include all that amounts to possession in law, and will include nothing else, and it is impossible to frame any definition from which the concrete law of possession can be logically deduced. Our task is merely to search for the idea which underlies this body of rules, and of which they are the imperfect and partial expression and application'. When Salmond says that there is no legal idea of possession, his statement is true only if the word 'idea' be taken to mean a single, neat, compact idea, capable of being expressed in a short sentence. It is perfectly true that there is no legal idea of possession of this kind. A complicated legal idea of possession there certainly is, though it varies from one branch of the law to another, and even within the same branch of the law, according to the purpose of the particular rule. It comes to this, therefore, that Salmond's theory of possession in fact is really a simplified and idealized theory of possession as he finds it in the legal system. It is the legal theory of possession with its inconsistencies smoothed away. Such a theory is not an adequate statement of the law, and it is very improperly called a statement of fact. It is either an elementary statement of the law, perhaps useful for the beginner but misleading if not carefully stated, or a statement of the ideal towards which in the writer's opinion the law ought to develop.[16]

[15] Salmond, Jurisprudence (7th ed.) § 94.

[16] The confusion above considered runs throughout Salmond's treatment of possession. Thus in § 95 (7th ed.) he debates the question whether incorporeal possession is possession 'in truth'. In § 104 he takes objection to Savigny's theory that possession at its

### (3) Intended, Comprehended and Ordinary Meaning.

Ogden and Richards seem to treat meaning as though it were a single relation. But 'meaning' is a word of many meanings, and to search for *the* meaning of meaning is (if it be not undue temerity in a lawyer to say so) to fall into error from the start. In the present division of this article it is proposed to examine three important varieties of meaning, and to show their importance for the work of the lawyer. They are: (1) the intended meaning, the meaning intended by the speaker or writer; (2) the ordinary meaning, the meaning that would be attached to the words by the ordinary hearer or reader; and (3) the comprehended meaning, the meaning actually attached to the words by a particular reader or hearer, *e.g.*, one to whom the words were particularly addressed. Where misunderstanding occurs, (1) differs from (3).

(1) It is not often that the law addresses itself purely and simply to meaning in the first sense, the intended meaning. It does so, however, in the law of deceit, for here the requirement of a fraudulent state of mind means that the Court must, where the words are equivocal, look to the sense actually intended.[17] It is submitted that meaning in sense (2), the ordinary or 'reasonable' meaning of the words, is not in issue, except as evidence of what the defendant probably intended and what the plaintiff probably understood. For, on the one hand, a defendant who has 'paltered in a double sense' cannot excuse himself by showing that the meaning applied by the plaintiff to his words, being the meaning that he hoped the plaintiff would apply, was an 'unreasonable' one.[18] And, on the other hand, however reasonable the plaintiff was in attaching the untrue meaning to the defendant's statement, if the defendant did not intend his words to be taken in that sense, there is no deceit because there is no guilty mind.

In wills, statutes, deeds, written contracts and other formal documents, the general theory is again that the Court is concerned with the meaning

commencement and possession in its continuance are made up of different elements, appearing to think that this is somehow a logical impossibility. 'Savigny's theory . . . tells us, at the most, how possession begins, and how it ceases; but we wish to know what it essentially and continuously *is*'. In § 101 he distinguishes between immediate and mediate possession; on his own previous statement this is a discussion of 'possession in fact'; yet he declares that 'a test of the existence of a true mediate possession is to be found in the operation of the law of prescription'. To a casual reader it is most confusing to be informed that rules of law are a test of what exists in fact.

[17] *Per* Lord Blackburn in *Smith* v. *Chadwick* (1884) 9 App. Cas. at 201; *per* Bowen L.J. in *Angus* v. *Clifford* [1891] 2 Ch. at 472; *per* Atkinson J. in *Halifax Building Society* v. *Salisbury* [1939] 4 A. E. R. at 452.

[18] *Contra*, Winfield, Text-Book of the Law of Tort (3rd ed.) § 116, who lays it down that 'if the statement is ambiguous, the true interpretation of the authorities seems to be that the plaintiff must prove (i) that the statement was reasonably capable of bearing the meaning which he attached to it; (ii) that he understood it in that sense; and (iii) that the defendant made use of the ambiguity with the express purpose of deceiving the plaintiff'. This implies that a plaintiff cannot succeed in deceit although the defendant meant him to understand the statement in the way in which he did understand it, unless he shows also that the statement was reasonably capable of bearing the particular meaning. It is respectfully submitted that there is not this requirement. Of course, the Court may be slow to believe that the defendant meant or hoped that his words would be understood in an 'unreasonable' way, and it may also be slow to believe that the plaintiff did understand them in an 'unreasonable' way. But if the evidence is clear, the question what was the reasonable interpretation of the words is surely irrelevant. What matters, ultimately, is what the parties in fact intended and understood respectively, not what a reasonable man would have intended or understood. The words of Lord Selborne L.C. in *Smith* v. *Chadwick*, 9 App. Cas. at p. 191, are, it is submitted, not inconsistent with this view.

of the author or authors, but this is seriously qualified by a refusal (in general) to look at certain classes of extrinsic evidence (that is, evidence outside the document itself) for the purpose of ascertaining the author's intention. The result is a tendency to look only at the meaning of the words *as words*—that is, not at the actual personal meaning of the author but at the usual meaning in which the words that expressed the actual meaning are commonly employed. But it is always the duty of the Court, within the limits set by the law of evidence, to go behind the dehumanized dictionary-meaning to what the assertor was actually trying to express. As F. C. S. Schiller put it (he was not speaking of legal interpretation, but his words have a strong interest for the lawyer) :—

> 'It is the desire to communicate meaning which dictates the choice of the words used, and ultimately controls their meaning. For the original compilers of dictionaries get the word's meanings from an examination of the passages in which it has been used in print. Nevertheless, the meaning (or meanings) as formulated in a dictionary never can be an absolute and infallible guide to actual usage. It represents merely the *average* meaning, with which the word has been used in the past, and the probable meaning, with which it will be used in the future; but it cannot prohibit its modification. To understand any particular sentence, we may have (as every schoolboy translator has painfully to discover) to go beyond anything we find in our dictionaries, and in any case we have to select the "right" meaning from those given, and to adjust their *dicta* to our special problem. No critic of a bad translation would allow the excuse that the wrong meanings given to the mistranslated words had been found in a dictionary.' [19]

On the whole the Courts realize pretty well the dangers of blind adherence to dictionaries. Thus it is laid down as one of the governing rules of interpretation that words are not to be looked at in isolation but their meaning is to be gathered from their context : *noscitur a sociis*. Moreover, in the case of wills and contracts, evidence is admissible, within certain limits, to show that words were used in a special meaning that is not their ordinary one. There are instances, however, where the Courts fall far short of the ideal of interpretation as the ascertainment of meaning. A striking case of this sort is *Re Gale* (1941),[20] where the testator, who had lived with an unmarried woman and had had four children by her, died leaving her certain property 'during her widowhood'. Farwell J. held that the gift failed, because a woman who had not been married could not be anyone's 'widow'. This astonishing refusal to exercise intelligence in the construction of language cannot fairly be said to represent the customary attitude of judges; yet, though not the rule, it may be said, without disrespect, to be too frequent an exception.

(2) There are some cases where the Court is concerned solely with the ordinary meaning of words, and frankly disavows any intention to look

[19] Formal Logic 17. At one place Ogden and Richards seem to deny that meaning in one sense of the word is a personal matter, for they say (p. 103) : 'A symbol refers to what it is actually used to refer to; not necessarily to what it ought in good usage, or is intended by an interpreter, *or is intended by the user* to refer to'. It is probably my deficiency, but I do not understand this, and the discussion that precedes and follows it seems in my humble opinion to confuse meaning with truth.

[20] *Re Gale, Gale* v. *Gale* [1941] Ch. 209.

at the meaning of the speaker or writer, or even at the understanding of those to whom the words were intended to be addressed. Illustrations occur in the law of defamation, but the precise rules are too complicated to be gone into here.

(3) We pass to the third kind of meaning, the meaning attached to language by the hearer or reader. There are several situations in which this is the kind of meaning that is important in law. Thus, the question whether an offer is made or acceptance given depends, at least in part, on the question what the other party reasonably understands. So also do the questions of innocent misrepresentation and estoppel. In such cases there are two matters to be considered : first, what the hearer understands by the words, and second, whether his understanding is 'reasonable'—*i.e.*, whether it conforms to what the ordinary person, or the judge himself, would have understood in the circumstances. Thus, this type of meaning is a compound of senses (2) and (3).

To say that the Court in a particular case is concerned with the ordinary meaning of words (sense (2)) does not solve all difficulties, for the Court may have to select between different ordinary meanings current in different circles; or, in the case of phrases, it may have to select between the meaning built up from a consideration of the words taken separately, and the meaning of the phrase as a whole. Good illustrations are supplied by two cases decided on the Merchandise Marks Act, 1887. By section 2 (1) (*d*) of the Act it is an offence to apply 'any false trade description' to goods; and similarly, under section 2 (2) it is an offence to sell goods to which a 'false trade description' has been applied. Now before a description can be pronounced to be true or false its meaning must be ascertained, and the ascertainment of meaning may depend upon the group of people whom one takes as interpreting the words. This is illustrated by *Lemy* v. *Watson* (1915),[21] where the Court had to choose between a meaning current among vendors and a meaning current among purchasers. The facts were that small fish caught off the coast of Norway were sold in tins under the description of 'Norwegian sardines'. The word 'sardine' had come to England from France, being the French name for a pilchard. English usage had confined it to small fish, *i.e.*, young pilchards. There were no pilchards in Norwegian waters, and the so-called Norwegian sardines were brisling. This was well known in the trade, but was not known to the purchasing public. The public was unaware that the fish so sold were different from the French sardine, and for the most part did not know that the French sardine was a pilchard. In these circumstances, was the epithet 'Norwegian sardines' false as applied to these fish? It was held that it was, and that an offence had been committed.

It is hardly necessary to point out that the decision is not an authority for saying that French usage, the usage of the country of the word's origin, is to be preferred to English usage, or that original usage must be preferred to current usage, or that the meaning built up from the words taken separately is necessarily to be preferred to the meaning of a phrase taken as a whole. All that the case decides is that under the Merchandise Marks Act the buyers' usage must be preferred to the sellers' usage. If this be the *ratio decidendi*, a *dictum* of Lord Reading C.J. in the course of

[21] [1915] 3 K. B. 731.

his judgment is open to some objection. Referring to the fish sold under the name of Norwegian sardines, he said : 'They were not sardines in fact because they were not the small pilchard which is the sardine proper, and even with the prefix "Norwegian" it was false in fact to say that these fish so prepared were Norwegian sardines. It is true they were Norwegian, but they were not sardines'. In criticism of this it may be said that when there is a conflict of linguistic usage, as there was in this case, it is begging the question to assert that the goods were or were not something or other. The question whether the goods were or were not $x$ is, in the absence of an agreed definition of $x$, a verbal, not a factual question, and it can be resolved only by deciding which usage is to prevail. Nor did it help to say that the goods were not sardines 'in fact', or not sardines 'proper', because this was true only on the assumption that the French (*i.e.*, the buyers') usage was to be adopted in preference to the sellers' usage. Finally, it was misleading to suggest that goods that are not 'sardines' *simpliciter* may not be 'sardines' qualified by an epithet like 'Norwegian'. They would be, if that were the understanding of the buyers. As Darling J. put it :

> 'There are many erroneous terms consecrated by common use. One which has been mentioned in the course of the argument, a glaring instance, is the term "Bombay ducks" as applied to an Indian fish, and it is agreed that if anybody ordered Bombay ducks and somebody supplied him with ducks from Bombay the contract to supply Bombay ducks would not be fulfilled. Another obvious instance is eau de Cologne. Whatever eau de Cologne may be, as to which I know nothing, it certainly is not water from the Rhine. If eau de Cologne were ordered and you simply supplied a gallon of water from Cologne that would not fulfil the contract. Another instance where anybody would understand what was meant is if you spoke of Roman pearls. They are not pearls with which any oyster has anything to do, nor do I know that they are Roman. They indicate something which is probably neither Roman nor a pearl, just as it was said by a well-known historian that the Holy Roman Empire had for its chief characteristic that it was neither holy nor Roman nor an empire. One other instance occurs to me of a term consecrated, if I may say so, by common user which does not indicate the true fact, and that is when people speak as they commonly do of the judicial ermine, meaning merely any white fur when worn by a judge. These expressions have become conventional terms, and are, I think, instances of a trade description lawfully and generally applied.' [22]

In the other case, *Fowler* v. *Cripps* (1906),[23] the substance sold possessed the qualities indicated by the descriptive words taken separately, but the description was nevertheless misleading to the ordinary purchaser. The facts were that Glauber's salt was sold under the name of 'soda crystals'. It was proved in evidence that both Glauber's salt and washing soda are salts of soda in crystalline form; but the description 'soda crystals' was by the usage of the trade of manufacturing chemists applied only to washing soda. It was therefore held that an offence had been committed. Wills J. said : 'The fact that a

[22] [1915] 3 K. B. at 752–3.
[23] [1906] 1 K. B. 16.

description as applied to particular goods is scientifically correct will not prevent it from being a false trade description'. While respectfully agreeing with this, it must be pointed out that the words 'scientifically correct' mean only 'in accordance with the linguistic practices of scientists'. They do not mean that a scientist can pronounce upon the 'correctness' of ordinary verbal conventions.

Similar problems arise under the Food and Drugs Act, 1938, s. 3 (1), whereby it is an offence to sell food that is not of the nature, substance and quality demanded. At first sight it may appear that the question whether an article of food is of the nature, substance or quality demanded is wholly a scientific one, for are not 'nature, substance and quality' matters of objective fact? But on further reflection it will be seen that the question is only partly scientific, being in part linguistic. The question 'What, in ordinary language (including scientific language) is the description of the article that has been sold?' is a scientific one, to be settled by examining the thing that has been sold. But the question 'What is the meaning of the words used by the purchaser, and does the thing sold (as already examined) conform to this meaning?' is linguistic. In practice, the difficulty that the judge experiences in deciding cases under the Act is always on the linguistic question, for the scientific one can be accurately answered by the evidence of analysts.

Particularly interesting as illustrations of the linguistic difficulty are the 'cordial' cases of the war now ended. Before the war it was the almost invariable practice of manufacturers of the drinks called cordials to put into them substantial quantities of sugar. It appears that the word 'cordial' originally signified what is now called a liqueur, but in the course of time it came to be applied to non-alcoholic beverages containing this substantial quantity of sugar. The sugar took the place of alcohol in giving the beverage the stimulating effect that justified its name. After the outbreak of the war, when sugar became scarce, so-called cordials were put on the market that contained no sugar or alcohol, being sweetened with saccharin, and the question accordingly arose whether they could properly be sold as 'cordials'. This question illustrates three of the perennial problems of interpretation. (1) In the first place, it illustrates the difficulty of choosing between 'essence' and 'accident' in definition. It was open to the vendors of the so-called cordials to admit that a very large proportion of the drinks sold as cordials before the war did contain sugar, and yet to argue that this fact was a logical accident, the essence of 'cordials' (as the term was understood immediately before the war) being that they were sweet; on this view a drink sweetened with saccharin is a cordial. (2) Second, it illustrates the difficulty caused by an incipient change of meaning. At the outbreak of the war a drink containing a large percentage of sugar was clearly a cordial, although that was not the original meaning of the word. Had the practice of selling saccharin 'cordials' gone on long enough without legal proceedings being taken, it would have been easy to hold that the word 'cordial' had undergone yet another change of meaning. The difficulty arose from the fact that the attempt to change the meaning of the word was nipped in the bud. (3) The third difficulty, which if satisfactorily solved might also for legal purposes solve the other two, is the difficulty of evidence. It is clearly settled that the question of the meaning of a word like ' cordial ' in cases under the Food and Drugs Act is not one of law to be decided exclusively by the judge's own view of language, but is a question of fact to be decided (chiefly) by evidence. It is true that the judge is entitled to use his own knowledge of the meaning of words, even if that knowledge is a specialized one [24]; also, he may look at dictionaries. But, in addition, it is always open to the parties to give evidence on the meaning of the words. What kind of evidence, then, is to be tendered? This is the crux of the difficulty in cases under the Food and Drugs Act. To formulate more precisely the question for decision in cases under the Act, it is what the hypothetical purchaser who demands (say) ' cordial ' expects to receive. To begin with, it would seem that the question is not what a particular actual purchaser expected to receive, for, on the one hand, his expectation may have been quite ' unreasonable ', *i.e.*, unusual, and, on the other, he may not have realised the full implications to the ordinary person of the word he was using. He is entitled to expect an article that he can himself properly resell as ' cordial ', and the fact that he does not know the ordinary meaning of the word, and is himself quite satisfied with what he gets, is immaterial. The question, then, turns on the expectation of the hypothetical purchaser. But the hypothetical purchaser is an abstraction, who cannot be put into the witness-box. How is the judge to be made to understand the mind of this abstract entity? Scientifically, the proper thing to do would doubtless be to issue a questionnaire to some hundreds or thousands of people who are likely to buy the commodity in question, carefully selected so as to be representative of the community as a whole, and to ask the judge to go by the majority of their answers. This method has not hitherto been suggested in a Court of law, and would quite possibly be regarded as violating the rules of evidence. An alternative method, less accurate but more in accord with ordinary Court practices, would be to draw a number of witnesses at random from the nearest Clapham omnibus; but again no attempt has been made to do this. In practice, the only evidence to which the Court listens is that of a few so-called experts. Thus, in *Sopers* v. *Johnston* (1944),[25] which was a civil action for breach of a warranty of compliance with the Food and Drugs Act, the judge listened to evidence of the meaning of the word ' cordial ' tendered by (among others) a public analyst and a manufacturer of ' soft drinks '. Neither of these persons can well be regarded as representing the ordinary member of the buying public.

In prosecutions under the Act a particular difficulty has arisen. By section 81 (1), ' in any proceedings under this Act, the production by one of the parties of a document purporting to be a certificate of a public analyst in the prescribed form . . . shall be sufficient evidence of the facts stated therein . . .' It might be thought that this provision was confined to statements of scientific fact made by the analyst, resulting from investigations that he has been trained as a scientist to make. However, the Courts have extended it to opinions given by the analyst as to the proper (*i.e.*, ordinary) use of words, such as the question whether a particular product is properly called a cordial.[26] One cannot help

[24] *R.* v. *Field* (1895) 64 L. J. M. C. 158; cp. Bell, Sale of Food and Drugs (11th ed.) 97.

[25] [1944] 2 A. E. R. 42, affirmed *ibid.* 586.

[26] *Broughton* v. *Whittaker* [1944] 1 K. B. 269, following *Bowker* v. *Woodroofe* [1928] 1 K. B. 217, where Avory J., at p. 225, characterized an analyst's certificate that a

feeling that this is a confusion between the scientific and the verbal question. The question what such-and-such a product contains is a scientific question, with which the analyst is fitted to deal; but the question whether, given the composition of the product, it is properly called by a certain name, is a verbal question, to answer which the analyst has frequently no better training than the ordinary educated person. Further complexity is caused by the decision in *Collins Arden Products* v. *Barking Corporation* (1943),[27] where it was held that the certificate of the analyst may be contradicted by witnesses, and that in the event of this happening the Court is left to frame its own opinion of what an ordinary person who goes into a shop would mean by the words under consideration in the case (*e.g.*, the word 'cordial'). Unfortunately, the type of evidence adduced in these cases frequently fails to provide an answer to this question.

### (4) Logical Implication.

One of the apparent puzzles of mathematics, which a philosopher is called upon to explain, is the almost uncanny way in which its pronouncements, if accurately worked out from correct premises, are verified by the facts of experience. The interior of a box measures 6″ x 6″ x 6″. It is desired to fit 1″ wooden cubes into this box. A mathematician, on being given these facts, predicts that 216 cubes, and no more, will fit into the box. Upon the experiment being performed, the prediction is invariably found to be correct. The mathematician is not surprised, for he asserts that, given the accuracy of the premises, by no possibility can his prediction ever be found to be wrong.[28] This looks like a standing miracle. What is the explanation of it? The answer is that the mathematician's prediction, if his reasoning has been accurate, is invariably correct because it was already contained in the premises from which he started. So long as the premises remain constant the conclusion must follow, because the conclusion is merely a restatement, complete or partial, of the premises. This holds for all mathematical deduction, and indeed for logical deduction in general. Statements of deductive logic are necessarily true for the simple reason that they are tautologies.

The interesting thing is that a person may be aware of certain premises, and understand their immediate 'meaning', without realizing the logical implication that, in fact, is necessarily contained in them. Thus, a person may know the dimensions of a box and know the dimensions of the cubes that are to go into it without knowing how many cubes will fit into the box. The logical deduction, when drawn, may come as a psychological surprise. Yet the proposition deduced was, in a sense, already contained in the known premises.

In some cases logical implication yields quite remarkable consequences.

particular article was not a meat and malt wine as a 'statement of fact'. It is submitted that it was not a statement of fact except in the sense that it was a statement (whether true or not) of the ordinary use of words.

[27] [1943] 1 K. B. 419, distinguished in *Broughton* v. *Whittaker*, last note.

[28] Cases are sometimes put in which the mathematician's result seems at first sight to be falsified in practice, but it will be found that the falsification is only apparent. For instance, it may be admitted that pouring a pint into a pint jug that is already full does not yield two pints in the jug; but the mathematician does not say that it will. He says only that the addition of one pint to one pint will, assuming the continued existence of both pints, result in a total of two pints somewhere.

Illustrations of this occur in geometry, where the acceptance of a few simple axioms involves acceptance of a complicated logical structure. To take one example : a circle is defined as being bounded by a line, every point in which is equidistant from a certain point within the circle. It is not an obvious consequence of this definition that the length of the circumference bears a constant ratio to the length of the diameter of 3·14159 to 1; yet such is the case. Similarly, it is not obvious to a person who knows the English language but has no mathematical knowledge that every triangle with sides in the proportion 3, 4, 5 is necessarily right-angled. In such cases the consequence follows from the premises and cannot be rejected without self-contradiction; yet the consequence is not, to an ignorant person, psychologically obvious from a bare statement of the premises.

This element of psychological surprise in logical implication is capable of presenting some awkward legal problems, particularly in the case of contracts, where the Courts are accustomed to reject the defence of unilateral mistake. For instance, suppose that *A* offers to employ *B* for a term of five years, commencing at £1,000 a year, with a rise of £100 every year. *B* considers this offer and then counters by proposing that he be paid by the half-year, starting at £475 for the first half-year and rising by £50 every half-year. *B* knows the mathematical implications of this, but shrewdly suspects that *A* does not. The suspicion is well founded, for *A* thinks, as most people would, that the counter-offer is substantially the same as the original proposal, and that the difference relates merely to the time of payment. *A* accordingly accepts the counter-offer. Actually the counter-offer is very much more beneficial to *B* than *A* thought, for it turns out that, by a freak of arithmetic, a rise of £50 every half-year is equivalent to a rise of £200 every year.[29] At the end of five years *B* will have pocketed £1,000 more under his counter-offer than he would have done under the original proposal. Will the Court hold the contract to be void for mistake on the part of *A*? An even more serious question arises in the case of a trick played with geometrical progressions. In *James* v. *Morgan* (1663),[30] a horse was delivered in return for a promise to pay a barleycorn for the first nail in the horse's shoes, doubling it for every nail to the total of thirty-two nails. This amounted to 500 quarters of barley, which was doubtless much more than the promisor expected. On action being brought for the non-delivery of the barley, Hyde J. held the contract to be good, but directed the jury to give only the value of the horse as damages. This solution means in effect that the contract is undone, for

[29] The amounts work out as follows :—

| | *A*'s offer. | *B*'s counter-offer. | | |
|---|---|---|---|---|
| | | January–June | July–December | Total |
| | £ | £ | £ | £ |
| 1st Year .. | 1,000 | 475 | 525 | 1,000 |
| 2nd Year .. | 1,100 | 575 | 625 | 1,200 |
| 3rd Year .. | 1,200 | 675 | 725 | 1,400 |
| 4th Year .. | 1,300 | 775 | 825 | 1,600 |
| 5th Year .. | 1,400 | 875 | 925 | 1,800 |
| Total .. | £6,000 | | | £7,000 |

[30] 1 Lev. 111; 1 Keble 569. Cp. *Thornborow* (*Thornborough*, *Thornburgh*) v. *Whitacre* (1706) 2 Ld. Raym. 1164; 6 Mod. 305; 3 Salk. 97, where the plaintiff accepted a similar recompense by way of compromise, and no judgment was given.

the so-called damages amount merely to quasi-contractual recovery in protection of the restitution interest. It is submitted that this is the desirable result, and that mistake as to the logical implications of a contract, if known to or suspected by the other, ought to have the same effect as a slip of the pen or of the tongue,[31] and render the contract void; at any rate, where the logical implication is substantially different from what was expected by the party under the mistake.

Exceptional cases apart, the Courts will enforce consequences logically implied in the terms expressed in contracts, statutes and other legal documents and transactions, as though they had been expressed *totidem verbis*. Also, consequences may be logically implied not only from the terms of the document taken alone but from those terms taken in conjunction with propositions of fact or rules of law. Thus, speaking of wills, Lord Westbury declared that implication may be founded upon ' a direction to do something which cannot be carried into effect without, of necessity, involving something else in order to give effect to that direction, or something else which is a consequence necessarily resulting from that direction '.[32]

### (5) Literal and Ulterior Meaning.

In division (3) of this section we considered the distinction between (1) the intended meaning, (2) the ordinary meaning, and (3) the comprehended meaning. Another distinction must now be made between (*a*) the literal or primary meaning of the words, and (*b*) the ulterior meaning, *i.e.*, the meaning, other than the literal meaning, intended to be conveyed by the speaker when he uttered the words, or the meaning, other than the literal meaning, attributed by a hearer to the speaker.

In some cases ulterior meaning may coincide with logical implication; but the meaning of the two phrases is different. Ulterior meaning is a matter of psychology, not of logic. On the one hand, the logical implication of statements may lie hidden for years, as did the truths of mathematics before they were discovered. On the other hand, the ulterior meaning of a proposition need not be logically entailed in its literal meaning.

The distinction between literal and ulterior meaning applies to each of the three meanings of ' meaning ' stated in division (3), this resulting in six possible combinations. For example, a tactless host looks out of the window and says to his guest : ' It has stopped raining '. The guest mistakenly takes this to be an oblique hint that he is desired to leave. Here it may be said that while the meaning of the words to the host is ' It has stopped raining ' (intended literal, 1*a*), the meaning to the guest is both this (comprehended literal, 2*a*), and also ' Please go ' (comprehended ulterior, 3*b*). If the host meant his guest to make this implication, there would be a fourth ' meaning ', namely, an intended ulterior meaning (1*b*). The facts are too scanty for a pronouncement on whether the ordinary onlooker would make the implication (ordinary ulterior, 2*b*), but he would of course understand the literal meaning (ordinary literal, 2*a*).

It may be contended that so-called ulterior meaning as explained above is not meaning at all. In support of this contention it may be

[31] *Webster* v. *Cecil* (1861) 30 Beav. 62; *Hartog* v. *Colin* [1939] 3 A. E. R. 566.
[32] *Parker* v. *Tootal* (1865) 11 H. L. C. 143 at 161.

said that when the guest reads (or thinks he reads) his host's mind from his words, he might equally have read it from his host's non-verbal acts, like the expression on his face or the impatient tapping of his toe. This kind of meaning is, therefore, not confined to symbols. Also, it may be said that the sentence 'It has stopped raining' does not mean the same as the sentence 'Please go'. In reply, it may be said that although the objections are true in a way they do not affect the proposition that the intention of the host (the state of affairs that he desires to bring about by his words) when he says 'It has stopped raining' may be the same as when he says 'Please go'. Whether or not ulterior meaning is called meaning is simply a question of words.

Ulterior meaning—or, as Wyclif called it, 'ghostly understandynge'—has given rise to a distinct literary form, namely, the parable or allegory. In legal matters it figures prominently in the defamatory innuendo and the construction of documents. To discuss the former in detail would take us off into too specialized a branch of the law, but something may be said upon the latter.

It has already been remarked that the Courts will generally enforce consequences logically implied in the language of contracts, wills, statutes, and other legal documents and transactions. The point now to be noticed is that the legal doctrine of implied terms goes much farther than this. Judges are accustomed to read into documents and transactions many terms that are not logically implied in them. As an academic matter non-logical implication may be classified into three kinds: (i) of terms that the parties (the plural shall throughout include the singular) probably had in mind but did not trouble to express; (ii) of terms that the parties, whether or not they actually had them in mind, would probably have expressed if the question had been brought to their attention; and (iii) of terms that the parties, whether or not they had them in mind or would have expressed them if they had foreseen the difficulty, are implied by the Court because of the Court's view of fairness or policy or in consequence of rules of law. Of these three kinds of non-logical implication (i) is an effort to arrive at actual intention; (ii) is an effort to arrive at hypothetical or conditional intention—the intention that the parties would have had if they had foreseen the difficulty; (iii) is not concerned with the intention of the parties except to the extent that the term implied by the Court may be excluded by an expression of positive intention to the contrary.

Concerning the three kinds of non-logical implication there are the following special remarks to be made. First, the name 'non-logical implication' is intended to indicate that this sort of implication has no *necessary* connection with logic. In any particular case it is possible for a term to be implied both logically and by what is here called non-logical implication. Second, although the line between the three cases can be made sharp as a matter of definition, in practice they merge imperceptibly into each other, because the distinguishing factor, that of probable intent, is a matter of degree. Third, only in case (i) does the implication amount to a declaration by the Court of ulterior meaning in the sense already defined; in the other two cases the so-called implication is in reality an addition by the Court to the meaning of the parties. The present discussion of ulterior meaning will therefore be concluded with some remarks on the attitude of the Courts towards non-logical implication of type (i).

Generally speaking it may be said that whenever the Court comes to the conclusion that the meaning of the parties has been incompletely expressed, and that the unexpressed meaning can be gathered from what has been expressed (simply because in the circumstances it is improbable that the parties meant their words to be a complete statement), the omitted words will be supplied. As Lord Westbury put it, 'implication may arise from an elliptical form of expression which involves and implies something else as contemplated by the person using the expression'.[33] But there are some few cases where the Court may refuse to make this form of implication: for instance, it may be excluded by a presumption. An important exclusion of it in the law of wills is in the rule that a will confers no interest by mere implication. Thus, in *Scalé* v. *Rawlins* (1892),[34] a testator devised property to his niece during her life, and after her death '(she leaving no child or children)' he gave the property to his nephews. The niece died leaving children. It was argued that the intention of the testator must have been that if the niece left children they were to have the property, for otherwise there could be no possible reason for making the gift over to the nephews depend upon the niece's not having children. However, it was held by the House of Lords that since no gift to the children was expressed in the will, effect could not be given to any unexpressed intention of the testator. The policy of this strict rule of construction may be doubted, and there is at least one case where it is departed from. If a testator leaves a sum of money 'after the death of *A*' to *B*, the person who would be entitled to the money if the testator died intestate, the Court will imply a life interest in *A*, for otherwise the testator's evident intention to postpone *B*'s enjoyment of the property would fail of effect.[35]

### (6) The Transition from Implied Terms to Rules of Law.

We pass to a consideration of non-logical implication of types (ii) and (iii). It is common form among judges to deny that they ever read into a contract or other document anything other than what, in their view, the parties actually intended[36]; and occasionally they have even gone so far as to say that the implication must be collected from the words of the

[33] *Parker* v. *Tootal* (1865) 11 H. L. C. 143 at 161; cp. Jarman, Wills (7th ed.) 601 ff.

[34] [1892] A. C. 342.

[35] Jarman, *op. cit.* 606 ff.

[36] 'An implied warranty, or, as it is called, a covenant in law, as distinguished from an express contract or express warranty, really is in all cases founded on the presumed intention of the parties and upon reason': *per* Bowen L.J. in *The Moorcock* (1889) 14 P. D. 64 at 68; and see the same judge in *Lamb* v. *Evans* [1893] 1 Ch. 218 at 229. 'The Court has no right to imply in a written contract any such stipulation, unless, on considering the terms of the contract in a reasonable and business manner, an implication necessarily arises that the parties must have intended that the suggested implication should exist. It is not enough to say that it would be a reasonable thing to make such an implication': *per* Lord Esher M.R. in *Hamlyn* v. *Wood* [1891] 2 Q. B. 488 at 491; and see the same judge in *Emanuel* v. *La Compagnie Fermière de l'Etablissement Thermal de Vichy* [1889] W. N. 150 at 151. 'Implied obligations in a contract must be governed by the common intention of the parties': *per* Lord Loreburn in *Lyttelton-Times Co.* v. *Warners* [1907] A. C. 476. 'The Court ought not to imply a term merely because it would be a reasonable term to include if the parties had thought about the matter, or because one party, if he had thought about the matter, would not have made the contract unless the term was included; it must be such a necessary term that both parties must have intended that it should be a term of the contract, and have only not expressed it because its necessity was so obvious that it was taken for granted':

document itself.[37] These statements cannot be taken seriously. It is true that the declaration of presumed actual intention is the commonest form of implication; but it is not the only form. Courts frequently import into a document terms that are not logically implied in it, and that the parties probably did not think about: or, to say the least, such terms are imported whether or not in the particular case it is probable that the parties thought about them. Examples of such terms 'implied' into contracts by rules of law are the implied conditions of reasonable fitness and merchantable quality on a contract of sale of goods, the rule that payment and delivery of goods are concurrent conditions, the implied warranty of seaworthiness, the implied condition on the letting of a furnished house that it is reasonably fit for habitation, the implied promise by one who agrees to build a house that the house will be reasonably fit for habitation, the implied promise by a servant not to disclose secret processes, not to hand over to a rival written work completed for the master, and not, while still in his master's employment, to solicit the master's customers to transfer their custom to himself, the implied promise by an employer (in some cases) to furnish work, the implied duty of care in the carriage of passengers and in looking after bailed goods, and the implied promise by a banker not to disclose the state of his customer's account.

The view may perhaps be held that this particular process is not very happily called 'implication'. It is not so much the interpretation of a pre-existing and expressed intent as legislation amending or supplementing the expressed intent. Terms so read into the contract might better be called 'constructive' than 'implied'.[38] However, this is simply a question of nomenclature; and in any case no fixed nomenclature can be maintained in practice, because terms of classes (i) (ii) and (iii) merge into each other. There is no legal difference between the three classes, and the only practical difference is that the Courts are more ready to imply terms of class (i) than of classes (ii) and (iii). Terms of classes (ii) and (iii) are mainly of specified types and are comparatively rarely added to, though it is always open to the Court to add to them.[39] Also, implication

---

*per* Scrutton L.J. in *Re Comptoir Commercial Anversois and Power* [1920] 1 K. B. 868; and see the same judge in *Reigate* v. *Union Mfg. Co. (Ramsbottom)* [1918] 1 K. B. 592 at 605, and *Guaranty Trust Co.* v. *Hannay* [1918] 2 K. B. 625 at 664. '*Prima facie* that which in any contract is left to be implied and need not be expressed is something so obvious that it goes without saying; so that, if, while the parties were making their bargain, an officious bystander were to suggest some express provision for it in their agreement, they would testily suppress him with a common "Oh, of course!" At least it is true, I think, that, if a term were never implied by a judge unless it could pass that test, he could not be held to be wrong': *per* MacKinnon L.J. in *Shirlaw* v. *Southern Foundries, Ltd.* [1939] 2 K. B. 206 at 227, affd. [1940] A. C. 702.

[37] *E.g. per* Lush, J. in *Churchward* v. *R.* (1866) L. R. 1 Q. B. 173 at 211. *Contra*, *per* Bowen L.J. in *Lamb* v. *Evans* [1893] 1 Ch. 218 at 230; *per* Vaughan Williams L.J. in *Krell* v. *Henry* [1903] 2 K. B. 740 at 749.

[38] So Restatement, Contracts, § 253; Williston, Contracts (revised ed.) § 668; Patterson, 'Constructive Conditions in Contracts' (1942) 42 Col. L. Rev. 903. There is much confusion of terminology. In *Re Cadogan and Hans Place Estate, Ltd., Ex p. Willis* (1895) 73 L. T. 387, Rigby L.J. seemed to say that terms of class (i) were express, and those of class (iii) implied. Cp. Salmond and Williams, Contracts, 2nd ed. 24. In *Williams* v. *Burrell* (1845) 1 C. B. 402, Tindal C.J. recognized that the phrase 'implied covenant', in one meaning, applied to terms of class (i), though he held that it differed in no respect from an express covenant.

[39] Thus in *Aerial Advertising Co.* v. *Batchelor's Peas* [1938] 2 A. E. R. 788, on a contract to advertise by an aeroplane towing trailers, there was held to be an implied promise not to fly during the two minutes' silence on Armistice Day.

of type (iii) is generally confined to the interpretation of bilateral or multilateral private transactions like contracts. Generally, it is not applied to the interpretation of wills, for the Courts disclaim any jurisdiction to reform wills,[40] except in the exercise of statutory powers. Generally, also, the doctrine of separation of powers prevents the Courts from interfering with legislation otherwise than by declaring the probable or (at most) hypothetical-probable intent of the Legislature. However, in declaring the probable or hypothetical-probable intent of a testator or Legislature the judge naturally tends (however much he may deny it) to go upon his own ideas of policy, convenience or justice. Further, there are certain rules of construction of wills and statutes that may, if desired, be thought of as implied (constructive) terms, such as the rule that 'children' does not include illegitimate children, or that statutes do not bind the Crown in the absence of express words or necessary implication. No doubt the ordinary lawyer would dislike hearing these referred to as implied terms, but they differ in no way from implied terms of classes (ii) and (iii).

This brings me to my last point, which is that it is a matter of taste whether implied terms of classes (ii) and (iii) be styled implied terms or rules of law. They are in fact merely rules of law that apply in the absence of an expression of contrary intent[41]: whether we choose to call them implied terms or not is simply a matter of terminology. Our terminology as we now have it is not consistent, for there are some rules of law that are indistinguishable from implied terms in their practical effect, yet which are never called implied terms. Such, for instance, are the rules of interpretation. So, also, we do not say that the rule that a contract is voidable for innocent misrepresentation is an implied term,[42] although it can be derogated from by agreement; yet some judges and writers have been known to declare that the law of frustration,[43] the duty to disclose in contracts *uberrimae fidei*,[44] and even part of the law of mistake in contract,[45] rest upon implied terms or conditions. With all respect to those who hold a contrary opinion, it is submitted that the question is purely terminological and has (or should have) no practical importance. This submission may be stated a little more fully for the first two of the three departments of law just mentioned.

---

[40] *Per* Knight Bruce V.-C. in *Bird* v. *Luckie* (1850) 8 Hare 301 at 306–7.

[41] Exceptionally, the rule that the Crown can dismiss its civil and military servants at will, though said to be a term implied into contracts of employment with the Crown, seems to be incapable of being excluded by contrary agreement. See D. W. Logan, 'A Civil Servant and his Pay' (1945) 61 L. Q. R. at 255, 262; *Rodwell* v. *Thomas* [1944] 1 K. B. 596. It would be better not to call it an implied term.

[42] See *per* Luxmoore L.J. in *Merchants' and Manufacturers' Insce. Co.* v. *Hunt* [1941] 1 K. B. 295 at 318; and cp. *Pennsylvania Shipping Co.* v. *Compagnie Nationale de Navigation* (1936) 155 L. T. 294.

[43] For a review of the *dicta* see L. J. Sturge, 'The Doctrine of Implied Condition' (1925) 41 L. Q. R. 170. Lord Wright has rejected the language of implied condition in frustration cases: *Denny, Mott & Dickson, Ltd.* v. *Fraser* [1944] A. C. 265 at 275–6; cp. his address in The Future of the Common Law, 112.

[44] *Per* Parke B. in *Moens* v. *Heyworth* (1842) 10 M. & W. 147 at 157; *per* Lindley L.J. in *Blackburn* v. *Vigors* (1886) 17 Q. B. D. 553 at 578; on appeal, *per* Lord Watson (1887) 12 App. Cas. 531 at 539–40, but see *per* Lord Halsbury L.C. *ibid.* at p. 536; *per* Atkinson J. in *Zurich Insce. Co.* v. *Morrison* [1942] 1 A. E. R. 529 at 535. *Contra*, *per* Fletcher Moulton L.J. in *Joel* v. *Law Union and Crown Insce. Co.* [1908] 2 K. B. 863 at 886.

[45] *Lever Bros. Ltd.* v. *Bell* [1931] 1 K. B. 557 at 584, 595–6, *per* Scrutton and Greer L.JJ.; on appeal [1932] A. C. 161 at 224–7, *per* Lord Atkin.

(*a*) A problem that may seem at first sight to give practical importance to the issue in the law of frustration is one concerning the interpretation of an arbitration clause. Suppose that a contract contains a clause referring to arbitration all disputes arising 'under' the contract, and suppose that a dispute arises over the question whether the contract has been frustrated: is that a dispute arising 'under' the contract within the meaning of the arbitration clause? In *Hirji Mulji* v. *Cheong Yue S.S. Co.* (1926)[46] the Privy Council held that it was not, but this decision was doubted, *obiter*, by the House of Lords in *Heyman* v. *Darwins* (1942),[47] and Viscount Simon L.C. put his dissent on the ground that discharge for frustration rested upon an implied term in the contract. 'If, . . . when parties have entered into a contract, circumstances arise before the performance of the contract is completed which, in the view of one party, bring the contract to an end by frustration, and, therefore, discharge both parties from further performance, but the other party does not agree, this is a difference about the applicability of the implied term, and is just as much within the arbitration clause as if it were a difference about an express term in the contract.'[48] Lord Wright, however, though he concurred in doubting the *Hirji Mulji Case*, expressly said that his criticism of it did not depend upon the implied term theory of frustration.[49] It is respectfully submitted that this is a perfectly tenable view. It can be held that a dispute as to frustration is a dispute arising 'under' the contract, because it is a dispute concerning the application of the law of frustration to the contractual situation; there is no need to bring in the implied term theory.

Although, as already said, the question is (or should be regarded as) purely one of terminology, there are certain reasons for rejecting the terminology of implied term in cases of frustration. In the first place, although the rubric 'implied term' is a convenient heading for some comparatively minor rules of law, like the implied conditions and warranties on a contract of sale of goods, it is not convenient as a matter of classification to include under it such a large subject as frustration. In the second place, to speak of the discharge of *both* parties on account of frustration as resting on an implied term or condition conceals the fact that their discharge is governed by different principles of law. The discharge of the party whose act becomes impossible of performance rests on the law of impossibility of performance or undue delay; that of the other party rests on the law of failure of consideration. That the principles are different is seen from the fact that sometimes one party is discharged and not the other.[50] A terminology that slurs this over cannot be accounted satisfactory. In the third place, the phrase 'implied term' (or 'condition') has a threefold signification. It is now clear that as applied to the law of frustration it refers to implication of type (iii), but there are some older *dicta* that make it seem to refer to implication of type (i), and this tends to create doubt and confusion in the law. For instance, it is sometimes suggested that a contract is discharged for frustration only where the frustrating event was not contemplated by the parties, for if it

[46] [1926] A. C. 497.
[47] [1942] A. C. 356.
[48] At p. 367.
[49] At pp. 382–3.
[50] Williams, The Law Reform (Frustrated Contracts) Act, 1943, 26–7.

was contemplated by them, and yet not referred to in the contract, no term relating to frustration can (according to this argument) be implied. This argument was rejected by Goddard J. (as he then was) in *W. J. Tatem* v. *Gamboa* (1939),[51] it is submitted rightly. Discharge for frustration, if we must state it as a matter of implication, rests upon constructive implication, not genuine implication.

(*b*) There appears to be only one case in which a practical consequence was purported to be attached to the so-called 'rule' that the duty to disclose in contracts *uberrimae fidei* rests on an implied term. This was the case of *Pickersgill* v. *London, etc., Insurance Co.* (1912),[52] where the question arose whether an insurer's defence of non-disclosure by the assured was a defence 'arising out of the contract' within the Marine Insurance Act, 1906, s. 50 (2). Hamilton J. held that it was, on the ground that the duty to disclose arose out of an implied condition in the contract. It is submitted that the decision is right but the reason unsatisfactory, for, granting that the duty to disclose can be said to be an implied condition, the implication belongs to type (iii), and is simply another name for a rule of law. The proper reason for the decision is that, on the construction of the section, a defence arising out of the combined effect of the contract (*i.e.*, the agreement) and the rules of law relating to the contract is a defence 'arising out of the contract'. Were the construction otherwise, the section would have no application, for every defence arising out of a contract is at the same time a defence arising out of a rule of law applicable to the contract, even if it be only the rule of law that a defence expressly given by the contract shall be a good legal defence.

In *Merchants' and Manufacturers' Insurance Co.* v. *Hunt* (1941),[53] it was argued that, on the assumption that the duty to disclose is an implied term, it is superseded by an express term covering the same ground as (or being inconsistent with) the implied term.[54] The Court of Appeal did not finally pronounce upon this argument, but Scott L.J. said : 'I am not satisfied that [the] argument on principle is sound. I realize that there are several reported cases in which judges have, in the course of their judgments, expressed an opinion that the duty of disclosure may be regarded as resting on an implied term, but I do not know of any case where the point has come up for actual decision.' It is submitted that in any event the argument has no bearing on the conclusion sought to be deduced from it. Whether or not the law of non-disclosure is stated in the language of implied term, it is evident that the parties are able, if they wish, to contract out of it; and whether they have so contracted out of it is a matter of construction that need not be affected by the terminological question whether or not the law is stated as an implied term.

(*To be concluded.*)

Glanville L. Williams.

---

[51] [1939] 1 K. B. 132. Criticisms of this decision are considered by Williams in McElroy, Impossibility of Performance, 246.

[52] [1912] 3 K. B. 614.

[53] [1941] 1 K. B. 295.

[54] Cp. the somewhat similar argument raised and rejected on the law of frustration in the *Fibrosa Case* [1942] 1 K. B. 12 at 25–6, affirmed on this point [1943] A. C. 32.

387

## LANGUAGE AND THE LAW—V.

*(Concluded from Volume 61, p. 406.)*

### § 7. The Emotive Function of Words.

So far we have been speaking chiefly of the use of words to indicate facts. There is a wealth of adjectives available to express this function of words: it has been variously described as referential, symbolic, indicative, factual, positive, informative, intellectual, representative, and scientific. In addition to this referential function words frequently have an emotive function, which in any particular context may pertain to them as well as or in place of the referential function. In the present section some general remarks will be made on the emotive function of words. The next section will consider the bearing of the emotive function on rules of law.

The distinction between the referential and emotive function is pointed out by Ogden and Richards, and has become a commonplace.[1] 'Emotive' as here used covers not only the affective but also the conative aspects of mind. It is a blanket term for every sort of pleasure-discomfort, will and desire; for every degree of instinct, sentiment and passion. It includes love, joy, hope, wonder, desire, reverence, obedience, amusement, sympathy, social, moral and religious feeling, rage, fear, grief, horror, disgust, and every other affective-volitional state. A word is said to perform an emotive function when it either expresses an affective or volitional attitude or arouses such an attitude in others. Thus an emotive word may be either an expression or an excitant of feeling or desire.

The emotive function is particularly pronounced in certain types of linguistic activity. To give some ill-assorted examples, one might instance swearing, advertising, oratory, poetry, love-making, and religion. This finding of a common element in attitudes so different may seem to some to be a depressing feat of abstraction; it links activities that are dissimilar in so many other respects. These differences are, of course, not denied, but for the moment we are concentrating on the one point of resemblance.

Apart from these specialised linguistic activities the emotive function is found also in ordinary speech and writing. All action is inspired ultimately by emotion. It is inevitable, therefore, that in our speech

---

[1] Ogden and Richards, *op. cit.* 123 ff.; Rignano, Psychology of Reasoning (London, 1923) 256–7; H. R. Huse, The Illiteracy of the Literate (New York and London, 1933), ch. 4; Karl Britton, Communication (London, 1939) 35–6; also bibliography on Logical Positivism in § 9. Other classifications attempt greater refinement. Ingraham, Swain School Lectures (London, 1903) 143 ff., distinguishes nine uses of language. Adrian Coates, A Basis of Opinion (London, 1938) 52–3, reduces these to three: the indicative, the expressive or affective, and the practical or conative. These three correspond to the three psychological attitudes, the cognitive, the affective (pleasure-pain) and the conative. The text above follows the other writers in lumping the expressive and conative functions under the term 'emotive', it being admitted that no exact line separates the two.

Hayakawa, in his entertaining book Language in Action (New York, 1941) 74–6, describes the emotive function as pre-symbolic and declares that words so used 'are the equivalent of screams, howls, purrs and gibbering'. He therefore divides emotive words into what he calls 'snarl-words' and 'purr-words'. This seems to be an unduly restricted classification.

we should both express our own emotion and attempt to satisfy our emotions by working upon the emotions of others. As Huse puts it, 'language is mainly a means to bring others to think, feel and act as we desire: it is a medium for interpsychological and social activity. The primary function is to influence: hardly anything would be said if there were no interest in others' beliefs and actions. Meaning is almost always subjected to practical aims which involve affective attitudes '.[2]

One result of this aspect of language is that every statement of fact can be put in such a way as to excite a feeling either of attraction or of repulsion, so far as language can do it. In particular, there exist in language many pairs of words that are capable of symbolizing the same referent but express emotionally opposite attitudes. While apparently expressing a trait of the thing referred to, they in fact express, at least in part, the attitude of the person making the reference. Hobbes noted this a long time ago. 'In reasoning', wrote Hobbes, 'a man must take heed of words; which besides the signification of what we imagine of their nature, have a signification also of the nature, disposition, and interest of the speaker; such as are the names of Vertues and Vices; For one man calleth *wisdome*, what another calleth *feare*; and one *cruelty*, what another *justice*; one *prodigality*, what another *magnanimity*; and one *gravity*, what another *stupidicy*, etc.'[3] The list could be greatly extended: from the language of law and politics one might instance such pairs as 'liberty' and 'licence', 'government' and 'bureaucracy', 'conservation' and 'conservatism', 'radicals' and 'reds', 'procedure' and 'technicality'. In addition to these eulogistic and dyslogistic words and phrases there are certain constructions particularly designed for emotive purposes: the imperative and (in Greek and Sanskrit) optative moods, and the auxiliaries 'must', 'may' (permissive) and 'ought'.

A distinction must now be drawn between the emotive function of particular words and the emotive function of sentences taken as a whole. An emotive sentence may contain some words that taken in themselves are not emotive. Thus, in the sentence 'You are a good boy', the words 'you' and 'boy' are purely referential, yet the sentence as a whole is emotive. It follows that when we say that a sentence is emotive we do not mean that it contains no referential words.

Conversely, a sentence may be referential as a sentence and yet contain emotive words. In such a case the sentence is both referential and emotive. Thus the sentence 'You are a good boy' is referential in so far as it asserts that the person addressed is a boy, though emotive in so far as it asserts that he is good. The statement 'You are a boy' is a statement of fact, and so referential; 'You are good' is an expression of emotion, and is not a statement of fact except in so far as it implies a standard of conduct to which the boy in fact conforms; 'you are a good boy' combines both these statements. Of course, it is the emotive element that is predominant in this particular sentence.

The commonest type of emotive sentence is the value-judgment. This is a statement of approval or disapproval, usually in the form of a generalization. Value-judgments are contrasted with referential statements, the distinguishing feature being that referential statements

[2] Huse, *op. cit.* 43.
[3] Leviathan i ch. 4.

purport to state past, present or future reality, while value-judgments merely express emotional reaction to reality. The same sentence may, however, be both a referential statement and a value-judgment.

To guard against possible misunderstanding, one should perhaps add that in speaking of the emotive function of words it is not intended to express disdain or distrust of emotion or of any of the attitudes here described as emotional. The word 'emotive' is not meant to be emotive of contempt for emotion. Emotion, that is, desire or feeling, is an inseparable part of our mental make-up. This is true not merely of some people but of all. The dispassionate scientific enquirer comes to mind as a type of person who appears on the surface to be devoid of emotion in his work; yet even he has a motive for working, and all motives belong to the emotional life. If it were possible to live at all without aim, purpose, and values, life would become empty and almost intolerable. Thus to be emotional is not to be irrational; the only irrationality is in failing to see the difference between emotion and objective fact.

It should also be pointed out that just as there is nothing to blame in emotion as such, so there is nothing to blame in the emotive use of language as such. The use of language for the purpose of stamping conduct with approval or disapproval, or of obtaining an affective response, is not necessarily objectionable. For example, it is of the highest social importance that people should react in words as well as in actions against anti-social conduct. But the emotive use of words is objectionable if, as so often, it hinders thought. The value-judgments that we make, though governed ultimately by our particular temperament, should proceed in the light of knowledge of the relevant facts. Only thus can we in the long run achieve the maximum of satisfaction of our desires. Now the use of emotive language in the presentation of facts may prevent the hearer or reader from examining the alleged facts critically. Again, language that is highly emotive but symbolically almost blank may be made a substitute for the presentation of facts. American publicists like Walter Lippmann and Thurman Arnold have declared that American politics is full of bogey words and catch phrases, which are imprecise in meaning and yet have an important influence upon the mind of the average voter. Instead of suggesting specific remedies for specific evils, political parties, according to these writers, frequently propose their policies only in terms of broad generality. Each then reviles the policy of the other, and the result is a series of sweeping condemnations and approvals, summed up in slogans and catcalls, upon which the electorate votes. How far this picture can be applied to English politics need not be considered, but that there would be an element of truth in such an application can hardly be denied. Nor can it be denied that an atmosphere of the kind described makes it difficult for the ordinary elector to think clearly and coolly about the issues involved.

These are two abuses of the emotive function of language. There is also a third, which occurs where the emotive use of words is strategically disguised as a referential statement. Instead of expressing emotion frankly in words customarily appropriated for that purpose (such as the 'ought' statement and the adjectives 'good' and 'bad'), we frequently find that it carries greater conviction if we use instead the terminology of the referential statement (such as the indicative 'is' and the adjectives 'true' and 'false'). It may even happen that the speaker is himself deluded by his own language into supposing that he is expressing a statement of fact. This tendency to dress emotive statements as referential statements is endemic in works on philosophy, sociology and jurisprudence. Just as this type of writing tends to confuse propositions of fact with definitions, so it tends to confuse propositions of fact with value-judgments. In particular, most of the subject known as political philosophy, political science, or legal theory, consists of elaborate definitions interspersed with value-judgments, the whole being disguised, usually, as a statement of fact. Much of the literature is polemical, each writer advancing his own set of definitions and value-judgments in opposition to the others. Since neither a definition nor a value-judgment is capable in the last resort of being logically refuted, no finality can be reached in such a subject.

One or two examples of this confusion must serve for many. The following is a typical sentence from a work professing to treat of sociology. 'Laws are in profession and principle enacted for the welfare of the whole community. . . . When [the majority] act on any other principle and legislate in view of a mere sectional, class or party good which is inconsistent with the good of the whole, their action is false to the nature of law and false to the spirit of obedience to law which rules in a community.'[4] Here the words 'false' and 'nature' give the appearance of a factual statement to what is in reality a value-judgment. Of course, there is no objection to a sociologist having a particular set of values—in fact, he must have them, and it is desirable that he should both express them and orient his studies in order to further them. But the reader has a right to object to these values being foisted upon him as scientific truths.

One of the commonest ways in which an emotive statement is disguised as a referential one is by means of the hypostasis of values. Thus, if a moralist who supports the retributive theory of punishment should argue that all moral wrongdoing ought to be punished, he is seen to be uttering only a personal opinion and it is perhaps unlikely that he will succeed in persuading others to accept his opinion in that unqualified form. But if he asserts that 'Justice requires all moral wrongdoing to be punished', he may appear to be stating some mysterious natural nexus between anti-social action and suffering, and this time an unreflecting person may be led into accepting the speaker's authority for what is thought to be a factual statement. Similarly, the language of natural law and natural rights is nothing more than an attempt to express values in terms derived from referential statements.

Of course, there is no harm in the hypostasis of values if it is realized on both sides that a figure of speech is being employed. But the trouble is that this is often missed. The language of Coates is not too strong when he says that the tendency to hypostasize values is 'one of the chief sources of human self-deception and irrationality, in the confusion of what is willed with what is true, the bodying forth of individual or corporate purposes and values into the structure of an eternal and transcendental Reality, the source of Creeds and Dogmas and Mytho-

[4] MacIver, Community (3rd ed., London, 1924) 143.

logies, national, economic and religious, for the sake of which as holding the one Truth, men will destroy each other and themselves, and turn their backs upon all reason and kindness '.[5]

An important aspect of the distinction between referential and emotive statements is indicated by Coates in the foregoing sentence, namely, that the criterion of truth or falsity is applicable only to the referential. If A says: 'Do not steal', it obviously makes nonsense to ask whether his command is true or false. Similarly, if A says: 'B has joined the Communist party: it is disgusting', the first statement is verifiable, so that one can intelligibly speak of it as being true or false, but the second statement is a value-judgment and is capable neither of proof nor of disproof. Value-judgments do not express observable facts, and it is impossible to deduce them from observations of facts.[6]

This proposition, that a value-judgment cannot be true or false, is so often denied that it is worth pausing to consider three sources of confusion that cause the terms 'true' and 'false' to be applied to such judgments. In the first place, a value-judgment may be true in the sense that it is a genuine expression of the feeling of the person uttering it. Although it is convenient to speak of emotive statements as though they were purely emotive, almost every emotive statement is also, in a sense, symbolic. Laughter expresses happiness and is non-symbolic, but the sentence 'Now I feel happy' expresses happiness and also symbolizes the mental state. If the mental state is as it is asserted to be, the statement can be said to be true. Similarly, in the sentence given above, the assertion 'It is disgusting' can be said to be a true statement inasmuch as it truly reflects the view of the person uttering it. However, this would here be a peculiar use of the word 'true'. In an action for defamation it would not be regarded as proving the 'truth' of a derogatory remark to show that the speaker actually entertained that value-judgment. Indeed, in all cases where it is meant to assert that a value-judgment is or is not entertained in fact, it is better to use the adjectives 'genuine' and 'feigned' than 'true' and 'untrue'.

There is another sense in which the words 'true' and 'false' are sometimes applied to value-judgments. Suppose that C, hearing the above remark of A, says: 'Your remark that B's conduct is disgusting is perfectly true'. He would mean that he himself agrees with the remark. He would be expressing emotional agreement with A. This, however, would not be verification of A's statement, in the ordinary sense of the word 'verification'. Nor would it be a verification if ten thousand other people expressed agreement with A. Yet it seems that in an action of defamation, if the issue is whether a derogatory value-judgment is true, the issue is settled by the jury making or refusing to make the same value-judgment themselves. It is clear that this is quite a different process from proving the truth of a derogatory factual statement.

[5] Adrian Coates, A Basis of Opinion (London, 1938) 54–5.

[6] The classic statement of this position is by Henri Poincaré in his Dernières Pensées (Paris, 1913) 224–5. He pointed out that a sentence in the imperative mood cannot be deduced from a sentence in the indicative mood. Since all ethical propositions are equivalent to imperatives, while the propositions of science are in the indicative mood, it follows that ethical propositions cannot be founded on science. To translate this into the language of the present article, a value-judgment cannot be deduced from a referential statement.

A third element of confusion results from a particular blend of referential and emotive statement that has been called by a recent writer an 'instrumental judgment'.[7] This writer divides judgments into three: value-judgments, existential judgments and instrumental judgments. (1) A value-judgment asserts that 'X is good or valuable in itself' (*i.e.*, without specific reference to its consequences), or that 'X ought to be done (for its own sake)', or that 'X is (intrinsically) better than Y'. (2) An existential judgment is a judgment of the form 'X exists, did exist, or will exist', 'X has property Y', 'X is a member of a class of real objects Y', or 'X causes Y'. (3) An instrumental judgment may take the verbal form of a value-judgment (such as 'X is good', or 'X ought to be done'), but its actual meaning is that 'X is good for Y', or 'X is good or valuable in that it produces Y', or 'X is more likely than Z to produce (the good) Y.' Such a judgment is the conclusion of an argument in which one of the premises is a value-judgment and one an existential judgment, thus:—

Y is good (as an end).
X causes Y.
Therefore X is good (as a means).

Here the second premise is capable of being true or false in respect of the element of causation, and so, in the same respect, is the conclusion. Many moral rules can be proved to be 'true' by showing that they tend to the preservation, happiness or welfare of humanity. But the proposition that the preservation, happiness or welfare of humanity is good, and that its extinction, or the infliction of suffering upon it, is bad, can never be proved or disproved. It is only if we take for granted a desire of the former that we can say that a moral rule is true as furthering that end, or untrue as impeding it. One can see that the dual character of instrumental judgments may easily lead to a misunderstanding of the difference between referential (existential) and value-judgments.

## § 8. The Emotive Function and the Law.

The emotive function of words has a three-fold importance for the lawyer. First, certain rules of law are so worded or designed as to avoid or make use of the emotions of those who are subject to the law. Second, all rules of law employ the emotive function as a means of social control. Third, certain rules make use of expressions the application of which to a given situation involves an emotional attitude on the part of the person making the application.

### (1) The Recognition of the Emotive Function in Particular Rules.

(a) *Legal euphemisms.* Human nature is a curious mixture of the inflammable and the sensitive. Words can engender storms of passion and shed oceans of blood; they can bring about tyranny, insurrection and war; but, without doing any of these things, the verbal pin-pricks of daily life and the subtle influence that words exercise on men's conduct can cause much silent grief. Hence the need for moderation of language, politeness, and euphemism. Every lawyer knows the verbal delicacy that

[7] E. Benoit-Smullyan, 'Value Judgments and the Social Sciences', (1945) 42 Journal of Philosophy 197.

has been maintained in lunacy matters,[8] which is now being extended to the poor.[8a] Before the late war the Depressed Areas were transformed by a stroke of the legislative pen into—the Special Areas. Then, adding a note of hope, they became 'Development Areas'.[9] The untouchables in Indian have become the 'Scheduled Castes'. In somewhat the same way the common process of 'finding a formula' is often in great part an effort to agree upon a form of words that will not arouse the susceptibilities of either of two disputing sides. Thus, in the Accession Declaration Act, 1910, Parliament, in view of the offence given to the Roman Catholic subjects of the Crown by the terms of the Declaration against Transubstantiation that the King was bound to make at his accession by the Bill of Rights, 1689, and the Act of Settlement, 1701, altered it to a milder form of words having substantially the same effect. In doing this Parliament was not itself acting out of word-superstition; it was recognizing the emotive power of words. It may be that some of the examples of apparently irrational legislation given in an earlier part of this article [10] can be justified on a similar ground.

In criminal law, the effort to destigmatize the probation order has been carried so far that it may cause difficulty in the working of legal concepts. Section 1 (1) of the Probation of Offenders Act, 1907, provides that 'where any person is charged . . . and the Court thinks that the charge is proved, . . . the Court may, without proceeding to conviction, make an order either (i) dismissing the information or charge, or (ii) discharging the offender conditionally on his entering into a recognizance'. This means that the term 'conviction' is not applied even though the offender is found guilty. In *Oaten* v. *Auty* [11] the question arose whether, when the justices have dismissed an information under the power given by this section, the defendant can appeal by way of case stated; and this in turn depended upon whether there had been a 'conviction, order, determination or other proceeding of a Court of summary jurisdiction' within section 33 of the Summary Jurisdiction Act, 1879. It was held by a majority of the Divisional Court that there had been no 'conviction' within the latter section, but the desirable outcome was reached by holding that the defendant was entitled to appeal under the concluding words ('or other proceeding') of the section. Darling J., in the course of considering the words of the Probation of Offenders Act, characterized them as 'unscientific, thoroughly illogical, and merely a concession to the modern passion for calling things what they are not'.[12] These epithets are perhaps open to some criticism, for an alteration in established usage is not itself either unscientific or illogical. The objection to

[8] Thus the Lunacy Act, 1890, is always officially referred to as 53 Vict. c. 5 (see the Schedule to the Act, Form A). The office of the Master in Lunacy is 'The Management and Administration Department' (Management of Patients' Estates Rules, 1934, No. 269, r. 8). A lunatic is a 'patient', or, at worst, a 'person of unsound mind' (cp. Mental Treatment Act, 1930, s. 20 (5)). An asylum is a 'mental hospital' (Mental Treatment Act, 1930, s. 20 (1)). The Criminal Justice Bill, 1939, proposed to change the designation 'criminal lunatic' to 'State mental patient'.

[8a] Thus by the Mental Treatment Act, 1930, s. 20 (4), a pauper lunatic is a 'rate-aided patient'. The Rushcliffe Report on legal aid for the poor recommends that the words 'assisted person' should be substituted for 'poor person' (Cmd. 6641 of 1945).

[9] Special Areas (Development and Improvement) Act, 1934; Distribution of Industry Act, 1945.

[10] (1945) 61 L. Q. R. 75.

[11] [1919] 2 K. B. 278.

[12] At p. 282.

the wording of the Act is, it is submitted, that in altering an established legal concept the draftsman ran the risk of causing difficulty in applying other rules of law that made use of that concept. In the instant case injustice was avoided only because of the lucky accident that the Summary Jurisdiction Act used alternative expressions to the term 'conviction'.[13]

If the Probation of Offenders Act had been skilfully drawn it would have declared that the word 'conviction' in any enactment should include a charge dismissed under the Act where the charge had been proved. A provision of this type is actually incorporated in the Children and Young Persons Act, 1933, s. 59. This enacts that the words 'conviction' and 'sentence' shall cease to be used in relation to children and young persons dealt with summarily, but it is added that any reference in any enactment to a person convicted, a conviction or a sentence shall, in the case of a child or young person, be construed as including a reference to a person found guilty of an offence, a finding of guilt or an order made upon such a finding.

(b) *Insult.* The irritant quality of words is recognized in certain rules relating to insulting language. As we have seen, the prohibition of blasphemy is now rested upon this ground. Insulting words or behaviour with intent to provoke a breach of the peace or whereby a breach of the peace is likely are an offence under the Public Order Act, 1936, s. 5. In contrast to these legal provisions for the shortness of human temper, it has now been settled that mere words are not, save possibly in circumstances of a most extreme and exceptional character, sufficient provocation to reduce a charge of murder to one of manslaughter: *Holmes* v. *D. P. P.*[14] As Viscount Simon expressed it, 'the proverb reminds us that hard words break no bones, and the law expects a reasonable man to endure abuse without resorting to fatal violence'. In this particular case the rule was applied not to mere words of abuse but to a referential statement having an incidental emotive effect, namely to a wife's confession of adultery.

Perhaps the most interesting legal recognition of the dual theory of linguistic meaning is in the law of defamation. A distinction is drawn between defamation and insult or abuse; the former is the legal wrong known as defamation, while the latter is not.[15] Although this distinction seems clearly to be connected with that between referential and emotive language, the exact correlation is a matter of some difficulty which cannot be gone into here.

(c) *The use of words as a stimulus.* The emotive function of words is of vast importance in social control. Present-day writers lay emphasis upon this. 'Speech', says Stern, 'is the great medium through which human co-operation is brought about.'[16]

---

[13] In another situation, similar to the above, injustice did actually occur. By s. 37 of the Criminal Justice Administration Act, 1914, the right to appeal from Petty Sessions to Quarter Sessions was confined to cases of 'conviction'; hence it did not cover persons released on probation. It was not till the Criminal Justice Act, 1925, s. 7 (1), that release upon probation was deemed to be a conviction for this purpose.

[14] [1946] 2 A. E. R. 124; 62 T. L. R. 466 (H. L.).

[15] Winfield, Text-Book of the Law of Tort, 3rd ed. § 73; Salmond, Torts, 10th ed. (ed. Stallybrass) § 99.

[16] Stern, Meaning and Change of Meaning (Göteborg, 1931) 20. Cp. Markey, Symbolic Process, ch. 12.

The marriage ceremony, designed by the church and adopted by the law, is one of the most powerfully emotive forms of words we possess. It would be wrong, of course, to say that the institution of the family depends entirely on the marriage service. The family has existed ever since animals mated and combined to protect their young. Speaking of the present day, it would be difficult to assess the relative importance of the various psychological factors that in most cases serve to keep a married couple together for life. However, it seems probable that the marriage ceremony with its mutual promises must be given a considerable part of the credit. Then there are titles of honour, the justification for which in modern society is that they are in fact highly prized and that the offer of them constitutes a cheap stimulus to the kind of effort that is considered socially desirable. Although a privilege to the few, they are not burden to the many. Finally, words, ceremonies and emblems (banners, robes, the panoply of kingship) are used to stimulate the emotion of loyalty to the established order of the community. 'From the totem pole to the national flag, from the wooden idol to God the Invisible King, from the magic word to some diluted version of Adam Smith or Bentham, symbols have been cherished by leaders, many of whom were themselves unbelievers, because they were the focal points where differences merged.' [17]

The use of emotional stimuli for the purpose of social control is not confined to particular institutions; as we shall now see, it is a characteristic of the legal system as a whole.

### (2) LEGAL RULES AS EMOTIVE STATEMENTS.

For the purpose of the following discussion propositions can be regarded as of three kinds.

(1) Referential statements or statements of fact. These are sentences that intend or pretend to state past, present or future reality. Examples are the sentences in a scientific or historical work or a work of fiction. Such sentences may or may not have an emotive element in addition to the referential.

With referential statements we may group instrumental statements, which, as we have seen, are referential in respect of the factor of causation.

(2) Tautologies, identical propositions, equations, definitions, analytical propositions—that is to say, statements that a certain symbol or group of symbols are used with the same meaning as, or with part of the meaning of, another symbol or group of symbols.

(3) Value-judgments, *i.e.*, statements of approval or disapproval. We may include with these imperatives, which are merely value-judgments expressed in a particularly forcible manner. In value-judgments there are always some individual words that are referential, but the statement as a whole does not purport to state past, present or future reality.

Let us now try to place legal rules within this scheme. A rule of law is not a referential statement. It is not meant to be a statement about what has actually happened or is happening in the world, nor is it meant exactly as a prophecy. Nor yet is it merely a tautology. There seems, then, to be only one other category in which it can fall: it must be a

[17] Walter Lippmann, Public Opinion (New York, 1922) 234.

value-judgment. This is what it turns out on inspection to be. Just as all ethics consists ultimately of value-judgments, so does all law. Every legal proposition is reducible in the last analysis to the affirmation or denial of an 'ought'; that is to say, it is reducible either to the statement that A ought to do or refrain from doing something, or else to the statement that there is no 'duty' (a hypostasized 'ought') that A shall do or refrain from doing something.[18] Thus the whole of the law consists of emotive statements. As with most other emotive statements there is a referential element, but not such as to make the statement a proposition of fact.

This is frequently denied. It is contended that the 'ought' can be eliminated by introducing into the statement a reference to the sanction behind the rule. Thus the rule against stealing can be resolved, it is said, into a threat or prophecy of punishment if the subject of the rule does steal. 'In substance always, and in form almost always, what the law says is not "Thou shall not steal", but "He that takes what isn't his'n, when he's caught will go to prison".'[19]

This does not seem to be the true view. What the law says in the case put is this (putting the matter in terms of procedure): '*If* a person steals and *if* he is prosecuted and *if* the facts are proved in the manner established by law, then the judge *ought* to pass sentence of the proper kind, and the appropriate officer *ought* to carry out the sentence.' This proposition is just as much a statement of 'ought' as the simpler proposition that people ought not to steal, only it is a conditional 'ought'. The 'ought' reappears in the sanction. Lawyers do not assert that the sanction is bound to operate. For all they know it will fail to take effect, *e.g.*, because no one happens to think of prosecuting, or because the case breaks down on some point of fact or law, or because the offender evades the punishment by escaping. In none of these cases will the lawyer be abashed in his statement of the legal rule. Nor is he even concerned to state a tendency that people who steal are usually punished. For example, he would not alter his statement of what the law 'is' (*i.e.*, of what men ought to do, according to the legal pattern) if a criminologist proved to him that more thieves escaped than were brought to justice. Finally, the legal rule 'Thou shalt not steal' cannot be translated into 'If you steal I will do my best to punish you', because a statement of a legal rule is not the same as a personal threat. There is therefore nothing for it but to say that legal rules are emotive statements. They are the particular kind of emotive statements known as value-judgments, and the particular kind of value-judgments known as normative judgments. Other normative judgments are the rules of ethics, religion and convention.

Instead of being thought of as an 'ought' statement, law is sometimes regarded as a kind of command. But even if it is so regarded, this makes no difference to the foregoing analysis. For a command is just

[18] To be explicit, Hohfeld's duties (and their correlative rights) are 'oughts', his privileges are denials of 'oughts', and his powers and immunities are reducible to statements of the way in which new 'oughts' can be created or destroyed, or assertions that they cannot be created or destroyed in particular ways.

No weight is to be attached to the objection that a rule of law is not an 'ought' but a 'must'. 'Must' is simply an emphatic 'ought'.

[19] Dowdall in (1926) 42 L. Q. R., at 456.

as much a combination of the symbolic and emotive function of words as an 'ought' statement. The nouns and verbs used may have referents, but the sentence as a whole is not a statement of fact but the expression of a wish. The words may also stimulate in the hearer the desire to obey; thus they may both express an emotion and stimulate an emotion. In fact, as already said, a command is simply a value-judgment in vigorous form.

It may be objected that to regard law as an emotive statement is false because one may state the law without feeling emotion. There is something in this objection, but not much. Take again the sentence 'It is legally wrong to steal'. Factually (*i.e.*, unemotionally), and apart from the operation of legal sanctions, all that this sentence does is to describe a state of affairs in which people do not steal. This state of affairs is linked with the conduct of the individual by the idea that the individual 'ought' to conform to the pattern so presented to him. This 'ought' can only be an expression of desire. It is true that it need not be the desire of the person stating the rule, but it must be, in some sense, somebody's desire, or else it is untrue that that is the law. For legal purposes the people whose desires are important are the judges and the law-enforcement officers. Law is a wish as to conduct maintained collectively by the judges and law-enforcement officers.

Another objection that may be advanced is that to describe both law and morality as 'oughts' is to run the two into one, and to fail to explain how a conflict can arise between them. If both law and morality are 'oughts', is it not contradictory to say that the legal 'ought' may go one way and the moral 'ought' another? The answer is that the word 'ought' represents a desire, and there may be conflicting 'oughts' in the same way as there are conflicting desires. Imagine the state of mind of a judge who regards himself as compelled by the law to give judgment against his own moral feeling. He may express himself as follows: 'In this case I regard myself as bound by the decision in *Blank* v. *Blank* to give judgment for the plaintiff, but I regard the case as one of great hardship for the defendant, and I hope that the matter may be considered by a higher Court.' Here there is evidently a conflict of desire in the mind of the judge. On the one hand he wishes to see the law observed, and thus feels himself impelled to give the judgment he does; on the other hand, he regrets the result, and wishes that the law were otherwise. Both desires arise from a feeling of public spirit, not from selfish considerations [20]; yet they are not logically contradictory.

Another case of split desire is where the law and public interest pull one way and private sympathy and interest the other. Strong as the private inclination may be, human beings are capable of subordinating it to the public interest.

> 'Be you content, fair maid;
> It is the law, not I, condemn your brother;
> Were he my kinsman, brother, or my son,
> It should be thus with him: he must die tomorrow.' [21]

[20] Where the law prevails, it is frequently because, though the judge does not approve of the law, he does desire compliance with it so long as it remains a law, because he believes that disregard of a bad law is harmful as tending to a noncompliance with law in general. There may also be less worthy reasons for a judge's preferring the law to morality—*e.g.*, his fear of the adverse opinion of his colleagues, or fear of dismissal.

[21] Measure for Measure, II, ii, 79–82.

What sort of a wish, then, is the wish expressed in the rule? It may perhaps be described as an 'official' wish. The judges and the other law-enforcement officers may not themselves feel the wish, but they have made up their minds to pretend to feel it, or at any rate to act for most purposes as though they feel it. The statement that 'it is the law, not I, condemn your brother' is only a poetic way of saying: 'Although I condemn your brother it is not because I desire his death in itself, but because I desire to act in accordance with the rules of law'.

To sum up: a rule of law is a pattern of conduct for the individual. Every member of the community may not desire this pattern to be followed, but some important members of the community (judges and other law-enforcement officers) either desire the pattern to be followed or at least conduct themselves as though they do desire it. In any case the rule of law, whatever the intention of its originator, does tend to produce an attitude of obedience in the subject; thus whether or not intended to *express* emotion, it certainly *arouses* it.

The foregoing view of the law as a system of 'oughts' gives the clue to the vexed question of the nature of legal rights and duties. Many attempts have been made to state in clearer language the nature of these concepts. In most cases the attempt has taken the form of equating rights and duties with empirical mental facts. For instance, Vinogradoff [22] regarded a legal right as a kind of claim. Now a claim is a psychological fact, a state of mind; but legal rights can 'exist' in people who do not know of their existence, and so have not the mental attitude of claim.[23] Thus the definition breaks down. Lundstedt [24] regarded a legal right as an 'actual situation', but that is clearly erroneous; factually, and apart from future legal proceedings, there is no difference between a person legally exercising a hotly-disputed right of way and a trespasser. Jhering and Salmond translated the word 'right' into the word 'interest', a legal right being an interest recognized by law [25]; but the meaning of the word 'interest' is so obscure that it does not help. If it refers to psychological desire, the trouble is that one may have rights that one does not desire. Holmes approached more nearly to the truth when he described a legal right as 'the hypostasis of a prophecy—the imagination of a substance supporting the fact that the public force will be brought to bear upon those who do things said to contravene it'.[26] One difficulty is, however, as already said, that lawyers who state a legal rule do not intend to prophesy that it will be enforced in any particular case. All these definitions are open to the objection that in attempting to define rights and duties in factual terms they neglect the emotive function of these words. The true view is that legal rights and duties are the hypostasis not of a factual prophecy but of the legal 'ought'. The sentence 'There is a legal duty not to steal' is the equivalent of the sentence 'There is a legal rule that one ought not to steal'; and this again is equivalent to 'It is legally wrong to steal'. Thus legal rules do not 'recognize' or 'create' or 'enforce' rights and

[22] 'The Foundations of a Theory of Rights' (1924), 34 Yale L. J. 60, reprinted in his Collected Papers ii 367.

[23] *Cooper* v. *Phibbs* (1867), L. R. 2 H. L. 149.

[24] Superstition or Rationality in Action for Peace? (London, 1925) 118.

[25] Jhering, Geist des römischen Rechts, 4th ed. iii 339; Salmond, Jurisprudence, 7th ed. § 72.

[26] Holmes, Collected Legal Papers (New York, 1921) 313. Cp. *ibid.* 167 ff.

duties; on the contrary, certain legal rules are themselves rights and duties. Rights and duties are mental states, but they are not states of mind of the subjects of the rights and duties; they are states of mind of the persons asserting the legal rules. The crux of the difficulty in understanding the words 'right' and 'duty' is that they express a desire by the grammatical means commonly used for the signification of a material thing.

### (8) The Uncertainty in the Application of Legal Rules Brought About by the Use of Emotive Words.

The words 'right', 'duty' and 'wrong' have an emotive function, but since they are merely auxiliaries for indicating that a standard of conduct is involved they do not in themselves blur the meaning of a sentence. However, there are other emotive terms, used in the formulation of rules of law, which purport to express the legal standard itself, and thus introduce an unusual amount of subjectivity into the interpretation of the rule. The possibility of attaching a relatively certain meaning to such emotive terms depends upon the extent to which different people react alike to the same situation.

Instances of this class of emotive terms are the words 'just' and 'justice', the former of which is coming into increasing favour among Parliamentary draftsmen.[27] Another is the phrase 'public policy'. The rule that a contract is void if against public policy, except so far as this rule has been crystallized into more specific rules, tells one comparatively little, for it is offset by the rule or proposition that the enforcement of contract is itself required by public policy. Thus the supposed rule is simply a warning that in certain cases the judge's value-judgment may be in favour of denying a remedy in contract rather than granting it. It is well known that, under cover of applying the so-called rule that a contract against public policy is void, judges' opinions have changed greatly during the passage of the years as to what public policy requires. Within limits, however, predictions can be founded upon the rule, because the judge's reaction to certain types of situation can be forecast, particularly where there are precedents in point.[28]

The same is true of the defence of necessity in tort and crime. In one sense of the term it is never 'necessary' to do a particular act; there is always an alternative, even though the alternative involves the death of oneself or somebody else. A person who breaks a general rule of law on the ground of necessity is really claiming to further some value that in the particular circumstances of the case contradicts the value of obedience to the general rule of law. For this reason the defence is looked upon with suspicion by the judges, but there are cases where it is recognized, and these cases, like cases of public policy in contract, provide neat illustrations of an unformulated social value-judgment prevailing over the formulated value-judgment that we call the law.

Certain rules of law and standard forms of contract require that a

[27] Law Reform (Married Women and Tortfeasors) Act, 1935, s. 6 (2); Inheritance (Family Provision) Act, 1938, s. 1 (1); Law Reform (Frustrated Contracts) Act, 1943, s. 1 (2), (3); Law Reform (Contributory Negligence) Act, 1945, s. 1 (1).

[28] It is indeed said that the Courts are no longer free to add to the heads of public policy. The authorities are collected in Cheshire and Fifoot, Law of Contracts 222–3. But the existing heads are sufficiently vague to leave much room for judicial discretion.

person shall not act 'arbitrarily',[29] and this word is used for conduct of which we disapprove. There seems to be no difference of significance, in general, between 'arbitrary' and 'discretionary', except that the former word has a hostile colouring whereas the latter may be entirely non-emotional.

Again, the contrast between 'important' and 'unimportant' is generally emotional. If A and B dispute which feature of an agreed situation is the more important, there is no scientific way of resolving the dispute, unless, of course, the parties agree to give the term 'important' some special referential meaning. In the absence of such agreement there is no objective test of importance; everything becomes important that we choose for the moment to regard as important.

The notion of importance appears in the law under all sorts of disguises. Thus the difference between conditions and warranties is that a condition is 'fundamental', 'essential', 'substantial', 'basic', and 'goes to the root' of the contract, while a warranty is 'collateral'. All these words are in this context simply synonyms for 'important' and 'unimportant' respectively.[30] Similarly, the rule is that a person who in breach of contract fails to perform the whole of his part can recover nothing, unless his failure is not substantial [31]—*i.e.*, is unimportantly small. The same meaning occurs in connexion with riparian owners, who are entitled to take water for riparian purposes provided, in general, that the stream is not thereby substantially diminished.[32] In patent law there is a distinction between the amendment of a patent specification and a substantially different claim;[33] and 'substantially different' means 'different in an important respect'. In the law of settlements of land, casual repairs must be paid for out of income but improvements can be debited to capital, and repairs are improvements if they substantially add to the value of the property.[34] We have already discussed the problems involved in applying these words of approximation,[35] and here it is necessary only to observe that their application is a matter of feeling, that is to say, of emotion.

In questions of causation lawyers distinguish one cause as 'the' cause of an occurrence, and give it a distinguishing name such as the 'direct' cause or the 'immediate' cause. None of the adjectives used can be taken in its usual meaning, and they all appear to be synonyms for 'important'. Scientifically, it is impossible to distinguish between causes merely in terms of importance; every event has several causes, and each of these causes has itself several causes, and so back to the beginnings

[29] Burrow's Words and Phrases, *s.v.*; *Roberts* v. *Hopwood*, [1925] A. C. 578 at 590.

[30] It is not asserted that they are so in all contexts. 'Essential' often means not important but indispensable. Again the proposition that the 'substance' and not the form of an instrument is to be regarded (*e.g.*, Alpe, Stamp Duties, 23rd. ed. 2) means that one must look at the meaning of the instrument as a whole, not at the usual meanings of particular words in it.

[31] *Dakin* v. *Lee*, [1916] 1 K. B. 566; *Harland & Wolff* v. *Burstall & Co.* (1901), 84 L. T. 324; *Wilensko, etc.* v. *Fenwick & Co.*, [1938] 3 A. E. R. 429 at 433; (1941) 57 L. Q. R. 493–4.

[32] *Per* Lord Cairns L.C. in *Swindon Waterworks Co.* v. *Wilts. & Berks. Canal Navigation Co.* (1875), L. R. 7 H. L. 697 at 704.

[33] *Per* Warrington L.J. in *Re British Thomson-Houston Co.'s Patent* (1919), 36 R. P. C. 251 at 264.

[34] *Re Smith*, [1930] 1 Ch. 88 at 101.

[35] (1945) 61 L. Q. R. 181 ff.

of time; and no one of these causes is objectively more 'important' than another. However, there are a few relatively definite legal rules for determining the legal cause, and to the extent that these rules apply the question is removed from the sphere of emotion to one of objective fact.

The legal distinction between principal and accessory is another form of the same distinction. We say that the button is accessory to the shirt because we regard the shirt as more important than the button; if we had a very expensive button we might regard the shirt as accessory to it. In *Yousoupoff* v. *Metro-Goldwyn-Mayer* (1934)[36] Slesser L.J. held that in a sound film the sound is ancillary to the vision. Possibly this was because the silent film was invented first. In the case of television, it may well be held that the vision is ancillary to the sound.

In general, a nuisance is not actionable unless unreasonable in degree. The word 'unreasonable' here is an appeal not so much to observation and reason as to emotion. There is a certain factual element in the rule, in that the application of it depends to some extent on our knowledge of how much discomfort the ordinary person puts up with. But it seems that the Court is not finally bound to enforce only the average standard of comfort, and thus, in the last resort, the application of the rule is a matter of emotion.

The law of negligence, despite the misleading language in the books about the 'reasonable man', seems to involve the application not of a fixed but of a variable subjective standard. The standard is not that of the average man determined statistically but (seemingly) that of the ideal man—in others words, it is the standard approved by the jury or judge in the circumstances.[37] The word 'reasonable' in this context certainly does not refer to selfish reason, for the reasonable man is expected to exert himself a great deal for the sake of others. It would express the conception more nearly to call him not the reasonable man but the ethical or moral man, though this would in turn be open to objection because the legal duty of care is in some respects lower than the generally-accepted ethical duty.

It will be seen from the last paragraph that a question of value-judgment may pass in legal terminology under the name of a 'question of fact' and be left to the jury to settle. The question in negligence depends not merely upon findings of fact but upon the evaluation of the findings; yet it is left to the jury. On the other hand, some value-judgments may be for the judge. Thus the question of public policy in contract involves the making of a value-judgment, and it is a question for the judge.

It is not surprising to find that these rules involving emotional attitudes are often uncertain and difficult to apply. This is because the emotional reaction of the lawyer who advises on their application is not necessarily the same as that of the judge or jury who finally determines the matter, and because the emotions of the judge or jury are not always predictable. Within limits, however, they are predictable, because within limits human beings make similar emotional responses.

[36] 50 T. L. R. 581 at 587.

[37] Cp. Salmond, Torts, 10th ed. (ed. Stallybrass) 437; Underhill, Torts, 15th ed. (ed. Sutton) 157; Wurzel in The Science of Legal Method 406–7.

## § 9. Syntactical Meaning.

Hitherto, apart from the discussion of value-judgments, we have been concerned chiefly with the meaning of individual words. It is now necessary to make some remarks upon syntactical meaning, the meaning of words taken together, as in phrases, propositions and questions.

It is possible to refer to the same referent in two phrases or sentences composed of quite different words. An illustration would be the phrases 'the King of England' and 'the owner of Buckingham Palace'. Whether these two phrases have the same meaning is a verbal question which does not admit of a monosyllabic answer. For a hearer who knows the relevant facts and so is able in each case to make the desired reference, it may be said that they have in a sense the same meaning, though the thought-process is different in each case. But if the hearer does not realize that the owner of Buckingham Palace is the King, the two phrases have not the same meaning for him, in the sense of leading him to the same referent. This is another illustration of the importance of considering not meaning in the abstract but only meaning in relation to a particular speaker or hearer.[38]

The fact that it is possible to make a reference by various routes underlies the lawyer's distinction between general and specific gifts in wills. If a testator devizes 'my house Crossways', this is a specific devize; but if he devizes 'all my real property' this is a general devize, even though Crossways is the sum total of his real property. The distinction between the two cases lies not in the intended referent but in the mode of reference. The general gift expressly refers to the whole of the testator's real or personal property, or to the whole of his property, and does not expressly say that the particular property in question constitutes the whole of such property. The specific gift refers to property that may on the wording of the will constitute only a part of the testator's real or personal estate.[39]

Ogden and Richards direct their main attention to the meaning of individual words. They appear to regard syntactical meaning as a product or synthesis of the meaning of the separate words employed, when interpreted in the light of rules of grammar. In some cases this is an adequate explanation, but there are difficulties. One difficulty is that some words used in a sentence have no referents, or, if they have referents, refer only to language itself. Examples are 'is', 'than', 'not', 'true', and 'false'.[40] Other writers, therefore, approach the problem differently. They occupy themselves with the meaning of complete questions and propositions. Of these writers the best-known belong to the vigorous and subtle school of thought that has become known as the Vienna Circle or the Logical Positivists.

Before coming to the work of this school it is convenient to mention the views of an American physicist, P. W. Bridgman, who seems to have arrived independently at the central tenet of Logical Positivism. In his book, *The Logic of Modern Physics* (1928), Bridgman urged that for the

[38] Ogden and Richards, from whose work the above illustration is taken (*op cit.* 92), seem to neglect this aspect of the question. They say merely that the two phrases have the same referent but do not symbolize the same reference. 'Reference' here seems to mean 'process of thought'.

[39] For a discussion of the technical complexities of this distinction see Jarman, Wills, 7th ed. ii 915 ff, 1001 ff.

[40] B. Russell, An Inquiry Into Meaning and Truth (London, 1940) 62 ff.

scientist (he was not pretending to speak for other people) a question has meaning only if it can be verified in sense-experience, *i.e.*, only if a physical operation can be performed that will give an answer to it. With many questions it is impossible as yet to perform any experiment or operation in order to test them, and so, until such an operation be discovered, the questions in his view remain without meaning. 'Many of the questions asked about social and philosophical subjects will be found to be meaningless when examined from the point of view of operations.'

This attitude has a certain practical merit in saving us from bothering our heads over questions that in the present state of knowledge are insoluble, but most of us would dissent from the idea that a question has meaning only if it can be experimentally tested. The question 'Are there craters on the other side of the moon?' is significant, even though no answer to it is yet possible. This is admitted by the Logical Positivists,[41] who weaken Bridgman's assertion by saying that it is enough if a sentence (whether question or statement) is *in principle* verifiable in sense-experience, even though it cannot actually be so verified, and even though it may be empirically false. At the same time, these writers strengthen Bridgman's theory in another respect, for apparently they do not adopt his limitation of the theory as a theory for scientists only. In general, they seem to take the view that it is valid for everyone. No sentence, by whomsoever uttered, says anything unless it be empirically verifiable, and it is verifiable if, and only if, we know the conditions under which the sentence would be true and the conditions under which it would be false.

This theory, in the hands of the Logical Positivists, becomes a weapon of tremendous destructive power. One of its consequences is that metaphysical discussion becomes regarded as nonsense, for it can never, in any conceivable circumstances, be put to the test of sensuous observation. Metaphysics claims to communicate knowledge about something that is beyond experience. As a result, it consists of 'sentences which fail to conform to the conditions under which alone a sentence can be literally significant'.[42] 'Metaphysicians cannot avoid making their propositions non-verifiable, because if they made them verifiable, the decision about the truth or falsehood of their doctrines would depend upon experience

[41] Logical Positivism was anticipated by writers like Hume, and also by Bentham in his Theory of Fictions, but in its modern form is generally attributed to the inspiration of Wittgenstein, who was himself influenced by Russell. The Vienna Circle was formed by Moritz Schlick in 1928, other members being Carnap, Frank, Hahn, Neurath and Waismann. An English exponent of the theory is A. J. Ayer. Mnch of the literature is extremely subtle, but Rudolf Carnap's Philosophy and Logical Syntax (London, 1935) and Ayer's Language, Truth and Logic (London, 1936) are readable. Among other publications in English are Carnap's Philosophy and Logical Syntax (London, 1935), Logical Syntax of Language (London, 1937), and his new series entitled Studies in Semantics (Cambridge, Mass., 1942– ); Carnap, 'Testability and Meaning' (1936) 3 Philosophy of Science 419, (1937) 4 *ibid.* 1; Ayer, Foundations of Empirical Knowledge (London, 1940), particularly pp. 92–112; also various articles in the International Encyclopaedia of Unified Science (Chicago, 1938– ). For critical discussions see L. S. Stebbing, 'Logical Positivism and Analysis', (1933) 19 Proceedings of the British Academy 53; J. R. Weinberg, An Examination of Logical Positivism (London, 1936); A. D. Ritchie, 'Errors of Logical Positivism' (1937) 12 Philosophy 47; Charles W. Morris, Logical Positivism, Pragmatism and Scientific Empiricism (Paris, 1937); W. M. Urban, Language and Reality (London, 1939) 208 ff.; Olaf Stapledon, Philosophy and Living (Pelican Books, 1939) ii 327–335.

[42] Ayer, Language, Truth and Logic 19.

and therefore belong to the region of empirical science. This consequence they wish to avoid, because they pretend to teach knowledge which is of a higher level than that of empirical science. Thus they are compelled to cut all connexion between their propositions and experience; and precisely by this procedure they deprive them of any sense.'[43] As an illustration, Ayer quotes Bradley's sentence: 'the Absolute enters into, but is itself incapable of, evolution and progress'. This, he says, being intended neither as a tautology nor as a proposition that is capable of being verified, must be unintelligible even to its author.[44] A lawyer may add that much continental literature passing under the name of legal philosophy becomes meaningless by the same test.[45]

In its rejection of metaphysics Logical Positivism is gratifying to the Anglo-American jurist because it confirms the strong suspicion that he has already felt regarding the value of metaphysical speculation, particularly metaphysical speculation about law. If the theory be accepted, it offers a means of escape from the perennial problems of philosophy, for it shows (1) that many statements of a philosophical or metaphysical character are neither true nor false but literally senseless, and also (2) that many statements that seem to be opposed to each other are identical in meaning and differ only verbally. Indeed, it has been a principal task of the Logical Positivists to expose the pseudo-problems, the *Scheinprobleme*, of philosophy, and many of their specific criticisms of these problems are extremely effective.

As against these advantages there is one consequence, or suggested consequence, of the Logical-Positivist theory that is not likely to be acceptable to the average lawyer, namely, its demolition of religion and ethics. Religion is a branch of metaphysics and thus falls with it, all propositions relating to a transcendent god, or even apparently to a life after death, becoming mere gibberish. Similarly, the statements of a moralist concerning what is 'good', 'right', or 'just', or about what one 'ought' to do, become either a statement of the moral feeling of a particular society, or else devoid of factual content, being in the latter case only expressions of emotion, devoid of what Carnap calls 'theoretical sense'.[46]

Attractive though it is in some respects, Logical Positivism is open to several objections. Some of these its exponents have endeavoured to answer, though without producing general conviction. One objection is that, even in the realm of physics, it is somewhat defeatist to pronounce a question meaningless merely because at the moment one cannot think of a way of answering it. At one time physicists considered it meaningless to ask for the weight of a single atom. Today the weight of an atom can be stated to within its ten-thousandth part.[47] On the whole, however, the theory works well enough for empirical propositions; the serious difficulty is in connexion with value-judgments. Suppose that A says to B: 'You ought to be honest'. It seems to be using words in a most

[43] Carnap, Philosophy and Logical Syntax 17–18.

[44] *Op. cit.* 22.

[45] The Logical Positivists are not the first to assert that metaphysics is a useless speculation. That had been asserted by the Comtists. The distinguishing feature of the Logical Positivists is that they assert metaphysics to be not merely useless but meaningless

[46] Philosophy and Logical Syntax 25.

[47] Max Planck, The Philosophy of Physics (London, 1936) 29.

unusual sense to say that this sentence is a meaningless noise. Even granting that it is an expression of emotion, it is not 'meaningless' in the usual meaning of that word. The effect of the sentence upon B might conceivably be to turn him from a career of crime and make him honest; it is an unusual and inconvenient use of words to say that a sentence designed to have a specific effect on the conduct of another, and actually having that effect, is meaningless.

The truth is that the Logical Positivists do not explain the meaning of the word 'meaning' in its present usage, but merely propose a new usage. Logical Positivism hinges upon an unusual definition of the word 'meaning' which, like every other definition, must be taken as a postulate and cannot be proved.[48] If anyone likes to deny the definition he immediately becomes free to say that the rules of ethics and the articles of religion are significant. Thus it turns out that the attempt of the Logical Positivists to legislate ethics and religion out of existence depends upon a mere juggling with definitions. It is somewhat odd that the very writers who take delight in unmasking the verbal controversies of philosophy should thus raise an issue as to the meaning of 'meaning' that is itself a verbal one. An even odder feature of the situation is that, as has been frequently pointed out, the empirical criterion of the Logical Positivists is itself by its own rule meaningless.

The interest of this for the lawyer is that law, like the rules of ethics and religion, is a statement of 'ought', and therefore the 'meaning' of a rule of law stands or falls with the 'meaning' of a rule of ethics or religion. Since it is obvious to every lawyer that a rule of law has meaning, in any ordinary sense of the word 'meaning', it follows that a lawyer must reject the definition of meaning advanced by the Logical Positivists as a complete definition of the word.

However, it needs only a slight modification of Logical Positivism to produce a theory that will concede meaning to a value-judgment, and therefore, to a rule of law. As already explained, a rule of law, like other value-judgments, contains two elements, a referential and an emotive. The referential element indicates the state of affairs that is desired or not desired, and this referential element can be separated from the desire and stated as a (probably false) proposition of fact. Thus the rule 'Do not steal' can be expressed as the (false) proposition of fact that people do not steal. If the rule against stealing is obeyed this proposition of fact will become true. Since the proposition of fact derived from the value-judgment is capable of being true or false, and is theoretically capable of being verified, it has meaning even on the strictest tenets of Logical Positivism. It is but a short step from this to admit that the value-judgment into which it is compounded has meaning also.[49]

This same argument can be put more vividly in another way. Suppose that a man were to write a book describing a Utopia. Such a work would have meaning in the same way as any other work of fiction; none

[48] The Logical Positivists seem sometimes to be conscious that their definition is unusual. Thus Carnap, though he usually treats of meaning *simpliciter*, when discussing ethical sentences contents himself with saying that they have no 'theoretical sense'. The use of the qualifying adjective seems to imply that they may have sense other than theoretical sense, but he does not clearly explain what this is. See also the same writer's remarks in The Unity of Science 26.

[49] Cp. Jörgen Jörgensen, 'Imperatives and Logic', (1938) 7 Erkenntnis 288 at 291, who reaches the same conclusion for sentences in the imperative mood.

the less so because the facts stated are untrue. Suppose that after writing it the author expressed a wish in the last sentence that it were all true. That would be the expression of an emotion. Now, if the book had been written with 'ought' throughout, instead of in the indicative mood, the expression of emotion would have been put into the book; but otherwise the analysis would be the same.

GLANVILLE L. WILLIAMS.

# [5]



## THE THEORY OF LEGAL INTERPRETATION.

THE paper upon the Principles of Legal Interpretation by Mr. F. Vaughan Hawkins, reprinted in Professor Thayer's recently published and excellent Preliminary Treatise on Evidence, induces me to suggest what seems to me to be the theory of our rules of interpretation, — a theory which I think supports Lord Wensleydale and the others whom Mr. Hawkins quotes and disapproves, if I correctly understand their meaning and his.

It is true that in theory any document purporting to be serious and to have some legal effect has one meaning and no other, because the known object is to achieve some definite result. It is not true that in practice (and I know no reason why theory should disagree with the facts) a given word or even a given collocation of words has one meaning and no other. A word generally has several meanings, even in the dictionary. You have to consider the sentence in which it stands to decide which of those meanings it bears in the particular case, and very likely will see that it there has a shade of significance more refined than any given in the wordbook. But in this first step, at least, you are not troubling yourself about the idiosyncrasies of the writer, you are considering simply the general usages of speech. So when you let whatever galvanic current may come from the rest of the instrument run through the particular sentence, you still are doing the same thing.

How is it when you admit evidence of circumstances and read the document in the light of them? Is this trying to discover the particular intent of the individual, to get into his mind and to bend what he said to what he wanted? No one would contend that such a process should be carried very far, but, as it seems to me, we do not take a step in that direction. It is not a question of tact in drawing a line. We are after a different thing. What happens is this. Even the whole document is found to have a certain play in the joints when its words are translated into things by parol evidence, as they have to be. It does not disclose one meaning conclusively according to the laws of language. Thereupon we ask, not what this man meant, but what those words would mean in the mouth of a normal speaker of English, using them in the circumstances in which they were used, and it is to the end of answering this last question that we let in evidence as to what the circumstances were. But the normal speaker of English is merely a special variety, a literary form, so to speak, of our old friend the prudent man. He is external to the particular writer, and a reference to him as the criterion is simply another instance of the externality of the law.

But then it is said, and this is thought to be the crux, In the case of a gift of Blackacre to John Smith, when the donor owned two Blackacres and the directory reveals two John Smiths, you may give direct evidence of the donor's intention, and it is only an anomaly that you cannot give the same evidence in every case. I think, on the contrary, that the exceptional rule is a proof of the instinctive insight of the judges who established it. I refer again to the theory of our language. By the theory of our language, while other words may mean different things, a proper name means one person or thing and no other. If language perfectly performed its function, as Bentham wanted to make it, it would point out the person or thing named in every case. But under our random system it sometimes happens that your name is *idem sonans* with mine, and it may be the same even in spelling. But it never means you or me indifferently. In theory of speech your name means you and my name means me, and the two names are different. They are different words. *Licet idem sit nomen, tamen diversum est propter diversitatem personæ.*[1] In such a case we let in evidence of intention not to help out what theory recognizes as an uncertainty of speech, and to read what the writer meant into what he has tried but failed to say, but, recognizing that he has spoken with theoretic certainty, we inquire what he meant in order to find out what he has said. It is on this ground that there is no contract when the proper name used by one party means one ship, and that used by the other means another.[2] The mere difference of intent as such is immaterial. In the use of common names and words a plea of different meaning from that adopted by the court would be bad, but here the parties have said different things and never have expressed a contract. If the donor, instead of saying "Blackacre," had said

[1] Bract. 190 *a*.

[2] Raffles *v.* Wichelhaus, 2 H. & C. 906. See Mead *v.* Phenix Insurance Co., 158 Mass. 124; Hanson *v.* Globe Newspaper Co., 159 Mass. 293, 305.

"my gold watch" and had owned more than one, inasmuch as the words, though singular, purport to describe any such watch belonging to the speaker, I suppose that no evidence of intention would be admitted. But I dare say that evidence of circumstances sufficient to show that the normal speaker of English would have meant a particular watch by the same words would be let in.

I have stated what I suppose to be our general theory of construction. It remains to say a few words to justify it. Of course, the purpose of written instruments is to express some intention or state of mind of those who write them, and it is desirable to make that purpose effectual, so far as may be, if instruments are to be used. The question is how far the law ought to go in aid of the writers. In the case of contracts, to begin with them, it is obvious that they express the wishes not of one person but of two, and those two adversaries. If it turns out that one meant one thing and the other another, speaking generally, the only choice possible for the legislator is either to hold both parties to the judge's interpretation of the words in the sense which I have explained, or to allow the contract to be avoided because there has been no meeting of minds. The latter course not only would greatly enhance the difficulty of enforcing contracts against losing parties, but would run against a plain principle of justice. For each party to a contract has notice that the other will understand his words according to the usage of the normal speaker of English under the circumstances, and therefore cannot complain if his words are taken in that sense.[1]

Different rules conceivably might be laid down for the construction of different kinds of writing. In the case of a statute, to turn from contracts to the opposite extreme, it would be possible to say that as we are dealing with the commands of the sovereign the only thing to do is to find out what the sovereign wants. If supreme power resided in the person of a despot who would cut off your hand or your head if you went wrong, probably one would take every available means to find out what was wanted. Yet in fact we do not deal differently with a statute from our way of dealing with a contract. We do not inquire what the legislature meant; we ask only what the statute means. In this country, at least, for constitutional reasons, if for no other, if the same legisla-

[1] In Nash *v.* Minnesota Title Insurance & Trust Co., 163 Mass. 574, I thought that this principle should be carried further than the majority of the court were willing to go.

ture that passed it should declare at a later date a statute to have a meaning which in the opinion of the court the words did not bear, I suppose that the declaratory act would have no effect upon intervening transactions unless in a place and case where retrospective legislation was allowed. As retrospective legislation it would not work by way of construction except in form.

So in the case of a will. It is true that the testator is a despot, within limits, over his property, but he is required by statute to express his commands in writing, and that means that his words must be sufficient for the purpose when taken in the sense in which they would be used by the normal speaker of English under his circumstances.

I may add that I think we should carry the external principle of construction even further than I have indicated. I do not suppose that you could prove, for purposes of construction as distinguished from avoidance, an oral declaration or even an agreement that words in a dispositive instrument making sense as they stand should have a different meaning from the common one; for instance, that the parties to a contract orally agreed that when they wrote five hundred feet it should mean one hundred inches, or that Bunker Hill Monument should signify Old South Church.[1] On the other hand, when you have the security of a local or class custom or habit of speech, it may be presumed that the writer conforms to the usage of his place or class when that is what a normal person in his situation would do. But these cases are remote from the point of theory upon which I started to speak.

It may be, after all, that the matter is one in which the important thing, the law, is settled, and different people will account for it by such theory as pleases them best, as in the ancient controversy whether the finder of a thing which had been thrown away by the owner got a title in privity by gift, or a new title by abandonment. That he got a title no one denied. But although practical men generally prefer to leave their major premises inarticulate, yet even for practical purposes theory generally turns out the most important thing in the end. I am far from saying that it might not make a difference in the old question to which I have referred.

*Oliver Wendell Holmes.*

[1] Goode *v.* Riley, 153 Mass. 585, 586.

[6]



## STATUTORY INTERPRETATION

ANGLO-AMERICAN law is in a fair way of becoming statutory, not by a great act of summation like the *Bürgerliches Gesetzbuch* or the Swiss Code, but piecemeal by the relentless annual or biennial grinding of more than fifty legislative machines. At any rate, in a constantly increasing number of litigated cases, the point of departure is as likely as not to be a statute, the effect of which is to be estimated, the meaning discovered, and the applicability affirmed or rejected.[1] That is, of course, particularly true in the United States courts, but it is evident that a great many states which speak as though the common law scarcely allowed of modification do in fact find themselves compelled to discuss the wording of enactments in more and more cases. That they do so reluctantly is a part of the older tradition, but it is hard to see how this attitude can be successfully maintained for any length of time.

When the work of the American Law Institute reaches its final stage and is available in printed volumes for lawyers and courts, there will be a huge body of quasi-statutory law to add to the bulk of our statutes. The fact that the Restatements are not statutory in form, that they make no pretensions to legislative authority and in fact deprecate any attempt to ascribe such authority to them, will probably be of little effect. Some courts will certainly apply to them whatever method or technique they have been accustomed to use in the case of statutes.

In Continental Europe, an accepted technique, as we might expect, has long been developed.[2] Even where "gaps in the law"

---

[1] If we omit the CENTURY DIGEST because the constant increase of jurisdictions before 1897 makes comparison difficult, we find that in the first DECENNIAL DIGEST (1897–1906), 88 columns were devoted to statutory construction, in the second (1907–1916), 194 columns, and in the third (1917–1926), 268 columns.

[2] It is next to impossible to list even the most important of the works of Swiss, German, French, and Italian jurists which present the Continental theories of statutory interpretation. Fortunately, almost any one contains full bibliographies. Much material is collected in: MANICK, *s.v. Auslegung* in 1 HANDWÖRTERBUCH DER RECHTSWISSENSCHAFT (1926) 429 *et seq.* In French, there is the almost classical book of GÉNY, MÉTHODE D'INTERPRÉTATION ET SOURCES EN DROIT PRIVÉ POSITIF (2d

are admitted and the completeness of the statute rejected,[3] it is assumed that the gaps will occur rarely, and that, for the most part, there will be a code provision applicable to the question before the court. The method, the professed method, of applying the code provision is somewhat as follows. The provision is quoted. If necessary, it is interpreted. That is to say, the "meaning" is discovered, generally by consulting the "materials," the debates in the legislature, the reports of commissions, and the like. These sources are declared necessary when there is an apparent or latent ambiguity. With the meaning thus clarified, the contentions of the two parties are examined, and it is shown that the statute by logical deduction will cover the one and not the other.

That this is not always the true order of events is evident even to those courts which announce their decisions somewhat in this form, or which imply a sequence of this sort. They scarcely conceal from themselves or from their readers that the order is in fact almost the reverse, that a choice has for one reason or another been made and that sections of the code have then been sought to justify that choice: that an ambiguity has been discovered and an interpretation selected after — rather than before — the effect of such an interpretation on the decision was known. This is called

ed. 1919). By the side of this critical study we may place the practical handbook of FABREGUETTES, LA LOGIQUE JUDICIARE (1914) 366–92, in which the precise judicial phrases used in interpretation are set forth. *Cf.* VAN DER EYCKEN, MÉTHODE POSITIVE DE L'INTERPRÉTATION JURIDIQUE (1907); JANSSEN, DAS WESEN DER GESETZESBILDUNG (1910); REICHEL, GESETZ UND RICHTERSPRUCH (1915); BONNECASE, L'ÉCOLE DE L'EXÉGÈSE EN DROIT CIVIL (2d ed. 1924); STERNBERG, EINFÜHRUNG IN DIE RECHTSWISSENSCHAFT (1912) 123–42; DEGNI, L'INTERPRETAZIONE DELLA LEGGE (2d ed. 1909). Perhaps, as a final reference, we may add the acute and sensible remarks in 1 PERREAU, TECHNIQUE DE LA JURISPRUDENCE EN DROIT PRIVÉ (1923) 260–374. The extent to which a sociologic theory of law can be developed under a system primarily statutory may be seen from the article of Professors Kantorowicz and Patterson, *Legal Science — A Summary of its Methodology* (1928) 28 COL. L. REV. 679–707. Indeed, the selections in THE SCIENCE OF LEGAL METHOD (IX Mod. Leg. Phil. Ser. 1917), from many Continental writers, are all illustrations of problems of interpretation under a law deemed for the most part to be statutory.

[3] For a fairly full statement of the "gap" theory and an ample bibliography, see COSENTINI, LA RÉFORME DE LA LÉGISLATION CIVILE (French transl. 1913) Pt. II, c. 1, at 223–78. The Italian original appeared in 1911 and is somewhat less complete. For American readers, reference may be made to Kantorowicz and Patterson, *supra* note 2, at 699–703.

cryptosociology, a term apparently invented by Ernst Fuchs.[4] It is not a very good description of the process of searching for a major premise, but the frequency of the act is beyond question.

Yet in a number of cases, the process of the application of statutes is quite likely to have been in the order which courts assume, and in almost every case it is recast into that order. And since what might be called judicial epistemology has a real importance in itself, the technique of interpretation is never negligible. We must remember that when a statute is as well known in its actual phraseology as the German, French, and Swiss Codes are known to judges and practitioners in those countries, a great many situations will almost automatically stimulate the recollection of some particular section, even if the resemblance between the situation to be judged and that contemplated by the code is only partial. In every case, however, the process of adjusting the statute to the case will be called good or bad according to the skill shown in the adjustment. It is idle to deny that to a trained profession, professional skill carries weight, and something of the approbation intended for the skill exhibited is carried over to the substance.

A very similar technical skill has been exhibited at various times in Anglo-American courts, but it is a skill which is professedly applied to deduction from principles.[5] Now, we sometimes like to

---

[4] FUCHS, DIE GEMEINSCHÄDLICHKEIT DER KONSTRUKTIVEN JURISPRUDENZ (1909) 2 *et seq.*; FUCHS, JURISTISCHER KULTURKAMPF (1912) 1, 37–50.

[5] The leading textbooks in English are MAXWELL, ON THE INTERPRETATION OF STATUTES (7th ed. 1929), and CRAIES, STATUTE LAW (3d ed. 1923) — itself founded on HARDCASTLE, STATUTORY LAW (1879). See especially Pt. I, at 65–203. Mr. C. K. Allen's excellent book on LAW IN THE MAKING (1927) has a good chapter on statutory interpretation, at 273–89. BLACK, CONSTRUCTION AND INTERPRETATION OF LAW (1896), lists the various "rules" that courts have asserted that they use in interpreting laws. The received litany is, of course, to be found in 1 BL. COMM. 88–91, and in 1 KENT, COMM. 460–68.

The usual textbooks on jurisprudence in English generally omit specific discussion of statutory interpretation. But GRAY, NATURE AND SOURCES OF THE LAW (1909) §§ 366–99, devotes a considerable space to the topic, and there is half a chapter in SALMOND, JURISPRUDENCE (7th ed. 1924) c. VII, § 53. Two older books may be noticed. DWARRIS, STATUTES (Potter's Am. ed. 1874) 122–24, gives nineteen maxims of interpretation, to which are appended in the American edition the forty-five maxims of Vattel. It may be added that it is hard to find Dwarris' text in the American edition which has omitted much and inserted much. Dwarris will be found in 9 LAW LIBRARY (1835).

It would hardly do to make no mention of the LEGAL AND POLITICAL HERME-

fancy that statutes also are statements of principles; at any rate we believe that generally phrased statutes are superior to particular determinations in favor of particular persons. But the principles as ascertained in the common law — aside from the question of how these principles are ascertained — differ from those declared in the statute in that we have no need in the former case to consider any particular form of expression.

Words are certainly not crystals, as Mr. Justice Holmes has wisely and properly warned us,[6] but they are after all not portmanteaus. We can not quite put anything we like into them. And we may not disregard them in statutes. The real question in statutory interpretation is just what we shall do with them.

The interpretation of words is a familiar technique of philology and theology, or, perhaps we might say, of theological philology. Words are found which in the case of the Bible are deemed to be the utterances of God. They are therefore unchangeable, eternal, and precise in content.[7] Inadvertence or mere approximation is excluded. In various theological systems, even if plenary and verbal inspiration is not asserted for the sacred texts, and absolute authority not predicated of any human interpreter, there is a gradation of beliefs which approximate this view more or less fully.

The term interpretation got into law when it already had a literary history; and when it was applied to modern European law, it had developed a large theological aura as well. It has a strong suggestion of making clear to an uninitiated group what an esoteric inner circle knows by some sort of exclusive transmission. This suggestion may be said to be the basis for that commonest of assertions about statutes, namely, that what we seek to know

NEUTICS (3d ed. 1880), of Francis Lieber, a man whose lofty spirit has had less than its due meed of recognition by his adopted country. There is a mass of well digested learning compacted into this book which gives it a permanent value. But for our present purpose, we can hardly do much with a system that begins with the proposition, "No sentence, or form of words, can have more than one 'true sense,' and this is the only one we have to inquire for." *Ibid.* at 74.

[6] Towne v. Eisner, 245 U. S. 418, 425 (1918).

[7] It is perhaps not improper to point out that certainty of the divine source of a statute has not always been accompanied with equal certainty as to its application. See THE FEDERALIST, No. 36. "When the Almighty himself condescends to address mankind in their own language, His meaning, luminous as it must be, is rendered dim and doubtful by the cloudy medium through which it is communicated."

is what the legislature or the "legislator" intended. In literature and theology, that is precisely what we have as our task. But both the literary and the theologic methods are irrelevant, or should be so, in the interpretation of statutes. We are not seeking to enter into the mind of an artist. We are not attempting to fathom a divine will, and it is not clear that a method developed under prepossessions of the kind indicated will be of service when our primary duty is to rid ourselves of these prepossessions.

The courts have recognized this, in effect, when they assert that there is no room for interpretation when the meaning is "plain."[8] *Cum in verbis nulla ambiguitas est, non debet admitti voluntatis quaestio.*[9] This would not necessarily be the case in theology or literature. There may be a dogma that the plain meaning of a sacred text is the wrong one, and that in every case, an esoteric or mystical meaning is the right one, even when no particular consequence is sought as the result of such an interpretation. Similarly in literature, the plain meaning may be plainly wrong in view of a known peculiarity of the writer. Courts therefore which will not interpret, when the meaning is "plain," have already, as it were, committed themselves to a non-theologic or non-literary technique. But there is implicit in the rule the notion that generally there is such a plain meaning, and that it is a meaning at once apparent to the simple, honest understanding of an ordinary sensible man.[10] Any other meaning is under suspicion.

At the risk of descending into pure metaphysics, we shall have to make sure of the meaning of meaning.[11] We may perhaps save

---

[8] The courts indulge themselves in many approximate synonyms. There is the word "plain" itself, Regina v. Poor Law Comm., 6 A. & E. 56 (1838); Lake County v. Rollins, 130 U. S. 662 (1889); Mulville v. City of San Diego, 183 Cal. 734, 192 Pac. 702 (1920); "unambiguous," People v. Long Island R. R., 194 N. Y. 130, 87 N. E. 79 (1909); Johnson v. Southern Pac. R. R., 196 U. S. 1 (1904); "natural, plain and ordinary," Southington v. Southington Water Co., 80 Conn. 646, 658, 69 Atl. 1023, 1030 (1908); "clearly shown," Miles v. Wells, 22 Utah 55, 61 Pac. 534 (1900); "explicit," Sutters v. Briggs, [1922] 1 A. C. 1, 8. *Cf.*, in general, MAXWELL, *op. cit. supra* note 5, at 3–24.

[9] DIG. 32, 25, 1. The reference in the Digest is to a will, but the citation is used as a general maxim by civilians.

[10] "'It is generally safe to reject an interpretation that does not materially suggest itself to the mind of a casual reader.'" Shulthis v. MacDougal, 162 Fed. 331, 340 (E. D. Okla. 1907).

[11] Lawyers will probably get little assistance from such a book as OGDEN, THE MEANING OF MEANING (1923), nor is this particular book the best example of meta-

ourselves from being compelled to wrestle with this terrifyingly difficult question by limiting it to the meaning of statutory meaning.

A statute is neither a literary text nor a divine revelation. Its effect is therefore neither an expression laden with innumerable emotional overtones nor a permanent creation of infallible wisdom. It is a statement of a situation, or rather of a group of possible events within a situation, and as such is essentially ambiguous. This word is a pejorative expression in the mouths of most persons and seems to suggest that an ambiguous sentence can have two contradictory meanings; that, for example, it can permit what it seems to forbid. But of course that is not what the word "ambiguous" ought to suggest. A statement is ambiguous if there are two possible meanings — any two — and it can make no difference whether or not they partially contradict each other.

If therefore a group of events is described in a statute, there must at least be two which will fit that description, and since events are unique, any description of a group is almost by definition ambiguous. But although "unambiguous" and "plain" have been equated, the equation is not quite justified. It is still possible to find a plain statute, even though its meaning involves several things rather than one.

Mr. W. E. Johnson, whose *Logic* [12] is one of the most considerable of recent contributions to this much-discussed subject, has given us in his differentiation of *determinables* and *determinates* a valuable instrument for presenting the meaning of statutes. The situation described in a statute is generally a determinable; that is to say, it is a statement which involves a number of possible events or individualizations, any one of which would be correctly described by that determinable. A determinable of this sort can be made more nearly determinate by reducing the number of possible individualizations, and it becomes quite determinate when it is so expressed that there is only one.

A statute which ratifies a particular past act by a named person deals with a determinate event. So does a private bill, granting a pension to a named person or divorcing a named couple. Such

---

physical handling of the subject. In a sense, every form of pragmatic or of naturalistic philosophy is vitally concerned with what "meaning" means.

[12] JOHNSON, LOGIC (1921) Pt. I, c. 11, at 173–86.

statutes are therefore themselves determinates. But they are very few compared with the statutes in general, and a still smaller number of such statutes are ever discussed in law. If they are so discussed, it certainly can be said of them that they are plain and unambiguous. But they may still be plain, though perhaps no longer unambiguous, if, being determinables, they are so nearly determinate that we can indicate almost at once all the ways in which they can become determinate. If there were a statute which provided that " when the President dies, the Vice-President shall at once *ipso facto* become President," it would be a determinable, because there might be an indefinite number of future presidents and vice-presidents, but it would be plain enough, because the number of cases is after all much smaller than in almost any other statutory determinable. It will hardly be necessary to say that most of our most specific statutes fall considerably short of this ready determinability, and consequently no great limitation is imposed by the self-denying ordinance which renounces " interpretation " when the statute is plain. As a matter of fact, in most cases when courts say that a statute is plain and therefore needs no interpretation, they do so in the inverted fashion which marks so much of the judicial process. They have already interpreted, and they then declare that so interpreted the statute needs no further interpretation.

The act of interpretation, however, is not that of rendering a determinable quite determinate. The determinate involved is the actual issue in litigation. As soon as it is made apparent that the statutory determinable does or does not cover this determinate event, the act of interpretation is finished. It consists therefore in making a determinable somewhat more nearly determinate. Our inquiry must then turn to the methods by which this is done.

It has frequently been declared that the most approved method is to discover the intent of the legislator.[18] Did the legislator in

[18] It was repeated by Lord Justice Turner in an often cited judgment, Hawkins v. Gathercole, 6 De G. M. & G. 1, 22 (1855); by Blackburn, J., in River Wear Comm'rs v. Adamson, 2 App. Cas. 743 (1877), and by Birkenhead, L. C., and Lord Wrenbury in Viscountess Rhondda's Claim, [1922] 2 A. C. 339. Tindal, C. J., called it the " only rule," in the Sussex Peerage Case, 11 Cl. & F. 85, 143 (1844), a phrase quoted by Lord Macnaghten in Vacher v. London Soc. of Compositors, [1913] A. C. 107, 118. *Cf.* BACON, ABRIDGEMENT Stat. I, (5). It comes in as the last phrase of the fourth of the things which the barons of the exchequer said must

establishing this determinable have a series of pictures in mind, one of which was this particular determinate? On this transparent and absurd fiction it ought not to be necessary to dwell. It is clearly enough an illegitimate transference to law of concepts proper enough in literature and theology. The least reflection makes clear that the law maker, *der Gesetzgeber*, *le législateur*, does not exist,[14] and only worse confusion follows when in his place there are substituted the members of the legislature as a body. A legislature certainly has no intention whatever in connection with words which some two or three men drafted, which a considerable number rejected, and in regard to which many of the approving majority might have had, and often demonstrably did have, different ideas and beliefs.

That the intention of the legislature is undiscoverable in any real sense is almost an immediate inference from a statement of the proposition. The chances that of several hundred men each will have exactly the same determinate situations in mind as possible reductions of a given determinable, are infinitesimally small. The chance is still smaller that a given determinate, the litigated issue, will not only be within the minds of all these men but will be certain to be selected by all of them as the present limit to which the determinable should be narrowed. In an extreme case, it might be that we could learn all that was in the mind of the draftsman, or of a committee of half a dozen men who completely approved of every word. But when this draft is submitted to the legislature and at once accepted without a dissentient voice and without debate, what have we then learned of the intentions of the four or five hundred approvers? Even if the contents of the minds of the legislature were uniform, we have no means of knowing that content except by the external utterances or behavior of these hundreds of men, and in almost every case the only external

be " considered for the sure and true interpretation of statutes." Heydon's Case, 3 Co. 8a (1584). They must advance the remedy " according to the true intent of the makers of the act." *Ibid.* It is the limitation on the golden rule of " plain " interpretation. Jervis, C. J., in Mattison v. Hart, 23 L. J. C. P. 108, 114 (1854). Kent thought the real intent of the legislature was controlling. 1 KENT, COMM. 460.

The American cases that have so declared run into the hundreds. One of the most recent is Takao Ozawa v. United States, 260 U. S. 178 (1922).

[14] He is no less a fiction if he is idealized as a presumed *bonus pater patriae* who wishes only the good of the people. *Cf.* REICHEL, *op. cit. supra* note 2, at 78.

act is the extremely ambiguous one of acquiescence, which may be motivated in literally hundreds of ways, and which by itself indicates little or nothing of the pictures which the statutory descriptions imply. It is not impossible that this knowledge could be obtained. But how probable it is, even venturesome mathematicians will scarcely undertake to compute.

And if it were discoverable, it would be powerless to bind us. What gives the intention of the legislature obligating force? In theology or in literature, that question answers itself; but in law, the specific individuals who make up the legislature are men to whom a specialized function has been temporarily assigned. That function is not to impose their will even within limits on their fellow-citizens, but to "pass statutes," which is a fairly precise operation. That is, they make statements in general terms of undesirable and desirable situations, from which flow certain results. As a rule, the statements must be made in the words of a specified language. A statute made in Latin[15] at the present time is no statute, although the intention of the legislature can be as well or as ill made out from Latin as from English. A statute which presented a photograph of two automobiles and printed the legend beneath it that drivers who get into the situation pictured above would be prosecuted would not be a statute, although intention would be no less easily, and perhaps more easily, discoverable in this way than in set words. When the legislature has uttered the words of a statute, it is *functus officio*, not because of the Montesquieuan separation of powers, but because that is what legislating means. The legislature might also be a court and an executive, but it can never be all three things simultaneously.

And once the words are out, recorded, engrossed, registered, proclaimed, inscribed in bronze, they in turn become instrumentalities which administrators and courts must use in performing their own specialized functions. The principal use is that of "interpretation." Interpretation is an act which requires an existing determinate event — the issue to be litigated — and obviously that determinate event can not exist until after the statute has come into force. To say that the intent of the legislature decides the interpretation is to say that the legislature interprets in ad-

---

15 *In re* Lockett, 179 Cal. 581, 587, 178 Pac. 134, 137 (1919).

vance by undertaking the impossibility of examining a determinable to see whether it can cover a situation which does not exist.

The courts in England and America have generally qualified the "golden rule" that intent governs the meaning of a statute, by saying that it must be the intent "as expressed in the statute."[16] In that case, it would obviously be better to use the expression alone, without reference to the intent at all, since if the intent is not in the expression, it is nowhere. If the doctrine means anything, it means that, once the expression is before the court, the intent becomes irrelevant.

A legislative intent, undiscoverable in fact, irrelevant if it were discovered, is the last residuum of our "golden rule." It is a queerly amorphous piece of slag. Are we really reduced to such shifts that we must fashion monsters and endow them with imaginations in order to understand statutes?

It may be that we shall fare better if we pursue the ordinarily hopeful course of examining history. As has been stated, this is the common practice in Continental countries, in which summaries of the legislative history of a statute are published with the statute itself. This is so much a matter of course that a different practice seems almost irrational.[17] In England, a very different practice has prevailed, at least in recent times. The legislative history of a statute is definitely excluded, even when adduced in support of an interpretation otherwise obtained.[18] And in Germany, there has been notable opposition to the process, which has been contemptuously denominated *Materialienkult*.[19] In the United States, there is no general agreement. In interpreting the Constitution, the debates in convention are frequently resorted to, and in construing a great many statutes as well; but in other cases, it is declared that the English rule will be adhered to.[20]

---

[16] Two citations may suffice for the many which could be made. United States v. Goldenberg, 168 U. S. 95 (1897); The Sussex Peerage, 11 Cl. & F. 85 (1844).

[17] Compare the discussion of the point in (1919) 43 Revue Générale du Droit 56–57.

[18] 1 Halsbury, Laws of England (1907) 141; Millar v. Taylor, 4 Burr. 2303, 2332 (1769); Rex v. Board of Education, [1909] 2 K. B. 1045, 1057, 1072.

[19] Poewe, Der Kampf um eine neue Rechtsprechung (1916) 10.

[20] We may contrast United States v. Trans-Missouri Freight Ass'n, 166 U. S. 290 (1897), with Standard Oil Co. v. United States, 221 U. S. 1 (1911), and Binns v. United States, 194 U. S. 486 (1904).

As far as successive drafts of the statute and the debates in the legislature are concerned, the English rule has much to commend it. Successive drafts of a statute are not stages in its development. They are separate things of which we can only say that they followed each other in a definite sequence, and that one was not the other. But that fact gives us little information about the final form, since we never really know why one gave way to any other. There were doubtless many reasons, some of them likely enough to be personal, arbitrary, and capricious — the fondness of the draftsman for a special locution, his repugnance to another, a misconception of the associations of some word, a chance combination, and often enough a mere inadvertence. That is not to say that some conclusions, principally negative ones, can not be drawn from the legislative history of a statute. But in the end, all that we know is that the final form displaced the others, and that fact is not disputed.

The legislative history[21] based on the "materials" does not therefore enable us to discover without more ado what determinate situations or events are included in the small or large group described by the statute. Technical devices have been resorted to, similar in theory to the processes by which, in mathematics or in the Aristotelian syllogism, propositions are reduced, simplified, transposed, and solved. Without examining the question whether these processes are abstractly applicable, it may be of interest to notice two such technical devices, both phrased in Latin and both widely employed. They are, *expressio unius est exclusio alterius*, and *ejusdem generis*.

The rule that the expression of one thing is the exclusion of another is in direct contradiction to the habits of speech of most persons. To say that all men are mortal does not mean that all women are not, or that all other animals are not. There is no such implication, either in usage or in logic, unless there is a very particular emphasis on the word *men*. It is neither customary nor

21 The "legislative history" of a statute is taken to mean the successive forms in which the statute is found from the first draft presented until its final passage. That is different obviously from the history of the agitation which resulted in the fact that such a statute was proposed at all. It is this latter history which is contained in the famous four considerations established by the barons of the exchequer in Heydon's Case, 3 Co. 8a (1584), and popularized by Blackstone, 1 COMM. 88 *et seq.*

convenient to indicate such emphasis in statutes, and without this indication, the first comment on the rule is that it is not true.

So far from being logical, as some courts have called it, it illustrates one of the most fatuously simple of logical fallacies, the "illicit major," long the *pons asinorum* of schoolboys.[22] And yet in a widely used cyclopedia, there are at least seven hundred cases cited in which the maxim has been "applied or explained."[23] It has been called an axiom by the House of Lords, and it has been said of it that no maxim is of more general and uniform application.[24] Yet in the same case in which the House of Lords called it axiomatic, it was disregarded; [25] and the first case of its "application" cited in *Corpus Juris* is a case in the United States Supreme Court in which it was rejected.[26]

It must be clear that the only value which such a maxim or axiom or rule could have would lie in the existence of an infallible or approximately infallible test of its applicability. Emphasis will help us in ordinary speech, but except for such inferred emphasis as the general purpose of the act will enable us to apply, no other stress on the words will be apparent in the printed page. The question will accordingly be in every case, not whether or not the expression of one thing excludes everything else, but whether we are to deny or affirm this rule in this particular case. We shall evidently deny it or affirm it for some other reason than its axiomatic force, and it will be necessary to search for that other reason.

The other rule, *ejusdem generis*, has a little greater foundation in logic and in ordinary habits of speech. But for that very reason it is of limited importance in discovering the determinates covered by the statute. There is no case in which the words "other" or "any other" are used and applied, in which the same result could not have been reached if these words were absent. And where the courts have found that the phrase "other" has the effect of enormously increasing the number of determinates, it is generally at

---

[22] *Cf.* JEVONS, ELEMENTARY LESSONS IN LOGIC (1918) 132.

[23] (1921) 25 C. J. 220.

[24] See Saunders v. Evans, 8 H. L. Cas. 721, 729 (1861); BROOM, LEGAL MAXIMS *s.v.*; Johnson v. Jordan, 2 Metc. 234, 261 (Mass. 1841).

[25] Saunders v. Evans, 8 H. L. Cas. 721 (1861).

[26] United States v. Barnes, 222 U. S. 513 (1912).

the cost of making redundant all the previously enumerated ones. Thus we have the dilemma that when a long list of categories of things is supplemented by the phrase "and other," we may either omit these words or omit the preceding list.[27] The rule of *ejusdem generis* would have some value in cases in which the doctrine of "strict construction" applied. But since this doctrine, as we shall see, is really no longer applied in any proper sense, those cases do not seriously qualify the considerations presented.

Our search for a method of finding a meaning in the statute will readily bring us to two which have at various times been employed or suggested, consideration of its purpose and consideration of its results. These are very different things, and any effort to combine them may lead to what was called in the case of Heck, "methodological bigamy,"[28] in which the offspring of the one or the other union must necessarily be illegitimate.

If by the purpose of a statute we mean the actual purpose entertained by those who framed it or voted it, the purpose is indistinguishable from the intention, and we should have the same difficulty already noted, that this purpose is practically undiscoverable and would be irrelevant if discovered. But the purpose of many entities may be something far simpler and more apparent, something which is evident in the character of the thing itself, the end or final cause in the Aristotelian sense as distinguished from its efficient or its material cause.[29] So, a razor is something to shave with, and we should know this without the least speculation

---

[27] This is less a criticism of the rule of *ejusdem generis* as a canon of interpretation than it is a criticism of the legislative practice of using the lazy phrase "and other." It serves no purpose whatever in the absence of a clear test of when the rule of *ejusdem generis* is to be used and when not, and just how large *idem genus* is. In the case of Matter of La Société Française, 123 Cal. 525, 56 Pac. 458 (1899), § 1276 of the Code of Civil Procedure, which read "any religious, benevolent, literary, scientific or other corporation," was construed to mean any corporation whatever, including a savings bank. If there had been no words "and other" this result could not have been reached, but there is scarcely a conceivable charitable corporation which would not have fallen within the enumerated list. The phrase "and other" is usually disingenuous. It professes to be a modest admission of human incapacity to be exhaustive. It is in reality a confession of human disinclination to think things through. The worst that could happen to a class not specifically included would be that its fate would be determined as though there were no statute, a situation which ought not to baffle common law lawyers.

[28] REICHEL, *op. cit. supra* note 2, at 67, n.1.

[29] ARISTOTLE, PHYSICS II, 3, 194b, 24, and METAPHYSICS 1013, a, 24.

as to the ideas which were in the manufacturer's mind when the razor was made. There are some objects the purpose or end of which we can not decide on so easily. Doubtless only a technical expert could tell from looking at one of many machine parts, what it was for, but in most concrete objects, the purpose is self-evident.

In the case of statutes also, it is rare indeed that we can not say positively what any particular statute is for, by reading it. A statute is quite generally a fairly specific statement. It asserts that something is to be done, and whatever uncertainty or vagueness or ambiguities may exist as to the conditions under which it should be done, as a rule there is none as to the situation which the conditions are to give rise to. A statute which declares gambling contracts to be void may need a deal of interpretation, but its obvious purpose is to discourage gambling.

But as a matter of fact, can we be quite sure about it? There are purposes and purposes. It is not so much that the same statute may be an obvious instrument to several ends simultaneously, which is, after all, unlikely, but that nearly every end is a means to another end. We distinguish in our conduct and our thinking between immediate and ulterior purposes. And in most cases we contemplate a final or ultimate purpose which is in all likelihood vague and remote enough but is certainly not to be disregarded.

If we then return to our gambling statute, can we say simply that its purpose is to discourage gambling? That is obviously a remoter purpose, but the immediate purpose is something less. It is to make it impossible to sue on gambling contracts, or at any rate to make their gambling character a defense. And it must be apparent that the immediate purpose will depend largely on the remoter purpose. Again, a statute making murder capital has as its immediate purpose the putting to death of murderers. But certainly a further purpose is to discourage murder. It may be said that its better and larger purpose is that its immediate one may never be effectuated.

When we recall that the avowed and ultimate purposes of all statutes, because of all law, are justice and security, we have an additional fact to keep in mind. Surely it is not open to us to say that these purposes are too remote to be regarded, and in some cases there are solemn constitutional declarations that they must be considered paramount. At all events, the long concatenation of means and ends leads to a final end or to a final group of ends, and if the immediately apparent or the " primary " purpose of a statute seems to point away from it, courts are quite properly and justly perturbed.

There could be no better example of all this than the Statute of Frauds. The original statute passed by Parliament in 1677 states its purpose in the very name. It is to prevent frauds and perjuries. The means whereby this was to be achieved make up the immediate purpose of the statute. It was to make invalid to some extent many groups of oral contracts. There has probably never been a statute in which the immediate purpose has so frequently defeated the ulterior purpose as has been the case in this statute, and there is scarcely a group of these oral contracts in which the court has not struggled vigorously to prevent such a result. As a consequence, the number of determinate situations to which each of the larger determinables described by the statute might be reduced, has been constantly lessened, and this has surely gone on without much attention to those which the framers of the statute might have imagined.

In fact, we must qualify the statement that the immediate purpose of the statute is generally apparent. It is commonly rather the ulterior purposes which are apparent. Only when we have made up our minds what the ulterior purpose really was shall we know, for example, the immediate purpose of a statute which makes gambling contracts " void."

A contradiction between the primary and the ulterior purposes of the statute or the ultimate purpose of all statutes, will become apparent, if at all, only when we actually carry out or attempt to carry out the primary purpose. The method of " interpreting " a statute by its results is therefore an almost inevitable consequence of the existence of a chain of purposes in every piece of legislation. If courts tell us, and they often do, that the result is never to be considered, they are announcing a psychological impossibility.

The immediate result of interpreting a statute is plain enough. The given determinate situation is or is not to be treated as one of the reductions of the larger determinable which the statute describes. But that can not be the result which will tell us how to interpret a statute, because we find this result only after we have interpreted. What we mean therefore when we use a result as a method of interpreting statutes, is that we ask ourselves what remoter results will follow if this immediate one is effected. Courts are fond of pointing to the dangers incident to the interpretation they reject. It is curious that an apprehensive glance at disastrous future consequences is likely to be the mark of a court which considers itself conservative and which would repudiate as a radical and intolerable innovation [80] a method of interpretation consciously based on results.

The method of results involves prophecy, which is in itself not a damning indictment. A certain amount of forecasting of probabilities is an essential element of human conduct; and there is no reason in the world to command judges not to indulge in it. Our difficulty lies in the skill with which the forecasting is done. When a court declares that a certain interpretation will lead to undesirable consequences and is therefore to be avoided, the striking quality of this declaration is usually the grave doubt it elicits as to the accuracy of the forecast.

We may sum up by saying that to interpret a law by its purposes requires the court to select one of a concatenated sequence of purposes, and this choice is to be determined by motives which are usually suppressed. To interpret it by its results is to prophesy probable consequences for one or another of several interpretations, and the basis of the calculus is equally undisclosed. And yet these two types of interpretation are not merely the commonest in actual operation but are in most cases imperfectly concealed under so-called technical interpretations.

It will be seen that so far as purposes or results are concerned, courts act in the case of statutes as they act when no statute is in question. But the necessity of considering precise words points to an important difference when a statute is to be applied, and imposes certain limitations in the application. Whether words be the skin of an idea, in the simile of Mr. Justice Holmes, or chameleons which take their color from their surroundings, in the figure occasionally used by Continental jurists, the skin, we must

---

[80] See Hammer v. Dagenhart, 247 U. S. 251, 385 (1918); Felts v. Edwards, 181 Ky. 287, 204 S. W. 145 (1918); Jersey City v. North Jersey St. Ry., 72 N. J. L. 383, 61 Atl. 95 (1905); Albermarle County Immigration Soc. v. Commonwealth, 103 Va. 46, 48 S. E. 509 (1904).

remember, is already half filled; the chameleon's natural gray shines through the red or green which it has assumed from its surroundings. Although we are convinced that hanging a murderer has no deterrent effect whatever, or has even a slight stimulating effect, we can scarcely recast the obvious immediate purpose of a statute which makes murder capital. Our manipulation of other elements of the judicial process, the ascertainment of the facts, the application of certain kinds of procedure, the attempt at securing pardon or commutation, will be affected by our selection of an ulterior purpose here, but hardly the "interpretation" of the statute itself. That, as far as its immediate purpose is concerned, takes little color from its ultimate purposes or from its probable consequences.[31] Similarly, the Statute of Frauds will permit of a considerable reduction of extension, but it is not possible to refuse to apply the statute in every case where there is hardship to the plaintiff or overreaching by the defendant. The immediate purpose after all is partially immutable, and a certain number of honestly made and just claims will be unenforceable, despite the fact that the announced purpose of the statute is to prevent only dishonest claims from being enforced.

Accordingly, the determinate situation posited by a statute has after all a maximum and a minimum of extension. These limits are either apparent to any intelligent person reading the statute or they will never be known at all, and the statute may be disregarded as completely meaningless and therefore useless. If we agree to call these limits the "plain meaning" of the statute, there can be no quarrel with that designation. But the famous rule that interpretation is inadmissible under such a plain meaning does not follow at all, since there is ample room within these limits for a choice of purposes and a selection of determinates to effect them.

That almost any determinable situation posited by a statute is capable of expansion or contraction is recognized in the frequent

[31] An even clearer case is presented by the many statutes in Western states granting a bounty for coyote scalps. The ultimate purpose was unquestionably that of extirpating coyotes, or, at any rate, of reducing them in number. It turned out that coyote farms were established and coyotes bred in order to collect the bounty. Yet the statute was so nearly determinate that it took little color from this remoter result, and it would have been an unlawful violation of duty for a court to disregard the sharp limitations of the statutory extensibility. Cal. Stat. 1891, 280, repealed by *id.* 1895, 1.

differentiation between restrictive and liberal constructions. On the lips of opponents, the terms "strict" and "liberal" become changed to "rigid" and "loose," but they are obviously instances in which a small number of determinates is preferred to a great number, or *vice versa*. A strict construction is resorted to when it is desired to exclude a determinate which might readily enough be included within the statute. Liberal construction, as a rule, merely means that no such effort of exclusion will be made.

These tendencies are perfectly intelligible, and to know when a strict interpretation is to be applied and when it is not, would be of distinct value. Unfortunately the statements made on this question do not help us. When we read that laws enacted "in the interest of the public welfare or convenience, for the construction of works of great public utility, for the protection of human life or in regard to the rights of citizenship; for the prevention of fraud; or providing remedies against public or private wrongs, should be liberally construed,"[82] we are not aided much by an enumeration which includes almost every type of legislation that we can imagine, particularly when we are almost immediately referred to a case in which liberal construction is to be restricted to an attempt at effectuating only the "specified" purposes and objects of the statute. Similarly, the rule that remedial statutes are to be liberally construed[83] has the qualification that this construction is never to be applied so as to extend the application of statutes to cases not within the contemplation of the legislature. The doctrine that statutes in derogation of the common law or common right, statutes conferring privileges, and all penal statutes are to be strictly construed[84] would be a little clearer and easier to deal with if it were not so often disregarded, and if logically indistinguishable precedents were not present for the application and the rejection of the rule of strict construction in these cases.

Nevertheless, every process of interpreting statutes is ultimately a choice between a strict or a slightly less strict construc-

[82] The enumeration is found in (1910) 36 CYC. 1173, and is in part derived from 1 BL. COMM. 87–89.

[83] *Ibid.* at 87; Hudler v. Golden, 36 N. Y. 446 (1867); Camunas v. New York & P. R. S. S. Co., 260 Fed. 40 (C. C. A. 1st, 1919).

[84] 1 BL. COMM. 89; Corrigan v. United States, 298 Fed. 610 (S. D. N. Y. 1923). But *cf.* Ash Sheep Co. v. United States, 252 U. S. 159 (1920).

tion. A determinate that is sought to be brought within a statute is almost always capable of being included if the statutory determinable is made as inclusive as the limits indicated by the words will allow. The question is whether the limits will be extended to include this determinate or not. Strict or liberal construction or interpretation is therefore the ordinary process of interpretation, *tout simple*. If in the cases where "strict" interpretation is said to be necessary, strict interpretation were taken to mean the least possible number of determinates, we should have a practicable, if unsatisfactory, rule. But it does not seem to mean this, and without a definite limit at which to stop and with a practice which frequently ignores the rule altogether, the terms lose most of their significance.

We are therefore still sadly to seek in attempting to discover on what basis a statutory determinable is made to stop just outside a particular determinate. The "plain meaning" of the statute offers us a large choice between a maximum and a minimum of extension. The "intent of the legislature" is a futile bit of fiction. The "purpose" requires a selection of one of many purposes. The "consequences" involve prophecy for which the courts are not particularly prepared, and in which, by any calculus of probabilities, several choices of results are open.

But since a choice implies motives, it is obvious that, somewhere, somehow, a judge is impelled to make his selection — not quite freely, as we have seen, but within generous limits as a rule — by those psychical elements which make him the kind of person that he is. That this is pure subjectivism and therefore an unfortunate situation is beside the point. It is hard to see how subjectivism can be avoided or how the personality of the judge can be made to count for nothing in his decision on statutory interpretation as on everything else.[85] The most deplorable results

[85] The contrast that sociologic jurists are fond of making between subjectivism and their own methods is based on the assumption that sociologic values or goals are clear and demonstrable. It may be doubted whether this is true. After all, a decision is a selection, and a selection must be motivated. A Tory will on sound sociologic principles select a result which will establish property, exalt conventional morality and repress malcontents. A Radical will be equally sociologic in being less concerned with these ends. It is highly likely that if statutes are couched in approved sociologic terminology, either type of sociologist will be given a free rein to secure his desired goal.

of subjectivism need not be apprehended, since the tendency to follow precedents in statutory interpretations as well as elsewhere [36] relieves the court of some of its burdens, and since judges are members of their several groups and, like all other citizens, exhibit more group traits than individual ones.

But it may well be said that the presence of so many confused, contradictory, and meaningless "theories" and "methods" of interpretation creates a turbid atmosphere about courts, which is not conducive to clear thinking. The best we can say about it is that the sound sense of many judges will frequently penetrate this smoke screen and reach results that seem satisfactory, but it is often done half-consciously and almost surreptitiously.

Clarity would manifestly be secured by singleness of avowed method. If we must select one, it is hard to see how we can avoid selecting that method which is the commonest in practice, if the least announced. The statute — the *lex lata* — creates limits on both sides of strictness and liberality. Within them, any decision to interpret strictly — that is, any decision to exclude a particular determinate — might with advantage be consciously rendered, as is so often done semi-consciously or covertly, on the basis of its probable consequences. Judges will perhaps have to seek special and expert guidance as to what those consequences will be — especially in those many cases in which a limited and highly specialized group of economic activities is involved.

When they have properly equipped themselves with the material competence necessary to make an intelligent conjecture of results, we shall doubtless find a considerable difficulty in making them desire one result rather than another. A judge may well be free from the *sophismes du coeur* which M. Fabreguettes has so eloquently described,[37] but he cannot be free from some preference. When he discovers that the exclusion of a given determinate will have a certain effect, he must decide whether he wishes that effect.[38] If the matter is one which is intimately connected

[36] I have deliberately omitted all discussion of the weight to be assigned to previous interpretations of statutes by the same court. That is a question of *stare decisis*, as ticklish a subject to revive as Yorkshire schools, and far too important to be discussed casually.

[37] Fabreguettes, La Logique Judiciare 436 *et seq.*

[38] Perhaps the best examples of this effect on interpretation are two much discussed cases. In Holy Trinity Church v. United States, 143 U. S. 457 (1892), the

with other elements of the social or economic order, it is worse than idle to profess that he will disregard the connection and select as a desirable consequence something which he does not wish to happen.

There would then be two questions of importance in the interpretative process. The first would be: Can the statutory determinable in the widest range be taken to include the determinate before the court? The more nearly determinate the statute is, the easier that question will be to answer. It is far easier to make a statute which contains large determinables than limited ones, but if we wish to see clearly and with brief consideration what the maximum and minimum of extension is, in any determinable, we

---

Court examined the contract labor law which forbade the encouragement of an alien to migrate to the United States in order to perform services of any kind, and asked itself whether the employment of an English clergyman by a wealthy and distinguished Protestant Episcopal church was an encouragement to migrate in order to perform services of any kind. It could easily be included, of course, in the large determinables of the statutory expression. The Court found a legislative intention, for which there was not an atom of evidence, that it was not to be included. The only obvious purpose of the statute was to prevent foreign labor from being imported to the United States in order to compete with local labor. But that was not the only purpose the statute might well have had. The narrowing of the determinable so that this determinate was not included was almost certainly motivated by the feeling of men trained to respect an established Christian denomination which by virtue of its history could hardly fail to look abroad frequently for its ministers.

In Caminetti v. United States, 242 U. S. 470 (1917), the so-called Mann Act came into question. 36 STAT. 825 (1910), 18 U. S. C. § 398 (1926). The act made it a felony to aid in the transportation of any woman or girl for the purpose of prostitution or debauchery, or for any other immoral purpose; the Court held it applicable to the case of a couple who had voluntarily crossed a state border and after having crossed it were guilty of an offense which in their own state would have been immoral but not criminal. The legislative intent was urged upon the Court and rejected. 242 U. S. at 484. One of the known purposes of the statute was to prevent traffic in prostitution. A great many persons certainly believed this was the sole purpose. The Court chose to make the determinable large enough to include this special case of illicit relations, and it can hardly be doubted that in doing so, it was influenced by the disinclination to seem to condone a moral dereliction. If the Court had considered probable consequences, it might perhaps have foreseen that such an interpretation made the statute a ready instrument of blackmail and did not appreciably decrease the instances of sexual irregularity. But the contrast between the two interpretations illustrates clearly the effect of social motives in deciding where the determinable is to be limited. The Court desired to support religion in every way. It did not desire to connive at sexual immorality in any way.

must avoid words like "just" and "reasonable" and "property" and similar almost indefinitely extensible terms. These words have so little color of their own that they can be made to take almost any hue we desire.

The second question would be: Will the inclusion of this particular determinate in the statutory determinable lead to a desirable result? What is desirable will be what is just, what is proper, what satisfies the social emotions of the judge, what fits into the ideal scheme of society which he entertains. The dangers, whatever they are, which are involved in a *Gefühlsjurisprudenz* can in no system be completely avoided. An attempt to avoid them by declaring that judges must be guided by broad principles and not by particular situations is inevitably futile, because the broader the principle, the wider the scope of the personal predilections of the judge. If there is a glaring contradiction between what the judge thinks desirable and what the great majority of the community so considers, the community must, in its legislative function, limit as carefully as it can by more easily determinable categories the range within which the judge shall select his desirables. But the legislature can not both have its cake and eat it. It can not indulge itself in using large, round, sonorous words and then complain that courts do not treat them as precise, definite, and unreverberant.

It is quite true that courts might deliberately go beyond the limits set within the determinables of the statute. They might decide *contra legem*. This is a constant reproach directed against those who make much of gaps in the law. One might say that under a clear theory of interpretation, courts will less frequently judge *contra legem* than they do now, because there will be fewer screens behind which they may do so. But if we lay aside the theologic prepossessions which make the humdrum instrumentality of statutes a fiat of semi-divine wisdom, we must also lay aside the awe which has surrounded the judge from the time in which their lordships on the bench represented sovereign power in an immediate fashion. A more pliable and manageable system of enforcing judicial responsibility than any we now have might effectively lessen the dangers of arbitrary action on the part of the courts. Judges who decide *contra legem* are under our present system impeachable. That method of discipline generally collapses by its own weight. But a disciplinary tribunal which could suspend, reprimand, remove, fine, or sentence to pecuniary reparation, might work, even though the suggestion causes a shudder to common law lawyers.

Obviously we can not reasonably hope that a unified and clear system of statutory interpretation by means of a competent calculus of probable consequences will be adopted in set terms. The murky terminology and the cardboard structures of technical devices are consecrated, and in all likelihood will need something like a juristic revolution to destroy. This fact will continue to be one of the chief sources of that unhealthy severance between legal thinking and any other thinking, which has already worked no inconsiderable mischief. On statutory interpretation, laymen feel themselves more nearly able to meet lawyers on equal terms than on questions of traditional legal principles. If judges refuse to discard such absurdities as *expressio unius*, if they will play fast and loose with "plain meanings" on which substantial judicial authorities can not themselves agree, if they will impute imaginary intentions to fictitious entities, if they will arbitrarily select purposes and equally arbitrarily forecast consequences, they can not hope to convince laymen that they are acting rationally or usefully. To act rationally and usefully and then to disguise the fact by a self-stultifying "technique"[89] is unfortunately likely to be, in the future as it has been in the past, the only method by which lawyers and courts can deal with the statutes from which communities so naïvely expect an efficacy *ex opere operato*.

*Max Radin.*

UNIVERSITY OF CALIFORNIA SCHOOL OF JURISPRUDENCE.

---

[89] The use of this technique is a sort of procedure into which legal argumentation must fit itself, at whatever cost to common sense or consistency, just as older forms of pleading gave a rigid mould into which judicial processes had to be cast. If it were recognized as purely procedural, the mischief would be slight.

[7]

Social Philosophy & Policy Vol. 4 Issue 1 ISBN 0265–0525

# CONSTITUTIONAL INTERPRETATION AND ORIGINAL MEANING*

BY DAVID LYONS

## I. CONSTITUTIONAL ORIGINALISM

> By "originalism" I mean the familiar approach to constitutional adjudication that accords binding authority to the text of the Constitution or the intentions of its adopters. At least since *Marbury*, in which Chief Justice Marshall emphasized the significance of our Constitution's being a written document, originalism in one form or another has been a major theme in the American constitutional tradition.[1]

Indeed, originalism can seem to be the only plausible approach to judicial review. One might reason as follows: "A court cannot decide whether an official decision conforms to the Constitution without applying its rules. The Constitution was written down to fix its content, and its rules remain unchanged until it is amended. Courts have not been authorized to change the rules. So courts deciding cases under the Constitution should follow the rules there laid down. By what right would courts decide constitutional cases on any other grounds?"

That challenge is conveyed by writings on judicial review that are regarded as originalist. But it is misleading. Most of the positions that are condemned by contemporary originalists accept the authority of the Constitution.[2] Although originalists present the issue as fidelity to the Constitution, it primarily concerns, I shall argue, how the Constitution is to be interpreted.

* This is a revised version of a paper presented on March 14, 1986 to the conference on philosophy and law sponsored by the Social Philosophy and Policy Center and held at the University of Michigan Law School. Earlier drafts of all or part were presented at the State of Washington Annual Judicial Conference, the University of Utah, the University of Saskatchewan, and the Cornell Law School. I am grateful for comments offered on those occasions as well as comments from Gary Simson, Sterling Harwood, and the editors of *Social Philosophy & Policy*. Research for this paper was supported in part by a Constitutional Fellowship from the National Endowment for the Humanities and a summer research stipend from the Cornell Law School, for which I am also grateful.

[1] Brest, *The Misconceived Quest for the Original Understanding*, 60 B.U. L. Rev. 204 (1980).

[2] At the same time, it seems that most if not all theorists hold that constitutional cases may sometimes be decided by rules that cannot be attributed to the Constitution. We shall touch on "nonoriginalism" in section III.

A distinctively originalist mode of interpretation assumes that the doctrinal content of the Constitution was completely determined when it was adopted and that constitutional doctrines can be identified by a value-free factual study of the text or of "original intent." It is part of my purpose to show that this type of theory is not only less plausible than its severest critics have suggested,[3] but that significant alternatives to it are available (sections II and III).

An approach to judicial review includes not only a theory of interpretation, which tells us how to understand the Constitution, but also a theory of adjudication, which tells us how to apply the Constitution so interpreted – how it should be used in constitutional cases. Originalist theory is not usually analyzed in this way, but we shall find that the distinction is needed when considering contemporary originalism.

One would expect a distinctively originalist approach to adjudication to hold that constitutional cases should be decided on the basis of doctrines in the "original" Constitution (that is, the Constitution interpreted in an originalist way), and on no other basis whatsoever. I shall show that contemporary theorists who present themselves as strict originalists accept rules for judicial review that cannot be found in or otherwise attributed to the "original" Constitution (sections IV–VI).

A third point I wish to make is that doctrines drawn from general philosophy – ideas about meaning and morals, for example – play a significant role in contemporary originalist theorizing. This point is important because these philosophical notions are dubious and controversial. It must be emphasized, however, that some of the same philosophical ideas have wide currency in legal theory generally.

Although originalism has relatively few defenders, its most prominent champions are highly placed within the federal government. These include Robert H. Bork,[4] Judge on the United States Court of Appeals for the District of Columbia Circuit, Edwin Meese III,[5] Attorney General of the United States, and William H. Rehnquist,[6] Associate Justice of the United States Supreme Court. It is important for us to recognize the quality of the constitutional theories that are embraced by these responsible officials.

This paper is, then, a critique of constitutional originalism. We need a

[3] See, e.g., John Ely, Democracy and Distrust, ch. 2 (1980); Brest, *The Misconceived Quest*; Dworkin, *The Forum of Principle*, 56 N.Y.U. L. Rev. 469–500 (1981); and Schauer, *An Essay on Constitutional Language*, 29 UCLA L. Rev. 797 (1982). MacCallum, *Legislative Intent*, 75 Yale L.J. 754 (1966) applies here too.

[4] Bork, *Neutral Principles and Some First Amendment Problems*, 47 Indiana L.J. 1 (1971).

[5] Meese, *Construing the Constitution*, 19 U.C. Davis L. Rev. 22 (1985).

[6] Rehnquist, *The Notion of a Living Constitution*, 54 Texas L. Rev. 693 (1976).

better theory. Although I shall not offer one here, I shall suggest some requirements for an adequate theory of constitutional adjudication.

## II. ORIGINAL INTENT

Paul Brest's definition of "originalism" mentions two variants – "textualism" and "intentionalism."[7] The difference between them is significant. This section deals with constitutional intentionalism, especially its need for justification and the difficulties of finding any.

An originalist mode of interpretation holds that the doctrinal content of the Constitution was fixed when (or by the time that) the Constitution was adopted,[8] and that constitutional doctrines can be identified by a value-free factual inquiry. An intentionalist version of originalism holds that we must understand the Constitution in terms of the "intentions" of its framers, adopters, or ratifiers,[9] such as the specific applications that they had in mind, those they would have been prepared to accept, or their larger purposes.[10]

Champions of "original intent" seem to regard that approach to constitutional interpretation as so obviously correct that it requires no justification; for none seems to be offered. So it will be useful to begin by noting some aspects of intentionalism that imply its need for justification.

Reference to "original intent" is inherently ambiguous. The following questions indicate some (but not all) of that ambiguity. Whose intentions count? The intentions of, for example, one who drafts a text or one who votes for it? Which intentions count? To establish as authoritative some particular text, or some text understood in a certain way, or to serve some identifiable larger purposes? Reference to original intent is problematic in other ways

[7] Brest also draws a distinction between "strict" and "moderate" originalism, which I take up below.

[8] On this view, the meaning of an amendment would presumably be fixed when (or by the time) it was ratified, and its incorporation into the Constitution would presumably modify (and in that sense fix anew) the doctrinal content of the Constitution as a whole.

[9] I shall occasionally use "author" to refer to such an exclusive subclass of the population.

[10] This covers both species of intentionalism in Brest's typology. "Strict intentionalism requires the interpreter to determine how the adopters would have applied a provision to a given situation, and to apply it accordingly." (Brest, *The Misconceived Quest*, p. 222) This permits "intentions" to include general principles, as most original intent theorists appear to accept. "A moderate intentionalist applies a provision *consistent with* the adopters' intent at a relatively high level of generality, consistent with what is sometimes called 'the purpose of the provision.'" (*ibid.*, p. 223) The words I have emphasized suggest the view that "intentions" are relatively concrete or specific whereas "purposes" are relatively abstract or general, so that an appeal to original intent, strictly speaking, should be limited to the former. Brest does not defend this view, which does not square with his definition of "strict intentionalism" and is not required by the concept of intent. On the relevance of abstract intentions, see Dworkin, *The Forum of Principle*.

too. While two or more individuals can share an intention, it is by no means clear how (or whether it is always possible) to aggregate the relevant attitudes of the members of a group so as to determine their collective intentions.[11]

The answer that one gives to such questions should affect originalist interpretation, so the selection of any particular criterion of original intent as the basis for interpreting the Constitution requires specific justification. In the absence of a satisfactory rationale, we should regard any particular criterion of original intent as theoretically arbitrary. Sad to say, original intent theorists generally ignore these fundamental problems, despite their having systematically been surveyed in law reviews for at least two decades.[12]

But the differences among the various versions of originalist intentionalism do not chiefly concern us now. The point I would like to emphasize is that *any* intentionalist approach requires substantial justification. Intentionalism is a special theory of constitutional interpretation, not a platitude.

Early in our constitutional career, the Supreme Court refused to apply the Bill of Rights to the several states, holding that the first ten amendments restricted only the federal government, although their language does not explicitly limit most of those amendments in that way.[13] In so deciding, the Court made some reference to the intentions of "the framers." Although the Court's grounds for its decision went far beyond original intent, its reference to framers' intent might suggest that the Court followed that criterion of constitutional meaning instead of the apparent meaning of the authoritative text. If that were so, the Court would have followed a special theory of constitutional interpretation, and one that requires substantial justification.

In general, we recognize that we do not always mean what we say or write; *we* may mean something different from the meaning *of the language* that we use. This is reflected in our reading of legal instruments such as wills and contracts. It has also been observed, by advocates as well as critics of intentionalism, that the surest guide to authors' intent is the authoritative constitutional text itself. This is possible only because the text is understood

[11] The most plausible criterion in such cases – which are, of course, most directly relevant here – would refer to the meaning of a text that has been adopted as authoritative. But that criterion would subordinate intentionalism to textualism and would make authors' intent a derivative rather than a basic determinant of meaning. I am here considering intentionalism as a basic general theory of constitutional interpretation. I am not considering, for example, the idea that considerations of original intent may for one reason or another properly play a secondary, subordinate, or supplementary role in constitutional interpretation.

[12] See Ely, Democracy and Distrust; Brest, *The Misconceived Quest*; Dworkin, *The Forum of Principle*; Schauer, *An Essay on Constitutional Language*; and MacCallum, *Legislative Intent*.

[13] Barron v. The Mayor and City Council of Baltimore, 7 Pet. 243, 8 L. Ed. 672 (1833).

to carry a meaning that stands on its own – that is independent of its authors' intentions.[14]

It follows that intentionalism is a special theory of constitutional interpretation, not a platitude. Either it derives from a failure to appreciate the distinction between the meaning of a text and what its authors meant to convey; or else it presupposes some reason for holding that the meaning of the constitutional text, unlike that of texts generally, is a matter of authors' intent. So intentionalism is either confused or else requires substantial justification.

What might justify intentionalist constitutional interpretation? Originalists might appeal to (1) the idea (not limited to law) that interpretation should generally be governed by authors' intentions; (2) a specifically legal canon of construction; or (3) some theory of political morality that implies that we are under an obligation to respect the intentions of the framers, adopters, or ratifiers.

(1) *Intentionalism as a general approach to interpretation.* The notion that textual interpretation seeks generally to determine authors' intentions is plausible when our primary concern is what some individual had in mind, as in the case of personal communications, studies of literary figures and, in law, wills and contracts. The question is whether our proper concern when interpreting an authoritative public text such as a constitution is to determine what its authors had in mind. The suggestion seems to me implausible.

I do not wish to deny that, just as a poem can be a political statement, law can be read as literature. But law's distinctive functions are significantly different from those of literature and personal communications. Law tells us what we must or must not do, threatening punishment for disobedience. It places the coercive power of the state behind some individuals' decisions. It quite literally regulates death and taxes, war and peace, debts and compensation, imprisonment, conscription and confiscation, and innumerable other matters of direct, vital interest to individuals, communities, and often all humanity. That is the explicit, normal business of the law, including the U.S. Constitution.

An important feature of law's normal business is that it requires justification. The same applies, of course, to judicial decisions, including those that turn upon legal interpretation. They require justification, too. The justification of judicial decisions, like the justification of the normal business of the law generally, cannot be understood in narrowly legalistic terms.

[14] This point does not presuppose a general theory of text meaning. The argument of section III would seem to imply, however, that the meaning of a text is not determined solely by linguistic conventions.

Adequate justification concerns not merely whether something is required or allowed by law but, also, whether what the law does is what I have elsewhere called "defensible."[15] All of this suggests that the need for justification may properly regulate matters of legal and specifically constitutional interpretation and, thus, that these matters turn on political morality.

(2) *Intentionalism as a theory of legal interpretation.* Could intentionalism be based on a general canon of construction for legal instruments? The possibility is suggested by the fact that statutory construction is said to seek out "legislative intent." But there are several difficulties here. Insofar as constitutional intentionalism relies upon a canon of construction that derives from precedent or common law, there will be some difficulty incorporating such a theory of interpretation into originalism, as I shall explain later.

Another problem is this. Conventions regulate the identification of "legislative intent," such as the authority given to official reports from legislative committees. Such conventions have only problematic application to the U.S. Constitution. The existence of such conventions suggests something else that seems important, namely, that the search for "legislative intent" is not a purely factual inquiry about a consensus that obtained at a particular historical moment. This is suggested also by the fact that statutory construction characteristically seeks to interpret legislation in as favorable a light as possible; for example, as a reasonable and legislatively legitimate means to a reasonable and legislatively legitimate end. Such a normative bias can be explained by the fact that statutory construction seeks to provide, if possible, a grounding for judicial decisions that are justified. If what counts as "legislative intent" is in fact shaped by normative considerations, it could not serve as a model for "original intent," for those who endorse the latter as the criterion of constitutional meaning regard it as a plain matter of historical fact, accessible to a value-free inquiry.

Originalists assume that the Constitution is a morally adequate basis for judicial decisions (as well as for our political arrangements generally). The normative bias within interpretation to which I refer requires that we interpret the Constitution in such a way that it is, if possible, capable of performing that function.

If statutory construction is no help to constitutional intentionalism, what about the interpretation of other legal instruments, such as wills and contracts? The first point made about "legislative intent" applies here, too: insofar as constitutional intentionalism relies upon a canon of construction that derives from precedent or common law, there will be some difficulty incorporating such a theory of interpretation into originalism.

[15] See my *Derivability, Defensibility, and the Justification of Judicial Decisions*, 68 The Monist 325 (1985).

It might nonetheless be thought that an intentionalist interpretation of contracts[16] could serve as a model for constitutional intentionalism. That is because political rhetoric often refers to the Constitution as the upshot of a "social contract." Now, the idea of a "social contract" is invoked to argue for obedience to law, however objectionable on other grounds it might be, so long as it does not violate constitutional restrictions. This means that a "social contract" basis for intentionalism is dependent on a theory of political morality. To accept intentionalism on this basis, we must establish the legitimacy of a "social contract" argument and its valid application to this case.

(3) *Intentionalism as a theorem of political morality*. Our discussion suggests that we should seek a rationale for constitutional intentionalism in the political morality of constitutional creation and application, that is, in principles that explain why the Constitution is worthy of respect and morally binding. Two ideas are provided by political rhetoric. One, already noted, refers to a "social contract." Another, asserted within as well as outside the Constitution, holds that it comes from "the people."

The latter idea is promising because contemporary originalists, like most constitutional theorists, emphasize the predominantly "democratic" character of our constitutional arrangements. Representative government nicely complements popular sovereignty. Political rhetoric suggests that "the people" knowingly and freely agreed to respect government so long as it conforms to the Constitution, and that "the people" are accordingly bound by that agreement. But this does not yet yield the constitutional theory of original intent, which requires that the Constitution be understood in terms of the "intentions" of a special subclass of "the people," namely, the framers, adopters, or ratifiers, as opposed to (say) the understanding that one might have of the Constitution based on text meaning.

The present line of reasoning requires us to suppose, then, (a) that "the people" *contracted to accept the intentions of the authors*, by reference to which the Constitution must therefore be understood, and (b) that *this* makes the Constitution binding on us now. The theory seems fatally flawed.

(a) In the first place, only a small minority of the people of that time and place were permitted to participate in the original adoption process. We lack precise figures, but it should suffice for present purposes to observe that the process excluded not only many adult white males (and, of course, children) but also women, chattel slaves, and Native Americans. It could not have included more than a small fraction of the total population, and willing contractors would have amounted to a smaller fraction still.

[16] Insofar as such interpretation is, in fact, intentionalist. It seems relevant that contractual interpretation is not purely a matter of actual intent, but is also regulated by legal norms.

In the second place, it is doubtful whether any such contractors would have been morally competent to create obligations to respect political arrangements that continued chattel slavery, second-class citizenship for women, and the subjugation of Native Americans. At the very least, those subject to such arrangements could not be bound by a constitution simply because it was agreeable to others.

(b) In the third place, it is unclear how contracts made by members of earlier generations can bind succeeding generations. This is not to suggest that law can bind only those who have given their consent. But the mere fact that some people some time in the past have accepted a political arrangement cannot by itself automatically bind others. More is required than that to show that later generations are bound.

But the rhetoric of popular sovereignty is nonetheless illuminating. It suggests a commitment to popular government, however narrowly that was at first conceived.[17] Furthermore, the Constitution is a piece of public, not private law. Our proper concern in interpreting it is not to implement the understanding of parties to a limited, private agreement or the personal wishes of a testator, but to establish the basis for political arrangements and justified judicial decisions that legitimately concern the community as a whole. Whatever else is needed for a theory of constitutional adjudication, the legitimate interest of the entire population strongly suggests that the primary criterion of constitutional meaning should be popular understanding, the basic index of which must be text meaning.

Consider the alternative. Interpretation in terms of the intentions of constitutional framers or ratifiers would seem to assume a conception of law like that of the classical legal positivists Bentham and Austin, according to which an exclusive subgroup of the population makes law for others to follow.[18] That is objectionable because of our interest in justification. Interpretation based on anything like that conception of the law will present formidable obstacles to justifying the Constitution, justifying compliance with morally deficient laws so long as they conform to the Constitution, and justifying judicial decisions that those laws require.

The upshot is that constitutional intentionalism is profoundly problematic. There is no obvious linguistic or moral basis for interpreting the Constitution by reference to the intentions of an exclusive political group, as opposed to the meaning of the text. When these considerations are combined with other substantial objections to intentionalism, the theory seems unpromising indeed.

[17] The idea of popular sovereignty was reflected in constitutional *rhetoric* from early on. It became increasingly reflected in the constitutional *system* as time passed, as major changes occurred in the Republic, including of course major constitutional amendments.

[18] This aspect of that theory is discussed by H. L. A. Hart, The Concept of Law 41–43 (1961).

## III. ALTERNATIVES TO INTENTIONALISM

In this section, I argue that intentionalism does not win out by default, despite its deficiencies. According to Brest's typology, the originalist alternative to intentionalism is textualism, which comes in two varieties. "A strict textualist purports to construe words and phrases very narrowly and precisely."[19] Brest appears to argue that this is untenable both as textual interpretation and as originalism: "An originalist would hold that, because interpretation is designed to capture the original understanding, the text must be understood in the contexts of the society that adopted it."[20] This means that textualism must be "moderate" to be plausible. "A moderate textualist takes account of the open-textured quality of language and reads the language of provisions in their social and linguistic contexts."[21]

In other words, Brest judges the only legitimate originalist alternative to intentionalism[22] to be a reading of constitutional language as "open textured."[23] Unfortunately, Brest does not explain what he takes this to mean. But his reference to the spurious precision of "strict" textualism suggests that we might understand "moderate textualism" by reference to Hart's use of "open-textured" when he introduced that technical term into legal theory.[24]

Following the received wisdom of the time, Hart held that all terms in "natural" languages (which include the language of the law) are "open-textured." An "open-textured" word has a core of determinate meaning, encompassing fact situations to which it uncontroversially applies, and a "penumbra" encompassing fact situations to which the term neither clearly applies nor clearly does not apply. The idea of "open texture" assumes that the meaning of a word is indeterminate whenever there are reasons both for and against applying the word. This aspect of the theory of "open texture" provides a theoretical rationale for a view that is widely accepted by legal theorists, namely, that legal language has indeterminate meaning insofar as its proper application is unclear.

On this understanding, to characterize constitutional language as "open textured" is to imply that the doctrines given by that language are incompletely formed. Provisions that many theorists seem to believe fit this description to an extreme degree include the so-called "vague clauses" guaranteeing "free speech," "due process," "just compensation," "equal

[19] Brest, *The Misconceived Quest*, p. 204.

[20] *ibid.*, p. 208.

[21] *ibid.*, p. 223.

[22] Actually, Brest seems to believe that moderate *textualism* amounts to the only plausible originalist alternative to "strict" *intentionalism*, as he says that "moderate textualism and intentionalism closely resemble each other in methodology and results." *ibid.*

[23] *ibid.*, pp. 205, 223.

[24] Hart, The Concept of Law, pp. 121–132.

protection," and the like. On the "open texture" model, these provisions are seen as having tiny cores of clear (and therefore determinate) meaning and relatively wide unclear (and therefore indeterminate) penumbras.

This is a politically significant idea. For it implies that, insofar as the judicial process of "interpreting" the Constitution makes its proper application clearer, the process really *changes* the Constitution by making its meaning more determinate. The clearer doctrines resulting from such "interpretations" could not then be attributed to the "original" Constitution. That is the view of constitutional language that Brest seems to regard as the ("moderate") originalist alternative to "strict" textualism.

Given this conception of the alternatives, we can better understand why originalists regard as most significant the dividing line between "strict" and "moderate" originalism. That is because moderate originalism appears to collapse into nonoriginalism.

Originalism regards the authority of the "original" Constitution as axiomatic, whereas nonoriginalism holds that adherence to the Constitution requires justification and that principles of political morality that are capable of providing such justification might also justify deviation from it.[25] To clarify this difference, we can distinguish two categories of doctrines that might be used in constitutional cases. Those that can and those that cannot truly be attributed to the Constitution may be called "constitutional" and "extra-constitutional," respectively. Nonoriginalism is prepared to consider using extra-constitutional doctrines in constitutional cases, whereas a distinctively originalist theory of adjudication would presumably reject any such use of them.

"Moderate" originalism regards unclear constitutional language as "open-textured," or inherently somewhat vague. It also accepts the judicial practice of deciding cases under unclear aspects of the Constitution. But it seems to regard the constitutional "interpretations" that are used as creating, and the resulting decisions as applying, doctrines that are extra-constitutional – judicial amendments to the "original" Constitution. On this view, "moderate" originalism's approach to deciding cases under unclear aspects of the Constitution *is equivalent to nonoriginalism*. Such decisions would be condemned by a "strict" originalist who holds that, as courts have no authority to amend the Constitution, they should refrain from doing so.[26]

It must be emphasized that the line of reasoning sketched in the last few paragraphs assumes that "moderate" textualism regards the Constitution as indeterminate insofar as its proper application is unclear. But we need not

[25] Compare Brest, *The Misconceived Quest*, p. 225. For a work that might be considered "nonoriginalist," see M. J. Perry, The Constitution, The Courts, and Human Rights (1982).

[26] We shall consider the originalist approach to this issue in section V.

assume this; we need not accept the dubious assumption that the meaning of a text is indeterminate whenever it is unclear, or whenever interpretation of it would be controversial, so that the discovery of text meaning is impossible precisely when it is needed.

Instead of discussing these issues in the abstract, it will be useful to consider an approach which agrees that such language in the "original" Constitution does *not* provide *complete* doctrines of just compensation, free speech, and the like. This approach nevertheless provides grounds for attributing the doctrines resulting from sound interpretations to the Constitution. This will provide us with all that we require for present purposes, namely, an alternative to "strict" intentionalism that might justifiably assign meaning to the Constitution and enable courts to decide cases on constitutional grounds.

It has been suggested[27] that the so-called "vague clauses" incorporate "contested concepts." It is the nature of such a concept to admit of competing "conceptions" and thus routinely to *require* interpretation. Contested concepts do not have built-in criteria of application; they are more abstract than that. As a result, different people can use the same (contested) concept while accepting and employing different standards for its application. It would seem, for example, that general normative concepts, such as "right" and "wrong," "good" and "bad," "right" and "obligation," as well as more specific normative concepts, such as particular virtues and vices, are "contested" in this way. When people agree about the "facts" but disagree in their evaluations, their disagreement concerns the principles that determine the proper application of those concepts to particular cases.

The notion of a "contested concept" is explicitly used, for example, in Rawls's theory of social justice, the relevant part of which can be explained as follows. Imagine that you and I disagree about the substantive requirements of social justice. We then differ as to how the concept of justice applies; we differ, that is, about the principles of justice. This is possible if the concept of justice admits of different interpretations, or competing conceptions. That seems to be the case.

Rawls maintains that the mere concept of justice determines no detailed, substantive criteria of justice, only the skeletal requirement that there be no "arbitrary distinctions" between persons but, rather, "a proper balance between competing claims."[28] The task of a theory of justice is to show (not merely to claim) the superiority of one conception (one principle or set of principles) over competing conceptions as an interpretation of this require-

[27] R. Dworkin, Taking Rights Seriously 132–137 (1977). This suggestion is independent of other aspects of Dworkin's legal theory.

[28] J. Rawls, A Theory Of Justice 5, 10 (1971).

ment. The possibility of a uniquely correct interpretation of a provision incorporating the contested concept of justice, then, depends on the superior justifiability of a particular conception of justice.

Now consider a constitutional example. Past judicial interpretations aside,[29] a court applying the just compensation clause would not necessarily decide a case as the original authors would have done, nor would it automatically follow a more popular consensus of the time (even if either were possible). Instead, a court would understand the Constitution to mean precisely what it says and thus to require *just compensation*. A court would need to defend a particular conception of just compensation (that is, it would need to defend principles of justice appropriate to compensation) against the most plausible alternatives. It would then apply that conception to decide the case at bar.

Someone might be skeptical about the possibility of justifying such an interpretation. Someone might believe it is impossible to provide a rational defense of, say, principles of just compensation and might therefore claim that a court adopting this approach would inevitably impose its own arbitrary conception of just compensation instead of the conception embraced by the authors of the Constitution or by a broader "original" consensus. (It should be emphasized that, on this view, an "original" conception of just compensation is completely arbitrary and indefensible.) Someone might hold, in other words, that all such principles are inherently arbitrary, so that courts cannot possibly do what is required to implement this approach to the interpretation of "vague" constitutional language.[30] I shall not offer a general critique of such skepticism,[31] but I shall suggest below why it is reasonable to believe that there can be a best conception among competing conceptions of some contested concepts. I shall later show how philosophical skepticism about values is, in this context, incoherent.[32]

Contested concepts do not seem confined to morality and law. Their properties are at any rate similar to those of concepts referring to natural

[29] If a court works under a doctrine of precedent, then the criterion of a justifiable interpretation cannot simply be fidelity to the "original" Constitution. In that case, past judicial interpretations can presumably affect the content of a justifiable interpretation, even when those past interpretations were mistaken. I ignore that complication here.

[30] We should distinguish such philosophical skepticism about values from concern about the difficulty a court might have trying to identify the best conception of a contested political concept (even when the alternatives are severely limited in number) and from an appreciation of the fact that any attempt to identify the best conception is likely to be controversial. We may also assume that reasonable judges can differ in their interpretations. It should be emphasized, however, that approaches to judicial review that seek to avoid controversial interpretations of the Constitution cannot be assumed to be justifiable by reference to the "original" Constitution. That is precisely one of the points at issue here.

[31] I address some aspects of this issue in Ethics and the Rule of Law, ch. 1 (1984).

[32] Section VI.

substances or phenomena, such as water and heat. On a plausible understanding of the development of science, for example, the caloric and kinetic theories of heat are (or at one time were) competing conceptions of the concept heat. This is suggested by the fact that "heat" refers to a physical phenomenon that is but partially and imperfectly identified by any prescientific verbal definition of the word, and that something very much like the idea of a contested concept is required to explain how there can be two theories of heat, that is, two different conceptions of the single concept heat.

If, as most people would agree, "heat" refers to a determinate physical phenomenon, there can be, in principle, a best theory of heat. This implies that there can be a best conception of a contested concept, at least in some cases. This suggests, in turn, that contested concepts in the Constitution might have best interpretations.

The kinetic theory of heat has displaced the caloric conception and is currently our best conception of heat. As this example implies, we may be justified in using *our* best conception even if it is not in fact *the* best. Similarly, just as our best conception of heat is liable to change, so we may expect change from time to time in our best conception of, say, just compensation. This involves no moral relativism.

Now if the idea that the Constitution includes contested concepts is correct, then to apply the Constitution in terms of their best interpretation is, in effect, to apply doctrines whose application is called for by the original Constitution. But, just as interpretation of the concept heat requires more than mere reflection, any interpretation of this type inevitably draws upon resources that are neither implicit in the text nor purely linguistic. It makes essential use of political argument, though at a relatively general or abstract level. So this alternative approach implies that a sound interpretation – one faithful to the meaning of the text – can include substantive doctrines that are not derivable from the text (even supplemented by its original social and linguistic context) but that are identifiable only by reasoning about political principles in the context of the federal system.

It is important to emphasize that this approach to constitutional interpretation, where applicable, requires that an interpreter go outside the "four corners" of the text, its strict linguistic implications, and the relatively specific intentions of its authors,[33] for interpretations and arguments supporting them. But, as this is done because it is understood to be required by the very nature of contested concepts found within the Constitution, both the strategy of argument and its results can claim fidelity to the Constitution. For this reason, the interpretive approach just sketched might reasonably be regarded as "originalist."

[33] Interpretation by reference to "original intent" also, of course, draws upon information outside the "four corners" of the text.

As usually understood, however, "originalism" assumes that constitutional doctrines must be identified by a value-free factual study of the text or of original intent and that doctrines that are not implicit in the "original" text or "understanding" cannot truly be attributed to the Constitution. It accordingly rejects without a hearing the possibility of attributing to the Constitution interpretations of those contested concepts that are in the Constitution. That possibility gives reason to withhold assent from the more familiar originalist theories.

## IV. ORIGINALIST ADJUDICATION

The Fourteenth Amendment says that no state "shall deny to any person within its jurisdiction the equal protection of the laws." The meaning of this provision is unclear. If (as some suggest) the provision does not have any determinate meaning, how should courts deal with cases under it? The Constitution does not tell us what we should then do.

As I have suggested, a comprehensive theory of judicial review can be understood as having two parts. A theory of interpretation purports to determine constitutional meaning. If well grounded, such a theory should be welcome when the text is unclear. Furthermore, anyone who holds the text to be misleading needs a good theory to justify such a claim.

But theories about judicial review go beyond straightforward interpretation; they include theories of adjudication, which purport to determine how the Constitution should be applied.[34] Such a theory is required if cases are decided when the meaning of the Constitution is undetermined, or to justify departure from the Constitution's implications.

To illustrate the latter possibility, consider Thayer's famous deferential doctrine.[35] Thayer argued that federal legislation should never be nullified by federal courts unless it cannot reasonably be doubted that the legislation violates the Constitution. He held that this judicial policy was needed to promote respect for federal law and to protect the courts from legislative interference.[36] Thayer did not assume that the Constitution has no determinate meaning when there is reasonable disagreement about its meaning. On the contrary, he insisted that the judiciary should not apply its best interpretation of the Constitution but should defer whenever it is possible to regard the legislature's actions as constitutional.

[34] A theory of adjudication would seem to presuppose an independently determined interpretation of the Constitution, to fix whatever is (or is not) to be applied.

[35] Thayer, *The Origin and Scope of the American Doctrine of Constitutional Law*, 7 Harv. L. Rev. 129 (1893).

[36] These are Thayer's chief arguments for judicial deference. Although he nods in the direction of democratic sentiments, he expresses little respect for the virtue, sense, or competence of legislators, but he fears their collective power.

> [W]hen the ultimate question is . . . whether certain acts of another department, officer, or individual are legal or permissible, . . . *the ultimate question is not what is the true meaning of the constitution, but whether legislation is sustainable or not.*[37]

Thayer recommends, in effect, that the courts should sometimes refrain from enforcing the Constitution, even when they have a good, justifiable, and perhaps sound idea of what it means. That amounts to a special theory of adjudication (and, incidentally, one that seems decidedly extra-constitutional).

The distinctively originalist approach to adjudicating constitutional cases would seem to hold that they should be decided exclusively by doctrines that can be found in the "original" Constitution, that is, interpreted in an originalist way. There is a problem here. It is by no means clear that originalist theory can be found within the "original" Constitution. If originalism itself includes extra-constitutional doctrines, then insofar as a court applied and was guided by this theory of adjudication, it would decide cases in a nonoriginalist way!

It may accordingly seem reasonable to revise the originalist theory of adjudication so that originalism does not prohibit its own application. It would be modified to say that a doctrine may be applied within judicial review if, but only if, the doctrine either is attributable to the Constitution (in the sense required by an appropriate originalist theory of interpretation) or else is a doctrine of originalism itself.

That problem seemed easily solved. But it may suggest how difficult it is to embrace originalism unqualifiedly. Take another example. Raoul Berger's attack upon judicial decisions that fail to respect "framers' intent" leads him to suggest that courts should repudiate all decisions that cannot be grounded upon the Constitution so construed, regardless of "undesirable consequences."[38] But Berger hastily retreats from this proposal, saying:

> It would, however, be utterly unrealistic and probably impossible to undo the past in the face of the expectations that the segregation decisions, for example, have aroused in our black citizenry – expectations confirmed by every decent instinct. That is more than the courts should undertake and more, I believe, than the American people would desire.[39]

Berger's retreat appears unprincipled. At best, he invokes an undefined and undefended extra-constitutional principle of constitutional adjudication, which clashes with his originalist pretensions.

[37] Thayer, *The Origin*, p. 150 (emphasis in the original).
[38] R. Berger, Government By Judiciary 412 (1977).
[39] *ibid.*, pp. 412–413.

Henry Monaghan appears sensitive to Berger's problem. He too says that the school desegregation decisions should not be undone. Unlike Berger, however, Monaghan suggests a judicial principle that would permit leaving those decisions undisturbed, even though he questions their constitutional warrant. His solution is to advocate a doctrine of judicial precedent.[40]

The question now is whether a doctrine of judicial precedent can be attributed to the "original" Constitution. Monaghan appears not to think so. But he believes that such a doctrine can be justified because it serves "the long-run values of stability and predictability for ordering our most fundamental affairs."[41]

Monaghan does not seem to appreciate the awkwardness of his position. In offering a justification for a doctrine of precedent based on its desirable consequences, he commits himself to holding that judicial review may be regulated by *any* principles whose use would serve the same "long-run values." That would permit the use in judicial review of an indeterminate class of useful extra-constitutional principles.[42]

One might, alternatively, suggest that a doctrine of precedent was in fact provided by the "original" Constitution. For the Constitution was grafted upon a system whose common law heritage includes, of course, a doctrine requiring courts to respect judicial precedent.[43] The trouble with this way of reasoning, from an originalist perspective, is that it would render the Constitution much less limited doctrinally than originalists tend to view it. It would imply that the Constitution contains a multitude of common law principles.

Monaghan's predicament suggests the instability of originalism. If an originalist believes that there is justification for respecting a judicial principle

[40] Monaghan, *Our Perfect Constitution*, 56 N.Y.U. L. Rev. 387–391 (1981); and *Taking Supreme Court Decisions Seriously*, 39 Maryland L. Rev. 1–12 (1979).

We are presumably concerned here with precedents on the same court level, as distinct from precedents that are binding due to the hierarchical structure of a layered court system.

[41] Monaghan, *Our Perfect Constitution*, p. 389; compare *Taking Supreme Court Decisions Seriously*, p. 7.

Lawyers seem to favor consequentialist arguments for precedent over the notion that precedent is grounded upon the fairness of treating like cases alike. For a discussion of this alternative, see Lyons, *Formal Justice and Judicial Precedent*, 38 Vanderbilt L. Rev. 495 (1985).

[42] Perhaps Monaghan would like to limit the use of consequentialist argument in some unexplained way. It will be difficult to show, however, that such limitations are not ad hoc. Indeed, Monaghan's consequentialist strategy of argument threatens to get completely out of hand. For his argument commits him to approving all principles whose use would serve *any* values that are as desirable as "stability and predictability." It may also be noted that insofar as originalist doctrine, such as strict intentionalism, appeals to past judicial practice, its originalist credentials must be as problematic as those of a doctrine of precedent.

[43] Monaghan distinguishes the doctrine of precedent that is needed for constitutional cases from "common law analogies" because of differences in details, and he may infer from these differences that the constitutional doctrine could not be based on common law traditions; *Taking Supreme Court Decisions Seriously*, p. 12. But that reasoning is dubious.

that is no more controversial than precedent, he not only runs the risk of agreeing that constitutional cases may properly be decided by doctrines that cannot be attributed to the Constitution; he may become committed to accepting a relatively indeterminate theory of judicial review, incorporating all the principles of constitutional adjudication that can be justified by the criteria that are needed to justify a doctrine of precedent.

This point is generalizable. Contemporary originalists are often preoccupied with "restraining" the federal judiciary in constitutional cases and tend to embrace theories of adjudication that are designed in part to limit judicial nullification of decisions made by elected officials. The relevant judicial principles require justification. If such principles cannot be found in the "original" Constitution, they require justification by reference to some principles of political morality. The considerations that are adduced or required to justify such doctrines are capable of justifying an indefinite class of other doctrines that are relevant to constitutional adjudication. To endorse an extra-constitutional principle is to commit oneself to endorsing any other principle that is justifiable on the same grounds that justify the one endorsed. Such an approach to constitutional adjudication is hardly consistent with the spirit of originalism.

## V. DEMOCRATIC SENSIBILITIES

Constitutional theorizing nowadays puts an emphasis upon "democracy" that we have so far neglected. It arises in contexts like the following. Intentionalists believe that our knowledge of constitutional meaning extends only so far as our knowledge of original intent. What remains unclear can be assigned no determinate meaning. If it is assumed that the "interpretation" and application of unclear aspects of the Constitution involves extra-constitutional doctrines, it would be natural for originalists to prefer that courts refrain from deciding such cases.

One who wishes to justify such a policy of "judicial restraint" might suggest that the defendant should win whenever law is unclear and therefore indeterminate, because then the burden of proof cannot effectively be shouldered by a plaintiff or appellant.[44] This reasoning seems warranted by the notion that courts should decide cases by reference to existing law. Not requiring extra-constitutional doctrines, it seems compatible with originalism.

But extensive use of the burden-of-proof rule would be problematic in our system. Suppose, for example, that district courts in different circuits,

[44] See, e.g., Van Alstyne, *Interpreting This Constitution: The Unhelpful Contributions of Special Theories of Judicial Review*, 35 U. Fla. L. Rev. 229 (1983).

believing they had adequate constitutional grounds for doing so, decided similar cases, but did so differently. Suppose, further, that their decisions involved aspects of the Constitution that their respective circuit courts regarded as indeterminate because unclear. If the circuit courts invoked the burden-of-proof rule, the result would in effect establish conflicting constitutional doctrines in different circuits. The federal courts would seem to require some extra-constitutional doctrine to extricate us from that predicament.

The alternative basis for a policy of "judicial restraint" is an argument from "democracy," which concludes that nonelected judges should not nullify decisions made by "electorally accountable" officials. The reasoning may be understood as follows. Insofar as political arrangements are subject to popular control through elections, they are regarded by many constitutional theorists as respecting democratic values. In addition, our system involves a division of political power under which popularly elected legislatures are authorized to make law and the judiciary is conventionally understood as authorized to interpret and apply, but not to make law.

One who assumes that unclear law is indeterminate will also believe that judges must "legislate" whenever they decide "hard cases." This practice is tolerable, or even desirable, when kept to a minimum, judges are elected and, most importantly, elected legislatures are able, if they wish, to modify the results by means of subsequent legislation. This would normally be the case except when courts must rule on limits to the legislature's authority.

From that perspective, judicial review by the federal courts of decisions made by elected officials is most problematic. In the first place, federal judges are not elected, but are appointed with indefinite tenure. Popular control is more limited over the federal judiciary than over elected officials (or, more generally, over those who are considered "electorally accountable" – those who, for example, are appointed but serve at the pleasure of elected officials). In the second place, such review concerns the constitutionality of nonjudicial decisions. Decisions made by electorally accountable officials are liable to be nullified by nonelected federal judges, and electorally accountable officials will be unable to override those judicial decisions. It is accordingly held by many constitutional theorists that such judicial review severely strains democratic principles.

These same democratic sensibilities are most seriously offended when judicial review is thought to be combined with "judicial legislation." Therefore, when constitutional cases turn upon the testing of nonjudicial decisions against unclear constitutional provisions, legal theorists tend to suppose that any substantive decision involves judicial revision of the Constitution itself. On the basis of such reasoning, contemporary originalists sometimes hold that decisions made by officials who are answerable to the electorate should not be nullified by nonelected judges unless it is clear that those decisions violate the Constitution.[45]

Some constitutional theorists are thought to lack such scruples. They are accused of claiming that courts may take it upon themselves to change the supreme law of the land. An example of such thinking is discussed by Justice Rehnquist, who quotes from a brief filed in federal court on behalf of state prisoners as follows:

> We are asking a great deal of the Court because other branches of government have abdicated their responsibility. . . . Prisoners are like other 'discrete and insular' minorities for whom the Court must spread its protective umbrella because no other branch of government will do so. . . . This Court, as the voice and conscience of contemporary society, as the measure of the modern conception of human dignity, must declare that the [named prison] and all it represents offends the Constitution of the United States and will not be tolerated.[46]

Rehnquist understands this to imply that "nonelected members of the federal judiciary may address themselves to a social problem simply because other branches of government have failed or refused to do so."[47] Federal judges would then have "a roving commission to second-guess Congress, state legislatures, and state and federal administrative officers concerning what is best for the country."[48] Rehnquist accordingly describes such a view as "a formula for an end run around popular government, genuinely corrosive of the fundamental values of our democratic society."[49]

Rehnquist's rhetoric is fired by "democratic" flames, so let us look more closely at this argument from democracy. It challenges the legitimacy of judicial review. If we were to formulate the argument rigorously, its conclusion would amount to the following proposition:

> Judicial review of a non-judicial decision violates democratic principles to the extent that the reviewing judiciary is less directly accountable to a popular electorate than is the non-judicial decision maker.

[45] This assumes, of course, that judicial review can be justified despite the argument from democracy. We shall return to that point presently.

[46] Rehnquist, *The Notion of a Living Constitution*, 54 Texas L. Rev. 695 (1976).

[47] *ibid.*

[48] *ibid.*, p. 698.

[49] *ibid.*, p. 706.

To reach this conclusion, a premise like the following is needed:

> Democratic principles imply that the more directly accountable an official decision maker is to a popular electorate, the greater the priority that should be given her official decisions.

This claim is dubious. It assumes that democratic standards apply directly to the several branches of a political structure, although the several branches are supposed to complement each other so as to yield a structure that is democratic overall. On the contrary, just as various amendments to the Constitution can be understood as promoting the system's respect for democratic values, rather than compromising that commitment, judicial review may be instrumental in securing that respect.

The sort of premise that seems to be needed by the standard argument against judicial review invokes "democracy" in a problematic way. It seems to invoke a theory of the Constitution. But no attempt is made to explain what relation such a view must have to the Constitution if the former is to qualify as a theory of the latter, no less how a particular theory might be defended. This is especially important because it is uncertain whether any view can both qualify as a theory of the Constitution, to be used in constitutional interpretation, and be reconciled with "strict" originalism.

More generally, the premise of the standard argument from democracy fails to reflect any appreciation of the values that might explain the importance of accountability to a popular electorate. It is implausible to suppose that "electoral accountability" is a fundamental value. That it is not is suggested, for example, by the qualifications that one would reasonably place on electoral accountability before it could serve in such a role; for example, that elections be free and fair. This strongly suggests that electoral accountability derives its importance from some more fundamental value, such as the right to participate in shaping the rules that may be enforced against oneself or, perhaps, political equality. These values and their relation to electoral accountability require clarification. Until we understand the basic values at stake, we can hardly determine the relation between judicial review and a commitment to democracy. And yet the literature on judicial review is silent on such matters.

Now, a federal judge might find it awkward to endorse the argument from democracy. For it suggests that the constitutional system is "democratic" in such a way as to make judicial review illegitimate. One who endorses such an argument might find it difficult to function honestly in the federal judiciary, where judicial review is firmly established.

It turns out, however, that the argument from democracy is used not to block judicial review but, rather, to establish a presumption against it. It is thought to counsel "restraint." This is illustrated by Rehnquist's response to the argument from democracy. He does not reject judicial review. He endorses it on the ground that the constitutional arrangements including judicial review are given by "the people."[50] Unfortunately, Rehnquist's version of this claim is no more plausible than the one we considered in section II. A specious argument receives a glib reply.

It should be observed, finally, that Rehnquist charges those he criticizes as favoring "the substitution of some other set of values for those which may be derived from the language and intent of the framers."[51] As this formulation suggests, his argument really turns on how the Constitution is to be understood. The quoted brief claimed, after all, that courts have a special responsibility to protect "discrete and insular minorities." This is a proposition with which some constitutional scholars agree.[52] They hold this responsibility to be based on the Constitution, not created by judicial fiat. Rehnquist disagrees with this interpretation and treats its proponents as if they recommend infidelity to the Constitution.

## VI. THE WAGES OF SKEPTICISM

An initially more promising argument regarding judicial review is presented by Professor (now Judge) Bork, who begins by rejecting the crude argument from democracy and by describing our constitutional system as "Madisonian":

> A Madisonian system is not completely democratic, if by "democratic" we mean completely majoritarian. It assumes that in wide areas of life majorities are entitled to rule for no better reason than they are majorities. We need not pause here to examine the philosophical underpinnings of that assumption since it is a "given" in our society. . . .[53]

Bork refrains from reflecting on the values that are at stake. This may be deliberate, for reasons that will emerge presently. But it is unfortunate because Bork, too, appears to offer us a theory of the Constitution.

Bork claims that "the Madisonian model" has two "premises." One is "majoritarian," the other "counter-majoritarian."

> The model . . . assumes there are some areas of life a majority should not control. There are some things a majority should not do to us no matter how democratically it decides to do them.[54]

[50] *ibid.*, p. 696.
[51] *ibid.*, p. 695.
[52] See, e.g., Ely, Democracy and Distrust.
[53] Bork, *Neutral Principles*, pp. 2–3.
[54] *ibid.*, p. 3.

To reconcile these "premises," we charge the Supreme Court to "define both majority and minority freedom through the interpretation of the Constitution."[55] Thus Bork accepts the legitimacy of judicial review. But, he says,

> the Court's power is legitimate only if it has, and can demonstrate in reasoned opinions that it has, a valid theory, derived from the Constitution, of the respective spheres of majority and minority freedom. If it does not have such a theory but merely imposes its own value choices, or worse if it pretends to have a theory but actually follows its own predilections, the Court violates the postulates of the Madisonian model that alone justifies its power.[56]

This passage suggests Bork's concern that the Court not impose its own "value choices."

He explains that concern in the course of an argument that appears more promising than Rehnquist's because it deals with the issues at a more fundamental level. Bork's argument may be summarized as follows:

1. Judicial decisions *should be* "principled."
2. Judicial decisions either *make* or *implement* "value choices."
3. Judicial decisions that *implement* "value choices" *can* be "principled."
4. There is *no* "principled" way to *make* a "value choice."
5. Judicial decisions *should implement*, rather than make, "value choices."
6. Law-creation, such as legislation or the framing of a constitution, involves *making* "value choices."
7. "Courts [reviewing legislation] must accept any value choice the legislature makes unless it clearly runs contrary to a choice made in the framing of the Constitution."[57]

This argument is originalist in spirit, if not entirely in content. An originalist theory of interpretation is suggested by the notion that certain "value choices" were made by the framers and are now available to be implemented by the courts. This corresponds to the idea that Constitutional doctrines are fixed when the document is framed. An originalist theory of adjudication is suggested too, as Bork comes near to claiming that only those doctrines embodying the "framers' value choices" should be applied by the Court.

Note that the last step in the argument appears to presuppose a nonoriginalist principle:

[55] *ibid.*
[56] *ibid.*
[57] *ibid.*, pp. 10–11.

> Whenever the Constitution is unclear, the Court should defer to the legislature.

What basis could there be for such a doctrine of "restraint"? Bork has no grounds for suggesting, for example, that the practice of judicial review should be confined because it suffers under a cloud of illegitimacy. For, as we have seen, he has rejected the dubious argument from democracy, endorsed the practice of judicial review, and assigned it an indispensable constitutional function.

Here is one possible explanation of that last step in Bork's reasoning. As we have observed, many legal theorists embrace assumptions about meaning which lead them to believe that law is indeterminate when it is unclear. As we shall presently see, Bork explicitly endorses an even more radical type of philosophical skepticism – about value judgments generally. It would therefore not be out of keeping for Bork to indulge in the semantical skepticism that leaps from "unclear" to "indeterminate." This would lead him to reason that, when (a) the Constitution does not *clearly* contain a doctrine that is violated by a piece of legislation, then (b) the Constitution contains *no* such doctrine, (c) the legislation does not violate the Constitution, and (d) the legislation should accordingly be accepted by the Court.[58]

But the most serious difficulty with Bork's reasoning derives from his value skepticism. To see this, we might begin by asking what is meant by a "value choice." This expression is so commonplace in constitutional theory that we may need to remind ourselves that it is an artifact of theory. Compare the expression with "value judgment." "Value choice" omits any reference to judgment, and so encourages the suggestion of arbitrariness and discourages any contrary suggestion of rational defensibility. The difference fits nicely into Bork's strategy of argument, which explicitly invokes a general philosophical doctrine of skepticism about the rational defensibility of value judgments.

As we have seen, Bork defines the central problem of "Madisonian democracy" as the need to strike a balance between "majority and minority freedom."[59] It is precisely in this context that he says, for example:

> Every clash between a minority claiming freedom and a majority claiming power to regulate involves a choice between gratifications of the two groups. When the Constitution has not spoken, the Court will be able to find no scale, other than its own value preferences, upon which to weigh the respective claims to pleasure.[60]

[58] This assumes the use of a burden-of-proof rule discussed in section V.
[59] Bork, *Neutral Principles*, p. 3.
[60] *ibid.*, p. 9.

Bork has two examples. One is *Griswold*, which he views as a judicial choice between two "claims to pleasure" and their respective "gratifications." Another is "a hypothetical suit by an electric company and one of its customers to void a smoke pollution ordinance as unconstitutional. The cases are identical."[61]

To make Bork's position perfectly clear, we should consider a different example. Prior to the Fourteenth Amendment, Bork would presumably respond to a suit seeking invalidation of a law banning Jews and Catholics from certain occupations, as follows:

> There is no way of deciding these matters other than by reference to some system of moral or ethical values that has no objective or intrinsic validity of its own and about which men can and do differ. Where the Constitution does not embody the moral or ethical choice, the judge has no basis other than his own values upon which to set aside the community judgment embodied in the statute.[62]

My point is not that a refusal to invalidate the statute would have been unfaithful to the law, for the contrary interpretation is, unfortunately, plausible. My point is that Bork's express reason for a judicial policy of "restraint" is that all opposing positions, including the rejection of bigotry, are rationally indefensible, so that, lacking constitutional warrant, a judicial decision favoring one would be "unprincipled" *just because* any "preference" for one side or the other *could not be* "principled." Value "choices" are required to adjudicate between any two opposing views, because moral and political positions are in Bork's view equivalent to preferences. The judicial vindication of a morally motivated claim is likewise equivalent, in his eyes, to favoring one person's gratification over another's. But:

> There is no principled way to decide that one man's gratifications are more deserving of respect than another's or that one form of gratification is more worthy than another.[63]

Such "value choices" might be made by judges or derived from the Constitution. If made by judges, Bork maintains, the judicial decisions in which

[61] *ibid.*

[62] *ibid.*, p. 10.

[63] *ibid.* Bork's note explains: "The impossibility is related to that of making interpersonal comparisons of utilities." He apparently assumes that if there is any morally defensible criterion for making decisions (including those adjudicating interpersonal conflicts of interest), it is that they should maximize (in Bork's terms) "gratifications." The alleged impossibility to which he refers would make that criterion impossible to satisfy. Normative welfare economics avoids the problem by giving up the maximizing requirement and replacing it with a conception of economic efficiency, such as Pareto's, that requires no interpersonal comparisons of utility. Bork's note suggests that he is unaware of or refuses to consider either economic or deontological alternatives to classical utilitarianism.

they are embodied are "unprincipled," because value judgments are in general "unprincipled."

> Where constitutional materials do not clearly specify the value to be preferred, there is no principled way to prefer any claimed human value to any other.[64]

But if the "value choices" are derived from the Constitution, then the judicial decisions implementing them are "principled."

It is important to emphasize that in these passages Bork is *not* simply asserting the standard originalist claim that judges reviewing legislation should not impose their own values, but should apply doctrines derived from the Constitution. For that is what he is trying to prove. He is arguing, in effect, that *when the Constitution is unclear and interpretation of it may seem to require moral reasoning*, judges should defer to the legislature. His philosophical skepticism is deployed to show that judges should make no value judgments when deciding constitutional cases.

That is relevant to an earlier argument of this paper. The alternative to "strict" originalism that was sketched in section III requires that courts applying "vague clauses" of the Constitution interpret "contested concepts," which requires reasoning about moral or political principles. Bork's view that judges should not make "value choices" seems to mean that courts should not engage in any such reasoning. Bork reasons: judicial review should be neutral, principled, and nonarbitrary; it is impossible to make value judgments that are neutral, principled, or nonarbitrary; so judges should not incorporate value judgments into their constitutional decisions.

Bork's value skepticism is assumed and applied without justification.[65] Needless to say, value skepticism cannot be found within the Constitution. Indeed, the two are clearly incompatible. Thus Bork invokes an *anti*-constitutional doctrine to significant effect.

It is worth noting that Bork's skepticism renders his overall position incoherent. Consider his claim that judges *should* decide constitutional cases in a certain way – that (as he seems to argue) they are *under an obligation* to do so. Bork writes as if he is providing a rational defense for that sort of conclusion about the responsible, legitimate use of judicial power. He appears to believe that his reasoning excludes contrary conceptions of judicial obligation. In his terminology, however, to embrace such a doctrine is to make a "value choice," which according to his value skepticism is irremediably "unprincipled," or rationally indefensible.

The result is a dilemma for Bork. If it is possible to provide good reasons

[64] *ibid.*, p. 8.
[65] But see note 63.

(as Bork purports to do) for his conception of the legitimate (justified, responsible) exercise of judicial power – reasons designed to show that his conception is superior to contrary conceptions – then "value choices" can be principled. On the one hand, the success of any argument for the attribution of an obligation to judges would refute his value skepticism and undermine his argument that value judgments have no legitimate place in constitutional adjudication. On the other hand, his wholesale value skepticism excludes the possibility that any conception of the legitimate exercise of judicial power might be rationally defensible; so his skepticism undermines his own argument for and resulting judgment about responsible adjudication.

Consider now Bork's notion that judges must rely upon the value judgments that are embedded in the Constitution if their decisions are to be "principled." Bork assumes that decisions involving the exercise of judicial review can be "principled" insofar as they are grounded upon constitutional doctrines. This apparently means that the decisions can be justified relative to, or conditional upon, those doctrines.

But conditional justification is only as good as its condition. Recall that one piece of Bork's argument goes as follows:

> Law-creation, such as legislation or the framing of a constitution, involves making "value choices."

Another piece says:

> There is no principled way to make a "value choice."

Put together, these pieces yield the conclusion that the "value choices" embodied in the Constitution and the corresponding doctrines are themselves "unprincipled" or, in other words, unjustifiable. But if the doctrines on which the justification of judicial decisions depends are themselves unjustifiable, then the same applies to those decisions.

This means that Bork is faced with another dilemma. On the one hand, if "value choices" are unjustifiable, then so are the "value choices" reflected in the Constitution, and the same applies to all that relies on them for justification. On the other hand, if some value judgments can be justified (such as the idea that the Constitution merits respect), then Bork's general value skepticism is unsound, and his main argument collapses.

Bork might seem to avoid this particular incoherence when he remarks that his value skepticism "is not applicable to legislation. Legislation requires value choice and cannot be principled in the sense under discussion."[66] Bork might seem to suggest that there is another sense of "principled" in which

[66] Bork, *Neutral Principles*, p. 8.

the "value choices" embodied in legislation (and thus the legislation itself) can be "principled." Bork might mean, for example, that, rationally defensible or not, legislation by popularly elected officials is *permissible* under both democratic principles and our constitutional system. He might also wish to infer from this that those subject to such laws are under an obligation to respect them.

But this interpretation would not enable Bork to avoid the dilemma. Either he accepts the idea that democratic standards *justify* political arrangements that satisfy them, or he rejects it, presumably because of his value skepticism. If he rejects the idea, then there is no apparent sense within Bork's skeptical system in which legislation or indeed our constitutional system can be justifiable; there is no apparent sense in which the Constitution can *truly* be said to merit respect, in which judges can *truly* be said to be under an obligation to respect it. If Bork believes that any of these value judgments can *truly* be justified, then he must forsake his objection based on value skepticism to the exercise of moral judgment within judicial review.

## VII. CONCLUSION

Originalism seems to derive its initial plausibility from a simplified conception of how written constitutions work. Interpretation in terms of original intent promises a stable, uncontroversial version of the Constitution. But intentionalism faces overwhelming difficulties and appears to lack compensating justification, either in political or linguistic terms. Seeing no promising alternatives, opponents of strict originalism have accepted the need for extra-constitutional doctrines in constitutional adjudication. Originalists appear to reject such heterodoxy, but they unselfconsciously embrace a variety of extra-constitutional doctrines. Their theorizing about the Constitution tends toward the superficially descriptive and has yet to face the substantive value commitments implicit even in ritualistic appeals to democracy. Just as the Constitution cannot be value-free, so our understanding of it must be informed by reflection on the principles it serves.

*Philosophy and Law, Cornell University*

# [8]

# ARTICLES

## AN ESSAY ON CONSTITUTIONAL LANGUAGE

Frederick Schauer*

Many contemporary constitutional scholars have explored the extent to which, if at all, judges should go "outside of" or "beyond" the constitutional text for decisional principles in constitutional cases.[1] Although the resulting discussions have been highly illuminating, I do not wish to deal directly with this controversy here. Rather, I propose to discuss what is logically a prior question. For before we can argue intelligently about whether to go outside of the text, we ought to explore the meaning of the words *inside* the text. Only then will we know what counts as going "outside," and until then, it is not clear that there even is an outside because "inside" and "outside" are relative terms.

---

* Cutler Professor of Law, College of William and Mary. A.B., 1967, M.B.A., 1968, Dartmouth; J.D., 1972, Harvard.

The research and writing of this essay were supported by a grant from the National Endowment for the Humanities. I am also indebted to Philip Devine, Kent Greenawalt, Margit Livingston, Mary Jane Morrison, Stanley Paulson, Martin Willard, and William Van Alstyne for their helpful comments on earlier drafts.

1. The contemporary jargon draws a distinction between "interpretivism" and "noninterpretivism," but this is merely one characterization of an issue that predates the current labels. *See generally* J.H. ELY, DEMOCRACY AND DISTRUST 1-14 (1980); Brest, *The Misconceived Quest for the Original Understanding,* 60 B.U.L. REV. 204 (1980); Grey, *Do We Have an Unwritten Constitution?,* 27 STAN. L. REV. 703 (1975) [hereinafter cited as Grey, *Unwritten Constitution*]; Grey, *Origins of the Unwritten Constitution: Fundamental Law in American Revolutionary Thought,* 30 STAN. L. REV. 843 (1978) [hereinafter cited as Grey, *Origins*]; Linde, *Judges, Critics and the Realist Tradition,* 82 YALE L.J. 227 (1972); Monaghan, *Of "Liberty" and "Property,"* 62 CORNELL L. REV. 405 (1977); Monaghan, *The Constitution Goes to Harvard,* 13 HARV. C.R.-C.L. L. REV. 117 (1978) [hereinafter cited as Monaghan, *The Constitution*]; Perry, *Substantive Due Process Revisited: Reflections on (and Beyond) Recent Cases,* 71 NW. U.L. REV. 417 (1976); Richards, *Human Rights as the Unwritten Constitution: The Problem of Change and Stability in Constitutional Interpretation,* 4 U. DAYTON L. REV. 295 (1979); *Constitutional Adjudication and Democratic Theory,* 56 N.Y.U. L. REV. 259 (1981); *Judicial Review versus Democracy,* 42 OHIO ST. L.J. 1 (1981).

We assume, perhaps too easily, that the language of the Constitution is neither the source of, nor the answer to, our problems, and we then head off into the forbidding jungles of history, political theory, moral philosophy, public policy, and what have you without any clear guide. An examination of the words in the Constitution has been merely the hors d'oeuvre, with high theory as the main course.

There is nothing unseemly about high theory in this sense. Nevertheless, we need to look at the words of the Constitution *as language,* and we need to examine closely some of our rarely questioned presuppositions about constitutional language. Although this examination logically is prior to any broader interpretation of the Constitution, it has received surprisingly little concentrated attention in the literature.[2]

Constitutional cogniscenti talk about "gaps," "great silences," "vague language," and "open texture" as if these were concepts of little controversy.[3] But what makes the requirement that the President be of "the Age of thirty five Years" specific and the requirement of "equal protection of the laws" vague? Why are there "loopholes" in the Internal Revenue Code, but not in the Constitution? In order to understand and to attempt to answer questions like these, we need a theory of constitutional language as much as we need theories of constitutional law.

The Constitution is, after all, a writing,[4] and at bottom we are

2. One notable exception is Munzer & Nickel, *Does the Constitution Mean What it Always Meant?,* 77 COLUM. L. REV. 1029 (1977). *See also* Alexander, *Modern Equal Protection Theories: A Metatheoretical Taxonomy and Critique*, 42 OHIO ST. L.J. 3, 4-16 (1981); Smith, *Rights, Right Answers, and the Constructive Model of Morality,* 5 SOC. THEORY AND PRAC. 409, 421-25 (1980). Philosophy is at the moment having a good run in the constitutional arena, but, with few exceptions, it is moral philosophy rather than the philosophy of language that is taken to be the most useful for constitional inquiries. Given that we have a *written* constitution, this lack of attention from the perspective of the philosophy of language seems a bit surprising. Although not directed specifically towards constitutional interpretation, there has been some recent attention to legal language from a philosophical perspective. Moore, *The Semantics of Judging*, 54 S. CAL. L. REV. 151 (1981); Stone, *From a Language Perspective*, 90 YALE L.J. 1149 (1981).

3. In addition to the works cited *supra* note 1, see L. TRIBE, AMERICAN CONSTITUTIONAL LAW at iii (1978) ("[T]he Constitution is an intentionally incomplete, often deliberately indeterminate structure for the participatory evolution of political ideals and governmental practices."); L. TRIBE, AMERICAN CONSTITUTIONAL LAW 2 (Supp. 1979) ("open-textured" provisions such as "equal protection" and "due process"; use of "broad terminology" in the Constitution). *See also* Baker v. Carr, 369 U.S. 186, 242 (1962) (Douglas, J., concurring) ("large gaps in the Constitution"); H.P. Hood & Sons, Inc. v. Du Mond, 336 U.S. 525, 535 (1949) (Jackson, J.) ("great silences of the Constitution"); Prudential Ins. Co. v. Benjamin, 328 U.S. 408, 413 (1946) ("great constitutional gaps").

4. Although it illustrates the focus both of this inquiry and of my conclusions, the phrase in the text is, at this stage, question-begging. For even if we note that the Constitution is written, what does this say about the constitution? This question can

interpreting the *words* of a written document. But how do we do this? What does it mean to "interpret" a constitutional provision? What do we mean when we say that a constitutional provision "means" something? How do we start such an analysis? These are hard and important questions, and we should not dismiss them as irrelevant philosophical speculation. Indeed, answers to these questions underlie any theory of constitutional adjudication, and this Essay attempts to bring some of these answers to the surface for closer inspection.

My intention here is not to offer a completely mature theory of constitutional language. Rather, I wish to explore the way in which the conventions of language affect constitutional theory. At the end of this Essay, I conclude that constitutional language acts as a significant restraint on constitutional decision, but I will not have developed a complete theory of constitutional language which directs any particular substantive outcomes. A complete theory will have to wait for another time.

## I. On the Supposed Uniqueness of Constitutional Language

In his pioneering work on legal language, H.L.A. Hart argued that legal language is fundamentally different from ordinary language.[5] According to Hart, if one fails to recognize the unique context and the distinct presuppositions of legal discourse, then one commits the errors of formalism or conceptualism—giving to words in the abstract an aura of authority and of unique reference inconsistent with the view of language as an activity determined and governed by social rules.[6] If, as Hart and his philosophical

---

be expressed in terms of how much of the constitution is contained or captured in the (written) Constitution. It is this question that this essay is intended to address. Positing the question in this way suggests the Continental distinction between a material constitution and a formal constitution. *See* H. Kelsen, The Pure Theory of Law 222-24 (M. Knight trans. 2d ed. 1967).

5. Hart's original foray into the field was *The Ascription of Responsibility and Rights*, in Logic and Language (First Series) 145-66 (A. Flew ed. 1955). Hart's later repudiation of this strictly performative view of legal language (H.L.A. Hart, Punishment and Responsibility v (1968)) was the result of the more complex, presupposition-oriented theory first put forth in Hart, *Definition and Theory in Jurisprudence*, 70 Law Q. Rev. 37 (1954) [hereinafter cited as Hart, *Definition and Theory*], and embellished in H.L.A. Hart, The Concept of Law 13-17 (1961). *See also* Cohen, *Theory and Definition in Jurisprudence*, 29 Proc. Aristotelian Soc. (Supp.) 213 (1955); Hart, *Theory and Definition in Jurisprudence*, 29 Proc. Aristotelian Soc. (Supp.) 239 (1955). *See generally* N. MacCormick, H.L.A. Hart (1981); Hacker, *Hart's Philosophy of Law*, and Baker, *Defeasibility and Meaning*, in Law, Morality, and Society: Essays in Honour of H.L.A. Hart 1, 26 (P. Hacker & J. Raz eds. 1977).

6. *See* H.L.A. Hart, *supra* note 5, at 126-27; Sartorius, *Hart's Concept of Law*, in More Essays in Legal Philosophy 131-61 (R. Summers ed. 1971). *See also* G.

contemporaries supposed, meaning is use,[7] then legal use ought to produce different meanings than a physicist's use, a sociologist's use, or the use of the man on the Clapham omnibus.[8] And, just as legal language is different in kind from ordinary language, constitutional language may be different from other legal language.[9] In fact, this hypothesis implicitly undergirds many different theories of constitutional interpretation.[10] The various theories of a "living" or "changeable" constitution each presuppose a view of the uniqueness of constitutional language, setting it off from the linguistic raw material with which lawyers normally deal.[11]

---

GOTTLIEB, THE LOGIC OF CHOICE 48 (1968); Hart, *Problems of Philosophy of Law*, in 6 ENCYCLOPEDIA PHIL. 266, 270 (P. Edwards ed. 1967); Stone, *Ratiocination Not Rationalisation*, 74 MIND 463 (1965).

7. *See* L. WITTGENSTEIN, PHILOSOPHICAL INVESTIGATIONS §§ 30, 43, 120, 138, 340, 532 (G. Anscombe trans. 1958). Although Wittgenstein was the guiding light of the "meaning is use" approach, that approach was in fact the standard under which most of Anglo-American philosophy operated in the 1950s and 1960s. *See, e.g.*, J. AUSTIN, HOW TO DO THINGS WITH WORDS (J.O. Urmson & M. Sbisa 2d ed. 1975) [hereinafter cited as J. AUSTIN, WORDS]; J. AUSTIN, PHILOSOPHICAL STUDIES (3d ed. 1979); Grice, *Meaning*, 66 PHIL. REV. 377 (1957); Strawson, *Propositions, Concepts, and Logical Truth*, 7 PHIL. Q. 15 (1957).

8. The man on the Clapham omnibus is most frequently taken to be the prototypical reasonable man for purposes of tort law, *see, e.g.*, Bolam v. Friern Hospital Management Committee, 1 W.L.R. 582, 586-87 (Q.B. 1957), but he is also the ordinary speaker of ordinary English. *See, e.g.*, Woodhouse A.C. Israel Cocoa Ltd. S.A. v. Nigerian Produce Marketing Co., 2 Q.B. 23, 63 (C.A. 1971). Although we need not recount Hart's arguments, those arguments do suggest that constitutional language may possess a uniqueness of its own. For summary and critique, see N. MACCORMICK, *supra* note 5; Baker, *supra* note 5; Hacker, *supra* note 5. *See also* Shuman, *Jurisprudence and the Analysis of Fundamental Legal Terms*, 8 J. LEGAL EDUC. 437 (1956).

9. "[I]t was by no means self-evident in 1789 that judges should use the same techniques in the construction of constitutional provisions as in the interpretation of ordinary statutory and decisional sources." H. Jones, *The Common Law in the United States: English Themes and American Variations*, in POLITICAL SEPARATION AND LEGAL CONTINUITY 134 (1976). *See also* Bridwell, Book Review, 1978 DUKE L.J. 907, 914-15 (reviewing R. BERGER, GOVERNMENT BY JUDICIARY: THE TRANSFORMATION OF THE FOURTEENTH AMENDMENT (1977)).

10. Thus, when John Marshall observed that "we must never forget that it is a *constitution* we are expounding," McCulloch v. Maryland, 17 U.S. (4 Wheat.) 316, 407 (1819), he was adopting the thesis discussed in the text, although *McCulloch* is significantly obscure in that Marshall did not explain in what way constitutional interpretation was unique. *See* Frankfurter, *John Marshall and the Judicial Function*, 69 HARV. L. REV. 217 (1955). For a sampling of the various theories that embody this view in one way or other, see C. BLACK, STRUCTURE AND RELATIONSHIP IN CONSTITUTIONAL LAW (1969); C. MILLER, THE SUPREME COURT AND THE USES OF HISTORY (1969); Llewellyn, *The Constitution as an Institution*, 34 COLUM. L. REV. 1 (1934); Murphy, *The Art of Constitutional Interpretation: A Preliminary Showing*, in ESSAYS ON THE CONSTITUTION OF THE UNITED STATES 130 (M. Harmon ed. 1978).

11. *See, e.g.*, R. DWORKIN, TAKING RIGHTS SERIOUSLY 131-49 (1980); H. MCBAIN, THE LIVING CONSTITUTION (1927); Brest, *supra* note 1; Grey, *supra* note 1; Munzer & Nickel, *supra* note 2; Perry, *supra* note 1; Miller, *Notes on the Concept of the "Living" Constitution*, 31 GEO. WASH. L. REV. 881 (1963); Reich, *The Living Constitution and the Court's Role*, in HUGO BLACK AND THE SUPREME COURT 133 (S. Strick-

There *seem* to be readily apparent differences between constitutional language and other legal language. Grandiloquent phrases like "freedom of speech," "equal protection of the laws," "due process of law," and "privileges and immunities of citizens of the United States" have few counterparts in the Internal Revenue Code or the Public Utility Holding Company Act of 1935. Indeed, many constitutional provisions are more than merely indeterminate. They have a powerful emotive component. The Constitution is more an eloquently written manifesto[12] than it is a code, and in many ways we are much better for that. But the eloquence and emotive force of the document further reinforce the view that the Constitution's words are as different as they are special. To construe its language too literally or too much like the language in a conventional statute would be both unrealistic and inconsistent with its deeper purposes. In some ways, the Constitution is a metaphor.[13]

Not unrelated to the Constitution's metaphorical quality is its permanence. Statutes are frequently amended, and the common law is continually changing, but the Constitution has a special sort of durability. Not only is amending the Constitution extremely difficult, but we also seem remarkably averse to doing so.[14] Many

---

land ed. 1967); Richards, *supra* note 1. *Contra* Rehnquist, *The Notion of a Living Constitution,* 54 TEX. L. REV. 693 (1976). In terms of a theory of meaning, some of the foregoing theses could be said to assume that the meaning of constitutional provisions changes over time, while others would hold that the meaning remains the same while the applications change. Exploring that distinction at this point would serve little purpose, because it and related issues are the focus of the balance of this Essay.

12. In this sense, the Constitution combines both argument and aspiration with a statement of existing principles, not unlike Joel Feinberg's "manifesto sense" of a right. J. FEINBERG, SOCIAL PHILOSOPHY 67 (1973). I derive some support for this view from the similarity between the largely enforceable American Constitution and the many largely unenforceable international treaties, declarations, and conventions dealing with human rights. Learned Hand, of course, treated this manifesto sense as virtually the *sole* function of some constitutional provisions. L. HAND, THE BILL OF RIGHTS 33-34 (1958).

13. One of the purposes of a metaphor is to get us to think in different ways, to block intentionally some of our routine thought processes. *See, e.g.,* I. HUNGERLAND, POETIC DISCOURSE 127 (1958); Black, *Metaphor,* in MODELS AND METAPHORS 25 (1962). It seems to me quite likely that this process is at least one of the implicit purposes of the Constitution, but proving that hypothesis is beyond the purview of this Essay.

14. Fear of the possible results of judicial interpretation may explain a large part of this aversion. It has been 114 years since any very broad language was added to the Constitution (the ratification of the fourteenth amendment), and the rough road travelled by both the Equal Rights Amendment and the various proposed "right to life" amendments suggests that we may never again add a constitutional provision of similar openness. Quite possibly, it is only a fortunate historical accident that aggressive judicial review arose only after the enactment of those constitutional provisions which now occupy most of the Supreme Court's time. Perhaps such active review has, for all practical purposes, foreclosed the possibility of ever again achieving the consensus necessary to add similar provisions to the Constitution.

have feared a constitutional convention because too much might be changed,[15] even though such changes would still require ratification by the states. On the other hand, we certainly do not suspend Congress or the state legislatures for fear that they might legislate too much—however appealing that suggestion may at times seem.

Despite these important differences, we would be mistaken to view constitutional language as a wholly unique creature. The seemingly intentional openness of many constitutional terms, upon which most of the supposition about the uniqueness of constitutional language is based,[16] has counterparts in other areas of law, especially in American law. The generality of "equal protection of the laws" or "the freedom of speech" differs little from the language in Rule 10b-5 of the Securities and Exchange Commission, which prohibits the employment of "any device, scheme, or artifice to defraud."[17] Likewise, the fourth amendment's prohibition of "unreasonable" searches and seizures provides no more guidance than the Sherman Act's ban on "[e]very contract, combination . . . or conspiracy, in restraint of trade or commerce . . . ."[18] As a result, the task of the courts in putting flesh on the skeleton of the Constitution is not wholly different from the task that courts have undertaken in developing the elaborate structure of tests, rules, and standards that surround and govern the application of the securities laws, the antitrust laws, and many other statutory schemes.[19]

---

15. *See generally* Dellinger, *The Recurring Question of the "Limited" Constitutional Convention,* 88 YALE L.J. 1623 (1979); Dellinger, *Who Controls a Constitutional Convention?—A Response,* 1979 DUKE L.J. 999; Fordham, *Some Observations Upon Uneasy American Federalism,* 58 N.C.L. REV. 289 (1980); Gunther, *The Convention Method of Amending the United States Constitution,* 14 GA. L. REV. 1 (1979); Tribe, *Issues Raised By Requesting Congress to Call a Constitutional Convention to Propose a Balanced Budget Amendment,* 10 PAC. L.J. 627 (1979); Van Alstyne, *Does Article V Restrict the States to Calling Unlimited Conventions Only?—A Letter to a Colleague,* 1978 DUKE L.J. 1295; Van Alstyne, *The Limited Constitutional Convention—The Recurring Answer,* 1979 DUKE L.J. 985; Note, *Good Intentions, New Inventions, and Article V Constitutional Conventions,* 58 TEX. L. REV. 131 (1979). The implicit theme of most of the recent literature, which has attracted an all-star lineup of constitutional scholars, is that an unlimited convention is fraught with danger.

16. *See supra* note 3. A pervasive problem in attempting to generalize about constitutional language is that constitutional language is hardly uniform in degree of generality, in purpose, or in historical origin. This recognition of the diversity of constitutional language is most prominently associated with Justice Frankfurter. *See, e.g.,* Malinski v. New York, 324 U.S. 401, 414-15 (1945). *See generally* H. THOMAS, FELIX FRANKFURTER: SCHOLAR ON THE BENCH 127-47 (1960).

17. 17 C.F.R. § 240.10b-5(a) (1981).

18. 15 U.S.C. § 1 (1976).

19. Note, for example, the intermingling of examples from both constitutional and statutory interpretation in E. LEVI, AN INTRODUCTION TO LEGAL REASONING (1949).

If the openness of constitutional language does not provide its uniqueness, perhaps the notion of presupposition,[20] which undergirds Hart's argument in "Definition and Theory in Jurisprudence,"[21] can explain the uniqueness. Statements of law, or *in* law (as opposed to statements *about* law), presuppose the existence of a legal system, and particular statements of legal rules themselves contain presuppositions.[22] Thus, the statement "the corporation is liable in damages" presupposes a body of law creating and defining a "corporation." But presupposition is hardly unique to law. When we use "home run" or "small slam," we presuppose the systems of baseball and bridge, respectively, and when we use "professor" or "hour examination," we similarly presuppose the existence of a college or university, which is in turn defined by a (probably looser) set of constitutive rules.[23] Legal language is not special because it contains presuppositions, but rather because it alone contains presuppositions which relate to the existence of a legal system.

In this sense, then, constitutional language is unique because it, and no other language, presupposes the existence of a constitution, and incorporates those particular presuppositions which concern the role of a constitution in a given legal system. But this is not going to get us very far, because the presuppositions of constitutionalism are themselves both vague and contested. Unlike the specific terms of a general legal system, which, to some extent, relate to relatively uncontroversial presuppositions about the way the legal system operates, the terms of a constitution *themselves* determine the differences between the constitutional presuppositions and other legal presuppositions. Therefore, an initial search for constitutional uniqueness reduces itself to circularity because the presuppositions of a constitutional system are dependent on our view of the language of a constitution. Perhaps constitutional language *is* unique. But we cannot articulate the differences which make it unique simply by examining the presuppositions of constitutionalism. Rather, we must examine the *language* in order to discover the differences between the presuppositions embedded

20. "When did you stop beating your wife?" contains a prototypical presupposition in that it presupposes, but does not assert, that you have a wife and that you have beaten her. Presuppositions are not asserted to be true or false, but undergird the thought and language of people. *See also* J. AUSTIN, WORDS, *supra* note 7, at 48-52; J. SEARLE, SPEECH ACTS (1969). *See generally* Strawson, *On Referring*, 59 MIND 320 (1950).

21. Hart, *Definition and Theory*, *supra* note 5, at 37. *See supra* note 5.

22. This notion is embodied in Hart's theory of the "internal" point of view. H.L.A. HART, *supra* note 5, at 54-60, 84-88, 97-107, 138-44.

23. *See* J. SEARLE, *supra* note 20, at 33-42, 184-87. *See also* Harris, *Do Performatives Still Exist?* (Paper presented at the Pacific Division of the American Philosophical Association, March, 1980) (copy on file at *UCLA Law Review*).

in that language and the presuppositions included in the language of statutes or the common law.

These observations on the presuppositional nature of constitutional language are neither interesting nor important enough to provide the touchstone for a theory of constitutional language. They show, however, that certain uses of language have distinct meanings because of the context in which they occur.[24] When an entomologist talks about "bugs," when a physicist describes something as "solid," and when a logician refers to "implication," each uses those terms in a more technical and precise sense than the ordinary person uses them. We know this because we know something about the special context in which entomologists, physicists, and logicians speak.[25] Similarly, the context in which lawyers talk determines their use of "real property" (which is not the opposite of "fake property") or "wrongful" (which refers to conduct that may have no moral counterpart in ordinary language). Unlike strictly technical legal terms, such as "habeas corpus," "demurrer," and "curtesy," which have no ordinary language meaning, the technical uses of "real property" and "wrongful" are parasitic on ordinary language.[26] If this phenomenon occurs in conventional (non-constitutional) legal language, then the equally parasitic nature of certain constitutional terms, such as "equal protection of the laws," "free exercise of religion," and "search and seizure" should not surprise us. These are expressions derived from ordinary language, but their constitutional meaning in the context of constitutional adjudication diverges in important ways from the ordinary meaning that first generated each expression. The constitutional presuppositions of constitutional language may not establish the complete uniqueness of constitutional language, but they do emphasize the context from which the words take their meaning.

## II. The Intentional Paradigm

Most discussion of constitutional language takes place within what I call the "intentional paradigm"—the assumption that any

24. On contextual definition, see J. AUSTIN, *supra* note 20; J. SEARLE, *supra* note 20; L. WITTGENSTEIN, *supra* note 7; Frankena, *Some Aspects of Language,* in LANGUAGE, THOUGHT & CULTURE 121-23 (P. Henle ed. 1958); Ryle, *Ordinary Language,* in ORDINARY LANGUAGE 24 (V. Chappell ed. 1964). For a somewhat controversial application of the notion of contextual definition to the problem of obscenity, see Schauer, *Speech and "Speech"—Obscenity and "Obscenity": An Exercise in the Interpretation of Constitutional Language,* 67 GEO. L.J. 899 (1979).

25. There has been surprisingly little discussion of technical language in the philosophical literature, but one noteworthy source is Caton, *Introduction* to PHILOSOPHY AND ORDINARY LANGUAGE at v (C. Caton ed. 1963).

26. *See generally* Morrison, *Technical Language (and the Law),* 10 COLONIAL LAW. 18 (1980).

interpretation of the constitutional text must comport with the explicit, implicit, reconstructed, or fictionalized intentions of the drafters. In its crudest and least plausible version, the intentional paradigm focuses on the results that the drafters specifically had in mind.[27] Thus, because we can show that the drafters of the due process clauses of the fifth and fourteenth amendments intended to invalidate lengthy imprisonment without trial, we can be confident that we are correct in applying those provisions to that end.[28] Conversely, because we can fairly clearly infer that those same drafters did not intend to invalidate prejudgment real estate attachment for the purpose of securing a potential money judgment,[29] we can be equally confident that we are correct in refusing to apply the due process clause to invalidate prejudgment real estate attachment. Use of the same methodology would support the

27. The nature of the ratification process makes the search for original intent in constitutional adjudication especially problematic. Are the states presumed to have ratified the intent of the drafters as well as the language those drafters wrote? What if legislative history from state legislatures shows that different states ratified for different reasons? What if the intent of the drafters is unavailable to the states? Given the nature of my conclusions, I need not attempt to answer these very troubling questions, but they cannot be avoided by any theory that is tied to original intent.

Even if we put the "whose intent?" question aside, we must still address two different questions. The first is "What results would the drafters have intended had they been confronted with the problems and context of today's world?" This question seems largely unanswerable, inviting the most speculative kind of historical psychoanalysis. This formulation of the issue has, however, attracted a substantial following. *See, e.g.,* L. LUSKY, BY WHAT RIGHT? 21 (1975); Murphy, Book Review, 87 YALE L.J. 1752, 1770 (1978).

The other question that could be asked is "What results did the drafters specifically intend?" This question is, at least, one that is possible to answer, although much of this Essay contends that it is still the wrong question. This question is at the heart of the much discussed theories of Raoul Berger. R. BERGER, GOVERNMENT BY JUDICIARY: THE TRANSFORMATION OF THE FOURTEENTH AMENDMENT (1977). The assumption that clear or unmistakable intent, as evidenced in historical documents, is the exact equivalent of a textual statement to that effect is central to Berger's thesis. *See, e.g., id.* at 368; Berger, *A Political Scientist as Constitutional Lawyer: A Reply to Louis Fisher,* 41 OHIO ST. L.J. 147, 162-63, 167 (1980). *See also* Oregon v. Mitchell, 400 U.S. 112, 203 (1970) (Harlan, J., concurring and dissenting in part); Harper v. Virginia Board of Elections, 383 U.S. 663, 677-78 (1966) (Black, J., dissenting); West Coast Hotel Co. v. Parrish, 300 U.S. 379, 402-03 (1937) (Sutherland, J., dissenting). Among current members of the Supreme Court, Justice Rehnquist most clearly subscribes to the view that original intent is dispositive. *See, e.g.,* Trimble v. Gordon, 430 U.S. 762, 777-86 (1977) (Rehnquist, J., dissenting); Sugarman v. Dougall, 413 U.S. 634, 649-64 (1973) (Rehnquist, J., dissenting in *Sugarman* and also in *In re* Griffiths, 413 U.S. 717 (1973)). Because, as should be apparent from all of this Essay, I disagree with Berger's assumption as to what is the proper question, I have no need to deal with the issue of whether Berger's own answers to his question are even correct. It is certainly not abundantly clear that they are. *See, e.g.,* Murphy, *supra,* at 1754-60.

28. *See* Palko v. Connecticut, 302 U.S. 319 (1937); Murray's Lessee v. Hoboken Land & Improvement Co., 59 U.S. (18 How.) 272 (1856).

29. *See* Sniadach v. Family Finance Corp., 395 U.S. 337, 344-51 (1969) (Black, J., dissenting); Ownbey v. Morgan, 256 U.S. 94 (1921).

first amendment's application to prior restraints and at the same time justify excluding its application to obscenity, defamation, commercial speech, and blasphemy.[30]

The specific intention theories of constitutional interpretation, of which the writings of Raoul Berger represent the most extreme example,[31] are the least plausible of any of the theories discussed in this Essay. They are implausible precisely because they ignore the distinction between the meaning of a rule (such as a constitutional provision) and the instances of its application.[32]

When we draft any rule, we envision certain particular applications of that rule, certain cases where the rule will produce a particular outcome. We do not merely list these outcomes in a series of specific commands because we do not see those particular outcomes as exhaustive. They are only instances of a more general problem, and we analyze the problem to discover some underlying unity in the instances that we wish to treat.[33] We then formulate the rule to deal with this general unitary problem. By formulating a rule in general terms, the rule extends, by the nature of language, further in time or space than those particular applications envisaged by the drafters of the rule.

This is a commonplace observation,[34] and we can easily im-

30. Patterson v. Colorado, 205 U.S. 454 (1907), is the Supreme Court's most explicit statement of the now-repudiated "prior restraints only" interpretation of the first amendment. *Id.* at 462. For references to other historical exclusions, see, e.g., Roth v. United States, 354 U.S. 476 (1957); *Ex parte* Jackson, 96 U.S. 727 (1877); L. LEVY, LEGACY OF SUPPRESSION: FREEDOM OF SPEECH AND PRESS IN EARLY AMERICAN HISTORY (1960).

31. *See supra* note 27.

32. "The provisions of the Federal Constitution, undoubtedly, are pliable in the sense that in appropriate cases they have the capacity of bringing within their grasp every new condition which falls within their meaning. But, their *meaning* is changeless; it is only their *application* which is extensible." Home Bldg. & Loan Assn. v. Blaisdell, 290 U.S. 398, 451 (1934) (Sutherland, J., dissenting) (footnote omitted). *See also* Village of Euclid v. Ambler Realty Co., 272 U.S. 365, 387 (1926) (Sutherland, J.); 1 T. COOLEY, CONSTITUTIONAL LIMITATIONS 124 (8th ed. 1927).

This distinction parallels the philosopher's related distinctions between connotation and denotation, and intension and extension. *See* W. ALSTON, PHILOSOPHY OF LANGUAGE 17 n.8 (1964); J.S. MILL, A SYSTEM OF LOGIC (8th ed. 1904); W. SALMON, LOGIC 122-29 (2d ed. 1973). *See also* J. HOSPERS, AN INTRODUCTION TO PHILOSOPHICAL ANALYSIS 40-54 (2d ed. 1967). The distinction also parallels those between sense and reference. *See* FREGE, *On Sense and Reference*, in TRANSLATIONS FROM THE PHILOSOPHICAL WRITINGS OF GOTTLOB FREGE 58 (P. Geach & M. Black eds. 1952) ("Sense" and "reference" are the generally accepted English translations of Frege's "*Sinn*" and "*Bedeutung.*"). But, not wishing to carry more philosophical baggage than I must, I will stick to a distinction between the meaning of a rule and the instances of its application.

33. "[A] principle to be vital must be capable of wider application than the mischief which gave it birth." Weems v. United States, 217 U.S. 349, 373 (1910), *quoted in* Gregg v. Georgia, 428 U.S. 153, 171 (1976) (opinion of Stewart, J. joined by Powell and Stevens, JJ.).

34. *See* Munzer & Nickel, *supra* note 2, at 1031; Bridwell, *supra* note 9, at 914-15.

agine examples of the distinction between meaning and instances of application in constitutional interpretation. For example, punishment by electric shocks to the genitalia falls plainly within the eighth amendment's prohibition of cruel and unusual punishments even though the drafters could not have imagined this particular procedure in 1791.[35]

This much is relatively uncontroversial, but it does not take us very far because, at some point, the new applications are so different that the meaning has changed.[36] The "meaning" of a cruel and unusual punishment clause prohibiting only painful and humiliating punishment is different from one prohibiting capital punishment.[37] The "meaning" of an equal protection clause prohibiting only racial discrimination is different from the meaning of an equal protection clause prohibiting discrimination on the basis of, say, gender,[38] alienage,[39] illegitimacy,[40] or wealth.[41] And the meaning of "the freedom of speech" that includes only political argument[42] is different from the meaning of "the freedom of speech" that includes the right to advertise pharmaceutical prices[43] or the right to display a "For Sale" sign on a front lawn.[44]

I am not contending that such shifts in constitutional meaning are constitutionally impermissible. I am saying only that they

---

On generality as part of the nature of law, see H.L.A. HART, *supra* note 5, at 20-23, 234.

35. *Cf.* United States v. Seeger, 380 U.S. 163 (1965) (broad extension of concept of religion for purposes of statutory exemption from conscription for conscientious objectors). *But cf.* Wisconsin v. Yoder, 406 U.S. 205 (1972) (emphasis on the historical legitimacy of the Amish church).

36. *See* Munzer & Nickel, *supra* note 2, at 1-31. This seems to have been Justice Sutherland's point. *See supra* note 32.

Whether there is a shift in meaning may depend on why a particular provision is in the Constitution. The narrower the reason, the more likely it is that a new application will be beyond the scope of that reason and will therefore constitute a shift of meaning. Conversely, the broader the reason taken to justify the provision in the text, the more likely it is that subsequent applications will still be within the scope of that reason, and therefore not represent a change of meaning.

37. *See supra* note 34. But if you define the first meaning differently, then the application may involve no shift.

38. *See* Craig v. Boren, 429 U.S. 190 (1976).

39. *See* Graham v. Richardson, 403 U.S. 365 (1971).

40. *See* Levy v. Louisiana, 391 U.S. 68 (1968).

41. *See* San Antonio Indep. School Dist. v. Rodriguez, 411 U.S. 1 (1973) (rejecting strict scrutiny).

42. *See* A. MEIKLEJOHN, FREE SPEECH AND ITS RELATION TO SELF-GOVERNMENT (1948), *reprinted in* A. MEIKLEJOHN, POLITICAL FREEDOM: THE CONSTITUTIONAL POWERS OF THE PEOPLE (1960); BeVier, *The First Amendment and Political Speech: An Inquiry into the Substance and Limits of Principle,* 30 STAN. L. REV. 299 (1978); Bork, *Neutral Principles and Some First Amendment Problems,* 47 IND. L.J. 1 (1971); Meiklejohn, *The First Amendment is an Absolute,* 1961 SUP. CT. REV. 245.

43. Virginia State Bd. of Pharmacy v. Virginia Citizens Consumer Council, Inc., 425 U.S. 748 (1976).

44. Linmark Associates, Inc. v. Township of Willingboro, 431 U.S. 85 (1977).

*are* shifts in meaning, and thus are neither explained nor justified by the distinction between the meaning of a rule and the instances of its application. For such explanation or justification we must look elsewhere.

The defects of the specific intention approach have been amply documented in the literature,[45] and there is little need for me to belabor these criticisms here. Intriguingly, however, even the most vehement critics of the specific intention approach still feel obliged to tether their arguments to some form of original intent. According to Laurence Tribe[46] and Ronald Dworkin[47], for example, the extremely general language in the Constitution conclusively proves the drafters' intent that subsequent generations should work out their own theories applying such phrases as cruel and unusual punishment, due process of law, equal protection of the laws, and so on. John Hart Ely implicitly criticizes wide excursions from the text as a whole,[48] but his argument is as revealing as it is interesting. Ely bases his deference to the text on the idea that the text constitutes *the best evidence* of the drafters' intent.[49] The text, for Ely as for the others, is still a way of bringing forward the intentions of the framers.

Those who argue within the framework of this "intentional paradigm" appear to operate on the model of the "convention" in the game of bridge. When bridge players reach a certain level of proficiency, they begin to use artificial conventions in bidding. These bids do not represent the intended contract, but rather aim at describing specific features of the bidder's hand or at asking questions about the partner's hand. The bids are in a *code* whose primary ordinary meaning ("clubs" means clubs) may be irrelevant to the specific contextual use. Most bridge players use simple conventions like Blackwood or Stayman, and more advanced players are likely to use complex systems containing a high percentage of so-called "artificial" bids. These systems and conven-

45. *See, e.g.*, Bridwell, *supra* note 34; Lusky, *"Government By Judiciary": What Price Legitimacy?*, 6 HASTINGS CONST. L.Q. 403 (1979); Munzer & Nickel, *supra* note 2, at 1030-33; Murphy, *supra* note 27; Nathanson, Book Review, 56 TEX. L. REV. 579 (1978); Perry, Book Review, 78 COLUM. L. REV. 685 (1978). Although it is possible that we have ignored the relevance of history and original intent, *see* Monaghan, *The Constitution*, *supra* note 1, at 117, it seems that we have more often succumbed to the error of ignoring Joseph Story's admonition that "Nothing but the text itself was adopted by the people." 1 J. STORY, COMMENTARIES ON THE CONSTITUTION OF THE UNITED STATES 300 (4th ed. 1873).

46. *See supra* note 3.

47. R. DWORKIN, *supra* note 11, at 133; Dworkin, *The Forum of Principle*, 56 N.Y.U. L. REV. 469 (1981).

48. J. H. ELY, *supra* note 1; Ely, *The Wages of Crying Wolf: A Comment on* Roe v. Wade, 82 YALE L.J. 920 (1973).

49. "[T]he most important datum bearing on what was intended is the constitutional language itself." J.H. ELY, *supra* note 1, at 16.

tions are languages designed in part, like other languages, to convey information. But the important feature of a bridge convention (or indeed the notion of bidding at all) is that the use of conventions is derived from and directed towards one quite simple fact—in the game of bridge, you are not permitted to look at your partner's cards. If a player could look at his partner's hand before arriving at the final contract, he could dispense with every convention yet devised.

Many people understand constitutional language in much the same way as a bridge convention. Under the intentional paradigm, constitutional language exists only because we are unable to know the specific intentions (the cards) of the drafters. If we could ascertain that specific intention, or if we knew how the drafters would treat the constitutional problems of the present, we would have no need for constitutional language. To the extent that we know that intention, then the importance of the text is diminished *pro tanto.*[50]

This is not a useful model, for it fails to capture the sense in which a text is authoritative *as a text.* No amount of looking into the minds of the framers, or constructing fictionalized intentions at various levels of abstraction, can render the text less authoritative.[51] The text is not only the starting point, but is also in some special way the finishing point as well. Constitutional language exists not only because the constitutional convention is not still sitting, nor because James Madison and his colleagues were not immortal. The text interposes itself between the intentions of the framers and the problems of the present, cutting off the range of permissible access and references to original intent, thereby reducing the extent to which original intent persists after the text's

50. This is implicit in any view that treats "unmistakable intention" as being equivalent to text. *See supra* note 27. The difficult question occurs, however, when the text and the legislative history are in some way inconsistent. On this point, the canons of interpretation are not helpful, because one canon suggests that we look at the legislative history only when the text is unclear, and another says that we can look at legislative history to reject a textual statement inconsistent with that history. *Compare* Caminetti v. United States, 242 U.S. 470, 490 (1917), *with* United Steelworkers v. Weber, 443 U.S. 193, 201-02 (1979). *See generally*, Note, *Intent, Clear Statements, and the Common Law: Statutory Interpretation in the Supreme Court*, 95 HARV. L. REV. 892 (1982).

It is unfortunately common for commentators to conflate textual and historical approaches to constitutional interpretation. *See, e.g.*, Bork, *supra* note 42, at 8; Grey, *Unwritten Constitution, supra* note 1, at 712-13; Perry, *Interpretivism, Freedom of Expression, and Equal Protection*, 42 OHIO ST. L.J. 261, 280-81 (1981). The two approaches are, however, fundamentally different. *See* Bobbitt, *Constitutional Fate*, 58 TEX. L. REV. 695, 707 (1980). *See also* Alexander, *supra* note 2.

51. J. STORY, *supra* note 45, at 300; Chafee, *The Disorderly Conduct of Words*, 41 COLUM. L. REV. 381, 399-402 (1941); Linde, *Judges, Critics, and the Realist Tradition*, 82 YALE L.J. 227, 254 (1972). *See also* Chevigny, *Philosophy of Language and Free Expression*, 55 N.Y.U. L. REV. 157, 174 (1980).

adoption. A theory of constitutional language is incomplete if it does not recognize the way in which a text is authoritative — the way in which we treat the Constitution, but not, for example, the Declaration of Independence or the Mayflower Compact, *as law.*

The authoritativeness of a text is by no means a peculiar feature of a written constitution. Although constitutional law is exciting and popular at the moment, we should not forget our basic law school contracts principles. One such basic principle requires that the parties be held to the reasonable meaning of the terms they have used, regardless of their subjective intent at the time they used those words.[52] And the considerations that led to acceptance of this "objective" theory of contracts[53] are the same as those that generated other common law rules, for example the "plain meaning" rule in the common law of defamation.[54]

What the analogy with contract law shows us, however, is not something about contracts, or even about law. The analogy illuminates, rather, something about language in general, of which the language of a written constitution and the language of a contract are subsets. In order to make sense of language, we presume

52. "If, however, it were proved by twenty bishops that either party, when he used the words, intended something else than the usual meaning which the law imposes upon them, he would still be held, unless there were some mutual mistake, or something else of the sort." Hotchkiss v. National City Bank of New York, 200 F. 287, 293 (S.D.N.Y. 1911) (Hand, L., J.).

53. *See, e.g.,* Ricketts v. Pennsylvania Ry. Co., 153 F.2d 757 (2d Cir. 1946) (Frank, J., concurring). *See also* Mansfield v. Hodgdon, 147 Mass. 304, 17 N.E. 544 (1888); Embry v. Hargadine, McKittrick Dry Goods Co., 127 Mo. App. 383, 105 S.W. 777 (1907); Smith v. Hughes, 6 Q.B. 597 (1871). *See generally* 1 A. CORBIN, CORBIN ON CONTRACTS § 106 (1963); 3 A. CORBIN, CORBIN ON CONTRACTS § 539, at 82 (1963); L. SIMPSON, HANDBOOK OF THE LAW OF CONTRACTS 10 (2d ed. 1965).

Corbin maintains that it is an "illusion" that words have meaning independent of those who use them. 1 A. CORBIN, *supra*, § 106, at 474. Were it not for that "illusion," however, we would have no way of understanding each other. This is the whole point of any theory of meaning that stresses language as a rule-governed form of behavior. *See, e.g.,* J. SEARLE, *supra* note 20, at 33-50; B. HARRISON, AN INTRODUCTION TO THE PHILOSOPHY OF LANGUAGE 165-258 (1979).

Moreover, Corbin's critique of a strictly objective view exposes an important ambiguity in our use of the term "objective." To the extent that "objective" suggests certainty or precision, then Corbin's criticism is well taken. But if "objective" suggests only that we interpret on the basis of external factors, including the conventions of language, but excluding the intentions of the language user, then a theory can be objective without making any claim of precision or certainty. It is the latter sense of "objective" that is at the heart of the objective theory of contracts and also at the heart of the theory of constitutional interpretation suggested in this Essay.

54. *See, e.g.,* Lorentz v. R.K.O. Radio Pictures, Inc., 155 F.2d 84, 87 (9th Cir. 1946), *cert. denied,* 329 U.S. 727 (1946); Lyman v. New England Newspaper Pub. Co., 286 Mass. 258, 260, 190 N.E. 542, 543 (1934); Roberts v. Camden, 103 Eng. Rep. 508, 509 (K.B. 1807). *See generally* W. ODGERS, A DIGEST OF THE LAW OF LIBEL AND SLANDER § 93, at 144 (2d ed. 1887); W. PROSSER, HANDBOOK OF THE LAW OF TORTS § 111, at 747 (4th ed. 1971).

that it represents the intentional acts of human beings.[55] But there is a difference between the intention of a text and the human thoughts that accompanied the creation of that text. Although the authority of a text is derived in part from the intention that it be authoritative, a text can have purpose without reference to the psychological condition of its creator, as we see in the attempts of courts to derive purpose from statutes themselves.[56] As one philosopher has put it, "[c]ommunication is a public, social affair and [the communicator] is not exempted from responsibility for aspects of his performance he failed to notice."[57] Thus, "a speaker is not the sole arbiter over what import his utterances have,"[58] and our touchstone must be the rules of language rather than largely futile explorations into the mind of the communicator. So long as the distinction between "what he said" and "what he meant to say" is meaningful, then we must recognize that the conventions of language use are superior, in the hierarchy of interpretive tools, to the intentions of the speaker. This is even more true when the language used has an authoritative embodiment, as in a statute or in a written constitution.

The intentional paradigm implicitly confuses a language with a code (as in "morse code" rather than in "Uniform Commercial Code"). Codes, such as bridge conventions, are only one form of language,[59] and it is wrong to assume that every language is a code. In theory, codes are dispensable, as the bridge example demonstrates, but language is not. Moreover, language operates only because *it* has meaning, quite apart from what the speaker may have *meant* to say.[60] Perhaps meaning is use,[61] but the inten-

55. In Gibbons v. Ogden, 22 U.S. (9 Wheat.) 1 (1824), John Marshall noted that those who ratified the Constitution "must be understood . . . to have intended what they have said." *Id.* at 188.

56. *See* Frankfurter, *Some Reflections on the Reading of Statutes,* 47 COLUM. L. REV. 527, 538-39 (1947). *See generally* P. BREST, PROCESSES OF CONSTITUTIONAL DECISIONMAKING: CASES AND MATERIALS 31-44 (1975).

57. P. JONES, PHILOSOPHY AND THE NOVEL 183-84 (1975). The dispute between the "intentionalists" and the "anti-intentionalists" is prominent in contemporary philosophy of literary criticism. The dispute is described and fully documented in P. JUHL, INTERPRETATION: AN ESSAY IN THE PHILOSOPHY OF LITERARY CRITICISM (1980). Juhl himself is an intentionalist. There is much in the corpus of writing about literary interpretation that is of great importance to the constitutional theorist, both for intentionalists and anti-intentionalists like myself.

58. P. JONES, *supra* note 57, at 183-84. *See also* S. CAVELL, MUST WE MEAN WHAT WE SAY? 32 (1969).

59. Perhaps the characteristic feature of a code is that it is perfectly translatable into some language. Natural languages, however, arising in the context of particular cultures, are not necessarily perfectly translatable into other natural languages. *See* W. QUINE, WORD AND OBJECT (1960).

60. *See generally* P. JONES, *supra* note 57, at 182-99; J. SEARLE, *supra* note 20; J. SEARLE, EXPRESSION AND MEANING: STUDIES IN THE THEORY OF SPEECH ACTS (1979). For a more intention-oriented theory of meaning, see Grice, *supra* note 7, at

tions of the user do not determine exclusively, or even mainly, the use.

In arguing for greater attention to the Constitution as an authoritative text, I do not urge a literalist, conceptualist, or formalist approach to constitutional adjudication.[62] The view that the text can be interpreted as self-defining, or as ordinary language,[63] or without reference to purpose[64] does not follow from the proposition that the text is authoritative. In many instances, we can derive purpose from a text,[65] and we can apply canons of interpretation peculiar to the nature of the Constitution itself. Working out the details of such a program is difficult, but it is a task that cannot be avoided if we are to develop a theory of constitutional interpretation that captures both the authoritativeness of the text and the necessity of contextual interpretation.

## III. Moral Theory and Constitutional Language

Many issues of constitutional interpretation concern the Constitution's incorporation or non-incorporation of moral values. We must, then, examine the way in which the text either mandates, prohibits, or permits the use of certain moral arguments. Thus, I will propose questions that are metaethical, but in a rather special way. For, unlike most of the others who have asked metaethical questions,[66] I will not ask how we reason about ethics, but rather *when* and *how much* we reason about ethics—at least in this constitutional law context.

---

377; Grice, *Utterer's Meaning and Intentions,* 78 PHIL. REV. 147 (1969). A more sophisticated version is found in S. SCHIFFER, MEANING (1972).

61. *See supra* note 7.

62. The term "literalism" is ambiguous, because it is unclear where the literal meaning of the term at issue comes from. In one sense, every textually oriented theory, including this one, is a version of literalism. But we more commonly equate literalism with the ordinary language definition of constitutional terms, or with the notion that the text provides clear answers to all of our problems. In this sense, literalism shares both the characteristics and the flaws of what we usually refer to as "formalism" or "conceptualism." *See* H.L.A. HART, *supra* note 6, at 126; J. STONE, THE PROVINCE AND FUNCTION OF LAW 149-65 (1946); Hart, *supra* note 6, at 270. On the distinction between literalism and interpretivism, see Grey, *supra* note 50, at 703, 706 n.9.

63. In addition to the authorities cited *supra* note 63, see Stone, *supra* note 6, at 466, 472.

64. On purpose-oriented interpretation, see Fuller, *Positivism and Fidelity to Law—A Reply to Professor Hart,* 71 HARV. L. REV. 630 (1958). *See also supra* note 56 & accompanying text.

65. *See* P. JONES, *supra* note 57, at 183-84, 194-95; Frankfurter, *supra* note 56.

66. Whether there is a distinction between ethics and metaethics (between substantive ethical principles and the methodology of ethical inquiry) is by no means clear, because some metaethical views, particularly versions of relativism and subjectivism, may tend to collapse the distinction. But the distinction serves tolerably well for my present purposes.

At the conclusion of his essay on "Constitutional Cases,"[67] Ronald Dworkin notes that the problem of rights against the state "argues for a fusion of constitutional law and moral theory, a connection that, incredibly, has yet to take place."[68] This statement is both revealing and ambiguous, for the key word "fusion" admits of a number of importantly different interpretations.[69] Two items may become fused in a strong sense when they are merged so that the two are no longer separately identifiable; or they may become fused in a weaker sense when, although tightly joined, we can continue to identify the originally separate components.

If we are to accept Dworkin's incredulity as justified, we must determine how much moral theory is to be merged into constitutional law, where and how that merger is to take place, and how much of the resultant product will be fused in the strong sense. I propose therefore to explore several "strategies of fusion," and their presuppositions about the Constitution and moral theory.

## A. *Moral Theory as Constitutional Command*

In his essay "Cruel and Unusual Punishments,"[70] Jeffrie Murphy introduces his argument by saying that "if one can mount a good argument that to treat a person in a certain way is gravely unjust or would violate some basic human right of his, this is also and necessarily a good argument that it is unconstitutional to treat him in this way."[71]

The import of Murphy's characterization of constitutional argument is that if he is correct, then he has, in the same forty-six words, *just written the Constitution?!* For if any good moral argument is *eo ipso* a good constitutional argument, the text becomes superfluous.[72] But surely the text must serve some purpose other than to offer a *carte blanche* for moral philosophizing. In fact, it defines the contours of permissible moral arguments. The authori-

---

67. R. DWORKIN, *supra* note 11, at 131-49.

68. *Id.* at 149.

69. I do not mean to take Dworkin to task for this one word. The rest of his essay, as well as Dworkin's use of the word "connection" in the same sentence, cautions us against taking Dworkin's metaphor as an argument.

70. J. MURPHY, *Cruel and Unusual Punishments,* in RETRIBUTION, JUSTICE, AND THERAPY 223-49 (1979).

71. *Id.* at 223.

72. The quoted sentence is hardly crucial to Murphy's fine analysis of the problem of punishment, and in that sense I suppose I am being unfair. But the sentence is there, and it provides a concise statement of a position that has at times surfaced in constitutional theory. *See, e.g.,* Thomas Grey's description of a now "moribund" first form of non-interpretivist review in Grey, *Origins*, *supra* note 1, at 844 n.8 (1978). For a powerful critique of theories that strive for congruence between constitutional law and "correct" moral theory, see Monaghan, *Our Perfect Constitution*, 56 N.Y.U. L. REV. 353 (1981).

tative nature of the text, and the existence of a substantive content beyond a mere formal authorization[73] for judges to philosophize, compels us to reject Murphy's notion of one-to-one fusion of constitutional law and moral theory. In addition, we can find counterexamples to Murphy's theory; there are moral arguments that appear good yet irrelevant to the Constitution (for example, rights to safety in the workplace). Conversely, there are constitutional issues, even in the Bill of Rights, that are only dimly illuminated by moral argument (for example, the right to trial by jury in civil cases,[74] and the right to keep and bear arms).

Murphy's statement erroneously suggests a model of constitutional law and moral theory as congruent circles. The more apt geometric metaphor is that of intersecting circles, which leaves areas of both constitutionally irrelevant moral argument and morally sterile constitutional argument. Viewed in this way, a good moral argument is no longer "necessarily" a good constitutional argument. That one has a moral duty to support one's parents in their dotage is fairly clear, but the Constitution does not deal with this duty, nor does it require that it be enforced or supplemented by the state. Conversely, a good constitutional argument is not necessarily a good moral argument, as for example the argument one would deploy in challenging the constitutional qualifications of an able and mature thirty-three year old to hold office as President of the United States. A good moral argument is therefore a good constitutional argument only if it falls within that area of moral theory embraced by the Constitution as relevant. The crucial task remains, then, to define the contours of this area, and to determine the manner in which the constitutional text identifies constitutionally relevant moral theory.

## B. *The General/Particular Theory*

A more plausible theory than an interpretation that takes the moral or political flavor of the Constitution as a mandate for rendering the text irrelevant is the "general/particular" theory of textual interpretation. This theory, which appears in various forms, takes the morally or politically oriented constitutional provi-

---

73. Without getting too deeply into the issue of the meaning and scope of judicial discretion here, I use formal authorization to refer to a norm that grants authority without specifying the substantive standards or constraints for the exercise of that authority. *See* Paulson, *Material and Formal Authorisation in Kelsen's Pure Theory*, 39 CAMBRIDGE L.J. 172 (1980).

74. U.S. CONST. amend. VII. My unargued assumption that this provision has little moral content derives some support from the fact that it remains one of the few provisions of the Bill of Rights that has not been incorporated by the fourteenth amendment. *See* Melancon v. McKeithen, 345 F. Supp. 1025 (E.D. La.), *aff'd sub nom*. Hill v. McKeithen, 409 U.S. 943 (1972).

sions—for example, freedom of speech, equal protection of the laws, and freedom of religion—not as discrete repositories of self-contained moral or political theories, but rather as instances, or more particularized expressions of the single moral or political theory embedded in the Constitution. The theory, as most commonly expressed, does not merely say that instantiated constitutional values are derived from higher and more general principles. It says that they are derived from *one* higher and more general principle. This theory is implicit in the work of theorists as diverse as David Richards[75] and John Hart Ely,[76] and is suggested in some parts of Ronald Dworkin's writings.[77] Its proponents view the text as the raw material from which to construct a general moral or political theory of the Constitution. Because the generated theory must encompass the more particularized values explicitly stated in the text, it is not totally unbounded, but can claim a mandate from the text itself.

The general/particular theory (or metatheory) is attractive because it evolves out of the text, while, at the same time, it is not constrained by the more uncomfortable moral or political gaps[78]

75. *See, e.g.*, D. RICHARDS, THE MORAL CRITICISM OF LAW 51-54 (1977); Richards, *Constitutional Privacy, The Right to Die and the Meaning of Life: A Moral Analysis*, 22 WM. & MARY L. REV. 327 (1981) [hereinafter cited as Richards, *Constitutional Privacy*]; Richards, *supra* note 1; Richards, *Sexual Autonomy and the Constitutional Right to Privacy: A Case Study in Human Rights and the Unwritten Constitution*, 30 HASTINGS L.J. 957 (1979); Richards, *Unnatural Acts and the Constitutional Right to Privacy: A Moral Theory*, 45 FORDHAM L. REV. 1281 (1977). For Richards, "the concept of human rights" is his "unwritten constitution," Richards, *supra* note 1, at 300-01, and it is this concept that he proceeds to use for the decision of particular cases. Richards acknowledges that there may be different conceptions of that concept, but that is not inconsistent with the theory that there is, for a particular analyst at a particular time, *one* unitary constitutional theory, and that is the methodology with which I take issue.

76. J.H. ELY, *supra* note 1. I have heard Professor Ely's theory of the Constitution described as "one big equal protection clause." His theory is far richer and more complex than that, but it is still *one* theory. For a quite different critique of unitary constitutional theories, including Ely's, see Gerety, Book Review, 42 U. PITT. L. REV. 35 (1980).

77. Dworkin's general theory of adjudication is similarly both unitary and reconstructive in that he would have judges construct the unifying theory that provides "the best justification . . . for the body of propositions of law already shown to be true . . ." Dworkin, *No Right Answer?*, in LAW, MORALITY, AND SOCIETY: ESSAYS IN HONOUR OF H.L.A. HART 58, 82 (P. Hacker & J. Raz eds. 1977). *See also* R. DWORKIN, *supra* note 11, at 81-130. Dworkin, however, explicitly recognizes the underdetermination problem discussed in the text. *Id.* at 64-68. *See* Alexander & Bayles, *Hercules or Proteus? The Many Theses of Ronald Dworkin*, 5 SOC. THEORY & PRAC. 267 (1980). It is questionable whether Dworkin's solution is really a solution. *Id.*. In any event, there is much in his theory that would provide support for any particular/general theorist.

78. The right to privacy, *see* Griswold v. Connecticut, 381 U.S. 479 (1965), and the right to travel, *see* Shapiro v. Thompson, 394 U.S. 618 (1969), are perhaps the most prominent of these gaps.

in the Constitution. Thus, if we use the mentioned particulars as the building blocks for a theory, and then apply that general theory directly to future cases, we can easily find a particular right to privacy,[79] a particular right to travel,[80] and so on, as well as even more particular rights derived from these rights.[81] So long as these rights are part of the general theory constructed from the mentioned particulars and are not inconsistent with the text, the absence of these particular rights in the text does not undermine their existence and application. The text operates somewhat like a ladder.[82] We use it to build the theory, or perhaps to reconstruct the theory that was implicit all along. Having built the theory, we can kick away the ladder and then apply the theory directly.

This methodology appeals to us because it captures, at a rather high level of abstraction, the intuitive feeling that the Constitution is incomplete. It also reflects the sense in which not only particular applications but also more general principles must change to accommodate changing circumstances.[83] Moreover, it justifies a wide range of morally or politically attractive results without totally rejecting the importance of the text.[84] Indeed, this methodology would be ideal but for the fact that it rests on two mistakes and one controversial assumption.

First, any general/particular theory mistakenly assumes that one general principle (or theory) can be uniquely, or at least most correctly, derived from a set of particulars, or instances. This assumption, however, ignores the extent to which any theory—scientific, moral, or interpretive—is underdetermined by any number of specific instances or observations.[85] Theory is underdetermined

79. The methodology under discussion here was most notable in Griswold v. Connecticut, 381 U.S. 479 (1965). In that case, the Court used specific particulars, embodied in the first, third, fourth, and fifth amendments, to construct a right to privacy and then applied that constructed right to the issue (contraception) at hand. *See* D. RICHARDS, *supra* note 75, at 81-109.

80. *See* J. H. ELY, *supra* note 1, at 177-79.

81. Thus, Richards talks about various specific rights being generated by the right of privacy. *See, e.g.*, Richards, *Constitutional Privacy*, *supra* note 75.

82. *See* L. WITTGENSTEIN, TRACTATUS LOGICO-PHILOSOPHICUS (D. Pears & B. McGuinness trans. 1961). I do not claim to be using Wittgenstein's ladder metaphor for the same purpose for which he used it.

83. *See* A. BICKEL, THE LEAST DANGEROUS BRANCH 63 (1962); A. BICKEL, THE MORALITY OF CONSENT 25-30 (1975); Munzer & Nickel, *supra* note 2; Richards, *supra* note 1.

84. *Griswold* did not generate nearly the avalanche of scholarly criticism that befell Roe v. Wade, 410 U.S. 113 (1973). *See, e.g.*, J. H. ELY, *supra* note 48, at 15, 66; Epstein, *Substantive Due Process By Any Other Name: The Abortion Cases*, 1973 SUP. CT. REV. 159. Part of the explanation might be that the statute at issue in *Griswold* was substantially more ridiculous than that in *Roe*. The more likely explanation, however, is that the reliance on specific textual provisions, rather than on general liberty/due process considerations, made *Griswold* seem more palatable.

85. The *loci classici* for the underdetermination thesis are P. DUHEM, THE AIM

in this sense because any number of empirical observations, or specific instances, can generate and be consistent with a large and perhaps infinite number of explanatory theories. Moreover, each such explanatory theory will yield different predictions or results for future cases.[86] For example, a given set of symptoms can be consistent with a number of different medical diagnoses, and to that extent the diagnosis is underdetermined by the observation of symptoms. Similarly, several different theories about the formation of the solar system might be equally consistent with our observations about the solar system. The principle of underdetermination of theory applies to a wide range of activities, and it has been frequently discussed in reference to the philosophy of science,[87] to literary criticism,[88] to historical explanation,[89] and so forth. In each of these disciplines, theory acquires a different role, but the point remains the same: specific examples, instances, observations, or events can produce more than one theory equally consistent with those examples, instances, observations, or events.

We see the same phenomenon in constitutional theorizing because a large number of different overarching theories would be consistent with the specific moral or political principles specified in the text. We may have good reasons to choose one theory rather than another, just as a doctor may have good reasons to choose one medical diagnosis over another that is equally consistent with the same symptoms. But the constitutional text does not determine the choice among theories equally consistent with it, and thus the argument that the theory is generated by the Constitution is seen to be a fake. Certainly we can require that the particular theory fit all of the textualized particulars as a necessary condition of its validity. But if this is taken to be a sufficient con-

---

AND STRUCTURE OF PHYSICAL THEORY (P. Wiener trans. 1954); W. QUINE, FROM A LOGICAL POINT OF VIEW (2d ed. 1961); W. QUINE, *supra* note 59.

86. One practical, rather than strictly logical, objection to the underdetermination thesis is that a large enough number of observations will cause "convergence" towards only one theory. *See* M. HESSE, REVOLUTIONS AND RECONSTRUCTIONS IN THE PHILOSOPHY OF SCIENCE at viii (1980). This seems to be the point implicit in Dworkin's references to "density." Dworkin, *supra* note 77, at 83-84. Apart from the fact that the convergence thesis itself has some logical difficulties, M. HESSE, *supra,* at viii-x, it seems plain to me that the constitutional *text* is hardly dense enough to rebut the problem of underdetermination in reference to constructing a theory from the text.

87. *See, e.g.,* C. GLYMOUR, THEORY AND EVIDENCE (1980); M. HESSE, *supra* note 86; M. HESSE, THE STRUCTURE OF SCIENTIFIC INFERENCE (1974); T. KUHN, THE STRUCTURE OF SCIENTIFIC REVOLUTIONS (2d ed. 1970).

88. *See* Rader, *Fact, Theory, and Literary Explanation,* 1 CRITICAL INQUIRY 245 (1974).

89. *See generally* R. ATKINSON, KNOWLEDGE AND EXPLANATION IN HISTORY (1978); R. MARTIN, HISTORICAL EXPLANATION: RE-ENACTMENT AND PRACTICAL INFERENCE (1977).

dition, then there is little limit on the extent to which quite different theories can find their source in the Constitution. If that is so, the text does not control the result in future cases and does not affect our decision of which competing coherent theory to accept. This does not mean that judges should be forbidden to construct moral or political theories,[90] but it does defeat the claim that the theory so constructed is either mandated by or derived from the text.

A general/particular theory makes its second mistake by presuming that the selection of particulars from which to construct or reconstruct the general theory is itself independent of theory. The process of selecting particulars is not and cannot be value-neutral.[91] Textually explicit particulars are analagous to observations from which we construct a theory, and we cannot lightly ignore the extent to which such observations are controlled by theory.[92] The instances are not just there waiting for us to build a theory around them. We have to select the particulars to use, and this selection process contains implicit judgments of value and importance.

Interestingly, in this connection, most people who seek to build unitary moral or political theories of constitutional rights select (i.e., observe) the same constitutional provisions—the first amendment, the due process clause, the equal protection clause, the prohibition on cruel and unusual punishment, the amendments extending the franchise, and so on. They thus impose a theory on the Constitution more than they extract one from it.[93] If the process of selection concentrates on different provisions, a different theory results. For example, John Hart Ely,[94] who concen-

90. Even though the actual theory constructed will not, in my view, be textually mandated, the process of theory construction still aids in assuring principled adjudication. Thus, theory construction serves methodological goals of the legal system that are independent of the substance of the theory. *See* Golding, *Principled Decision-Making and the Supreme Court,* 63 COLUM. L. REV. 35 (1963); Greenawalt, *The Enduring Significance of Neutral Principles,* 78 COLUM. L. REV. 982 (1978).

91. In this sense, "values" incorporates not only particular views about particular subjects, but also the experiences and training of the selector. Imagine an automobile accident observed by a surgeon, a tort lawyer, and an automotive engineer. If we asked each of them the question "What happened?," we would get fundamentally different answers which varied in the particular facts reported and the language used to describe the reported facts.

92. *See generally* P. ACHINSTEIN, CONCEPTS OF SCIENCE: A PHILOSOPHICAL ANALYSIS (1968); M. HESSE, *supra* note 86; K. POPPER, UNENDED QUEST 52 (1976) ("There is no such thing as a perception except in the context of interests and expectations . . . .").

93. The story of the blind men and the elephant suggests just how easy it is to generalize on the basis of preselected and incomplete versions of the evidence. Saxe, *The Blind Men and the Elephant: A Hindoo Fable,* in STORY POEMS 267 (L. Untermeyer rev. ed. 1961).

94. J. H. ELY, *supra* note 1, at 87-101.

trates on the majoritarian provisions of the Constitution, derives a theory quite unlike the theories derived by Dworkin and Richards, who concentrate on individual rights and anti-majoritarian aspects of the Constitution.[95] And imagine the theory we might derive if we concentrated on the property-protecting provisions of the Constitution,[96] perhaps including the second amendment as well?! Our selection depends on what we think is most important, and what we think is most important is pre-textual. Although some of these theories might be better than others, any theory based on something less than *all* of the constitutional text is selective,[97] and the process of selection is hardly value-neutral. We see what we want to see and ignore what we want to ignore, and theories that purport to "explain" the Constitution usually explain only those portions of the Constitution that the theorist finds, for non-textually based reasons, to be most significant.

The controversial assumption contained in any particular/general theory is that the morally or politically loaded clauses of the Constitution are particulars instead of more general irreducible principles, and also that they are particulars of the same general principle.[98] Some constitutional provisions, of course, are derived from higher principles. For example, the first amendment's protection of freedom of speech might be plausibly derived from the political principle of popular sovereignty,[99] and the equal protection clause is plausibly derived from some sort of "golden rule" or universalization principle.[100] But in order to construct *a* theory of the Constitution, we must assume that all of the textual provisions are reducible to one overarching principle. Thus, the methodology of a particular/general theory presupposes a unitary moral or political theory (albeit perhaps a highly complex one[101]) that explains and unites all but the purely structural constitutional provisions.

---

95. *See* R. Dworkin, *supra* note 11; D. Richards, *supra* note 75.

96. Art. I, § 10; amend. III; amend. IV; amend. V; amend. XIV.

97. Even if all of the text is used, the weighting is selective. It is a mistake to assume that even "equal" weighting would be value-neutral, because the notion of equality is dependent upon the context. How would we react to a constitutional law casebook that devoted as much space to the third and twenty-third amendments as it did to the first and fourteenth?

98. *See supra* notes 75-76. For Professor Dworkin the principle is that of "equal concern and respect." Dworkin, *Liberalism*, in Public & Private Morality 113, 126 (S. Hampshire ed. 1978).

99. *See* A. Meiklejohn, *supra* note 42.

100. On universalization, compare R. Hare, Freedom and Reason 7-50 (1963) to Schwartz, *Against Universality*, 78 J. Phil. 127 (1981).

101. There are, in fact, two kinds of unitary theories. One kind involves only one ultimate principle, such as Dworkin's principle of "equal concern and respect." *See supra* note 98. Other theories have two or more principles, but incorporate theories that relate those principles to each other in a priority relationship. *See, e.g.*, J. Rawls,

In order to evaluate this presupposition, we must question whether such an overarching theory can conceivably exist. If we follow Rawls,[102] Richards,[103] Dworkin,[104] Gewirth,[105] and others in believing that such a theory exists or can be constructed, then the search for a unifying theory of constitutional morality is highly plausible. But if one accepts ethical pluralism[106] as a more accurate reflection of reality, then freedom of speech, fair procedure, equality, and so on may be ultimate and irreducible primary values with no necessarily coherent relationship.[107] If this is true, then we need not tie these values together nor fill the gaps between them. If there is a plurality of first principles, then that, of course, means that in some cases they will conflict.[108] The pluralist would not wish to deny this, but would deny the existence of any conflict-resolving higher theory.[109] This makes constitutional intepretation more difficult than it would be under a single unifying principle, but one cannot validly move from "it would be nice if it did" to "therefore it must," despite the prevalence of this move in many arguments for non-pluralist ethical theories.[110]

---

A THEORY OF JUSTICE (1971). The distinction is therefore best expressed in terms of the complexity of the single ultimate principle.

102. *Id.* at 34-53.

103. D. RICHARDS, A THEORY OF REASONS FOR ACTION (1971).

104. Dworkin, *supra* note 98.

105. A. GEWIRTH, REASON AND MORALITY (1978) ("Principle of Generic Consistency").

106. Perhaps the foremost pluralist of modern times is Isaiah Berlin. Berlin's most important works are collected in I. BERLIN, AGAINST THE CURRENT: ESSAYS IN THE HISTORY OF IDEAS (H. Hardy ed. 1980); I. BERLIN, CONCEPTS AND CATEGORIES: PHILOSOPHICAL ESSAYS (H. Hardy ed. 1979); I. BERLIN, FOUR ESSAYS ON LIBERTY (1969); I. BERLIN, RUSSIAN THINKERS (H. Hardy & A. Kelly eds. 1978). *See also* B. WILLIAMS, PROBLEMS OF THE SELF 166-86 (1973); Feinberg, *Rawls and Intuitionism,* in READING RAWLS: CRITICAL STUDIES ON RAWLS' *A Theory of Justice* 108 (N. Daniels ed. 1975); Williams, *Conflicts of Values,* in THE IDEA OF FREEDOM: ESSAYS IN HONOUR OF ISAIAH BERLIN 221 (A. Ryan ed. 1979). *See generally* B. BARRY, POLITICAL ARGUMENT (1965); R. BRANDT, ETHICAL THEORY (1959); H.L.A. HART, PUNISHMENT AND RESPONSIBILITY (1968).

107. The relation of coherence is stronger than the relation of consistency. Two propositions, such as "It is snowing today" and "Napoleon lost at Waterloo" may be consistent with each other, although not possessing the relation of mutual entailment implicit in the idea of coherence. *See generally* A. WOOZLEY, THEORY OF KNOWLEDGE 129-75 (1949). A claim of coherence in any normative philosophy—moral, political, or legal—is a claim that in some way all of the norms of the system "fit together." Thus, coherence requires consistency, but the reverse is not true. I am now in the process of developing a fuller analysis and explication of the notion of coherence in the philosophy of law, and my remarks here are a specific and tentative embodiment of this larger project.

108. J. RAWLS, *supra* note 101, at 34-40.

109. *Id. See also* B. BARRY, THE LIBERAL THEORY OF JUSTICE 5-6 (1973).

110. Rawls, concedes, however, that the desirability of having conflict-resolving higher principles is not *eo ipso* evidence of their existence. J. RAWLS, *supra* note 101, at 39.

I do not wish here to join further the debate between the pluralists (Rawls' "intuitionists"[111]) and the coherence theorists.[112] But that dispute exists, and we must recognize that the argued mandate for constructing unitary moral theories around or through the Constitution derives from only one side of a highly contested deontological debate. Moreover, this one-sided view presupposes not only that ethical pluralism is wrong, but it must presuppose as well that pluralism is totally implausible despite the structure of the constitutional text which suggests plurality rather than unity. The arrangement of the text, with particular and discrete provisions and with no expressed unifying principle save a vacuous Preamble,[113] appears to be the embodiment of pluralistic ethics. Thus, the task of the constitutional coherence theorist is not only to show that ethical pluralism is wrong, but also to refute the appearance of ethical pluralism in the text of the Constitution.

## IV. Language and Theory

In a much more promising start toward constructing a theory of constitutional language, Ronald Dworkin distinguishes "concepts" and "conceptions."[114] His theory is incomplete, but its gaps can direct us toward a more satisfactory formulation.

Despite its similarity to ordinary language associations, Dworkin's distinction between concepts and conceptions does not parallel the distinction between connotation and denotation, or between intension and extension. Rather, his distinction admits the existence of, and is derived from, differences in meaning rather than various applications of an agreed meaning.[115] A con-

111. Because "intuitionism" has been used to refer to a method of identifying moral values rather than the relation among them (and in this sense Rawls, Richards, Dworkin, and Gewirth may all be intuitionists), Rawls' terminology is a trifle misleading. It has been suggested that "pluralism" would be a better appellation, as a plurality of values is used. B. Barry, *supra* note 109, at 6.

112. I use "coherence theorist" to refer to anyone who holds that there is one ultimate system of moral values, whether they be monists like Dworkin or priority-ranked pluralists like Rawls. *See supra* note 101.

113. *See* Monaghan, *Our Perfect Constitution*, 56 N.Y.U. L. Rev. 353, 371 (1981).

114. R. Dworkin, *supra* note 11, at 134-37; Dworkin, *The Forum of Principle*, 56 N.Y.U. L. Rev. 469 (1981). *See also* J. Rawls, *supra* note 101, at 10. For commentary on the distinction, see Munzer & Nickel, *supra* note 2, at 1037-41; Saphire, *Professor Richards' Unwritten Constitution of Human Rights: Some Preliminary Observations*, 4 U. Dayton L. Rev. 305 (1979). *See also* D. Richards, *supra* note 75, at 44-56.

115. This is so, except to the extent that changes in meaning (different conceptions) are built into what Dworkin means by a concept. R. Dworkin, *supra* note 11, at 103, 134-37. In this sense, the meaning of a concept never changes, but this is only because in another sense the concept itself has no meaning apart from some conception of it. The real problem is that there is an inevitable tension between open concepts and most traditional theories of meaning. *See generally* M. Weitz, The Opening Mind 25-48 (1977).

ception in Dworkin's scheme is a particular (but not necessarily particularized, in the sense of highly detailed) theory which is thought to explain the meaning of a concept.[116] A concept, therefore, allows competing theories of its meaning, and no one of these theories is necessarily more or less correct as a definition or explanation of the concept.[117] A concept is something[118] whose definition requires references to a theory, but no theory provides a uniquely correct definition. If only one plausible theory existed, then that theory would provide the definition of the concept, and there would be no need for the distinction between concept and conception. In order for the distinction to survive, then, there must be at least two competing conceptions (theories), neither of which is demonstrably better or more correct than the other as a definition of the concept.

This distinction seems to hold great potential for a theory of constitutional interpretation, because, as Dworkin maintains, it enables us to argue alternative conceptions within the framework of the existing concepts set forth in the constitutional text. But the utility of the distinction rests on the exact nature of a "concept." In order for any word, including a concept, to have a potential use, it must have some meaning which allows us to understand its use in the face of competing theoretical conceptions. One candidate for "some meaning" is the existence of a paradigm, or exemplar. W.B. Gallie contrasted "essentially contested concepts"[119] (the notion from which Dworkin derives his distinction[120]) with those words whose use was merely "radically confused."[121] For Gallie, the existence of an exemplar makes it possible to meaningfully use words whose essential characteristics are contested.[122]

Gallie offers the concept of a "champion" to demonstrate the

---

116. R. DWORKIN, *supra* note 11, at 103, 134-37.

117. *Id.*

118. I use the word "something" deliberately, because there is a long tradition of philosophical debate about just what concepts are, some claiming they are words of a particular sort, some claiming they are mental images, and so on. *See generally* M. WEITZ, *supra* note 115, at 3-24; N. CAMPBELL, FOUNDATIONS OF SCIENCE 45 (1957).

119. Gallie, *Essentially Contested Concepts,* 56 PROC. ARISTOTELIAN SOC. 167 (1955). *See also* W.B. GALLIE, PHILOSOPHY AND THE HISTORICAL UNDERSTANDING (1964). For commentary, see Kekes, *Essentially Contested Concepts: A Reconsideration,* 10 PHIL. & RHETORIC 71 (1977); Garver, *Rhetoric and Essentially Contested Arguments,* 11 PHIL. & RHETORIC 156 (1978). *See also* Booth, *"Preserving the Exemplar" or, How Not to Dig Our Own Graves,* 3 J. CRITICAL INQUIRY 407 (1977); McIntyre, *The Essential Contestability of Some Social Concepts,* 84 ETHICS 1 (1973). Also useful is C. STEVENSON, *Persuasive Definitions,* in FACTS AND VALUES 32 (1963).

120. R. DWORKIN, *supra* note 11, at 103.

121. Gallie, *supra* note 119, at 178-79.

122. *See id.* at 176-86. Munzer and Nickel are cautious about taking up the question of the ultimate validity of the concept/conception distinction and presumably are equally cautious about Gallie's original notion of essentially contested concepts. Munzer & Nickel, *supra* note 2, at 1039 n.46.

operation of an exemplar.[123] Modifying this example, we might contend that the New York Yankees of 1927 were the exemplar of a "great" baseball team. If, in this context, "great baseball team" marks an essentially contested concept, we nonetheless understand the use of the concept because we recognize the authority and unattainable standards[124] of the exemplar. Thus, if one baseball team's hitting and depth were stronger than that of the 1927 Yankees, but its pitching was weaker, and if another team's pitching and depth were stronger but its hitting was weaker, we could contest whether either or both of these teams were entitled to the "great baseball team" designation. Although the concept is contested, it retains meaning through a core of settled meaning, the exemplar, which allows us to debate about the shape and extent of the fringe.

A more plausible candidate than the "exemplar," for "some meaning" that makes understanding of a contested concept possible, could be a "family resemblance."[125] Unlike the unattainable standards of the exemplar, the family resemblance has no set of necessary and sufficient defining characteristics,[126] but rather is an interlocking relationship among the appropriate uses of a term. Although the Wittgensteinian "family resemblance" does not admit of a core and fringe characterization,[127] it still contains exemplars. While we might debate whether some novel form of amusement is "really" a game, we have no doubt that Olympic games and party games are games, despite the absence of identifiable shared features. Without the existence of exemplars of some kind, we have not a contested concept, and perhaps not even Gallie's "radically confused" concept, but perhaps just loose talk, or, even worse, vacuous talk.

If this is so, then Dworkin's concepts have run into heavy weather. Almost certainly exemplars for freedom of speech, equal protection, and many other similar constitutional concepts have

---

123. Gallie, *supra* note 119, at 176-79.

124. The standard of being unattainable is important, although neglected by Gallie, for if the exemplar were attainable there would be little to contest. The question would only be whether one had attained identity in all respects with the exemplar, in which case the concept would apply—or had not, in which case the concept would not apply. But if the exemplar is unattainable, then we can argue about which features are necessary in order for the concept to apply.

125. L. Wittgenstein, Philosophical Investigations §§ 65-72 (3d ed. G. Anscombe trans. 1958). Wittgenstein's famous example is that of games. *Id.* at § 66.

126. *Id.*

127. *See* G. Pitcher, The Philosophy of Wittgenstein 215-27 (1964); Chandler, *Three Types of Classes*, 3 Am. Phil. Q. 77 (1966). Hart has claimed that all legal terms could fit into the core and fringe characterization. Hart, *Scandinavian Realism*, 1959 Cambridge L.J. 233, 239-40. This seems mistaken, however, because it ignores the existence of terms, such as family-resemblance terms, that do not have a single core.

never existed. There are exemplars for some, and Dworkin properly points out that an exemplar exists for cruel and unusual punishment.[128] But surely no exemplar for "the freedom of speech" shares the common agreement implicit in Gallie's original formulation of the essentially contested concept. Is imprisonment of a newspaper editor for publishing criticism of the government the exemplar of a free speech violation? It is not if we understand an aversion to prior restraint to be the essential feature of the meaning of the "freedom of speech,"[129] or if we take individual self-expression through communication as the paradigm.[130] The identification of an exemplar in the absence of general agreement is dependent upon a particular theory. In the absence of an exemplar, however, it is difficult to see how a particular theory or conception is or is not related to the concept at hand.

From this perspective, constitutional adjudication *builds* exemplars. But we encounter difficulty in locating the foundation on which to build the exemplar or theory. Though the words of the Constitution are the starting point, they give us very little guidance.

Perhaps we should forget about concepts and conceptions, and look instead at *words*, but words of a certain sort. Here, we encounter a particular variety of words that cannot be understood without reference to a theory.[131] Not all words share this characteristic equally, but some words or terms, such as "anal-retentive personality" or "kinetic energy" or "wave function,"[132] can only be understood with reference to a theory. When we use terms such as these, we presuppose the existence of some theory, even though we do not explain the theory every time we use the terms. If theory-laden words can appear in non-legal texts, then similar terms ought to be able to appear in legal texts, and it seems promising to look at terms such as "the freedom of speech" and "equal protection of the laws" as such theory-laden words, except that

128. R. DWORKIN, *supra* note 11, at 136 n.1.

129. *See supra* note 30.

130. *See, e.g.*, Baker, *Scope of the First Amendment Freedom of Speech*, 25 UCLA L. REV. 964 (1978). The focus is similar in Richards, *Free Speech and Obscenity Law: Toward a Moral Theory of the First Amendment*, 123 U. PA. L. REV. 45 (1974).

131. Most of the existing literature is in the philosophy of science, although the point has much more universal application. *See generally* P. ACHINSTEIN, CONCEPTS OF SCIENCE 157-201 (1968); N. HANSON, PATTERNS OF DISCOVERY (1958); C. HEMPEL, PHILOSOPHY OF NATURAL SCIENCE 75 (1966); G. RYLE, DILEMMAS 90-91 (1956). Philosophers of science refer to theory-ladenness in reference both to terms of this type and to observation, *see supra* note 91 & accompanying text, but it is important to keep the two ideas distinct.

132. For a discussion of the theories to which these terms refer, see generally P. ACHINSTEIN, *supra* note 131, at 180-83; N. HANSON, *supra* note 131, at 60.

here the use of the term precedes the development of the theory, rather than following after it.

If the use of the terms precedes the development of the theory, the terms themselves may have no meaning other than some ordinary language associations and some syntactic meaning. Notwithstanding this fact, they are still in a text which we take to be authoritative. Their irremovable presence in the text must then be taken as a mandate for the development of a theory that will give content to the terms used. Significantly, the mandate does not derive from the personal intentions or states of the mind of the drafters of the document. It derives from the conventions that govern language use, conventions that operate without regard to the intentions of the user.[133] We argue unnecessarily and misleadingly when we argue that the use of such terms provides evidence of an original intent by the framers that the underlying theories be developed and changed, an intent we can assume from the failure to use more specific terminology.[134] The constructed intent here is unnecessary, because the rules and conventions of language cut off the necessity and possibly even the permissibility of looking behind them into the mind of the speaker or writer.

Philosophers commonly argue that if a speaker says $p$, and $p$ logically entails $q$, then the speaker is committed to $q$ even if he had never thought of $q$ and never would have intended to say $q$.[135] A similar convention of language use appears applicable to the use of theory-laden terms. When a speaker uses a theory-laden term, the speaker is committed to the theory that may at any time surround the use of the term, even if the speaker did not intend that result. If, for example, I accuse someone of having an anal-retentive personality, my use of that term commits me to accusing him of having whatever an anal-retentive personality entails as a matter of psychiatric theory. And if I use terms such as "equal protection of the laws," that too commits me to having authorized the incorporation (and, if necessary, the creation) of a theory without which the term's meaning is incomplete.

Given that theories change, we can legitimately commit the user of theory-laden terminology to the possibility of change implicit in any theory. Thus, the users of theory-laden language such as "the freedom of speech" and "privileges and immunities

133. *See supra* notes 27-65 & accompanying text.

134. *See supra* notes 46-49 & accompanying text.

135. P. Jones, *supra* note 57, at 182. *See also* S. Barker, The Elements of Logic 7 (3d ed. 1980). The notion of commitment in this sense is central in the writings of John Searle. *See* J. Searle, *supra* note 20. For an interesting application, see Finnis, *Scepticism, Self-Refutation, and the Good of Truth*, in Law, Morality, and Society: Essays in Honour of H.L.A. Hart 247 (P. Hacker & J. Raz eds. 1977).

of citizens of the United States" are committed to the theory whose construction they have authorized by their choice of words. Whether or not the user of those terms intended to be so committed does not matter. It's just part of the rules of the game. Theory-laden terms are incomplete, and the use of an incomplete term commits the user to the fact that the completion is going to come from somewhere else. The interpreter of the Constitution is thus, in some sense, like a musician working with a score that is not complete until it is interpreted; and in some sense like a trial lawyer who is expected to make the best case possible with the available evidence. An interpretation becomes an explication rather than an explanation,[136] and we can hope for no more.

Additionally, we can argue that all of ordinary language is theory-laden,[137] and indeed this is the assumption of much of Western metaphysics, embodied, for example, in the categories of Aristotle[138] and Kant.[139] But even if not all of ordinary language is theory-laden, it is fairly uncontroversial that at least much of it is. In some sense, the word "lunch" is theory-laden, at least as compared to "eating" or "placing organic matter in one's mouth for the purpose of introducing it into the digestive system." So, too, are terms like "time," "space," "hailing" a cab, "playing" a game, "sending" a letter, and "understanding" a book. We constantly use expressions which presuppose or incorporate theories that do more than identify a physical object or activity.

Thus, when we say that a term is theory-laden, we presuppose a particular point of view of the speaker with respect to which a term is theory-laden. I cannot explain to a person ignorant of baseball what a "home run" is without explaining a great deal of baseball, but it seems strange to describe "home run" as theory-laden when one baseball player is talking to another. Similarly, I cannot explain a "trick" to a non-bridge player without explaining at least the rudiments of the game of bridge, even though "trick"

136. "*Explication,* when not simply a synonym for 'explanation,' is the process whereby a hitherto imprecise notion is given a formal definition, and so made suitable for use in formal work. The definition does not claim to be synonymous with the original notion, since it is avowedly making it more precise." A. LACEY, A DICTIONARY OF PHILOSOPHY 66 (1976). The idea of *explication* is usually attributed to Carnap. R. CARNAP, MEANING AND NECESSITY 7-8 (2d ed. 1956). *See also* W. QUINE, *supra* note 59, at 258-59. I am using "explication" in a slightly looser sense. We explicate when we work out a theory, and when we explicate we put something in, rather than just pulling something out.

137. *See* Hesse, *Theory and Value in the Social Sciences,* in ACTION AND INTERPRETATION 1, 1-2 (C. Hookway & P. Pettit eds. 1978). *See also* P. FEYERABEND, AGAINST METHOD 66 (1975). Whether there is or can be a value-free or theory-free observation language has been one of the perennial problems in the philosophy of science.

138. *See* G. ANSCOMBE & P. GEACH, THREE PHILOSOPHERS 5-63 (1961).

139. *See* J. HOSPERS, *supra* note 33, at 184-86.

is not highly theory-laden in conversations between bridge players. But suppose that after a sequence of bidding I explain to my opponents at the bridge table that a particular bid was an "impossible negative." I must then explain a bidding system or theory known as "Precision," without which the term "impossible negative" cannot be understood.

We can clarify things by distinguishing between two forms of theory-ladenness. In the weaker sense, many of the terms of ordinary language are theory-laden. But in a stronger sense, terms are only theory-laden if they force us to go outside the domain of discourse in which they are used. Thus, "lunch" and "time" are theory-laden in the weaker sense but not in the stronger, because the theory that they presuppose is as much a part of ordinary language as is the language itself. But "straight flush" or "anal-retentive personality" or "habeas corpus," if used in ordinary conversation, are theory-laden in the stronger sense because they presuppose theories outside the domain of ordinary discourse.[140]

Therefore, we can say that terms are theory-laden in a strong sense only when they require us to go outside the context in which we are speaking. And that is why "habeas corpus" may be theory-laden in ordinary language but not in law, as is even more true for terms like "pleading," "statute of limitations," or "appeal."

This distinction applies directly to constitutional language. The requirement that the President shall have attained "the Age of thirty-five years" is theory-laden in the weak sense because it presupposes a theory of determining age. It also presupposes the deeper idea of determining growth with reference to chronology. But it is not theory-laden in the strong sense because it is uncontroversially known to all participants speaking *within* the domain. A reference in the Constitution to "habeas corpus," or "Congress," or "amendment" is similar. But a term in the Constitution is theory-laden in the strong sense when it sends us outside the legal domain. "Freedom of speech" and "equal protection of the laws" are different from "habeas corpus" or "Congress," because they send us outside of the legal domain and into the moral or the political. That is also why the use of terminology that lacks meaning within the domain in which it is used can be said to commit

140. "[O]ne must always specify the theory with respect to which a given term is or is not 'theory-laden.'" P. ACHINSTEIN, *supra* note 131, at 183. Although we often talk, especially in the context of constitutional theory, about vague or general terms, it is important to remember that vagueness is relative as well, and the degree of vagueness will depend on the particular context in which a term is used and the particular purposes for which it would or would not be vague. *See* I. SCHEFFLER, BEYOND THE LETTER: A PHILOSOPHICAL INQUIRY INTO AMBIGUITY, VAGUENESS AND METAPHOR IN LANGUAGE 49-50 (1979).

the user to whatever meaning may appear in or be provided by another domain.

# [9]

VOLUME 69 NUMBER 4 JULY 1989

BOSTON UNIVERSITY LAW REVIEW

# RECONSIDERING THE RULE OF LAW

MARGARET JANE RADIN*

## I. INTRODUCTION

The ideal of "the rule of law, not of men"[1] calls upon us to strive to ensure that our law itself will rule (govern) us, not the wishes of powerful individuals. According to this traditional ideal, government must be by "settled, standing Laws," not by "Absolute Arbitrary Power."[2] Although the Rule of Law ideal is central to our legal tradition, it is deeply contested. Among those who affirm the traditional ideal there is no canonical formulation of its meaning, and critical theorists argue that the Rule of Law is mere ideology that should be jettisoned. In this essay I suggest that it is too soon to throw out the Rule of Law

---

* Carolyn Craig Franklin Professor of Law, University of Southern California Law Center.

This article is an expanded and revised version of my lecture at Boston University School of Law presented on March 3, 1988. Earlier versions were presented to law faculty workshops at Tulane, Southern California, Michigan, and Yale. I am grateful to the hearers on these occasions; many of their comments range beyond the scope of the present essay, but they will continue to motivate me in further work. I am grateful, as well, to the many colleagues and friends whose sharp insight and critical honesty keep me trying to dispel the haze.

[1] For obvious reasons, because I am considering the Rule of Law in today's context, I shall rephrase the ideal as "the rule of law, not of individuals." Yet we must not forget that when the ideal developed, and during most of its long history, it was inconceivable that any individuals who were not "men" could be a part of political life.

[2] J. LOCKE, *Of the Extent of the Legislative Power*, § 137 in TWO TREATISES OF GOVERNMENT (P. Laslett rev. ed. 1970) (3d ed. 1698) (emphasis omitted). The formulation of the term "the Rule of Law" is sometimes credited to the nineteenth-century British jurist Albert Venn Dicey, who elaborated upon three characteristics of "the rule or supremacy of law": absence of arbitrary power on the part of the government; ordinary law administered by ordinary tribunals; and general rules of constitutional law resulting from the ordinary law of the land. *See* A.V. DICEY, INTRODUCTION TO THE STUDY OF THE LAW OF THE CONSTITUTION 179-92 (1908).

wholesale, but that at minimum the concept should be reinterpreted.

By way of concrete introduction to the complex of problems I mean to examine, consider *Robinson v. Diamond Housing Corporation.*[3] *Robinson* was one of Judge J. Skelly Wright's famous decisions remaking modern landlord-tenant law in the early seventies. Judge Wright decided that the landlord, Diamond Housing Corporation, could not end Mrs. Robinson's month-to-month tenancy if its termination was motivated by retaliation against Mrs. Robinson for having successfully asserted the habitability defense of "illegal contract."[4] The result was that if a tenant lives in housing that seriously violates the housing code, he or she has a right to stay there, rent-free, until the landlord either fixes up the premises or proves economic compulsion to exit the landlord business. As Judge Wright put this, perhaps not fully mindful of the irony, precedent and the housing code "guarantee the right of a tenant to remain in possession without paying rent when the premises are burdened with substantial housing code violations making them unsafe and unsanitary."[5] In a ringing peroration, Wright declared that this result is "required . . . by respect for the separation of powers and the rule of law."[6]

It is this claim about the underlying ideal of the Rule of Law that prompts me to bring up the *Robinson* case here.[7] My guess is that a great number of legal observers thought the Rule of Law required the case to come out the other way, in favor of the landlord's previously unquestioned right to end a month-to-month tenancy on proper notice. Can the Rule of Law impose any limitation on the "arbitrary power" of individual decision makers? Is the Rule of Law a good way to go about trying to achieve government by law?

I begin with an attempt to make clear exactly what *is* the Rule of Law, and the way in which its meaning is contested because of differences in emphasis of its instrumental and substantive aspects. Having noticed the fact that the main formulations of the Rule of Law do agree upon an assumption that law consists of rules, I move on to an inquiry into the nature of rules. Specifically, I consider a social practice conception of rules, commonly attributed to

---

[3] 463 F.2d 853 (D.C. Cir. 1972).

[4] The District of Columbia Court of Appeals had recently recognized the "illegal contract" defense in Brown v. Southall Realty Co., 237 A.2d 834, 837 (D.C. 1968). Successful assertion of this defense meant that a tenant's promise to pay rent was unenforceable.

[5] *Robinson*, 463 F.2d at 865. Wright conceded that he would be "deeply troubled" if his ruling led to "many families living indefinitely in substandard housing without paying rent," *id.* at 869, but he apparently believed that giving the landlord the legal choice of either repairing the premises or being unable to charge rent would result in an increase in habitability at no increase in rent.

[6] *Robinson*, 463 F.2d at 871.

[7] Perceptive law students ask me, "If Wright wanted to protect a tenant's right to safe and sanitary housing, why didn't he enjoin the landlord to repair the premises, rather than holding that the tenant could remain indefinitely without paying?" This is an excellent (and complex) question, although answering it would lead me afield here. *See infra* p. 818.

Wittgenstein,[8] which holds that rules can only be claimed to exist when there is community agreement in practice. To put this conception roughly, agreement in action does not *follow* from there being a pre-existing rule; agreement in action is the only basis for claiming that there *is* a rule.

I then consider the implications for the Rule of Law once this social practice conception of rules is accepted. First, I show how the traditional ideal of the Rule of Law is connected with a certain traditional conception of the nature of rules, which I shall call "formalist." Then I ask the more specific question which is the main focus of this essay: Does the social practice conception of rules render the Rule of Law impossible? I argue that the social practice conception of rules does indeed render the traditional Rule of Law impossible, because of the link between the Rule of Law and the traditional conception of rules. I believe the Rule of Law can survive as a coherent ideal if it receives a modern interpretation, however, and I conclude by suggesting a possible avenue for such reinterpretation.[9]

## II. THE RULE OF LAW AS A CONTESTED CONCEPT

Before reconsidering the Rule of Law in light of a social practice conception of rules, we must try to define the elements of the Rule of Law. The complex of ideas thought to comprise the Rule of Law is not completely canonical. We can, in fact, readily distinguish two main contested views: a primarily instrumental version and a more substantive version. The instrumental version holds that the Rule of Law is a prerequisite for any efficacious legal order. The substantive version holds that the Rule of Law embodies tenets of a particular political morality.[10] These versions are illustrated by two of the best modern

[8] The view I discuss is often attributed to Wittgenstein, but no view can be attributed to him uncontroversially. As I discuss below, *see infra* pp. 797-810, my reading of Wittgenstein is broad and neo-pragmatic in character, but a narrower, more analytic reading is preferred by many.

[9] The task of working out the required reinterpretation in detail, and exploring its connections with reinterpreted central aspects of political theory, awaits further work. The complete analysis would involve theories of the person, the state, and community, and theories of the proper roles of citizens, legislators, and judges in the well-developed polity. For another piece of the picture, see Michelman, *Law's Republic*, 97 YALE L.J. 1493 (1988) (presenting a modern interpretation of government by law through reinterpretation of the political theory of civic republicanism and exploration of the conundrum of government-of-laws versus government-by-the-people).

[10] To avoid possible misunderstanding, I should say here that the view I refer to as substantive is substantive only in an attenuated sense. As elaborated below, *see infra* notes 22-33 and accompanying text, the view I call substantive merely asserts that having a system of rules of a certain type by itself serves substantive values, such as fairness and respect for persons. On its face, at least, the view I call substantive does not make the stronger claim that, in addition, in order to fulfill the Rule of Law ideal the rules must themselves be good rules. Ronald Dworkin's recent view of the Rule of Law is indeed "substantive" in this more robust sense, but I believe Dworkin's view departs from the main parameters in which the Rule of Law has previously been con-

attempts to address the Rule of Law, those of Lon Fuller[11] and John Rawls.[12] Although labels oversimplify, I think it will be appropriate to characterize Fuller's version as instrumental[13] and Rawls's version as substantive.[14]

### A. *The Instrumental Conception of the Rule of Law, or "How to do Things with Rules"*

Lon Fuller claimed that the Rule of Law is part of the "internal" morality of law.[15] I interpret this to mean that the complex of ideas associated with the term "Rule of Law" is essential for the efficacy of any system of legal rules. This instrumental conception of the Rule of Law is presented in Fuller's engaging parable of King Rex,[16] who failed to make law by ignoring the eight elements of the Rule of Law. These eight elements compromise "the morality

---

ceived. *See* R. Dworkin, A Matter of Principle 11-12 (1985) (the "rights conception" of the Rule of Law "requires, as part of the ideal of law, that the rules in the rule book capture and enforce moral rights").

[11] *See* L. Fuller, The Morality of Law 33-94 (rev. ed. 1969).

[12] *See* J. Rawls, A Theory of Justice 235-43 (1971).

[13] I do risk mischaracterizing Fuller's view by calling it instrumental, because Fuller himself apparently believed that his formulation embodied other values besides instrumental efficacy. *See infra* note 17. For another account of the instrumental conception of the Rule of Law, see J. Raz, *The Rule of Law and Its Virtue*, in The Authority of Law: Essays on Law and Morality 210-29 (1979), although Raz in the end turns toward the substantive conception in important respects. *Cf.* Michelman, *Justification (and Justifiability) of Law in a Contradictory World*, in Justification in Law, Ethics, and Politics 71, 72 (J. Pennock & J. Chapman eds. 1986) (XXVIII) (characterizing legalist justification as implying a law that is general, external to the case to be decided, rationally applicable to cases, and transcending individual deciders).

[14] Other accounts that stress the substantive aspect of the Rule of Law are F. Hayek, The Political Ideal of the Rule of Law (1955) (characterizing the liberty produced by the Rule of Law in terms of the laissez-faire market regime—private property and freedom of contract); J. Lucas, The Principles of Politics §§ 24-25 (1985); R. Sartorius, Individual Conduct and Social Norms (1975). *Cf.* Moore, *The Semantics of Judging*, 54 S. Cal. L. Rev. 151, 293 (1981) [hereinafter Moore, *Semantics*]; Moore, *A Natural Law Theory of Interpretation*, 58 S. Cal. L. Rev. 277 (1985) [hereinafter Moore, *Theory of Interpretation*]. For a discussion of Moore's ideas, see *infra* notes 100-10 and accompanying text.

[15] Fuller entitled his chapter on the Rule of Law "The Morality That Makes Law Possible." He did not explicitly elaborate on why he thought his analysis rested on anything properly called morality. He did seem to think that government by rules is necessary before the question of justice can be meaningfully posed:

> The internal morality of the law demands that there be rules, that they be made known, and that they be observed in practice by those charged with their administration. These demands may seem ethically neutral so far as the external aims of law are concerned. Yet, just as law is a precondition for good law, so acting by known rule is a precondition for any meaningful appraisal of the justice of law.

L. Fuller, *supra* note 11, at 157.

[16] For the parable of King Rex, see *id.* at 33-38.

that makes law possible":

1. Generality. Roughly, there must be rules, cognizable separately from (and broader than) specific cases, such that the rules can be applied to specific cases, or specific cases can be seen to fall under or lie within them.

2. Notice or publicity. Those who are expected to obey the rules must be able to find out what the rules are.

3. Prospectivity. The rules must exist prior in time to the actions being judged by them.

4. Clarity. The rules must be understandable by those who are expected to obey them.

5. Non-contradictoriness. Those who are expected to obey the rules must not simultaneously be commanded to do both A and not-A.

6. Conformability. The addressees must be able to conform their behavior to the rules.

7. Stability. The rules must not change so fast that they cannot be learned and followed.

8. Congruence. The explicitly promulgated rules must correspond with the rules inferable from patterns of enforcement by functionaries (e.g., courts and police).

I believe this list can be boiled down to two principles: first, there must be rules; second, those rules must be capable of being followed.

The requirement that there must be rules encompasses what Fuller meant by generality. Generality implies that the rules are broader (more general) than specific cases or particulars, which can be brought within them, or seen to be comprehended, subsumed, or covered by them. All particulars of specific cases that fall under the rule are covered by the rule. If a rule commands, "No one under 21 is allowed in a saloon," then it applies necessarily to all people under 21 and to all saloons.

Thus, here the familiar idea that like cases ought to be treated alike (consistency) is seen to be an attribute of the formally general nature of rules. Consistency here means simply that every particular item that *is* within the extension of the operative words in the rule must be ***recognized*** as being within the extension of the words, and hence within the purview of the rule. We are not allowed to pick out only certain people under 21 or only certain saloons and say our rule applies only to them, simply because the rule's general nature precludes this. Similarly, the familiar idea that the discretion of judges and other functionaries should be limited in applying or interpreting the rules is, in Fuller's view, likewise seen in a formal guise. The generality of rules (that is, their very status as rules) is negated if functionaries are able to treat one item that comes within the extension of the operative words—hence falls under the rule—differently from another. If functionaries can treat different minors or saloons differently (without showing that they aren't "really" minors or "really" saloons), then we don't have the "rule" we thought we had.

The requirement that the rules must be capable of being followed encompasses all the rest of Fuller's list. In order to be capable of being followed by the addressees, rules must have certain characteristics, which I think can also be boiled down to two. Let me colloquially call these two requirements "know-ability" and "perform-ability." In order for those to whom the rules are addressed to *know* what they are commanded to do, the commands must be public, congruent, and non-contradictory, clear enough to understand, and they must not change too fast. In order for the addressees to *do* what is commanded of them, in response to the commands, the commands must be prospective (not retroactive), not contradictory or non-congruent, and not physically, mentally, or circumstantially impossible for the human beings addressed to follow.

This is indeed an instrumental conception of the Rule of Law,[17] which could more colloquially be called "how to do things with rules."[18] All of Fuller's requirements are directed toward there being rule-like commands that can successfully induce desired behavior (whatever it is) in the addressees.[19] Substantive ideals, like fairness or democracy, and autonomy or dignity of persons, are not explicitly raised. Neither are democratic procedural traditions, like the separation of powers or the access to courts and jury trials. It seems that if a Nazi regime wanted to accomplish its heinous goals by means of rules, it would perforce make its commands conform to these requirements.[20]

---

[17] It is apparent, however, that Fuller himself objected to the type of instrumentalist reading I have given his work, for he chose to reply to the instrumentalist reading of his early reviewers in the revised edition of *The Morality of Law*. *See* L. FULLER, *supra* note 11, at 187-244 (chapter V is titled "A Reply to Critics"). Fuller tried to clarify his views after all of his reviewers argued that "the alleged internal morality of law is merely a matter of efficacy." *Id.* at 201. In his attempted clarification he spoke about the law as a "*facility* enabling men [sic] to live a satisfactory life in common," *id.* at 223 (emphasis in original), and about " 'an interactional theory of law' " that characterizes law as a joint normative enterprise of lawmakers and law-followers. *Id.* at 237. Fuller's concluding plea for legal philosophy to turn away from conceptualism and positivism and toward "the social processes that constitute the reality of law," *id.* at 242, makes clear that he was groping for a pragmatic theory of law.

[18] After so dubbing the instrumental conception, I discovered that there is a book with this title. *See* W. TWINING & D. MIERS, HOW TO DO THINGS WITH RULES: A PRIMER OF INTERPRETATION (1982).

[19] What motivates the addressees to conform their behavior to these rule-like commands is a separate issue. Traditionally, of course, a primary motivator is penal sanctions.

[20] *See, e.g.*, J. RAZ, *supra* note 13, at 211 ("A non-democratic legal system, based on the denial of human rights, on extensive poverty, on racial segregation, sexual inequalities and religious persecution may, in principle, conform to the requirements of the rule of law better than any of the legal systems of the more enlightened Western democracies."). It should be noted that Fuller was unwilling to commit himself unequivocally to this implication of the instrumentalist conception. He often noted that the Nazi

This conception of the Rule of Law assumes that law consists of rules. In Ronald Dworkin's terms, this conception is premised upon a model of rules.[21] Implicit in the understanding of law as rules, and of the Rule of Law as a guide to the efficacy of those rules, are two sets of philosophical problems. The first focuses on the individual as a rule-follower. Fuller's instrumental conception of the Rule of Law presupposes that the law controls its subjects by providing incentives to structure behavior. Thus, although not included on Fuller's list, it is clear that there must be a ninth and tenth requirement: (9) addressees of rules must be rational choosers; (10) addressees must be suitably motivated, perhaps by penal sanctions, perhaps by opportunities for reward. The addressees must be such as *can* respond by following the rules, if the rules have the two characteristics of know-ability and perform-ability. The addressees must further be such as *will* respond, if they are motivated to do so by their desires to obtain rewards or avoid punishment. The problems of choice and motivation are not my concern here, however, and I set them aside.

Instead, my focus will be on the second set of philosophical problems. These revolve around the very concept of rules itself. Does it make sense to think, as Fuller apparently did, that rules are general in the sense of being logically prior to action, and that they apply formally to particular actions that fall under them? These are the issues raised by the social practice conception of rules. But before addressing these issues, it will be helpful to examine the substantive conception of the Rule of Law.

### B. *The Substantive Conception of the Rule of Law, or "How to Foster Liberty and Constrain Leviathan"*

John Rawls claims that the Rule of Law is an aspect of his overall scheme of "justice as fairness." The Rule of Law is formal justice—"the regular and impartial administration of public rules"[22]—applied to the legal system. It promotes liberty, the prime value in justice as fairness. Indeed, perhaps Rawls may be read as making the stronger claim that the Rule of Law is *required* for liberty.

Rawls proposes a rationalist model of law, from which he draws out one version of the traditional complex of ideas that comprise the Rule of Law. Here is his seminal definition of a legal system: "A legal system is a coercive order of public rules addressed to rational persons for the purpose of regulating their conduct and providing the framework for social cooperation."[23] This

---

regime itself was not law-like, *see, e.g.*, L. FULLER, *supra* note 11, at 40-41, and he may have thought that truly bad regimes would never be law-like.

[21] R. DWORKIN, TAKING RIGHTS SERIOUSLY 14-80 (1977) [hereinafter R. DWORKIN, RIGHTS]. In his later work, Dworkin refers to the "rulebook model of community." *See* R. DWORKIN, LAW'S EMPIRE 209-15 (1986). Although he does not elaborate on the connections between this model of community—roughly, a positivist social contract position—and the notion that law consists of rules, they seem to be related.

[22] J. RAWLS, *supra* note 12, at 235.

[23] *Id.*

conception encapsulates many of the traditional precepts of the Rule of Law, in that, as Rawls explains, the precepts are derivable from it.[24] A lot is packed into these carefully chosen words. In the following paragraphs I shall unpack them slightly.

"A legal system is a coercive order of public rules": In Rawls's conception (as in Fuller's), the law consists of rules. To regulate conduct, and thereby achieve the social cooperation necessary for justice, rules must have certain characteristics associated with the Rule of Law:

1. "Ought implies can." The addressees must have the ability to conform, and the authorities must act in good faith. Impossibility of conformance, therefore, must be recognized as a defense.

2. Similar treatment of similar cases. This includes the requirement of consistency, and imposes limitations on judicial discretion.

3. "*Nullum crimen sine lege*" (no crime without law). Laws must be known and expressly promulgated, with clear meaning. There must be no retroactivity. Laws must be general and not bills of attainder. Severe offenses must be narrowly construed.

4. Natural justice. There must be structures for achieving truth and correct enforcement: trials, hearings, rules of evidence, due process. Judges must be impartial and independent. Trials must be fair, open, and not "prejudiced by public clamor."[25]

Rawls advances two arguments for a connection between these precepts of the Rule of Law and the fundamental substantive value, liberty. First, he argues that absence of these characteristics will cause a chilling effect. To the extent that rules are vague, or that like cases are not treated alike, or that judicial process is irregular, "the boundaries of our liberties are uncertain." And when these boundaries are uncertain, "liberty is restricted by reasonable fear of its exercise."[26] Hence, if rational persons in the original position are choosing a legal structure to promote their paramount value—liberty—they will choose the Rule of Law because of the need for predictability, determinateness, and certainty of legal consequences.

The second argument advanced by Rawls for a connection between the Rule of Law and liberty is characterized by Rawls as "Hobbes's thesis."[27] The scheme of social cooperation, which has as its purpose the enhancement of liberty over the conditions prevailing in the state of nature, requires the precepts of the Rule of Law. This is so because, under Hobbesian assumptions, the problem of social cooperation is the problem of the "n-person prisoner's dilemma." It benefits each person to restrain herself if all others cooperate, but it benefits her even more to act in self-interest while all others cooperate. Hence, there are strong incentives for each to act against the scheme of social

[24] *Id.* at 236.
[25] *Id.* at 239.
[26] *Id.*
[27] *Id.* at 240.

cooperation, but only if she thinks she can get away with it while everyone else cannot. (If all can cheat and get away with it, the system reverts to the state of nature, which is everyone's least preferred choice.) A coercive sovereign is necessary to remove the incentives of self-interested individuals to break the rules that all should see are in their interest so long as all obey. "The existence of effective penal machinery serves as men's [sic] security to one another."[28] Hence, even an "ideal theory" of justice requires an account of penal sanctions as a stabilizing device.[29] Once the rational choosers in the original position have recognized the necessity of a coercive sovereign that can enforce penal sanctions, they must also recognize the necessity of restraining this Leviathan. In order to control Leviathan, the Rule of Law is needed: "the dangers to liberty are less where the law is impartially and regularly administered in accordance with the principle of legality."[30]

Moreover, the principle of liberty leads to the principle of responsibility, which in turn leads again to the Rule of Law. The principle of responsibility requires the Rule of Law to include all the traditional defenses in the criminal law, not just the instrumental aspects of notice and non-retroactivity needed for instrumental efficacy of rules. "[U]nless citizens are able to know what the law is and are given a fair opportunity to take its directives into account, penal sanctions should not apply to them."[31]

This description should make clear why I refer to Rawls's argument as a substantive conception of the Rule of Law (even though he too is "doing things" with rules). His conception of liberty—the negative liberty of traditional liberalism—is held to be required for achieving justice in society; the precepts of the Rule of Law are held to be strongly connected with that substantive value. Although the list of precepts—generality, consistency, notice,

---

[28] *Id.* In later work, Rawls makes clear his view that if a liberal political order is to be stable over time, it must rest on moral consensus and not be merely a Hobbesian "*modus vivendi.*" Rawls, *The Idea of an Overlapping Consensus*, 7 OXFORD J. LEGAL STUD. 1, 9-12 (1987). It is unclear, however, whether this development of Rawls's views would modify his treatment of the Rule of Law in *A Theory of Justice.* J. RAWLS, *supra* note 12, at 235-43.

[29] Rawls characterizes his theory of justice as an "ideal theory" in the sense that everyone is presumed to act justly. In general, this means that all principles dealing with the errors, complexities, and injustices of the real world are not properly a part of the theory. This excludes civil disobedience and revolution, as well as the theories of corrective justice and punishment. J. RAWLS, *supra* note 12, at 8-9. I have expressed doubts elsewhere that "ideal theory" is a good way to reason about justice. *See* Radin, *Risk-of-Error Rules and Non-Ideal Justification*, in JUSTIFICATION IN LAW, ETHICS, AND POLITICS 33 (J. Pennock & J. Chapman eds. 1986) (Nomos XXVIII); Radin, *Justice and the Market Domain*, in MARKETS AND JUSTICE 165 (J. Chapman ed. 1989)(Nomos XXXI).

[30] J. RAWLS, *supra* note 12, at 241.

[31] *Id.* According to Rawls, the principle of responsibility is not based on the idea that punishment is primarily retributive or denunciatory, but that punishment exists for the sake of liberty itself. *Id.*

perform-ability, and congruence—is roughly the same as in the instrumentalist conception, the justification offered is quite different. The Rule of Law is grounded not on the bare claim of efficacy of behavioral control, but on the specific political vision of traditional liberalism. Liberty is the core value; over-reaching by Leviathan is the danger on one hand, and disintegration of social cooperation because of the prisoner's dilemma is the danger on the other.[32]

There is one traditional element of the Rule of Law in its substantive guise that is not explored by Rawls, yet it looms large in American jurisprudence. This element is the commitment to the separation of powers, and the connected ideas about judicial review and the constrained role of the judge. This commitment also figures in the instrumental conception from the instrumental point of view: rules as applied must not differ from the rules as made (Fuller's precept of "congruence"). Otherwise, the system gives conflicting commands and fails in its purpose of guiding behavior of the addressees. In a system committed to the institutions of courts and judicial review as ways to apply law, this instrumental point takes the form of insisting that judges be constrained so that they strictly "apply," and do not "make," the law. In the substantive conception of the Rule of Law the constrained judicial role is more central because it is held to be required for democracy, a core substantive value.

The point is put in typical fashion by Rolf Sartorius:

> If courts were to have the authority to make law, they would constitute a

---

[32] For Rawls, the substantive connection between the Rule of Law and the core value of liberty is so strong that he seems to make the claim that evil rules are preferable to rulelessness: justice as fairness is served to some extent by having rules, even apart from the justice of the rules themselves. Rawls says that "other things being equal, one legal order is more justly administered than another if it more perfectly fulfills the precepts of the rule of law." J. Rawls, *supra* note 12, at 236. This means that "[i]t will provide a more secure basis for liberty and a more effective means for organizing cooperative schemes." *Id.* Rawls does recognize, of course, the tension between this position and the need for justice in substantive law. He goes on to say that because the Rule of Law precepts "guarantee only the impartial and regular administration of rules, whatever these are, they are compatible with injustice." *Id.*

Perhaps Rawls's apparent claim that there is some increment of justice in merely being rule-bound, wholly apart from the justice of the rules, is a momentary lapse in his commitment to "ideal theory." In a fully ideal theory one would think we should assume that rules are just. No need or opportunity to make claims about the justice of unjust, but rule-bound, regimes would arise. It seems more intuitively attractive to think that once we are in a non-ideal situation, we cannot say a priori or in the abstract whether rule-boundedness will make it worse or better. Rawls seems to turn towards this more pragmatic position when, a few pages later, he mentions the moral dilemmas of "partial compliance theory." In arguing that these dilemmas are to be resolved with the priority of liberty in mind, he notes that "[s]ometimes we may be forced to allow certain breaches of [the Rule of Law] precepts if we are to mitigate the loss of freedom from social evils that cannot be removed, and to aim for the least injustice that conditions allow." J. Rawls, *supra* note 12, at 243.

> legislative elite in a very pure form indeed. But the very arguments which favor majority rule as the form of legislative decision procedure as against some form of nondemocratic elitism imply that the law-making power should be the exclusive province of the majority. They militate against entrusting a judicial elite with the awesome power to make the law as well as apply it.[33]

Those who are versed in the debate surrounding judicial review in American jurisprudence will recognize that this strong statement is simplistic and leaves untouched many famous puzzles. One is the counter-majoritarian difficulty—the problems surrounding the idea that the majority in creating a constitution can be understood to have constrained its own quotidian legislative actions by a broader vision, to be guarded by the judiciary. Another is the working-out of the idea that where there are "gaps" in the law, judicial law-making (subject to legislative override) may be perfectly consistent both with congruence and democracy. A third is the curious tendency to emphasize limiting the power of the judiciary rather than the equally nondemocratic organs of the executive branch. Nevertheless, Sartorius's statement well captures the force of the distinction between "making" and "applying" law, and the constrained conception of the judicial role, in the substantive conception of the Rule of Law.

### C. *A Contested Concept*

At this point I hope it is clear that much of the complex of ideas called the Rule of Law is two-faced. My discussion so far has shown that the central precepts of the Rule of Law can be defended either instrumentally, as necessary to make a legal system work to structure behavior, or substantively, as necessary to fairness, human dignity, freedom, and democracy. The ambiguous precepts include generality (no bills of attainder); treat like cases alike (consistency); notice; non-retroactivity; perform-ability (no impossible or conflicting commands); and congruence (limit discretion of enforcement functionaries). Hence, the Rule of Law itself is deeply ambiguous, a contested concept. Someone who stresses the instrumentalist aspect might affirm that a rule-bound dictatorship evidences the Rule of Law; someone who stresses the substantive aspect would not.

Having elaborated the instrumentalist and substantive conceptions, we can also see the connection between the Rule of Law and liberal legalism. As far as I can tell, legalism means the decision of particular cases by means of general pre-existing rules.[34] Then liberal legalism is the variety of legalism exhibited by liberalism, or found in liberal ideology. If this is correct, the instru-

---

[33] R. Sartorius, *supra* note 14, at 175-76.

[34] *See* R. Unger, Law in Modern Society 52-57, 176-81 (1976); *cf.* J. Shklar, Legalism 1 (1964) (defining legalism as "the ethical attitude that holds moral conduct to be a matter of rule following, and moral relationships to consist of duties and rights determined by rules").

mental conception of the Rule of Law is simply legalism, and the substantive conception is the (or a) liberal form of legalism.

Aside from the surface correlation in the lists of precepts, it is apparent that the two conceptions do have much philosophical underpinning in common, including five important assumptions: (1) law consists of rules; (2) rules are prior to particular cases, more general than particular cases, and applied to particular cases; (3) law is instrumental (the rules are applied to achieve ends); (4) there is a radical separation between government and citizens (there are rule-givers and appliers, *versus* rule-takers and compliers); (5) the person is a rational chooser ordering her affairs instrumentally.[35]

Nevertheless, the two conceptions *are* different. The instrumental conception is a model of government by rules to achieve the government's ends, whatever they may be. The substantive conception is a model of government by rules to achieve the goals of the social contract: liberty and justice. The instrumental conception purports to be more general and ahistorical; the substantive is more clearly bound up with our particular modern ideological heritage.[36]

## III. Traditional Formalism and the Rule of Law

Now I can zero in on the connection between the Rule of Law and traditional formalism—roughly the view that a unique answer in a particular case can be conclusively derived from application of a general rule. I begin by recounting several traditional senses of formalism, and considering their connection with traditional conceptions of the Rule of Law. Then I review the social practice ("Wittgensteinian") critique of the traditional conception of rules as formally or logically prior to particulars. This will bring me to the crucial issue of whether a switch to a Wittgensteinian view of rules makes any difference to our conception of the Rule of Law.

---

[35] As I have said, in this essay I am concentrating on the first two assumptions. As the modern reconsideration of the Rule of Law unfolds, however, they will all have to be considered together. Then the issue will arise whether these five assumptions imply each other or bear strong affinities to each other. I have not begun to argue this here; but I am sure the reader can infer that my intuition is that they are strongly related, though probably not by entailment. If that is right, then if we drop (2) the traditional conception of rules, and (1) the notion that law consists of [such] rules, we would also drop (3) the means/ends or process/substance distinction, (4) the public/private distinction, or what I like to call the "we-they" theory of government, and (5) the individualist/instrumentalist view of the person.

[36] If one is convinced that only those who embrace the particular substantive values of traditional liberalism would embrace the idea that law is a system of rules—as well as the other assumptions associated with the model of rules mentioned earlier—then the two conceptions ultimately coalesce. In such a view, the historical and ideological context that gives rise to the model of rules is what unites the two conceptions of the Rule of Law.

### A. *Senses of Traditional Formalism*

1. Formal connection between rule and particulars

Traditionally, legal "formalism" is the position that a unique answer in a particular case can be "deduced" from a rule, or that application of a rule to a particular is "analytical." (The scare quotes indicate that philosophical arguments about language have made the traditional understanding of these concepts just as problematic as "rule" itself. I shall return to this issue in the next section.) The connection between the rule and its application is, in other words, formal. Pejoratively, this is mechanical jurisprudence, or the computer model of judging. In this model, judges do not judge; they are only black boxes, who function to juxtapose the rule and the particular so the formal connection can be declared.[37]

2. Formal connection between foundations and rules

There is another way that the term "formalism" traditionally has been used. This "formalism" is the view that there exists a mind-independent reality consisting of certain first principles either of fact or value. These first principles form a logical, analytical, "foundation" for the law. A natural law theory would be formalist in this sense if it claimed that legal and moral rules are real and are there for us to discover, for example, or if it claimed that legal rules are deducible from a foundational set of real values. In this foundationalist kind of formalism, the crucial formal connection is between the structure of the universe and the rules of law. It is thus different from the mechanical jurisprudence kind of formalism, where the crucial formal link is between rules and the application of those rules to particulars.

3. Formal connection between words and things

In a famous metaphor, H.L.A. Hart suggested that legal rules have a

[37] A commitment to traditional formalism in the sense of mechanical jurisprudence is compatible either with legal positivism or natural law, as a general theory of law. It doesn't matter where the rules come from—from the sovereign, or from revelation or natural reason—it only matters that their application to particulars is a matter of deduction or formal analytical connection. It seems, however, that this kind of formalism is in practice especially allied with legal positivism. Positivists assert that law and ethics inhabit radically separate domains. The underlying motivation for maintaining such a thesis may be an ethical skepticism: the conviction that values are subjective or arbitrary. The traditional Rule of Law ideal carries an implied aspiration toward objectivity in law; it is the alternative we must pursue to avoid the evils of arbitrary power. For the skeptical positivist who desires to be able to affirm the Rule of Law by treating law as objective, then, law must be kept on the fact side of the fact/value dichotomy, which also keeps it on the objective side of the subjective/objective dichotomy. If the rules are formally derived from facts and the particulars are facts, as they are in positivist views, formalism is the obvious way to connect rules and facts without an admixture from a subjective domain.

"core" of certainty and a "penumbra" of uncertainty.[38] Hart declared that in the penumbra, judges must "legislate." A common understanding of the core/penumbra distinction—although probably not Hart's own understanding of it—is that in the core, formal deductive application of rules to particulars is possible.[39] If we do assume that formal application to particulars is possible within the core of a rule, then we can characterize a third sense of traditional formalism: formalism in semantics.[40] If there is a set of particulars, comprising the core meaning, to which a rule is applicable analytically or through deduction, it must be true that the *words* in the rule have an analytic connection with at least a subset of the particulars falling within these words' extensions. For example, if a rule contains the word "vehicle," then for the rule ever to be formally applicable there must be some subset of cases involving objects that are seen to be vehicles through deduction or some sort of analytic connection alone.[41]

The notion of an analytic connection between a word and its extension raises thorny problems in the theory of reference.[42] Yet some logical positivists may have thought word-meaning could be analytic in this way. Formalism in semantics may assume that the extension of a word can be logically determined by connection with a list of necessary and sufficient criteria, and thus that there is a formal connection between a word and the things to which it applies once the criteria are known. The necessary and sufficient criteria could be conventional artifacts of language. For a thorough reductionist, however, the criteria would be deducible from foundational sense-data, and formalism in se-

---

[38] Hart, *Positivism and the Separation of Law and Morals*, 71 HARV. L. REV. 593, 607 (1958).

[39] Hart said that "[i]f a penumbra of uncertainty must surround all legal rules, then their application to specific cases in the penumbral area cannot be a matter of logical deduction," *id.*, leaving it open to question whether logical deduction is what we do in core cases. Hart's general view of rules and language should more likely be interpreted, however, as incorporating the Wittgensteinian critique. *See, e.g.*, Hart, *Definition and Theory in Jurisprudence*, 70 LAW Q. REV. 37 (1954). *See infra* notes 76-77 and accompanying text.

[40] *See* Moore, *Semantics*, *supra* note 14, at 152, 157.

[41] The example of the word "vehicle" appearing in a statute was debated by Hart and Fuller in their *Harvard Law Review* exchange in 1958. *See* Hart, *supra* note 38, at 607; Fuller, *Positivism and Fidelity to Law*, 71 HARV. L. REV. 630, 662-63 (1958). It is drawn from the case of McBoyle v. United States, 283 U.S. 25, 26-27 (1931) (reversing defendant's conviction for theft of an airplane under the National Motor Vehicle Theft Act because the word "vehicle" as used in the statute could be read to include only those contrivances "capable of being used 'as a means of transportation on land' ").

[42] Of course, we can retain our common understanding that words have a core of certain meaning (some objects are unmistakably vehicles) without a formalist explanation of the source of this certainty. One way to do this is through Wittgenstein's essentially pragmatic view that words have meaning by virtue of being embedded in a form of life.

mantics would lead back to formalism in metaphysics.

4. Formal realizability and the formalist conception of rules

In the traditional conception of the nature of rules, a rule is self-applying to the set of particulars said to fall under it; its application is thought to be analytic. It is often said that rules are logically prior to the particular cases that fall under them. Another way of putting this is to think that somehow the applications to particulars are already present in the rule itself. For example, if a rule says that no one under 21 is allowed in a saloon, then the application of the rule to Sally, who is in Joe's Saloon on her sixteenth birthday, is analytic or formal. The result that Sally must be excluded follows immediately from the rule itself and Sally's specific circumstances, and is unaffected by any other previous applications of the rule or other circumstances.

Under the traditional conception of rules, the property of analytic self-application, thought to inhere in rules, is sometimes called "formal realizability."[43] When a directive or command is formally realizable, its application is deductive or analytic. In other words, it deserves to be called a "rule." To the extent that legal directives are formally realizable they are to be implemented by mechanical jurisprudence. In my view, rules would be formally realizable to the extent that the words in them are formally realizable. Thus, traditional formalism in the conception of rules leads back to traditional formalism in semantics. Formal realizability is an asserted characteristic primarily of words, and only secondarily of rules.

B. *Traditional Formalism and the Rule of Law*

The traditional understanding of formal realizability correlates with the demand for clarity in both the instrumentalist and substantive versions of the Rule of Law. The traditional view has been that in order for people to know what the law is so that they can conform their behavior to it, it is necessary for the law to consist, to the fullest extent possible, of formally realizable rules. Directives that are not formally realizable are sometimes called "standards."[44]

---

[43] The notion of formal realizability is rooted in German jurisprudential thought. Duncan Kennedy finds the term in Rudolph von Ihering's *Spirit of Roman Law*. Kennedy, *Form and Substance in Private Law Adjudication*, 89 HARV. L. REV. 1685, 1687-89 (1976), *citing* R. VON IHERING, DER GEIST DES ROMISCHEN RECHT 50-55, 84 (1883). Though Kant did not use the term "formal realizability," he apparently thought that law could not exist without it. *See, e.g.*, I. KANT, *Perpetual Peace*, in KANT ON HISTORY 85, 91-92 n.4 (L. Beck ed. 1963) ("[T]he possibility of a formula similar to those of mathematics is the only legitimate criterion of a consistent legislation.").

[44] This use of the term "standard" was apparently introduced by Duncan Kennedy, Kennedy, *supra* note 43, at 1688, and has been adopted by a number of critical writers. *See, e.g.*, Schlag, *Rules and Standards*, 33 UCLA L. REV. 379, 382 n.16 (1985). Unfortunately it causes confusion because other writers do not use the term "standard" in

If in the previous example of the rule about presence in saloons we substituted the words "no one who has not reached maturity and responsibility" for "no one under 21," it would be deemed a "standard" and not a "rule." The prevalence of "standards" in the law poses problems for the notion that clarity of commands depends upon formal realizability.

The traditional understanding of formal realizability as the crucial property of rules also correlates with the traditional conviction that the Rule of Law demands that judges "apply" rather than "make" the law. If rules do not tie judges' hands with their logical or analytic application, the traditional view is that judges will have personal discretion in how to apply the law. This will undermine congruence and confuse those who are supposed to follow the rules. It will diminish the efficacy of the system (in the instrumental view) and the liberty of the rule-followers (in the substantive view). It will also confer on judges a realm of "arbitrary power" and undermine democracy.

The Rule of Law as it comes down to us in the liberal tradition is committed to the model of rules, and this means, under the traditional conception of rules, that it is committed to traditional formalism. One reason for this, as Rawls saw, is that this model of law readily connects with aspects of the Hobbesian view of the nature and purposes of social cooperation. Because everyone is always motivated to "defect," government by majority rule reduces to accommodation among shifting coalitions of self-interested individuals. The government is a Leviathan to be restrained. Yet, if judges can ignore the legislative "bargains" of these shifting coalitions, then judges are even more in need of restraint than are legislatures. Hence, the role of the judges is tightly constrained. Judges should be mere tools of implementation of the underlying "contract" that guarantees social cooperation and prevents "defection" and degeneration into the state of nature.

The underlying "contract," that justifies the existence of government at all, can be thought of as a "constitution." Most of the time judges should function as tools to implement what the legislature enacts, but when legislatures overstep the bounds of justified government, judges must function as tools of the underlying constitutional "contract" and intervene to strike down the offending legislation. In view of the very great danger posed by judges, the Hobbesian theorist needs an ironclad system of rules to restrain them. Rules, in the traditional formalist sense, must determine the decisions of judges to the fullest extent possible, on pain, otherwise, of losing the underlying justification for the whole legal system.

Although Rawls is not a thoroughgoing Hobbesian theorist by any means, his conception of a legal system coheres with this motivation for commitment to the model of rules.[45] It appears that any form of traditional liberalism, with

---

this way. *See, e.g.*, R. Dworkin, Rights, *supra* note 21, at 22 (using "standard" as a general term referring to rules, principles, policies, and others). *See infra* note 83 and accompanying text.

[45] Recall Rawls's quintessential definition: "A legal system is a coercive order of public rules addressed to rational persons for the purpose of regulating their conduct

its commitment to means/ends rationality and to methodological individualism, will be drawn to the traditional conception of rules as the means to structure incentives so as to achieve maximally the individual behavior desired by the state.[46]

## IV. The Wittgensteinian Conception of Rules and Its Consequences (If Any)

### A. *The Wittgensteinian Social Conception of Rules*

A Wittgensteinian view of words, and of the rules containing them, suggests that there is no such thing as traditional formal realizability, or in other words, that the traditional formalist conception of rules is wrong. The Wittgensteinian view of rules may be characterized as both a social and a practice conception. It is a social conception because in this view rules depend essentially on social context, and it is a practice conception because rules also depend essentially on reiterated human activity.

If we assume that the traditional formalist conception of rules is what we mean by the word "rule," the Wittgensteinian perspective may also be characterized as a species of rule-skepticism. A number of assertions may be encompassed in skepticism about rules in the traditional formalist conception of them. These assertions are skeptical answers to a set of problems about rules and rule-governed action. One problem is in determining when it can be said that someone is "applying" a rule. How do we *know* the rule is being "applied"? The skeptic says, "We can't really tell." We cannot identify any formal or logical criterion by which we can determine whether or not someone is following a rule. The problem is important for a distinction that is crucial to the Rule of Law—the distinction between the existence of the rules and their application by rule-appliers, such as judges.

A second problem is how we should understand the notion that rules are "binding." In what consists the "binding-ness" of rules? The skeptic says, "This bond cannot be shown." We cannot demonstrate any formal or logical nexus between the rule and the rule-follower's behavior in response to it. The problem is important for the coherence of the conception of a legal system as a

---

and providing the framework for social cooperation." J. Rawls, *supra* note 12, at 235.

[46] I am not attempting to treat fully in this essay the broader connections between the Rule of Law and theories of politics and the person. It seems apparent, however, that the traditional conception of rules that apply self-evidently of their own logical force to one person in one particular set of circumstances can be connected to methodological individualism. Additionally, it appears that the reduction of self-government to the following of rules laid down by legislative representatives follows from the traditional liberal tendency to think of government and citizens as radically separate; and it appears that the model of the rational person as chooser of action based upon external incentives for bettering her own welfare can—as many devotees of law and economics have argued—be connected to a need for structuring her activities by clear rules laid down by an authoritative entity.

"system of coercive rules" binding on citizens.

A third problem is how we should understand "ruleness" itself. I have suggested that traditional formal realizability is a conception of rules that asserts that rules are analytically applicable to particulars insofar as they contain words with precise, determinate extensions. The skeptic says, "Traditional formal realizability cannot be shown to exist." We cannot demonstrate that application of a rule is analytic or deductive. This problem is important for the idea that a rule is logically prior to particulars falling under it and can be seen to apply of its own force to any individual cases falling under it.

I think Wittgenstein in *Philosophical Investigations*[47] is fairly read as rejecting the traditional conception of rules in favor of a social practice conception in which agreement in responsive action is the primary mark of the existence of a rule.[48] I also think Wittgenstein is fairly read as a rule-skeptic in the three senses I just suggested.[49] There is no way to tell deductively or analytically when a rule is being followed; there is no special state that describes the binding-ness of rules; and traditional formal realizability is not the right way to conceive of the nature of rules.

The relevant passages in *Philosophical Investigations* are three sequences of remarks: on continuing an arithmetic series according to a certain formation rule; on reading; and on obeying a rule.[50] The questions Wittgenstein addresses are both internal and external. That is, with respect to continuing a series, he is interested both in what happens when someone can say, "Now I can go on" and what happens when others can say, "Now she's got it." Likewise with

---

[47] L. WITTGENSTEIN, PHILOSOPHICAL INVESTIGATIONS (G.E.M. Anscombe trans. rev. ed. 1968) [hereinafter L. WITTGENSTEIN, PHILOSOPHICAL INVESTIGATIONS]. *See also* L. WITTGENSTEIN, REMARKS ON THE FOUNDATIONS OF MATHEMATICS 391-437 (G.E.M. Anscombe trans. rev. ed. 1978) (another version of Wittgenstein's investigation on rules).

[48] The proper reading of Wittgenstein's later work is hotly disputed in the secondary literature. Among those whose readings seem most congenial to me are Peacocke, *Reply: Rule-Following: The Nature of Wittgenstein's Arguments*, in WITTGENSTEIN: TO FOLLOW A RULE 72 (C. Leich & S. Holtzman eds. 1981); P. STRAWSON, SKEPTICISM AND NATURALISM: SOME VARIETIES 75-95 (1983); S. KRIPKE, WITTGENSTEIN ON RULES AND PRIVATE LANGUAGE (1982). For opposing readings, see G. BAKER & P. HACKER, SKEPTICISM, RULES & LANGUAGE (1984); C. MCGINN, WITTGENSTEIN ON MEANING (1984).

[49] In characterizing Wittgenstein as a rule-skeptic, we must remember that he does not say there can be no such thing as a rule, only that the traditional formalist conception is the wrong way to think about how rules work. Wittgenstein's skepticism about rules has been compared with Hume's skepticism about induction. *See* P. STRAWSON, *supra* note 48, at 14-21; S. KRIPKE, *supra* note 48, at 62-68. In a reading that seems to me reasonable and interesting, Kripke understands Wittgenstein's *Philosophical Investigations* as propounding a skeptical paradox about rules. *See also* Yablon, *Law and Metaphysics* (Book Review), 96 YALE L.J. 613 (1987) (reviewing Kripke for a legal audience).

[50] L. WITTGENSTEIN, PHILOSOPHICAL INVESTIGATIONS, *supra* note 47, §§ 143-242.

reading: What licenses "Now I am reading" or "Now she's reading"? The discussion of rules in the third sequence is a generalization of these two examples. The internal questions are: What is the inner experience of obeying a rule? In what consists the determined-ness or binding-ness on me? The external questions are: How can other people tell when someone is obeying a rule? In what consists the knowledge or recognition of rule-application?

To all of these questions Wittgenstein gives skeptical answers. In the introspective portions of his analysis, Wittgenstein considers suggestions that the binding-ness might be a mental state or process or disposition,[51] a special experience or feeling or inner sensation,[52] a kind of derivation or being guided,[53] a causal or "super-strong" connection,[54] or a way of grasping in a flash or in a direct sense.[55] Wittgenstein rejects these attempts to capture the essence of the rule-follower's subjective experience of binding-ness. His conclusion is that the rule-follower acts without reasons,[56] without choice,[57] blindly, as a matter of course.[58] Following the rule is "simply what I do."[59]

In external portions of his analysis, Wittgenstein replies to his introspective suggestions, from the point of view of how we observe someone else following a rule. His conclusions are similarly skeptical. All we can say when we think someone is following a rule is that it seems natural.[60] For someone to apply a rule correctly is simply to do it "as we do it."[61] The decisive factor in knowing whether someone has followed a rule "is not his [the rule-follower's] inner experience but the *circumstances* under which he had it."[62]

The result of this skeptical deconstruction of the formalist notion of rules is that rule-following must be understood to be an essentially social phenomenon. Rule-following can only be understood to occur where there is reiterated human action both in responding to directives and in observing others respond. Only the fact of our seemingly "natural" agreement on what are instances of obeying rules permits us to say there are rules. The rules do not cause the

---

51 *Id.* §§ 146, 152-154.

52 *Id.* §§ 155, 157, 159-160.

53 *Id.* §§ 162-163, 172-173, 175.

54 *Id.* §§ 169, 176-177, 197.

55 *Id.* §§ 191-192.

56 *Id.* § 211. That there is no identifiable reason for one's experience of "binding-ness," no essence of "binding-ness," should of course not be misunderstood to mean that one cannot have reasons for following a rule.

57 *Id.* § 219. Similarly, that there seems to be no choice about whether or not one has the experience of "binding-ness" should of course not be misunderstood to mean that one cannot choose whether to follow a rule or to disobey it.

58 *Id.* § 238.

59 *Id.* § 217.

60 *Id.* § 185. *Cf.* S. Kripke, *supra* note 49, at 92-96; P. Strawson, *supra* note 48, at 75-80.

61 L. Wittgenstein, Philosophical Investigations, *supra* note 47, § 145.

62 *Id.* § 155 (emphasis in original). *Cf. id.* § 180 (calling words a "signal" of mental state, not a description of it).

agreement; rather, the agreement causes us to say there are rules.[63] As Wittgenstein says, "The word 'agreement' and the word 'rule' are *related* to one another, they are cousins."[64] As Wittgenstein also says, this is "not agreement in opinions but in form of life."[65] Rules are not logically prior to uniformity of action in response to them; rather, uniformity of action is prior to the existence of rules.

This view of rules is irreducibly social and rejects the traditional formal, logical, analytic, or deductive understandings of rule-application.[66] The form of life called rule-following is a practice, and the practice is a form of agreement among members of a social group. It is not possible to obey a rule "privately,"[67] nor is rule-following something that can be done by "only *one* man, only *once*."[68]

In the Wittgensteinian view, an action is *determined* by a rule when the action seems a "matter of course,"[69] and "disputes don't break out."[70] How do I know when I am following a rule? When I feel the answer is automatic or self-evident. But my subjective feeling of "binding-ness" could be mistaken.[71] How do I know when I'm *really* "applying" a rule? When everybody else also would have felt compelled to do as I did. How do we know someone else is following a rule? When we all would have felt bound to do as she did.

Although the Wittgensteinian view thus certainly admits that there can be action determined by a rule, it is not the kind of determined-ness required by the traditional concept of formal realizability. Formal realizability (the traditional formalist conception of the nature of rules) asserts that only the words of the rule and the action of one person with regard to one set of particulars are relevant in questions of rule-following. This Wittgenstein denies. If formal realizability would allow for the possibility of obeying a rule privately or only once, then formal realizability is merely what Wittgenstein would call a "phil-

---

[63] S. KRIPKE, *supra* note 49, at 96.

[64] L. WITTGENSTEIN, PHILOSOPHICAL INVESTIGATIONS, *supra* note 47, § 224 (emphasis in original).

[65] *Id.* § 241. *Cf.* S. KRIPKE, *supra* note 49, at 96-98.

[66] I believe the appropriate Wittgensteinian conclusion is that, along with the concept of rules, the concepts of formality, logic, analyticity, and deduction cannot mean what we have thought them to mean; even these categories are irreducibly social. *See infra* note 77 and accompanying text.

[67] L. WITTGENSTEIN, PHILOSOPHICAL INVESTIGATIONS, *supra* note 47, § 202. Wittgenstein also notes that "to think one is obeying the rule is not to obey the rule." *Id.*

[68] *Id.* § 199 (emphasis in original).

[69] *Id.* § 238.

[70] *Id.* § 240: "Disputes do not break out (among mathematicians, say) over the question whether a rule has been obeyed or not. People don't come to blows over it, for example. That is part of the framework on which the working of our language is based (for example, in giving descriptions)." *Id.*

[71] *See supra* note 67 and accompanying text (rule-following does not depend solely on one's private experience of it).

osophical superlative."[72]

There are still rules, of course; rules are an important practice of ours. But traditional formal realizability is not the right way to understand "rule-ness."

### B. *Consequences (if any) for the Model of Rules and the Rule of Law*

#### 1. Does Our Conception of Rules Matter?

One might say, "So what?" Under the Wittgensteinian view there are still obvious cases of rules and rule-following; whether we hold the traditional view of rules or the Wittgensteinian view makes no difference for our conceptions of the model of rules and the Rule of Law.[73] The "So what?" response is particularly appealing to those who read Wittgenstein more narrowly than I do. I take a view that aligns him with modern pragmatism. His insistence that meaning cannot be separated from "use"—from reiterated human activity, *practices*, embedded in and helping to constitute a "form of life"—seems, when given the central weight I believe it deserves, to make clear his intellectual affinity with pragmatism.[74] Yet those who read Wittgenstein more narrowly understand him merely to have been making an analytic point about language, and rules couched in language, to the effect that no rule can determine the scope of its own application. They deny that Wittgenstein means that there is something essentially social or "communitarian" about rules.[75]

If we thus interpret Wittgenstein narrowly we might think that everything remains the same. Law still consists (entirely or in important part) of a set of rules authoritatively laid down and implemented by judges who apply, but do not make, the rules. The only difference would be conceptual: we just change the way philosophers, inside their own heads, understand rules. In other words, if we think that all we change is our internal philosophical view of *rules* when we become Wittgensteinian, then the "So what?" response seems initially plausible.

The "So what?" response also seems initially plausible under a broader view of the role of practices. If one is inclined to treat practices as so "brute" and

---

[72] L. WITTGENSTEIN, PHILOSOPHICAL INVESTIGATIONS, *supra* note 47, § 192.

[73] For a sophisticated view of rules that has fully incorporated the Wittgensteinian perspective, and yet sees no important practical effects for our conceptions of law and the Rule of Law, see F. SCHAUER, PLAYING BY THE RULES: A PHILOSOPHICAL ANALYSIS OF RULE-BASED DECISION-MAKING (unpublished manuscript 1989).

[74] This view of Wittgenstein is explicit in the work of Richard Rorty, *see* R. RORTY, PHILOSOPHY AND THE MIRROR OF NATURE 367-68 (1979) [hereinafter R. RORTY, MIRROR OF NATURE], and is implicit in the views of many other modern critics of foundationalism and the traditional dichotomies of fact and value, theory and practice, and the like. What may be distinctive in the modern wave of pragmatism is the degree of emphasis placed on the social construction of reality. For a lucid description of the basic tenets of pragmatism, as well as some elaboration of a modern pragmatic view of law, see Grey, *Holmes and Legal Pragmatism*, 41 STAN. L. REV. 787 (1989).

[75] See G. BAKER & P. HACKER, *supra* note 48, at viii (arguing against Kripke); C. MCGINN, *supra* note 48, at 9 (same).

"given" that they cannot be interpenetrated by what we say or think about them, then the practice we call philosophy (or theory, or conceptual schemes) is radically separate from every other practice. When we reconceive meaning in terms of practice, all our practices (except philosophy) remain unchanged. So again, as with the narrow analytic view, any Wittgensteinian change is internal to philosophy.[76]

Wittgenstein's statement that we know there are rules when "disputes don't break out" provides a way to reinterpret the idea that rules have a "core" of certain application, as well as a "penumbra" of doubt, without resort to traditional formal realizability. In this reinterpretation, the core signifies our observance of rule-responsive behavior that feels compelled or blind or "a matter of course"; the penumbra signifies our observance of disputes breaking out or the absence of the feeling of compulsion. The core is roughly coextensive with our ability to say, "We all think that's self-evident." We can all recognize action under a rule when we eject sixteen-year-old Sally from Joe's saloon in response to the directive, "No one under 21 is allowed in a saloon." Under the Wittgensteinian view someone who doesn't see this result as self-evident will be considered insane or from Mars; and this is just as strong a form of social control as being thought irrational or deficient in deductive powers.

Even if we accept a slightly broader view of Wittgenstein, the philosophical change might still seem not to imply any significant differences in practice. A Wittgensteinian reinterpretation is just as possible, and just as necessary, for all the concepts allied with the traditional conception of "rule" as it is for the conception of "rule" itself. If the traditional conception of a "rule" amounted to a mistaken "philosophical superlative," then so too have our conceptions of "formal connection," "analyticity," "deduction," and so on. But it is possible to think of "formalism" not in the traditional sense of a logical connection

---

[76] The most vociferous exponent of this view, at least in law reviews, is Stanley Fish. *See, e.g.*, Fish, *Dennis Martinez and the Uses of Theory*, 96 YALE L.J. 1773, 1775 (1987) (discussing the dichotomy between theory and practice and arguing that the two cannot interact). Fish is clearly wrong that judging is a "brute" practice of this kind; judging as a practice also includes ideals about judging, critiques of judging, understandings about the role of judging in the polity, etc. *See infra* notes 89-90 and accompanying text (interaction between rhetoric and the world). I even think that Fish is wrong about the practice of baseball. Part of the reason Orel Hersheiser is a better pitcher than Dennis Martinez is his attention to "theory"; his detailed notes about hitters' propensities and past performances enable him to make better decisions about how to pitch to them, and these decisions are a part of the practice of baseball.

The primary complaint against these Fish-like views is that if practices are so "brute," so always-already given, we cannot make space for critique and social progress. On this reading, Wittgenstein seems like an apologist for the status quo. *See, e.g.*, R. UNGER, PASSION: AN ESSAY ON PERSONALITY 11-12 (1984). *But cf.* H. PITKIN, WITTGENSTEIN AND JUSTICE 46 (1972). Maybe, in the end, whether we read Wittgenstein in the broad, holistic way I prefer, in which the theory/practice dichotomy is dissolved and the practices of conceptualization and critique can interpenetrate many (all?) others, is perhaps a matter of personal temperament.

existing independent of a social setting and history of application, but instead as decisionmaking by uncontroversial reasoning.[77] It is possible to think of "analyticity," "deduction," and "logical connection," all as similarly embedded in an ongoing practice in which completely uncontroversial results are reached by what we "naturally" think of as rational procedures under the circumstances.

Does a Wittgensteinian reinterpretation of all of these concepts prevalent in the traditional Rule of Law change anything? At least, doesn't it leave untouched everything practical, everything that we can observe or that has significance for us and our lives? When the phlogiston theory was rejected, it did not change the fact that fire will burn us. Even if we admit that the formally realizable rules required by the Rule of Law rest on a social practice, a brute unquestionable agreement in a form of life, don't all our reasons for requiring formally realizable rules (clarity, notice, congruence, stability, prospectivity, restraint of judges) remain the same?[78]

Perhaps Wittgenstein himself would say, if we could ask him, that this is the correct way to understand his reinterpretations. After all, he was not one to think that the form of life called philosophy had much influence on our larger forms of life. Nevertheless, if this would be his position, I think it too modest.[79] We should not hastily conclude that commitment to the Wittgensteinian understanding of rules, at least to the broader, neo-pragmatist view of Wittgenstein I prefer, would be irrelevant for our views about law and the Rule of Law. But neither should we hastily conclude that because there is no such thing as traditional formal realizability, everything is indeterminate or up for grabs. We shall have to proceed in a more cautious and more piecemeal manner. As Wittgenstein might say, we must "look and see."

We can begin by noticing that the Wittgensteinian limitation of rules to situations in which "disputes don't break out" does not help lawyers much. Disputes *do* break out among lawyers and judges, and litigants *do* come to blows, at least metaphorically. If our only way to find out what result is compelled by a rule is to be part of a community that recognizes action as rule-following, then there is no way to bring any truly disputed cases—in which neither side changes its position even after being confronted by what the other side believes to be completely uncontroversial reasoning—under pre-existing rules, as the Rule of Law requires.

Perhaps a Wittgensteinian would not want to think of law as consisting *only* of rules. Of course, truly disputed cases can indeed come under reasonable judgment, or whatever faculty our practice recognizes as making appropriate judgments in disputed cases. But if by "our practice," we mean "our *legal*

---

[77] *See* Grey, *Langdell's Orthodoxy*, 45 U. PITT. L. REV. 1, 8 (1983) (characterizing formalism in this way).

[78] For a thoughtful argument to this effect, see F. SCHAUER, *supra* note 73, §§ 8.5, 8.6.

[79] In other words, if Wittgenstein professed this Fish-like view, *see supra* note 76, he would be untrue to himself.

practice," then our practice is at odds with the Rule of Law ideal that is supposed to describe and govern it.

A stubborn commitment to the model of rules as essential to the Rule of Law explains why legal theorists go to such lengths to try to show that even "hard cases" have pre-existing determinate answers.[80] Hart's declaration that judges "legislate" in hard cases is unorthodox in the liberal tradition because it tends to undermine the commitment to the model of rules. It is not surprising that Hart urges us to think such hard cases are few and far between. To the extent that law, when we "look and see," is the terrain of "disputed" cases, the pragmatic Wittgensteinian view seems to tell us we had better find another model (other than rules) for what law "is."

2. Compromise Positions on the Model of Rules

Perhaps, then, a Wittgensteinian reinterpretation requires us to divide law into domains, consisting of rules and other things, and to reconceive the Rule of Law in light of this complexity. A number of prevalent views (although they may have rested originally on the traditional conception of rules) present themselves as candidates for appropriate reinterpretation. The challenge, of course, is to characterize those "other things"—the domain of law that does not consist of rules—as "lawlike" in a sense that is politically acceptable to us.

The Wittgensteinian interpretation of the core/penumbra distinction can divide legal directives into domains of formal realizability vel non, but, as Dworkin complains, waving one's hand at the penumbra and simply announcing that we should recognize that judges "legislate" is not politically acceptable.[81] One who believes that rules (and words) have cores and penumbras would argue that we need all attributes of the Rule of Law to make sure that in at least the core cases, the formalist result is properly implemented. This strategy supposes that part of the legal realm instantiates formalism and the precepts of the Rule of Law, while the balance is given over to the "discretion"—the "Absolute Arbitrary Power"—that the traditional Rule of Law, in both its instrumental and substantive conceptions, decries. In the "discretionary" areas we cannot be manipulating behavior by means of known pre-existing rules (the instrumentalist view) nor can we be fixing the structure that enhances negative liberty (the substantive view). Unless we declare by fiat that the penumbra is insignificant compared to the core,[82] this strategy gives up a good deal to the abyss of absolute arbitrary power, the elimination of which is supposed to be the *raison d'être* of the social contract.

Ronald Dworkin's bifurcated model of law is aimed at answering this kind of criticism of Hart. When Dworkin attacked the model of rules he attributed to legal positivism, he did so by dividing up the general category of "standards" into "rules," on the one hand, and "principles, policies and other sorts

[80] *See, e.g.*, R. DWORKIN, RIGHTS, *supra* note 21, at 81-130.
[81] *Id.* at 44-45.
[82] This appears to be Hart's approach. *See* Hart, *supra* note 38, at 614-15.

of standards" that "do not function as rules," on the other.[83] His argument was that the model of rules does not fully describe what the law is, because law also consists of principles; and that rule-application does not fully describe what judges do, because judges also use principles.[84] Moreover, the use of principles determines one right answer to legal questions even though principles lack formal realizability, because in using principles the judge should apply the best interpretation of the entire body of past legal authoritative acts, where that interpretation rests on the best political theory available to explain and justify law as an enterprise.

Can Wittgensteinian reinterpretation stop with this reinterpreted version of Dworkin? There are a number of important objections, only two of which I raise here.[85] First, in actual practice, in the form of life we call the law, it makes no sense to say that right answers are available in principle when in reality there is no agreement on the answers; the disputes stubbornly remain

---

[83] *See* R. DWORKIN, RIGHTS, *supra* note 21, at 22.

[84] Dworkin asserted that there is a "logical difference" between rules and principles. Rules are applicable either/or, all-or-nothing, whereas principles have "weight." *Id.* at 26-27. Further, rules set out necessary conditions for their application but principles do not; in theory, a rule can be completely stated with all exceptions, but a principle cannot. *Id.* at 25-26. Although the notion of a "logical difference" can be given a Wittgensteinian reinterpretation, references to "logical difference" in conjunction with the idea of a complete statement of a rule with all its exceptions strongly suggest that Dworkin held the traditional conception of rules. In Dworkin's more recent work, LAW'S EMPIRE, *supra* note 21, he has turned toward interpretive theory, which renders shaky the idea that any rules could be self-evidently applied in the way assumed by the traditional conception of rules. As far as I know, however, Dworkin has not explicitly reinterpreted his rules/principles distinction.

[85] There is by now a large secondary literature on Dworkin and it is not my aim to add to it. In that literature, the lines of critique of Dworkin that I think are most significant are those relating to (1) the role of community and dialogue in legal meaning and decision making, *see, e.g.*, Michelman, *Foreword: Traces of Self-Government*, 100 HARV. L. REV. 4, 66-73 (1986); (2) the role of political practice in law, *see, e.g.*, Bruns, *Law as Hermeneutics*, in THE POLITICS OF INTERPRETATION 315 (W. Mitchell ed. 1983); and (3) the problem posed for coherence theory by indeterminacy and widespread conflict in the law. *See, e.g.*, Altman, *Legal Realism, Critical Legal Studies, and Dworkin*, 15 PHIL. & PUB. AFF. 205, 217 (1986). I am sympathetic also to Stanley Fish's critique, suggesting that Dworkin's dimensions of "fit" and "soundness" take apart fact and value in a way Dworkin acknowledges should be rejected along with the old paradigm supporting positivism. *See* Fish, *Working on the Chain Gang: Interpretation in the Law and in Literary Criticism*, in THE POLITICS OF INTERPRETATION 271, 284-85 n.5 (W. Mitchell ed. 1983).

In addition I believe there is an important critique that is underrepresented in the Dworkin literature. Contrary to the Critical Legal Studies critique that law is indeterminate and incoherent, it seems to me that law and its institutions may indeed exhibit integrity or coherence—for example, as they did with respect to racism and sexism—and yet be coherently wrong. A main task for nonfoundationalist theory is to find room for this kind of judgment.

when all the arguments are done. If those who are subject to judicial decisions cannot confidently predict the outcome, then Dworkin has not succeeded in preserving the Rule of Law virtues for the area in which "disputes break out"; he is susceptible to the same criticism he leveled against Hart. Second, when we really do "look and see" what law is like as a practice or a form of life, it is much more complicated than simply applying authoritative directives that are either rules or not-rules.

At this point we might turn to the distinction between "rules" and "standards" described by Duncan Kennedy and adopted by a number of critical writers.[86] Kennedy's claims are more complex than Dworkin's because Kennedy "continuum-izes" the dichotomy.[87] A directive can tend toward "rule-ness" (formal realizability) or be relatively standard-like. Thus the semantic underpinning of the formal realizability dimension must be complex: we must assume that words vary along a continuum from extremely vague (or otherwise indeterminate) to completely determinate.[88] This vision may be adequately Wittgensteinian in its understanding of language (or may be reinterpreted to be), but it still seems to leave out something important in its conception of law as consisting of verbal directives of one kind or another. In order to be true Wittgensteinians, at least on the neo-pragmatic understanding of him, we must find a way to say things about law as an activity or form of life containing practices other than the giving and following of verbal directives.

---

[86] *See supra* note 44 and accompanying text; Kennedy, *supra* note 43, at 1687-1701; *see also* Schlag, *supra* note 44, at 429-30 (accepting the rules/standards distinction and arguing that the distinction has been institutionalized in legal argument so as to form a dialectic incapable of resolution).

[87] *See* Kennedy, *The Stages of the Decline of the Public/Private Distinction*, 130 U. Pa. L. Rev. 1349, 1352-53 (1982).

[88] Kennedy further claims that individualism is associated with rules and altruism with standards. This claim is obscure for various reasons we need not elaborate here. Although Kennedy asserts that we all know intuitively that individualism and altruism are associated with rules and standards respectively, polls among my first-year students show that this is not a widespread intuition. Standards may be associated with individualism because they allow decision-makers to treat persons as unique individuals; rules force decision-makers into a "collectivist" straight-jacket. From the communitarian point of view, one vice of standards is that an individualist judge might prefer the power of discretion a standard gives; a communitarian judge might count it a virtue of rules that they make her a rule-bound functionary. *See* Schlag, *supra* note 44, at 399-426.

If we press beyond Kennedy's critique of formalism in this article, so that even the conception of a "rule" cannot include the notion of traditional formal realizability, then we may be remanded to a social practice conception of rules that blurs the distinction that Kennedy made here. All rules are in a sense other-directed. In later work, Kennedy adopts a more Wittgensteinian view of rules and takes a more pragmatic view of law. *See, e.g.*, Kennedy, *Toward a Critical Phenomenology of Judging*, in The Rule of Law: Ideal or Ideology? 141 (A. Hutchinson & P. Monahan eds. 1987). *See infra* notes 97-99 and accompanying text.

3. On the connection between philosophy and normative social activity: the repercussions of reconceiving rules

Although I speculated earlier that perhaps Wittgenstein himself wouldn't have thought that philosophical changes in our conception of rules would make much difference to us in real life, I think that view is too simplistic. At least on the pragmatic view of Wittgenstein that I find congenial, theory and practice cannot remain so separate; our conceptual schemes and human activity cannot be held apart.[89] Deep inner shifts in theoretical practices (like the "conversation" of philosophy[90]) must have repercussions in other kinds of practices (like legal decisionmaking). In this section I suggest how far-reaching the inner shifts must be if we accept the Wittgensteinian view of rules. Later I speculate on how those shifts might be allied to a more pragmatic reinterpretation of the Rule of Law.

The philosophical consequences we must accept if we accept the pragmatic Wittgensteinian view of rules are, I think, these: the tendency of "applying" rules to coalesce with "making" rules; the tendency of the "rule" to coalesce with the "particulars falling under it"; the idea that rules are contingent upon whole forms of life and not just specific acts of a legislature; and the essential mutability of rules.

From a Wittgensteinian perspective, making rules and applying rules cannot be radically separate activities. A rule would cease to exist if we (the relevant community) stopped apprehending it as a rule and stopped recognizing ourselves and others as acting under it. This view of legal rules would contrast with one aspect of the positivist view formulated by H.L.A. Hart. Hart drew a sharp distinction between primary rules of obligation, which can be valid whether or not people obey them, and the rule of recognition, whose existence depends upon the observed actions and public commitments of the legal community.[91] For a Wittgensteinian it seems the distinction cannot be quite so sharp. The rule of recognition itself certainly depends upon community agreement in practice, but so too (even if in a less direct sense) must the notion of validity. If a primary rule were never followed, at some point it would become questionable whether we were justified in thinking it to be a rule.

If we fail to follow a rule we undermine its existence as a rule. Thus when we do follow a rule we reaffirm its existence. Every time we apply a rule we also make it. Moreover, because a rule depends upon the existence of a social practice, it seems that an essential part of rule-application in a legal context is predicting the behavior of the community of judges and other legal actors,

---

[89] *See* H. Putnam, Reason, Truth and History 66-69 (1981); Radin, *Market-Inalienability*, 100 Harv. L. Rev. 1849, 1884-87 (1987) (exploring the consequences of using only market rhetoric to talk about human affairs).

[90] R. Rorty, *Pragmatism, Relativism, and Irrationalism*, in Consequences of Pragmatism 160 (1982) [hereinafter R. Rorty, *Pragmatism*]; R. Rorty, Mirror of Nature, *supra* note 74, at 389-94.

[91] *See* H.L.A. Hart, The Concept of Law 97-107 (1961).

including (it seems) one's own behavior if one is a legal actor. (At least this is true for the kind of rules Hart collectively called rules of recognition.) This is a very different picture of rule-application than the one embedded in the traditional formalist conception of rules, where the point of a rule is to close off contingencies related to one's own or others' behavior.

If we accept the Wittgensteinian view of rules, there can also be no radical distinction between a rule and the particulars falling under it. This seems to deny the generality (in Fuller's sense) of rules. In a Wittgensteinian view, rules depend upon the practice of decisions that the relevant community accepts as rule-like. Rules do not wholly pre-exist the particular applications of them in practice, because people must actually follow rules before we can say rules exist.

More broadly, a switch to the Wittgensteinian view of rules must profoundly affect our views about law and the Rule of Law because the Wittgensteinian view makes the existence of legal rules contingent not just upon the acts of legislatures or other authoritative entities, but also upon the surrounding social context, the content of an entire form of life. Of course, rules can come into being partly because we have specific practices (legislation, judging, agency promulgation) that formulate them. In order to find out what rules exist by virtue of these practices, we must "look and see" what the practice is.[92] But that which makes any directive rule-like relates not only to its promulgation according to an essentially social existing practice, but also to the content of surrounding social activities and understandings.[93] Rules are created and continue to exist not only because a legislature says so, but also by virtue of their being embedded in our *nomos*.[94] A judge's decision in response

[92] According to Hart, for example, we would look and see if our rule of recognition validated the particular rules in which we were interested. Hart's rule of recognition, which has its being only in the acceptance of legal actors as manifested in their actions and in their continuing public commitments, is essentially pragmatic. (In fact, Hart wondered whether it even should be thought of as a "rule." *See* H.L.A. Hart, *supra* note 91, at 107-14.)

[93] Ultimately whether or not a rule exists for us depends upon a social commitment that is not rule-based. *Cf.* F. Schauer, *supra* note 73, § 6.2 stating:

> But regardless of *why* a person might treat the existence of a rule as a reason for action . . . the process of taking a rule to be applicable is a function of something external to that rule. It may be another rule, but that process ultimately runs out, and at that point we face the realization that something *other* than a rule, any rule, will determine the applicability of a rule, thus, to say that a rule exists for any agent is to say that that agent treats the rule, for non-rule-based reasons, as supplying a reason for action. And to say that a rule exists within some decisional environment is similarly to say that the decision-makers in that environment, again for ultimately non-rule-based reasons, treat the rule as relevant to the decisions they are called upon to make.

(emphasis in original).

[94] This use of the term "*nomos*" stems from the work of Robert Cover. *See* Cover, *Foreword*: Nomos *and Narrative*, 97 Harv. L. Rev. 4 (1983).

to a rule responds necessarily to the community as a whole and not just to what the legislature has said.[95]

Finally, if we accept the Wittgensteinian view we must recognize that rules are not immutable. Whether an activity is seen as rule-like is contingent upon material social context and agreement. Over time the "same" action in response to the "same" directive can go from being compelled by a rule to not being compelled by a rule, or vice versa.[96] The traditional notion of law as rules cannot readily accommodate the idea that the contours of the law may shift through no legislative or official act but merely through social change. At what point in the process of coming-to-be-rule-like do we treat something as law?

The point of "the Rule of Law, not of individuals" is that the rules are supposed to *rule*. The easiest (most "natural") way to achieve that in our historical and philosophical context is to assume that rules apply to particular cases in an analytical or self-applying way. "Individuals"—judges, police, administrators—are needed to make sure these self-evident applications are carried out, but these individuals are not supposed to *rule*. They are to be rule-bound, merely instrumental functionaries.

Once we admit that rules are mutable and inextricable from material social practice, we will at least experience a psychological change in the way we perceive our roles as legal actors. This alone may have subtle but pervasive consequences in our practices. For example, suppose the majority of lawyers and judges come to see legal decisionmaking as pragmatic work in the sense described by Duncan Kennedy.[97] Kennedy describes the interaction between the views and desires of the legal actor and the "normative power of the field."[98] Even though the actor will sometimes find the field to be "impacted"—perceive it to be stubbornly rule-like—this cannot be read from the face of the legal materials. Often what looks at first to be rule-like will turn out not to be. I agree with Kennedy that on some not-quite-conscious level

---

[95] And because acting under a rule re-affirms the *nomos* that treats any particular directive as binding, judging can never be choice-less or value free. When rules exist only because we continue to apprehend them as rules, it can be argued that we are morally responsible even for "mere" rule-application. Cover explored this responsibility in R. COVER, JUSTICE ACCUSED (1975), and Cover, *supra* note 94, at 53-68.

[96] Compare this passage from Dworkin:

> We think the question whether someone may legally drive faster than the stipulated speed limit is an easy one because we assume at once that no account of the legal record that denied that paradigm would be competent. But someone whose convictions about justice and fairness were very different from ours might not find that question so easy; even if he ended by agreeing with our answer, he would insist that we were wrong to be so confident. This explains why questions considered easy during one period become hard before they again become easy questions —with the opposite answers.

R. DWORKIN, LAW'S EMPIRE, *supra* note 21, at 354.

[97] *See* Kennedy, *supra* note 88, at 150-67.

[98] *Id.* at 157.

good lawyers know this. But if conscious awareness of this malleability in response to legal work—this non-pre-existing-ness of the law—replaces the prevailing positivist rhetoric about decisions predetermined by the plain meaning of rules, the character of our practice will change in ways we cannot now predict very well.[99]

If we do come to think of rules in a different way—anti-formalist, non-foundationalist, contingent, socially constructed—I think the change in thought would not be irrelevant, but rather would be incompatible with the traditional ideal of the Rule of Law. Will this shift in our conception of rules allow us to form a better conception or interpretation of the Rule of Law? Or will it force us to abandon the concept of the Rule of Law altogether? I think it is too soon to counsel abandonment.

## V. TOWARD REINTERPRETATION OF THE RULE OF LAW

### A. *Liberal Legalism and Non-Formalist Natural Law*

In this section I consider a recent scholarly attempt to affirm the traditional Rule of Law while denying traditional formalism. In my view the attempt collapses back into liberal legalism and fails. Michael Moore has recently argued for a "natural law" theory of legal interpretation and use of precedent, while denying the possibility of formalist rule-application.[100] Moore's theory is not the "natural law" of traditional foundationalism, but rather a reincarnation in terms of coherence theory. His claims are "(1) that there is a right answer to moral questions, a moral reality if you like; and (2) that the interpretive premises necessary to decide any case can and should be derived in part by recourse to the dictates of that moral reality."[101]

The connection between these notions and the Rule of Law is Moore's claim that "the rule of law virtues" constitute morally real values that must be part of judicial decisionmaking if judges are to reach morally right answers.[102] The six "virtues" Moore lists are: separation of powers, equality, liberty, substantive fairness, procedural fairness, and utility.[103] Although he cites Lon Fuller in this passage, it is clear that Moore's version of the Rule of Law is close to Rawls's substantive conception. Moore gives a liberal legalist gloss for each of his "virtues." For example, Moore intends the separation of powers virtue to refer to the traditional idea that judges should apply, not make, the law. He intends the equality virtue to refer to the idea of treating like cases alike ("formal justice"), and the liberty virtue to refer to curbing the chilling effect of

---

99 *Cf.* R. RORTY, *Pragmatism, supra* note 90, at 174-75 (discussing the unforeseeability of the consequences of pragmatism).

100 *See* Moore, *Theory of Interpretation, supra* note 14, at 286-88; Moore, *The Interpretive Turn in Modern Theory: A Turn for the Worse?* 41 STAN. L. REV. 871 (1989) [hereinafter Moore, *Interpretive Turn*].

101 *See* Moore, *Theory of Interpretation, supra* note 14, at 286.

102 *Id.* at 313-18.

103 *Id.* at 314.

legal uncertainty.

Moore characterizes these "rule of law virtues" as "basic values that justify judges in a democratic society . . . in accepting a humbler, more constrained mode of decisionmaking than that which they adopt when they view themselves as persons and not as functionaries of some kind."[104] According to Moore, "these six rule of law virtues together demand that judges give up some of the decisional freedom we each have as persons when deciding what, all things considered, it is best to do."[105]

There are two salient results of coupling the claim of moral reality with the six asserted "rule of law virtues." First, the judge is to behave differently as a "functionary" than as a "person," the difference being "constraint." Second, because these morally real values underlie *stare decisis*, sometimes a judge as "functionary" is morally required to stick with the wrong answers of the past (embodied in legal precedent) rather than what she as a "person" otherwise knows to be morally right. For Moore the Rule of Law "virtues" are not only "real," they are strong enough to turn (real) wrong into (real) right.

Moore's theory echoes the traditional formalist model of rules in which it is the *rules* that are to "rule" or decide, not the person. Without satisfactory argument to show how the judge as "functionary" is simultaneously a responsible moral chooser (a "person"), this theory—in spite of itself—does not distance itself much from the traditional notion that the judge is a functionary who implements the pre-existing connection between a rule and a set of particulars "falling under" it.[106]

Moreover, because Moore's theory requires the judge as "functionary" to implement what she as a "person" knows to be wrong, his theory of the judge's role echoes the positivist separation of law and morals that he is at great pains to deny.[107] Without satisfactory argument about how the liberal legalist virtues turn wrong into right, the functionary judge's position suggests that whether the law is right or wrong is of no concern to the judge. Inherent

---

[104] *Id.*

[105] *Id.* at 318.

[106] It might be thought that there is room for the person to be a moral chooser because of the moral leeway afforded by the necessity of interpreting legal texts. In *Theory of Interpretation*, *supra* note 14, at 318 n.80, Moore distinguished legal reasoning from moral reasoning by saying that moral reasoning "does not involve the kind of textual exegesis involved in law, literary criticism, and theology." Because the Rule of Law virtues "demand that judges justify their decisions with reference to legal texts," legal reasoning "is more like dream interpretation, literary criticism, and theology than unconstrained moral reasoning." *Id.* at 318. According to Moore's view of moral reality, moral rules are there to be "discovered," whereas legal rules are not. But Moore believes that even though law is an interpretive activity, there can be authoritatively correct interpretations of it because texts have a metaphysically real meaning. "[T]o interpret dreams or statutes is to seek true explanations and evaluations, where 'true' is not a term internal to our practice but brought to it from general metaphysical and epistemological positions." Moore, *Interpretive Turn*, *supra* note 100, at 957.

[107] *See* Moore, *Semantics*, *supra* note 14, at 153.

in this theory is a deep force toward conservatism, legitimation of the status quo, by the time-honored "natural law" strategy of writing it into the fabric of the universe. In spite of Moore's scorn for conventionalism, he does not adequately explain why the values we have inherited from liberal legalism are to be taken as "real" other than the fact that they are part of our legal culture.

I am suggesting, in essence, that Moore's theory is at odds with itself. The tension at its heart is caused by his commitment both to a version of liberal legalism and to non-foundationalist views of meaning and justification. Ultimately these cannot coherently co-exist. The underlying commitment to liberal legalism—the traditional substantive conception of the Rule of Law—causes the traditional formalist characteristics of the judge's role as functionary and the traditional formalist interpretation of rules and precedent to re-assert themselves even as the non-foundationalist views of meaning and justification are destroying these ideas about rigidity of role and application of rules and precedent. It is no wonder that Moore argued—in an early article attacking all formalist theories of meaning—that formalism seems to be *the* theory of adjudication required by the Rule of Law.[108] For Moore the unstated problem is, how can we deny formalism and affirm the Rule of Law? His answer was that because formalism (by which he meant the traditional conception of formalism, not a Wittgensteinian reinterpretation) is impossible, and we wish to affirm the Rule of Law, the task for theory is to come "as close to formalism as knowledge of language will allow."[109] Apparently the strength of Moore's own commitment to liberal legalism does not allow him to see that his own arguments against traditional formalism also render meaningless the notion of coming "close to" it. If formalism is impossible, there is no "it" to which one can come close.[110]

### B. *The Rule of Law and Interpretive Community: Toward a Pragmatic View*

Suppose we drop both the notion that law is mediated through formal rules in the traditional sense (accepting Wittgensteinian reinterpretation of formal-

---

[108] *Id.* at 153-58.

[109] *Id.* at 167.

[110] Could a Wittgensteinian reinterpretation of formalism rehabilitate Moore's argument? One could contend that brute agreement on results, the socially evident compulsion of acting under a rule, does "come as close to formalism as knowledge of language will allow," and that, for all the traditional Rule of Law reasons—especially the separation of powers and constrained judicial role—we should formulate legal directives to maximize formal realizability (as reconceived). *See, e.g.*, Schauer, *Formalism*, 97 Yale L.J. 509 (1988). Moore himself would not accept any Wittgensteinian view; to him Wittgenstein's reliance on human practice seems merely "conventionalist," the category his perspective opposes to the realism he espouses. *See* Moore, *Theory of Interpretation*, *supra* note 14, at 291-301. Nevertheless, the Wittgensteinian move here seems plausible. It leads, however, to the view that liberal legalism remains the same when we alter its philosophical underpinnings, a view I find too simplistic.

ism), and the broader idea that law consists essentially of verbal directives like rules and standards, apart from the practice in which they are embedded (accepting a more far-reaching reinterpretation). We will still find it deeply normatively appealing to conceive of ourselves as a people governed by its law rather than by arbitrary individual power, because conceiving of ourselves this way I take to be constitutive of ourselves as a political community.[111] The enduring normative appeal of the Rule of Law is the reason I pursue reinterpretation. The reinterpretation I want to pursue (barely beginning in this essay) turns toward a view of law that emphasizes practice as well as words. It is a view that turns toward pragmatism, seeking to view law as a pragmatic normative activity. In this view, hermeneutics—the view of interpretation and meaning as holistic and practice-based—forms the epistemology of law.

The work of Robert Cover is suggestive for the reinterpretation I seek. Cover is perhaps the quintessential modern anti-positivist. He claims that the role of judges is rightly law-creating ("juris*generative*"). Thus, he stands on its head the traditional slogan that judges should apply rather than make law.[112] When judges slip into the old rhetoric and claim to act not as people but as functionaries whose hands are tied, they "substitut[e] the hermeneutic of jurisdiction for the hermeneutic of the text."[113] In other words, they refuse to take responsibility for their actions by taking refuge in their role as rule-followers. "Judges are people of violence"[114]; one way of being violent is to disavow responsibility for the consequences of their functionary behavior.

In Cover's view, judges are not functionaries but rather constitute an interpretive community. Law-creation is not unique to them; it inheres in all interpretive communities. In interpretive communities, "applying" and "making" law coalesce. As a community applies its law, it continuously [re-]makes it.[115] Law is not the creature of the state but the mark of an interpretive community. Law is not made by legislatures (or judges) alone. Under the sway of the positivist model of law as rules, the role of the state has been to crush all law contrary to that of the state. This Cover deplores. For Cover, to act rightly as a judge is to refuse to use the violence of one's office to enforce the law of the state against the law of various dissenting communities, while at the same time recognizing and taking responsibility for the fact that the law of the community of judges can come into conflict with, and is not intrinsically privileged

---

[111] *See* Michelman, *supra* note 9, at 1499-1503 (discussing the way we conceive self-rule and law-rule).

[112] Cover, *supra* note 94, at 53-60.

[113] *Id.* at 58.

[114] *Id.* at 53.

[115] Even the new Dworkin of LAW'S EMPIRE, *supra* note 21, would, it seems, readily acquiesce to this last statement. "[Hercules] does not amend out-of-date statutes to suit new times. . . . He recognizes what the old statutes have since become." *See, e.g., id.* at 350. (Unlike Cover, however, Dworkin is resolutely statist; he seems to write on the heroic assumption that we are one interpretive community expressing itself through the state.)

over, the law of other interpretive communities.

Like Cover's theory of law, hermeneutic social theories have rejected foundationalism, formalism, and the idea that a rule could be applied by one person, only once, apart from a group in whose interpretive practice the rule is embedded. Hermeneutic theories have also rejected the notion that there can be application without interpretation, or interpretation without politics and value, or politics and value without commitment.[116] These theories view interpretation as holistic, pragmatic, and historically situated. Because of these features, hermeneutic theory bears an affinity with the turn toward coherence theories and pragmatism in ethics and metaphysics. Hermeneutic theory thus seems more promising than the new non-foundationalist "natural law" for legal theorists who seek to exorcise formalism.

A pragmatic reinterpretation of the Rule of Law would at least deny that law consists of formally realizable rules in the traditional sense. More controversially, perhaps, I believe such a reinterpretation would deny that law consists quintessentially of rules at all, as well as the notion that rules are separate from cases and logically pre-exist their application. Such a reinterpretation would also deny the strict division of people into rule-givers and rule-followers, and the conception of judges as rule-appliers rather than rule-makers.

How would these broad theoretical features play out into a substantive conception of the Rule of Law that can supersede the traditional one? One task in answering this question is the one I left aside in this essay: the remaking of the supporting theories of the person and of politics.[117] In the meantime, we can set out to "look and see," readjusting our theory and thus the interpretation of our practice at each step along the way. Thus I suggest that we explore how each precept of the Rule of Law might be reinterpreted. If we can retain the entire complex, or most of it, but with new philosophical underpinnings, we shall retain the Rule of Law as a central normative commitment of our legal system. For those who accept the new interpretation, however, its meaning and import for the form of life we call law may be very different.

I suggest we begin by reconsidering the Rule of Law precepts clustering around notice, non-retroactivity, and the separation of powers.

In the instrumental view of the traditional model of rules, a law must not be retroactive because it cannot be the cause of conforming behavior unless it precedes the behavior. A law must be made public because it cannot be the cause of conforming behavior if the addressees do not know about it. In the substantive view of the traditional Rule of Law, fairness is the value underlying the requirements of non-retroactivity and notice. These precepts both rest

---

[116] *See* Hermeneutics and Praxis xiii-xvi (R. Hollinger ed. 1985); R. Rorty, Mirror of Nature, *supra* note 74, at 315-21; Garet, *Comparative Normative Hermeneutics: Scripture, Literature, Constitution*, 58 S. Cal. L. Rev. 35, 38-39 (1985).

[117] *See supra* notes 9-46 and accompanying text. *See also* Michelman, *supra* note 9, at 1502 (arriving at something close to the same point as I do through reinterpretation of politics).

on the idea that it is unfair to base adverse government interference with individual interests on the individual's failure to conform to rules the individual cannot fairly be charged to have known in advance of the non-conforming behavior, either because the rule has not properly been made public (the notice precept) or because the rule has not yet been enacted at the time of the conduct (the non-retroactivity precept). What the pragmatic approach can add to this traditional view is a broader understanding of what constitutes sufficient publicity or notice, and a reinterpretation of retroactivity in light of the idea that rules are not made merely by legislatures or other authoritative entities.

In the pragmatic view, a rule will be public whenever strong social agreement exists in practice, regardless of whether a legislature or a court has spoken.[118] Similarly, if a rule exists normatively even without specific legislative enactment (as, for example, would a rule against intentional homicide), then later legislative confirmation would not necessarily mean that it would be unfair retroactive application to punish earlier transgressions.[119] Moreover, where the line of evolution of legal interpretation is clearly foreseeable, it would not be unfair to hold people to what they can see is the emerging interpretation.[120]

The Rule of Law precepts concerning separation of powers and the nature of the judicial role pose a more complex issue. If we accept the Wittgensteinian view of rules, we must reject the conception of the separation of powers that pictures a rigid distinction between the legislature as rule-maker and the judges as rule-appliers; indeed, we must reject, as well, the more general

---

[118] In Keeler v. Superior Court, 2 Cal. 3d 619, 470 P.2d 617, 87 Cal. Rptr. 481 (1970), the California Supreme Court decided that a man who assaulted his ex-wife when she was nine months pregnant and killed the fetus, with intent to do so, could not be prosecuted for murder because common-law judicial precedent did not clearly give notice that killing an unborn baby could result in a murder prosecution. *Id.* at 636, 470 P.2d at 628, 87 Cal. Rptr. at 492. A pragmatic view would make us confront the unspoken social context—an abortion issue the Court did not wish to discuss—by asking: is our contemporary *nomos* one in which the killing of an unborn nine-month fetus by assault on the mother recognizable to us as murder?

[119] For example, if defendant assaults with intent to kill and the victim dies fourteen months later, it is fair to abolish the common-law year and a day rule and prosecute defendant for murder. The defendant can be fairly charged with knowing that if the victim dies the crime is murder, and we do not mind the "chilling effect" on people's liberty to assault with intent to kill. *See* United States v. Jackson, 528 A.2d 1211, 1216-20 (D.C. 1987).

[120] An interesting passage in the Hart and Sacks materials suggests that Buick Motor Co. could not object on notice and non-retroactivity grounds to Cardozo's decision in MacPherson v. Buick, 217 N.Y. 382, 389, 111 N.E. 1050, 1053 (1916) (holding the manufacturer liable to the ultimate consumer for injury caused by its negligence), because Buick could not reasonably maintain that it was justified in behaving negligently in light of the old (and decaying) doctrine limiting recovery to those in privity of contract with the manufacturer. H. HART & A. SACKS, THE LEGAL PROCESS 575 (tent. ed. 1958).

distinction between government as rule-maker and citizens as rule-followers. But this does not mean that there is no difference between the judicial role and the legislative role. The pragmatic view must certainly accept that the distinction is normatively important in the political tradition of our community.

In the pragmatic normative understanding, our constitution is not merely a document but rather that which "constitutes" us as a political community.[121] We are constituted both by commitment to majority rule and by counter-majoritarian commitments. One way to understand this constitutional dualism is to see it as a reflection of the tension between our understanding of our present state and our understanding of social ideals toward which progress is possible. In this pragmatic view of politics, we are always attempting to accomplish a transition from today's nonideal world to the better world of our vision, and it is a transition that never ends.[122] Moreover, our visions and our nonideal reality paradoxically constitute each other: what we can formulate as being better depends upon where we are now, and the way we understand where we are now depends upon our vision of what should be.

To the extent we live in present imperfect reality, majority rule is normatively appealing, and so is conventionalism in our understanding of morals and politics. To the extent we live in our visions of a better world (even though such visions must be contingent upon our present circumstances), judgment against the majority is normatively appealing where the majority has transgressed those visions, and so is some form of transcendence of conventionalism in our understanding of morals and politics. Because our constitutional tradition partakes of both tendencies, we constitute ourselves both by conventional reality and by vision. Our understanding of the separation of powers can be reinterpreted in light of this constitutive tension.

We might say that often legislatures are responsible for fidelity to convention, and judges for fidelity to vision. More important, perhaps, is recognition that legislatures and judges must interact in pursuing our vision. Consider, for example, civil rights in the modern era. The Court led the way in *Brown v. Board of Education*,[123] but in *Bell v. Maryland*,[124] it was able to let civil rights legislation carry the weight of progress toward the vision of social equality. The interaction of courts and legislatures in the modern development of the

---

[121] An important issue is whether "we" are indeed one political community. *See infra* note 127. It seems to me that "we" are one community on the issue of whether 2 + 2 = 4, but perhaps we are many diverse communities on other issues more readily regarded as ethical, religious, or political. The pragmatic normative significance of our having a constitution is to deny at least the furthest reaches of such pessimistic irreconcilable pluralism. We are one in at least some sense(s).

[122] *See* Radin, *supra* note 89, at 1875-76.

[123] 347 U.S. 483 (1954). It is important to recall that traditional concerns about neutral principles and the Rule of Law made *Brown* controversial when it was decided. For an eloquent pragmatic defense of the Court's decision, see Black, *The Lawfulness of the Segregation Decisions*, 69 YALE L.J. 421, 424-28 (1960).

[124] 378 U.S. 226 (1964).

law of landlord and tenant is an equally good although less celebrated example. Judges like J. Skelley Wright could move forward on their understanding of fair treatment of tenants in principle, but it was for legislatures to tell us what exactly might count as retaliatory eviction or breach of the implied warranty of habitability.[125]

Independence and impartiality are traditional aspects of the judge's role as a functionary separate from the legislative power; these elements of the Rule of Law are supposed to ensure that judges stay within their task of rule-applying. But independence and impartiality can refer to moral autonomy and a commitment to judgment in light of one's own moral understanding of the nature of community—not just to formal separation from the interests of the legislature or the litigants. Robert Cover, for example, regards independence for a judge in the same way as the independence characterizing a person of moral integrity who faces choices that impact on other people's lives, not as merely formal independence of a functionary whose hands are tied.[126]

In such an anti-formalist view of the judge's role, judges are an interpretive community conscious of their obligation to act as independent moral choosers for the good of a society, in light of what that society is and can become.[127] The law, as long as it is part of a viable and developing community, is neither "found" nor "made," but continuously re-interpreted. There are still rules. But there are no rules that can be understood apart from their context; nor are there rules that can be understood as fixed in time.[128]

---

[125] When Judge Wright decided Robinson v. Diamond Housing Co., 463 F.2d 853 (D.C. Cir. 1972) (the case with which I introduced the problem of the Rule of Law in this essay), he could point to legislation enacted subsequent to the events at issue to support his result. The legislation Judge Wright looked to was in turn based upon earlier court decisions. *Id.* at 857 n.1. For many other examples of pragmatic interaction between legislatures and courts, see G. CALABRESI, A COMMON LAW FOR THE AGE OF STATUTES (1982).

[126] *See, e.g.*, Cover, *supra* note 94, at 58-59 (advocating a "natural law of jurisdiction" which "implies the articulation of a legal principle according to an independent hermeneutic"); R. COVER, *supra* note 95, at 171 (exploring the moral predicament of anti-slavery judges who nevertheless enforced the fugitive slave laws in the era before the Civil War). *See especially id.* at Part III ("The Moral-Formal Dilemma").

[127] There are problems I gloss over here that must be taken very seriously. Is it appropriate to think of ourselves in any sense as only one community or does that do violence to heterodox groups that are less powerful, hence less able to say who "we" are? And is it intolerable elitism to think of judges as exercising moral autonomy on behalf of the rest of us? *See* Sullivan, *Against Republicanism*, in AFTER THE BICENTENNIAL (M. Tushnet ed.) (forthcoming); and Sullivan, *Rainbow Republicanism*, 97 YALE L.J. 1713, 1716-18 (1988).

[128] Indeed, this feature of continuous reinterpretation by an interpretive community of judges and those who argue to and with them help us understand the dynamic adaptability of the common law. It explains why the common law is traditionally characterized by organic metaphors like life and growth, and why it has resisted all theoretical attempts to bring it satisfactorily within a model of rules.

## VI. CONCLUSION

In *Robinson v. Diamond Housing Corporation*, Judge Wright did not see himself as a functionary implementing pre-existing formal rules. Yet he did see himself as acting in accord with the Rule of Law. If we are receptive to the reinterpretation I have begun to sketch, I think we may now see at least how he was trying to act in accord with the Rule of Law. Judge Wright recognized that in order even to know what his own prior cases "held" and their bearing on the case before him, he had to formulate a normative understanding of what the legislature and courts were doing by promulgating and enforcing a housing code. What they were doing depended not just on the words of the code, but also on the social context of housing in the District of Columbia community at the time, where (it seemed to Judge Wright, at least) landlords were commercial enterprises controlled by powerful groups and tenants were poor and powerless. What the code meant depended also on the broader social context of the Vietnam era.[129]

Within this context, Judge Wright understood the normative force of the law as affirming not only that there should be safe and sanitary housing for people, but also that people themselves should be involved in bringing this about by enforcing their housing rights in court. If he had allowed a situation to continue in which tenants would immediately lose their homes whenever they tried to invoke the law to improve those homes, the aspect of the law calling for community participation would be a cruel hoax, and the group upon whom it was perpetrated would become even more alienated from the community as a whole. In light of his obligation to support his community, Judge Wright saw the law as working against this alienating result. The Rule of Law ideal itself persuaded Judge Wright to see the law this way.

One could fault Judge Wright for not going further and enjoining the landlord to repair the house, rather than arriving at the ironic result that the tenant's right to habitable housing meant she could stay indefinitely in uninhabitable housing for free. Perhaps even the iconoclastic Judge Wright could not imagine bucking the traditional disfavor for affirmative injunctions. Perhaps it was relevant that in this particular case there was no need for such an injunction because Mrs. Robinson had in fact stopped living in the unsafe and unsanitary house before final disposition on appeal. One could also fault Judge Wright for taking too sanguine a view of the economic situation, if he thought that market forces would necessarily prevent landlords from sticking tenants with the increased costs of making housing habitable.[130]

---

[129] In a letter to Professor Edward H. Rabin, Judge Wright said, "I was indeed influenced by the fact that, during the nationwide racial turmoil of the sixties and the unrest caused by the injustice of racially selective service in Vietnam, most of the tenants in Washington, D.C. slums were poor and black and most of the landlords were rich and white." Rabin, *The Revolution in Residential Landlord Tenant Law: Causes and Consequences*, 69 CORNELL L. REV. 517, 549 (1984).

[130] The citation of Bruce Ackerman's theoretical article on the economic effects of

I do not think, however, that we should fault Judge Wright merely because he did not adhere to the traditional conception of law as static formal rules. His action in trying to keep open tenants' avenues of redress and thereby keep the community open to tenant participation, while at the same time not depriving landlords of the expected monetary gain afforded by property ownership, seems quite law-like. It seems so, that is, when law is understood to mean not just a set of rules laid down but rather to include an evolving complex of political commitments to the flourishing of the community and the individuals in it.

In the view of law as a pragmatic normative practice, law does not disappear. But it is always open to people to recognize, in various ways, that the law in the statute books is not the real law.[131] Some practices are so deeply accepted that they seem like immutable rules. Life according to rules is not impossible but quite routine, as Wittgenstein saw. It is only that, if we take the pragmatic and hermeneutic view of law, our understanding of rule-following must be reconstituted so that we know that rules are neither formal in the traditional sense, nor eternal, nor existing independently of us; and so that we know that every application of them is a reinterpretation. We must know that each time we feel ourselves to be rule-followers we are rule-creators as well.

Whether or not the term "the Rule of Law" should be dropped becomes another pragmatic question, a matter of judgment about its ideological baggage. Is the term indelibly linked in our usage with the ideas that law is instrumental and consists of pre-existing formal rules applied in a value-free manner? Or can its precepts be reinterpreted in the way I have begun to suggest? If we can use the term in this new way, it seems that we would at least have to drop the slogan, "the Rule of Law, *not* of individuals." If law cannot be formal rules, its people cannot be mere functionaries.

---

housing code enforcement as if it were an empirical study of the D.C. housing market is indeed a weakness in Judge Wright's opinion. *See Robinson*, 463 F.2d at 860, *citing* Ackerman, *Regulating Slum Housing Markets on Behalf of the Poor: Of Housing Codes, Housing Subsidies and Income Redistribution Policy*, 80 YALE L.J. 1093 (1971).

[131] Even Dworkin now allows for this possibility by claiming that the Rule of Law includes fulfillment of moral rights even if they are not enacted as positive law. *See* R. DWORKIN, *supra* note 10, at 11-13 (contrasting this rights conception with the "rulebook" conception); *cf.* R. DWORKIN, LAW'S EMPIRE, *supra* note 21, at 211-15 (the model of community as commitment to political integrity includes recognition that rights and duties are not exhausted by particular institutional decisions and enactments).

[10]



# Rules and the Rule-Following Argument

Frederick Schauer

Sparked by books by Saul Kripke and Crispin Wright, the last several years have seen a renewal of interest in Wittgenstein's remarks on rules. A large part of the contemporary discussion centers on what it is to follow a rule, how it is that human beings come to follow them, and what facts, mental or otherwise, determine or explain why some but not other logically equivalent extensions of a rule are deemed to constitute a *following* of the rule.

I have no reason to believe I have anything to contribute to the debate that has engaged not only Kripke and Wright, but also many others, including G.E.M. Anscombe, G.P. Baker & P.M.S. Hacker, Paul Boghossian, Robert Fogelin, Colin McGinn, and Guy Stock. Yet regardless of who has the better of the debate, it remains the case that the debate itself has an obvious relevance to those of us who think about regulative rules, the rules governing our moral conduct, our manners, our religious practices, and, perhaps most obviously, our conduct as citizens in a nation of laws. Moreover, the debate about rule-following has even more relevance in thinking about regulative rules as influencing the behavior and decisions of various officials, including judges, administrative officials, and the cop on the beat.

As is unfortunately all too often the case, legal scholars who have perceived the relevance of Wittgenstein and the debate about rule-following to legal theory have proceeded to apply misunderstood or simply erroneous readings of the lessons of the issue in the service of their own pre-philosophical jurisprudential inclinations. Two varieties are particularly egregious.[1] The first sees Wittgenstein's interlocutor as the chief player in the drama, rather than as Thrasymachus-like philosophical foil. Consequently, the challenges posed by the interlocutor are taken to be unanswerable and thus sound. The result of reading Wittgenstein in this way, of course, is the generation of a profoundly skeptical conclusion about the possibility of following any rule, including a legal rule. If it is the case, according to this reading of the lessons of the interlocutor, that a rule can be anything the so-called rule-follower wants it to be, then judges, for example, cannot be expected to and thus should not do anything other than follow their own rule-independent personal, psychological, moral, or political preferences. If the lesson of the rule-following argument is that constraint by rule is illusory, then the accompanying lesson is that constraint by legal rule is equally illusory.[2]

The second variety of spectacular misreading of the rule-following argu-

Earlier versions of this article have been presented at the Dartmouth College Department of Philosophy, Washington University Department of Philosophy, and University of Alberta Faculty of Philisophy.

1. References are omitted to protect the guilty.
2. This is not to say that there are not interesting and important issues surrounding the legal-rule-skepticism commonly referred to as Legal Realism. Indeed, if the rule-skepticism of Legal Realism is a claim that legal decisionmakers are not in fact constrained by rules in the way in which they purport to be in their articulated justifications (such as judicial opinions), or a claim that legal decisionmakers are constrained by rules other than the rules they claim constrain them, then it is in many domains true. But if Legal Realism is true, it is because some decisionmakers do not in fact follow the rules they claim to follow, and not because it is impossible to follow a rule.

ment consists of the conclusion that meaning, including the meaning of a rule and its constituent terms, is solely a function of the particular context in which the language of a rule is applied. Starting from the "meaning is use" slogan, this argument moves from this slogan to the conclusion that meaning is therefore coextensive with how language is used on a particular occasion—that the particular context of utterance is the sole determinant of meaning. This approach, rejecting semantics in favor of pragmatics as the exclusive determinant of meaning, and collapsing sentence meaning into utterance meaning, has the effect of rejecting the idea that the language of a legal or other regulative rule can have a meaning independent of the meaning it has when applied to a particular event or a particular dispute. As should be obvious, the result is to collapse rule-based constraint into a determination of what, all things considered, should be done on this occasion. And as with the argument described in the previous paragraph, the upshot is to embed an entirely plausible theory of judicial empowerment in an entirely implausible theory of meaning.[3]

Take as an example the standard jurisprudential chestnut, a "No vehicles in the park" rule. Now suppose the question arises whether a police car is to be excluded pursuant to that rule.[4] A number of responses are possible. One is to say that the enforcer or interpreter of the rule ought not to follow it when it would produce an absurd or otherwise undesirable result, just as we would not expect the authorities to enforce a speed limit against someone rushing a critically injured person to the hospital. A related response would say that it is a desirable or even a necessary characteristic of law that it authorize or even require its officials to refuse to follow the literal indications of the rule in such cases, and still another would recognize that other rules in the system might explicitly authorize such refusal to follow this rule. But none of these responses denies that a police car is still literally a vehicle, that this rule is still literally violated by the police car, and that it is conceptually possible to imagine a system in which even desirable violations of the rule would be treated as violations. Such a system may or may not be worth having, but it is not impossible. The question of whether the police car should be excluded is thus distinct from the question whether it is a vehicle, and it does not become less of a vehicle just because it would be undesirable to exclude it from the park.

* * *

Now that we have disposed of some of the less plausible applications of the rule-following argument to questions about regulative rules, let us make a new start. In doing so I will retrace some quite familiar terrain, but doing so

3. "The meaning of an expression cannot be identified with the object it is used, on a particular occasion, to refer to. The meaning of a sentence cannot be identified with the assertion it is used, on a particular occasion, to make. For to talk about the meaning of an expression or sentence is not to talk about its use on a particular occasion, but about the rules, habits, conventions governing its correct use, on all occasions, to refer or to assert." P.F. Strawson, "On Referring", (1950), 59 *Mind* 327. See also William Alston, "Meaning and Use", (1963), 13 *Philosophical Quarterly*, 107-24.
4. See David Brink, "Legal Theory, Legal Interpretation, and Judicial Review", (1988), 17 *Philosophy and Public Affairs*, 105-48.

will expose the foundations and therefore the potential weaknesses in the argument.

Let us start with the example of the numerical series 1000, 1002, 1004, 1006, and put it in the form of the question, "What number comes next in the series 1000, 1002, 1004, 1006, ____?" It is central to the Wittgensteinian point, as well as part of what has passed into the commonplace of mathematical theory, that there is no uniquely correct logical answer to that question. A rule could be constructed to make any answer to the question correct.[5] For example, the rule, "If *n* is less than 1006, add 2, but if *n* is equal to or greater than 1006, add 13," would explain all members of the existing series, but would generate and justify the answer 1019, rather than the answer 1008. The point of this, of course, is that something other than the prior numbers in the series makes 1008 correct and 1019 incorrect, with the debate being about just what that "something other" is, with Kripke and Wright talking about community practices, McGinn suggesting some natural inclination, and Baker and Hacker urging that faithfulness to Wittgenstein's conception of Wittgenstein's project would lead us to understand why we ought not even to be asking the question.[6]

But now suppose that the same question—"What number comes next in the series 1000, 1002, 1004, 1006, ____?"—were accompanied by the linguistically and canonically formulated instruction, "always add 2." If "always add 2" were an *instruction* incorporated within the question, then 1008 would become the right answer, and 1019 would be simply wrong. "If *n* is less than 1006, add 2, but if *n* is equal to or greater than 1006, add 13" is a permissible rule extracted from the series standing by itself, but it is not a permissible interpretation of "always add 2," and it is thus not a permissible rule if "always add 2" is one of the parameters determining which results are permissible.

Before you, the reader, tear up this paper in disgust, I know that at first it appears that what I have said just misses the point entirely. Why is it, Wittgenstein's skeptical interlocutor asks, that "always add 2" is inconsistent with "if *n* is less than 1006, add 2, but if *n* is equal to or greater than 1006, add 13?" Why can't we ask the same skeptical questions about each component term that we did about the question in its entirety? Why, therefore, couldn't the word "always" mean "in every case except those in which a series ending in a number equal to or greater than 1006 is involved, in which case all instructions inconsistent with 'add 13' are void"?[7]

To ask these questions, however, is to conflate two quite different inquiries.

---

5. It was in fact Leibniz who first made this point. "[I]f someone draws an uninterrupted curve which is now straight, now circular, and now of some other nature, it is possible to find a concept, a rule, or an equation common to all the points of the line, in accordance with which the very changes must take place. . . . Thus we may say that no matter how God might have created the world, it would have always been regular and in a certain general order." *Discourse on Metaphysics*, trans. R.H.D. Martin and S. Brown, (Manchester: Manchester Univ. Press, 1988) at 304.
6. No one but the skeptic claims that there is nothing that serves this purpose, for "if it were *always* possible ... to give a rule to justify any answer, a rule to make any answer *correct*, then there is no sense of the idea of 'incorrect,' and thus no sense of operating according to a rule at all." Guy Stock, "Leibniz and Kripke's Sceptical Paradox", (1988), 38 *Philosophical Quarterly*, 326-29.
7. "And besides, what about quaddition?" "And what about '2'?"

The reason that "always" does not mean something other than always is the very topic of the debate about what it is that supplies the benchmark for following or breaking a rule *of language*, where the very characterization of that bedrock question makes it circular and question-begging to answer the question in terms of the existence of rules of language. Community practices, to refer (without endorsement) to just one possible answer to the skeptic, is what and only what makes "always" mean always. Yet once something, whatever it is, *has* determined that "always" means always, the word "always" can *then* be used to refer to always. That is, skeptical questions about the foundations of language and the foundations of mathematics do not suggest that the techniques of language or of mathematics are non-existent, nor even that those techniques cannot themselves provide the foundation for practices other than those of language and mathematics. Thus, a practice of following rules articulated *in* language is not rendered problematic by the difficulty in explaining why it is that language operates in the way in which it plainly does operate. Our difficulty, to use Kripke's example, in explaining *why* 68 + 57 equals 125 and not 5 does not mean that the right answer to the question, 68 + 57 = ?, today and in this linguistic and mathematical community, is not 125. And if 68 + 57 does in fact, today in this world, equal 125, then *that* fact can provide the basis, today in this world, for some number of other practices, such as building bridges, calculating bank balances, and making change at the supermarket.

The question about rules other than the rules of language, therefore, is not why the rules of language work, but whether the rules of language, which *do* work (whether we can explain why or not), enable *other* rules to work. If we presuppose the ability of the rules (or conventions, or whatever) of language to generate meaning, then "1000, 1002, 1004, 1006, ____?," supplemented by the formulated instruction "always add 2" is crucially different from the question "1000, 1002, 1004, 1006, ____?," without that linguistically formulated direction. Adding the specific instruction makes all the difference. Thus, the question whether a sign reading "No dogs allowed" excludes seeing eye dogs is not a question whose answer requires direct reference, even according to Kripke and Wright, to community practices. Instead, the rule builds on and refers the rule-follower to the phrase "No dogs allowed," a phrase whose meaning exists apart from the question whether the community believes that seeing eye dogs should be allowed in restaurants.

* * *

That an account of prescriptive or regulative rules *builds on* the existence of language, and therefore does not itself engender the same kind of skepticism as do theories that seek to explain the operation of language, does not mean that this form of Wittgensteinian inquiry has little relevance for those interested in regulative rules. Two groups of issues are most important.

First, Wittgenstein's skeptical interlocutor compels us to wonder what it takes to constrain or at least to guide future behavior, and the message is now clear: The ability to explain the constraints *of an unformulated or unformulatable rule* is highly problematic. All agree that if *any* answer is correct to the question, "1000, 1002, 1004, 1006, ____?," then there is no rule. Suppose the restaurant I referred to above had no sign on its door, but had in the past excluded a Scottish terrier, a bulldog, and a cocker spaniel. When the question now arises whether an Irish wolfhound is to be excluded, the past instances themselves do not logically compel the first rather than the second and third of the following three rules, any of which would explain all of the previous decisions: "No dogs allowed"; "No short dogs allowed"; "No animals weighing less than 60 pounds allowed." Rule construction in cases such as this is like the process of theory construction in science, and burdened with the same problems of underdetermination. As a result, only an authoritative formulation of a rule will privilege the first over the others, and thus it appears to be precisely the authoritative formulation of a rule that makes it possible to say that some acts conform to the rule and others do not. The "No dogs allowed" rule, when formulated, acts just as "always add 2," when formulated, acts, building on the workability of language to exclude some otherwise eligible candidates as successors in the series. Without the formulation, it appears as if any rule could be constructed consistent with the previous decisions, and thus without the formulation there appears to be no rule at all.

This appears highly relevant to thinking about the common law, characterized, in theory, precisely by its absence of canonical formulations, and by the way in which a given common law decision is an extension of a previous series of decisions. What we now see, however, is not that there is no basis for preferring one extension over another, but that the basis is not something contained *in* the previous decisions in the series. Just as the existing categorial and conceptual apparatus of the human mind is likely to extract "No dogs allowed" rather than "No short dogs" or "No animals under 60 pounds" from the series of previous exclusions of specific dogs, so too might an array of community practices, subcommunity practices, and categorial presuppositions lead a legal decisionmaker to extend a series of previous decisions in one direction rather than another. But once we recognize that any number of extensions are logically compatible with the previous decisions in the series, we are led to examine those undisclosed assumptions and practices that make some extensions permissible and others not, and we are led as well to question the extent to which claims of compulsion with respect to some extensions are claims that mask the degree of choice actually available to the extender.

Second, examining regulatory rules through a Wittgensteinian lens enables us to see that even linguistically formulated regulatory rules owe their ruleness to a process by which those rules are internalized as reasons for action by some putative rule-follower. I have shown above that the logically prior rules of language make the internalization of formulated rules possible, but thinking in this way leads us to look at the rules that themselves influence and facilitate the internalization of formulated rules. A formulated rule may be internalized according to the rule, "Treat the indications of the ordinary language meaning of the formulated rule as a reason for acting (or deciding) in accordance with those indications," but other rules *of* internalization are possible as well. Another might substitute technical meaning within a linguistic subcommunity for ordinary meaning, another might incorporate an "except where doing so would be absurd" qualification, and still another might mandate that the rules should be viewed only as rules of thumb transparent to their background justifications.[8] All of these are possible, and thus the ruleness of a regulative rule can be seen to be a function not only of the fact of its internalization by some decisionmaker, but also of the *conditions* of its internalization. By recognizing that rules do not determine their own application, we are thus led not to reject the possibility of rule-based constraint, and not to reject the importance of rule-formulations in supplying the meaning that is at the heart of ruleness, but to acknowledge that the tools of language as embodied in a rule-formulation are necessary but not sufficient conditions for treating a rule as a reason for action. And when we look for the other conditions that contribute to the existence of a regulative rule, we see both the importance and the incompleteness of focusing on the formulation of that rule.

8. On the distinction between "real" rules and rules of thumb, and on the relation between rules and both their formulations and their background justifications, see my forthcoming *Playing By the Rules: A Philosophical Examination of Rule-Based Decisionmaking in Law and in Life* (Oxford: Clarendon Press, 1991).

# [11]



## Realist Semantics and Legal Theory

Dennis M. Patterson

### 1. Introduction

In "Legal Theory, Legal Interpretation, and Judicial Review",[1] David O. Brink advocates a central role in legal interpretation for considerations of human purpose. He states:

> It is important to remember that the primary objects of legal interpretation – statutes, constitutional provisions, and precedents – like most objects of interpretation, are human artifacts, the products of purposeful activity. In interpreting the products of purposeful activity, we must appeal to the purposes which prompted and guided the activity whose product we are trying to understand.[2]

The view that the meaning of human activities is best discerned from the point of view of the participants in the activity is one that is shared by philosophers from both the analytic and continental traditions.[3] Like others who argue for consideration of purpose in the interpretation of law,[4] Brink recognizes that no account of the purposive nature of law as a human activity can be complete without considering problems of meaning. In jurisprudence, this recognition finds specific focus in the problem of legal indeterminacy. Given the 'open texture' of legal norms, no theory of law can be adequate without some account of how problems of contextual indeterminacy are to be resolved. Indeed, without such an account, we cannot even make sense of the notion of 'disagreement' in law.[5]

As Brink reads its history, contemporary jurisprudence has attempted to solve problems of indeterminacy with an inadequate tool, that being an empiricist semantic theory.[6] As Brink sees it, proponents of this theory make the following two claims:

> (i) the meaning of a word or phrase is the set of (identifying) properties or descriptions which speakers associate with it, and
>
> (ii) the meaning of a word determines its reference.[7]

1. David O. Brink, "Legal Theory, Legal Interpretation, and Judicial Review, (1988), 17 *Philosophy and Public Affairs* 105 [hereinafter referred to by page number alone].
2. p. 125.
3. See Hans-Georg Gadamer, *Truth and Method*, translation ed. Garrett Barden and John Cumming (New York: Crossroad, 1975): Alasdair MacIntyre, "The Intelligibility of Action", repr. in J. Margolis M. Krausz & R.M. Burian eds., *Rationality, Relativism and The Human Science* (Dordecht: Martinus Nijhoff, 1986): 63-80.
4. This theme is illustrated in the work of, for example, both H.L.A. Hart and Ronald Dworkin. See H.L.A. Hart, *The Concept of Law* (New York: Oxford University Press, 1961): 121-32. Ronald Dworkin, *Law's Empire* (Cambridge: Harvard University Press, 1986) (hereinafter LE), 54-55, 64-65, 71.
5. p. 114.
6. p. 112. H.L.A. Hart is identified as a proponent of this view. *Id.*, 113.
7. p. 113.

Brink believes that traditional empiricist semantic theory[8] is flawed.[9] The nature of the flaw can be simply stated: empiricist semantic theory fails to draw a distinction between the meaning of a term and anyone's belief about its meaning.[10] By confusing meaning with belief, so Brink argues, legal theorists who embrace traditional semantic theory cannot account for the phenomenon of conceptual disagreement nor can they illuminate the connection between meaning and reference.[11]

The inadequacies of traditional semantic theory can be avoided, so Brink argues, by a realist semantics. Following Saul Kripke[12] and Hilary Putnam,[13] Brink urges legal theorists to adopt a semantics of natural kinds,[14] whereby the meaning of general terms is determined not by anyone's beliefs about their meaning but by reference to properties in the world. As he puts it: "natural kind terms . . . are general terms which refer to properties."[15]

Brink's programme is grounded in a metaethics of moral realism.[16] As he states: "[d]etermination of the meaning and reference of legal standards will often require reliance on theoretical considerations [the metaethics of moral realism] about the real nature of the referents of language in the law . . . ."[17] This is potentially a powerful claim if true, for it means that disputes over the meaning of general legal terms are irresolvable by traditional legal methods, which are clearly institutional.[18]

Despite the appeal of the argument, I think legal theorists would do well to avoid Brink's call to develop a general program of interpretation grounded in a realist semantics.[19] The meaning and reference of legal terms is not reducible to a natural kinds analysis because law is an institutional and not a scientific practice. Contrary to Brink's claims for the felicity of a natural kinds analysis, the meaning of general legal terms cannot be divorced from the beliefs of institutional participants in legal discourse nor can the meaning of general

---

8. Brink describes two versions of traditional semantic theory. He states the following:

   An individualistic theory makes the meaning of a word depend upon the criteria which *the speaker* associates with the word, while the conventionalistic theory makes the meaning of the word depend upon the criteria with which the word is *conventionally* associated or with which it is associated by a *majority*. p. 113.

9. As he describes it, I think he is right. But the strength of Brink's critique of the theory he identifies as 'traditional' depends upon the degree to which it is shared by linguistic philosophers as a whole. I don't believe the theory Brink denominates 'traditional' is the sort of theory advocated by, for example, Wittgenstein (Kripke's claims to the contrary notwithstanding).

   Therefore, I believe that the claims made against the theory Brink labels 'traditional' leave untouched positions that challenge the claims he makes for a realist semantics. Brink admits as much in his statement that his "discussion of these semantic issues will, of necessity, ride roughshod over many interesting details", p. 113.

   Given the focus of this critique of Brink's argument, I will not here defend a traditional theory that avoids the criticisms Brink advances. I have done that elsewhere. See Dennis M. Patterson, "Interpretation in Law: Toward a Reconstruction of the Current Debate," (1984), 29 *Villanova Law Review* 671; Dennis M. Patterson, "Wittgenstein and the Code: A Theory of Good Faith Performance and Enforcement Under Article Nine of the Uniform Commercial Code", (1988), 137 *University of Pennsylvania Law Review* 335. The cogency of my remarks on the semantic theory advanced by Brink do not depend on any alternative semantic theory I may hold.

10. pp. 117, 118, 121. Brink argues that legal theorists give up the claim of traditional semantic theory that meaning determines reference and follow a realist semantics whereby reference determines a meaning. *Ibid.*, 117.

11. p. 113.

12. See Saul Kripke, *Naming and Necessity* (Cambridge: Harvard University Press, 1980).

13. Hilary Putnam, "Meaning and Reference, repr. in *Naming, Necessity, and Natural Kinds*, ed. S. Schwartz (Ithaca: Cornell University Press, 1977), and "The Meaning of 'Meaning,'" repr. in Hilary Putnam, *Mind, Language and Reality* (New York: Cambridge University Press, 1975). It is not entirely clear that Putnam can still be classified as a realist. See Ian Hacking, *Representing and Intervening: Introductory Topics in the Philosophy of Natural Science* (New York: Cambridge University Press, 1983), 95-96.

14. p. 118.

15. p. 120.

16. Brink's metaethical program does not figure directly in his arguments for the assimilation of general legal terms into a natural kinds analysis. The arguments in support of a metaethics of moral realism are advanced in David O. Brink, *Moral Realism and The Foundation of Ethics* (New York: Cambridge University Press, 1989).

17. p. 121.

18. These include appeals to legislative intent, common law principles, and the like. It would also rule out methodological proposals such as Dworkin's model of "constructive interpretation" (L.E. 52-53).

19. pp. 147-148.

legal terms be discerned without reference to the beliefs and purposes embodied in legal institutions.

**2. Not All General Terms are Natural Kind Terms**

Brink asserts that the realist semantics of Kripke and Putnam advance "claims for the semantics of both proper names and general terms, such as natural kind terms."[20] As Brink reads Kripke and Putnam, there is no *in principle* distinction between natural kinds and artificial kinds. As with scientific terms, the meaning and reference of legal terms "is given by the way the world is."[21] Like 'atom,' 'neutrino,' and 'mass,' "'[f]air' and 'cruel' are natural kind terms . . . they are general terms which refer to properties."[22] Therefore, the meaning of, say, constitutional terms is not 'created,' it is discovered.[23]

The meaning of a natural kind term is fixed in the following way; "the substance is defined as the kind instantiated by (almost all of) a given sample. . . . the identity fixes a reference: it therefore is *a priori*."[24] As mentioned previously, Brink does not limit his realism to the domain of science or natural (as opposed to artificial) kinds. His semantic realism is presented in the form of a general argument for the meaning of all general terms.

To demonstrate the shortcomings of Brink's wide-ranging claims for realism, it is not necessary that one prove false the claim of Kripke and Putnam that there are natural kinds: it is only necessary to show that not *all* general terms refer in the way Kripke and Putnam claim that natural kind terms refer.[25]

Consider the meaning of the general legal term 'negotiable instrument.' This term is central to the conventions of drawing, assigning, and paying what are ordinarily referred to as 'checks.'[26] What counts as a check, the legal rights and obligations of the parties to a check, and the manner by which checks are processed for collection are all known by virtue of human conventions. If there were no human beings, or no interest in a system of payment by means other than gold and silver, there would be no negotiable instruments.

Like the vast majority of general legal terms, 'negotiable instrument' is an artifact, a creature of convention. The meaning of 'negotiable instrument' is not "given by the way the world is";[27] there is no "real nature"[28] of a negotiable instrument. We do not "discover"[29] the meaning of 'negotiable instrument' by discerning objects in the world having rigidly designated natural properties. It is only in and through the institutional conventions of commerce that 'negotiable instrument' has its meaning. To know the meaning of this general legal term, one must consult the conventions for its use, for it is solely against that background that participants in legal discourse frame interpretive arguments. Those arguments are shaped through and through by institutional conventions that are constitutive of the discursive practice of law.

---

20. p. 118. Brink also states that "Kripke and Putnam have defended these semantic claims for the semantics of general terms, such as natural kind terms." *Id.*, 120.
21. p. 123.
22. p. 120.
23. p. 123.
24. Saul Kripke, *supra*, note 12 at 136.
25. For a fuller demonstration of this claim, see T.E. Wilkerson, "Natural Kinds", (1988), 63 *Philosophy* 29-42.
26. The rules governing negotiable instruments are found in Articles Three and Four of the Uniform Commercial Code (hereafter U.C.C.).
27. p. 123.
28. p. 121.
29. p. 123.

### 3. Natural Kinds and Statutory Intent

I shall maintain my neutrality on the question of the possible existence of natural kinds, for that neutrality is convenient to the argument I wish to advance here.

One of Brink's central claims about interpretation is that the meaning and reference of legal terms is a function of the way the world is and is not dependent upon the beliefs of anyone.[30] When this claim is brought to bear on the question of how far, and to what extent, legislative purpose determines statutory meaning, the results are problematic.

According to traditional semantic theory, close attention must be paid to the intentions of constitutional or statutory framers[31] because "their intentions place constraints upon constitutional interpretation independently of the plausibility of the framer's moral or political beliefs."[32] But proponents of traditional semantic theory fail to distinguish between specific and abstract intent. An abstract intent takes the form of a policy or principle that is the impetus for particular legislation.[33] Specific intent reduces the extension of abstract intent to "certain actions and not others."[34]

Brink claims that specific intent is less important than proponents of traditional semantic theory take it to be.[35] The nub of his argument is that the meaning of statutory terms should not be tied to the intentions of their authors but is properly determined by our best current theory of the meaning of those terms.

Brink's example is a statute passed in 1945 imposing "strict standards of due care"[36] in the handling of toxic substances. If a court is today to decide a case under the statute involving a substance that, according to the best available theory in 1945, would not be considered toxic, is the court to decide the case on the basis of the best theory in 1945 or today's best theory? According to Brink, if one follows the traditional semantic theory, the court must decide the issue on the basis of the best theory in 1945.[37] On a realist semantics, the court's obligation is to decide the question of toxicity relative to our current best theory of the matter.

A realist semantics runs into trouble when we alter the facts of the hypothetical. Consider a statute written in 1945 that prohibited all fishing within fifty miles of shore. Assume that at the time the statute was promulgated, Congress mistakenly believed that whales and dolphins were fish. In the preamble to the text of the statute Congress announced that the statute was passed to prevent the extinction of all forms of fish "including whales and dolphins." Our best current theory shows that whales and dolphins are not fish but mammals. Is it now the case that the clear meaning of the statute is to be ignored because Congress mistakenly classified whales and dolphins as fish?

---

30. p. 123. ("The meaning and reference of our terms is given by the way the world is ...."); p. 117 ("Beliefs do not determine reference.")
31. Brink explicitly rejects a 'global' distinction between constitutional and statutory interpretation. See p. 119, n. 20.
32. p. 123.
33. p. 122. An example would be the U.C.C.'s purpose to simplify, clarify, and modernize the law governing commercial transactions. See U.C.C. 1-102(2)(a).
34. To continue with the U.C.C., an example of a specific intention is the drafters' particular desire to repeal the common law that firm offers are not enforceable without consideration. See U.C.C. 2-205 (firm offers need not be supported by consideration).
35. p. 122. ("Proponents [of traditional semantic theory] ... insist that the correct interpretation of any legal provision must be guided by, or at least violate, the framers' (specific) intentions.")
36. p. 122.
37. I must confess that the cogency of this claim escapes me, but I will not pursue the matter here. For a powerful argument to the effect that statutory meaning is a function of changing social conditions, see William N. Eskridge, Jr., "Dynamic Statutory Interpretation," (1987), 136 *University of Pennsylvania Law Review* 1479.

The problem for a realist semantics is plain: ignoring Congress' 'mistake' in classifying animals comes at the price of direct frustration of Congress' power to regulate 'fishing.' Obviously, Congress intended to include whales and dolphins within the purview of the statute and did so on the basis of a mistaken theory of classification. But if the court applies the statute to preclude the fishing of whales and dolphins, it can only do so on the basis of an inadequate semantic theory (the traditional theory). The meaning of 'fish' is not determined "by the way the world is":[38] it is determined on the basis of the way Congress then thought the world was. In other words, it is the *belief* of Congress, not natural kind predicates, that determines the interpretive obligations of the court.

## 4. Conclusion

In this article I have argued for two claims. The first is that Brink's claim that all general terms are natural kind terms cannot be sustained. Institutional practices such as law are replete with general terms the meaning of which can only be discerned by investigation of the beliefs and attitudes of participants in the practice.

My second claim is that a realist semantics is itself not free from difficulty when we are invited to adopt it as an exclusive semantic theory for legal interpretation. It is frequently the case that the meaning of a statute in a present context cannot be determined by direct consultation of the specific intentions of the drafters of a statute. But it is sometimes the case that to do otherwise would be to elide the distinction between legislation and adjudication. Disregard of the limitations of a realist semantics leads to just such undesirable outcomes.

38. p. 123.

# [12]



# Semantics and Legal Interpretation (Further Thoughts)

David O. Brink

In my article "Legal Theory, Legal Interpretation, and Judicial Review"[1] I tried to do three main things. First, I tried to establish a link between familiar issues within legal theory about the nature and determinacy of the law and familiar issues within constitutional theory about the scope and record of judicial review via their common dependency on assumptions about the nature of legal interpretation. Second, I argued that a proper theory of interpretation has at least two important components: a theory of the semantics of legal terms and a theory about how best to characterize the purposes or intentions underlying legal provisions. Third, I sketched my own account of these two components of legal interpretation and then explored their implications for these familiar disputes within legal theory and constitutional theory. In particular, the semantic claims that I outlined require us (a) to distinguish between the meaning or reference of legal terms and people's beliefs about the extension of those terms and (b) to rely on theoretical considerations, of various kinds, in ascertaining the extension of general terms occurring in legal provisions. The account of underlying purpose that I sketched requires legal interpreters to identify the purpose of a legal provision with the abstract values that the framers of that provision sought to implement, rather than with the specific activities that they sought to regulate, and then to determine the extension of these values (i.e., the activities that these provisions, properly understood, do regulate) by appeal to theoretical considerations about the nature of these principles and policies. These interpretive claims, I argued, tend to vindicate a belief in the determinacy of the law in hard cases and the style, if not the content, of the Court's exercise of judicial review in cases concerning individual rights, against worries that in these cases it has exceeded the scope of legitimate judicial review.

As this summary indicates, this was (and is) a large project, many aspects of which I was forced to ignore or treat programmatically. Dennis Patterson's reply to my article forces me to clarify and develop some of these programmatic remarks and arguments. I shall discuss the two criticisms Patterson makes of my claims about the semantics of legal interpretation (sections 1 and 2) and conclude by clarifying some of my remarks about legal interpretation and determinacy in the law (section 3). My discussion will assume that readers of the present article have read the earlier one and recall at least the main arguments for the claims summarized above.

## 1. REALISM AND THE SEMANTICS OF LEGAL INTERPRETATION

Patterson thinks that my suggestions about the appropriate semantics for legal interpretation require realist metaphysical assumptions and argues that, even if such assumptions are acceptable as applied the natural sciences, they are inappropriate assumptions as applied

I would like to thank Alan Sidelle for helpful comments on an earlier draft.

1. David O. Brink, "Legal Theory, Legal Interpretation, and Judicial Review" (1988), 17 *Philosophy & Public Affairs* 105. Parenthetical references in the text are to pages in this article.

to the sort of social institutions and other social artifacts with which the law deals. Patterson's reasoning seems to be something like this.

(1) My claims about the semantics of legal interpretation require me to accept what is sometimes called "the theory of direct reference" (e.g., Kripke-Putnam semantics) as applied to legal terms.

(2) The theory of direct reference requires the truth of metaphysical realism.

(3) Metaphysical realism about some subject matter *x* requires that there be facts or truths about *x* that are mind-independent.

(4) Law, like many social sciences, is concerned with artifactual objects (e.g., institutions, relations, and instruments), and artifactual objects are the product of minds, not mind-independent.

(5) Hence, my semantic claims do not apply to legal terms and legal interpretation.

On one reading, this argument is valid but not sound; on no reading is it sound. (1) is false. (2)'s status is unclear; it may depend upon how we understand 'realism'. (3) is problematic until we know more about how to understand 'mind-dependent': on a broad reading, (3) is false; on a narrower reading, it may be true. (4) is uncontroversial only on the broad reading of 'mind-independent' (on which (3) is clearly false); it's much more problematic on the narrow reading that makes (3) true. This fact about the two readings of 'mind-independent' by itself suggests that the argument is either invalid, because it equivocates between two distinct senses of 'mind-dependent', or unsound, on either univocal reading of 'mind-independent'. Let me explain these claims.

After rejecting certain aspects of the traditional empiricist semantic theory, which I take to underlie common views in legal theory and constitutional theory, on the ground that that theory cannot adequately represent phenomena of disagreement, I sketched two constraints that any adequate semantic theory should meet and explained how Kripke-Putnam semantic claims meet these constraints. My interpretive project will work on any semantic theory that meets two constraints for general terms that function as natural kind terms: an adequate theory must (a) deny that the descriptions conventionally associated with such terms determine the extension of those terms and so distinguish appropriately between changes in speakers' beliefs and changes in the meaning and reference of their terms, and (b) recognize the role of theoretical considerations in ascertaining meaning and reference. Patterson is certainly right that I discuss and make some use of the semantic claims of the theory of direct reference (TDR) and that I am sympathetic to these claims. But he is wrong to suppose that my interpretive theory requires TDR. As I indicated in the article (116-9, esp. 118), TDR is *one* way to meet the two constraints. As I will shortly explain, nothing Patterson says prevents application of TDR to legal terms. But my position does not depend upon this; it requires only that (a) and (b) apply to the semantics of legal terms.

TDR assumes that language users interact with their natural and social environment in certain ways; in particular, they introduce terms (e.g., names and general terms) to pick out interesting features of their environment. In the idealized case, a group of speakers introduces a term in this way; what their term refers to is that bit of the environment (e.g., that object, property, or relation) that explains what they found interesting and intended to pick out. Subsequent speakers borrow this term with the intention of referring to the same thing; their use of the term inherits reference to the same features of the environment via a historical-causal chain extending from their use of the term, through the original "dubbing ceremony," to the relevant aspects of the environment. Thus, for example, the term 'water' was introduced to pick out the colorless, odorless, stuff found in lakes, rivers, etc. that is suitable for drinking, bathing, supporting life, etc. This liquid is actually made of $H_2O$, and it is this chemical composition that allows it to serve these various functional roles. TDR claims that this fact implies that past, and present use of 'water' refers to $H_2O$. Since people have not always realized that the chemical composition of water is $H_2O$ or even that water has a chemical composition, TDR implies that people can use terms meaningfully while being quite ignorant, perhaps mistaken, about the extension of their terms. It is also this feature of TDR that allows us to see how people with quite different beliefs about the extension of a term can be using it univocally, and so how they can be in genuine disagreement (as people who use terms in different senses are not).[2] This is perhaps enough by way of explanation of TDR for us to begin to evaluate Patterson's criticisms of its applications to the semantics of legal interpretation.

Since we cannot decide whether TDR requires metaphysical realism without knowing what the latter doctrine involves, we cannot evaluate (2) prior to (3). No doubt, (3) represents a common initial formulation of realism. Realism, say, about the external world seems to be the view that there is a world external to cognizers that exists independently of their experiences of it or their beliefs about it, correspondence with which makes their beliefs about the world true (if they're true). Realism about the external world contrasts with various anti-realist views (e.g., idealism or phenomenalism) that seem to deny that there is a world independent of our experiences or beliefs. But the formulation of the realism/anti-realism debate in terms of mind-independence/dependence doesn't take us very far; those who have tried to formulate the debate in global terms (i.e., terms that apply correctly to all disciplines about which we want to formulate realist and anti-realist theses) know how difficult this is.[3]

First, we need to be clear about the kind of *dependence* that is involved in the anti-realist's claim about mind-dependence and the realist's claim about mind-independence. One thing is clear: it cannot be causal dependence. Everyone admits that some objects – artifacts – are causally dependent on human minds; they are the causal products of, among other things, their designers' beliefs and desires. Admitting this obvious fact does not make one an anti-realist about artifacts. So the dependence in question is not causal; rather, it must be something like logical, conceptual, or metaphysical dependence. The anti-realist claims, and the realist denies, that facts, say, about an external world are literally constituted by our beliefs or experience.

Even if we understand 'dependence' as something like logical or metaphysical dependence, *mind*-dependency cannot be the issue; it's too broad. For instance, most philosophers assume that there are realist and anti-realist theses about psychology and psychological states, but nearly all parties to the dispute (including the realists) agree that psychological states are mind-dependent. (Indeed, one form of psychological anti-realism – behaviorism – might actually be thought to deny this!) It seems we need something narrower than simple mind-dependency. One suggestion that would seem to work for some debates is that the issue is one of *evidence*-dependency. That is, a realist thinks that facts and truths about *p* are independent of those beliefs that are our evidence that *p*, while anti-realists either deny that there are facts or truths about *p* or think that facts or truths about *p* are in some

2. Compare this sketch with Saul Kripke, *Naming and Necessity* (Cambridge, MA: Harvard University Press, 1980) and Hilary Putnam, "The Meaning of 'Meaning'" reprinted in his *Mind, Language, and Reality: Philosophical Papers, Vol. 2* (New York: Cambridge University Press, 1975).

3. See, e.g., Elliot Sober, "Realism and Independence" (1982), 16 *Nous* 369 and my *Moral Realism and the Foundations of Ethics* (New York: Cambridge University Press, 1989), pp. 14-19.

way constituted by our beliefs about *p*. Thus, the philosopher who claims that *p* is true for those who believe it is an anti-realist. And so is the more sophisticated philosopher who claims that the truth of a belief about *p* consists in its being part of an ideally justified system of beliefs. I doubt that even this narrower reading of the realism/anti-realism dispute in terms of belief-dependence or evidence-dependence can provide the basis for a global characterization of that dispute, but it seems more helpful than the initial, broad reading in terms of simple mind-dependence.

Does TDR presuppose realism, as (2) claims? Obviously, TDR does not imply realism under the broad reading. Whether TDR presupposes realism under the more sensible, narrow reading is less clear. We might suppose TDR is agnostic as between realism and anti-realism if we think that it makes claims only about how (as they say) "words hook onto the world" and not about what metaphysical story to tell about the world. If we take one of the points of TDR to be to explain how it is possible for speakers, as individuals or as groups, to be ignorant of or mistaken about the real nature of the referents of their terms, then we might suppose that TDR is incompatible with those forms of anti-realism that think truth is constituted by a cognizer's beliefs or the beliefs of a group of cognizers. But *this* need not show that TDR requires realism; a sophisticated form of anti-realism, say, that identified truth with belief that would be accepted by people at the limit of rational inquiry could presumably accept TDR's claims that particular speakers and particular groups of speakers could be mistaken about the nature of the referents of their terms. So whether TDR requires realism, even when it is understood in this narrower way, seems quite unclear. Certainly, a great deal more needs to be said about TDR and the realism/anti-realism dispute before we should accept (2).

We've seen that (3) is plausible only on some narrow interpretation of 'mind-dependence' – such as belief-dependence or evidence-dependence, where the dependence in question is logical or metaphysical, not causal. If the argument is to be valid, then (4) must be true on this same, narrow reading of 'mind-dependent'. But there's the rub. It's only on the much broader, implausible reading of 'mind-dependent' that (4) is uncontroversially true. It's uncontroversial that artifacts, including social institutions and practices, are the causal products (in part) of people's beliefs, desires, and other mental states. It's often *claimed* that there is some more intimate, constitutive relation between people's beliefs, desires, and understandings, on the one hand, and their social institutions and practices, on the other. But it's very unclear that these claims can be made precise and plausible in a way that an intelligent formulation of realism would deny. No doubt, our understanding of our practices can influence our behavior and so can change the nature of our practices over time, but this does not seem to show that the social facts in question are constituted by our conceptions of them (certainly not if 'influence' and 'change' can be understood causally). Certainly, there's nothing obviously wrong with the realist claim that there are facts about social institutions, practices, and relations that are independent of particular people's conceptions of those institutions, practices, and relations in the following senses: (i) those social phenomena are the *object of* people's conceptions and so antedate those conceptions; (ii) people's conceptions about those phenomena can be mistaken about the real nature of the phenomena; (iii) when people's conceptions of those phenomena are correct it is in virtue of correctly describing the nature of those institutions, practices, and relations. Whether realism is committed to anything more controversial about the nature of artifacts and social facts than (i)-(iii) is unclear. The matter obviously cannot be settled here; but then precisely for this reason Patterson has not succeeded in making (4) plausible on a reasonable interpretation of 'mind-dependent'.

In some ways, this debate about (4) is unimportant, since neither my semantic constraints nor TDR seems to require realism. All these semantic claims presuppose is the kind of objectivity and fallibility in social domains secured by claims (i)-(iii) in the previous paragraph. If (i)-(iii) amount to realism about social artifacts, then these semantic claims may require realism, but this is no indictment of those semantic claims. If, on the other hand, (i)-(iii) are compatible with sophisticated forms of anti-realism, then so are these semantic claims.

It is somewhat surprising that Patterson thinks it so clear that TDR cannot provide a semantics for artifactual terms, since Putnam has explicitly defended it for artifactual terms.[4] Insofar as TDR applies to general terms, it is usually defended for natural kind terms. Perhaps Patterson has in mind a contrast between what is natural and what is artificial or artifactual; with this contrast in mind, one might suppose that TDR does not apply to terms for (certain) social kinds. But as I suggested in my article (120-1), and as discussions of TDR reflect, the relevant sense of 'natural' in the claim that TDR offers a semantics for natural kind terms is not 'natural scientific' or 'non-artifactual' but something like 'theoretical' or 'explanatory'.[5] Roughly, the idea is that a natural kind is a property or universal that figures in laws and explanatory generalizations. If so, it seems that social and, in particular, legal kinds will be natural kinds every bit as much as are chemical and biological kinds. Singular explanatory claims referring to legal instruments, entities, or institutions are justified only if there are interesting explanatory generalizations about individuals and society involving relations, roles, and institutions of that sort.

TDR implies that the meaning and reference of legal terms is given by the real nature of the institutions, practices, and relations with which speakers have interacted and continue to interact and is not determined by the descriptions conventionally associated with those terms or by people's beliefs about the extension of their terms. In particular, people can hold more or less mistaken beliefs about the real nature of the social institutions, practices, and relations that the law concerns. These semantic claims are all perfectly compatible with recognition of the obvious fact that the real nature of these institutions, practices, and relations *is social*, viz. that they not only are the product of social organization but themselves involve certain psychological relations holding among people (e.g., certain forms of mutual trust and mutual expectation).

I draw the following conclusions. First, my semantic claims do not commit me to all the details of TDR; TDR is one semantic theory that meets my constraints. Second, TDR does not obviously require metaphysical realism, though this will depend upon how we understand realism. Third, on no reasonable understanding of realism is it clear that one cannot be a realist about artifactual, social, or legal facts. Fourth, my semantic constraints and TDR do seem to apply to social kinds of the sort the law deals with. I hope these conclusions are enough to vindicate the hope expressed in my article (112-3) that the programmatic character of the semantic claims discussed there conceals no significant or relevant distortion.

---

4. See Putnam, "The Meaning of 'Meaning'", supra note 2 at 242-4.
5. Of course, I don't care about the *word* 'natural'. If one likes, one can insist on the narrow reading of 'natural kind'; my claim will then be that TDR and my own semantic constraints apply to social and legal kind terms as well as natural kind terms.

## 2. SEMANTICS AND LEGISLATIVE PURPOSE IN STATUTORY INTERPRETATION

Here things get a little less abstract. Patterson thinks that my claims about the semantics of legal interpretation lead to absurd interpretive conclusions. He considers a case involving the interpretation of a somewhat dated environmental protection statute drafted under the mistaken belief that whales are fish. The statute prohibits all fishing within fifty miles of shore *and* expresses in its preamble the purpose of preventing the "extinction of all forms of fish, including whales and dolphins." According to Patterson, my semantic claims commit me to what he takes to be the absurd view that the statute should be interpreted so as to allow the fishing of whales and dolphins within the fifty mile limit – contrary to the plain intentions of the legislature. I guess that I agree that *this* would be an absurd interpretive conclusion, but I see absolutely no reason to suppose that I'm committed to it. Patterson both misinterprets my interpretive claims and misapplies them to his own case.

Patterson mistakenly assumes, here and at other points in his discussion, that I take my claims about the semantics of interpretation to provide a complete theory of legal interpretation. In this case, he assumes that I must think that the correct interpretation of the statute consists entirely in determining what (on my semantic view) the extension of 'fishes' is and, in particular, that I must ignore the evident legislative intent to protect marine life generally. He defends this assumption by noting my argument against *semantic* reliance on *specific* intent (121-4). But this does not show that I reject interpretive appeal to underlying purpose. Indeed, one of my central aims in that article is to argue that semantic content and underlying purpose are *both* components of interpretation; they are distinct and comparatively autonomous, though not completely independent, aspects of interpretation that can, in some cases, conflict (124-9). I argue that in the interpretive appeal to underlying purpose we must often decide how best to characterize this purpose or intent and, in particular, that we must choose between the *abstract* intent or purpose (i.e., the kind of principle, policy, or value that the framers of the legal provision were trying to implement) and the *specific* intent or purpose (i.e., the particular activities that the framers expected the provision to regulate). In the article I appealed to a counterfactual test to determine which kind of purpose is dominant and argued that, by this test, abstract intent is typically dominant. Now it seems to me that application of this counterfactual test to this situation would establish the dominance of abstract intent and support identifying the relevant abstract intent as something like the preservation of marine life. Had the legislators' collateral beliefs been somewhat different, in particular, had they realized that whales are not fish, they would have redrafted the statute in terms of marine life, rather than fish. My interpretive theory claims we must interpret the statute in light of this abstract intent, as well as in light of the meaning of the language in which the statute is expressed, and do so in light of our own collateral beliefs about the extension of this abstract purpose. Since it is reasonable to claim that whales are a kind of marine life, even if they are not fish, interpretive appeal to underlying purpose argues in favor of regulating the "fishing" of marine mammals as well as fish. And since appeal to underlying purpose can override semantic content, if these conflict (124-5, 129), my interpretive views allow the interpretive conclusion that Patterson endorses – even if the semantic content of the statute pulls in the other direction.

Nor is it clear that the semantic content of the statute (even on my semantic views) pulls in the other direction; certainly, it does not pull unequivocally in that direction. First, notice that, though the statute contains a preamble that expresses a purpose underlying the legislative rule, the *legislative rule* itself prohibits all fishing within fifty miles of the shore and not just the fishing of certain species,genera or classes. Here, I assume that the gerund 'fishing' has within its extension the catching of marine animals or marine life and not simply the catching of fish; I don't see anything about my own semantic claims or TDR that prevents this. To make this point clear, we might distinguish fishing and *fish*ing and insist that 'fishing' and '*fish*ing' are not synonymous. If this assumption is right, then the statutory rule requires the regulation of whaling within the fifty mile limit, even if the *express* purpose for this rule is in a way narrower. (And, after all, a statutory rule of this sort need only bear a *rational* relation to a legitimate legislative purpose.) Since the express reference to fish is in the preamble, it seems that even the semantics of the statutory rule supports the desired interpretive conclusion.

Moreover, even if we assume (contrary to what I have just claimed) that the use of 'fish' in the express preamble is part of the rule, no untoward interpretive conclusions follow. *Insofar as* 'fish' is part of the statutory rule, the rule will not apply to whaling.[6] But *insofar as* (a) the rule is formulated in terms of 'all fishing' (and my semantic assumptions about 'fishing' in the previous paragraph are sound), and (b) 'including whales and dolphins' is part of the rule, the rule does apply to whaling within the fifty mile limit. This is just to say that insofar as we're concerned only with the semantic content of the statute and insofar as we include the language of the preamble as part of the statutory rule, then we should think that the statute is internally inconsistent. But I see nothing odd or absurd about *this* interpretive claim. And, of course, this interpretive claim does not commit me to the absurd interpretive claim that the statute is correctly interpreted as allowing whaling within the fifty mile limit, since I do not think semantic content exhausts interpretation and also since I think that we may legitimately doubt that the express preamble is part of the statutory rule.

But let's not focus on peripheral or unintended features of Patterson's example and discussion. Consider two cleaner examples. Consider the text of two preambleless statutes against the same legislative background Patterson assumes.

> S1: There will be no catching of fish (i.e., no *fish*ing) within fifty miles of shore; this regulation includes whales and dolphins.

Does S1 commit me to the absurd interpretive conclusion that, correctly interpreted (by my lights), the statute permits whaling within the fifty mile limit? I claim that S1 is *semantically* inconsistent, and (again) I think that *this* is a plausible interpretive claim. This does not require me to say that S1 is *interpretively* indeterminate; interpretation requires appeal to the abstract intent to preserve marine life, and so the correct interpretation requires the regulation of fishing as well as *fish*ing.

Consider the semantically consistent statute S2.

> S2: There will be no catching of fish (i.e., no *fish*ing) within fifty miles of shore.

I admit that I am committed to claiming that the *semantic content* of S2 implies that whaling within the fifty mile limit is not prohibited. But semantic content does not exhaust inter-

---

6. Even this, I think, is not required either by TDR or by my own semantic constraints [(a) and (b)]. Since there may be different important explanatory features underlying the use of kind terms in different communities (e.g. the biological community and the "fishing" community), there may be reason to recognize different dialects corresponding to the use of these terms by different communities. If so, then we couldn't decide what the extension of 'fish' is independently of specifying which dialect the term occurred in. As I say, I think these claims are perfectly compatible with my claims in the article and TDR, but since they do muddy the waters a bit, it may be best to ignore them for the present purposes.

pretation; interpretation requires appeal to underlying purpose also. And, as before, the underlying purpose is the abstract intent to preserve marine life, and so abstract intent (again) requires the regulation of fishing as well as *fish*ing. This is a case where my two components of interpretation – meaning and purpose – conflict. It was an explicit part of my theory to recognize the possibility of such conflicts and to allow that abstract intent can often predominate in such situations (124-9); this seems to me to be such a case. I offered no algorithm for resolving such interpretive conflicts, though I did sketch a general account of the structure of legal interpretation within which such conflicts would be adjudicated (129-33). It is within such a framework that I would have to defend the interpretive preference for abstract intent over semantic content in this case if I was challenged; as far as I'm concerned, this is as it should be.

## 3. SEMANTICS AND INTERPRETIVE DETERMINACY

In explaining the dependence of familiar disputes within legal theory on interpretive assumptions, I argued that belief in the determinacy of the law, even in so-called hard cases, of the sort that appeals to people like Ronald Dworkin and Rolf Sartorius (see 106), cannot be defended against H.L.A. Hart's arguments for judicial discretion (see 106-7) without rejecting his semantic assumptions about the open-texture of legal language (111-4). I also argued that my own alternative semantic claims block Hart's argument for legal indeterminacy and judicial discretion (119-20). I'd like to clarify these claims a little and discuss the more general issue about the relation between my interpretive theory and debates about legal determinacy.[7]

My position was not and is not that my semantic claims establish the strong determinacy thesis that there is a uniquely correct (non-tie) legal answer in even the hardest of hard cases. Rather, my claim is that my semantic claims block the standard argument for legal indeterminacy and judicial discretion, because they show that that standard argument rests on mistaken semantic assumptions. Now it may be that Hart's basic argument can be understood or perhaps reformulated in ways that do not rest on the suspect semantic claims. Here's one suggestion.

Hart's argument, as I reconstructed it, argues for semantic indeterminacy and, hence, legal indeterminacy, from disagreement over the application of a legal provision, via his semantic assumptions about open-texture. I argued that, given the dialectical role that these semantic assumptions serve, they seem best understood as relying on the traditional empiricist semantic theory (TEST) according to which (i) the meaning of a term or phrase is the set of descriptions conventionally associated with it, and (ii) meaning determines reference. TEST implies that in hard cases in which legal disagreement reflects the fact that legal principals associate different criteria with the legal terms in question the legal provision in question is semantically indeterminate. This kind of *criterial* disagreement is certainly one kind of open-texture that concerns Hart and that motivates his argument for indeter-

7. The thoughts in this section were prompted by some of the reactions to the original article by my MIT colleagues Dick Cartwright, Paul Hoffman, and Judy Thomson.

minacy and discretion.[8] And my objections to TEST and my alternative semantic claims do block the argument from criterial disagreement to indeterminacy.

But a friend of indeterminacy and discretion might reply that TEST connects only one kind of disagreement and one kind of open-texture with indeterminacy. If so, rejection of TEST may not block all of Hart's arguments for open-texture and indeterminacy. While some legal disagreement is between people who disagree about the criteria for applying the legal terms in question (these are the criterial disputes), some disagreement is between people that agree on the criteria for applying the term but disagree over whether the case in question satisfies those criteria. If such a dispute is to support a finding of open-texture and indeterminacy, it cannot be that one of the parties to the disagreement is just mistaken about the facts of the case. Instead, the suggestion is that there are disputes like this that concern *borderline* or *fuzzy* cases. A paradigm of a fuzzy property would be, say, an extremely dark charcoal shade. Is it gray or black? It seems natural to say that this shade falls within the open-texture of the terms 'gray' and 'black'; it is semantically indeterminate which predicate applies to the shade, and it is metaphysically indeterminate whether it is black or gray. Suppose, artificially, that some statute regulated all and only *x*s that are black. It seems natural to claim that this statute is open-textured, that for this reason its application to an *x* that is this dark shade of charcoal is indeterminate, and that for this reason the law in such a case is indeterminate. *This* kind of open-texture and indeterminacy does not seem to presuppose TEST, and so my semantic claims do nothing to block this kind of open-texture and indeterminacy in the law.

I agree with this, and it may be sufficient to block the claim for strong determinacy that there is a right (non-tie) answer for every possible case at law,[9] but I doubt very much that it reinstates the standard view about the indeterminacy of hard cases. I take Hart's view and the standard view to be that we are in the open-texture of a legal provision and that the law is, hence, indeterminate whenever there is fairly widespread disagreement over the application of the language of the provision to a case that does not depend upon some misunderstanding or ignorance about the facts of the case. If my rejection of TEST is correct, the standard view can be maintained, then, only if the vast majority of these disputes involve fuzzy cases, rather than criterial disputes. But, as a friend of moderately strong determinacy, I submit that this claim is implausible and, moreover, that it would in any case be insufficient to establish indeterminacy if my interpretive claims are correct.

It just seems incredibly implausible that most cases that are controversial in this sense are fuzzy cases. Consider some constitutional issues that I imagine proponents of the standard view must take to be legally indeterminate. Surely when people disagree over whether due process requires the exclusionary rule, whether the death penalty is cruel and unusual punishment, or whether there is a right to privacy and, if so, whether it generates rights to get abortions in certain circumstances (free from governmental interference), it is not the case that they accept the same criteria of due process, justifiable punishment, constitutional interpretation, or privacy and disagree only about the degree to which the practices

8. Cf. H.L.A. Hart, *The Concept of Law* (New York: Oxford University Press, 1961) [hereafter *CL*], esp. pp. 121-35, 200. Hart's discussion of open-texture does not explicitly mention disagreement; he talks more about uncertainty and lack of guidance (e.g. *CL*: 123, 124, 127). But it nonetheless seems right to see serious disagreement as signalling open-texture. First, we would expect uncertainty when there are competing arguments about the meaning of a provision, and Hart himself often speaks of the discretionary resolution of open-texture as concerned to address *competing* interests (*CL*: 126, 128). Second, I rely on Hart's belief that the rule-skeptics among the Legal Realists were right insofar as they recognized the limited determinacy of legal rules (e.g. *CL*: 135), and I take the rule-skeptics to be (over) impressed by the phenomena of legal disagreement.

9. It may be worth noting that, as far as I know, no one – including Dworkin and Sartorius - has made *this* claim.

in question satisfy these criteria.[10] Rather, their disagreement about these issues results from their having and employing quite different beliefs about the nature of these controversial moral and political issues. Nor do I see reason to suppose that disputes within civil (e.g., tort, contract, or probate) or criminal law are much different. For example, debates about whether a particular manufacturer was negligent in the manufacture of its product or the disposal of its waste typically reflect disagreement over the appropriate standards of care in the particular industry given available technology and knowledge and over the care that the manufacturer actually took, not debates about whether – given agreement on all these issues – what the manufacturer did crossed the threshold between sufficient care and negligence. I'm not claiming that no legal disputes concern fuzzy cases; I'm claiming only that this seems to be more the exception, than the rule. Only a closer analysis of an extremely wide range of cases could begin to settle this issue. But if the question is whether we should accept significant legal indeterminacy solely on the basis of fuzzy cases, then I think we have good prima facie reason to doubt an affirmative answer.

Moreover, it is worth noting that on my account of legal interpretation, legal indeterminacy does not follow from the semantic indeterminacy of legal provisions. This is because (a) the interpretation of a legal provision must also be guided by appeal to its underlying purpose (abstract intent) (124-9), and (b) what the law requires in a particular case is the decision that coheres best with the total body of legal standards, and not just what the correct interpretation of the closest legal provision, considered by itself, dictates (129-33). These two aspects of legal interpretation imply that a (fuzzy) case involving a provision that is semantically indeterminate may nonetheless be interpretively determinate.[11]

We can illustrate the influence of (a) with another usefully artificial example. Consider the interpretation of a public safety statute that expressly prohibits bicyclists from wearing black clothing while bicycling at night unless they also wear reflective equipment. The statute may be semantically indeterminate as applied to Spike who was caught bicycling alongside the highway at night, clad in dark charcoal clothes, and wearing no reflective equipment. But assuming that the (abstract) purpose underlying the statute is to prevent traffic accidents involving bicyclists, it would be reasonable to claim that, properly interpreted, the statute applies to Spike. Here we have semantic indeterminacy (involving fuzzy cases) without interpretive indeterminacy.

(b) can resolve semantic indeterminacy (involving fuzzy cases) if general, structural principles apply to the case and favor one side or the other. Such principles would include

---

10. Proponents of the standard view who also accept what Dworkin calls the "strict doctrine of precedent," according to which judges are obliged to follow past decisions of certain courts even when they believe those decisions to be interpretively mistaken, may think that the Supreme Court has, in some instances, resolved these indeterminancies in constitutional law by having exercised judicial discretion. (Cf. Ronald Dworkin, *Law's Empire* (Cambridge, MA: Harvard University Press, 1986), 24-6). For example, they might hold that *Mapp v. Ohio* (367 U.S. 643 (1961)) resolved the indeterminacy that there was concerning whether due process requires the exclusionary rule. This need not affect my point. First, I think that the strict doctrine of precedent is least plausible as applied to the Court itself in important constitutional matters. Whereas, in some civil matters it is arguably more important to adopt some rule than it is to adopt any particular rule (think of rules of the road), this is presumably not true in weighty constitutional matters; here it is arguably more important to get the rule right than it is to adhere to the same rule. Second, the strict doctrine of precedent, if defensible, is itself a principle of the legal system and figures in, among other things, constitutional interpretation; therefore, its relevance to constitutional interpretation could be acknowledged without supposing that it resolves the indeterminacy in the particular constitutional provisions (e.g. due process and cruel and unusual punishment clauses) themselves. Finally, even if we accept the strict doctrine of precedent and suppose that precedents can resolve indeterminancies in constitutional provisions, we could focus on the indeterminacy in the constitutional provisions *prior* to their resolution by the Court's exercise of judicial legislation.

11. It's true that Hart sometimes recognizes these extra-semantic aspects of interpretation; but (a) it's not clear that he thinks they're ever sufficient to resolve semantic indeterminacy, and (b) in any case, he seems to think of these aspects of judicial decision-making as extra-legal (cf. *CL*: 200).

what we might call *closure principles*. Closure principles would remove the indeterminacy of fuzzy cases in the following way. Consider a provision that regulates all and only *x*s that are F and its application to a fuzzy case involving an *x* that is G, where G is somewhat F but not fully F. A *strict* closure rule would require that G*x* be regulated as F*x*, while a *lenient* closure rule would imply that G*x* not be regulated as F*x*. There might be reasons to accept different kinds of closure principles for different kinds of laws. For instance, a common concern for individual liberties might lead to adoption of both a strict closure principle for the interpretation of constitutional constraints on the state that are designed to protect individual rights (e.g., due process, equal protection) and a lenient closure rule for the interpretation of provisions of the criminal law. Indeed, I think that our legal system does embody these two closure principles in this kind of principled way, though it would require much more argument to defend this claim adequately. (Some evidence for the lenient closure rule in the criminal law is the evidentiary principle that assigns to the prosecution the strong burden of proof that guilt be established beyond a reasonable doubt.)

These are reasons to think that the extra-semantic components of interpretation will often resolve those semantic indeterminacies that remain after we reject TEST. My interpretive claims, therefore, do not vindicate the strong determinacy claim that there is a uniquely correct (non-tie) legal answer to every possible case at law, but they do support healthy skepticism that there is significant indeterminacy in the law.

[13]



# What Was Realism?: A Reply to David Brink

Dennis M. Patterson

## Introduction

Professor Brink's response to my critique of his essay both raises and clarifies a number of questions that I wish to pursue further. In this response to his rebuttal to my critique, I shall discuss three issues: (1) the traditional meaning of realism; (2) the meaning of 'real' in Brink's arguments; and (3) Brink's resort to *purpose* as a tool in statutory interpretation.

## 1. What Was Realism?

Are meanings in the mind or in the world? This is the frame within which the realism/nominalism[1] debate has proceeded since its inception. In the twentieth century, proponents of realism have made many things the object of their attention.[2] Brink, himself a realist,[3] advocates a realist approach to legal theory, specifically of the objects of legal interpretation (whatever they may be). At least that is what I took him to be saying when I read his original essay.[4]

I say that I *thought* Brink made his arguments from a realist perspective because the central claim of his essay seemed to be that the meaning of legal terms is determined by *the way the world is* and not by anyone's beliefs about the world.[5] In short, Brink's overall perspective seemed to be consistent with the posture of traditional realism: that there are indeed entities in the world which do not depend for their meaning on any particular language we use to refer to them. After reading his reply to my comments on his essay, I am not now certain where to place his arguments.

## 2. The Meaning of 'Real'

I think the meaning of 'real', as employed by Brink, changes. In my view, this equivocation produces a fundamental ambiguity in his argument. 'Real' has two different senses for him: a. "true" or "correct" nature of the meaning of '*X*' as determined by some theory of *X*; b. "real in the world," as explained in Section 1 above. I read Brink's original essay as advocating the second of these two senses of 'real'.[6] In his reply, he seems clearly to be employing the first sense of 'real'.

---

I wish to thank Barry Hoffmaster for conversation on the issues considered in this reply and Jeff White for his editorial and substantive suggestions.

1. In framing the dichotomy "realism/nominalism", I am aware that the right side of the dichotomy could just as easily be filled in with "psychologism" and "idealism". The basic point of the realism/nominalism distinction, which is the role of universals in thought will, I hope, become clear.
2. These include linguistic entities (Frege), moral states or properties (Moore) and, of late, scientific entities (Kripke, Putnam).
3. See David O. Brink, *Moral Realism and the Foundations of Ethics* (Cambridge: Cambridge U.P. 1989).
4. David O. Brink, "Legal Theory, Legal Interpretation, and Judicial Review," (1988), 17 *Philosophy and Public Affairs* 105.
5. *Id.* at 123 ("The meaning and reference of our terms is given by the way the world is ...."); p. 117 ("Beliefs do not determine reference").
6. In "Legal Realism and Legal Theory" I document the many places in Professor Brink's original essay where such a reading is supported.

On page 184 of his reply to me, Brink describes the following three claims as realist:

> [T]here are facts about social institutions, practices, and relations in the following senses: (i) those social phenomena are the *object of* people's conceptions and so antedate those conceptions; (ii) people's conceptions about those phenomena can be mistaken about the real nature of the phenomena; (iii) when people's conceptions of those phenomena are correct it is in virtue of correctly describing the nature of those institutions, practices, and relations.[7]

In reading this paragraph, one gets the impression that the second sense, b., of 'real' is intended.[8] In the next paragraph, Brink signals that he does not mean to make the bolder claim for realism at all. He says, "[a]ll these semantic claims presuppose is the kind of objectivity and fallibility in social domains secured by claims (i)-(iii) in the previous paragraph."[9] Following this caveat, Brink confirms one's suspicion that 'real' does not mean *real in the world* at all but something roughly equivalent to a., "what our best theory of *X* is." Consider: "[T]he relevant sense of 'natural' in the claim that TDR offers a semantics for natural kind terms is *not* 'natural scientific' or 'non-artifactual' but something like 'theoretical' or 'explanatory'."[10] This definition (explication) of real shows Brink distancing himself from the definition of 'real' in Section 1 above.

Brink's use of the word 'real' hides more than it reveals. If the meaning of '*X*' is co-extensive with some theory of '*X*''s denotation, then I fail to see what is added by the claim that "there is a real meaning of '*X*'." If 'real *X*' simply means *the best theory of* X, then 'real' is idle; it just obscures the discussion.

### 3. Does 'Real' Do Any Work?

I do not see that appeals to the "the way the world *really* is" do any work in Brink's reformulation of his position. Perhaps the best evidence for my claim that 'real' does no work in his arguments is in the second and third sections of his reply. At no point in these two sections does Brink make any claims about the way the world *really* is.

What he does offer is further elaboration of his theory of statutory interpretation. In response to my Mammalian counterexample to his original claims for the theoretical power of semantic realism, Brink advances a purposive theory of interpretation. The key to the theory is in the distinction between abstract and concrete intent. As he puts the matter:

> [I]n the interpretive appeal to underlying purpose, we must often decide how best to characterize this purpose or intent and, in particular, that we must choose between the *abstract* intent or purpose (i.e. the kind of principle, policy, or value that the framers of the legal provision were trying to implement) and the specific intent or purpose (i.e. the particular activities that the framers expected the provision to regulate).[11]

I do not see that this distinction supports Brink's contention that his "semantic claims block the standard argument for legal indeterminacy and judicial discretion because they show that that standard argument rests on mistaken semantic assumptions."[12] What Brink

7. David O. Brink, "Semantics and Legal Interpretation (Further Thoughts)," (1989), II *Canadian Journal of Law and Jurisprudence* 184 [hereinafter "Further Thoughts".]
8. At least I get that sense that the use of the phrase "real nature of the phenomena".
9. "Further Thoughts", p. 185.
10. *Id.* (emphasis added).
11. *Id.* at 186.
12. *Id.* at 188.

needs to show is how "the way the world is" connects up with the judicial construction of "abstract intention". The reason this is so important is that any statute or line of cases is amenable to more than one purposive reconstruction. If purpose can be theoretically overdetermined, then appeals to realism must demonstrate how choice among competing purposive interpretations of legal materials is accomplished. For a realist this is no small task. I wish Professor Brink well in this venture.

# Part III
# Contemporary Debates about Indeterminacy

# [14]

Texas Law Review

Volume 60, Number 3, March 1982

## Law as Literature

Sanford Levinson*

### I

> [T]he process of reading is not a half-sleep, but, in highest sense, an exercise, a gymnast's struggle; . . . the reader is to do something for himself, must be on the alert, must himself or herself construct indeed the poem, argument, history, metaphysical essay—the text furnishing the hints, the clue, the start or framework. Not the book needs so much to be the complete thing, but the reader of the book does. That were to make a nation of supple and athletic minds, well-train'd, intuitive, used to depend on themselves, and not on a few coteries of writers.
>
> Walt Whitman, *Democratic Vistas*[1]

> Ultimately, man finds in things nothing but what he himself has imported into them: the finding is called science. . .
> Is meaning not necessarily relative meaning and perspective? All meaning is will to power (all relative meaning resolves itself into it).
>
> Friedrich Nietzsche, *The Will to Power*[2]

"Law," said Christopher Columbus Langdell, "considered as a science, consists of certain principles or doctrines. To have such a mastery of these as to be able to apply them with constant facility and certainty to the ever-tangled skein of human affairs is what constitutes a true lawyer."[3] Langdell's argument was two-fold; his conceptualiza-

* Professor of Law, The University of Texas. A.B. 1962, Duke University; Ph.D. 1969, Harvard University; J.D. 1973, Stanford University. This essay is dedicated to the memory of Arthur Leff.

1. W. WHITMAN, *Democratic Vistas*, in WALT WHITMAN: POETRY AND PROSE 992-93 (Library of America ed. 1982).

2. F. NIETZSCHE, THE WILL TO POWER 327, 323 (W. Kaufmann & R. Hollingdale trans., W. Kaufmann ed. 1967).

3. C. LANGDELL, A SELECTION OF CASES ON THE LAW OF CONTRACTS vii (2d ed. 1879), *quoted in* Stevens, *Two Cheers for 1870: The American Law School*, in 5 PERSPECTIVES IN AMERICAN HISTORY 435-36 (1971).

tion of law as a science was only the first. The other was his assertion that "all of the available materials of that science are contained in printed books."[4] Both of these principles are crucial to his approach to law. For Langdell law was essentially a literary enterprise, a science of extracting meaning from words that would enable one to believe in law as a process of submission to the commands of authoritative texts (the rule of law) rather than as the creation of willful interpreters (with submission concomitantly producing the rule of men).

To an extent never sufficiently acknowledged by his many detractors, Langdell was altogether correct in linking the legitimacy of the law to the mastery of texts, whether of cases, statutes, or the Constitution. However much legal positivism justifiably emphasizes the origins of law in social facts,[5] the ordinary language of all developed legal systems includes constant recourse to texts that authorize specific conduct. One does not have to accept the entire Langdellian system (indeed, I most certainly do not) in order to recognize the centrality of textuality to the lawyer's enterprise.

Perhaps the easiest way to confirm this point is simply to note that most controversial decisions of the past three decades, especially those of the United States Supreme Court, rest on purported interpretations of the United States Constitution. And the authority of the written Constitution is a prominent theme in American political thought. John Marshall, after noting the "reverence" with which Americans viewed written constitutions, went on to label such creations the "greatest improvement on political institutions" made by the citizenry of the new country.[6] And Marshall deftly asserted the power of the "obvious meaning" of the constitutional text to undergird his claim for the primacy of judicial review. "The powers of the legislature are defined, and limited; and *that those limits may not be mistaken*, or forgotten, the constitution is written."[7]

4. Address by Christopher Langdell, Harvard Law School Association Meeting (Nov. 5, 1886), *quoted in* Stevens, *supra* note 3, at 436 n.50.

5. *See* H.L.A. HART, THE CONCEPT OF LAW (1961).

6. Marbury v. Madison, 5 U.S. (1 Cranch) 137, 178 (1803).

7. *Id.* at 175-76 (emphasis added). Marshall goes on to say, "To what purpose are powers limited, and to what purpose is that limitation committed to writing, if these limits may, at any time, be passed by those intended to be restrained?" *Id.* Marshall, however, undercut (dare one say "deconstructed"?) his argument in *Marbury* when he decided McCulloch v. Maryland, 17 U.S. (4 Wheat.) 316 (1819). So far are words from having obvious meanings that Marshall reminds us that "Such is the character of human language, that no word conveys to the mind, in all situations, one single definite idea; and nothing is more common than to use words in a figurative sense." *Id.* at 414. And the "writtenness" of the Constitution becomes a far more complicated issue once one supplements the textualism of *Marbury* with the "texturalism" of *McCulloch*: "There is no express provision for the case, but the claim has been sustained on a principle which so entirely pervades the constitution, is so intermixed with the materials which compose it, so interwoven

## Law as Literature

No sense can be made of even present-day American political discourse without recognizing the power of constitutional writtenness within our language. Thus Senator Dale Bumpers of Arkansas attacked a bill pending before the Senate, which would have stripped the federal courts of their power to order busing as a remedy for unconstitutional segregation, by calling it part of a "continuing, sinister, devious attack" on the Constitution. "We will today begin the erosion," announced Senator Bumpers, "of *the only document* that stands between the people and tyranny."[8] Anyone familiar with English political discourse, on the other hand, knows that it is almost impossible to imagine similar language there; debate in England centers on the right or wrong of a particular bill, not on its fidelity to a presumptively authoritative text that stands above parliamentary activity.[9]

Citizens of the United States, however, retain within their active political language the purported commands of an allegedly comprehensible Constitution.[10] Comprehensibility is nothing peculiar to constitutions, however, for its possibility arises from the presumed attributes of writtenness. "The physical presentation of a text," the literary theorist Jonathan Culler points out, "gives it a stability . . . . Writing has something of the character of an inscription, a mark offered to the world and promising, by its solidity and apparent autonomy, meaning which is momentarily deferred."[11] In a more ominous vein, the late French critic Roland Barthes described writing as "a hardened language." Writing, he went on to say, "manifests an essence and holds the threat of a secret."[12]

with its web, so blended with its texture, as to be incapable of being separated from it without rendering it into shreds." *Id.* at 426. *See* Levinson, *Judicial Review and the Problem of the Comprehensible Constitution* (Book Review), 59 TEXAS L. REV. 395, 397-98 (1981). Indeed, the very multiplicity (if not promiscuity) of Marshall's approaches to constitutional interpretation, *see* P. BREST & S. LEVINSON, PROCESSES OF CONSTITUTIONAL DECISIONMAKING 35, 114 (2d ed. 1982), calls into question whether interpretation for Marshall (or for anyone else) ever transcended a desire to achieve specific political results.

8. N.Y. Times, Mar. 3, 1982, at A18, col. 4 (emphasis added); *see also* Broder, *Assault on Constitution*, Dallas Times Herald, Mar. 17, 1982, at A29.

9. I became especially aware of this difference in modes of discourse during a sojourn in Great Britain in the fall of 1979, when the Thatcher government put before Parliament several bills regarding rights of non-native-born Englishpersons that struck me (and many others) as racist in the extreme. Many letter writers pointed out the evils of the bills, but none claimed that the proposals violated the English constitution, since, of course, that notion—in its *Marbury* sense—makes no sense within the English language. The description of Great Britain and the United States as two countries separated by a common language never seemed more apt, for the two countries speak two entirely different constitutional languages, even if the words used sometimes seem deceptively similar.

10. *See* Levinson, *supra* note 7, at 418.

11. J. CULLER, STRUCTURALIST POETICS 131, 134 (1975).

12. R. BARTHES, WRITING DEGREE ZERO 19-20 (A. Lavers & C. Smith trans. 1978).

Constitutions, of the written variety especially, are usefully viewed as a means of freezing time by controlling the future through the "hardness" of language encoded in a monumental document, which is then left for later interpreters to decipher. The purpose of such control is to preserve the particular vision held by constitutional founders and to prevent its overthrow by future generations. The very existence of written constitutions with substantive limitations on future conduct is evidence of skepticism, if not outright pessimism, about the moral caliber of future citizens; else why not simply enjoin them to "be good" or "do what you think best"? Writers of constitutions must have a very high confidence in the ability of language both to "harden" and to control.

One form of "hardness" that any reader of written texts quickly becomes aware of, paradoxically, arises from the propensity of language to change, so that understanding past speech recorded in texts requires a "historical" dictionary. Consider, for example, the vicissitudes of the description of a person as "sentimental." The *Oxford English Dictionary* tells us: "Of persons, their dispositions and actions; characterized by sentiment. Originally in favourable sense: Characterized by or exhibiting refined and elevated feeling. In later use: Addicted to indulgence in superficial emotion; apt to be swayed by sentiment."[13] What had been a term of praise became one of mild reproach. What would be the task of a lawyer, then, if asked to construe a trust instrument written in 1720 establishing scholarships for "sentimental" youths?

Any writer, including a framer of constitutions, presumably imagines the following relationship between text and reader: "The reader sets himself to make out what the author has designed and signified through putting into play a linguistic and literary expertise that he shares with the author. By approximating what the author undertook to signify the reader understands what the language of the work means."[14] And, of course, in the case of those particular texts called legal, by understanding the meaning the conscientious adjudicator-reader becomes authorized to enforce it.

The remark just quoted comes from an essay vigorously attacking certain strains of contemporary literary criticism that Abrams finds in-

13. 2 OXFORD ENGLISH DICTIONARY 2730 (compact ed. 1971).

14. Abrams, *How to Do Things with Texts*, 46 PARTISAN REV. 566 (1979). I owe my familiarity with this comment to Richard Rorty. *See* R. RORTY, *Nineteenth-Century Idealism and Twentieth-Century Textualism*, in CONSEQUENCES OF PRAGMATISM 139 (1982), *reprinted from* 64 MONIST 155 (1981).

sufficiently respectful of determinate meanings allegedly generated by disciplined study of texts. The disputes currently raging through literary criticism precisely mirror some of the central problems facing anyone who would take law seriously; the basis of this parallelism is the centrality to law of textual analysis.[15] If we consider law as literature, then we might better understand the malaise that afflicts all contemporary legal analysis, nowhere more severely than in constitutional theory.

## II

The example given above regarding "sentimental" presents no shattering difficulty, for it rests on the notion that the word has a determinate meaning at a specific historical moment. But the emphasis of much contemporary theory is an attack on the stability of meaning (or, concomitantly, on the possibility of establishing techniques by which to retrieve meaning) at *any* given moment. Moreover, our increasing propensity to view all social activity as embedded within linguistic codes has universalized the scope of the inquiry regarding the difficulties of reading texts, whether formally written or not. Indeed, much contemporary writing and painting is explicitly self-referential in its demand that the reader-viewer confront the extent to which language and image are unavoidably ambiguous, and its assertion that any given ascription of narrative line or meaning is the product of an interchange between object and viewer rather than an attribute of the object itself.

There is less of a gap between contemporary legal theory and literature than we might suppose, for many practitioners of each are united by a pervasive anxiety generated by what has been well described as "the loss of the sense of doing and speaking in the name of someone or something recognizable and unquestionably valid."[16] This loss undercuts the confidence in one's ability to ground description or analysis in a purported reality beyond the descriptions or analyses themselves.

15. The best short treatment of these disputes is Culler, *Issues in Contemporary American Critical Debate*, in AMERICAN CRITICISM IN THE POSTSTRUCTURALIST AGE 1-18 (I. Konigsberg ed. 1981). A very illuminating book-length study is F. LENTRICCHIA, AFTER THE NEW CRITICISM (1980). The commonality of some of the problems of law and literary analysis are touched on in Abraham, *Three Fallacies of Interpretation: A Comment on Precedent and Judicial Decision*, 23 ARIZ. L. REV. 771 (1981); Abraham, *Statutory Interpretation and Literary Theory: Some Common Concerns of an Unlikely Pair*, 32 RUTGERS L. REV. 676 (1980); Michaels, *Against Formalism: The Autonomous Text in Legal and Literary Interpretation*, 1 POETICS TODAY 23 (1979), *reprinted with minor changes as* Michaels, *Against Formalism: Chickens and Rocks*, in THE STATE OF THE LANGUAGE 410 (1980); and Yeazell, *Convention, Fiction, and Law*, 13 NEW LITERARY HIST. 89 (1981).

16. M. Robertson, Language as Hero in Post-Modern Formalist Fiction 180 (1979) (unpublished Ph.D. dissertation, Department of English, University of Wisconsin). I am greatly indebted to this thesis (and its author) for many of the ideas contained in this essay.

For American lawyers the primary example, as already suggested, is constitutional law and its relationship to (something recognizable as) the Constitution. Paul Brest has recently noted that little contemporary constitutional doctrine explicitly relies on "originalist sources," i.e., on close analysis of the text or of the presumed intentions of the framers. Instead what is increasingly important is "the elaboration of the Court's own precedents." So far as the documentary Constitution is concerned, "It is rather like having a remote ancestor who came over on the Mayflower."[17] Brest's image brilliantly conveys the sense of a distant Constitution which can be seen, if at all, only "through a glass darkly." To view it as a genuine source of guidance is naive, however heartbreaking this realization might be.

Two classic approaches to understanding a written constitution involve emphasizing either the allegedly plain words of the text or the certain meaning to be given those words through historical reconstruction. I think it fair to say that these particular approaches are increasingly without defenders, at least in the academic legal community.[18]

17. Brest, *The Misconceived Quest for the Original Understanding*, 60 B.U.L. REV. 204, 234 (1980).

Brest, of course, is not unique in his perception. *See, e.g.*, Sandalow, *Judicial Protection of Minorities*, 75 MICH. L. REV. 1162, 1183 (1977) ("[T]he evolving content of constitutional law is not controlled, or even significantly guided, by the Constitution, understood as an historical document."). And Michael Perry emphasizes that "[v]irtually all of modern constitutional decisionmaking by the [Supreme] Court—at least that part of it pertaining to questions of 'human rights,' [i.e. the rights individuals have, or ought to have, against government] . . . must be understood as a species of policymaking, in which the Court decides, ultimately without reference to any value judgment constitutionalized by the framers, which values among competing values shall prevail and how those values shall be implemented." M. PERRY, THE CONSTITUTION, THE COURTS, AND HUMAN RIGHTS 2 (1982). Perry tries to defend this policymaking role in his book.

18. One certainly does not have to be an academic in order to repudiate one or another of these approaches. See, for example, Justice Traynor's opinion in Pacific Gas & Elec. Co. v. G.W. Thomas Drayage & Ry. Co., 442 P.2d 641 (1968), concerning the application of the parol evidence rule. Traynor dismisses "a judicial belief in the possibility of perfect verbal expression" as "a remnant of a primitive faith in the inherent potency and inherent meaning of words." *Id.* at 643-44.

> If words had absolute and constant references, it might be possible to discover contractual intention in the words themselves and in the manner in which they were arranged. Words, however, do not have absolute and constant referents . . . . The meaning of particular words or groups of words varies with the ". . . verbal context and surrounding circumstances and purposes in view of the linguistic education and experience of their users and their hearers or readers (not excluding judges) . . . . A word has no meaning apart from these factors; much less does it have an objective meaning, one true meaning."

*Id.* at 644-45, *quoting* Corbin, *The Interpretation of Words and the Parol Evidence Rule*, 50 CORNELL L.Q. 161, 187 (1965). It is clear that the parol evidence rule is philosophically indefensible. *See also* Michaels, *supra* note 15.

Traynor does, however, seem to retain faith in the ability to ascertain satisfactorily the context of any given speech act. As we become ever more aware, though, of the myriad difficulties standing in the way of contextual understanding, *see, e.g.*, C. GEERTZ, THE INTERPRETATION OF CULTURES (1973), the threat of chaos looms ever larger. See the remarkable review by Gordon Wood, *Star-Spangled History*, THE NEW YORK REVIEW OF BOOKS, Aug. 12, 1982, at 4-9, for a

Law as Literature

Even so capable an analyst as Professor Monaghan, who is eager to return to the confines of a knowable "originalist" Constitution, admits that he has no way of handling the authority of judicial precedents that (he argues) violate initial understandings.[19]

There is not time in this essay to canvass the problems of originalism. Suffice it to say that the plain meaning approach inevitably breaks down in the face of the reality of disagreement among equally competent speakers of the native language. Intentionality arguments, on the other hand, face not only the problem of explaining why intentions of long-dead people from a different social world should influence us,[20] but also, perhaps more importantly, the problem of extracting intentions from the collectivity of individuals and institutions necessary to give legal validity to the Constitution.[21] Even literary critics most committed to the existence of objective meaning through recovery of authorial intent, like E.D. Hirsch, admit that their approach applies only to individually authored works, and therefore cannot be used to analyze a document like the Constitution.[22]

As Richard Rorty has pointed out, however, there are at least two options open to critics who reject the two approaches outlined above but who, nonetheless, remain interested in interpreting the relevant texts. The first option involves the use of an allegedly more sophisticated method to extract the true meaning of the text. Thus Rorty refers to "the kind of textualist who claims to have gotten the secret of the

thoroughgoing attack on the possibility of continuing to write traditional narrative history, which relies for its cogency on the ability to embed events (and words) within a specific linear story. To the extent that cases are themselves narrative structures, there is disturbing relevance to the dilemma sketched by Wood. *See also infra* note 58.

It is not surprising that judges are ultimately limited in their skepticisms, at least so long as they continue to engage in their responsible tasks of judging. Academics, being irresponsible (and often socially marginal), are freer to follow ideas out to their most destructive limits.

19. Monaghan, *Our Perfect Constitution*, 56 N.Y.U. L. Rev. 353, 382 (1981). Like Raoul Berger, *see* R. Berger, Government by Judiciary 412-13 (1977), Monaghan does not really counsel turning back the clock by instantly overruling all putatively misdecided cases. Both offer what might uncharitably be regarded as an "adverse possession" approach to constitutional interpretation, whereby precedents that should at one time have been properly overruled (as wrongly decided) become entitled to recognition as authoritative after the passage of enough time and after the citizenry has come to rely on them. Neither offers the slightest guidance for recognizing the terms of such possession. To be fair, no other theorist of precedent does any better. Perhaps the central difference between law and literature is the lack in the latter of the notion of stare decisis.

20. *See* Cover, Book Review, New Republic, Jan. 14, 1978, at 26 (reviewing R. Berger, Government by Judiciary (1977)). *See also* M. Perry, *supra* note 17, at 75 ("I prefer to let the framers sleep. Just as the framers, in their day, judged by their lights, so must we, in our day, judge by ours.").

21. *See* Brest, *supra* note 17, at 214-15.

22. *See* E. Hirsch, Validity in Interpretation 123 & n.53 (1967); *see also* E. Hirsch, The Aims of Interpretation 1-13 (1976).

text, to have broken its code," as a "weak" textualist,[23] where the term is seemingly a metaphor for the power of the individual critic. Whatever pyrotechnics might come from a critic who "prides himself on not being distracted by anything which the text might previously have been thought to be about or anything its author says about it,"[24] there remains the infatuation—110 years after Langdell—with the possibility of a science of criticism. A "weak" textualist "is just doing his best to imitate science—he wants a *method* of criticism and he wants everybody to agree that he has cracked the code. He wants all the comforts of consensus, even if only the consensus of readers of the literary quarterlies" (or law reviews).[25]

Perhaps the best current example of such a "weak" textualist is John Hart Ely, whose *Democracy and Distrust*,[26] however radical some of its criticisms of so-called "interpretivism" purport to be, is merely the latest effort to crack the code of the United States Constitution and discover its true essence. As James E. Fleming pointed out in a recent review, Ely is engaged in a "quest for the ultimate constitutional interpretivism" which would in effect foreclose further debate about the genuine meaning of the Constitution.[27]

Like Charles Black,[28] Ely is savagely critical of those who seek constitutional meaning in the isolated words of the clauses themselves. And, like Black, Ely looks instead to the overall structure of the Constitution for guidance. If the lines themselves are no longer a plausible source of meaning, there is still a Constitution to be discovered "between the lines," as it were, in the interplay of conceptual structures—states, nation, citizens, republican government—that are undoubtedly present in the constitutional text. Consequently, Ely's structuralism is no less addicted to a search for the "one-and-only truth" about the Constitution than are its discredited competitors. He continues to presuppose what Rorty calls a "*privileged vocabulary*, the vocabulary which gets to the essence of the object" and "expresses the properties which it has in itself as opposed to those we read into it."[29]

No one can read Ely and miss his anger at those who merely read their own views into the Constitution. Indeed, most of Ely's reviewers

23. R. RORTY, *supra* note 14, at 152.
24. *Id.* at 151-52.
25. *Id.* at 152 (emphasis in original).
26. See Levinson, *supra* note 7, for an extended review of J. ELY, DEMOCRACY AND DISTRUST (1980).
27. Fleming, *A Critique of John Hart Ely's Quest for the Ultimate Constitutional Interpretivism of Representative Democracy* (Book Review), 80 MICH. L. REV. 634 (1982).
28. *See* C. BLACK, STRUCTURE AND RELATIONSHIP IN CONSTITUTIONAL LAW (1969).
29. R. RORTY, *supra* note 14, at 152 (emphasis in original).

agree with him at least on this last point, even as they criticize him for reading *his* preferred views into the Constitution. What unites Ely and most of his critics, though, is the continued belief that there is something "in" the Constitution that can be extracted if only we can figure out the best method to mine its meaning.

Against such weak textualists—the decoders, whatever the fanciness of their methods of decoding—Rorty posits "strong" textualists, who reject the whole notion of questing for the essential meanings of a text. "Strong," it should be emphasized, refers to the power of the critic, not the power of the text (or of its author). According to Stanley Fish, one of the leading proponents of this approach, "Interpretation is not the art of construing but the art of constructing. Interpreters do not decode poems; they make them."[30] Fish has argued that "[t]he objectivity of the text is an illusion and, moreover, a dangerous illusion, because it is so physically convincing. The illusion is one of self-sufficiency and completeness. A line of print or a page is so obviously *there* . . . that it seems to be the sole repository of whatever value and meaning we associate with it."[31]

Instead Fish emphasizes the reader's active role and concomitant inability to measure any given interpretation against the "actual" text. He correctly insists that the debate about what it means to read a text is of more than academic interest:

> [D]ifferent notions of what it is to read . . . are finally different notions of what it is to be human. In [one] view, the world, or the world of the text, is already ordered and filled with significances and what the reader is required to do is get them out (hence the question, "What did you get out of that?"). In short, the reader's job is to extract the meanings that formal patterns possess prior to, and independently of, his activities. In my view [on the other hand], these same activities are constitutive of a structure of concerns which is necessarily prior to any examination of meaningful patterns because it is itself the occasion of their coming into being.[32]

30. S. Fish, Is There a Text in This Class? 327 (1980); *cf.* Marcel Duchamp's statement, "It is the Observers who make the pictures," *quoted in* M. Caws, The Eye in the Text: Essays on Perception, Mannerist to Modern 135 (1981). *See generally* the valuable anthologies Reader-Response Criticism: From Formalism to Post-Structuralism (J. Thompkins ed. 1980); The Reader in the Text: Essays on Audience and Interpretation (S. Suleiman & I. Crosman ed. 1980). An excellent recent study is S. Mailloux, Interpretive Conventions: The Reader in the Study of American Fiction (1982).

31. S. Fish, *supra* note 30, at 43. For vigorous criticism of Fish and other radical literary critics, see Crews, *Criticism Without Constraint*, Commentary, Jan. 1982, at 65.

32. S. Fish, *supra* note 30, at 94. Professor Graff argues that the depiction of the controversy itself has ideological implications. Fish's statement might well be assessed against what Graff calls a "rhetorical scorecard":

As Fish notes, "The difference in the two views is enormous." The first one regards "human beings as passive and disinterested comprehenders of a knowledge external to them (that is, of an *objective* knowledge)."[33]

| Bad | Good |
|---|---|
| representation | creation |
| text as determinate object | text as open, indeterminate "invitation" |
| boundaries and constraints | voyages into the unforeseen |
| docility, habit | risk |
| truth as correspondence | truth as invention, fiction |
| meaning as "product" | meaning as "process" |

G. GRAFF, LITERATURE AGAINST ITSELF: LITERARY IDEAS IN MODERN SOCIETY 23 (1979).

33. S. FISH, *supra* note 30, at 94. It occurs to me, as I dutifully footnote Fish's statement, that the act of footnoting is itself a bow toward the notion of objective knowledge, for I am purporting, even as I describe Fish's reader-response theories, to be giving you (the reader) an "accurate" rendition of those theories. Indeed, the point of footnotes, especially if "cite-checked" by law review editors, is to suggest that the proof of my accuracy is that you would arrive at the same conclusions by reading the same material.

This generates an obvious, albeit important, paradox, one only made worse because I of course also expect you to grasp "my" argument and to be able to state it correctly (as Graff basically does), even if you (like Graff) reject it. I suppose, therefore, that I can be accused of being one of those "newreaders" who introduce their "own interpretive strategy when reading someone else's text, but tacitly relying on communal norms when undertaking to communicate the methods and results of [their] interpretations to [their] own readers." *Id.* at 303 (*quoting* Abrams, *supra* note 14, at 587). A similar point is made in Hirsch's review of H. GADAMER, WAHRHEIT UND METHODE (1960), *reprinted in* E. HIRSCH, VALIDITY IN INTERPRETATION 245 (1967); *see also* Graff, *Politics, Language, Deconstruction, Lies, and the Reflexive Fallacy: A Rejoinder to W.J.T. Mitchell*, SALMAGUNDI, Winter-Spring 1980, at 78.

Professor Graff is correct in his own contribution to this Symposium when he notes that I do on occasion use the word "correct" to refer to an interpretation, *see* Graff, *"Keep off the Grass," "Drop Dead," and Other Indeterminacies: A Response to Sanford Levinson*, 60 TEXAS L. REV. 405, 412 (1982), so that I cannot be the arch-indeterminist that I sometimes appear to be. I am not sure how far apart he and I actually are, for there is relatively little in his response that I genuinely disagree with. I do agree, as does Fish for that matter, that our ordinary speech acts are full of meanings instantly grasped by listeners, given the standard contexts in which they occur. I would further agree that the Constitution is not entirely incomprehensible, that, e.g., the President must take office on January 20. U.S. CONST. amend. XX, § 1. There are circumstances in which this might be problematic (what if Congress changed the calendar year), but it would be perverse to say that the ordinary reader would not be expected to give a single response to the question, "When does a newly elected President take office?" (Nor do I disagree with the Fifth Circuit that it was "quite incredible" to argue that ".82165" is not the equivalent of "82.165%." Oil & Gas Futures, Inc. of Texas v. Andrus, 610 F.2d 287, 288 (5th Cir. 1980), *reversing* [!] an unreported decision by the Honorable Finis E. Cowan of the United States District Court for the Southern District of Texas. Yet (presumably) competent lawyers and a (presumably) competent judge did not find even this proposition compelling.)

The problem, of course, is that constitutional litigation almost never concerns such clauses. Professor Graff recognizes the multiplicity of ambiguity that *can*, even if not *must*, be present in literary or legal texts. He seems to chide me for emphasizing power, rather than authority, in resolving conflicting interpretations, but this seems to be the principal explanation for why one legal result, rather than its equally plausible (indeed, on occasion more plausible) alternative, is imposed on the parties. Even here, I will quickly concede that courts and other constitutional interpreters operate within constraints. That is the importance of Fish's own distinction between "on-the-wall" and "off-the-wall" arguments; but the point is that whatever constraints exist are not constant over time.

Finally, I agree with Professor Graff that the alternative to determinacy (certainty) is not an anything-goes indeterminacy. However, especially from the perspective of the losers in a necessarily coercive legal system, a court decision that remains even within the ambit of "on-the-

Law as Literature

It is worth noting, I believe, that Felix Frankfurter's favorite single word was "disinterested,"[34] and that the ideology of the Harvard Law School, from Langdell's time to the days of Hart and Sacks and afterward, can be regarded as centered around the search for a "disinterested," impersonal approach to legal analysis.

The view endorsed by Fish regards "human beings as at every moment creating the experiential spaces into which a personal knowledge flows."[35] Meaning is created rather than discovered, though the source of creative energy is the particular community within which one finds him- or herself. Critics more Emersonian in their inspiration, like Harold Bloom, are willing to credit individual acts of creativity, though Bloom's emphasis on the ubiquity of "misreadings," rather than "truthful" renderings of what is inside texts, links him to Rorty's "strong" textualists.[36] All such readers could well join the Whitmanian anthem, where all readings, whether of life or of texts, become songs of oneself.

The patron saint of all strong textualists is Nietzsche:

> [W]hatever exists, having somehow come into being, is again and again reinterpreted to new ends, taken over, transformed, and redirected by some power superior to it; all events in the organic world are a subduing, a *becoming master*, and all subduing and becoming master involves a fresh interpretation, an adaptation through which any previous "meaning" and "purpose" are necessarily obscured or even obliterated.[37]

And the argument of Fish, Bloom, and other strong textualists, whether American or continental, is *not* that they prefer to do their thing as an alternative to the more banal work of "truthseekers" like Abrams or Hirsch, but rather that the project of ultimate truth-seeking is based on philosophical error. At the very least it presumes a privileged foundation for measuring the attainment of truth, and it is precisely this foundation that Nietzsche and most of the more radical literary theorists

wall" arguments may appear to be arbitrary (though not "whimsical"), given the presence of other available arguments that would have generated more palatable results.

34. *See* Levinson, *The Democratic Faith of Felix Frankfurter*, 25 STAN. L. REV. 430, 434 (1972) (author's student Note). No single citation, of course, can support the assertion that "disinterested" was Frankfurter's favorite word, but I challenge any reader of Frankfurter's prose to name a more oft-used and emotionally charged word in his vocabulary. (Proper nouns like Holmes or the Harvard Law School do not count.)

35. S. FISH, *supra* note 30, at 94. "Personal," incidentally, is a tricky word in this context, for Fish, like most structuralists and post-structuralists, rejects the meaningfulness of genuinely individualistic idiosyncracies, and instead emphasizes the inevitable membership of such "individuals" in communities of shared discourses which, indeed, ultimately supply any person's own sense of self. *See id.* at 338-55.

36. *See, e.g.*, H. BLOOM, A MAP OF MISREADING (1975).

37. F. NIETZSCHE, ON THE GENEOLOGY OF MORALS 77 (W. Kaufmann trans. 1967) (emphasis in original).

deny. Like Rorty, they do not substitute a new candidate for a winning method of how to recognize literary truth when one sees it; rather, they reject the very search for finality of interpretation.

To be sure, none of the radical critics defend the position that any interpretation is just as good as any other. Stanley Fish, for example, notes that he genuinely believes in the validity of any given view that he happens to hold, and he can present reasons for rejecting the views of his opponents on the interpretation of a given text.[38] In this regard Fish seems similar to Ronald Dworkin, who views judging as including the phenomenological experience of feeling oneself to have achieved the uniquely correct solution even to a hard case.[39] But Fish, more candid than Dworkin on this point, admits that his own conviction of rightness will provide no answer at all to anyone who happens to disagree with him, and that there is no way to resolve the dispute. It is at this point that he retreats to his Kuhnian[40] emphasis on communities of understanding and shared conventions. It may be true that these communities will share, at any given moment, a sense of what distinguishes "on the wall" from "off the wall" arguments,[41] but Fish is acutely aware of the contingency of such judgments. They describe only our own temporal sense of what is currently acceptable, rather than anything genuinely mirroring the essential characteristics of the texts being discussed.[42]

## III

Presumably only those professionally interested in literature are forced to wrestle with the issues presented by Abrams, Culler, and Fish regarding poetics or the interpretation of fiction. But if law is, in some meaningful sense, a branch of literature, then the problems discussed above take on new and bothersome implications. And nowhere is this more true within our own culture than in constitutional interpretation and its emphasis on writtenness.

The role of our Constitution is not only to enable us to pretend that past linguistic acts can control future action. It is also presumably to prevent the rise of Nietzschean "masters." Nietzsche seems to sug-

38. S. FISH, *supra* note 30, at 338-71.

39. *See* R. DWORKIN, TAKING RIGHTS SERIOUSLY 279-90 (1977); Levinson, *Taking Law Seriously: Reflections on "Thinking Like a Lawyer"* (Book Review), 30 STAN. L. REV. 1071 (1978) (reviewing Dworkin).

40. *See* T. KUHN, THE STRUCTURE OF SCIENTIFIC REVOLUTIONS (2d ed. 1970).

41. S. FISH, *supra* note 30, at 356-57.

42. For the importance of the "mirroring" image, see R. RORTY, PHILOSOPHY AND THE MIRROR OF NATURE (1979). Rorty's basic mission is the criticism of the possibility of mirroring.

gest, however, that a massive exercise in social deception is necessary if we are not to recognize the way that "interpretation" inevitably implies a struggle for mastery in the formation of political consciousness. For a Nietzschean reader of constitutions, there is no point in searching for a code that will produce "truthful" or "correct" interpretations; instead, the interpreter, in Rorty's words, "simply beats the text into a shape which will serve his own purpose."[43]

E.D. Hirsch, perhaps the most consistent opponent of the radical critics, notes that, "With a numinous document like the Constitution or the Bible, the principles and methods of correct interpretation are as important as they are problematical."[44] If one takes seriously the views articulated by Nietzsche, Rorty, and Fish (among others), one must give up the search for principles and methods of constitutional interpretation. Instead, one assesses the results of an interpretive effort by something other than the criterion of adherence to an inner essence of the text being interpreted. Indeed, Robert Cover addresses this point directly in his remarkable review of Raoul Berger's *Government by Judiciary*, in which Berger vigorously attacks judges for allegedly straying from the original meaning (which is equated with the true meaning) of the Constitution. Cover himself quotes Nietzsche's comment that "[t]he knowledge of the past is desired only for the service of the future and the present"[45] and emphasizes that it is up to us, the living, to decide for our own reasons what we wish the Constitution to mean.

To put it mildly, there is something disconcerting about accepting the Nietzschean interpreter into the house of constitutional analysts, but I increasingly find it impossible to imagine any other way of making sense of our own constitutional universe. For some years I have organized my own courses in constitutional interpretation around the central question, "But did the Court get it right?", as if one could grade any given opinion by whether or not it measured up to the genuine command of the Constitution. Answering such a question, of course, requires the development of a full set of "principles and methods of correct interpretation," and my courses have involved a search for such principles and methods.

I still spend a great deal of time examining various approaches, ranging from the linguistic to the historical, from the structural to what my colleague Philip Bobbitt calls the "ethical,"[46] but I have less and

43. R. Rorty, *supra* note 14, at 151.
44. E. Hirsch, The Aims of Interpretation 20 (1976).
45. Cover, *supra* note 20, at 27.
46. See P. Bobbitt, Constitutional Fate (1982), for an extraordinarily subtle survey of

Texas Law Review Vol. 60:373, 1982

less confidence that this is a sensible enterprise. At the very least there is no reason to believe that the community of persons interested in constitutional interpretation will coalesce around one or another of these approaches. Moreover, insofar as one accepts the plausibility of an analysis like Rorty's, there is no reason to regret this, for it is the result of a genuine plurality of ways of seeing the world, rather than of the obdurate recalcitrance of those who refuse to bend to superior argument.

Yet there are obvious difficulties in adopting Rorty's metaphor of the conversation (rather than the argument),[47] for the principal social reality of law is its coercive force vis-à-vis those who prefer to behave other than as the law "requires." As Chairman Mao pointed out, a revolution is not a tea party, and the massive disruption in lives that can be triggered by a legal case is not a conversation. The legal system presents a conversation from which there may be no exit, and there are certainly those who would define hell as the vision of their least favorite constitutional interpreter, whether the Court or a benighted law professor.

What does one do, then, when studying opinions, if one gives up the enterprise of determining whether or not they are "correct"? Are cases simply historical fragments which should be studied for insight into the ideology of the time?[48] One no longer would say, for example, that *Dred Scott*[49] or *Lochner v. New York*,[50] or any other case, was "wrongly" decided, for that use of language presupposes belief in the knowability of constitutional essence. One *can* obviously show that constitutional tastes and styles shift over time, but this retreat into historicism has nothing to do with the legal science so desperately sought by Langdell and his successors.

A study of shifts in legal styles, moreover, may force us to come to grips with the fact that there may be no guiding criteria to enable us to state with confidence that any given piece of writing is "legal" writing, as opposed to writing about a subject of interest to the legal system.

various modes of constitutional argumentation. A shorter version of the book was published as Bobbitt, *Constitutional Fate*, 58 TEXAS L. REV. 695 (1981).

47. See R. RORTY, *supra* note 42, at 389.

48. This seems to be the approach taken by some of the most fruitful practitioners of "critical legal studies." *See, e.g.*, M. HORWITZ, THE TRANSFORMATION OF AMERICAN LAW, 1780-1860 (1977); M. TUSHNET, THE AMERICAN LAW OF SLAVERY 1810-1860 (1981).

49. Dred Scott v. Sandford, 60 U.S. (19 How.) 393 (1856).

50. 198 U.S. 45 (1905). There is obviously not space here to consider in depth the complexity of our responses to these two cases. One might begin, though, by asking whether Taney's or Peckham's arguments in the two cases are really "off-the-wall" in terms of the conventions of American legal discourse; it seems clear that the answer is no.

## Law as Literature

Jonathan Culler has studied the ways in which readers use conventions to constitute something as a poem or a short story and to give it meaning.[51] It would be interesting to see what, besides identification of a particular piece of writing as emanating from a court, allows one with confidence to label it as peculiarly "legal."[52] Fish, as one might imagine, insists that poetry is anything we conventionally posit as such.[53] Is

51. J. CULLER, *supra* note 11, at 113-238.

52. Indeed, it is not even clear that material emanating from a court can, except by stipulation, be described as "legal writing." *See, e.g.,* Flood v. Kuhn, 407 U.S. 258, 260-64 (1972) (Justice Blackmun's ode to baseball).

53. S. FISH, *supra* note 30, at 322. One notes again the linkage between Fish and Duchamp, one of whose most famous artistic achievements was the transformation of a urinal into art by the mere act of placing it in a museum. We might have our individual favorite candidates for transforming dubious arguments into law through the aegis of placing them in a judicial opinion.

Indeed, yet further theoretical questions are suggested by the text of the paragraph to which this footnote is addressed. Consider, for example, the problem of parody, an extraordinarily sophisticated literary construction which depends for its force on the competence of the reader to know the "proper" or "conventional" style that serves as the background to the foreground of the parody itself. *See* J. CULLER, *supra* note 11, at 152-54; Culler, *Convention and Meaning: Derrida and Austin*, 13 NEW LITERARY HIST. 15, 22 (1981). The May 15, 1978, issue of the *New Yorker* featured, among its offerings, "Supreme Court Roundup," one example of which is the report of a first amendment decision in which "the Court ruled unanimously in favor of a twelve-year-old plaintiff who sought damages on account of being denied the chance to audition" for a movie. "The Court's opinion, written by Chief Justice Happ, argued that exclusion of the little girl was 'rotten, beastly, a crying shame—really makes the Court sick.' The case was not decided, as had been expected, on the ground of sex discrimination; rather, the Justices invoked the First Amendment's guarantee of freedom of expression. The Court thus affirmed for the first time the constitutional right to a screen test." Geng, *Supreme Court Roundup*, NEW YORKER, May 15, 1978, at 31. This is clearly parody, right? But then what is the genre of, say, Justice Douglas' opinion for the majority in Griswold v. Connecticut, 381 U.S. 479 (1965) ("the specific guarantees in the Bill of Rights have penumbras, formed by emanations from those guarantees that help give them life and substance"), or of Justice Brennan's description of "the give-and-take negotiation common in plea bargaining between the prosecution and the defense, which arguably possess relatively equal bargaining power," Parker v. North Carolina, 397 U.S. 790, 809 (1970), *quoted approvingly in* Bordenkircher v. Hayes, 434 U.S. 357, 362 (1978). And consider Justice Stevens' remark in Young v. American Mini Theatres, 427 U.S. 50 (1976), that "few of us would march our sons and daughters off to war to preserve the citizen's right to see 'Specified Sexual Activities' exhibited in the theaters of our choice." *Id.* at 70. Justice Stevens' "marching-off-to-war" standard garnered only three additional votes; perhaps the replacement of the dissenting Justice Stewart by Justice O'Connor will enable it to receive the fifth vote necessary to enshrine it in our constitutional litany as a certifiably serious approach to constitutional analysis.

One of the general problems facing so-called "post-modernist" writers is the impossibility of satirizing patterns of ordinary life and talk which themselves are bizarre. *See, e.g.,* the work of Donald Barthelme. Or, as Calvin Trillin has put it, "Someone who writes what has been officially labeled a 'humor column' about the American scene lives in constant danger of being blindsided by the truth." C. TRILLIN, UNCIVIL LIBERTIES 2 (1982). One sometimes wonders about the genre status not only of certain judicial opinions, but also of scholarly articles purporting to analyze them. *See, e.g.,* Michelman, *States' Rights and States' Roles: Permutations of "Sovereignty" in* National League of Cities v. Usery, 86 YALE L.J. 1165 (1977) (arguing that Justice Rehnquist's majority opinion requires states to provide essential services to their citizens); Tribe, *Unraveling* National League of Cities, 90 HARV. L. REV. 1065 (1977). For general reviews of the status of so-called constitutional scholarship, see Tushnet, *Legal Scholarship: Its Causes and Cures*, 90 YALE L.J. 1205 (1981); *Tushnet, Truth, Justice, and the American Way: An Interpretation of Public Law Scholarship in the Seventies*, 57 TEXAS L. REV. 1307 (1979).

Perhaps the best response to the issues raised in this footnote is to say that one should have a

the same thing true of legal writing?[54]

These remarks have obvious implications for legal education. Here, too, there are parallels to literary education. Some of Culler's most convoluted paragraphs are spent defending the enterprise of specialized undergraduate and graduate education in literature in the face of the attack by radical critics on the very notion of a science of criticism.[55] It is tempting to paraphrase Dostoyevski by saying that if there is no science, there is no truth, and if there is no truth, then anything is permitted. How does one describe education in such a climate of skepticism? As already indicated, Culler's major project is identifying the structured conventions by which readers supply meaning to texts; his own reference to only "*apparent* autonomy" in the remarks quoted earlier[56] indicates the limit of the extent to which he rejects reliance on the independent status of the language. It is we who establish what the monuments mean by ascribing content to them.

Insofar as Culler seeks the conventions that differentiate "competent" readers from incompetent ones, he faces the difficulty of establishing as well how one distinguishes "off-the-wall" readings that are the product of genuine incompetence from those that are simply brilliantly ahead of their time and in cadence with the next paradigm coming down the pike. Legal education too could devote itself more formally to studying the conventions of reading law and legal opinions, though such a move would face great hostility not only from students but from most present faculty members as well. I note the debate that raged in England over the appointment of Colin MacCabe to the English faculty at Cambridge.[57] MacCabe, with his interests in contemporary structuralism and post-structuralism, is fundamentally antagonistic to the view that the only task of students is to read set texts, without ever systematically reflecting on the notion of "reading" itself. Indeed, most constitutional law courses avoid discussing the as-

good sense of humor if teaching constitutional law these days, but this response works, of course, only if one has attained enough ironic distance so as not to care about the implications for living beings of the material analyzed.

54. Indeed, is *this* essay legal writing? If it is not, then why is it being published in the *Texas Law Review*?

55. *See, e.g.*, J. CULLER, *supra* note 11, at 258; *see also* J. CULLER, THE PURSUIT OF SIGNS: SEMIOTICS, LITERATURE, DECONSTRUCTION 210 (1981) ("Literary Theory in the Graduate Program").

56. *See* text accompanying note 11.

57. For descriptions of the MacCabe controversy, see *Unquiet Flow the Dons*, NEWSWEEK, Feb. 16, 1981, at 95-96; *Controversy at Cambridge*, TIMES LITERARY SUPPLEMENT, Jan. 30, 1981, at 112. The *TLS* also published an interesting symposium sparked by the MacCabe flap, *Modern Literary Theory: Its Place in Teaching*, TIMES LITERARY SUPPLEMENT, Feb. 6, 1981, at 135, with contributions by George Steiner, John Bayley, Denis Donoghue, C.J.E. Ball, L.C. Knights, Malcolm Bowie, Malcolm Bradbury, and Roger Scruton.

sumptions not only that there are standard cases that must be read, but also that the act of reading itself is, when all is (un)said and done, unproblematic.[58]

Consider also the way we treat the innovative judges of our legal tradition, particularly as they appear in law school courses. Do we really wish to argue that John Marshall or Earl Warren (or the most recent dynamic innovator, William Rehnquist)[59] got the essence right in their interpretations of the Constitution, or do we recognize instead the extent to which we have been subdued by their political visions?

Perhaps the most significant example of this dilemma is John Marshall himself, or rather I should say our response to Marshall. I have little trouble stating that I consider his major opinions to run the gamut from the intellectually dishonest[60] to the majestically visionary,[61] and rarely to contain the only (or even the most) plausible rendering of the Constitution. Yet there is also a profound irrelevance to such a criticism. Not only does it assume the existence of a privileged discourse that allows me to dismiss Marshall as "untruthful" rather than merely different, it also ignores the fundamental fact that John Marshall is as much a "founder" of the American legal system as those who wrote the Constitution he purported to interpret. He is, perhaps, the great Nietzschean judge of our tradition.

Indeed, Marshall is a worthy successor to the founders of 1787, for they too were aware of the awesome role they played as visionary leaders. When it was pointed out to the Philadelphia Convention that it was without authority to "revise" the Articles of Confederation by obliterating them, the response was candid and to the point. "There are great seasons when persons with limited powers are justified in exceeding them, and a person would be contemptible not to risk it."[62] So spoke Edmund Randolph, later the Attorney General in the Washington administration. Even James Madison, who gamely insisted that the

58. For all of the alleged emphasis on cases in American legal education, there is little systematic attention paid to what, beyond agreement with the teacher's own emphasis, constitutes "legal competence." Perhaps the most notorious example of the lack of reflection concerning case-reading is the bland assumption transmitted to generations of law students that cases can be "briefed." Exactly how it is that one distills "essence of case" from the full opinion, or why it was that the writer thought it necessary to write as fully as he or she did, is not usually brought to the student's attention.

59. *See* Fiss & Krauthammer, *The Rehnquist Court*, NEW REPUBLIC, Mar. 10, 1982, at 14.

60. *See* Marbury v. Madison, 5 U.S. (1 Cranch) 137 (1803) (presentation and construction of § 13 of the Judiciary Act of 1789).

61. *See* McCulloch v. Maryland, 17 U.S. (4 Wheat.) 316 (1819) (invocation of American nationalism).

62. M. FARRAND, 1 RECORDS OF THE FEDERAL CONVENTION 262 (1937) (speech of June 16, 1787, Yates transcription).

Texas Law Review Vol. 60:373, 1982

Convention was behaving properly, was reduced to arguing, in *The Federalist No. 40*, that the Philadelphia delegates "must have borne in mind, that as the plan to be framed and proposed, was to be submitted *to the people themselves* . . . its approbation [would] blot out all antecedent errors and irregularities."[63]

Madison's argument is significant, to be sure, and it serves to distinguish the Founders from twentieth-century authoritarians unconcerned with popular ratification of their acts. Nonetheless it establishes a powerful precedent for the general proposition that the people themselves can give their approval to what was arguably illegal conduct by visionary leaders, including judges who break the bonds of confining legal conventions and ultimately transform our vision of ourselves as a nation. Under this theory the difference between hero and villain is found not in fidelity to preexisting legal norms and adherence to their "correct" meaning, but in the ability of a hero-founder to impress the new understanding of the political order on the popular consciousness. And, in our particular culture we graft these new understandings, particularly if found in judicial opinions, on to something called "the Constitution" and pretend that the leader-judge has merely seen more deeply into its essence, rather than bent it to a new vision.

63. THE FEDERALIST No. 40, 265-66 (J. Madison) (J. Cooke ed. 1961) (emphasis in original).

Compare Madison's argument with Lincoln's defense of his policy of military arrests and suspension of habeas corpus:

> The constitution contemplates the question as likely to occur for decision, but it does not expressly declare who is to decide it. By necessary implication, when Rebellion or Invasion comes, the decision is to be made, from time to time; and I think the man whom, for the time, the people have, under the constitution, made the commander-in-chief, of their Army and Navy, is the man who holds the power, and bears the responsibility of making it. If he uses the power justly, the same people will probably justify him; if he abuses it, he is in their hands, to be dealt with by all the modes they have reserved to themselves in the constitution.

THE POLITICAL THOUGHT OF ABRAHAM LINCOLN 262 (R. Current ed. 1967).

There is a similarity between these arguments and the one made by Richard Nixon in his interview with David Frost:

> *Mr. Frost:* So what in a sense you're saying is that there are certain situations . . . where the President can decide that it's in the best interests of the nation or something, and do something illegal.
>
> *Mr. Nixon:* Well, when the President does it, that means that it is not illegal.
>
> *Mr. Frost:* By definition.
>
> *Mr. Nixon:* Exactly. Exactly. If the President, for example, approves something because of the national security, or in this case because of a threat to internal peace and order of significant magnitude, then the President's decision in that instance is one that enables those who carry it out, to carry it out without violating a law. Otherwise they're in an impossible position.

Transcript of Frost-Nixon Interview, N.Y. Times, May 20, 1977, at A16, col. 5.

Paradoxically, it may be that what most differentiates Nixon from the founders and Lincoln, beyond obvious differences in their breadth of vision, is his unwillingness to submit his deeds to the populace for their approbation. There is a public quality to the acts of Marshall and the others that is wholly lacking in those of Nixon, as revealed by the very term "cover up."

## Law as Literature

This description, of course, works only when a "strong" judge, like one of Harold Bloom's "strong" poets, successfully misreads the past to establish his or her own vision of reality as one for the writer's own time. But an age without such judges, or with contending candidates, can recognize only the existence of the competing visions themselves, with no recourse to the foundation document—the Constitution—being genuinely possible. It would obviously be nice to believe that *my* Constitution is the true one and, therefore, that my opponents' versions are fraudulent, but that is precisely the belief that becomes steadily harder to maintain. They are simply *different* Constitutions. There are as many plausible readings of the United States Constitution as there are versions of *Hamlet*,[64] even though each interpreter, like each director, might genuinely believe that he or she has stumbled onto the one best answer to the conundrums of the texts. That we cannot walk out of

64. Since writing the statement in the text, I have benefitted from an important article by Knapp and Michaels, *Against Theory*, 8 CRITICAL INQUIRY 723 (1982), which attacks similar arguments in S. FISH, *supra* note 30, at 367-69. Briefly, the authors argue that a statement like "There are as many plausible readings of the United States Constitution as there are versions of *Hamlet*" implies knowledge about the underlying nature of reality, whereas the general argument of Fish (and of this essay) is that we can never have confidence that we have such knowledge. Furthermore, they note that neither Fish nor any other critic, whether literary or legal, could actually live by such a view, since stands are constantly taken in the confidence, merited or not, that one's own views are indeed better than the alternatives. *See* Knapp & Michaels, *supra*, at 738-41. Indeed, I have written that Buckley v. Valeo, 424 U.S. 1 (1976), is "perhaps the worst decision . . . in the past forty years." Levinson, *supra* note 7, at 415. Such an assertion clearly entails at least a momentary rejection of the view that all constitutional approaches are equal, though I remain troubled as to how one could ever genuinely establish the superiority of any given constitutional theory.

Professor Fish himself, in his reply to this essay, emphasizes the degree to which we make judgments regardless of (some of) the implications of the anti-Realist philosophy he endorses, though I do not know if he would concede the legitimacy of Knapp and Michaels' general argument. In any event, *Against Theory* promises to provoke an important debate among literary theorists which will have obvious relevance for legal analysts. *See also infra* note 87. (I am grateful to Gerald Graff and Steven Mailloux for calling my attention to the Knapp and Michaels essay and for emphasizing its implications for the argument of this essay.)

Professor Bobbitt's inquiry, CONSTITUTIONAL FATE, *supra* note 46, is also highly relevant to the question of the intersection of theory and practice, since he finds our theories *in* our practices, rather than *underlying* them as a foundation.

One might, incidentally, be tempted to avoid the whole set of dilemmas raised in this Article by taking refuge in a simple "the Constitution is what the Court says it is" argument. Putting aside the usual responses to this argument (who or what authorizes the Court to say what the Constitution is?), there is an equally fundamental problem in relying on judicial precedent. Even if we ignore the fact that the Court itself does not feel bound by its own precedents, so that it regularly overturns them, there remains the question of how one figures out what a precedent means, and that of course brings us quickly back to the central problem of this Article. See, for example, Deutsch, *Harvard's View of the Supreme Court: A Response*, 57 TEXAS L. REV. 1445 (1979), which emphasizes "that our society is forced to live with an awareness of the *essentially uncertain nature* of the precedent contained in a judicial opinion." *Id.* at 1454 (emphasis added). Thus Deutsch argues that "[t]he reading of a holding as not only unintended, but as something contrary to the intent of the opinion's author, is a permissible one, since a later Court might so construe the earlier holding, and the meaning of a precedent is what is held by that later Court." *Id.* at 1453.

offending productions of our national epic poem, the Constitution, may often be anguishing, but that may be our true constitutional fate.

IV

Professor Owen Fiss has recently directed several arguments against the views expressed in an earlier version of the present essay.[65] Fiss forthrightly labels these views as "nihilism." He concludes his article by identifying what is at stake in the debate: "[T]his nihilism calls into question the very point of constitutional adjudication; it threatens our social existence and the nature of public life as we know it in America; and it demeans our lives." It is no surprise, then, that he goes on to state, "It must be combated and can be, but perhaps only by affirming the truth of that which is being denied—the idea that the Constitution embodies a public morality and that a public life founded on that morality can be rich and inspiring."[66]

In this section I shall first lay out what I perceive as the view of constitutional adjudication defended by Fiss. I shall then consider his response to those critics, like myself, who are unable to share it. I should emphasize at the outset that I share both Fiss' basic social and political values, even if not his theory of the Constitution, and his unhappiness about the implications of "nihilism." But a desire, however understandable, to combat it does not equal the ability to do so.

Professor Fiss first elaborated his views in a *Harvard Law Review* "Foreword."[67] For the purposes of this essay, the key paragraph is as follows:

> The rightful place of courts in our political system turns on the existence of public values and on the promise of those institutions—because they are independent and because they must engage in a special dialogue—to articulate and elaborate the true meaning of those values. The task [is] discovering the meaning of constitutional values such as equality, liberty, due process, or property . . . .[68]

A concomitant of "the meaning-giving enterprise implicit in constitutionalism itself"[69] is the judge's duty to be concerned with designing effective remedies. "The desire to be efficacious need not be seen as an assertion of will, but as a willingness of the judge to assume re-

65. Fiss, *Objectivity and Interpretation*, 34 STAN. L. REV. 739 (1982).
66. *Id.* at 763.
67. Fiss, *The Supreme Court, 1978 Term—Foreword: The Forms of Justice*, 93 HARV. L. REV. 1 (1979).
68. *Id.* at 51.
69. *Id.* at 57.

sponsibility for practical reality and its consonance with the Constitution." Indeed, "[t]he judge might be seen as forever straddling two worlds, the world of the ideal and the world of the practical, the world of the public value and the world of subjective preference, the world of the Constitution and the world of politics." It is the judge among all officials of government who "is in the best position to discover the *true meaning* of our constitutional values."[70]

Fiss more recently has spoken of the judicial duty to interpret legal texts; in doing so the judge "gives meaning and expression to the values embodied in that text."[71] Like Ronald Dworkin,[72] Fiss seems to assert the existence of uniquely valid ("true") solutions to the conundrums about the implications of our "public values," assuming in the first place that such values exist and can be ascertained. Moreover, like Dworkin's, Fiss' Constitution turns out to contain only the good, the true, and the beautiful.

Fiss takes pains to distinguish himself from that "arid and artificial conception of interpretation" which some label " 'interpretivism,' but [is] more properly called 'textual determinism.' "[73] He links this conception with that form of legal positivism that emphasizes "the 'written constitution' and stresses factors like the use of particular words or the intent or beliefs of the framers, all of which have little or no moral relevance."[74] The problem with this mode of interpretation goes well beyond any theoretical difficulty in ascertaining the true meaning of the text or the intentions of its authors.[75] As Fiss notes, even if one assumes the theoretical coherence of positivism, there remains the problem that "[a] too rigid insistence on positivism will inevitably bring into question the ultimate moral authority of the legal text—the justness of the Constitution."[76] Thus he concedes that an all-too-comprehensible Constitution might well be read to have protected slavery, and this fact alone would justify raising the question as to why the Constitution is worthy of respect and obedience. Indeed, the mere presence of such a question indicates "[a] moment of crisis in the life of a constitution."[77]

A resolution to any such crisis is close at hand, however. A judge

70. *Id.* at 58 (emphasis added).
71. Fiss, *supra* note 65, at 755.
72. *See* Levinson, *supra* note 39.
73. Fiss, *supra* note 65, at 743.
74. *Id.* at 753. For an example of that form, see Monaghan, *supra* note 19.
75. *See* Brest, *supra* note 17.
76. Fiss, *supra* note 65, at 753.
77. *Id.* at 754.

must be willing "[t]o read the moral as well as the legal text. The judge quickly learns to read in a way that avoids crises."[78] Indeed, Fiss accords the judiciary a "[s]pecial competence to interpret a text such as the Constitution, and to render specific and concrete the public morality embodied in that text."[79]

This assignment of authority to the judiciary is, allegedly, not a blank check, i.e., not an invitation to become a Nietzschean creator of meaning. Instead the judicial interpreter "is disciplined by a set of rules that specify the relevance and weight to be assigned to the material (e.g., words, history, intention, consequence), as well as by those that define basic concepts and that established the procedural circumstances under which the interpretation must occur."[80] There is, to be sure, no uniformity of rules of interpretation. Not only are the rules for interpreting poems different from those for interpreting legal texts, but, "even within the law, there may be different rules depending on the text—those for contractual interpretation vary from statutory interpretation, and both vary from those used in constitutional interpretation."[81] But in no case is an "interpreter . . . free to assign any meaning he wishes to the text," for the rules discipline the interpreter and thus succeed in "transforming the interpretative process from a subjective to an objective one, and they furnish the standards by which the correctness of the interpretation can be judged."[82] The disciplining rules derive from "an interpretive community consisting of those who recognize the rules as authoritative."[83]

Fiss' notion, of course, is very close to Fish's emphasis on the importance of interpretive communities,[84] and both have been influenced by the work of Thomas Kuhn.[85] It is easy enough to see why Fish and I find Kuhn's notions attractive, rooted as they are in the tradition of the sociology of knowledge and its rejection of the correspondence between ideas believed to be true and the external world itself.[86] It is harder to understand Fiss' embrace of Kuhn, given that the key element in Fiss' program is his defense of the objective truthfulness of

78. *Id.*
79. *Id.* at 755.
80. *Id.* at 744.
81. *Id.*
82. *Id.* at 745.
83. *Id.*
84. Indeed, the full title of Fish's book is IS THERE A TEXT IN THIS CLASS? THE AUTHORITY OF INTERPRETIVE COMMUNITIES.
85. *See* T. KUHN, THE ESSENTIAL TENSION: SELECTED STUDIES IN SCIENTIFIC TRADITION AND CHANGE (1977); T. KUHN, *supra* note 40.
86. Rorty, too, draws on Kuhn as an ally in his attack on the meaningfulness of seeking conceptions that "mirror nature." *See* R. RORTY, *supra* note 42, at 322-42.

claims about public and constitutional values.[87] The notions of "truth according to the conventions of my community" and "objective knowledge as determined by my reference group" differ substantially from notions of unmodified "truth" or "objective knowledge." The former exist within the language of skepticism, including that most virulent form castigated as nihilism. It was Nietzsche, after all, who emphasized the reduction of "truth" to the views of one's own perspective (and who thus went on to assert the possibility of changing our world by adopting different perspectives).

Fiss is aware, of course, that legal adepts argue vigorously among themselves over the meaning of the Constitution; he does not seriously suggest that legal academicians are significantly more in agreement with one another than are professors of literature debating the meaning of a poem or a novel. His most interesting (and dubious) move, however, is to differentiate the lawyer from the literary critic by asserting the significance of the membership of the former in an interpretive community presided over by authoritative courts and judges. The legal system offers procedures that can resolve disputes through, "for example, pronouncements by the highest court and perhaps even legislation and constitutional amendments. The presence of such procedures and a hierarchy of authority resolving disputes that could potentially divide or destroy an interpretive community is one of the distinctive features of legal interpretation."[88] Ultimately, then, the judge is "a combination of literary critic and moral philosopher. But that is only part of the picture. The judge also speaks with the authority of the Pope."[89]

This last assertion is directly relevant to an earlier essay of mine, in which I posited the existence of "protestant" and "catholic" ap-

87. In fairness to Fiss, I should note that he does not specifically endorse a correspondence theory of truth and, indeed, he specifically recognizes the participation of a reader-judge in bestowing meaning upon textual materials. "The idea of objective interpretation accommodates *the creative role* of the reader." Fiss, *supra* note 65, at 744 (emphasis added). Yet Fiss' article is replete with the tension generated by the joint embrace of creativity and objectivity.

The implications of Kuhn's thought for resolution of this tension are themselves the subject of an important scholarly debate. To be a critic of Kuhn does not seem to require a commitment to a correspondence (or context-independent) notion of truth, nor, apparently, does being a supporter entail commitment to radical indeterminacy. *See, e.g.*, H. PUTNAM, REASON, TRUTH AND HISTORY 113-19 (1981) (presenting criticisms of Kuhn within the context of a larger argument criticizing correspondence theories). Nonetheless it is clear that Kuhn has been most warmly embraced by critics of the notion of objectivity (and, beyond that, even of rationality) and that any theory which emphasizes the relevance of interpretive communities must confront the difficult sociological tasks of accounting for their composition and relationship to one another. *See* Brest, *Interpretation and Interest*, 34 STAN. L. REV. 765 (1982) (comments on Fiss). See the Fall 1982 issue of *Critical Inquiry* dealing with the politics of interpretation. 9 CRITICAL INQUIRY 1 (1982).

88. Fiss, *supra* note 65, at 747.

89. *Id.* at 755.

proaches to the Constitution.[90] That Fiss embraces a "catholic" Constitution, in the senses of looking to unwritten norms and accepting the institutional authority of the judiciary, tells us a great deal about him but only a little about the interpretive community. Indeed, a recent article co-authored by Fiss, attacking Justice Rehnquist, manifests all too well the problems faced by those seeking to slay the nihilist dragon.[91]

## V

The March 10, 1982 issue of *The New Republic* had as its cover story "The Rehnquist Court." The illustration of the cover is worth noting: A Sphinx-like head of Justice Rehnquist perches atop the "body" of the Supreme Court building. Reaching out on each side of the steps are the menacing paws of Sphinx-Rehnquist. The head, incidentally, is gazing with an ominous serenity into the distance. The phrase "Equal Justice Under Law" does not appear on the building. Finally, the magazine places the tag line ". . . and what it's doing to the Constitution" opposite the title. Fiss and his co-author, Charles Krauthammer, claim to have decoded the riddle of this particular sphinx, however, and it is the purpose of their article to bring the alarming news to the public. Whether or not the reader is convinced by the argument that the intellectual leader of the current Court is Justice Rehnquist, the specific way Rehnquist is described and criticized in the article gives great insight into the operation of Fiss' overall approach to legal analysis.

According to the article, Rehnquist's "opinions fall radically short of the ideals of the profession. He repudiates precedents frequently and openly, and if that is impossible (because the precedent represents a tradition that neither the Court nor society is prepared to abandon), then he distorts them."[92] The "failings of craft," however, pale before the real problem, which "is substance. Rehnquist has a constitutional program for the nation: he wants to free the states from the restrictions of the national Constitution, particularly those emanating from the

90. Levinson, *"The Constitution" in American Civil Religion*, 1979 SUP. CT. REV. 123, 132.

91. Fiss & Krauthammer, *supra* note 59.

92. *Id.* at 15. I confess myself mystified, incidentally, by what it means to say that "society" (rather than the Court) is or is not prepared to abandon a precedent, since the only relevant evidence we have is the Court's behavior. That behavior may indeed be based on its assessment of what society would tolerate, but it is also possible that a judge's attitude toward a precedent would be based on internal legal considerations, leading to a vote to overturn a (putatively mistaken) precedent even though society generally endorses the extra-constitutional decision.

Civil War Amendments and the Bill of Rights."[93] Thus Rehnquist rejects the incorporation doctrine as it has been used by the Court in the past two decades to "nationalize" the Bill of Rights.[94] Moreover, Rehnquist has led the way in questioning the extent to which Congress may legislate the behavior of the states.[95] And, the authors point out, Rehnquist has scarcely shown himself a textualist in his theory of constitutional interpretation, for he has proved skillful in adopting structural arguments to defend his particular theory of federalism.[96] Rehnquist "is no conservative, as that term is ordinarily understood in the law, but rather a revisionist of a particular ideological bent. He repudiates precedents; he shows no deference to the legislative branch; and he is unable to ground state autonomy in any textual provision of the Constitution."[97]

Yet the authors point out that Rehnquist claims more than his personal views as authority for his opinions. Indeed, he disparages those who emphasize contemporary social needs or morality as authorizing a "living Constitution";[98] instead Rehnquist is an "originalist,"[99] who sees the Court's task as enforcement of the goals of the framers themselves. Although Fiss and Krauthammer mention their doubts about the cogency of originalism,[100] they prefer to challenge Rehnquist on his own ground, for their argument is that he ignores the intent of the authors of the Civil War Amendments to diminish the state autonomy that concededly might have been the vision of at least some of the framers.[101] These amendments were not, they argue, "merely technical modifications to what Rehnquist claims to be the understanding at Philadelphia, corrections that assured all persons formal equality before the law. Rather, these amendments represent a second starting

93. *Id.* at 16.

94. *See, e.g.,* First Nat'l Bank v. Bellotti, 435 U.S. 765, 823 (1978) (Rehnquist, J., dissenting) (rejecting equal application of first amendment standards to state and national government).

95. Fiss and Krauthammer discuss Pennhurst State School v. Halderman, 457 U.S. 1 (1981), and National League of Cities v. Usery, 426 U.S. 833 (1976). They also mention Rizzo v. Goode, 423 U.S. 362 (1976), which severely limited the power of federal courts to impose effective remedies on state agencies. In *Rizzo* "a small percentage" of members of the Philadelphia police department had been found by a lower court to have systematically deprived people of their constitutional rights. Council of Organizations on Philadelphia Police Accountability and Responsibility v. Rizzo, 357 F. Supp. 1289, 1318 (E.D. Pa. 1973), *aff'd in part and rev'd in part sub nom.* Goode v. Rizzo, 506 F.2d 542 (3d Cir. 1974), *rev'd*, 423 U.S. 362 (1976).

96. *See* National League of Cities v. Usery, 426 U.S. 833, 845-52 (1976) (arguing that Congress cannot infringe on a state's sovereign power and that imposition of minimum wage laws on municipalities infringes on essential sovereign functions).

97. Fiss & Krauthammer, *supra* note 59, at 18, 20.

98. *See* Rehnquist, *The Notion of A Living Constitution*, 54 TEXAS L. REV. 693 (1976).

99. *See* Brest, *supra* note 17.

100. Fiss & Krauthammer, *supra* note 59, at 20.

101. *Id.*

point, a basic change in the postulates of our constitutional system. Any appeal to history which ignores that is a sham."[102]

I have no trouble agreeing that Rehnquist's jurisprudence is questionable in theory and pernicious in practice. But the terms of this attack, derived as they are from the allegedly internal professional norms of the legal interpretive community, present the occasion for embarrassment, if not incoherence. For, as the authors recognize, "the Marshall Court (in its affirmation of nationalism) and the Warren Court (in its affirmation of equality) also repudiated strict constructionism and practiced judicial activism."[103] Indeed, for Fiss and Krauthammer, "[t]he most plausible interpretation of *Brown*[104] is that it simply repudiated *Plessy*,[105] in an attempt to reflect a truer understanding of the fourteenth amendment. For the Warren Court, as for Rehnquist, precedent had less force than the framers' original understanding of the text they wrote."[106] It is clear from Fiss' earlier comments, though, that he would defend *Brown* even if he were convinced beyond a reasonable doubt that the framers of the fourteenth amendment did not understand that amendment to bar school segregation.[107]

If Rehnquist were simply a conservative law professor, like Robert Bork,[108] Ralph Winter,[109] or Richard Posner,[110] then it would be easy to dismiss his views by noting the extent to which they require the modification or abandonment of many of our "papal edicts" from the Warren Court. But the very point of the article, of course, is based on the proferred fact that Rehnquist is rapidly becoming the chief declarer of

102. *Id. But see* Benedict, *Preserving Federalism: Reconstruction and the Waite Court*, 1978 SUP. CT. REV. 39, 47-48 (footnotes omitted):

> Historians now recognize that every Reconstruction-era effort to protect the rights of citizens was tempered by the fundamental conviction that federalism required that the day-to-day protection of the citizen had to remain the duty of the States . . . . As to the permanent protections for Americans' rights, despite arguments to the contrary by those modern legal scholars who write in the tradition of a new nationalism, all the evidence of the congressional discussions, the ratification debates, and the public controversy indicates that Republicans intended the States to retain primary jurisdiction over citizens' rights. They attempted to write into the Constitution an obligation that antislavery theorists already believed incumbent on the States: the requirement that they protect all citizens equally in fundamental human rights. They did not intend the national government to replace the States in fulfilling that obligation.

Benedict builds on the important book by Harold Hyman, A MORE PERFECT UNION (1973).

103. Fiss & Krauthammer, *supra* note 59, at 20.

104. Brown v. Board of Educ., 347 U.S. 483 (1954).

105. Plessy v. Ferguson, 163 U.S. 537 (1896).

106. Fiss & Krauthammer, *supra* note 59, at 20 (footnotes added).

107. *See supra* text accompanying notes 73-79.

108. Now Judge Bork of the Court of Appeals for the District of Columbia.

109. Now Judge Winter of the Court of Appeals for the Second Circuit.

110. Now Judge Posner of the Court of Appeals for the Seventh Circuit.

Law as Literature

what the Constitution requires, and that the Court-directed interpretive community will increasingly revolve around him.

It is hardly likely, of course, that Professor Fiss (or I) will start teaching students the (normative) Constitution according to Rehnquist, even as we make our students aware of the existence of the appalling Rehnquist *oeuvre*. But will Professor Fiss argue that the interpretive community has been taken over by a false pope, a usurper, against whom the truly faithful must rally? Moreover, given the willingness of the voting public to elect a President and a majority of the Senate who share many of Rehnquist's values, how will Fiss (or anyone else) show that they contravene the public values embodied in the Constitution, especially given the undoubted interest of our Constitution-writers in protecting at least some measure of both state autonomy and the rights of private property owners?

Fiss' approach to the Constitution, like that of Professor Dworkin, ultimately rests on the premise that there is no genuine conflict among the values that animate the different parts of the public.[111] But, as Bray Hammond put it in his analysis of the early dispute in our history about the power of Congress to charter the Bank of the United States, "The controversy demonstrated at the very outset that the Constitution had not displaced rival principles or reconciled them but had become their dialectical arena."[112] This last term may bring to mind either the

111. See Levinson, *supra* note 39, at 1083-84, for a critique of Dworkin on this point. See also J. Ely, Democracy and Distrust 43-72 (1980), for a comprehensive attack on the "fundamental values" approach that Fiss in fact is defending.

112. B. Hammond, Banks and Politics in America 120 (1957). See also Paul Bator's reminder that "the Constitution itself contains a multiplicity of various sorts of values, many in tension with each other: process values as well as substantive values, structural and institutional values as well as those embodying individual rights." Bator, *The State Courts and Federal Constitutional Litigation*, 22 Wm. & Mary L. Rev. 605, 633 (1981). Indeed, Professor Bator argues eloquently for the desirability of a role for state court participation in constitutional adjudication precisely in terms of the ability of state judges to recognize values that federal judges are prone to overlook. In contrast to an argument which assumes "that the Constitution contains only one or two *sorts* of values: typically, those which protect the individual from the power of the state, and those which assure the superiority of federal to state law," Bator presents a different view:

> But the Constitution contains other sorts of values as well. It gives the federal government powers, but also enacts limitations on those powers. *The limitations, too, count as setting forth constitutional values*. Will the federal judge be more sensitive than the state judge in insuring that these limitations are complied with? Whose institutional "set" is likely to make one more sensitive to the values underlying the tenth amendment? . . . Why don't these sorts of issues even seem to count?

*Id.* at 631-32 (emphasis in original). Though I suspect I share more of Fiss' political values than I do those of Professor Bator, I have little hesitation in saying that I think Bator presents a more plausible view of the Constitution. That view, however, offers no guidance as to the dilemmas generated by recognizing the multiplicity (and contradictions) of constitutional values.

Resolving the dialectical tension, of course, is a central dilemma. See, for example, Tushnet, *Darkness on the Edge of Town: The Contributions of John Hart Ely to Constitutional Theory*, 89 Yale L.J. 1037 (1980), for an argument that value conflict cannot be resolved within the frame-

controversy of the seminar table or warfare in which each side claims adherence to the "true" meaning of the disputed document. It is the latter mode of dispute resolution that is suggested by Justice Black's comment that "the fundamental issues over the extent of federal supremacy had been resolved by war."[113] But surely there is something peculiar about the assertion that fundamental ideological issues are "resolved" by war, even if we concede that political power indeed often comes from the barrels of guns, and even if it is possible to identify clearly the doctrinal position that won or lost a particular battle. Indeed, Fiss and Krauthammer may even be correct that Rehnquist's views, taken to an extreme, reopen the dilemmas that ultimately led to the outbreak of war. But if that be so, it is only because of the continuing tension in American values and the inability of either armed victory or judicial articulation to settle the dispute firmly one way or another. Perhaps Rehnquist is attempting to resolve what he sees as a genuine legal crisis by reasserting certain traditional moral and legal values. That he cannot achieve resolution says more about the pervasiveness of the fundamental conflicts than it does about his mistake in reading our fundamental values.

The American wish is that one can avoid having to answer the political question posed by a Harlan County labor song, "Which side are you on?", by responding that one stands by the Constitution and that, in turn, the Constitution itself stands for the proper values. The transformation of political questions into legal questions, first emphasized by de Tocqueville,[114] allows the "adjudication" of disputes. As Fiss notes, however, "The idea of adjudication requires that there exist constitutional values to interpret, just as much as it requires that there be constraints on the interpretive process. Lacking such a belief, adju-

work of traditional liberal constitutionalism. See also the remarkable article by Frank Easterbrook, *Ways of Criticizing the Court*, 95 HARV. L. REV. 802, 811-31 (1982), which demonstrates by the use of social choice theory the extreme unlikelihood (indeed, impossibility, given the most likely empirical conditions) of the existence of a procedure for legal decisionmaking adequate to generate "definitive" decisions over time by the Supreme Court (let alone by the community at large). Easterbrook's article is a major challenge to those who look to the Supreme Court for clear articulation of basic legal precepts, especially if one accepts the proposition that there are at least three values contending in Hammond's "dialectical arena." Whether or not Easterbrook is accurately described as a "nihilist," his conclusions are in their own way every bit as hopeless as any in Tushnet's writings or the instant essay.

113. Testa v. Katt, 330 U.S. 386, 390 (1947).

114. 1 A. DE TOCQUEVILLE, DEMOCRACY IN AMERICA 290 (Vintage ed. 1945). It should be noted that de Tocqueville specifically stressed the tendency of a political question to be "resolved, sooner or later, into a judicial question." *Id.* For the importance of the emphasis on the judiciary as institutional resolver, see Levinson, *Fidelity to Law and the Assessment of Political Activity*, 27 STAN. L. REV. 1185, 1190-91 (1975).

dication is not possible, only power."[115]

As he portrays the bleakness of a world that rejects belief in the possibility of principled adjudication, Fiss speaks with much of the same eloquence and vigor as does Gerald Graff. It is worth noting that Richard Rorty, whose work has much influenced me, has indicated his own empathy with the attacks of Graff and others on the new literary criticism. What is at stake is a conception of the possibility of a shared moral life. Rorty refers to "the view that, in the end, when all the intellectuals have done all their tricks, morality remains widely shared and available to reflection—something capable of being discovered rather than created, because already implicit in the common consciousness of everyone."[116] Critics with this view "want criticism to bring an antecedent morality to light, enlarge upon it and enrich it," and they consequently "resist the suggestion that there is no common vocabulary in terms of which critics can argue with one another about how well this task has been performed."[117] No one with a democratic sensibility can easily reject the vision of a common discourse described by Rorty and evoked by Fiss.

Empathy, however, does not equal agreement. It would be contradictory to say that the historicist pragmatism celebrated by Rorty is "true," or that philosophy has "disproved" the possibility of true and certain knowledge about the natural world, including its moral component. But those who do not already share Fiss' faith are unlikely, I suspect, to be persuaded by his attack on positions like the one articulated in the present essay. The inability of Fiss and his co-author to mount a persuasive attack on Justice Rehnquist in anything other than political terms reveals the parlous state of contemporary constitutional discourse. The united interpretive community that is necessary to Fiss' own argument simply does not exist.[118] What one does in the absence of such a community is, of course, a problem of more than merely theoretical import. The decreasing propensity of the body politic to accord

115. Fiss, *supra* note 65, at 763.

116. R. Rorty, *supra* note 14, at 157.

117. *Id.* Indeed, responding to an earlier version of the present essay, Rorty wrote,

> I confess that I tremble at the thought of Barthian readings in law schools . . . . I suspect that civilization reposes on a lot of people who take the normal practices of the discipline with full "realistic" seriousness. However, I should like to think that a pragmatist's understanding of knowledge and community would be, in the end, compatible with normal inquiry—the practitioners of such inquiry reserving their irony for after-hours.

Letter from Richard Rorty to author (Apr. 28, 1981) (copy on file with the *Texas Law Review*). It is not clear, then, what Rorty's stance would be to those who would attempt to make his own thought central to their regular daily work.

118. *See supra* text accompanying note 111.

the Supreme Court ultimate authority in constitutional interpretation may portend an ever deeper constitutional crisis, especially if any of the jurisdiction- and remedy-limiting bills now before Congress had passed and received presidential signature.[119]

## VI

Even poets who emphasize the contingency of perception nevertheless continue to write their poems. "Even the linking of stars is a lie./ But for a while now let's be happy/ to believe the symbol. That's enough."[120] And so we who take the constitutional firmament seriously continue as well to write our articles and dispute with one another.[121] And, just as constellations are human attempts to link the separate stars, so are doctrinal analyses likely to serve as similar attempts to demonstrate that the cases themselves are meaningfully linked and intellectually patterned. All such writing (and reading) is a supreme act of faith. We can hope that some future conjunction of author and reader will provide a common language of constitutional

119. *See, e.g.,* S. 158, 97th Cong., 1st Sess. ("Human Life" bill) (1981); S. 481, 97th Cong., 1st Sess. (1981) (depriving federal courts of jurisdiction over cases regarding voluntary prayers in public schools). Although both of these bills were ultimately defeated in the Senate, conservative forces have indicated their intention to raise both issues again early in the next Congress. It is therefore unlikely that Congress has definitively resolved these conflicts. *See* N.Y. Times, Sept. 17, 1982, at A19, col. 1.

120. R. Rilke, Duino Elegies and the Sonnets to Orpheus 105 (A. Poulin trans. 1975) (Sonnets to Orpheus, First Series, No. 11).

121. Grant Gilmore has noted the existence in an earlier generation of "nihilist" individuals who were led by their own arguments to eschew writing itself. *See* G. Gilmore, The Ages of American Law 80-81 (1977) (discussing Wesley Sturges). Although the peculiar traditions of law schools in regard to tenure have meant that there have always been a relatively high number of nonwriters on law school faculties, *see* Ackerman, *The Marketplace of Ideas*, 90 Yale L.J. 1131, 1132-35 (1981), it may be that at least some of the failure to write is based on a conviction of having "nothing to say" in the profoundest sense of that term. It is not a coincidence, I suspect, that a substantial amount of the writing of scholars Fiss would be likely to view as "nihilists" is in the area of legal history and, more particularly, the ideological analysis of legal thought, whether expressed in cases, classic legal writings, or the work-product of scholars. In addition to the works cited *supra* note 48, see, e.g., Gordon, *Historicism in Legal Scholarship*, 90 Yale L.J. 1017 (1981); Katz, *Studies in Boundary Theory: Three Essays in Adjudication and Politics*, 28 Buffalo L. Rev. 383 (1979); D. Kennedy, The Rise and Fall of Classical Legal Thought 1850-1940 (1976) (unpublished manuscript); Kennedy, *The Structure of Blackstone's Commentaries*, 28 Buffalo L. Rev. 209 (1979); Schlegel, *American Legal Realism and Empirical Social Science: From the Yale Experience*, 28 Buffalo L. Rev. 459 (1979); Schlegel, *American Legal Realism and Empirical Social Science: The Singular Case of Underhill Moore*, 29 Buffalo L. Rev. 195 (1980). This (greatly truncated) list belies any genuine notion that persons alienated from a traditional stance of reverence (or even respect) for law have nothing to say. But it is fair to say that no one who defines his or her task as the search for "certain principles or doctrines," *see supra* text accompanying note 2, is prepared to listen. Few today would admit that they *are* engaged in such a search, for all of us portray ourselves as post-Realists, focusing on "policies" underlying the law. But see Gordon, Book Review, 1974 Wis. L. Rev. 1216 (reviewing G. Gilmore, The Death of Contract (1974)), for an analysis of the desiccated nature of the so-called policy analysis that occurs in American law schools.

discourse fit for "a nation of supple and athletic minds,"[122] but for now we can only await its coming and make do with the fractured and fragmented discourse available to us.[123]

122. W. WHITMAN, *supra* note 1, at 545.
123. *See* Leff, UNSPEAKABLE ETHICS, UNNATURAL LAW, 1979 DUKE L.J. 1229, 1249:

> All I can say is this: it looks as if we are all we have. Given what we know about ourselves and each other, this is an extraordinarily unappetizing prospect; looking around the world, it appears that if all men are brothers, the ruling model is Cain and Abel. Neither reason, nor love, nor even terror, seems to have worked to make us "good," and worse than that, there is no reason why anything should. Only if ethics were something unspeakable by us, could law be unnatural, and therefore unchallengeable. As things now stand, everything is up for grabs.
>
> Nevertheless:
>
> Napalming babies is bad.
>
> Starving the poor is wicked.
>
> Buying and selling each other is depraved.
>
> Those who stood up to and died resisting Hitler, Stalin, Amin, and Pol Pot—and General Custer too—have earned salvation.
>
> Those who acquiesced deserve to be damned.
>
> There is in the world such a thing as evil.
>
> [All together now:] Sez who?
>
> God help us.

# [15]

# "Keep off the Grass," "Drop Dead," and Other Indeterminacies: A Response to Sanford Levinson

Gerald Graff*

> In legal practice it is usually all right to treat laws as if they were solid things whose effects have definite spatial boundaries and material consequences. When a semiotician starts examining laws as a patterned system of meanings their insubstantiality becomes evident, and the inquiry presses on both jurisprudence and epistemology.
>
> —Mary Douglas[1]

The anthropologist Mary Douglas' point here seems to me right, and insofar as Professor Levinson's paper echoes her point, it seems to me right too. Not only lawyers but most people harbor superstitions about the nature of language and meaning. These superstitions assume that meanings reside "in" language somewhat the way furniture resides in rooms—securely "there" where the interpreter can see, identify, and grasp them the way we can see, identify, and grasp tables and chairs. Holding this conception of language, one is naturally going to be disturbed when a semiotician or some other new-style theorist of language comes along and says it isn't so at all, and points out that meanings have nothing like the substantiality of tables and chairs. Even worse, this theorist says that the words by which we signify "tables" and "chairs" are only somewhat arbitrary sounds, that even the visible "furniture" of the world is insubstantial, for the language we use to describe that world segments it in culturally conditioned ways. The more vertiginous the theorist makes things appear, the more inclined we are to cling to what's left of the "common sense" view of language, according to which words are essentially names of things and the meanings of words are securely fastened like barnacles onto the things the words denote. Those professionally concerned with the law may feel an especially strong need to cling to such superstitions lest the stability of their occupation, not to mention the stability of the law itself, be threatened.

I suspect that the legitimate inspiration of Sanford Levinson's pa-

* Professor of English, Northwestern University. B.A. 1959, University of Chicago; Ph.D. 1963, Stanford University.

1. Douglas, *The Future of Semiotics*,—SEMIOTICA—(forthcoming 1982).

per, *Law as Literature*,[2] was in some such view of why lawyers, judges, and other professional students of the law hold these superstitions. Levinson observes—rightly, I would guess, though I haven't his inside knowledge—that much thinking about meaning and interpretation among legal professionals is badly outmoded, and that it remains intact only for fear of the Pandora's box that would be opened if more up-to-date theories were admitted into court.[3] He writes to unmask this outmoded thinking, and to that extent I find no fault with his project. The belief that meaning is a substance or spirit reposing *in* language can't be exploded too soon to suit me. But it makes some difference *how* one goes about exploding this belief and what one puts in its place. Here I find serious flaws in Levinson's argument.

That argument rests on a good many non sequiturs, most of which, however, can be reduced to a single major one: Levinson assumes throughout his paper that once the fallacy of semantic immanence which I've described above is discarded, our practical ability to make sense of texts and utterances is somehow endangered or impaired. He falsely assumes, in other words, that our ability to decipher a text—whether that text be a legal document or some other text need not concern us here—depends on our ability to grasp what he calls "some presumed inner essence" that reposes *in* the "text being interpreted."[4] Judging quite correctly that no such inner essence exists, Levinson leaps to several illogical conclusions: that legal and other texts are therefore marked by a radical indeterminacy,[5] that there is no real truth in interpretation and "anything is permitted,"[6] and that what eventually gets construed as the correct interpretation in any given instance is a function merely of the institutional fiat or "coerciveness" of the interpreter.[7]

Levinson actually makes the same mistake committed by those whom he is attacking. Like them, he believes that if meaning is not an inner essence in utterances, meaning is then indeterminate and disputes over meaning aren't susceptible to rational procedures of adjudication. The difference between Levinson and those he opposes is merely a tactical or political difference: whereas they would presumably keep the cat in the bag, Levinson would let it out. The mistake of both parties is

2. Levinson, *Law as Literature*, 60 TEXAS L. REV. 373 (1982).

3. *See* Levinson, *Legal Realism and the Return of the Repressed: Some Notes on the Contemporary Status of Legal Thought*, __ AMER. Q. __ (forthcoming 1983).

4. Levinson, *supra* note 2, at 385.

5. *Id.* at 391 & n.64.

6. *Id.* at 388.

7. *Id.* at 386.

Response to Sanford Levinson

in supposing that there is any radical consequence in letting the cat out, or indeed that there is any cat in the bag to begin with.

Instances of Levinson's faulty reasoning could be cited from many pages of his essay, but I'll content myself with one or two of the more glaring. Levinson asks whether meaning "is to be found *within* a case or do we as analysts participate in creating the meaning of a given case?"[8] If there's a right answer to this question (which I would not like to encounter in a true/false test), it would have to be "neither." The alternatives are misleadingly formulated. Any sophisticated theorist of language would point out that the meaning of an utterance isn't a function of the words themselves or even of sentences, but of the *use* to which the words and sentences are put by speakers and writers. The notion of meaning as something "to be found *within* a case," which is, again, Levinson's "inner essence," is wrong to begin with. Meaning is an affair of the use of words and sentences, not of words and sentences considered as things-in-themselves which somehow bear meanings within them. This use can be *inferred* from words and sentences, because words and sentences have recognizably conventional uses, which are the "meanings" listed in dictionaries. But strictly speaking, no word or sentence means anything determinate until it is used in a specific situation by somebody, until it is employed in a speech act.

To be sure, we can talk of what words or even sentences mean apart from their uses. Speech act theorists like John Searle and H.P. Grice distinguish between "sentence meaning" and "utterance meaning" to distinguish between the kind of understanding we can have of a context-free sentence like "keep off the grass" and of the same sentence when actually used by somebody to commit a speech act, say, of warning.[9] One might suppose that the expression "keep off the grass" is sufficiently familiar that we know what it means independent of any situation in which it may be used. In fact, the expression's familiarity probably depends on our imagining a standard situation with which we associate the words—a sign seen on a well-manicured lawn, say, or the cry of a gardener working on such a lawn while somebody is walking across it. "Keep off the grass" would *mean* something entirely different if we overheard the expression uttered by a narcotics-counselor, in appropriate circumstances, to a person known to us as a convicted mari-

8. This quotation is from an earlier draft of Professor Levinson's article, *id.*; and, although it is not in the final version of that article, Professor Levinson acknowledges that the quotation accurately reflects his views.

9. *See* J. Searle, Expression and Meaning: Studies in the Theory of Speech Acts 117-36 (1979); Grice, *Utterer's Meaning and Intentions*, 78 Phil. Rev. 147 (1969).

Texas Law Review Vol. 60:405, 1982

juana-user. Even sentences that lack the same potential for ambiguity as the example I've chosen ("Keep off the tulips") can be used to mean a great variety of things. Though we can say that certain utterances "normally" are used to mean one thing rather than others they might potentially be used to mean (and it's such normal expectations that enable us to make educated guesses of what is meant in particular cases), this fact itself demonstrates that interpretation is concerned not with what words or sentences mean "in themselves" but with how speakers actualize the semantic potential of words and utterances in particular speech acts.

In this sense, meaning is not a substance but an activity and has the determinacy of an activity rather than of a physical object. Guessing the meaning of a text or utterance is inferring what a writer or speaker was or is *doing* with language and not what some linguistic object essentially was or is. Now what writers and speakers may be doing with words is as open to more or less reliable inference, according to the kinds of evidence that guides such inference, as is any other kind of human action. The question of what any text means, then, is neither more nor less open to "determinate" inference than the question of whether a person did or didn't commit a particular act, or whether a historical event occurred or didn't occur. Just as we have reason to believe that we know a lot about some historical occurrences, less about others, and so little about still others that their very occurrence may be conjectural, so it is with texts: the degree to which we can be confident about our inferences depends on the amount of evidence available, evidence which itself is open to criticism and may well be fallible.

Consider, for example, the problem of interpreting the words "drop dead." We would interpret these words in one way if we heard them shouted by the driver whose car we had just cut in front of on the freeway, and quite a different way if we heard them spoken—even with the same intensity and tone of voice—by a friend whom we knew well, or one whom we knew to be a frequent kidder. Again, the example points up the fact that meaning doesn't reside *in* the expression "drop dead," an expression which has acquired certain standard meanings only because of a history of use that has established those meanings as normal and conventional. And apart from some inferable situation in which "drop dead" is used to commit a speech act, whether it be to insult a passing motorist or to chide a friend gently, "drop dead" doesn't mean anything in particular. But Levinson, were he to remain faithful to the logic of his argument, would be obliged to conclude that since "drop dead" doesn't mean anything in particular in itself, it is therefore a radically indeterminate expression.

There are, to be sure, instances in which "drop dead" might very well be indeterminate. Suppose, for example, someone were to send Levinson an unsigned note with those words printed on it. How would he be able to guess whether the note constituted a serious expression of ill will, a threat, a joke, a put-on, or a message intended for another recipient mistakenly sent to him? The first thing most people would do on receiving such a note is start inventing circumstances to explain it. If by coincidence Levinson had just had a run-in with an ill-tempered student, he might be tempted to attribute the note to that student and thus to interpret it as an expression of ill will or as a threat, if not a literal wish for his extinction.[10] But if no such explanation came to Levinson's mind, he would not know what to make of such a note; its meaning, in this instance, would be indeterminate. Similarly, imagine a situation in which Levinson is told to "drop dead" by a colleague whom he doesn't know very well, or one suspected of psychological instability. Was the remark meant as a serious expression of malice or as badinage? Was it, in the case of the unstable colleague, perhaps meant in both ways at once, expressing ambivalence in that colleague's attitude toward Levinson, or in his attitude toward all his colleagues or the world?

Given the absence of sufficient evidence in such cases, evidence helping us identify the situations in terms of which speech acts are recognized, Levinson is not going to be able to interpret that note. But this kind of frustration, stemming from relative lack of evidence, doesn't introduce any *radical* indeterminacy into the practice of interpretation, except insofar as it means we can never be *certain* we understand what any text or utterance means. The older a text is and the more alien the culture that produced it, the more difficult it is likely to be to reconstruct the conventional situations in terms of which interpreters fix the meanings of speech acts. What might count for us as a "normal" or "standard" contextual indicator of a threat, say, or of a warning, or of praise or blame, may not have so counted in the convention-system of the culture that produced the text we are trying to decipher. A text produced by a culture in which masochism or sadism was the normal morality would be difficult for us to grasp, since we might mistake cer-

10. Though we can imagine situations in which "drop dead" can be used to express a literal wish for someone's extinction and would be interpreted as such, conventional use decrees that unless otherwise indicated we do not take it as that.

tain expressions of approval for disapproval.[11] There may in some instances be so little commonality between the convention system of the interpreter and that of another culture that it's not possible to crack the code of that culture's texts at all. There's no reason to suppose that all texts can be interpreted, that every hieroglyphic can be deciphered. Insofar as we take interpretation to be possible at all, however, we assume there is at least sufficient commonality (or commensurability) between different convention systems for areas of disparity and misunderstanding to be detected and defined.

What I think Levinson has failed to understand about interpretation is that it's essentially a messy business of guesswork predicated on practical knowledge of language, conventions, and the situations in which they operate. Levinson begins with an unrealistic expectation about interpretation and then adopts an unnecessary scepticism when the expectation isn't met. He supposes either that interpretations have the unchallenged authority of divine commandments, or else that they have no authority whatsoever except the coercive authority of institutional force. Again, to illustrate this charge fully would be tedious, so I'll content myself with a few flagrant examples. Levinson adverts to the "search for finality of interpretation"; he doubts the possibility of "final interpretive authority"; and he endorses "the proposition that there can be no ultimately provable right answer in legal discourse."[12] Just as Levinson had offered a false choice between understanding meaning as immanent in language and understanding it as indeterminate or determined only by whim or fiat, so here he offers another false choice between total absolutism and total uncertainty. In both cases, the choice is one of All or Nothing.

The problem is that the practice of interpretation doesn't depend on interpreters' possessing godlike power to arrive at an "ultimately provable right answer" that closes the books on further argument about the meaning of a text. Therefore the lack of such godlike power doesn't entail indeterminacy in Levinson's sense of that word. (The statement that law and mathematics have "the same" indeterminacy "as literature" is question-begging, since it assumes that the indeterminacy of literature is already well-established, which of course it isn't.) Levinson has merely inverted the gesture of the interpretive absolutist, who in-

11. The large element of redundancy in any communication is what tends to prevent our getting far with such mistakes and forces us to try more workable interpretive hypotheses. One just would not get very far in processing the sadistic text according to anti-sadistic conventions of morality.

12. *Supra*, note 8.

Response to Sanford Levinson

sists that there is One True Meaning and that he alone possesses it. Levinson turns this absolutism upside-down and comes out with an equally prescriptive No True Meaning. The alternatives he gives are simply unreal.

There are, to be sure, special problems attending the interpretation of legal texts, or the interpretation of texts from a legal point of view. Interpretations of statutes and legal documents have to carry authority in a way that a literary critic's interpretation of a poem or a bystander's interpretation of a remark in the street do not. Judges have to resolve ambiguities in statutes on one side or another even when there may be no very good reason to prefer one interpretation over conflicting ones. From a legal point of view, certain speech act conventions that operate in ordinary situations may have to be disregarded. I noticed in an airport recently a posted warning that persons who make jokes about having weapons in their possession as they pass through the inspection line may be prosecuted, meaning that from the legal point of view the frivolous or pretended claim to be packing a gun may be equivalent to a serious claim. For obvious practical reasons, the distinction between different kinds of speech acts has to be suspended in this case, as it might have to be in the case of somebody who only jokingly shouted fire in a crowded theatre. In short, the practical concerns of the law occasion the imposition of a number of *artificial* restrictions on interpretive procedure, restrictions that do not apply outside the legal context. These restrictions arise from practical, ethical considerations rather than epistemological ones, a distinction that is especially important if we want to grapple with the many serious problems that are posed by the interpretation of statutes and constitutions. Let me explain this last point more fully.

Questions of what the drafters of the United States Constitution may have meant or intended can be highly debatable and difficult to resolve. But it's a different kind of question from that of how the Constitution ought to be *applied* in a particular case of jurisprudence. Thus even where agreement is possible over what the Founding Fathers probably intended with respect to questions such as slavery or private possession of weapons, there may still be debate over how that intention ought to be applied to later circumstances, circumstances the drafters of the document didn't or couldn't foresee. Thus there may arise strong ethical or practical reasons for choosing to disregard the inferred intentions of the Founding Fathers, or for choosing to let one set of intentions override a conflicting set, or even for choosing to construe those original intentions in a sense at odds with their inferred original import. Debates that arise over all these choices may prove difficult to resolve, but my point is that such debates are distinguishable from debates over what the original intentions of the Founding Fathers were, and that the latter only are interpretive debates whereas the former are debates over the proper application of interpretations. What complicates such debates in practice, of course, is that both kinds of problems are often at issue—the intentions of the Founding Fathers are open to dispute, thus making it all the more difficult to negotiate disagreements over how those intentions should be applied. In any case, the special problems occasioned by legal interpretation in the area of application are essentially, as I have said, problems of ethical and political application. They are not epistemological problems, problems of how we are able to determine what texts mean.

To confuse the problem of what a text may be interpreted to mean with the problem of what application ought to be made of that interpretation (assuming the interpretation can be agreed on) is to plunge ourselves into a hopeless muddle. Levinson is trapped in this muddle necessarily, since his argument forbids him to distinguish between the search for interpretive truth and the forms of power and self-interest that for him determine the truth. Yet Levinson begins to recognize by the end of the paper that he's trapped himself in a contradiction. On the one hand, he wants to say that interpretation in general is radically "problematic," since it's determined not by considerations of truth or good reasons but merely by institutional power;[13] on the other hand, this argument proves inconvenient when he needs to give weight to his own interpretations. For example, Levinson says that the structuralist literary critic, Colin MacCabe, "is *correctly viewed* as fundamentally antagonistic to the view that the only task of students is to read set texts, without ever reflecting on the notion of 'reading' itself."[14] But according to what set of interpretive procedures is MacCabe "correctly viewed" the way Levinson says he's viewed? And why should the notion of correctness that's operating in such a judgment be taken seriously if, as Levinson has been arguing, such notions of correctness are the products of an institutional power that we ought to be trying to get out from under? What permits Levinson to appeal so selectively to an interpretive standard which, to this point, he has presented as an authoritarian fiction? One could cite other examples of Levinson's selective reliance on norms he appears to have discredited, but again I see no point in multiplying instances.

13. *Id.* at 385.
14. *Id.* at 388-89 (emphasis added).

Response to Sanford Levinson

I say "*appears* to have discredited" because finally Levinson's views are just as slippery as those of his mentors, Richard Rorty and Stanley Fish,[15] when one asks what precise consequences for interpretative practice these views are supposed to have. What these theorists insist on over and over again is the Nietzschean idea that interpretations are *made* by us and not found, that it is we who have created the standards and norms of interpretive truth that we so confidently attribute to the nature of things, and that we must recognize our personal and political responsibility for this creation.[16] But taken merely this far, such an assertion is merely a platitude, to which the proper reply is not, "No, that's not the case," but rather, "Yes, that's true, but *so what?*" Does the knowledge that we've in a sense "created" our interpretive norms compromise our interpretations in practice or doesn't it? If it does, what are we supposed to do? What alternative to current interpretive practices ought we take up? From what alternative standpoint (not contaminated by dependence on those current practices) is this critique of current practices being offered? If, on the other hand, the fact that our interpretive norms are conventional and man-made doesn't compromise them, or if any ideological criticism of some of these norms would depend on accepting others, then what is all the fuss about?

As I stated at the outset, I can well believe (though without firsthand knowledge) that the linguistic fallacies Levinson's paper sets out to overturn are widely held by theorists of legal interpretation. The beliefs that meanings are inherent in utterances and texts and that interpretation is a business of scooping them out and claiming a degree of certainty about them that's immune to counterargument, revision, and refutation—these beliefs die hard. But the remedy for bad theories of interpretation is better theories; replacing one set of superstitions with another, however "radical" or "subversive," just isn't the way.

15. *See id.* at 376 n.14, 380-84.

16. *Id.* at 383-84. Of course, Levinson may have taken Fish and Rorty to be more radical than they mean to be.

# [16]

# Deconstructive Practice and Legal Theory

J. M. Balkin†

*The stone that the builders rejected has become*
*the chief cornerstone.*

—*Psalms* 118:22

The purpose of this Article is to introduce legal readers to the ideas of the French philosopher Jacques Derrida, and to his philosophical practices regarding the interpretation of texts, sometimes known as deconstruction.[1] The term "deconstruction" is much used in legal writings these days,[2] and in this Article I propose to explain its philosophical underpinnings. Many persons who use the word "deconstruction" regard it as no more than another expression for "trashing," that is, showing why legal

---

† Assistant Professor of Law, University of Missouri-Kansas City. Harvard University A.B., 1978, J.D. 1981. I would like to thank my research assistants, Linda Talley, Suzanne Bardgett, and Jan Dodd, for their help in the preparation of this Article, and my colleagues, Joan Mahoney and James Kushner, for their comments on a previous draft.

1. Derrida has developed his ideas in several books and essays dating from 1967, some of which have only recently been translated into English. J. DERRIDA, DISSEMINATION (B. Johnson trans. 1981) [hereinafter DISSEMINATION]; J. DERRIDA, MARGINS OF PHILOSOPHY (1982) [hereinafter MARGINS OF PHILOSOPHY]; J. DERRIDA, OF GRAMMATOLOGY (1976) [hereinafter OF GRAMMATOLOGY]; J. DERRIDA, POSITIONS (1981) [hereinafter POSITIONS]; J. DERRIDA, SPURS (1979) [hereinafter SPURS]; J. DERRIDA, SPEECH AND PHENOMENA (1973) [hereinafter SPEECH AND PHENOMENA]; J. DERRIDA, WRITING AND DIFFERENCE (1978) [hereinafter WRITING AND DIFFERENCE]; Derrida, *The Law of Genre*, 7 GLYPH 202 (1980); Derrida, *Limited Inc abc* . . ., 2 GLYPH 162 (1977) [hereinafter *Limited Inc abc*].

The best general introduction to Derrida's thought is J. CULLER, ON DECONSTRUCTION (1982). Other good sources are H. STATEN, WITTGENSTEIN AND DERRIDA (1984) (suggesting Anglo-American philosophical approach to deconstruction); Johnson, *Translator's Introduction* to DISSEMINATION, *supra*, at vii; Rorty, *Philosophy as a Kind of Writing: An Essay on Derrida*, 10 NEW LITERARY HIST. 141 (1978); Spivak, *Translator's Preface* to OF GRAMMATOLOGY, *supra*, at ix (essay requires familiarity with continental philosophers and Freud). None of these has considered the relevance of Derrida's thought to legal theory.

2. *See, e.g.*, Dalton, *An Essay in the Deconstruction of Contract Doctrine*, 94 YALE L.J. 997 (1985); Frug, *The Ideology of Bureaucracy in American Law*, 97 HARV. L. REV. 1276, 1288–99 (1984) (citing Derrida's notions of "dangerous supplement"); Hegland, *Goodbye to Deconstruction*, 58 S. CAL. L. REV. 1203 (1985); Spann, *Deconstructing the Legislative Veto*, 68 MINN. L. REV. 473 (1984); Tushnet, *Critical Legal Studies and Constitutional Law: An Essay in Deconstruction*, 36 STAN. L. REV. 623 (1984); Note, *Overshooting the Target: A Feminist Deconstruction of Legal Education*, 34 AM. U.L. REV. 1141 (1985); Hutchinson, *From Cultural Construction to Historical Deconstruction* (Book Review), 94 YALE L.J. 209, 229–35 (1984).

doctrines are self-contradictory, ideologically biased, or indeterminate.[3] By the term "deconstruction," however, I do not have in mind merely stinging criticism, but specific techniques and philosophical ideas that Derrida and his followers have applied to various texts. These techniques often do involve teasing out the hidden antinomies in our language and thought, and that is primarily how I came to be interested in them.[4] However, I hope to demonstrate that "deconstruction," as I use the term, is not simply a fancy way of sticking out your tongue, but a practice that raises important philosophical issues for legal thinkers.

Lawyers should be interested in deconstructive techniques for at least three reasons. First, deconstruction provides a method for critiquing existing legal doctrines; in particular, a deconstructive reading can show how arguments offered to support a particular rule undermine themselves, and instead, support an opposite rule. Second, deconstructive techniques can show how doctrinal arguments are informed by and disguise ideological thinking. This can be of value not only to the lawyer who seeks to reform existing institutions, but also to the legal philosopher and the legal historian. Third, deconstructive techniques offer both a new kind of interpretive strategy and a critique of conventional interpretations of legal texts.

Although Derrida is a philosopher, his work has been applied mainly to problems of literary criticism; as a result much of the literature on deconstruction is written by literary critics and scholars.[5] Adapting the work of Derrida and other literary critics to the problems of legal and political thought is not, however, as difficult as might first appear. Derrida is above all interested in the connection (and misconnection) between what we want to say and the signs we use to express our meaning. In short, he is interested in the interpretation of texts, and that is hardly strange territory for lawyers, who spend most of their time trying to understand what other lawyers have said in legal texts. On the other hand, explaining deconstructive practice is no small undertaking. Like many French intellectuals of his day, Derrida was schooled in the continental

3. For example, Spann associates deconstruction with a critique of formalism in legal reasoning, or with the more general project of demonstrating that legal reasoning is indeterminate. Spann, *supra* note 2, at 536-43. *But see* Hegland, *supra* note 2, at 1203-05 (uses term "deconstruction" in same way, but argues that premise of deconstruction is wrong; principles can be determined).

4. I have argued that legal and moral thought in general is antinomal though not irrational. Balkin, *The Crystalline Structure of Legal Thought*, 39 RUTGERS L. REV. 1 (1987); Balkin, *Taking Ideology Seriously: Ronald Dworkin and the CLS Critique*, 55 U.M.K.C. L. REV. (forthcoming).

5. *E.g.*, H. BLOOM, P. DE MAN, J. DERRIDA, G. HARTMAN & J. MILLER, DECONSTRUCTION AND CRITICISM (1979); J. CULLER, *supra* note 1; B. JOHNSON, THE CRITICAL DIFFERENCE (1980); V. LEITCH, DECONSTRUCTIVE CRITICISM (1983); P. DE MAN, ALLEGORIES OF READING: FIGURAL LANGUAGE IN ROUSSEAU, NIETZSCHE, RILKE, AND PROUST (1979); P. DE MAN, BLINDNESS AND INSIGHT (1983).

Deconstructive Practice

tradition of philosophy, whose major influences are Hegel, Husserl, and Heidegger. None of these philosophers is known for clarity of exposition, and Derrida often does little better than his intellectual predecessors.[6] For this reason, I will attempt to translate his ideas into a form that can be more easily understood by those familiar with the Anglo-American schools of philosophy.

The use of the term "translation" is quite deliberate. It is now commonplace to suggest that a translation can never fully capture the sense of the original. However, this point is especially significant in discussing Derrida's work. Derrida has chosen a self-consciously obscure and self-referential style, overflowing with concealed allusions and counterallusions. As I will discuss more fully later, his style may reflect his critique of Western thought's emphasis on unambiguous and foundational concepts.[7] I am thus put in an especially precarious position because my goal is to represent clearly and simply the ideas of a philosopher who eschews clarity and simplicity in his own work. My explanation must involve a kind of alteration—I must simplify, interpret, and reinterpret Derrida as much as I explain him.[8]

I also engage in translation in the sense that Derrida does not write about legal, but rather about philosophical and literary, texts. In explaining Derrida's practices to a legal audience, I will focus on those areas of his work that have the most relevance to legal writing and thought. This too, requires selection, editorial judgment, and reinterpretation. What interests me most about Derrida's work is the possibility that deconstruction can shed light on theories of ideological thinking: how people form and use ideologies, consciously or unconsciously, in legal discourse. Derrida's work is not primarily about epistemology or the sociology of knowledge, but his work has relevance to these disciplines. For that reason, I emphasize some points in Derrida's writings that others (including Derrida) might not choose to emphasize.

A final obstacle to explaining deconstruction comes from the nature of Derrida's project. Because Derrida and his followers insist that decon-

6. At least one writer believes that structuralist and post-structuralist thinkers, most of whom were French, deliberately adopted an obfuscatory style in reaction to the bourgeois French preference for *la clarité*: a simple, clear, and elegant style in accordance with the "narrower stylistic bounds of orthodox academic discourse" expected of French intellectuals. Sturrock, *Introduction* to STRUCTURALISM AND SINCE 16–17 (J. Sturrock ed. 1979). The style of modern French philosophical writers, such as Jacques Lacan, Roland Barthes, Michel Foucault, and Derrida, was designed to challenge that paradigm of "proper" philosophical expression. *Id.* If this were in fact the goal of these writers, it bears noting that one can always have too much of a good thing.

7. *See infra* text accompanying notes 12–16.

8. Indeed, a deconstructionist might argue that the process of repetition alters as it repeats, so that any explanation involves alteration of some sort. *See infra* note 53. This point takes on a special urgency with a writer as elusive as Derrida, whose very work celebrates the gap between that which represents and that which is represented.

struction is not a philosophical position but rather a practice,[9] it is neither possible nor desirable to state a deconstructionist creed. Thus, my goal in this Article is to offer ways of bringing the concerns and methods of deconstructionists to the study of legal issues. Instead of describing what a deconstructionist believes, I will explain what a deconstructionist does and will attempt to show how one does "it" to legal texts. Not surprisingly, underlying deconstructive activities are philosophical presuppositions about language, thought, and the world. Such presuppositions are implicated in Derrida's work, even if he himself would not admit to them as a statement of a "position." I will try to make clear these hidden assumptions as the need arises.[10]

The two deconstructive practices that this Article will address are the inversion of hierarchies and the liberation of the text from the author. I believe these issues have the most relevance to what legal thinkers do when they analyze legal texts. They also have the most relevance to the study of ideology and the social and political theories underlying our legal system.

## I. The Inversion of Hierarchies

### A. *The Metaphysics of Presence*

Described in its simplest form, the deconstructionist project involves the identification of hierarchical oppositions, followed by a temporary reversal of the hierarchy. Thus, to use Derrida's favorite example, if the history of Western civilization has been marked by a bias in favor of speech over writing we should investigate what it would be like if writing were more important than speech. We should attempt to see speech as a kind of writing, as ultimately parasitic upon writing, as a special case of writing, rather than the other way around. In so doing, we reverse the privileged position of speech over writing, and temporarily substitute a new priority. This new priority is not meant to be permanent, for it may in turn be reversed using identical techniques. The point is not to establish a new conceptual bedrock, but rather to investigate what happens when the

9. *E.g.*, J. Culler, *supra* note 1, at 95 (deconstruction as philosophical strategy); C. Norris, Deconstruction: Theory and Practice 31 (1982) ("Deconstruction is . . . an activity of reading which remains closely tied to the texts it interrogates, and which can never set up independently as a self-enclosed system of operative concepts."); C. Norris, The Deconstructive Turn: Essays in the Rhetoric of Philosophy 6 (1983) ("It has become almost a ritual gesture among writers on deconstruction to insist that what they are doing is in no sense a species of conceptual exegesis or analysis. Deconstruction is first and last a textual *activity*.").

10. In doing so, my descriptions may well be seen by literary theorists, for example, as untrue to their understanding of deconstruction. However, just as deconstructive theorists take pride in the inability of others to systematize their work, I take comfort in the fact that an "orthodox deconstruction" is a contradiction in terms.

Deconstructive Practice

given, "common sense" arrangement is reversed. Derrida believes that we derive new insights when the privileging in a text is turned on its head.

For Derrida, hierarchies of thought are everywhere. They can be found in the following assertions: A is the rule and B is the exception; A is the general case and B is the special case; A is simple and B is complex; A is normal and B is abnormal; A is self-supporting and B is parasitic upon it; A is present and B is absent; A is immediately perceived and B is inferred; A is central and B is peripheral; A is true and B is false; A is natural and B is artificial. Indeed, my labelling of these ideas as A and B involves a hierarchical move because the letter A *precedes* B in the alphabet.

For Derrida, any hierarchical statements about a set of ideas A and B is an invitation for a deconstructive reversal—to show that the property we ascribe to A is true of B and the property we ascribe to B is true of A. Our deconstruction will show that A's privileged status is an illusion, for A depends upon B as much as B depends upon A. We will discover, then, that B stands in relation to A much like we thought A stood in relation to B. Indeed, it is possible to find in the very reasons that A is privileged over B the reasons that B is privileged over A. Having reversed the hierarchy, we are able to see things about both A and B that we had never noticed before.[11]

Any hierarchical opposition of ideas, no matter how trivial, can be deconstructed in this way. For Derrida, however, deconstruction is more than a clever intellectual parlor game. It is a means of intellectual discovery, which operates by wrenching us from our accustomed modes of thought. In fact, Derrida was led to this practice of deconstruction by his dissatisfaction with Western philosophical practice from Plato's time to our own.[12]

Derrida sees his major project as exposing the bias in Western philosophy he calls the "metaphysics of presence."[13] Each of the above oppositions privileges a kind of "presence" over a corresponding kind of "absence." To Derrida, Western conceptions of philosophy proceed from the hidden premise that what is most apparent to our consciousness—what is

11. The word "hierarchy" probably has political connotations to many legal readers. These connotations are unfortunate, for they may lead to a misunderstanding and oversimplification of Derrida's critique. Derrida's work is not concerned with the privileging of certain social groups over others (although it can be so applied), but with the privileging of certain *ideas* over others. We may, in fact, discover as we deconstruct legal texts that the privileging of ideas (as occurs in an ideology) has a connection to the privileged place that certain social groups enjoy. However, this connection is not a direct one. Our first task is to investigate the connections among ideas.

12. *See* J. CULLER, *supra* note 1, at 92-94, 100; OF GRAMMATOLOGY, *supra* note 1, at 3, 10-18, 46; *see also* Rorty, *supra* note 1, at 145.

13. *See* OF GRAMMATOLOGY, *supra* note 1, at 49 (metaphysics of presence is irrepressible desire for transcendental signified presence, the thing itself, or truth); *see also* J. CULLER, *supra* note 1, at 92 ("Philosophy has been a 'metaphysics of presence,' the only metaphysics we know.").

most simple, basic, or immediate—is most real, true, foundational, or important.

For example, the philosophical positions of an empiricist like Hume indicate a bias in favor of immediately perceived sense data.[14] This is a privileging of "presence" in Derrida's sense of the word. However, what Derrida means by "presence" need not be the presence of sense data to the mind, for a philosopher like Plato would argue that it is a Form or Essence which the mind grasps most immediately[15] and which is therefore most "present." Rather, Derrida sees the theories of Western philosophers as expressing, at various times, a series of different metaphysical valuations: subject over object, normal over abnormal, good over evil, positive over negative, identity over difference, being over non-being, ideal over non-ideal. Western philosophy has used the preferred concept as a ground for theorizing and has explained the other concept in terms of it. In each case, the preferred concept constitutes a belief in "presence," a self-sufficient, immediately cognizable existence.[16]

Three examples may help to demonstrate how Derrida hopes to reverse these oppositional hierarchies. I will begin with perhaps the most fundamental concept in Western thought—the notion of identity. Philosophers have regarded identity as a basic ground for metaphysical thought: Anything that exists is identical to itself. Difference is a derivative concept based upon identity: Two things are different if they are not identical. The deconstructionist wants to show that the notion of identity, which seems so basic, so "present," actually depends upon the notion of difference. Self-identity depends upon difference because a thing cannot be identical to something unless it can be different from something else. Identity is only comprehensible in terms of difference, just as difference can only be understood in terms of identity. We have just deconstructed the opposition identity/difference by showing the mutual dependence these ideas have upon each other. In doing so, we show that what was thought to be foundational (identity) is itself dependent upon the concept it was privileged over (difference).

It is true that having reversed this hierarchy, we could then show that difference cannot be a foundational term for metaphysics; difference depends upon identity as much as identity depends upon difference. This outcome is not a refutation of our previous deconstructive reading. The conclusion that neither term is foundational, but that both are mutually

14. *See generally* D. HUME, A TREATISE OF HUMAN NATURE (L. Selby-Bigge 2d ed. 1888) (all knowledge derived from sense data).

15. *See* PLATO, THE COLLECTED DIALOGUES OF PLATO 40, 575 (E. Hamilton & H. Cairns eds. 1961) (theory of Forms in *Phaedo* and *Republic*).

16. *See* WRITING AND DIFFERENCE, *supra* note 1, at 278–79; *Limited Inc abc*, *supra* note 1, at 236.

dependent upon each other, is precisely the conclusion that Derrida wants us to reach.

Next consider the opposition between serious discourse and non-serious discourse.[17] This opposition also involves the metaphysics of presence, although at first glance the connection is not quite as obvious. When I am speaking seriously, I mean what I say to you, so that my true intentions are immediately present in the meaning of what I say. On the other hand, when I am not being serious, for example, when I am joking, lying, or reciting lines in a play, I do not really intend what I say. There is a divergence between my true thoughts and intentions and what you hear me saying. Now philosophers naturally are more concerned with serious discourse than non-serious, for serious discourse is, obviously, to be taken seriously. A philosopher would use the paradigm of serious communication as the foundation either for a theory of meaning or for a theory of performative speech acts like promising, warning, or marrying. Non-serious discourse, such as jokes, lies, or dramatic readings, is an aberration, an additional feature of discourse that one would explain in terms of serious discourse after one has worked out the basic theory of serious communication.

The opposition between the serious and the non-serious can be deconstructed in the same manner as the opposition between identity and difference. Once again, the goal is to subvert the notion that serious discourse is a self-contained, self-supporting ground upon which we can base a philosophical theory of meaning or promising.

To deconstruct this opposition, we must introduce the notion of iterability. Iterability is a property of signs. If one makes a sign, one can make the sign again at another time, in another place, in another context. In a simple sense, words are like signs. We are able to communicate because we can use words and combinations of words over and over again. If we had to create new signs to express our thoughts every time we attempted to communicate, we would never be able to communicate with anyone. Thus, iterability, or the property of being able to be repeated in many different contexts, is essential to any form of communication.

When I say "It is raining outside" or "I promise to pay you thirty dollars for that coat," the statements I make are iterable. They can be repeated many different times, in many different places, and in many different contexts. I can say them when in fact I believe it is raining, or when I do intend to make a promise. But the feature of iterability means that I can also say them when I am merely joking or reciting lines in a

17. The discussion that follows is loosely based on Derrida's deconstruction of J.L. Austin's work in MARGINS OF PHILOSOPHY, *supra* note 1, at 307, 321–29, and in *Limited Inc abc*, *supra* note 1, at 162.

play. Indeed, we are brought to the surprising conclusion that we could not use words to express ourselves seriously unless we could use the same words non-seriously. The same property of words that allows us to express what we mean requires that we also be able to express what we do not mean.

Serious discourse thus depends on the ability to make statements whether or not they conform with our true intentions. That is to say, the serious ultimately depends upon the prior existence of the non-serious. Indeed, we can go further. If we now reconceptualize "non-serious" statements as those statements in which there is no necessary connection between the statement and real intention, we may describe serious statements as merely a special case of iterable non-serious statements in which what we say happens to coincide with what we really intend.[18]

The work of the Swiss linguist Ferdinand de Saussure presents a third example of deconstruction. Saussure distinguished between *langue*, the background system of linguistic rules, and *parole*, the set of speech acts made by members of a linguistic community.[19] Saussure argued that *langue* was the more important element in the understanding of language because the system of relations among various signs is what constitutes a language. Specific examples of *parole*, that is specific speech acts by speakers in a linguistic community, are only possible because of the preexisting *langue* that speakers unconsciously rely upon to understand each other. Thus, the word "cat" is possible in English because English speakers can distinguish it from "mat," "cot," and "cad." In this sense, languages are systems of differences; when an English speaker uses English words, those words carry with them the system of differences that makes them intelligible to other English speakers. In Derrida's terminology, English words carry the "traces" of other words from which they are distinguished and in opposition to which they possess intelligibility.[20]

However, Saussure's privileging of *langue* over *parole* as the basis of language leads to an historical paradox: How did language begin at a time in which there was no established system of differences that constituted a language? As Jonathan Culler explains, "If a cave man is successfully to inaugurate language by making a special grunt signifying 'food,'

18. In this last statement, I have used the word "non-serious" in a new sense. Originally, I used it to mean "not serious." By the end of the deconstruction, however, it has taken on a new meaning, namely, "stated without regard to whether the statement conforms to real intention." In reversing the serious/non-serious opposition, I have created a broader notion of non-serious speech upon which both the serious and the non-serious (in the former sense of the word) depend. This is a common practice in a deconstructive reversal and involves the creation of a paleonym, a new concept with an old name that recalls the previously subordinated concept. *See infra* text accompanying notes 42-44.

19. F. de Saussure, Course in General Linguistics 9, 13-15, 17-20, 77 (3d ed. 1959).

20. *See infra* note 25 and accompanying text.

Deconstructive Practice

we must suppose that the grunt is already distinguished from other grunts and that the world has already been divided into the categories 'food' and 'non-food.' "[21]

Language must have begun with speech acts, and through history the collection of past speech acts (*parole*) was consolidated to create a linguistic system (*langue*). On the other hand, speech acts could not have been understood without some pre-existing structure that made others understand that certain primordial grunts signified "This is a rock," rather than "I am in pain." No matter how far back we go in history, each speech act seems to require a pre-existing linguistic and semantic structure in order to be intelligible, but any such structure could not come into being without a history of pre-existing speech acts by past speakers. Neither *langue* nor *parole* could be a foundational concept in a theory of language because each is mutually dependent upon the existence of the other.[22]

## B. Différance *and Trace*

The three examples of privileging that I have given all have a single feature in common. Once the hierarchy of the more basic term over the less basic term is deconstructed, we see that the more basic term depends upon the less basic. Because we already know that the less basic term depends upon the more basic, we end up asking the proverbial question: "Which came first, the chicken or the egg?" This question neatly summarizes what Derrida is trying to show in deconstructing hierarchical oppositions. He is not attempting to show that we were wrong in thinking that difference is dependent upon identity, that the non-serious is dependent upon the serious, or that *parole* is dependent upon *langue*. Rather, he wants to expose what we have forgotten: that identity is also dependent upon difference, the serious is also dependent upon the non-serious, and *langue* is also dependent upon *parole*. In other words, neither term of the opposition can be originary and fundamental because both are related to each other in a system of mutual dependences and differences. Each is continually calling upon the other for its foundation, even as it is constantly differentiating itself from the other.

---

21. *See* J. Culler, *supra* note 1, at 96.

22. *See* J. Derrida, *Semiology and Grammatology*, in Positions, *supra* note 1, at 15, 17, 28 [hereinafter *Semiology and Grammatology*]. Culler refers to this as the paradox of structure and event. J. Culler, *supra* note 1, at 94-96. The same problem arises for theorists who explain obligations in terms of the existence of "practices." *See* Rawls, *Two Concepts of Rules*, 64 Phil. Rev. 3 (1955). Promissory obligations, for example, are explained by the practice of promising. *See* H.L.A. Hart, The Concept of Law 42-43 (1961). By arguing that acts of promising could not come into being before the creation of a practice of promising, these thinkers face the problem of showing how a practice of promising could have arisen before there were any specific acts of promising.

Derrida has a special term for the chicken-and-egg quality of mutual dependence and difference that the terms of hierarchical oppositions have for each other: *differance*. *Differance* is a pun based upon the French word *differer*, which means both to differ and to defer. Derrida replaces an "e" with "a" in *difference* to make it *differance*; the two words sound exactly the same in French.[23] *Differance* simultaneously indicates that (1) the terms of an oppositional hierarchy are differentiated from each other (which is what determines them); (2) each term in the hierarchy defers the other (in the sense of making the other term wait for the first term), and (3) each term in the hierarchy defers *to* the other (in the sense of being fundamentally dependent upon the other).

From *differance*, we can understand the idea of "trace." Both of the terms in a hierarchical opposition rely for their coherence on the differentiation between them. The relation between identity and difference, serious and non-serious, *langue* and *parole*, is one of mutual dependence and difference, or *differance*. However, Derrida would also say that in each case the first concept bears the traces of the second concept, just as the second concept bears the traces of the first.

The word "trace" is a metaphor for the effect of the opposite concept, which is no longer present but has left its mark on the concept we are now considering.[24] The trace is what makes deconstruction possible; by identifying the traces of the concepts in each other, we identify their mutual conceptual dependence.[25]

One might ask whether the ideas of *differance* and trace between two opposed concepts could form a new ground for explaining both. However, *differance* and trace are not stable conceptions; they simply represent the play of differences and dependences between two mutually opposed concepts. Neither *differance* nor trace could serve as a foundational concept.[26]

23. *See* MARGINS OF PHILOSOPHY, *supra* note 1, at 3; J. DERRIDA, *Positions*, in POSITIONS, *supra* note 1, at 39-40 [hereinafter *Positions*]; *Semiology and Grammatology*, *supra* note 22, at 26-28.

24. *See* OF GRAMMATOLOGY, *supra* note 1, at 46-47.

25. *See id.* at 62-63. The phoneme /b/ is a sound in English because of its differentiation from the set of other available sounds in that language. The idea of "trace" may be compared to the way in which speakers are able to distinguish /b/ from other phonemes, while simultaneously being able to identify the /b/ spoken by one person with the /b/ spoken by another. In a similar way, the concepts in hierarchical oppositions create the possibility for each other's existence; they form, shape, or identify each other by their absence. This necessary conceptual support is the "trace" of the absent concept.

26. *See Positions*, *supra* note 23, at 39-40. Note that this statement is itself deconstructible. The concept of *differance* is essential (hence foundational?) to Derrida's own thought, at least as I present it here.

Two points follow from this deconstruction. First, if we attempted to give concepts like "*differance*" and "trace" a special status, whether as foundations for deconstruction or as ineffable concepts that escape analysis, we would fall into the very trap that Derrida seeks to avoid. Rorty, *supra* note 1, at 151-53. Thus, trace cannot be "divinized," as Rorty says, *id.* at 153, and neither can *differance*. These conceptions must simply describe the situation of foundationlessness, provisionality, or revers-

## Deconstructive Practice

Having seen one originary concept after another fall under the deconstructionist sword, the reader might be tempted to ask whether Derrida means to deny that there is any self-sufficient, originary foundation for a system of thought. This is precisely the point of the deconstructionist critique of Western philosophy. Proposed foundational terms all depend ultimately upon the subordinate concepts we would like to depend upon those foundational terms. Derrida is denying the validity of the Cartesian project of discovering an unquestionable, self-sufficient ground for philosophy.[27]

The notions of *differance* and trace suggest a revolutionary theory of how people grasp abstract ideas. Our commonsense view is that one holds an idea in one's mind, and that idea is immediately present as one conceives it. Thus, when I think about the idea of identity, I am thinking about it, and not about another idea (difference). When I think about speech, I am thinking about speech and not about writing. But we can read Derrida's work as challenging this commonsense conception. When we hold an idea in our minds, we hold both the idea *and its opposite*; we think not of speech but of "speech as opposed to writing," or speech with the traces of the idea of writing, from which speech differs and upon which it depends.[28] The history of ideas, then, is not the history of individual conceptions, but of favored conceptions held in opposition to disfavored conceptions.[29]

---

ibility. The second point is that this lack of foundational concepts puts any expositor of Derrida's thought in an unfortunate situation. These concepts are important to understanding Derrida, and one cannot do justice to his work without discussing them. I therefore present them as essential, although Derrida would not approve. This dilemma merely demonstrates the impossibility of giving a fully deconstructionist account of deconstruction. *See infra* note 54.

27. *See* Rorty, *supra* note 1, at 159. I use the term "Cartesian" because in many ways Descartes is the high priest of the metaphysics of presence: Descartes believed that one could ultimately base a philosophical system upon the indubitable truth that one's existence is *immediately present* to one's own consciousness. R. DESCARTES, *Meditations on First Philosophy*, in THE PHILOSOPHICAL WORKS OF DESCARTES 131 (E. Haldane & G. Ross trans. 1911).

The *cogito* of Descartes attempted to ground philosophy on a metaphysics of presence. Derrida did not need to deconstruct the assertion because David Hume had already performed the task. Hume argued that one's sense of identity is dependent upon the continuous flow of thoughts that one experiences. Thus, instead of thought being dependent upon the self's identity, identity is dependent upon the experience of thought. When Descartes said, "I think, therefore I am," he believed that he had demonstrated the privileged nature of existence over thought (I must be, in order to be thinking at all). Instead, Hume showed that Descartes' conclusion made knowledge of identity only an inference from the continuous experience of thought (I know that I exist because there is a continuous stream of thoughts). D. HUME, *supra* note 14, at 6. A deconstructive reading of Descartes' *cogito*, then, demonstrates that identity and thought are mutually dependent upon each other in a relation of *differance*.

28. *See Semiology and Grammatology*, *supra* note 22, at 26. What speech is opposed to, of course, depends upon the context.

29. This is an epistemological interpretation of Derrida. Derrida does not purport to offer a theory specifically about epistemology, metaphysics, or any traditional field of philosophy. Indeed, Derrida would probably resist the idea that his theories were "about" anything in particular, although it is my belief that they have many applications in such fields as literary criticism, philosophy, psychology, and law. I offer my interpretation because of the connection I am about to make between

It might seem at first that deconstructive practice is less important to lawyers than to philosophers. Derrida's critique of foundational thinking might be of great concern to philosophers searching for ultimate truth. Philosophy usually involves a search for ultimate groundings, and so the power of Derrida's critique is troubling. On the other hand, we do not expect that all or even most legal doctrines can be proven to have a basis in objective moral truth. Law is a much more pragmatic enterprise than philosophy. However, Derrida's critique is not simply directed at metaphysics. Derrida's point is that the privileging of presence may be found in everyday thought as much as in abstract philosophy. *Any* system of thought that proceeds by marking out the fundamental, the essential, the normal, or the most important—in short, virtually any rational system—can be analyzed from the standpoint of deconstructive practice.

Our understanding of legal ideas may indeed involve, as Derrida says of speech and writing, the simultaneous privileging of ideas over their opposites. Legal doctrines are based upon a group of foundational concepts and principles. Thus, in tort law, one learns the basic concepts of fault, intent, or causation, and more recently, the notions of cost-benefit analysis and economic efficiency. Such concepts are building blocks for further development. Using Derrida's methods, we discover that each legal concept is actually a privileging, in disguise, of one concept over another. By revealing the opposition, and deconstructing it, we are brought to an entirely different vision of moral and legal obligation.

One example of legal doctrines' reliance on privileging is the Supreme Court's doctrine of standing. By holding that the Constitution requires a plaintiff to show "actual" injury in order to sue,[30] the Court has created a privileging of plaintiffs who have actual injury over plaintiffs whom the Court classifies as purely "ideological."[31] One way to deconstruct this opposition would be to show how arguments in favor of the actual injury requirement "undo" themselves. The goal would be to examine the standard arguments for the actual injury requirement: Plaintiffs with actual injury are more reliable, more adversarial, and more likely to present a concrete record for decision. We could then use these arguments against themselves to demonstrate that ideological plaintiffs also possess these de-

privileging and ideological thinking. If we apply Derrida's work to the way people formulate and use legal concepts, we are making a point about human psychology and the sociology of knowledge. An epistemological interpretation is consistent with the work of Derrida's structuralist predecessors, such as Saussure and Levi-Strauss. These thinkers argue that human consciousness is structured in terms of mutually defined oppositions. *See generally* T. HAWKES, STRUCTURALISM AND SEMIOTICS 19-58 (1977).

30. *See, e.g.*, Warth v. Seldin, 422 U.S. 490 (1975).

31. *See, e.g.*, Schlesinger v. Reservists Comm. to Stop the War, 418 U.S. 208 (1974); Sierra Club v. Morton, 405 U.S. 727 (1972).

Deconstructive Practice

sired traits. Conversely, we could show how plaintiffs who possess actual injury, but who lack ideological zeal, are less dependable, less adversarial, and less likely to produce a concrete record for decisionmaking than their ideological counterparts.[32]

This example suggests that law provides a fertile field of discourse for deconstructive readings. Lawyers are continually involved in establishing principles of regulatory behavior, whether in contract law, constitutional law, or other areas, and this project necessitates the privileging of concepts. Deconstruction can serve another purpose. The law reflects social visions that involve privilegings of particular conceptions of human nature. As we deconstruct legal principles, we deconstruct the ideology or world view that informs them. Although we can use deconstruction to show that doctrines are incomplete, or that the arguments for a given doctrine "undo" themselves, we can also use deconstruction as a tool for ideological and historical analysis.

### C. *Arguments that Undo Themselves*

Deconstructive reversals show that the reasons given for privileging one side of an opposition over the other often turn out to be reasons for privileging the other side. The virtues of the first term are seen to be the virtues of the second; the vices of the second are revealed to be true of the first as well. This undoing of justifications for privileging is part of the deconstructionist aim of "ungrounding" preferred conceptions by showing that they cannot act as self-sufficient or self-explanatory grounds or foundations.

The most famous example of this "ungrounding" is Derrida's treatment of speech and writing in *Of Grammatology*.[33] Derrida finds in the texts of several writers, including Rousseau, Saussure, and Levi-Strauss, a consistent valuing of speech over writing as a form of communication.[34] Derrida argues that this preference is not accidental; it relates to the general "logocentric" bias of Western thought.[35] By "logocentric," Derrida means centered on the concept of *logos*, which he often equates with the idea of presence. Derrida believes that a privileging of speech over writing is a symptom of a more general bias in favor of presence as a foundational term in Western philosophical thought.[36]

---

32. For examples of deconstruction of this doctrine, see Tushnet, *The Sociology of Article III: A Response to Professor Brilmayer*, 93 HARV. L. REV. 1698 (1980); J. Balkin, Deconstructing Article III (Sept. 27, 1986) (unpublished manuscript on file at Yale Law School Library).

33. OF GRAMMATOLOGY, *supra* note 1, at 34-43, 166-67.

34. *Id.* at 29-44 (discussing Saussure); *id.* at 101-268 (discussing Levi-Strauss and Rousseau).

35. *Id.* at 3; *see infra* text accompanying notes 53-55.

36. Derrida also speaks of "phonocentrism," or the privileging of voice. *See, e.g.*, OF GRAMMATOLOGY, *supra* note 1, at 11-12. Phonocentrism normally appears in discussions of the privileging

One might ask why speech is more "present" than writing, and why it is more highly valued. Derrida considers several plausible arguments to explain the privileging. First, writing is only a method of representing speech. It was invented as a means of recording what people said.[37] Writing consists of a series of signs that stand for spoken words. Thus, writing is only a substitute for speech, and an imperfect substitute at that. For example, written language often uses non-phonetic spellings. People who have encountered certain words in writing but not in speech often mispronounce them, and written language occasionally leads to corruptions and alterations in natural forms of speech.

Second, speech is connected more closely to the immediate thoughts of the communicator than is writing. When one hears a person talk, that person's intention is immediately communicated by her speech.[38] Our understanding is derived not only from words, but also from inflections and tone of voice. Sarcasm, enthusiasm, and a hundred other nuances are immediately apparent when we listen to a person; they are less discernible when the text of a speech has been transcribed.[39] Thus, the preference for speech over writing is a privileging of presence: The immediacy of meaning in speech is privileged over the mediation of thought that occurs in writing.[40] Speech is immediate, unambiguous, and sincere; writing is distant, ambiguous, and potentially misleading.[41]

---

of speech over writing.

37. Speech is prior to writing both culturally and historically. J. GREENBERG, ANTHROPOLOGICAL LINGUISTICS 22-23 (1968). Spoken language arrives in a culture before written language, and to this day there are primitive cultures that have no written language. *Id.* at 22; *see also* S. MULLER, THE WORLD'S LIVING LANGUAGES 107, 119 (1964) (most languages in Africa, Indonesia, and New Guinea still unwritten). Thus, speech is a prior, and therefore more fundamental, development in the creation of cultures and civilizations than writing.

38. Derrida argues that the direct temporal connection between speech and thought leads us to this conclusion. He points out that in French, the expression *s'entendre parler* means both to hear oneself and to understand oneself. OF GRAMMATOLOGY, *supra* note 1, at 98.

39. An old joke illustrates this point. A man walks past a laundry which bears a sign reading: "My name is Fink /and what do you think /I'll do your wash for free." Thinking he has spotted a bargain, the man takes his laundry there. The next day, when he returns to pick up his laundry, the proprietor, Mr. Fink, asks for a payment of five dollars.

"Five dollars?" asks the man. "What about your sign?"

"Can't you read?" replies Fink. "The sign says: " 'My name is Fink, and what do you think, I'll do your wash for *free*?' "

The joke seems to demonstrate the capacity of writing to mislead and the superior expressive abilities of speech. However, this joke also undermines the very point that the phonocentrist (the privileger of speech) wants to make, because it *was* possible, in writing, to express inflection and avoid misunderstanding by using the correct punctuation. Indeed, were it otherwise, no one would understand the joke in its written form. Conversely, if Mr. Fink had spoken his lines in a monotone, he still might have been misunderstood.

40. Indeed, many people prefer to receive information from a lecture rather than by reading because they find it easier to comprehend and assimilate meaning from what a person is saying than from what she has written. The belief that speech is a privileged way of understanding the "true meaning" of communication is connected to Derrida's notion of logocentrism, or the privileging of presence.

41. Barbara Johnson sums up the privileging of speech over writing:

Deconstructive Practice

There are additional connections between speech and presence. Normally, a speaker is physically present when she talks to you; in contrast, you may be reading the words written by a person who is far away and perhaps no longer even alive. A person who is speaking to you can be interrupted and asked to clarify what she means. The same cannot be done with the author of a text one is reading. The author is not present, and only the representations of her past thoughts remain on the page.

After identifying all of the characteristics that define writing, and after arguing how they make writing inferior to speech, one can deconstruct the opposition of speech to writing by showing how the arguments "undo themselves." One can demonstrate that each identified characteristic of writing is true of speech as well; in other words, speech is a kind of "writing" that suffers from the same inadequacies attributed to writing.

First, speech itself is only a sign of what is present in a person's mind; it too is only a signifier of thought. A person's true thoughts and real meanings must be mediated through the use of speech. Furthermore, speech can be as unclear and ambiguous as writing, as most persons who have attended a law school lecture can testify.

Second, for speech to function as a signifier, as a sign, speech must be iterable. It must be possible to speak when one does not mean what one says. Speech also can be separated from the speaker and the moment of intention, in both space and time. One can listen to a politician speak over a radio or television, with no chance to stop the speaker and ask for clarification. One can play a recording of a speech by Martin Luther King over and over again; the sounds one hears are no longer connected to the thoughts of a living person. The emotional impact of recorded speech does not come from the presence of living thought in the speech, but only from its efficacy as a signifier of past thoughts, which have long ago faded away.

Derrida thus shows that speech, as a signifier of thought, shares all of the properties that we had associated with writing. Speech is merely a special case of a generalized idea of writing. This "arche-writing"[42] is the iterable representation of a signified by a signifier. Speech and writing (in the normal sense of the word) are both varieties of this more generalized form of "writing."

Derrida uses the word "writing" in this broader sense to stand for three

---

> The spoken word is given a higher value because the speaker and listener are both present to the utterance simultaneously. There is no temporal or spatial distance between speaker, speech, and listener, since the speaker hears himself speak at the same moment the listener does. This immediacy seems to guarantee the notion that in the spoken word we know what we mean, mean what we say, say what we mean, and know what we have said.

Johnson, *supra* note 1, at viii.

42. *See* Of Grammatology, *supra* note 1, at 56–57.

basic properties of signification: (1) the substitution of the signifier for what it signifies; (2) the mediation of the experience of the signified by the signifier, and (3) the iterability of the signifier at different times and in different contexts.[43] "Writing," as used by Derrida, is a *paleonym*[44]—a word with an old meaning which has had a new meaning grafted on to it. "Writing" in Derrida's general sense recalls the reversal of the hierarchy of speech over writing from which the broader conception arises. Derrida's project, at least in its initial incarnation, was a call for a science of "writing," or a Grammatology, which would investigate and expose the hidden logocentric biases of Western thought.[45]

### D. *The Logic of the Supplement*

Derrida also deconstructs the hierarchy of speech over writing through the "logic of the supplement." The term "supplement" comes from Rousseau, who describes writing as a "supplement" to speech.[46] Writing is a supplement to speech in that it represents speech. The "natural" condition of language is spoken; writing is merely added later:

> [S]peech being natural or at least the natural expression of thought, . . . writing is added to it, is adjoined, as an image or representation. In that sense, it is not natural. It diverts the immediate presence of thought to speech into representation and the imagination. This recourse is not only "bizarre," but dangerous. It is the addition of a technique, a sort of artificial and artful ruse to make speech present when it is actually absent. It is a violence done to the natural destiny of the language . . . .[47]

However, the word "supplement" has many meanings. First, it can mean something added to an already complete or self-sufficient thing. For example, I teach out of the latest edition of a constitutional law casebook. The book is finished, complete in itself, but every year the publisher distributes a supplement adding cases decided by the Supreme Court after the date of the casebook's publication. However, the fact that the publisher provides a supplement to my casebook indicates that the casebook is incomplete as a teaching aid—it needs supplementation to make it com-

43. *See id.* at 44-45, 55-57; H. STATEN, *supra* note 1, at 60-61, 121; *Limited Inc abc*, *supra* note 1, at 189-90.

44. *See supra* note 18.

45. *See Semiology and Grammatology*, *supra* note 22, at 35-36.

46. *See* OF GRAMMATOLOGY, *supra* note 1, at 144. Similarly, Rousseau speaks of culture as a supplement to nature and masturbation as a supplement to normal sexual relations. The latter supplement Rousseau refers to as a "dangerous supplement," a phrase Derrida seizes upon as characteristic of all supplementation. *See infra* text accompanying notes 47-48.

47. OF GRAMMATOLOGY, *supra* note 1, at 144.

plete. This is the second meaning of "supplement"—something added to something lacking in order to complete it, as one takes vitamin supplements to achieve a healthy diet.

If writing is a supplement to speech, in the sense that it is added to speech, it may well be dangerous. Writing may infect the naturalness of speech, alter speech, or even supplant it. Some people may begin to speak in the same stylized way in which they write. Writing may lead to mistakes in pronunciation. For example, uneducated French people occasionally pronounce the silent consonants in their language. As time passes, writing may become so important that all official acts are recorded, certain types of oral promises are no longer enforced, and storytellers and town criers are replaced by authors and journalists. Rousseau's life provides an example of the displacement of speech by writing. Rousseau, who exalted the naturalness of speech, was a writer by profession; he is now best remembered not for what he said, but for what he wrote.[48]

Yet, Derrida would argue, writing can only supplement speech in the first sense (representation of speech) if speech can be supplemented in the second sense (having a lack that could be fulfilled). By now we know what that lack is: Speech is not thought made present to the listener, but aural symbols that represent thoughts. Speech only appears to possess "presence," or a direct connection to the mind of the speaker because of the fortuity that people speak and think simultaneously. In reality, however, speech-as-thought is a sham; like writing, speech is a mediation of thought, a delaying through representation. It is for that reason that writing can supplement, or take the place of, speech.

Thus, we see a new meaning of the term "dangerous supplement." Writing is indeed a dangerous supplement, not because, as Rousseau feared, it might infect the purity of speech, but because the supplementary capacity of writing demonstrates that speech already possesses that which we dislike about writing. It is as if one met a lover's relatives and saw for the first time unpleasant qualities common to the whole family.

From this Derrida wants to make a larger claim: If we thought that speech was present and writing a mere representation of speech, we now see that speech, too, is only a mediation of something more present. Speech, like writing, is a supplement. (Note the crucial move in Derrida's argument: A signifier supplements that which it signifies.) But if speech is a supplement, that which it supplements must also be lacking, for otherwise speech could not represent it. That new thing must, in turn, be a

48. Writing may be dangerous in still another way. Derrida argues that both Rousseau and Levi-Strauss identified speech with nature and writing with culture. The invention of writing and its introduction to primitive peoples brought a moral and spiritual decline that is closely associated with the corrupting influence of culture upon nature. *See id.* at 101–40.

supplement (signifier), which represents something further; and so on. The result is a chain of supplements, reaching towards an unmediated, complete, self-sufficient presence.[49] To speak the language of signs, the result is a chain of signifiers, each pointing to the next, each reaching towards a pure, unmediated signified.[50]

But now comes the great irony of this logic. The Real Thing, Presence Itself, must, by definition, be something that could not be supplemented or represented by a sign, for it is self-sufficient, and could not serve as a signifier or supplement. The world as we know it is only a world of representations, and representations of representations, ad infinitum. Every signified is actually a signifier in disguise. Derrida describes the ultimate deconstruction of presence:

> *There is nothing outside of the text* . . . . What we have tried to show by following the guiding line of the "dangerous supplement," is that in what one calls . . . real life . . . there has never been anything but writing; there have never been anything but supplements; substitutive significations which could only come forth in a chain of differential references. . . . [T]he absolute present, Nature, . . . ha[s] always already escaped, ha[s] never existed . . . .[51]

"Writing" is all there is. This conclusion follows from Derrida's argument that a sign can only represent still another sign. Derrida's famous aphorism *il n'y a pas de hors-texte* (there is nothing outside of the text) is a metaphor which proclaims that all understanding is metaphorical.[52] The "text" of which Derrida speaks is not merely words, but life itself: "[O]ur very relation to 'reality'. . . functions like a text."[53]

Derrida's critique can be viewed as nihilistic because it appears to deny the existence of objective truth. On the other hand, Derrida's own arguments subtly rely on the notion of truth. The basic claim is that a signifier only *imperfectly represents* the thing it signifies. This is not a mistake of logic, or an oversight on Derrida's part. We speak in logocentric terms, so that our critique of logocentrism must rely on suspect categories of thought. This is the case with all deconstructions; each uses the conceptual apparatus of the very thing that it wishes to subvert.[54]

---

49. *Cf. id.* at 152-57 (describing chain of supplements involved in Rousseau's love object).

50. *Id.* at 49-50.

51. *Id.* at 158-59.

52. *Id.* at 158.

53. Johnson, *supra* note 1, at xiv.

54. Derrida demonstrates the precarious position of the deconstructionist by placing certain concepts *sous rature* ("under erasure"). For example, he uses the word "is" with a line through it to show that the word is logocentrically biased ("being" is the ultimate expression of presence) yet necessary for expression. OF GRAMMATOLOGY, *supra* note 1, at 19.

It should now become clear why explanations of deconstruction necessarily involve a modification of

Deconstructive Practice

Derrida's seemingly nihilistic conclusion must be understood in the context of his method of reaching it. Derrida does not deny the existence of objective truth as much as he affirms the interpretative character of our attempts to comprehend truth. Our "truth"—the conceptual apparatus we create to explain the world to ourselves—is only a sign or metaphor for an endless succession of still other signs and metaphors, and we have forgotten that it is only that. Thus, the Real Truth seems always beyond our grasp, outside the dominant conceptual apparatus, because that apparatus is necessarily always incomplete and capable of further supplementation.

Our frustation in our attempts to experience the Real Thing, whether we call it "truth" or "presence," stems from the desire in Western philosophy to foundationalize. Here is the agenda of traditional Western philosophy: One can only seek truth if one discovers fundamental principles and builds upon them.[55] We should recognize this "agenda" by now as privileging. The act of privileging requires the privileged term to be foundational, complete, self-sufficient; however, it is none of these things. It is related to the non-privileged term in a system of mutual differentiation and dependence, or *differance*.

The privileged concept is incomplete; it is only a supplement, a signifier, a metaphor. For that reason, we are able to use it against itself, to deconstruct it. The act of privileging, of asserting that one of two mutually dependent concepts is really foundational, is like drinking from the springs of the mythical river Lethe, after which we forget our past. Once we have accepted the privileging, we forget that the foundational concept was only a metaphor, a supplement. Deconstruction awakes us from our dogmatic slumber, and reminds us that our "truth" is only an interpretation.

## E. *Deconstruction and Ideology*

Although these issues seem metaphysical, we can translate Derrida's concerns into a legal setting.[56] Legal doctrines both reflect and regulate

---

it. My attempt at explanation is a logocentric project. I seek to present the foundations of Derrida's thought in a clear, easily comprehensible, logical progression, beginning with simple ideas and then working to more complicated results. Obviously, there is something paradoxical about using logocentric methods to develop a critique of logocentrism. However, to argue that a logocentric presentation of deconstruction is suspect because it misstates the "true" content of Derridean thought is simply to engage in another logocentric move, that is, that there is a privileged reading of Derrida, a true unmediated presence, of which all interpretations are inferior copies.

55. Of Grammatology, *supra* note 1, at 97 (history of metaphysics is history of logocentrism); J. Culler, *supra* note 1, at 92-93 (logocentric practice in Western philosophy moves from fundamental ideas to elaboration of ideas); *Limited Inc abc*, *supra* note 1, at 236 (single recurrent gesture in Western metaphysics is move from good, positive, pure, simple, and essential to evil, negative, impure, complex, and accidental).

56. Note that I am presenting my interpretation of Derrida, which is my own "dangerous supplement" to his work and my own metaphor.

social life. The choice of protected rights and of enforcement techniques reflect views, whether obvious or obscure, about social relations. Law tells a story about what people are and should be.[57]

To give an obvious example, laws that permit (or enforce) discrimination on the basis of race or sex tell a different story about people than laws that prohibit such discrimination. The principles of a social theory like Liberalism tell a story about human nature, which some accept and others criticize.[58] Even the seemingly most insignificant or neutral doctrines and rules, taken as a whole, have a story to tell, if we are willing to listen to them.[59]

We can think of a system of law as a community's attempt to realize human ends. This presupposes a description of the good and bad in human nature: what people want from their lives and what their limitations are. This description necessarily involves privilegings of certain aspects of human nature over others. Later, we justify our system by claiming that it is the best, given the natural constraints of the human condition. For example, an advocate of laissez-faire might argue that, given the natural self-interestedness of people, unregulated market transactions are the best way to realize human goals. But the deconstructive critique reminds us that our social vision and system of laws are not based upon human nature as it really is, but rather upon an interpretation of human nature, a metaphor, a privileging. We do not experience the "presence" of human nature; we experience different versions of it in the stories we tell about what we are "really like." These stories are incomplete; they are metaphors and can be deconstructed. Too often we forget that our systems of law are based upon metaphor and interpretation; we mistake the dominant or privileged vision of people and society for real "present" human nature, as Rousseau confused speech with the presence of thought.

57. Clare Dalton uses this metaphor in her deconstruction of contract doctrine. Dalton, *supra* note 2, at 999.

58. For example, it is often asserted that Liberalism's emphasis upon individual autonomy ignores other aspects of human nature, such as the need for communal sharing of values. The vision of human personality and responsibility that Liberalism poses is disputed both by the right and the left. Libertarians argue that Liberals violate principles of self-determination and autonomy by asking people to contribute to a common good, while Marxists argue that Liberal capitalism hides the real nature of relations between worker and capitalist under a veneer of free exchange. Of course, one also can criticize each of these alternatives to Liberalism as portraying a fundamentally false picture of human nature.

59. In her deconstruction, Dalton argues that the ideology of contract law, which privileges the view of contracts as the "neutral facilitator of private volition," and is "concerned at the periphery with the imposition of social duties," Dalton, *supra* note 2, at 1014, is also present in the doctrines of implied contracts, parol evidence, and consideration. *Id.* at 1014-24, 1048-52, 1066-95. She concludes that although these doctrines in contract law may seem less overtly political in nature than others, such as duress and unconscionability, the same tensions are at work: "[In] contract doctrine . . . a comparatively few mediating devices are constantly deployed to displace and defer the otherwise inevitable revelation that public cannot be separated from private, or form from substance, or objective manifestation from subjective intent." *Id.* at 1113.

Deconstructive Practice

At that point, the metaphor becomes mistaken for what it describes. But latent within the metaphor is a countervision that can be located and brought to the surface through deconstruction. It exists within the privileged conception because the latter ultimately depends upon it in a relation of *differance*.

The argument of the laissez-faire advocate presupposes a vision of what is most important about people, and necessarily relegates other aspects of the human condition, such as altruism and community, to marginal status. We could deconstruct this vision of humanity by showing how economic individualism ultimately depends upon social cooperation and the sharing of values. We could show the incompleteness of this vision of human nature, its poverty in describing what people are like and the nature of their relations to each other. A part of humanity will always escape this vision because it is only a metaphor, a signifier. The vision suffers from a lack that needs to be supplemented, and the supplement is a countervision that has been relegated to the periphery. This supplement is indeed "dangerous," for it threatens to subvert the picture of human nature posed by the dominant conception.[60]

The deconstruction of legal concepts, or of the social vision that informs them, is not nihilistic. Deconstruction is not a call for us to forget about moral certainty, but to remember aspects of human life that were pushed into the background by the necessities of the dominant legal conception we call into question. Deconstruction is not a denial of the legitimacy of rules and principles; it is an affirmation of human possibilities that have been overlooked or forgotten in the privileging of particular legal ideas.

Any social theory must emphasize some human values over others. Such categorizing necessarily involves a privileging, which in turn can be deconstructed. But the goal of deconstruction is not the destruction of all possible social visions. By recalling the elements of human life relegated to the margin in a given social theory, deconstructive readings challenge us to remake the dominant conceptions of our society. We can choose to accept the challenge or not, but we will no longer cling to our social vision blindly. Nor can we assume that this vision is the "real essence" of human

60. *See supra* notes 46–48 and accompanying text (discussing danger in supplementation). The deconstruction of the philosophy of economic individualism is a favorite topic of the Critical Legal Studies movement. For a classic discussion of the *differance* between individualism and altruism, see Kennedy, *Form and Substance in Private Law Adjudication*, 89 HARV. L. REV. 1685 (1976). Kennedy's famous statement of the "fundamental contradiction" of social life is a more general expression of *differance*. Kennedy, *The Structure of Blackstone's Commentaries*, 28 BUFFALO L. REV. 209, 211–13 (1979) ("[T]he goal of individual freedom is at the same time dependent on and incompatible with the communal coercive action that is necessary to achieve it. . . . [R]elations with others are both necessary to and incompatible with our freedom.").

nature because that would be a claim to have experienced presence, an experience that Derrida denies that we can ever have.

As Robert Gordon has observed, people "build structures, then act as if (and genuinely come to believe that) the structures they have built are determined by history, human nature, economic law."[61] Deconstruction allows us to see that ideologies are signs or metaphors that describe social life. They are privileged conceptions of social reality; they are supplements, which can in turn be supplemented. Like Derrida's signs, they are not self-sufficient, but ultimately depend upon the very aspects of human life that they deny and from which they differentiate themselves. Every ideology suffers from an elementary lack: its dependence on what it denies, on what it is exalted over. This lack, this *differance*, is what we seize upon and exploit in a deconstructive reading.

We now see that the legal deconstructor deconstructs *ideologies*, which are manifested in particular legal doctrines. By challenging what is "given," deconstruction affirms the infinite possibilities of human existence. By contesting "necessity," deconstruction dissolves the ideological encrustations of our thought.

## F. *Deconstruction as a Critical Theory*

One might object that a deconstructive reassessment of our legal and social institutions offers us no logical stopping point. If the results of a deconstructive reading can themselves be deconstructed, deconstruction threatens to become an endless series of reversals and counter-reversals. Once again, nihilism seems an unavoidable consequence.

To answer this charge, I would like to compare deconstructive practice (or at least my interpretation of it) to psychoanalysis. Such an analogy is not at all farfetched. The psychoanalyst engages in a process similar in many ways to deconstruction. The psychoanalyst reverses the privileging of the conscious over the unconscious as the explanation of human behavior.[62] The psychoanalyst also performs a deconstructive reversal by focusing on seemingly marginal or unimportant elements of the patient's experience, such as everyday events, free associations of ideas, and dream material, to understand the deeper connections that are the key to unconscious motivation.[63]

61. Gordon, *New Developments in Legal Theory*, in THE POLITICS OF LAW 289 (D. Kairys ed. 1982).

62. Michels, *The Basic Propositions of Psychoanalytic Theory*, in INTRODUCING PSYCHOANALYTIC THEORY 12 (S. Gillman ed. 1982) (psychoanalysis reverses emphasis on outer world as determinant of human behavior and concerns itself with inner dispositions of individual).

63. *See* L. KOLB & H. BRODIE, MODERN CLINICAL PSYCHIATRY 750-55 (10th ed. 1982); *see also* F. REDLICH & D. FREEDMAN, THE THEORY AND PRACTICE OF PSYCHIATRY 276 (1966) ("*Free association* [involves] full and unedited reporting of mental events, including seemingly trivial

Deconstructive Practice

Furthermore, both deconstruction and psychoanalysis offer critical theories.[64] A critical theory may be distinguished by three characteristics. First, the goal of a critical theory is not to develop a series of true factual propositions, but to achieve enlightenment and emancipation.[65] Second, a critical theory is self-referential; it may be applied to itself or to the process of its application.[66] Third, a critical theory is confirmed not by a process of experimentation and empirical verification, but through a more complicated process of self-reflection. The critical theorist determines whether she has achieved enlightenment and emancipation in terms of knowledge and beliefs she has developed in the course of applying the critical theory.[67]

Psychoanalysis possesses all of the characteristics of a critical theory. Its goal is emancipation of the patient from unfulfilling behavior patterns caused by unconscious repressed material.[68] This emancipation is achieved by a process of progressive enlightenment: The patient learns how her behavior patterns have been caused by unconscious forces and this, in turn, alters her behavior.[69] Psychoanalysis is potentially self-referential because the process of analysis itself can be understood and criticized in terms of hidden motivations and desires of the analyst.[70] Finally, the success of analysis often can only be judged through a process of self-reflection by the patient, aided by the therapist.[71]

Like psychoanalysis, deconstructive readings of texts offer the possibility of emancipation from customary ways of thinking. Deconstruction operates by a momentary reversal of privileging. This reversal alters our

---

or obnoxious details.").

64. In this discussion of critical theory, I follow the ideas developed in R. Geuss, The Idea of a Critical Theory 55-95 (1981).

65. *Id.* at 55.

66. This distinguishes critical theories from other types of theories. For example, Newton's theory about particles in motion is not itself a particle in motion, and therefore, does not refer to or explain itself. *Id.* By contrast, Marxism as a social theory is potentially self-referential. *Id.* at 56. It tries to explain not only the connections between a person's beliefs and her relation to various economic classes in society, but also why a Marxist holds the beliefs that she does.

67. *Id.* at 55-56, 85-86.

68. L. Kolb & H. Brodie, *supra* note 63, at 748-49.

69. *Id.* at 749, 755.

70. For example, psychoanalytic psychotherapy applies the techniques of analysis to the analyst herself when it addresses mistakes and failures in therapy due to countertransference:

> [C]ountertransference reactions arise in the therapist as a result of the patient's influence on the physician's unconscious feelings and have their origin in the latter's irrational projections and identifications. The therapist must not permit his own unconscious feelings and attitudes, aroused during phases of treatment, to intrude in his relations with the patient.

*Id.* at 752; *see also* S. Lorand, Technique of Psychoanalytic Therapy 209-22 (1946) (discussing countertransference); Peters, *Transference*, in Introducing Psychoanalytic Theory, *supra* note 62, at 99-101 (same).

71. *See* M. Basch, Doing Psychotherapy 36-37, 52, 178 (1980).

view of the privileging, just as the act of uncovering repressed material liberates the psychoanalytic patient.

As a critical theory, deconstruction can also be a self-referential activity because it can be performed on previous deconstructive readings indefinitely. It is this very property that leads to the charge of nihilism. However, the analogy to psychoanalysis shows us why this charge is ill-founded. We do not think that psychoanalysis is futile because a patient can be psychoanalyzed indefinitely or because the act of psychoanalysis can itself be investigated psychoanalytically. Rather, we believe that the psychoanalyst is performing a meaningful function even though her own work is potentially subject to further psychoanalysis. More importantly, the psychoanalyst and patient may properly decide that the patient has progressed sufficiently to end analysis. Similarly, deconstruction need not continue indefinitely if it has achieved the goals of emancipation and enlightenment.

On the other hand, how is one to tell when these goals have been achieved? There is no foolproof answer to this question for deconstruction, but the same may be said for psychoanalysis. There is simply no mechanical method for the analyst and patient to identify when analysis should end. The decision is an act of self-reflection on the part of both that the patient has been sufficiently enlightened and emancipated from the burdens of repressed material.[72] Of course, this decision may be questioned on the grounds that it is subjective, that one person's "enlightenment" may be another's neurosis. However, the analyst and patient are entitled to employ a personal judgment based upon a vision of normalcy and good mental health developed in the course of the analysis.[73]

In the same fashion, the deconstructionist must engage in a process of self-reflection to determine when the insights provided by deconstruction have produced sufficient enlightenment with respect to a view of law, legal doctrine, or human society previously accepted as privileged, natural, or complete. This decision is, of course, a political and moral choice, but it is one informed by insights gained through the activity of deconstruction itself. At the moment the choice is made, the critical theorist is, strictly speaking, no longer a deconstructionist. However, the purposes of engaging in the deconstruction have been served. In both psychoanalysis and deconstruction, the justification of when one should cease analysis may

72. *Id.*

73. *Cf.* F. Redlich & D. Freedman, *supra* note 63, at 277 ("Analysis is essentially an educational process. . . . After a successful analysis, the patient will take with him the ability to introspect . . . with candor and to apply such insights . . . to life problems.").

Deconstructive Practice

appear self-supporting, and so it is. But such justification is a characteristic of any critical theory.[74]

## G. *An Example of a Legal Deconstruction*

At this point it might be useful to give an example of a deconstructive argument in a legal context. I will use an argument by the noted British legal scholar P.S. Atiyah, who is not generally known as a deconstructionist. There is nothing unusual about the appearance of deconstructive arguments in the texts of non-deconstructionists; recall Hume's deconstruction of Descartes' *cogito*.[75]

In his *Promises, Morals, and Law*,[76] Atiyah argues against a theory of contract that bases obligation upon individual will or intention. Atiyah notes that the commonsense view of promissory obligation is that promises are binding because of the intent of the party and its objective manifestation by the act of promising. He suggests that the explicit promise, with its deliberate manifestation of intent, is usually viewed as the paradigmatic case of contractual obligation. The law then attempts to explain the binding nature of implied promises in terms of the standard case of promising:

> In law and, I think, with most contemporary writers on philosophy, the traditional explanation of an implied promise assumes that the explicit promise is the paradigm case. The implied promise is then treated as a case where no explicit promise is made in so many words, but where, from his words and conduct, it is plain that the party intends to bind himself. Simple examples . . . concern contracts made by boarding a bus . . . or ordering a meal in a restaurant. . . . The lawyer explains these obligations by saying that there are implied promises.[77]

We can already see the hierarchical relationship at work. The paradigmatic case of promissory obligation concerns explicit promises, in which intention is manifested by specific promissory words. Implicit promises are parasitic upon explicit promises: The intention to be bound is mani-

74. *See* R. GEUSS, *supra* note 64, at 85–88. *Compare* Unger, *The Critical Legal Studies Movement*, 96 HARV. L. REV. 561, 580 (1983) ("Legal doctrine rightly understood and practiced is the conduct of internal development through legal materials.") *with* J. RAWLS, A THEORY OF JUSTICE 48–51 (1971) (sense of justice comes from matching initial convictions with proposed reconceptions in attempt to achieve reflective equilibrium). Note that the establishment of a "reflective equilibrium" creates a new privileging. The defense of the new privileging is a constructive, and not a deconstructive, activity.

75. *See supra* note 27.

76. P. ATIYAH, PROMISES, MORALS, AND LAW (1981) [hereinafter PROMISES, MORALS, AND LAW].

77. *Id.* at 173 (footnote omitted).

fested (and thus implied) not by the defendant's words of promise, but by her conduct. Thus, one explains the legal obligation of ordering a meal in a restaurant in terms of previous cases in which people have intended to purchase a meal and have said: "If you serve me food, I will pay you the price listed on the menu," or words to that effect. But basing the obligatory nature of implied promises upon explicit promises opens the way for a deconstructive reversal of the hierarchy, a reversal that may tell us something new about why promises are binding:

> [T]here are difficulties with this traditional explanation. What of the person who does not intend to pay his fare on boarding the bus, or pay for the meal supplied to him in the restaurant? The lawyer brushes aside this difficulty, appealing to what he calls the "objective test" of promise or assent. There is the appearance of a promise and that is enough. But this explanation is not very satisfying. For it dismisses what is—on the traditional view—the very central requirement of a promise. If a person who intends to steal a ride on a bus is liable to pay his fare in exactly the same way as the person who intends to pay his fare, it seems odd to say that it is the intention which creates the liability in both cases.[78]

Atiyah's argument calls into question whether it is really the intention that creates the obligation. Indeed, even in the case of explicit promises, we may wonder whether intention creates obligation. Imagine the person who walks into the restaurant and says "I promise to pay for the food I consume," when he has no intention of paying. Will his intention not to be bound shield him from moral culpability or legal liability? Indeed, it is precisely because he lacks the intention that he should be made to pay. Atiyah notes that there is something strange about a theory of contractual liability based upon intent:

> [T]o imply a promise suggests that it is because of the promise that the relevant party is bound by an obligation. He is obliged to pay for the meal or pay the bus fare *because* he has promised. However, it seems quite plausible to suggest that the truth is the other way round. It is because he is bound by an obligation that we generally feel impelled to imply a promise. Naturally, if that is right, the source of the obligation cannot lie in the implied promise itself, but must be sought elsewhere. . . . [I]t is often, perhaps always, the case that the conduct itself justifies the creation of the obligation. . . . In the great majority of cases of this nature . . . the intention to pay will exist, and so will the intention to assume or accept the legal obligation. But we must never forget the defaulter.

78. *Id.*

Deconstructive Practice

> Occasionally people do order meals in restaurants without any intention of paying. Nobody doubts—least of all the lawyer—that this makes not the slightest difference to the obligation to pay.[79]

We may translate this argument into Derrida's terminology. The classical theory of contract involves a privileging of explicit promises over implicit promises because in explicit promises the thing that makes the contract binding—the intention of the actor to enter into an agreement and be bound by it—is in some sense more "present." The speaker's explicit promise gives evidence of her "real" intentions. In the case of an implied promise, these intentions are hidden, and can only be inferred from the circumstances. A theory of implied promises supplements the will theory, which explains the binding nature of explicit promises. The supplementary theory explains why there is a binding obligation when the promisor's present intent is not immediately known to the promisee.

Following the logic of the supplement, however, we can argue that a theory of explicit promises can only be supplemented if explicit promises also defer presence (the present intention of the promisor at the moment of promising). Explicit promises are binding because they manifest intent, but the objective manifestation of intent in an explicit promise is only binding because it acts as a signifier for presence (the promisor's actual will or intent). However, as a sign, the explicit promise must be iterable. Thus, an explicit promise could only bind a promisor if it could bind regardless of the promisor's intent, that is to say, only if the dishonest promisor also could be bound.

Atiyah has argued that this is how the law treats the dishonest promisor.[80] Promises are binding even if there is no connection between the objective manifestation and the presence of subjective intention. The "presence" of the promisor's intent at the moment of promising does not create the moral obligation. Rather, we explain the obligation of explicit promises in terms of the reasons implicit promises are binding: They confer a benefit on the promisor that it would be unjust not to repay, or they induce justified reliance on the part of the promisee.

This argument leads to a broader generalization. The privileging of a will theory of contract over a theory based upon effect (unjust enrichment or reliance) involves a relation of *différance*—of mutual differentiation and dependence. A theory that postulates the will of the promisor as binding must explain the moral obligation involved in cases in which the promisor does not will herself to be bound, but accepts a benefit or creates

79. *Id.* at 173–74.
80. *Id.*

detrimental reliance to the promisee. Thus, a will theory ultimately depends upon the theory over which it is privileged.

Of course, the relation between privileging of ideas and construction of ideologies gives Atiyah's deconstruction additional importance. Atiyah is an historian as well as a legal theorist, and he recognizes the connection between the will theory and the ideology of the nineteenth century.[81] Indeed, he argues that a consequence of the privileging of the will theory of contract was the emphasis on purely executory contracts as the paradigmatic case of moral and legal obligation (in contrast to cases of detrimental reliance or unjust enrichment) and the emphasis on the expectation interest as the paradigm of what the law of contracts was designed to protect (as opposed to the reliance or restitution interest).[82]

Needless to say, the law has moved a considerable distance from the nineteenth century model in both respects. What is important for our purposes is that the deconstruction of a privileging in a limited area of contract doctrine exposes a more pervasive underlying ideology, which gave rise to the privileging. Ironically, it also gives us the chance to investigate the unquestioned ideological assumptions in our current doctrines. Thus, the techniques of deconstruction, as a tool for the analysis of past and present ideological thinking, are especially valuable to the legal philosopher or historian.

Atiyah has used the tools of deconstructive practice to criticize the classical will theory of contract. A deconstruction of an opposition, however, cannot by itself establish a new hierarchy in place of an old one, because the new hierarchy also could be deconstructed. This is a point Atiyah neglects, for he wants to argue that reliance and benefit are the "real" sources of promissory obligation.[83] In so doing, he wants to establish a new hierarchy. However, a theory of contract based wholly upon benefit or reliance must explain why promises are binding immediately after the parties enter into them, before detrimental effects have developed. Atiyah has great difficulty explaining the binding nature of these promises, and concludes that if they are binding (which he doubts they should be), there are only weak grounds for enforcing them.[84] His conclusion is not surprising, because the best explanation for the binding nature

81. *Id.* at 4-5, 7, 33. *See generally* P. ATIYAH, THE RISE AND FALL OF FREEDOM OF CONTRACT (1979) [hereinafter THE RISE AND FALL OF FREEDOM OF CONTRACT] (historical treatment of nature of contractual and promissory liability).

82. *See* THE RISE AND FALL OF FREEDOM OF CONTRACT, *supra* note 81, at 424-29, 441-43, 456; PROMISES, MORALS AND LAW, *supra* note 76, at 33.

83. More specifically, he argues that the social group has determined that reliance and benefit are the conditions for promissory obligation. PROMISES, MORALS, AND LAW, *supra* note 76, at 129, 166-67, 193-94.

84. *Id.* at 208-12.

of these promises is the intent of the two parties to bind themselves, an explanation Atiyah has already rejected. In essence, Atiyah's benefit/reliance theory of promissory obligation must admit its own "dangerous supplement" to explain mutually unrelied upon executory promises. This "dangerous supplement," of course, is a disguised version of the will theory.

Note the irony: In the classical theory, the purely executory promise was the paradigm case; the implied promise was the exception, and the classical theory had to be supplemented with a theory explaining the binding nature of implied obligations. However, this supplement was a dangerous one, as Atiyah has shown. One might view explicit promises as merely a special case of implied promises; that is, promises whose binding nature lies in socially imposed norms and not in the assumption of individual will. On the other hand, under Atiyah's benefit/reliance theory, the acceptance of benefits or the creation of reliance becomes the paradigmatic case of promissory obligation and the purely executory unrelied upon promise becomes the exception, which must be explained by the use of a supplementary theory of obligation.

Similarly, even Atiyah's basic premise, that promises are binding if there is a pre-existing obligation in the form of a benefit received or detrimental reliance incurred, must smuggle in the will theory through the back door:

> Suppose, for example, that *A* and *B* "agree" on the sale of *B's* house to *A* for £ 20,000. *A* promises to pay the price, and *B* promises to convey the house. . . . The promises do not simply create obligations, on their own as it were. *A's* obligation to pay the price will not arise just because he has promised: it will arise if and when he receives a conveyance of the house. *B's* obligation to convey does not arise just from his promise: it arises if and when he receives the price. . . . If [*A*] gets the house, he surely has an obligation to pay, irrespective of the promise: ***it is not A's house, and B has no intention of making a gift*** . . . .[85]

Atiyah argues that A is obligated because B has conferred a benefit on him (and therefore A would be unjustly enriched if he did not perform). This raises the question of how we know that A would be unjustly enriched. Atiyah responds that B did not ***intend*** to make a gift of the house. Thus, Atiyah's benefit/reliance theory of obligation turns upon the intent of B, and we are back to a version of the will theory.

I have not refuted Atiyah's skeptical arguments regarding the will the-

85. *Id.* at 189–90 (emphasis added).

ory of contract. On the contrary, Atiyah's deconstruction of the will theory of contract is quite successful. Atiyah is wrong, however, in thinking that he has shown that a new ground of explanation will succeed where the old one has failed. Rather, he has demonstrated that the will theory and the benefit/reliance theory of promissory obligation exist in a relation of *differance*, that is, of mutual differentiation and dependence. This conclusion is unsatisfying to someone who seeks an ultimate ground for contractual obligation, but Derrida's work suggests that this is the best that can be done.

## II. The Liberation of Text from Author

### A. *Readings and Misreadings*

Derrida's conclusion that there is only "writing," that there are only signs and metaphors for still other signs and metaphors, has interesting consequences for a theory of interpretation. These consequences are important to lawyers, who are greatly concerned with the interpretation of texts.

I want to introduce these ideas with a simple paradigm of textual interpretation. According to this simple paradigm, a text is a representation of an author's intent. Thus, a novel represents a story (and artistic ideas) that a novelist wishes to express. A philosophical treatise represents ideas that a philosopher wishes to convey. A judicial opinion stands for the principles of decision that are used to decide a case. The goal of interpretation is understanding the meaning of the text, that is, the author's intent. If we interpret correctly, we grasp the author's intent; if we interpret incorrectly, we miss the author's intent.

This simple paradigm of interpretation is not a popular theory of interpretation among literary critics these days.[86] However, the simple paradigm of interpretation continues to be well-respected among legal thinkers as a preferred method of interpreting legal texts. Indeed, if most lawyers or judges were asked how statutes or judicial decisions should be interpreted, they would probably respond that the author's intent is the most

86. Indeed, the reader-response movement in literary criticism has championed the role of the reader in constructing the meaning of texts. *See generally* S. Fish, Is There A Text In This Class? (1980); S. Mailloux, Interpretive Conventions: The Reader in the Study of American Fiction (1982); The Reader in the Text (S. Suleiman & I. Crosman eds. 1980); Reader-Response Criticism (J. Tompkins ed. 1980). Only a few literary critics, such as E.D. Hirsch, still hold to the view that the author's intent is the primary source of interpretation. *See, e.g.*, E.D. Hirsch, The Aims of Interpretation (1976); E.D. Hirsch, Validity in Interpretation (1967).

Of course, the argument that the primary source of meaning lies in the reader's response rather than in the author's intention involves a privileging as much as the reverse claim, and therefore, is equally subject to deconstruction. The relation between author and reader is one of *differance*.

Deconstructive Practice

important factor.[87] As I shall argue later, the strong hold that the theory of authorial intent has upon legal thinkers probably arises from its association with the principle of the Rule of Law.[88]

I would now like to give a particular example of how the simple paradigm of interpretation operates in a legal setting. Suppose that *Brown v. Board of Education*[89] had just been decided. A black janitor files suit in a federal district court in Mississippi, contesting a "coloreds only" seating section in a cafeteria at a municipal office building. The district court must decide whether *Brown* (and the text of the Fourteenth Amendment that it interprets) outlaws the maintenance of "separate but equal" dining facilities in an establishment operated by a municipal government. According to the simple paradigm of interpretation, if the court holds one way, it has read *Brown* correctly, while if it holds another way, it has misinterpreted or misapplied *Brown*.[90]

It is possible to distinguish *Brown* on the ground that it applies only to schools, where impressionable children will be greatly affected by the perception of separate treatment. This is a possible interpretation of *Brown*, and I mention it because it is important to understand that distinguishing a case is as much an interpretation as following it. On the other hand, following the simple paradigm of interpretation, this reading may misinterpret *Brown* because the authors of *Brown* intended that all separate but

---

87. "Although there have been occasional heretics, it is an article of faith among American lawyers that the function of a court when dealing with a statute is to ascertain and effectuate the intent of the legislature." Murphy, *Old Maxims Never Die: The "Plain-Meaning Rule" and Statutory Interpretation in the "Modern" Federal Courts*, 75 COLUM. L. REV. 1299, 1299 (1975) (footnote omitted); *see also* R. DICKERSON, THE INTERPRETATION AND APPLICATION OF STATUTES 36 (1975) (same); J. HURST, DEALING WITH STATUTES 32-40 (1982) (fundamental principle of statutory construction is inquiry into legislative intent); 2A N. SINGER, STATUTES AND STATUTORY CONSTRUCTION § 45.05, at 20-22 (Sands 4th ed. 1984) ("An overwhelming majority of judicial opinions considering statutory issues are written in the context of legislative intent."). Although Professor Murphy expresses the prevailing view, the number of "heretics" is greater than his quotation suggests. *See, e.g.*, Radin, *Statutory Interpretation*, 43 HARV. L. REV. 863 (1930) (legislative intent fictional and irrelevant concept); H. Hart & A. Sacks, The Legal Process 1410 (tent. ed. 1958) (unpublished manuscript) (legislative purpose created by courts and not identical with intent).

In constitutional law, where there is perhaps the greatest controversy about proper methods of textual interpretation, the simple paradigm remains surprisingly strong. *E.g.*, R. BERGER, GOVERNMENT BY JUDICIARY (1977); Bork, *Neutral Principles and Some First Amendment Problems*, 47 IND. L.J. 1 (1971); Monaghan, *Our Perfect Constitution*, 56 N.Y.U. L. REV. 353 (1981). Even more liberal authors often pay lip service to the principle of authorial intent. Ronald Dworkin, who argues that the Framers' intent is not a psychological fact to be discovered but only something to be invented, still makes an obeisance to the simple paradigm when he proposes that one should look to the Framers' general abstract concepts of "due process" and "equal protection," rather than to specific concrete conceptions of these ideas in practice. Dworkin, *The Forum of Principle*, 56 N.Y.U. L. REV. 469, 477, 488-91, 497 (1981).

88. *See infra* text accompanying notes 108-09.

89. 347 U.S. 483 (1954).

90. This statement is true not only of the simple paradigm. Many other theories of interpretation label readings as proper or improper, although they might reach different results in individual cases.

equal public facilities for blacks and whites should be considered presumptively unconstitutional.

The simple paradigm of interpretation involves a privileging. There are many possible readings of *Brown v. Board of Education*, and these readings can take place in a multitude of different factual and legal contexts. However, some of these readings are correct, and others are incorrect. Incorrect readings are mistakes of legal reasoning, which should be eliminated from a legal system to the greatest extent possible. The commonsense understanding of legal reasoning, then, is premised upon a distinction between readings and misreadings of legal materials. Therefore, the goal of good legal interpretation is to separate the correct readings from the incorrect readings.[91]

Now this privileging of readings over misreadings can be deconstructed. Culler's treatment of the subject, although it does not specifically concern legal texts, is excellent:

> When one attempts to formulate the distinction between reading and misreading, one inevitably relies on some notion of identity and difference. Reading and understanding preserve or reproduce a content or meaning, maintain its identity, while misunderstanding and misreading distort it; they produce or introduce a difference. But one can argue that in fact the transformation or modification of meaning that characterizes misunderstanding is also at work in what we call understanding. If a text can be understood, it can in principle be understood repeatedly, by different readers in different circumstances. These acts of reading or understanding are not, of course, identical. They involve modifications and differences, but differences which are deemed not to matter. We can thus say, in a formulation more valid than its converse, that understanding is a special case of misunderstanding, a particular deviation or determination of misunderstanding. It is misunderstanding whose misses do not matter. The interpretive operations at work in a generalized misunderstanding or misreading give rise both to what we call understanding and to what we call misunderstanding.
>
> The claim that all readings are misreadings can also be justified by the most familiar aspects of critical and interpretive practice. Given the complexities of texts, the reversibility of tropes, the extendability of context, and the necessity for a reading to select and organize, every reading can be shown to be partial. Interpreters are able to discover features and implications of a text that previous interpreters neglected or distorted. They can use the text to show that previous readings are in fact misreadings, but their own readings

91. Again, even if one did not subscribe to the simple paradigm of interpretation, it still might make sense to speak of correct and incorrect interpretations of legal texts. One would not even have to claim that there was only one correct interpretation to speak in this way.

Deconstructive Practice

> will be found wanting by later interpreters, who may astutely identify the dubious presuppositions or particular forms of blindness to which they testify. The history of readings is a history of misreadings, though under certain circumstances these misreadings can be and may have been accepted as readings.[92]

Lawyers' readings of cases are partial in two senses of the word. First, they are partial in Culler's sense, in that they represent only some aspects of the meaning of texts. They are also partial in a second sense, in that they are interpretations that benefit (and thus are partial *to*) the position they advocate. Certainly, the second kind of partiality is likely to lead to the first. The interpretations of judges are no less partial in either sense of the word. The materials of the law—cases, constitutions, and statutes—take on new meanings as legal contexts change. Throughout history, interpretations are constantly offered, some of which are later labelled misreadings. The history of the law is iteration; the development of law is the development of legal materials, which are subjected to new interpretations as we read them over and over again in different factual, historical, and political contexts.

The deconstruction of the opposition of readings and misreadings is at first troubling to lawyers because our legal system seems to depend upon the ability to distinguish readings from misreadings. If all readings of legal materials are actually misreadings, then law cannot be a rational enterprise and the Rule of Law is impossible to achieve. Before reaching this conclusion, however, we should consider exactly what the deconstruction of the understanding/misunderstanding privileging has accomplished. Once again, Culler's thoughts on the matter prove instructive:

> Attacks on deconstructionists . . . frequently emphasize that if all reading is misreading, then the notions of meaning, value, and authority promoted by our institutions are threatened. Each reader's reading would be as valid or legitimate as another, and neither teachers nor texts could preserve their wonted authority. What such inversions do, though, is displace the question, leading one to consider what are the processes of legitimation, validation, or authorization that produce differences among readings and enable one reading to expose another as a misreading. In the same way, identification of the normal as a special case of the deviant helps one to question the

92. J. CULLER, *supra* note 1, at 176. The same arguments may be applied to my interpretation of Derrida in this Article. By interpreting Derrida, I present his ideas in a necessarily selective and ordered fashion. My reading of Derrida is partial, and therefore, may be classified as a "misreading" in the more general sense Culler describes. However, to use Culler's phrase, I would argue that it is a misreading whose misses do not matter much.

> institutional forces and practices that institute the normal by marking or excluding the deviant.
>
> In general, inversions of hierarchical oppositions expose to debate the institutional arrangements that rely on the hierarchies and thus open possibilities of change—possibilities which may well come to little but which may also at some point prove critical.[93]

Put another way, the deconstructive reversal has not demonstrated that all readings of *Brown v. Board of Education* are equally legitimate, but rather has called into question the ways in which we decide that a given interpretation of *Brown* is illegitimate. This issue is important for two reasons. First, our justifications of what are "proper" interpretations of a text are not always consistent.[94] Second, our method of privileging interpretations as appropriate or inappropriate is often tantamount to deciding a legal issue. It becomes the process by which we formulate legal doctrine, and will serve to foster or foreclose later doctrinal developments.

We may make a comparison here with the use of deconstruction to privilege legal concepts informed by ideological thinking. Just as deconstruction does not prove the bankruptcy of all social visions but rather affirms the many possible characterizations of social life, so too the decon-

93. *Id.* at 179.

94. For example, there are clauses of the Constitution we would probably read quite literally, confining our interpretations to the plain meaning of the words. *E.g.*, U.S. CONST. art. II, § 1, cl. 5 (president must be at least 35 years old). Other clauses, like the equal protection clause, are more ambiguous and require a fuller theory of interpretation, which would no doubt be more controversial. In still other cases, we read the Constitution in ways clearly at odds with the ordinary meaning of its language. The Eleventh Amendment, for example, literally bans all suits, in law or equity, against a state by citizens of another state. U.S. CONST. amend. XI. Yet the amendment is most often invoked to bar suits by citizens against their own state, *e.g.*, Edelman v. Jordan, 415 U.S. 651 (1974). Suits in equity against a state are permitted through the fiction of suing a state officer in her official capacity, *e.g.*, *Ex Parte* Young, 209 U.S. 123 (1908); suits for monetary damages are permitted if the relief sought is prospective rather than retrospective, *e.g.*, *Edelman*, 415 U.S. at 664, 668. Even suits for retrospective relief in the form of damages are permitted, if the state is held to waive its immunity. *Id.* at 671-74.

Ironically, the rule for determining waiver is that a state will be deemed to have waived its immunity "only where stated 'by the most express language or by such overwhelming implications from the text as [will] leave no room for any other reasonable construction.' " *Id.* at 673 (quoting Murray v. Wilson Distilling Co., 213 U.S. 151, 171 (1909)). This interpretative principle is quite at odds with the principles used to interpret the Eleventh Amendment itself.

Our use of different methods of reading constitutional and statutory texts does not necessarily mean that we are contradicting ourselves. We could defend different hermeneutical principles for interpreting waiver under the Eleventh Amendment and for interpreting the amendment itself on the grounds that the rules for statutory interpretation must be different from those for divining the meaning of the Constitution. A similar explanation could be developed to show why the Eleventh Amendment should be interpreted differently than other clauses of the Constitution. Rather, deconstruction calls these interpretative practices into question and requires us to articulate a political and legal theory to explain the differences. This process also may cause us to reevaluate our hermeneutical practices. *Compare* Atascadero State Hosp. v. Scanlon, 105 S. Ct. 3142 (1985) (defending current Eleventh Amendment doctrines on general grounds of preserving federalism) *with Edelman*, 415 U.S. at 687-88 (Brennan, J., dissenting) (Eleventh Amendment immunity should be restricted to cases falling within its literal meaning: suits against a state brought by citizens of another state).

struction involved here is designed to create possibilities for interpretation rather than to foreclose them. In introducing deconstructive strategies to texts it cannot be stressed too much that freedom and nihilism are not the same thing.

The deconstructive critique of the privileging of readings over misreadings does have a further consequence, which may at first prove unsettling to lawyers: The simple (or intent-based) theory of interpretation of legal texts is necessarily incomplete. However, as I will now show, this consequence is actually necessary for the Rule of Law to operate in the manner we think it should.

### B. *The Free Play of Text and the Rule of Law*

> Someone says to me:
>
> "Shew the children a game." I teach them gaming with dice, and the other says "I didn't mean that sort of game." Must the exclusion of the game with dice have come before his mind when he gave me the order?[95]

One of the most important ideas that Derrida's work demonstrates is that if (as everyone thinks) we mean more than we say, we also say more than we mean. Our words seem to perform tricks that we had not intended, establish connections that we had not considered, lead to conclusions that were not present to our minds when we spoke or wrote. Students of statutory construction and the law of contracts are no doubt familiar with many examples of this phenomenon. This curious habit of our words to burst the seams of our intentions and to produce their own kind of logic is what Derrida labels the free "play" of text.[96]

For Derrida, what we did not intend to say is as interesting as what we did intend. That is why so much of his work makes use of puns, or investigates how what a text says refers to itself or what it does. Much of deconstructive criticism involves the discovery of unintended connections between words. One reason for looking for such connections is that they may condense or crystallize important ideas that are already present in a text. (This is one reason we find slogans and aphorisms so effective in conveying ideas.) But there is a more important reason to investigate the unintended connections between the words in our texts. It is simply a

95. L. WITTGENSTEIN, PHILOSOPHICAL INVESTIGATIONS § 70 (1953).

96. *See, e.g.*, WRITING AND DIFFERENCE, *supra* note 1, at 292 ("Play is the disruption of presence."). A more trivial, yet classic, example of unexpected connections between words is the common pun. Derrida's work often relies on puns to emphasize connections among ideas in a text. *See, e.g.*, DISSEMINATION, *supra* note 1, at 65-171, 173-285 ("Plato's Pharmacy" and "The Double Session").

logocentric bias on our part to think that the most important meanings in a text are those the author intended to put there.

In literature, the critic does not think less of her interpretation of *Moby Dick* because Melville did not see the same connections as he composed his work. A philosopher does not think less of her critique of the *Phaedo* when she discovers a connection between ideas that Plato did not recognize in his text. Indeed, there is generally great critical importance in discovering that a text says more than the author meant it to say, or that the logic of a text leads to an unexpected difficulty or contradiction. Often, hidden flaws or strengths in a work of literature or philosophical treatise only become apparent over time. Legal texts, like other texts, often present later readers with new meanings, connections, and difficulties that their creators did not contemplate. These meanings are uncovered by the interpretations of successive readers in different historical and cultural contexts.

There are two different reasons that one might be concerned with unintended connections. The first is not Derrida's purpose, although the second is. One might use unintended meanings in a legal text to criticize the reasoning of the author. In her dissent in *City of Akron v. Akron Center for Reproductive Health*,[97] Justice O'Connor argued that the viability-based doctrine of *Roe v. Wade*[98] would self-destruct as the point of the fetus' viability came earlier and earlier during pregnancy while technology assured that the time at which abortions were virtually risk free to the mother came later and later.[99] This consequence of the *Roe* decision was not envisioned by its author, Justice Blackmun, and Justice O'Connor believed that this unintended consequence was an important criticism of the logic of Justice Blackmun's opinion.

On the other hand, the discovery of unintended connections and difficulties may not involve any criticism of the author at all. A good example is our current understanding of the equal protection clause. The drafters of the equal protection clause probably did not contemplate that one day its words would strike constitutional scholars and judges as requiring equality between men and women. However, when we read the equal protection clause today, with an expansive notion of equality that would have greatly upset the framers of that amendment, we do not mean to

97. 462 U.S. 416, 458 (1983) (O'Connor, J., dissenting).

98. 410 U.S. 113 (1973).

99. The *Roe* framework . . . is clearly on a collision course with itself. As the medical risks of various abortion procedures decrease, the point at which the State may regulate for reasons of maternal health is moved further forward to actual childbirth. As medical science becomes better able to provide for the separate existence of the fetus, the point of viability is moved further back toward conception.

462 U.S. at 458.

Deconstructive Practice

criticize their choice of words. Indeed, we demonstrate how their linguistic commitment to equality has brought us to a deeper political commitment to equality. We celebrate the manner in which the authors' words have worked themselves pure in spite of the authors' intentions.

When Derrida hunts for unseen connections in a text, he is usually not attempting to discover errors in the thought of the author. His is not the sort of task that Justice O'Connor undertook in the *Akron* case. Instead, he is looking for the type of connections that no author can avoid because no author intends them. Derrida seeks to understand the gap between what the author commands by her language and what the language performs—the uncontrollable incongruity in human language and thought. As Barbara Johnson explains, "the deconstructive reading does not point out the flaws or weaknesses or stupidities of an author, but the *necessity* with which what he *does* see is systematically related to what he does *not* see."[100]

There is an important connection between the principle of the "free play" of text and Derrida's theory of the sign. For Derrida, a sign can only signify to the extent that it can signify repeatedly, in a number of different contexts. The essential property of the sign is its iterability. It follows from Derrida's theory of the sign that we can use signs if and only if they are separable from our intent—if and only if they "mean" whether or not they mean what we intend. Thus, if I write a heartfelt love letter to my girlfriend, in order to communicate my most deeply felt sentiments through language, it must also be possible for the same words to be written insincerely, in jest, or even through random creation by a computer program. Language can signify only if it can escape the actual present meaning it had to the person who used it.[101]

This surprising conclusion stems from the fact that signs can only be used for communication if they are public. They must be capable of repetition and manipulation by any possible user.[102] But the public nature of communication necessitates that signs signify repeatedly, regardless of the presence or absence of a present meaning that informs them. A piece of graffiti continues to signify as long as it remains on the wall. Thus, to the extent that B can understand A, it is A's (iterable) signs, and not A's intention, which permits this understanding.

Moreover, the essence of the sign, iterability, carries with it the notion of a repetition of the same in a different context. Language can only operate to the extent that it is repeatable, but language is repeatable only to

100. Johnson, *supra* note 1, at xv.
101. *See* MARGINS OF PHILOSOPHY, *supra* note 1, at 317.
102. *Id.* at 315.

the extent that what A says means something, albeit not identical to what A meant, to another person B. According to Derrida:

> [I]t belongs to the sign to be legible, even if the moment of its production is irremediably lost, and even if I do not know what its alleged author-scriptor meant consciously and intentionally at the moment he wrote it, that is[,] abandoned it to its essential drifting . . . . [B]y virtue of its essential iterability[,] one can always lift a written syntagma from the interlocking chain in which it is caught or given without making it lose every possibility of functioning, if not every possibility of "communicating," precisely.[103]

The structural precondition of the sign is its ability to break free from the author, and to mean other than what the author meant. The very act of "meaning" something creates a chasm between the sign and the producer's intention. This detachability makes iterability, and thus intersubjective meaning, possible. The repetition of the sign in the new context is simultaneously a relation of identity and difference; the repeated sign is syntactically identical, yet semantically different. The result is that the text, as it is repeatedly understood, takes on a life of its own in a relation of *differance* with the person who "meant" it:

> [A]t the very moment when someone would like to say or to write, "On the twentieth . . . etc.," the very factor that will permit the mark (be it psychic, oral, graphic) to function beyond this moment—namely the possibility of its being repeated *another* time—breaches, divides, expropriates the "ideal" plenitude or self-presence of intention, of meaning (to say) and, *a fortiori*, of all adequation between meaning and saying. Iterability alters, contaminating parasitically what it identifies and enables to repeat "itself"; it leaves us no choice but to mean (to say) something that is (already, always, also) other than what we mean (to say) . . . .[104]

Derrida's aphorism, "iterability alters,"[105] is a shorthand way of saying that once the signifier leaves the author's creation and is let loose upon the world, it takes on a life of its own in the other contexts in which it can be repeated.[106] The liberation of the text from the author at the moment of creation results in the free play of the text.

103. *Id.* at 317.

104. *Limited Inc abc*, *supra* note 1, at 200.

105. *Id.* Derrida also makes a pun on the two possible origins of the word "iterable": "iter-," or "again," comes from the Sanskrit "itera," or "other." The philological ploy suggests that repetition differentiates even as it imitates. *Id.*

106. Under the simple theory of interpretation, we might still insist that the text has a meaning independent from its context: a clearly definable "core" of meaning that cannot be varied by context. According to this theory, context affects only the "peripheral" meanings of the text while preserving

Deconstructive Practice

Moreover, if the meaning of a signifier is context bound, context is boundless—that is, there are always new contexts that will serve to increase the different meanings of a signifier.[107] This should come as no surprise to a legal thinker: The words in a statute or in a case used as precedent take on new meanings in new factual contexts, and cannot be confined to a limited number of meanings. There are an indefinite number of possible contexts in which a given legal text could be read. For this reason, a text is always threatening to overflow into an indefinite number of different significations.[108]

Most of us assume that the Rule of Law requires that legal materials will be essentially determinate in meaning; that there will be a privileged interpretation of a legal text. If a text had many meanings, and no one "authentic" or privileged meaning, it would be impossible to treat like cases alike according to general and knowable universal principles equally applicable to all citizens. Moreover, if a text had many equally valid interpretations, no interpretation could have an exclusive claim to legitimacy and command the respect of all citizens.

The simple theory of interpretation seems to offer us just such a privileged interpretation. It provides that the privileged interpretation of a legal text is the one consistent with the intention of the author who created it. The simple theory has two advantages. First, it avoids the uncertainty and arbitrariness that would follow if all interpretations were equally valid. It creates the possibility of a single, knowable interpretation of legal materials, which can be applied in a non-arbitrary fashion to all citizens.

---

the "core." Thus, context is only supplementary to the basic, unchanging meaning of the text.

The "core/periphery" distinction can be deconstructed by noting that the "core" depends as much on the context as the "periphery" does. Both the core and the periphery are context dependent. The core meaning of the word "cow" provides a simple example. If two parties have adopted a code for contracts involving livestock where "cow" means "horse," the core meaning of "cow" will shift radically. This may look like a trick, but it is the "normal" context in which we use the word "cow" that gives us its "core" meaning.

In Derrida's terminology, context is a dangerous supplement to the meaning of a text. "Context" indicates both that which accompanies the text (con- as in convocation) and that which is posed against the text, or which the text is read against (con- as in contra). Both readings are important, for the text is both dependent upon and differentiated from its context. Text and context thus exist in a relation of *differance*. There is no text without a context.

107. *See* J. CULLER, *supra* note 1, at 123-28.

108. I use the word "indefinite" and not "infinite." What is important is not the number of possible new contexts, but their unexpectedness. Theoretically, it always should be possible to derive an infinite number of meanings from a text if we are willing to acknowledge all sorts of bizarre ways of reading the text. However, some of these contexts are probably irrelevant in the further context of our legal institutions. (For example, one might look for meanings in a legal text by searching for hidden anagrams that stated a rule.) Although we can be sure that some contexts will be irrelevant, we cannot predict which contexts *will* be relevant in the future. The number of such contexts may not be infinite, but it is indefinite. We cannot create an all-inclusive list in advance. To use an earlier example, what makes the equal protection clause uncanny in its moral force is the unexpected nature of classifications we may come to see in time as requiring equal treatment or permitting differential treatment.

Second, the simple theory establishes the legitimacy of the interpretation, for it adopts the meaning of the author (judge, framer, or legislator) who had the authority to create the legal text in the first place. Thus, at first glance, the Rule of Law appears to reject the idea of the free play of text and to embrace instead the simple theory of interpretation: The meaning of a legal text is the meaning of its author, which does not change as the text is introduced into new factual situations or contexts.

However, the grounding of the Rule of Law on the privileging of the author's intent can be deconstructed, and then we see that the relation of the Rule of Law to the author's intent is not so unambiguous. We discover that the Rule of Law must also depend upon the free play of legal texts, an idea which bears a relationship of *différance* to the simple theory of interpretation.

Let us consider, as an example, a published opinion of a judge appearing in a case reporter. What is the legal effect of this opinion on subsequent cases? The simple theory of interpretation would suggest that (if the precedent is binding) what the judge/author intended is the principle that controls succeeding cases. However, this will not do. The intent of the author does not control, but rather the interpretation of the author's intent as derived by subsequent readers of the text controls. It is the text as read, and not the text as written, that becomes the law.

The principle of iterability explains this result. The Rule of Law cannot operate unless legal materials (which in theory, are what bind persons) are iterable. The Rule of Law presupposes that the same corpus of legal materials will be applied to case A as to case B. If a different rule were applied in each case we would not have the Rule of Law.[109] However, the author's present intent when she creates legal materials is not iterable; it is forever lost at the moment of creation. All that remains is the sign, the existence of which makes intersubjective communication possible. The iterability of the sign of the author's intent, and not the intent itself, is essential to the operation of the Rule of Law.

In addition, the Rule of Law is based upon the premise that it is not the individual wills of people that control, but laws passed by elected representatives or case law construed and developed by judges. Rule by the arbitrary will of persons would violate the Liberal principle of autonomy;[110] social coercion is not achieved according to arbitrary will, but ac-

109. I pass over the obvious difficulty that the corpus of laws is constantly changing, so that if case B appears later in time than case A, different legal rules may apply to it. This is a problem for the theory of the Rule of Law, not for my deconstruction.

110. The principle of autonomy holds that persons should be free from coercion by the arbitrary will of another. *See* F. HAYEK, THE CONSTITUTION OF LIBERTY 139-40 (1960). Recognition of legal rights according to the Rule of Law preserves this principle by preventing inconsistent and arbitrary treatment of persons. *Id.*

cording to general, equally applicable rules. Once the rules are established by the governing authority, the rules constitute the authority for deciding cases. Thus, the Rule of Law presupposes that texts rule, and not the persons who created them.

Of course, in deciding the proper application of the rule, we look to the purpose of the governing body that created it. However, that body may not have had a single purpose or it may not have explicitly considered the factual situation at issue. Indeed, many of the legislators may not have read the measure thoroughly before voting on it.

The "purpose" used by a legal interpreter or decisionmaker is not the pure present purpose of the creator of the legal text. Instead, it is a constructed purpose: a reading of the text (a statute or decision) and of other texts (legislative history) in a particular context. The "purpose" that we discover and use in the application of a legal rule comes from texts, and not from the author.

Moreover, the Rule of Law *requires* that a legal text be separated from the purpose present in the mind of the creator of the text. As an example, suppose that airlines lobby for the passage of a law that sets minimum prices for airfares. Assume that legislator A voted for the bill in return for a favor from legislator B. This is not the kind of purpose that a judge can use to construe a statute's operation in a particular context. Nor could A's intent to receive a bribe in exchange for a vote be properly considered. The Rule of Law ultimately relies upon a distinction between proper and improper interpretive purposes. This distinction, in turn, can be deconstructed, but my point here is that the decisionmaker who seeks a purpose must reconstitute, reconstruct, or interpret a purpose from still other interpretations or signs. She must separate those purposes which are "appropriate" from those which are inappropriate. This act of discovery is an interpretation and deferral of "presence," i.e., the purpose "present" to the mind of the creator of the legal text at the time of its creation, and indeed, may even be a rejection of it.

Another example may prove instructive. Assume that the sole purpose of price control regulation is to benefit the airline industry. After intense lobbying, the legislators are convinced that they need to outlaw "cutthroat competition" among the airlines. Suppose that economic conditions then change, and the airlines will lose revenue unless they can increase volume by dropping their prices below the minimum price levels. We would not read the statute to mean that minimum prices no longer control, even though that would achieve the authors' purpose of benefiting the airline industry. Rather, we must admit that the text of the statute has taken on a life of its own, apart from the original purpose of the legislators who created it.

The statute's claim to legal authority is derived not from the intent of its framers, but from its present signification. The institutional rules that give binding authority to acts of government recognize the sign (the text) and not the signified (the purpose). The Rule of Law presupposes that the only legitimate solution to the change in economic conditions is to pass a new statute repealing the old price support legislation.[111]

The simple theory of interpretation is a logocentric theory, relying upon the "presence" of the author's intent at the moment of textual creation. By deconstructing, or "ungrounding" it, we see that the Rule of Law depends upon the free play of text, as much as it depends upon the author's intent. From this deconstruction emerge two mutually differentiated and dependent visions of interpretative practice:

> The one seeks to decipher, dreams of deciphering a truth or an origin which escapes play and the order of the sign, and which lives the necessity of interpretation as an exile. The other, which is no longer turned toward the origin, affirms play and tries to pass beyond [the] man . . . who . . . [—]throughout his entire history—has dreamed of full presence, the reassuring foundation, the origin and the end of play . . . .
>
> There are more than enough indications today to suggest we might perceive that these two interpretations of interpretation—which are absolutely irreconcilable even if we live them simultaneously and reconcile them in an obscure economy—together share the field which we call, in such a problematic fashion, the social sciences.
>
> For my part, although these two interpretations must acknowledge and accentuate their difference and define their irreducibility, I do not believe that today there is any question of *choosing*—in the first place because here we are in a region (let us say, provisionally, a region of historicity) where the category of choice seems particularly

111. The same arguments apply to the interpretation of judicial opinions. If the simple theory of interpretation were required by the Rule of Law, we might be tempted to try to solve today's difficult problems of constitutional law by communicating with the spirit of Chief Justice Marshall, and by asking him what exactly he meant in Marbury v. Madison, 5 U.S. (1 Cranch) 137 (1803). However, I hope that the reader will find something odd about this solution, aside from the idea that judges should be performing seances or raising the dead. Like the Constitution itself, *Marbury* as text has meanings that live on independently of the meanings of its creator. Therefore, even the author of the text, were he here to communicate with us, would not have a monopoly on the "real" meaning of *Marbury*. Rather, we understand intuitively that the author has already had his "bite at the apple." Once he has expressed himself, it is the opinion that binds future judges. This, too, is a necessary consequence of the Rule of Law.

Of course, if a Supreme Court Justice writes an opinion, she does, in a sense, have a "second bite at the apple" because she will be able to vote for subsequent applications of the original opinion. But her interpretation of her own writing will not be conclusive; she will have to convince four other Justices. The point is easier to understand if one considers a Justice who retires after writing a given opinion. In subsequent cases, it would be inappropriate to ask her what she meant in her opinion and to accept her views as binding.

Deconstructive Practice

> trivial; and in the second, because we must first try to conceive of the common ground, and the *différance* of this irreducible difference.[112]

The purpose of the deconstruction is not to establish that any interpretation of a text is acceptable, but that the yearning for originary meaning in the simple theory of interpretation is incomplete and cannot serve as a foundation for interpretation. We must, to some degree, acknowledge the free play of the text. However, as Derrida notes above, there can be no question of choosing the free play of legal texts as a new ground for interpretative practice, a fact that critics of original intent theory may too easily forget. The intent theory and a theory of free play must coexist in an uneasy alliance in which neither can be master nor servant. The relation of *différance* between them prevents either from serving as an originary ground of interpretative practice.

Of course, I have only considered two possible approaches to interpretation: one that looks to the intent of the author, and one that acknowledges the free play of the text. Derrida's critique, however, extends much further. As soon as the author's original intent is displaced as the foundation of interpretative practice, the critic finds that she must substitute a new ground for her interpretative theory, and this theory too, must depend upon and define itself in terms of that which it excludes. Thus, the critic who replaces "original intent" by "intersubjective meaning," "historical development," or "shared consensus of values," must reinstitute a new form of presence, which is subject to further deconstruction.[113]

---

112. Writing and Difference, *supra* note 1, at 292–93.

113. Consider, for example, theorists who advocate using tradition, moral consensus, or conventional morality as the basis of constitutional interpretation. *See, e.g.*, Lupu, *Untangling the Strands of the Fourteenth Amendment*, 77 Mich. L. Rev. 981, 985, 1040–41 (1979); Perry, *Substantive Due Process Revisited: Reflections on (and Beyond) Recent Cases*, 71 Nw. U.L. Rev. 417, 425 (1976); Wellington, *Common Law Rules and Constitutional Double Standards: Some Notes on Adjudication*, 83 Yale L.J. 221, 284 (1973). Such a proposal involves a privileging of traditional over non-traditional values, of non-controversial over controversial attitudes, and of conventional over non-conventional morality. Dean Ely deconstructs this privileging by showing that arguments for this interpretative theory undo themselves: "[P]art of the point of the Constitution is to check today's majority . . . . 'If the Constitution protects only interests which comport with traditional values, the persons most likely to be penalized for their way of life will be those least likely to receive judicial protection.'" J. Ely, Democracy and Distrust 62 (1980) (quoting Karst, *The Supreme Court, 1976 Term Foreword: Equal Citizenship Under the Fourteenth Amendment*, 91 Harv. L. Rev. 70, 136 (1977)). Thus, the argument for enforcing the privileged concept, traditional values, becomes an argument for enforcing the excluded concept, non-traditional values. Similarly, one can show that the argument for enforcing values agreed upon by a majority of the public deconstructs itself. As Ely notes, "it makes no sense to employ the value judgments of the majority as the vehicle for protecting minorities from the value judgments of the majority." *Id.* at 69.

The Yale Law Journal Vol. 96: 743, 1987

## III. Conclusion

Deconstruction by its very nature is an analytic tool and not a synthetic one. It can displace a hierarchy momentarily, it can shed light on otherwise hidden dependences of concepts, but it cannot propose new hierarchies of thought or substitute new foundations. These are by definition logocentric projects, which deconstruction defines itself against. Deconstruction is thus revelatory, and what the legal theorist does with the revelation is not dictated by the deconstruction itself, nor could it be.

In theory then, deconstructive readings of legal texts can be a tool of analysis for the right as well as for the left. In practice, left legal scholars will probably make more use of deconstructive techniques for two reasons: first, because of the historical connection between continental philosophy and left political thought, and second, because the left usually has more to gain from showing the ideological character of the *status quo* than does the right.[114]

Deconstructive readings, at least in the sense used in this Article, do not demonstrate that legal thought is incoherent any more than they demonstrate that all forms of logocentric practice are incoherent. Similarly, deconstructive readings do not demonstrate that legal thought is any more irrational than any other form of logocentric thought. Rather, what deconstruction demonstrates is the *differance* between what is privileged and what is excluded in legal thought. Deconstruction thus reveals the antinomal character of legal thought, a characterization which is at first disturbing, but in the end is the best description of our actual experience in using legal concepts.

114. On the other hand, an economic libertarian might well use deconstructive techniques to criticize the modern welfare state on the grounds that it rests upon a false privileging of certain aspects of human nature.

[17]

The Yale Law Journal
Volume 97, Number 4, March 1988

Article

# Formalism

**Frederick Schauer***

*Legal decisions and theories are frequently condemned as formalistic, yet little discussion has occurred regarding exactly what the term "formalism" means. In this Article, Professor Schauer examines divergent uses of the term to elucidate its descriptive content. Conceptions of formalism, he argues, involve the notion that rules constrict the choice of the decisionmaker. Our aversion to formalism stems from denial that the language of rules either can or should constrict choice in this way. Yet Professor Schauer argues that this aversion to formalism should be rethought: At times language both can and should restrict decisionmakers. Consequently, the term "formalistic" should not be used as a blanket condemnation of a decisionmaking process; instead the debate regarding decision according to rules should be confronted on its own terms.*

With accelerating frequency, legal decisions and theories are condemned as "formalist" or "formalistic." But what *is* formalism, and what is so bad about it? Even a cursory look at the literature reveals scant agreement on what it is for decisions in law, or perspectives on law, to be

* Professor of Law, University of Michigan. I am grateful to audiences at Brooklyn Law School, Cornell Law School, DePaul University College of Law, Duke University School of Law, Indiana University at Bloomington School of Law, New York University School of Law, and the American Political Science Association for helping me to clarify some of my good ideas and jettison some of my bad ones. I am also indebted to Alex Aleinikoff, Bruce Frier, Leo Katz, James Krier, William Miller, and Richard Pildes for commenting on earlier versions of this article with just the right blend of hostility and sympathy.

formalistic, except that whatever formalism is, it is not good.[1] Few judges or scholars would describe themselves as formalists, for a congratulatory use of the word "formal" seems almost a linguistic error. Indeed, the pejorative connotations of the word "formalism," in concert with the lack of agreement on the word's descriptive content, make it tempting to conclude that "formalist" is the adjective used to describe any judicial decision, style of legal thinking, or legal theory with which the user of the term disagrees.

Yet this temptation should be resisted. There *does* seem to be descriptive content in the notion of formalism, even if there are widely divergent uses of the term. At the heart of the word "formalism," in many of its numerous uses, lies the concept of decisionmaking according to *rule*. Formalism is the way in which rules achieve their "ruleness" precisely by doing what is supposed to be the failing of formalism: screening off from a decisionmaker factors that a sensitive decisionmaker would otherwise take into account. Moreover, it appears that this screening off takes place largely through the force of the language in which rules are written. Thus the tasks performed by rules are tasks for which the primary tool is the specific linguistic formulation of a rule. As a result, insofar as formalism is frequently condemned as excessive reliance on the language of a rule, it is the very idea of decisionmaking by rule that is being condemned, either as a description of how decisionmaking can take place or as a prescription for how decisionmaking should take place.

Once we disentangle and examine the various strands of formalism and recognize the way in which formalism, rules, and language are conceptually intertwined, it turns out that there is something, indeed much, to be said for decision according to rule—and therefore for formalism. I do not argue that formalism is always good or that legal systems ought often or

---

1. *See, e.g.*, H.L.A. Hart, The Concept of Law 124-30 (1961) (formalism as refusal to acknowledge necessity of choice in penumbral area of rules); M. Horwitz, The Transformation of American Law 254 (1977) (formalism as refusal to recognize instrumental functions of law); K. Llewellyn, Jurisprudence: Realism in Theory and Practice 183-88 (1962) (formalism as excessive reliance on canonically written language of rules); R. Unger, The Critical Legal Studies Movement 1-2 (1986) (formalism as constrained and comparatively apolitical decisionmaking); Kennedy, *Legal Formality*, 2 J. Legal Stud. 351, 355 (1973) (formalism as view that rule application is mechanical and that mechanical rule application is just); Strauss, *Formal and Functional Approaches to Separation-of-Powers Questions—A Foolish Inconsistency?*, 72 Cornell L. Rev. 488, 489 (1987) (formalism as refusal to acknowledge practical consequences of judicial decisions); Tushnet, *Anti-Formalism in Recent Constitutional Theory*, 83 Mich. L. Rev. 1502, 1506-07 (1985) (formalism as artificial narrowing of range of interpretive choices).

One can avoid the confusion of multiple usage by simply stipulating a meaning for the term "formalism." *See, e.g.*, Posner, *Legal Formalism, Legal Realism, and the Interpretation of Statutes and the Constitution*, 37 Case W. Res. L. Rev. 179, 181-82 (1986). This tack, however, evades most of the interesting problems. Having stipulated that "formalism" means deductive logical reasoning, Judge Posner proceeds easily to the conclusion that formalist reasoning has no application to the interpretation of canonical texts. That conclusion, however, follows, if at all, only from the narrowness of the stipulated definition. By not stipulating a meaning in advance of the analysis, I intend to focus on a broader range of issues. In the process, I will explore the way in which deduction, even in Posner's sense, may be related to the interpretation of canonical texts. *See infra* note 48.

even ever be formalistic. Nevertheless, I do want to urge a rethinking of the contemporary aversion to formalism. For even if what can be said for formalism is not in the end persuasive, the issues should be before us for inspection, rather than blocked by a discourse of epithets.

## I. Formalism as the Denial of Choice

### A. *Choice Within Norms*

Few decisions are charged with formalism as often as *Lochner v. New York*.[2] But what makes Justice Peckham's majority opinion in *Lochner* formalistic? Surely it is not just that the Court protected an unrestricted privilege of labor contracting against the first stirrings of the welfare state. For the Court to make such a political decision under the rubric of broad constitutional clauses like "liberty" is a far cry from what seems to be meant when decisions are criticized as being formal. To the extent that the charge of formalism suggests narrowness, *Lochner* is hardly a candidate. We criticize *Lochner* not for being narrow, but for being excessively broad.

Although *Lochner* is criticized for the length of its reach, a closer look reveals that it is not the result that is condemned as formalistic but rather the justification for that result. The formalism in *Lochner* inheres in its *denial* of the political, moral, social, and economic choices involved in the decision, and indeed in its denial that there was any choice at all. Justice Peckham simply announced that "[t]he general right to make a contract in relation to his business is part of the liberty of the individual protected by the Fourteenth Amendment"[3] and that "[t]he right to purchase or to sell labor is part of the liberty protected by this amendment."[4] To these pronouncements he added the confident statement that "[o]f course the liberty of contract relating to labor includes both parties to it."[5]

Justice Peckham's language suggests that he is explaining a precise statutory scheme rather than expounding on one word in the Constitution. It is precisely for this reason that his opinion draws criticism. We condemn *Lochner* as formalistic not because it involves a choice, but because

2. 198 U.S. 45 (1905). For condemnations of *Lochner* (and the era of which it is taken to be archetypal) as formalistic, see Gordon, *Critical Legal Histories*, 36 Stan. L. Rev. 57, 99 (1984); Peller, *The Metaphysics of American Law*, 73 Calif. L. Rev. 1151, 1193, 1200-01 (1985); Seidman, *Public Principle and Private Choice: The Uneasy Case for a Boundary Maintenance Theory of Constitutional Law*, 96 Yale L.J. 1006, 1006-07 (1987); *Developments in the Law—Immigration Policy and the Rights of Aliens*, 96 Harv. L. Rev. 1286, 1292 (1983); Note, *The Constitutionality of Rent Control Restrictions on Property Owners' Dominion Interests*, 100 Harv. L. Rev. 1067, 1077 (1987); Note, *Formalism, Legal Realism, and Constitutionally Protected Privacy Under the Fourth and Fifth Amendments*, 90 Harv. L. Rev. 945, 951 (1977); Powers, Book Review, 1985 Duke L.J. 221, 232; Rotenberg, *Politics, Personality and Judging: The Lessons of Brandeis and Frankfurter on Judicial Restraint* (Book Review), 83 Colum. L. Rev. 1863, 1875 n.60 (1983).

3. 198 U.S. at 53.

4. *Id.*

5. *Id.* at 56.

it attempts to describe this choice as compulsion.[6] What strikes us clearly as a political or social or moral or economic choice is described in *Lochner* as definitionally incorporated within the *meaning* of a broad term. Thus, choice is masked by the language of linguistic inexorability.

When I say that pelicans are birds, the truth of the statement follows inexorably from the meaning of the term "bird." If someone disagrees, or points at a living, breathing, flying pelican and says "That is not a bird," she simply does not know what the word "bird" means.[7] We criticize *Lochner* as formalistic because it treats the word "liberty" (or the words "life, liberty, or property, without due process of law") as being like the word "bird" and the privilege of contracting as being like a pelican, i.e., subsumed in the broader category. According to the reasoning in *Lochner*, if you don't know that contracting for labor without governmental control is an example of liberty, then you just don't know what the word "liberty" means.

*Lochner* is condemned as formalistic precisely because the analogy between pelicans (as birds) and unrestricted contracting (as liberty) fails. One can understand much about the concept of liberty and about the word "liberty" and yet still deny that they include the privilege of unconstrained labor contracting.[8] Thus, a decisionmaker who knows or should

6. This was noted by Holmes in his now-famous observation, "General propositions do not decide concrete cases." *Id.* at 76 (Holmes, J., dissenting).

7. Of course when I use the term "inexorable," I do not mean that the world and our language could not have been otherwise; the word "bird" could have referred to frogs instead of pelicans, or to only puffins, robins, and sparrows, but not pelicans, ostriches, and condors. Definitions are contingent and subject to change, and therefore the word "bird" might yet come to be the word that speakers of English use to refer to frogs, or only to small and not to large birds. Yet although there remains a possibility that the word "bird" will come to mean these things, this is only a possible world—it is not *our* world. In our world, the exclusion of frogs and the inclusion of large birds is definitionally part of the meaning of the word "bird." As I argue below, *see infra* notes 56-57 and accompanying text, the contingency of definition hardly entails the view that it is within the province of any one actor, legal or otherwise, to change it. Neither you nor I have the power to make it proper to use the word "bird" to refer to a frog, even though the word "bird" could in another world be used to refer to frogs.

8. The extent to which this is true for morally and politically loaded words such as "liberty" is likely to vary with time, place, and culture. Take, for example, the transformation of the "honor codes" at various venerable universities. These codes were phrased in quite general terms at their inception in the 18th and 19th centuries because these schools contained homogeneous student bodies who shared a common conception of the type of conduct definitionally incorporated within the word "honor." If a person thought that purchasing a term paper from a professional term paper service was consistent with being honorable, then that person simply did not know what "honor" meant. As values have changed and as student bodies have become less homogeneous, however, shared definitions of terms such as "honor" have broken down. Some people now *do* think that buying a term paper can be honorable, and this breakdown in shared meaning has caused general references to "honor" to be displaced in such codes by more detailed rules. There may now be little shared agreement about what the precept "be honorable" requires, but there is considerable agreement about what the rule "do not purchase a term paper" requires.

Thus, the criticism of *Lochner* and its ilk as "formalistic" in the sense discussed in the text is ambiguous. The critic could mean that the term we *now* take to be susceptible to debate was not as debatable at the time of the relevant decision. But this would hardly explain the pejorative, unless we want to condemn an entire era and the conceptual and linguistic apparatus that reflected its understandings. The alternative is that the term "formalism" charges that there was *at the time* room for debate about the application of the general term to the particular case, but the relevant decisionmakers either did not recognize that fact (perhaps because they refused to look outside their own socioeco-

know that such a choice is open, but treats the choice as no more available than the choice to treat a pelican as other than a bird, is charged with formalism for treating as definitionally inexorable that which involves nondefinitional, substantive choices.[9]

*Lochner* is merely one example in which a false assertion of inexorability is decried as formalistic. Much contemporary criticism of Blackstone, Langdell, and others of their persuasion attacks their jurisprudence on similar grounds.[10] They stand accused of presenting contestable applications of general terms as definitionally incorporated within the meaning of the general term. It is important, however, to understand the relationship between the linguistic and the ontological questions for those of Blackstone's vision. Blackstone's view that certain abstract terms definitionally incorporate a wide range of specific results is tied intimately to his perception of a hard and suprahuman reality behind these general terms. If the word "property," for example, actually describes some underlying and noncontingent reality, then it follows easily that certain specific embodiments are necessarily part of that reality, just as pelicans are part of the underlying reality that is the universe of birds. These instantiations might still follow even if the general term is not a natural kind whose existence and demarcation is beyond the control of human actors. There is nothing natural or noncontingent about the term "basketball," but it is nevertheless an error in this culture at this time to apply that word to a group of people hitting small hard balls with one of a collection of fourteen different sticks. Still, linguistic clarity and rigidity are both facilitated insofar as the words track the natural kinds of the world. To the extent that Blackstone and others believed that categories like liberty, property, and contract were natural kinds rather than human artifacts, they were less likely to perceive the choices we would now not think to deny. When one believes that a general term reflects a deep reality beyond the power of human actors, the view that certain particulars are *necessarily* part of that reality follows with special ease.

Thus, one view of the vice of formalism takes that vice to be one of deception, either of oneself or of others. To disguise a choice in the lan-

---

nomic and political class) or intentionally chose to hide it.

9. Formalism may be more broadly viewed as extending to any justification that treats as inexorable a choice that is not. In this broader sense, the claimed inexorability might come from something other than rule formulations. To mask, for example, a political, moral, or social choice in the language of "original intent" when original intent in fact does *not* provide a uniquely correct answer to the issue might be considered formalistic in the same way that masking a political, moral, or social choice in the language of the meaning of a rule is considered formalistic when that language does not provide a uniquely correct answer. Similarly, masking choice in the language of mathematical economic derivation or in the language of a unique solution to some "balance" might be considered formalistic *if* these methods are in fact comparatively indeterminate.

10. *See, e.g.*, Grey, *Langdell's Orthodoxy*, 45 U. Pitt. L. Rev. 1 (1983); Hart, *Positivism and the Separation of Law and Morals*, 71 Harv. L. Rev. 593, 610 (1958); Kennedy, *The Structure of Blackstone's Commentaries*, 28 Buffalo L. Rev. 205 (1979); Lyons, *Legal Formalism and Instrumentalism—A Pathological Study*, 66 Cornell L. Rev. 949, 950 (1981).

guage of definitional inexorability obscures that choice and thus obstructs questions of how it was made and whether it could have been made differently. Use of the word "formalism" in this sense hinges on the existence of a term (or phrase, sentence, or paragraph[11]) whose contested application generates the choice. Some terms, like "liberty" and "equality," are *pervasively indeterminate*. It is not that such terms have no content whatsoever; it is that *every* application, every concretization, every instantiation requires the addition of supplementary premises to apply the general term to specific cases.[12] Therefore, any application of that term that denies the choice made among various eligible supplementary premises is formalistic in this sense.[13]

More commonly, however, the indeterminacy to be filled by a decisionmaker's choice is not pervasive throughout the range of applications of a term. Instead, the indeterminacy is encountered only at the edges of a term's meaning. As H.L.A. Hart tells us, legal terms possess a core of settled meaning and a penumbra of debatable meaning.[14] For Hart, formalism derives from the denial of choice in the penumbra of meaning, where applying the term in question is optional. Thus, Hart conceives of formalism as the unwillingness to acknowledge in cases of doubtful application, such as the question of whether a bicycle is a vehicle for purposes of the prohibition on vehicles in the park, that choices must be made that go far beyond merely ascertaining the meaning of a word.

Hart's conception of formalism[15] is closely aligned with that undergirding those who criticize both Blackstone and *Lochner*.[16] Hart's formalist takes the penumbra to be as clear as the core, while the *Lochner* formalist takes the general term to be as determinate as the specific. Both deny the extent of actual indeterminacy, and thus neither admits that the application of the norm involves a choice not determined by the words of the norm alone.

---

11. *See infra* note 85.

12. For a discussion of the often-ignored necessity of relying on such supplementary premises in the application of the term "equality," see Westen, *The Empty Idea of Equality*, 95 HARV. L. REV. 537 (1982). I disagree, however, with Westen's argument that the necessity of adding those supplementary premises to give the primary term meaning renders the primary term superfluous. Because a term is not self-standing does not mean that it serves no purpose, even if it needs external assistance in order to serve that purpose.

13. On the choices necessitated (but often denied) by general terms, see Cohen, *Transcendental Nonsense and the Functional Approach*, 35 COLUM. L. REV. 809 (1935); Dewey, *Logical Method and Law*, 10 CORNELL L.Q. 17 (1924); Horwitz, Santa Clara *Revisited: The Development of Corporate Theory*, 88 W. VA. L. REV. 173, 175-76 (1985); Singer, *The Player and the Cards: Nihilism and Legal Theory*, 94 YALE L.J. 1, 9-25 (1984).

14. Hart, *supra* note 10, at 608-12; *see also* H.L.A. HART, *supra* note 1, at 121-50.

15. H.L.A. HART, *supra* note 1, at 121-50; Hart, *supra* note 10, at 608-12.

16. *See, e.g.*, Gordon, *supra* note 2; Grey, *supra* note 10; Peller, *supra* note 2.

B. *Choice Among Norms*

Implicit in Hart's conception of formalism is the view that in the core, unlike in the penumbra, legal answers are often tolerably determinate. Even if this is true, and I will examine this claim presently, the possibility remains that a decisionmaker has a choice of whether or not to follow a seemingly applicable norm even in its core of meaning. The question in this case is not whether a bus is a vehicle, or even whether the core of the rule excludes buses from the park, but whether the rule excluding vehicles must be applied in this case. At times a decisionmaker may have a choice whether to apply the clear and specifically applicable norm. In such cases we can imagine a decisionmaker having and making a choice but denying that a choice was in any way part of the process. Thus, a variant on the variety of formalism just discussed sees formalism as involving not denial of the existence of choices within norms, but denial that there are frequently choices about whether to apply even the clear norms.

As an example of this type of formalism, consider the unreported and widely unknown case of *Hunter v. Norman*.[17] Hunter, an incumbent state senator in Vermont seeking re-election, filed his nominating petition in the Windsor County Clerk's office on July 21, 1986 at 5:03 p.m. In doing so he missed by three minutes the petition deadline set by title 17, section 2356, of the Laws of Vermont.[18] The statute provides, in its entirety, that "Primary petitions shall be filed not later than 5:00 p.m. on the third Monday of July preceding the primary election prescribed by section 2351 of this title, and not later than 5:00 p.m. of the forty-second day prior to the day of a special primary election."[19] The Windsor County Clerk, Jane Norman, duly enforced the statute by refusing to accept Hunter's petition, observing that "I have no intention of breaking the law, not for Jesus Christ himself."[20] Hunter's name, consequently, was to be withheld from appearing on the September Democratic primary election ballot.

Hunter, not surprisingly, took his disappointment to the courthouse and filed an action in equity against Norman for extraordinary relief.[21] He asked that the court order her to accept his petition and to ensure that his name would appear on the primary ballot. At the hearing, Hunter alleged that he had called the clerk's office earlier on the date in question and been told that he was required to deliver the petition in person because of

17. No. S197-86-WrC (Vt. July 28, 1986). The following account of the case is drawn from Judge Cheever's brief opinion, the pleadings, news accounts in the *Rutland Herald* of July 22, 23, 24 and 26, 1986, and a conversation with Marilyn Signe Skoglund, Assistant Attorney General in the Office of the Attorney General, State of Vermont.

18. VT. STAT. ANN. tit. 17, § 2356 (1982).

19. *Id.*

20. Rutland Herald, July 23, 1986, at 5, col. 4.

21. The petition is unclear as to whether Hunter was seeking the extraordinary legal remedy of mandamus or a mandatory injunction in equity.

the necessity of signing forms consenting to his nomination. In fact, these consent forms were not due until a later date. Hunter claimed that had he not been led to appear in person by receiving this erroneous advice, the petition would have been filed earlier in the day. He argued that in light of the erroneous information given to Hunter by the Clerk's office, the clerk (and the state) were estopped from relying on the statutory deadline. In support of this proposition, Hunter offered *Ryshpan v. Cashman*,[22] in which the Vermont Supreme Court, on similar facts, held that because "reliance on erroneous actions on behalf of the State has put . . . its citizens in inescapable conflict with the literal terms of one of the time requirements instituted by that same sovereignty . . . [t]he statutory time schedule must . . . as a matter of equity . . . yield."[23]

Ultimately, Hunter prevailed, and it appears that *Ryshpan v. Cashman* saved the day—or at least saved Hunter's day. *Ryshpan* therefore seems to have operated as an escape route from the rigors of the statute. Suppose, however, that everything in Hunter's case had been the same, including the existence of *Ryshpan*, but that the judge had ruled against Hunter solely on the basis of the statutory language. Had this hardly unrealistic alternative occurred, it would seem but a small step from the brand of formalism discussed above to a formalist characterization of this hypothetical decision. As long as *Ryshpan* exists, the judge has a choice whether to follow the letter of the statute or instead to employ the escape route. To make this choice and merely cite the statute as indicating the absence of choice would therefore deny the reality of the choice that was made. The crux of the matter is that this choice was present as long as *Ryshpan* existed, whether the judge followed that case or not. The charge of formalism in such a case would be but a variation of formalism as the concealment of choice: Instead of a choice within a norm, as with either pervasively indeterminate language or language containing penumbras of uncertainty surrounding a core of settled meaning, here the choice is between two different norms.

This variation on *Ryshpan* reveals the reasons we condemn the masking of choice. When the statute and *Ryshpan* coexist, neither determines which will prevail. Thus, the choice of the escape route represented by *Ryshpan* over the result indicated by the statute, or vice versa, necessarily would be made on the basis of factors external to both. These factors might include the moral, political, or physical attractiveness of the parties; the particular facts of the case; the judge's own views about deadlines; the judge's own views about statutes; the judge's own views about the Vermont Supreme Court; the judge's own views about clerks of courts; and so on. Yet were any of these factors to cause a particular judge to decide that

22. 132 Vt. 628, 326 A.2d 169 (1974).

23. *Id.* at 630-31, 326 A.2d at 171.

the statute should prevail, mere citation of the statute as inexorably dictating the result would conceal from the litigants and from society the actual determinative factors. Insofar as we expect the reasons for a decision to be open for inspection (and that, after all, is usually the reason judges write opinions),[24] failure to acknowledge that a choice was made can be criticized because knowing how the choice was made helps to make legitimate the products of the system.

### C. *Is There Always a Choice?*

*Ryshpan v. Cashman* is a trifle obscure, but it is hardly unique. Consider the number of *Ryshpan* equivalents that allow decisionmakers to avoid the specific mandates of a particular rule. A decisionmaker may determine that the literal language of a rule does not serve that rule's original intent, as the Supreme Court has interpreted the Civil Rights Act of 1964,[25] the contracts clause of the Constitution,[26] and the Eleventh Amendment.[27] Or a decisionmaker may apply the "mischief rule" or its variants to determine that a literal application of the rule would not serve the rule's *purpose*.[28] Or a decisionmaker may apply a more general rule that denies relief to a claimant entitled to relief under the most locally applicable rule;[29] for example, she might apply the equitable principle of

24. Although it is generally accepted that judges should write opinions explaining their actual reasons for decision, *see, e.g.*, Shapiro, *In Defense of Judicial Candor*, 100 Harv. L. Rev. 731 (1987), some scholars have suggested that there may be reasons to avoid a candid explanation of the reasoning process. *See* sources cited *id.* at 731 n.4. Thus an opinion might be equated with a statute, whose message legitimately may depart from a reflection of the process that generated it. While recognizing that reasons going to the symbolic, guiding, and persuasive function of opinions may urge against candid explanation of the decision process, I address here only opinions in which honesty is deemed appropriate.

25. *See, e.g.*, California Fed. Sav. & Loan Ass'n v. Guerra, 107 S. Ct. 683, 691 (1987); United Steelworkers v. Weber, 443 U.S. 193, 201 (1979).

26. *See, e.g.*, Keystone Bituminous Coal Ass'n v. DeBenedictis, 107 S. Ct. 1232, 1251 (1987).

27. *See, e.g.*, Monaco v. Mississippi, 292 U.S. 313, 329-30 (1934); Hans v. Louisiana, 134 U.S. 1, 10-11 (1890).

28. Heydon's Case, 76 Eng. Rep. 637 (Ex. 1584), phrases the rule as deriving from original legislative intent. *See infra* note 68. However, limitation of the purpose of a rule to the intent of the legislature that passed it unnecessarily restricts the meaning of the term "purpose." Purpose gleaned from the words of a rule itself should not be confused with the psychological intentions of the drafters. Consider a rule which specifically excludes from a park children, radios, musical instruments, dogs but not cats, and cars and trucks but not bicycles. One might conclude from reading this rule that its purpose is to prevent noise. Even if the drafters of the rule intended to promote safety rather than prevent noise, their psychological intentions would not negate this reading of purpose from the rule's words themselves, any more than a person, having said "stop," could deny the import of that phrase because she in fact meant "go."

29. *See* Singer, *supra* note 13, at 17-18. The most "locally" applicable rule (or statute) is that which most narrowly pertains to the situation at hand. "Dogs should be leashed" is, in a case involving a dog, more locally applicable than "animals should be restrained." Similarly, "beneficiaries named by the testator are to inherit according to the will" is more locally applicable than "no person should benefit by his own wrong." The idea of *local* applicability distinguishes the rules in each of these pairs, for in each pair both rules might apply to the same situation. Local applicability captures our intuition that a more specifically applicable rule is somehow *more* applicable than a less specifically applicable, but still applicable, rule.

unclean hands or laches,[30] the legal principle of *in pari delicto*,[31] or the civil law principle of abuse of right.[32] Any reader of this article could easily add to this list.[33]

Yet, what if none of these established routes were available in a particular case—would a judge then be forced to apply the specifically applicable rule? To answer this question, let us examine another variation on *Hunter v. Norman*. Suppose that *Ryshpan v. Cashman* did *not* exist, but that everything else about the facts and the applicable law in *Hunter* remained the same. What choices, if any, would be open to the judge? The judge could, of course, simply hold that the statute applied and rule against Hunter. But must he? Could the judge instead "create" *Ryshpan* by concluding that Hunter should win because he was misled by the clerk's office?

This option of creating *Ryshpan* does not seem inconsistent with the way the American legal system operates. Despite the lack of any specific statute or case authorizing such a result, allowing Hunter to win because he was misled would raise no eyebrows in American legal circles. No one would call for an investigation of the judge's competence, as someone might had the judge ruled for Hunter because Hunter was a Capricorn and Norman a Sagittarius. If the creation of such an escape route would be consistent with American judicial traditions, then the judge can be seen to have had a choice between deciding for Hunter and deciding for Norman even without *Ryshpan*. Thus a judge who ruled against Hunter on the basis of the statute would be denying the extent to which there was still a choice to create *Ryshpan* and thereby rule for Hunter.

Of course, a judge who decided to "create" *Ryshpan* would probably not simply assert that Hunter should win because he relied on erroneous information from a state official. Rather, the judge would justify this conclusion by reference to general principles that lurk in various corners of the legal system. For example, the judge might say that, as a general principle, parties are estopped from relying on laws whose contents they have

30. *See, e.g.*, Brenner v. Smullian, 84 So. 2d 44 (Fla. 1955) (unclean hands); Gorham v. Sayles, 23 R.I. 449, 50 A. 848 (1901) (laches).

31. *See, e.g.*, Rozell v. Vansyckle, 11 Wash. 79, 39 Pac. 270 (1895). Riggs v. Palmer, 115 N.Y. 506, 22 N.E. 188 (1889), made famous in R. DWORKIN, LAW'S EMPIRE 15-20 (1986) [hereinafter LAW'S EMPIRE] and R. DWORKIN, TAKING RIGHTS SERIOUSLY 23 (1977) [hereinafter TAKING RIGHTS SERIOUSLY], presents a similar issue. *Riggs* is significant because the most locally applicable legal rule, the relevant statute of wills, would allow the murdering heir to inherit. Only the imposition of the less locally applicable general principle that no person should profit from his own wrong allowed the court to avoid the result indicated by the most directly applicable legal norm. From the perspective of the result dictated by the most immediately applicable legal rule, *Riggs* is not a hard case, but an easy one. Understanding Dworkin's enterprise requires an understanding of his attempt to explain the ways in which the result "easily" dictated by the most locally applicable rule frequently yields to less locally applicable legal and nonlegal norms. *See* Schauer, *The Jurisprudence of Reasons* (Book Review), 85 MICH. L. REV. 847 (1987).

32. *See generally* Gutteridge, *Abuse of Rights*, 5 CAMBRIDGE L.J. 22 (1935) (discussing possibility of incorporating principle forbidding exercise of legal rights for purposes of malevolence).

33. *See* Singer, *supra* note 13, at 17-18.

misstated to the disadvantage of another; a decision against the clerk would be merely a specific instance of the application of that general principle. Or, the judge might cite other particular principles, such as the principle of reliance in securities law, and analogize this case to those.[34] Under either analysis the judge would attempt to ground the new principle in some already existing principle.

On the basis of these variations, we can distinguish three possible models of escape route availability. Under one model, the existing escape routes in the system represent an incomplete list of principles to ameliorate the rigidity of rules, and the judge may add to this list where amelioration is indicated but no applicable ameliorative principle exists. In such instances, the judge might discuss justice or fairness or some other general value and explain why this value supports the creation of a principle like that in *Ryshpan v. Cashman.* The implicit ideal of this system is the availability of an ameliorative principle whenever the circumstances demand it. Thus the judge who creates a new ameliorative principle on an appropriate occasion furthers the goals of this system.

Alternatively, we could develop a model of a system in which there is already a more or less complete stock of ameliorative principles. In such a system, a judge would *always* have some escape route available if all the circumstances indicated that the applicable norm was not the best result to be reached in that case. If *Ryshpan* itself did not exist, the judge would be able to pick other extant ameliorative principles that would get Hunter's name on the ballot.

Both the first model, which resembles Dworkin's account of the law,[35] and the second, which borrows from Llewellyn's,[36] acknowledge the pervasiveness of judicial choice in their recognition of the judge's opportunity (or perhaps even obligation) to avoid the arguably unjust consequences of mechanical application of the most directly applicable legal rule. If either of these models is an accurate rendition of some legal system, then a decisionmaker within such a system who simply applies the most directly applicable legal rule without further thought or explanation either denies herself a choice that the system permitted or required, or denies to others an explanation of why she chose not to use the escape routes permitted by the system. This failure to explain the choice to apply the most locally applicable rule is simply a variation on the more egregious forms of formalism as denial of choice.[37]

34. Use of precedent is not as simple as I make it out to be here, but these subtleties of precedential reasoning need not detain us here. For a discussion of precedent, see Schauer, *Precedent*, 39 STAN. L. REV. 571 (1987).

35. *See* LAW'S EMPIRE, *supra* note 31; TAKING RIGHTS SERIOUSLY, *supra* note 31. *See also* discussion of Dworkin, *supra* note 31.

36. See especially Llewellyn, *Remarks on the Theory of Appellate Decision and the Rules or Canons About How Statutes Are To Be Construed*, 3 VAND. L. REV. 395 (1950).

37. Whether a system allows judges to create norms of rule avoidance where none exist, whether

These two models—one allowing the creation of rule-avoiding norms, and the other presenting a complete list of such norms for use[38]—must be contrasted with a third model. Under this third model, the stock of extant rule-avoiding norms is not temporarily incomplete but completable, as in the first model, nor is it complete, as in the second. Instead, it is both incomplete and closed. A decisionmaker will therefore be confronted with situations in which the immediately applicable rule generates a result the decisionmaker wishes to avoid but for which the system neither contains an escape route nor permits one to be created. Under this model, a judge who followed the rule—rather than the course she otherwise would have taken on the basis of *all* relevant factors—would not have acted formalistically in the sense now under discussion. Where there was no choice, a decisionmaker following the mandates of the most directly applicable norm could not be accused of having a choice but denying its existence.

If we can imagine a model in which a rule-avoiding norm is both nonexistent and precluded in some instances, then we can also imagine a model in which no rule-avoiding norms exist at all. In such a system, a decisionmaker would be expected simply to decide according to the rule when there was a rule dealing specifically with the situation. Because there was no choice to be made, the decisionmaker could not be charged with masking a choice.

This third model presents the conceptual possibility of a different type of formalism than that which has been the focus of this section. In this third model, the charge of "formalism" would possess a different significance than in the other two models, for the decisionmaker accused of being formalistic might not be denying a choice made in the decisionmaking process, but might never have had a choice at all. To investigate the possibility of this type of formalism we must determine whether a system can truly foreclose choices from the decisionmaker. It is to this issue that I now turn.

## II. Formalism as the Limitation of Choice

### A. *Can Language Constrain?*

Each of my variations on *Hunter v. Norman* presupposed that the judge reached a conclusion that was not influenced by the language of the

judges in fact create such norms, and whether a sufficient stock of rule-avoiding norms exists such that judges need only apply them are all unavoidably empirical questions. *See* Kennedy, *Toward a Critical Phenomenology of Judging*, 36 J. Legal Educ. 518, 547–48, 562 (1986); *see also* Trubek, *Where the Action Is: Critical Legal Studies and Empiricism*, 36 Stan. L. Rev. 575 (1984). There is no reason, of course, to presume that the answers to these empirical questions will remain consistent across all decisional domains within a legal system. For example, no logical necessity dictates that the stock of rule avoidance norms applicable to administrative determination of individual social security claims be identical to that applicable to Supreme Court adjudication of constitutional questions.

38. There need not be any conceptual inconsistency between the two models. The second can be conceived of as the end product of the first.

rule.[39] This rule-independent conclusion presents the possibility that the results required by the most locally applicable statute may diverge from the result the judge considers to be the optimal result for this case in light of a range of factors wider than that specifically mandated by the statute. In cases of such divergence between a judge's unconstrained judgment and the result indicated by the most locally applicable statute, a rigid requirement that the decision follow the statutory language would limit the choices open to the judge.[40]

Insofar as rigid adherence to the most locally applicable statute is required, either by the norms governing a decisional domain or by a judge's understanding of her role, a judge following that requirement would not be formalistic in the sense discussed in the previous section. Nevertheless, legal theorists condemn this type of decisionmaking as formalistic because it requires that a decisionmaker allow her best judgment about what should be done in *this* situation to yield to the dictates of a mere rule. In particular, it is the language of the rule that is perceived as binding the decisionmaker;[41] critics therefore condemn this decisionmaking process as formalistic because it appears to be a commitment to constraint by mere words on a printed page, words chosen and perpetuated without consideration of the exact situation now at hand. Formalism in this sense is not the denial of choice *by* the judge, as above, but the denial of choice *to* the judge. To be formalistic, it is said, is to be enslaved by mere marks on a printed page.[42]

---

39. I need not consider here which factors the judge actually used to reach a conclusion, for I am not trying to catalog the considerations comprising an ideal decisionmaker's totally particularized decisionmaking process. Instead, I seek merely to distinguish the concept of a complete array of factors that any particularizing decisionmaker would take into account, regardless of the source of the particularizing norms, from the more limited array of factors available to a decisionmaker inhibited by rules.

40. I assume here a distinction between internal and external constraint. A host of factors defining what I am and how I got that way constrain me from appearing unclothed in a football game at Michigan Stadium. Some of these are internal constraints—the factors that shape my very existence. These internal constraints may be psychological, ideological, or economic, but all shape what I *am* internally up to the moment of decision to appear clothed rather than naked at the football game. Even if I could overcome these internal constraints, however, external ones, such as social disapproval and a formal rule against such behavior, still might deter me from that action. Similarly, all sorts of internal factors influence the decision a judge might reach about the optimal result in this case. But these influences are distinguishable from external constraints, such as rules, that come from outside the judge's personal determination of what should be done.

Rules are only one possible example of external constraints. A decisionmaker also may believe herself to be externally constrained by statutory *purpose*. As I will demonstrate below, however, *see infra* text accompanying notes 77-79, statutory purpose is an external constraint when, and only when, it operates as a *rule* in the sense central to my argument. That is, purpose is an external constraint only when some *formulation* of that purpose, on paper or in the mind, operates in substantially the same way that a canonically formulated rule operates.

41. I explore this issue in depth below. *See infra* Section II-C.

42. For an example of this common use of the term "formalism," see Levinson, *What Do Lawyers Know (and What Do They Do with Their Knowledge)? Comments on Schauer and Moore*, 58 S. CAL. L. REV. 441, 445 (1985) (erroneously concluding that Schauer "is much too sophisticated a theorist to endorse . . . linguistic formalism"). This usage of the term "formalism" parallels that of other disciplines. *See, e.g.*, Michaels, *Against Formalism: The Autonomous Text in Legal and Literary Inter-*

Formalism as the linguistic limitation of choice can be illustrated in a number of ways. Think of the judge who evicts the destitute widow and her family on Christmas Eve because "the law" permits no other result. Consider the classic, fictional case of *R. v. Ojibway*,[43] in which the judge determines that a pony with a down pillow on its back is a small bird because it literally fits a statutory definition of a small bird as a two-legged animal covered with feathers.[44] And recall Justice White's dissent in *Bowsher v. Synar*,[45] in which he accuses the majority of being "formalistic" for taking its narrow reading of article II to be more important than the practical consequences of striking down attempts to deal with the deficit problem.[46]

These cases exemplify a decisionmaking process that, by distinguishing the literal mandates of the most locally applicable legal norm from some arguably better result reachable by considering a wider range of factors, reinforces the systemic isolation, or closure, of the legal system.[47] Those who condemn such an outlook as formalistic criticize the perception of law as a closed system, within which judgments are mechanically deducible from the language of legal rules.[48] Note that this description of formalism

---

*pretation*, 1 POETICS TODAY 23 (1979).

43. Pomerantz & Breslin, *Judicial Humour—Construction of a Statute*, 8 CRIM. L.Q. 137 (1966).

44. Note, of course, that four-legged animals have two legs—and more. *Id.* at 138.

45. 478 U.S. 714, 106 S. Ct. 3181, 3205 (1986) (White, J., dissenting).

46. The plausibility of Justice White's dissent indicates that the majority opinion may also have been formalistic in the first sense considered in this article, *see supra* Section I, for it suggests that the majority had a choice. Yet by phrasing the opinion largely in terms of the clear mandate of the Constitution, the majority denied the existence of that choice and thus denied its audience the benefit of knowing how that choice was made. *See* Strauss, *supra* note 1.

47. On the relationship between the idea of systemic isolation and the more familiar terminology of legal positivism and its opponents, see *infra* note 81.

48. *See, e.g.*, M. HORWITZ, *supra* note 1, at 250-51. After defining formalism as syllogistic deduction, Judge Posner concludes that formalism is inapplicable to statutory rules (rules with a canonical embodiment) because the decision to take these rules literally is itself a choice. Posner, *supra* note 1. Posner stumbles, however, in taking this preliminary choice to distinguish rule interpretation from common law adjudication. He offers the following as an instance of a common law deduction: "So if an enforceable contract is a promise supported by consideration, and *A*'s promise to *B* was supported by consideration, the promise is a contract." *Id.* at 182. He then contrasts that example with the following requirement: "[O]ne must be at least thirty-five to be eligible [to be President], X is not thirty-five, therefore X is not eligible." *Id.* at 188. The latter case, says Posner, is not deductive, superficial appearances to the contrary, because interpreting the text to produce the premise is not deductive. According to Posner, the text could have been interpreted nonliterally; thus interpretation of the text to require that a President actually be at least thirty-five years old, rather than some less determinate measure of maturity, involves a nondeductive choice.

Posner's conclusion is correct, but only because of Posner's sleight of hand in drawing the preliminary distinction between statutory rule application and common law adjudication. Posner builds into the common law case a hardly noticeable "if." Thus, although the statutory case is not deductive because the generation of the major premise involves an interpretive *choice*, neither is the common law case deductive, because its major premise is also a choice. Note that although both are equally nondeductive, both can be equally deductive once the major premise is generated. We therefore can reformulate the issue this way: If we make the original determination that the language of a rule is to be interpreted literally, then the process of rule application is indeed deductive in any case in which a putative application is definitionally incorporated within the scope of the rule as set forth in its major premise.

conjoins two different elements: mechanical deducibility and the existence of a closed system. Neither element on its own necessarily implies the other, however. Mechanical deducibility need not entail closure. If we had a legal rule prohibiting all actions specifically condemned by the United Nations, for example, the coverage of the rule would be readily determinable, even if the answers were found outside the legal system (narrowly construed). Conversely, nonmechanical judgments can be made within the boundaries of a single system.[49] Consider the questions of whether there should be a three-point shot in basketball or a designated hitter in baseball. These are not easy questions (nor are they important ones), but their answers are *internal* to the games at issue; they involve a determination of whether the proposed change serves the goals of the game.[50] Although mechanical deducibility is thus analytically severable from systemic isolation, the two are commonly conjoined when critics deride legal decisions or theories as "formalistic," because both limit the domain of choices available to a decisionmaker.[51]

Having posited a model in which the decisionmaker's choice is limited by rules, we now must determine whether this model is descriptively accurate and normatively sound. The descriptive question, which I will take up first, is whether such limitation of choice by the words on a printed page is possible. To put it differently, and to distinguish this version of formalism from that considered in the previous section, the question is whether choice can be constricted by a canonical set of words on a printed page, or whether the choices open to a seemingly constrained decisionmaker are in fact virtually the same as those available to an unconstrained decisionmaker. This descriptive question in turn has both conceptual and psychological aspects. Even if it may be conceptually possible for language to constrain choice, it may still be beyond the psychological ca-

---

49. For an important defense of this variety of formalism, see Weinrib, *Legal Formalism*, 97 YALE L.J. (forthcoming 1988).

50. My point here parallels Dworkin's notion of "fit." As Dworkin illustrates the point, the determination whether the existence of a homosexual relationship between David and Steerforth best fits *David Copperfield* is by no means mechanical, but its resolution takes place largely within the boundaries of the novel. Dworkin, *No Right Answer?*, in LAW, MORALITY AND SOCIETY: ESSAYS IN HONOUR OF H.L.A. HART 58 (P. Hacker & J. Raz eds. 1977). A slightly different version of this article appears under the same title in 53 N.Y.U. L. REV. 1 (1978) and as *Is There Really No Right Answer in Hard Cases?*, in R. DWORKIN, A MATTER OF PRINCIPLE 119 (1985). In a later work, LAW'S EMPIRE, *supra* note 31, Dworkin broadens the systemic boundaries with which he is concerned to encompass those norms commonly understood as legal, political, and moral. The expansion of these boundaries is a separate issue, however; one could agree with Dworkin that it is possible to look for fit *within* a domain while disputing the size of the relevant domain.

51. The mechanical aspects of formalism are stressed in the important discussion in Kennedy, *supra* note 1. The concept of formalism as not necessarily mechanical but involving significant limitations on otherwise eligible results is the focus of Tushnet, *supra* note 1. *See also*, Grey, *The Constitution as Scripture*, 37 STAN. L. REV. 1, 4 n.8 (1984) (distinguishing between "operative" textual norms that guide decisions themselves and "non-operative" textual norms that tell decisionmakers to use decisive norms outside text).

pacity of those who make decisions to abide by these constraints. But let us turn first to the conceptual question.

Is it possible for written norms to limit the factors that a decisionmaker considers? At first glance, the answer to this question seems to be "no." Language is both artificial and contingent and therefore appears insufficiently rigid to limit the choices of the human actors who have created it. The word "cat," for example, could have been used to refer to canines, and the English language could have followed the language of the Eskimos in having several different words to describe the varieties of snow. Yet this answer confuses the long-term mobility of language with its short-term plasticity, and is a conclusion comparable to taking the ponderous progress of a glacier as indicating that it will move if we put our shoulders against it and push. Of course language is a human creation, and of course the rules of language are contingent, in the sense that they could have been different. It is also beyond controversy that the rules of language reflect a range of political, social, and cultural factors that are hardly *a priori*. But this artificiality and contingency does not deny the short-term, or even intermediate-term, noncontingency of meaning. If I go to a hardware store and request a hammer, the clerk who hands me a screwdriver has made a mistake, even though it is artificial, contingent, and possibly temporary that the word "hammer" represents hammers and not screwdrivers. Similarly, a rule requiring candidates to file nominating petitions at a certain place by a certain time on a certain day is violated by filing in the wrong place or after the specified time. Whatever the real judge *did* say in *Hunter v. Norman*, and whatever some judge might have said in any of my hypothetical variants, none of them would be that Hunter, in filing at 5:03 p.m., had filed at or before 5:00 p.m.

The questions about the possibility of linguistic constraint can be clarified by considering again the rule prohibiting vehicles in the park. But now let us turn from its peripheral applications to the central applications—whether cars and trucks are excluded. Hart assumed that, whatever else the rule did, it excluded cars and trucks. This was the rule's "core" of settled meaning and application.[52] Against this, Fuller offered the example of a statue of a truck erected as a war memorial by a group of patriotic citizens. According to Fuller, the example challenges the idea that a rule will have a settled core of meaning which can be applied without looking at the rule's purpose. Fuller argues that it cannot be determined whether the truck, which is a perfectly functional vehicle, falls into the rule's periphery or core unless one considers the purpose of the rule.[53] Fuller's challenge is ambiguous, however; there are three variant interpre-

52. Hart, *supra* note 10, at 607.

53. Fuller, *Positivism and Fidelity to Law – A Reply to Professor Hart*, 71 HARV. L. REV. 630, 663 (1958).

tations of his challenge to the theory of linguistic constraint.[54] One interpretation of Fuller's challenge is that legal systems necessarily incorporate rule-avoiding norms such as those discussed earlier.[55] Legal systems must provide some escape route from the occasional absurdity generated by literal application because applying the literal meaning of a rule can at times produce a result which is plainly silly, clearly at odds with the purpose behind the regulation, or clearly inconsistent with any conception of wise policy. Insofar as a legal system offers its decisionmakers no legitimate escape from unreasonable consequences literally indicated by the system's norms, the system is much less a *legal* system, or is at least not a legal system worthy of that name. This argument, however, asserts a normative point about how legal systems should operate, rather than any necessary truth about how the norms themselves operate. Moreover, the argument itself admits the potential binding authority of rules: If rules require an escape route to avoid the consequences of literal application, then it must be that literal application can generate answers different from those which a decisionmaker would otherwise choose. Thus, this interpretation fails to challenge the possibility of linguistic constraint; it merely points out the undesirability of employing it too rigorously in certain domains.

Alternatively, Fuller might be arguing that legal systems necessarily require the interpretation of regulatory language in light of the purpose of the regulation. As with the first interpretation of the challenge, however, this interpretation focuses on whether a rule should bind, and it leaves the claims of linguistic determinacy untouched. We still can imagine a system in which decisionmakers do not interpret clear regulatory language according to its purpose if its purpose diverges from the regulatory language. The outcome in some instances might seem absurd, but it is question-begging to use the existence of the absurd result as an attack on the possibility of a core of literal meaning.

Finally, Fuller might be interpreted as making a point about language itself: He might be arguing that meaning cannot be severed from the speaker's purpose and that meaning must be a function of the specific context in which words are used. Fuller's argument that the idea of literal meaning is incoherent, an argument also made by other critics,[56] reveals a

54. Fuller's example and other illustrations of seemingly absurd results generated by applying a rule without attention to the circumstances of its creation figure prominently in criticism of formalism. *See, e.g.*, Moore, *A Natural Law Theory of Interpretation*, 58 S. Cal. L. Rev. 277, 386–88 (1985); H. Hart & A. Sacks, The Legal Process: Basic Problems in the Making and Application of Law 1148–78 (tentative ed. 1958) (unpublished manuscript); *see also* Dworkin's use of *Riggs v. Palmer*, *supra* note 31.

55. This use of the term "necessarily" to describe the essential features of anything properly called a legal system would be consistent with the general tenor of Fuller's jurisprudence. *See* L. Fuller, The Morality of Law (1964); R. Summers, Lon L. Fuller 27–31, 36–40 (1984).

56. *See, e.g.*, Boyle, *The Politics of Reason: Critical Legal Theory and Local Social Thought*, 133 U. Pa. L. Rev. 685, 708–13 (1985) [hereinafter *The Politics of Reason*] (arguing that words do not

mistaken view of the nature of language. Fuller and his followers fail to distinguish the possibility and existence of meaning from the *best* or *fullest* meaning that might be gleaned from a given communicative context. In conversation, I am assisted in determining what a speaker intends for me to understand by a number of contextual cues, including inflection, pitch, modulation, and body language, as well as by the circumstances surrounding the conversation. That such contextual cues assist my understanding, however, does not imply that the words, sentences, and paragraphs used by the speaker have *no* meaning without those cues. The "no vehicles in the park" rule clearly points to the exclusion of the statue from the park even if we believe that the exclusion is unnecessary from the point of view of the statute's purpose.

If I come across an Australian newspaper from 1827, I can read it because I understand, acontextually, the meaning of most of the words and sentences in that newspaper, even though with better historical understanding I might understand *more* of what was written by a colony of transported English convicts. This example does not demonstrate that language is unchanging, nor that language can be perfectly understood without attention to context, but rather that some number of linguistic conventions, or rules of language, are known and shared by all people having competence in the English language. Linguistic competence in a given language involves understanding some number of rules also understood by others who are linguistically competent in the same language. When individuals understand the same rules, they convey meaning by language conforming to those rules.[57] Members of the community of English speakers,

have essences or core meanings); Boyle, *Thomas Hobbes and the Invented Tradition of Positivism: Reflections on Language, Power, and Essentialism*, 135 U. PA. L. REV. 383, 408-19 (1987) (discussing Hobbes' rejection of notion of linguistic essences). In passing, I note my disagreement with those who describe as "post-Wittgensteinian" the view that meaning cannot be separated from the particular context of a particular utterance. *E.g.*, Boyle, *The Politics of Reason*, *supra*, at 708. A footnote in a law review article is hardly the place to debate interpretations of Wittgenstein, including whether Wittgenstein can even plausibly be interpreted to support a pragmatist/particularist theory of meaning. Yet I would briefly note that a fair reading of Wittgenstein reveals that he argued that the meaning of a word is a function of how that word is contingently used in an existing linguistic community, but emphatically not a function of how the word is used on a particular occasion by a particular member of that community.

It is crucial to recognize the seductive quality of phrases like "post-Wittgensteinian," which suggest that if the reader acknowledges Wittgenstein's genius, then she must agree with the point described in those terms. It is better to discuss the point at issue without attempting to lean on the argumentative props of associations with philosophers whose names are currently fashionable in legal circles. In light of the still-raging disputes about the most foundational questions in the philosophy of language, to substitute Wittgenstein's name for an argument is unwarranted even if the use of his name is accurate. When that use is mistaken or at the very least contested, the dangers of facile borrowing from other disciplines are compounded.

This criticism of the presentation of Boyle's argument has no bearing on its underlying validity, however. Although I disagree with much of what he and Fuller argue, those arguments raise central questions about the nature of law which I believe should be confronted directly. Boyle's useful perspectives are ill-served by clothing them in what appears to me to be an idiosyncratic misreading of Wittgenstein.

57. For a particularly insightful and influential articulation of the view that meaning exists inde-

for example, possess shared understandings that enable them to talk to all other members of the community.

Among the most remarkable features of language is its compositional nature, i.e., the way in which we comprehend sentences we have never heard before. We can do this because rules, unspecified and perhaps unspecifiable, allow us to give meaning to certain marks and certain noises without having to inspect the thought processes of the speaker or the full context in which words appear. Words communicate meaning at least partially independently of the speaker's intention. When the shells wash up on the beach in the shape of C-A-T, I think of small house pets and

---

pendent of speaker's purpose or other related aspects of context, see J. SEARLE, SPEECH ACTS: AN ESSAY IN THE PHILOSOPHY OF LANGUAGE 42-50 (1969). This view also seems to be the import of paragraphs 489-512 of L. WITTGENSTEIN, PHILOSOPHICAL INVESTIGATIONS (G.E.M. Anscombe trans. 3d ed. 1953). A similar interpretation of Wittgenstein, relying on different passages, is G. BAKER & P. HACKER, WITTGENSTEIN: RULES, GRAMMAR AND NECESSITY 329-38 (1985). Indeed, even those who are rightly concerned with the foundational rule-following questions posed by Wittgenstein would not dispute that "communal language constitutes a network of determinate patterns." Wright, *Rule-Following, Objectivity and the Theory of Meaning*, in WITTGENSTEIN: TO FOLLOW A RULE 99, 105 (S. Holtzman & C. Leich eds. 1981).

Interpretations of Wittgenstein apart, acceptance of the possibility of literal meaning has passed into the commonplace of contemporary analytical philosophy of language, even while philosophers hotly dispute the source or explanation of that phenomenon. *See, e.g.*, W. ALSTON, PHILOSOPHY OF LANGUAGE 74-75 (1964); M. BLACK, *Meaning and Intention*, in CAVEATS AND CRITIQUES: PHILOSOPHICAL ESSAYS IN LANGUAGE, LOGIC, AND ART 109 (1975); S. CAVELL, *Aesthetic Problems of Modern Philosophy*, in MUST WE MEAN WHAT WE SAY? 73, 80-82 (1969); S. CAVELL, *Knowing and Acknowledging*, *id.* at 238, 248-49; D. DAVIDSON, INQUIRIES INTO TRUTH AND INTERPRETATION xix, 243-64 (1984); D. HOLDCROFT, WORDS AND DEEDS: PROBLEMS IN THE THEORY OF SPEECH ACTS 122-23 (1978); R. MARTIN, THE MEANING OF LANGUAGE 217 (1987); M. PLATTS, WAYS OF MEANING: AN INTRODUCTION TO A PHILOSOPHY OF LANGUAGE 130-32 (1979); I. SCHEFFLER, BEYOND THE LETTER: A PHILOSOPHICAL INQUIRY INTO AMBIGUITY, VAGUENESS AND METAPHOR IN LANGUAGE 81 (1979).

In one philosopher's words:

> It is a platitude—something only a philosopher would dream of denying—that there are conventions of language, although we do not find it easy to say what those conventions are. If we look for the fundamental difference in verbal behavior between members of two linguistic communities, we can be sure of finding something which is arbitrary but perpetuates itself because of a common interest in coordination. In the case of conventions of language, that common interest derives from our common interest in taking advantage of, and in preserving, our ability to control others' beliefs and actions to some extent by means of sounds and marks. That interest in turn derives from many miscellaneous desires we have; to list them, list the ways you would be worse off in Babel.

D. LEWIS, *Languages and Language*, in 1 PHILOSOPHICAL PAPERS 163, 166 (1983).

Obviously some tension exists between the way that language is discussed in analytic philosophy of language and the way that it is discussed in other circles, including literary theory. Part of the difference between the terms of the debate in these two circles can be explained by the different extent to which the two disciplines focus on "difficult" interpretations. This may also explain the extent to which *some* branches of legal theory, with their focus on difficult interpretations in linguistically hard cases, have been drawn to literary theory. Moreover, insofar as literature exists primarily to illuminate, inspire, and transform, its very existence encourages attempts to pierce literal meaning. The relationship between the enterprise at issue and the view of literal meaning adopted suggests an important question: Might the purposes of the legal enterprise be so different from those of interpreting literature that literal meaning is no longer an obstacle but instead a tool? I have no answer to this question, nor do I intend to offer a few easy citations to suggest a familiarity I do not possess. Nevertheless, the very differences in focus between analytic philosophy of language and literary theory may suggest that it is a bit too easy, for me or for those who draw on literary theory or other perspectives on language, to assume that the applications of these perspectives to law cannot take place without some theoretical slippage.

not of frogs or Oldsmobiles precisely because those marks, themselves, convey meaning independently of what might have been meant by any speaker. Of course there can never be *totally* acontextual meaning.[58] The community of speakers of the English language is itself a context. Yet meaning can be "acontextual" in the sense that that meaning draws on no other context besides those understandings shared among virtually all speakers of English.

Given that the meaning of words may be acontextually derived from our understandings of language, the central question becomes whether enough of these understandings exist to create the possibility of literal language. In other words, we must ask whether words have sufficient acontextual import so that communication can take place among speakers of English in such a way that at least a certain limited range of meaning, if not one and only one meaning, will be shared by all or almost all speakers of English. The answer to this question is clearly "yes." As with the shells that washed up on the beach in the shape of C-A-T, words strung together in sentences point us toward certain meanings on the basis of our shared understandings. At times these sentences may be descriptive, but at other times these comprehensible sentences may be general prescriptions—rules. Because we understand the rules of language, we understand the language of rules. Contextual understanding might be necessary to determine whether a given application does or does not serve the purposes of a rule's framers. Yet the rule itself communicates meaning as well, although that meaning might depart from the purposes behind the rule or from the richer understanding to be harvested from considering a wider range of factors than the rule's words. That we might learn more from considering additional factors or from more fully understanding a speaker's intentions does not mean that we learn nothing by consulting the language of rules themselves.

Of course, certain obvious, accessible, and by and large undisputable features of rules distinguish the meaning we cull from them from our interpretation of other types of communications. For example, when we interpret a rule of law, we understand that it is a law and that it is to be interpreted in light of surrounding language in the same law. In addition, ordinary "lawspeak" (habeas corpus, certiorari, party, appeal) can be viewed as a language for a subcommunity in the community of English speakers, capable of doing within the subcommunity what ordinary language does within the larger community of English speakers. Thus, although all those reading a statute come to that task with certain shared

58. *See* J. Searle, *Literal Meaning*, in Expression and Meaning 117 (1979) (literal meaning exists albeit only against a set of background assumptions about contexts in which sentence could appropriately be uttered); Moore, *supra* note 54, at 304–07 (arguing that minimal context allows and is required for fixing references to singular terms).

assumptions, it is probable that almost all lawyers add to these an additional set of assumptions which are shared mainly by lawyers.[59]

Both those within the legal community and those within the larger linguistic community are capable of deriving the literal import of rules, even though the literal lawyer's meaning may occasionally diverge from the literal lay meaning of the same term. A law that limits membership in Parliament to those who take an oath "on the true faith of a Christian" literally excludes Jews by its language.[60] A statute requiring that the master of a vessel shall record in the log book "[e]very birth happening on board, with the sex of the infant, and the names of the parents,"[61] can be understood by virtually any speaker of English as requiring the master to take certain actions.[62] In these and countless other cases, statutes can be wrenched from most of the context of their enactment and application and still be read and understood.

---

59. Note that I am talking about language and about two different embellishments on the main theme of literal meaning. First, ordinary people within a given linguistic culture might share, as linguistic conventions, knowledge about how to interpret the language of rules, including conventions relating to the difference between normative and descriptive language and conventions telling them to interpret words in light of surrounding language in the same rule or statute. This suggests only that all competent speakers of the language in which the text is written have access to a certain minimal amount of noncontroversial information about what kind of text it is.

Second, literal meaning is not necessarily ordinary meaning, because linguistic conventions may exist within a technical or professional subcommunity of a larger community. For example, photographers may have a literal sense of the meaning of the term "burning in," physicians may have a literal sense of the meaning of the term "Cushing's Syndrome," and lawyers may have a literal sense of the meaning of the term "assumpsit," even though none of these are terms used at all or in the same way by ordinary English speakers. This second embellishment, however, must be sharply distinguished from other notions of "conventionalism" that build in much more than linguistic meaning. *See, e.g.*, S. Burton, An Introduction to Law and Legal Reasoning (1985); Fiss, *Conventionalism*, 58 S. Cal. L. Rev. 177 (1985); Fiss, *Objectivity and Interpretation*, 34 Stan. L. Rev. 739 (1982). The conventionalist legal literature talks merely about the conventions of permissible legal argument and does not confront the question of the relationship between the conventions of permissible legal argument and the conventions of literal meaning, whether ordinary or technical. Thus, legal conventionalists such as Fiss avoid questions regarding whether and why certain literal readings of legal rules are or are not permissible arguments within the legal interpretive community. It is these questions, in some sense more foundational, that concern me here, because my aim is to locate the particular permissible arguments in the legal interpretive community, rather than merely to assert the existence of permissible arguments.

60. Salomons v. Miller, 8 Ex. 778, 155 Eng. Rep. 1567 (1853); Miller v. Salomons, 7 Ex. 475, 155 Eng. Rep. 1036 (1852).

61. 46 U.S.C. § 201 (1958), *repealed by* Pub. L. No. 98-89, 97 Stat. 600 (1983).

62. "When you come tomorrow, bring my football boots. Also, if humanly possible, Irish water spaniel. Urgent. Regards. Tuppy."

"What do you make of that, Jeeves?"

"As I interpret the document, sir, Mr. Glossop wishes you, when you come tomorrow, to bring his football boots. Also, if humanly possible, an Irish water spaniel. He hints that the matter is urgent, and sends his regards."

"Yes, that's how I read it, too . . . ."

P.G. Woodehouse, *The Ordeal of Young Tuppy*, *quoted in* S. Blackburn, Spreading the Word: Groundings in the Philosophy of Language 3 (1984).

B. *Does Language Constrain?*

The conceptual question of whether literal meaning is possible can therefore be answered affirmatively. Rules may point to results that diverge from those that a decisionmaker would have reached apart from the literal meaning of the rule. When there is such divergence, however, the psychological question remains: Is it possible in such cases for decisionmakers to follow the literal meaning of the rule rather than their own judgment regarding how the case should be resolved?

The psychological challenge to formalism involves the claim that decisionmakers will usually take all factors they believe to be relevant into account, or at least that they will usually feel compelled to reach "reasonable" results whether or not the language of the rule points in that direction.[63] When expressed this way, it is obvious that the psychological question is an empirical one. Accordingly, it cannot be answered by mere argument. Yet despite legal scholarship's sorry failure to take the psychological challenge seriously,[64] the possibility that judges usually obey their own rule-independent judgment is, on its face, quite plausible. We can easily imagine a world in which decisionmakers consider everything that they feel relevant and ignore, or at least slight, any inconsistent external instructions in making their decisions. The question is whether that is the world of the law.

Certainly some legal decisionmakers conform to this model. Although one may dispute as excessive the generalizations of the more extreme Realists, it is difficult to deny the existence of decisionmakers who consult the rules only to create *post hoc* rationalizations. Indeed, to the extent that legal systems resemble the model in which a rule-avoiding norm is always available, such behavior is encouraged. Insofar as the view ever prevailed that there were few decisionmakers who rejected, ignored, or bent the plausibly determinate mandates of governing rule, it is important that that view be shown for the optimistic fantasy it is. Yet to accept that some judges arrive at decisions without considering rules does not imply that all or most decisionmakers act in such a way as either an inevitable feature of human nature or even as a contingent feature of judicial behavior.

Just as it is a mistake to assume that because some judges ignore rules most judges do so, it is also a mistake to assume that because rules sometimes constrain, they usually constrain. The truth, an empirical rather than a logical one, plainly lies between the extremes of always and never, or even between the lesser extremes of rarely and usually. Although this is not the place to examine the rudimentary empirical work that has been

63. *See* Aleinikoff, *Constitutional Law in the Age of Balancing*, 96 YALE L.J. 943, 985, 1004 (1987).

64. Noteworthy exceptions are J. FRANK, LAW AND THE MODERN MIND (1930), and Kennedy, *supra* note 37. However, legal scholarship still must systematically investigate the important issues that Frank, Kennedy, and others have raised in an impressionistic way.

done on the question, it is sufficient for my purposes to note that this research has, not surprisingly, yielded the result of "sometimes."[65] In some settings, decisionmakers sometimes apply instructions external to their own decisional process even if those instructions diverge in outcome from the results the decisionmakers otherwise would have reached. This conclusion should cause no surprise as long as we recognize that people often do what *others* think best. If privates in the army often follow orders instead of making autonomous choices, and if privates might behave in this way with respect to general orders in addition to particularized commands, we can imagine judges doing the same with respect to rules.[66]

We have seen that, as a descriptive and conceptual matter, rules can generate determinate outcomes; that those outcomes may diverge from what some decisionmakers think ought to be done; and that some decisionmakers will follow such external mandates rather than their own best particularistic judgment. The normative question of formalism now remains: To what extent *should* a system legitimate the avoidance of literal meaning when avoidance seems to be the optimal outcome to the decisionmaker? To put it simply, now that we have established that formalism—in the sense of following the literal mandate of the canonical formulation of a rule—is conceptually and psychologically possible, we must ask whether it is desirable. Before turning to that question, however, I want

65. *See* D. BLACK, THE BEHAVIOR OF LAW (1976); L. FRIEDMAN, THE LEGAL SYSTEM: A SOCIAL SCIENCE PERSPECTIVE (1975); Hogan & Henley, *Nomotics: The Science of Human Rule Systems*, 5 LAW & SOC'Y REV. 135 (1970); Johnson, *Law, Politics, and Judicial Decision Making: Lower Federal Court Uses of Supreme Court Decisions*, 21 LAW & SOC'Y REV. 325 (1987); Scandura, *New Directions for Theory and Research on Rule Learning*, 28 ACTA PSYCHOLOGICA 301 (1968).

66. There is something unrealistic about all of this, because it erroneously assumes that my paradigm "easy" cases are representative of the kinds of decisions that come before decisionmakers. They are not, at least when we take "decisionmaker" in a somewhat narrow sense to refer to formal decisionmakers such as judges sitting in courts of law. In most legal systems, various screening devices ensure that cases at the center of decisional determinacy will not enter the formal adjudicative process. The time and expense of litigation and the widespread inclination to avoid futile battles are such that decisions at the core of settled meaning seldom confront any formal decisionmaking process. *See* Priest, *Reexamining the Selection Hypothesis: Learning from Wittman's Mistakes*, 14 J. LEGAL STUD. 215 (1985) (develops selection hypothesis to determine which cases are settled and which are litigated); Priest and Klein, *The Selection of Disputes for Litigation*, 13 J. LEGAL STUD. 1 (1984) (presents model to predict whether litigation will be resolved by suit or settlement).

This, however, is but a contingent feature of modern legal systems. It is possible to imagine a legal system closer to a sporting event, where umpires call "safe" or "out" on every play, or where officials with red penalty flags in their back pockets patrol the social landscape, ready to throw the flag and call "tort," or "crime," or "breach of etiquette" whenever there is a transgression of the rules. Obvious logistical problems prevent such a system from being a reality, but it is a useful *Gedankenexperiment* for thinking about the innumerable instances in which rules are followed or clearly broken without coming to the attention of the judicial system.

Many legal systems, unlike those with "roving umpires," operate largely in the area of linguistic indeterminacy, generated either by vagueness of the governing norm or by open texture when previously clear norms confront the unexpected. And in some systems, such as that of the United States, the likelihood of success is sufficient to make it worth litigating cases in which linguistic determinacy produces a politically or morally uncomfortable result. But that is exactly our question, because the weight the system gives to literal meaning will determine the extent to which it is worth litigating against literal meaning.

to answer an important counterargument to the possibility of the type of formalism defined in this section.

## C. *Language and Rules*

Until this point my argument may appear to create a false dichotomy. I have counterpoised the vision of decisionmakers who follow the literal language of a rule with that of decisionmakers who follow the dictates of their own externally unguided opinions. But are these the only alternatives? Although *rules* can and do constrain, is it not possible that these rules need not be equated with the literal meaning of the language in which they happen to be articulated? In other words, is portraying the vice of formalism as the vice of literalism actually confusing rules with the literal meanings of their explicit formulations?

The argument that rules can be distinguished from the language in which they are written has a distinguished lineage in Anglo-American legal thought. We see, for example, Ronald Dworkin urging interpreters to search for or to construct the "real" rule lying behind the mere words on a printed page.[67] Somewhat less explicitly, the "mischief rule" of the common law compels the literal language of a rule to yield to the purpose behind a rule when application of the literal language would frustrate the rule's purpose.[68] Indeed, the mischief rule and related principles urging the primacy of purpose over text are features of the thinking of Fuller, of Hart and Sacks, and also of Llewellyn's "Grand Style" of judging.[69] As a matter of fact, Llewellyn distinguished the Grand Style from the Formal Style because he believed that formalism, as the obeisance to the literal language of a rule, could frustrate the rule's purpose and lead to difficulties where the practical consequences of the decision would indicate a different result.

The language in which a rule is written and the purpose behind that rule can diverge precisely because that purpose is plastic in a way that literal language is not. Purpose cannot be reduced to any one canonical formulation, for when purpose is set down canonically, that canonical formulation of purpose may frustrate the purpose itself. It is because purpose is not reduced to a concrete set of words that it retains its sensitivity to novel cases, to bizarre applications, and to the complex unfolding of the human experience. Thus, for the recourse to purpose to "solve" the problem of formalism, the purpose must not be imprisoned in the rigidity of

---

67. LAW'S EMPIRE, *supra* note 31, at 16-17.

68. The standard references for this rule are Heydon's Case, 76 Eng. Rep. 637 (Ex. 1584), and Church of the Holy Trinity v. United States, 143 U.S. 457 (1892); see discussion *supra* note 28. *See also* J.G. SUTHERLAND, STATUTES AND STATUTORY CONSTRUCTION §§ 45.05, 45.09 (N. Singer rev. ed. 1984).

69. K. LLEWELLYN, *supra* note 1, *passim*; *see* W. TWINING, KARL LLEWELLYN AND THE REALIST MOVEMENT 210-11 (1973).

words. This unrigidified purpose can be explained, clarified, and enriched as new examples and applications come to our attention. The purpose behind the "No vehicles in the park" regulation is not embarrassed by the statue of the truck exactly because purpose can bend to the circumstances of the moment in a way that language, with its acontextual autonomy of meaning, cannot. In contrast, the term "vehicles," at least at the core, literally refers to vehicles;[70] if it turns out that the prohibition of some vehicles does not serve the purpose of the regulation, then the embarrassment is unavoidable.[71]

If adhering to concretized language causes this embarrassment, then why not adhere to the purpose of the rule rather than the words of the rule? To do so would conform with the models advocated by Fuller,[72] Hart and Sacks,[73] Dworkin,[74] and Llewellyn[75] and would match what can be called, with only negligible exaggeration, the current paradigm of American statutory interpretation.[76] Yet locating the idea and the force of a rule in its purpose rather than in its formulation poses the same problem posed by concretized rules, except at one remove. To illustrate the point, suppose the purpose of the "no vehicles in the park" regulation is the preservation of peace and quiet in the park. Suppose, as well, that this purpose derives from an even deeper purpose of maximizing the pleasure of the residents of the town. Now imagine that a town native who has just

70. Note that the "No vehicles in the park" example may be a flawed illustration of the problem Hart, Fuller, and I explore, because locomotive capacity may now be definitional of a "vehicle." Insofar as this is true, the statue is not a vehicle, and no conflict arises between literal meaning and purpose. This is a defect only in the example, however, rather than in the general formulation of the issue. I will therefore stipulate, for the purposes of this argument, that a statue of a vehicle *is* a vehicle, just as a lion in a cage is still a lion. Consider a rule prohibiting "live animals on the bus" and whether it would prohibit carrying on the bus three live goldfish in a sealed plastic bag.

71. My point about the plasticity of purpose should not be confused with claims, often correct, about the indeterminacy of purpose. *See, e.g.*, Easterbrook, *Foreword: The Court and the Economic System*, 98 HARV. L. REV. 4, 15-18 (1984); Easterbrook, *Statutes' Domains*, 50 U. CHI. L. REV. 533, 537-38 (1983); Kennedy, *supra* note 1; Posner, *Statutory Interpretation—In the Classroom and in the Courtroom*, 50 U. CHI. L. REV. 800, 819-820 (1983). Insofar as purpose becomes both concrete and determinate, as when everyone agrees what the purpose is, the argument that "ruleness" resides in purpose becomes more plausible. But when some conception of purpose is determinate, noncanonical purpose itself can operate formalistically. Conversely, if purpose is comparatively indeterminate, then it looks especially odd to say that the rule exists not in the specific rule-formulation, but in the quite different and nonspecific purpose. Thus, those who argue for the indeterminacy of purpose make claims consistent with mine.

72. L. FULLER, *supra* note 55, at 81-91; Fuller, *supra* note 53; Fuller, *The Speluncean Explorers*, 62 HARV. L. REV. 616, 620-26 (1949) ("opinion" of Foster, J.).

73. H. Hart & A. Sacks, *supra* note 54.

74. LAW'S EMPIRE, *supra* note 31.

75. K. LLEWELLYN, *supra* note 1.

76. *See* Wellman, *Dworkin and the Legal Process Tradition: The Legacy of Hart & Sacks*, 29 ARIZ. L. REV. 413 (1987); Note, *Intent, Clear Statements, and the Common Law: Statutory Construction in the Supreme Court*, 95 HARV. L. REV. 892 (1982). Recent manifestations of this paradigm include G. CALABRESI, A COMMON LAW FOR THE AGE OF STATUTES (1982); Eskridge, *Dynamic Statutory Interpretation*, 135 U. PA. L. REV. 1479 (1987); Langevoort, *Statutory Obsolescence and the Judicial Process: The Revisionist Role of the Courts in Federal Banking Regulation*, 85 MICH. L. REV. 672 (1987). *But see, e.g.*, United States v. Locke, 471 U.S. 84 (1985) (failure to file timely claim deprives petitioner of right, irrespective of statutory purpose).

won six gold medals in the Olympic Games is returning to this park, the scene of her youth, along with a widely popular President of the United States. Suppose as well that the park with the "no vehicles in the park" regulation is the only suitable place for the motorcade, which must be a motorcade because the President is disabled and cannot walk. Under these circumstances, the purpose behind the "no vehicles in the park" rule would be served by excluding the motorcade, but the purpose behind *that* purpose would be frustrated. Thus the same logic that requires the formulation of a rule to be defeasible in the service of its purpose would also require that purpose to be defeasible in the service of the purpose behind *it*.

As the example reveals, the potential tension between the general goal and its concretized instantiation exists at every level. At one level, the tension is between language and purpose; at the next, it is between that purpose and the deep purpose lying behind it; at the next, between the deep purpose and an even deeper purpose; and so on. When we decide that purpose must not be frustrated by its instantiation, we embark upon a potentially infinite regress in which all forms of concretization are defeasible.

The view that rules should be interpreted to allow their purposes to trump their language in fact collapses the distinction between a rule and a reason, and thus loses the very concept of a rule.[77] Rules are by definition general. They gather numerous known and unknown particulars under headings such as "vehicles," "punishment," "dogs," and "every person who is directly or indirectly the beneficial owner of more than 10 per centum of any class of any [registered] equity security (other than an exempted security)." After identifying a category of items or events to which the rule applies, in the *protasis*, rules then prescribe what shall be done with these particulars in the *apodosis*.[78] Occasionally, however, not all of the particulars comprising the rule's category of coverage are suitable for the prescribed treatment; the generalizations that are a necessary part of any rule treat all members of the class in a manner that may be appropriate only for *most* members of the class. What, then, is to happen when a case arises in which the generalization does not apply to this particular? When a rule's prescribed treatment is unsuitable, if the decisionmaker

77. Note, however, that this claim is not inconsistent with the view that rules should be interpreted to further their purposes when several interpretations of the rule are possible *and all are supported by the language of the rule*. In such cases, it is not only possible but positively desirable to choose the interpretation that will serve the rule's purpose. *See* H.L.A. HART, *Introduction*, in ESSAYS IN JURISPRUDENCE AND PHILOSOPHY 1, 8 (1983).

78. On this terminology for the structure of rules, which distinguishes the part of the rule specifying its operative facts from the part describing the consequences flowing from the existence of those facts, see W. TWINING & D. MIERS, HOW TO DO THINGS WITH RULES 136-40 (2d ed. 1982). *See also* Friedman, *Legal Rules and the Process of Social Change*, 19 STAN. L. REV. 786, 786-87 (1967) (same distinction with different labels); Schlag, *Rules and Standards*, 33 UCLA L. REV. 379, 381-83 (1985) (same).

were to ignore the rule, the rule would not be a real rule providing a reason for decision but would be a mere rule of thumb, defeasible when the purposes behind the rule would not be served. If every application that would not serve the reason behind the rule were jettisoned from the coverage of the rule, then the decision procedure would be identical to one applying reasons directly to individual cases, without the mediation of rules. Under such a model, rules are superfluous except as predictive guides, for they lack any normative power of their own. By contrast, if in cases in which the particular application would not serve the reasons behind the rule, the rule nevertheless provides its own reason for deciding the case according to the rule, the rule itself has a normative force that provides a reason for action or decision.

In summary, it is exactly a rule's rigidity, even in the face of applications that would ill serve its purpose, that renders it a rule.[79] This rigidity derives from the language of the rule's formulation, which prevents the contemplation of every fact and principle relevant to a particular application of the rule. To be formalistic in Llewellyn's sense is to be governed by the rigidity of a rule's formulation; yet, this governance by rigidity is central to the constraint of regulative rules. Formalism in this sense is therefore indistinguishable from "rulism," for what makes a regulative rule a rule, and what distinguishes it from a reason, is precisely the unwillingness to pierce the generalization even in cases in which the generalization appears to the decisionmaker to be inapposite. A rule's acontextual rigidity is what makes it a rule.

## D. *The Idea of a Closed System*

We now are in a position to reconsider the charge that formalism embodies the erroneous view that law (or any other decisional domain) is a closed system. We have seen that rules can generate answers or exclude otherwise eligible answers from consideration. We also have seen that there are rules, such as one prohibiting the shooting of pelicans, whose application throughout much of their range requires recourse only to the rule and to uncontroversial judgments of meaning and identification of discrete particulars. There can therefore be systems whose operations require recourse only to the norms of the system and to accepted linguistic and observational skills.

Such a system would be closed, but it would not necessarily be complete. Closedness and completeness are different properties. Closedness refers to the capacity of a system to decide cases within the confines of that

79. This is not to say that rules are always or even ever good things to have. My aim now is to distinguish a form of decisionmaking in which generalizations have independent normative power from a form of decisionmaking in which the full richness of the particular event always is open to consideration. The questions of whether rules should be employed, in which domains, and to what extent, are addressed below. *See infra* Section III.

system, while completeness refers to the extent to which a system deals with those cases at all. A mathematical system is closed insofar as the rules of mathematics provide an answer to the question "What is the sum of 97 and 53?" But that same system is incomplete insofar as it provides no answer to the question "What should the United States do about the problem of poverty?" The dimension of completeness, although perhaps unimportant for mathematics, is important for law precisely because most modern legal systems claim the ability to deal with a wide range of issues. Insofar as the human experience is especially complex and fluid, the legal system is likely to be frustrated by its incompleteness, its frequent inability to answer the questions it wants to answer. Commonly, we plan for these frustrations by rendering the norms of the law less determinate and thereby using vagueness as the tool by which we plan for the open texture of experience.[80] As a result, legal systems, to avoid the consequences of widespread incompleteness, often employ norms sufficiently indeterminate to accommodate much that is important in the world at large, and in doing so sacrifice the occasional virtues of closedness. Such systems are more open even at the expense of being less predictable and less constraining of their decisionmakers.

Thus, legal systems often reject closedness because they must deal with a large array of problems presented by a complex and fluid world. But this is to say that comparatively closed systems may sometimes be undesirable, not that they are not possible. The importance of drawing this distinction is to stress that the degree of closedness may vary, and that closedness is a tool that might be usable in some domains even if, in untempered form, it is not the *only* tool we would want to use for an entire system of social control.

When applied to individual norms rather than to entire systems, closedness is merely another word for ruleness. By limiting access to the reasons behind the rule, rules truncate the array of considerations available to a decisionmaker.[81] Rules get in the way. They exclude from consideration factors that a decisionmaker unconstrained by those rules would take into

80. *See* Schauer, *Authority and Indeterminacy*, in AUTHORITY REVISITED: NOMOS XXIX 28 (1987).

81. The closed system/open system dispute merely recasts the debate about legal positivism in different terminology. Any version of legal positivism is premised on what Ronald Dworkin, no positivist, has felicitously referred to as "pedigree." TAKING RIGHTS SERIOUSLY, *supra* note 31, at 17. Positivism posits that *legal* norms are identified by reference to some other norm, rule, or standard that distinguishes legal from non-legal norms. Hart's "rule of recognition" serves this purpose, H.L.A. HART, *supra* note 1, as does the "next higher norm" for Kelsen. H. KELSEN, THE PURE THEORY OF LAW 193-278 (M. Knight trans. 1967). The positivist conceives of the set of norms so pedigreed as constituting some sort of a closed system, although that system will not necessarily decide all or even most cases that come before the courts. Kelsen, for example, sees every law-applying act as only partially determined by law. *Id.* at 233-36, 244-45. By contrast, the opponents of positivism, most notably Dworkin, attack the pedigreeability thesis by arguing that in no case is the distinction between pedigreed and nonpedigreed norms dispositive and consequently the characterization of law in terms of pedigreed norms is descriptively inaccurate.

account. Understanding the way in which rules truncate the range of reasons available to a decisionmaker helps us to appreciate the distinction between formalism and functionalism, or instrumentalism.[82] Functionalism focuses on outcomes and particularly on the outcome the decisionmaker deems optimal. Rules get in the way of this process, and thus functionalism can be perceived as a view of decisionmaking that seeks to minimize the space between what a particular decisionmaker concludes, all things considered, should be done and what some rule says should be done. Rules *block* consideration of the full array of reasons that bear upon a particular decision in two different ways. First, they exclude from consideration reasons that might have been available had the decisionmaker not been constrained by a rule. Second, the rule itself becomes a reason for action, or a reason for decision.

The notion of a rule as a reason for decision requires further exploration. What makes formalism formal is this very feature: the fact that taking rules seriously involves taking their mandates as reasons for decision independent of the reasons for decision lying *behind* the rule.[83] If it were otherwise, the set of reasons considered by a decisionmaker would be congruent with the set of reasons behind the rule, and the rule would add nothing to the calculus. Rules therefore supply reasons for action *qua* rules. When the reason supplied by a rule tracks the reasons behind the rule, then the rule is in a different way superfluous in the particular case. Rules become interesting when they point toward a different result than do the reasons behind the rule—when they indicate, for example, that statues of vehicles ought to be excluded even though the reasons behind the rule indicate that the statues ought not to be excluded. To take these occasionally perverse reasons as always relevant and therefore sometimes dispositive is condemned as "formalistic" because it abstracts the mandates of a rule from the reasons behind it. Yet that is what rules do. Refusal to abstract the rule from its reasons is not to have rules. This refusal reduces rules to rules of thumb, useful but intrinsically unweighty indicators of the results likely to be reached by direct application of reasons.

Thus, the essential equivalency of formalism and "ruleness" is before us. Viewing formalism as merely rule-governed decisionmaking does not make it desirable. Yet recognizing the way in which formalism is merely a way of describing the process of taking rules seriously allows us to escape

82. *See, e.g.*, R. Summers, Instrumentalism and American Legal Theory 136-75 (1982); Aleinikoff, *supra* note 63, at 985; Summers, *Professor Fuller's Jurisprudence and America's Dominant Philosophy of Law*, 92 Harv. L. Rev. 433 (1978).

83. Insofar as a system permits recourse to the purpose behind a rule's formulation but does not permit departure from *that* purpose when adhering to it will produce unfortunate results or will frustrate the even deeper purpose behind it, that system will still be formal in the sense I am now using that term. It will also be rule-bound, because the less than totally plastic purpose (although more plastic than the rule-formulation) will operate as a rule vis-a-vis the higher order reasons that generated that particular purpose.

the epithetical mode and to confront the critical question of formalism: What, if anything, is good about the unwillingness to go beneath the rule and apply its purpose, or the purposes behind that purpose, directly to the case before the decisionmaker?

## III. Should Choice Be Restricted?

Let me recapitulate. One conception takes the vice of formalism to consist of a decisionmaker's denial, couched in the language of obedience to clear rules, of having made any choice at all. Yet rules, if followed, may not leave a decisionmaker free choice. Rules *can* limit decisional choice, and decisionmakers *can* abide by those limitations. Those limitations come in most cases from the literal language of a rule's formulation, for to take a rule as anything other than the rule's formulation, or at least the meaning of the rule's formulation,[84] is ultimately to deny the idea of a rule.

Thus, formalism merges into ruleness, and both are inextricably intertwined with literalism,[85] i.e., the willingness to make decisions according to the literal meaning of words or phrases or sentences or paragraphs on a printed page, even if the consequences of that decision seem either to frustrate the purpose behind those words or to diverge significantly from what the decisionmaker thinks—the rule aside—should be done. But does dem-

84. In a trivial sense, rules differ from their formulations. *See, e.g.*, G. Baker & P. Hacker, *supra* note 57, at 41–52; M. Black, *The Analysis of Rules*, in Models and Metaphors: Studies in Language and Philosophy 95 (1962); D. Shwayder, The Stratification of Behaviour 241 (1965); G. vonWright, Practical Reason 68 (1983). "Do not walk on the grass," "Walking on the grass is prohibited," and "No walking on the grass" constitute one and not three rules. Referring to these three formulations as formulations of only one rule, however, presupposes that all have the same meaning, that the differences are syntactical and not semantic. Thus, the distinction between a rule and its formulation is like the distinction between a proposition and a sentence. When I discuss a rule and equate it with its formulation, I therefore mean that a rule is that set of semantically equivalent rule formulations.

85. My references to "literalism" are slightly metaphorical. As noted above, *see supra* note 59, literalism includes those aspects of context, such as the appearance of words in a statute rather than in a poem, that are accessible to all or most readers. Moreover, although I often use single words as examples, statutes are not read word by word, but instead by sentences, paragraphs, and larger units of text. This is not to deny, however, that the ability to assign meanings to individual words is what enables us to understand a sentence we have never seen before. *See* D. Davidson, *Truth and Meaning*, in Inquiries into Truth and Interpretation 17 (1984). This assertion, however, superficially in conflict with Frege's assertion that only in the context of a sentence does a word have any meaning, *see* G. Frege, The Foundations of Arithmetic (J.L. Austin trans. 1959), is not without its detractors and complexities. *See, e.g.*, Wallace, *Only in the Context of a Sentence Do Words Have Any Meaning*, in Contemporary Perspectives in the Philosophy of Language 305 (P. French, T. Uehling, Jr., & H. Wettstein eds. 1979).

Still, *pace* Fuller, *supra* note 53, at 662–63, sentences and paragraphs can have literal and even acontextual meaning insofar as an entire sentence or paragraph may supply enough context to make its meaning comparatively clear. As texts become lengthier and richer it is often *more* possible to understand those texts without departing from them and thus *more* possible for them to have acontextual meaning.

Moreover, literal meaning need not always be ordinary meaning. Where some aspect of the minimal and uncontested context makes it plain that a settled specialized or technical meaning of a term or phrase applies, that technical meaning, rather than the ordinary usage of the man on the Clapham omnibus, is controlling.

onstrating that formalism is ruleness rescue formalism? Restated, what is so good about decision according to rules?

The simple answer to this question, and perhaps also the correct one, is "nothing." Little about decision constrained by the rigidity of rules seems intrinsically valuable. Once we understand that rules get in the way, that they gain their ruleness by cutting off access to factors that might lead to the best resolution in a particular case, we see that rules function as impediments to optimally sensitive decisionmaking. Rules doom decisionmaking to mediocrity by mandating the inaccessibility of excellence.

Nor is there anything essentially *just* about a system of rules. We have scarce reason to believe that rule-based adjudication is more likely to be just than are systems in which rules do not block a decisionmaker, especially a just decisionmaker, from considering every reason that would assist her in reaching the best decision. Insofar as factors screened from consideration by a rule might in a particular case turn out to be those necessary to reach a just result, rules stand in the way of justice in those cases and thus impede optimal justice in the long term. We equate Solomon's wisdom with justice not because Solomon followed the rules in solving the dispute over the baby but because Solomon came up with exactly the right solution for that case. We frequently laud not history's rule followers, but those whose abilities at particularized decisionmaking transcend the inherent limitations of rules.

Still, that rules may be in one sense unjust, or even that they may be inappropriate in much of what we call a legal system, does not mean there is nothing to be said for rules. One of the things that can be said for rules is the value variously expressed as predictability or certainty. But if we pursue the predictability theme, we see that what most arguments for ruleness share is a focus on disabling certain classes of decisionmakers from making certain kinds of decisions.[86] Predictability follows from the decision to treat all instances falling within some accessible category in the same way. It is a function of the way in which rules decide ahead of time how *all* cases within a class will be determined.

Predictability is fostered to the extent that four different requirements are satisfied. The first of the factors contributing to predictability is the capacity on the part of those relying on a rule to identify certain particulars as instances of a given category (for example, that pelicans are birds). When there is a more or less uniform and uncontroversial ability to say

86. *See generally* A. KOCOUREK, AN INTRODUCTION TO THE SCIENCE OF LAW 165-85 (1930); R. WASSERSTROM, THE JUDICIAL DECISION: TOWARD A THEORY OF LEGAL JUSTIFICATION 60-66 (1961); Marsh, *Principle and Discretion in the Judicial Process*, 68 LAW Q. REV. 226 (1952). Along with Wasserstrom, *supra*, at 61, I object to the use of the word "certainty" in this context because, unlike the term "predictability," it suggests that no doubt is involved. I can predict that it will snow in Vermont this winter and rely on that prediction in making winter plans, yet still not be *certain* that it will snow. Although one usage of "certain" does recognize variability, I prefer the term "predictability" because its common usage implies such variability.

that some item is a member of some category, little in the way of potentially variable judgment clouds the prediction of whether the rule will apply to this particular item. This relates to the second factor: that the decisionmakers in the system will perceive those particulars as being members of the same category perceived by the addressees and will be seen as so perceiving by those affected. That is, people perceive pelicans as birds; decisionmakers perceive pelicans as birds; and people know that decisionmakers will perceive pelicans as birds. Third, the rule must speak in terms of an accessible category. Predictability requires that a rule cover a category whose denotation is substantially noncontroversial among the class of addressees of the rule and common to the addressees of the rule and those who apply it. Finally, the rule must treat all members of a category in the same way. Only if the consequences specified in the apodosis of the rule are as accessible and noncontroversial as the coverage specified in the protasis can a rule produce significant predictability of application. Thus, predictability comes from the knowledge that if this is a bird a certain result will follow, and from the confidence that what I now perceive to be a bird will be considered a bird by the ultimate decisionmaker.

This predictability comes only at a price.[87] Situations may arise in which putting this particular into that category seems just too crude—something about this particular makes us desire to treat it specially. *This* vehicle is merely a statue, emits no fumes, makes no noise, and endangers no lives; it ought to be treated differently from those vehicles whose characteristics mesh with the purpose behind the rule. Serving the goal of predictability, however, requires that we ignore this difference, because to acknowledge this difference is also to create the power—the *jurisdiction*—to determine whether this vehicle or that vehicle actually serves the purpose of the "no vehicles in the park" rule. It is the jurisdiction to determine that only some vehicles fit the purpose of the rule that undermines the confidence that *all* vehicles will be prohibited. No longer is it the case that anything that is a *vehicle*, a moderately accessible category, is excluded. Instead, the category is now that of *vehicles whose prohibition will serve the purposes of the "no vehicles in the park" rule*, a potentially far more controversial category.

Thus, the key to understanding the relationship of ruleness to predictability is the idea of decisional jurisdiction.[88] The issue is not whether the statue serves the purpose of the "no vehicles in the park" rule. It is whether giving some decisionmaker jurisdiction to determine what the

87. *See, e.g.*, H.L.A. HART, *supra* note 1, at 121–32.

88. On jurisdiction in this sense, see Schauer, *Slippery Slopes*, 99 HARV. L. REV. 361, 367–68 (1985). *See also* Fried, *Two Concepts of Interests: Some Reflections on the Supreme Court's Balancing Test*, 76 HARV. L. REV. 755, 759–65, 771 (1963) (noting that courts define their competencies in the process of making substantive decisions); Rawls, *Two Concepts of Rules*, 64 PHIL. REV. 3, 10 (1955).

rule's purpose is (as well as jurisdiction to determine whether some item fits that purpose) injects a possibility of variance substantially greater than that involved in giving a decisionmaker jurisdiction solely to determine whether some particular is or is not a vehicle. Note also that the jurisdictional question has a double aspect. When we grant jurisdiction we are first concerned with the range of equally correct decisions that might be made in the exercise of that jurisdiction. If there is no authoritative statement of the purpose behind the "no vehicles in the park" rule, granting jurisdiction to determine that purpose would allow a decisionmaker to decide whether the purpose is to preserve quiet, to prevent air pollution, or to prevent accidents, and each of these determinations would be equally correct. In addition to increasing the range of correct decisions, however, certain grants of jurisdiction increase the likelihood of erroneous determinations. Compare "No vehicles in the park" with "The park is closed to vehicles whose greatest horizontal perimeter dimension, when added to their greatest vertical perimeter dimension, exceeds the lesser of (a) sixty-eight feet, six inches and (b) the greatest horizontal perimeter dimension, added to the greatest vertical perimeter dimension, of the average of the largest passenger automobile manufactured in the United States by the three largest automobile manufacturers in the preceding year." The second adds no inherent variability, but it certainly compounds the possibility of decisionmaker error. Creating the jurisdiction to determine whether the purposes of a rule are served undermines predictability by allowing the determination of any of several possible purposes; in addition, the creation of that jurisdiction engenders the possibility that those who exercise it might just get it wrong.

Grants of decisional jurisdiction not only increase permissible variance and the possibility of "computational" error, they also involve decisionmakers in determinations that a system may prefer to have made by someone else. We may believe that courts are less competent to make certain decisions than other bodies; for example, we may feel that certain kinds of fact-finding are better done by legislatures. There may also be moral or political reasons to restrict the judge's discretion, for decisionmaking implicates profound questions of just who in a given domain may legitimately make certain decisions. It is, for example, a plausible position that the public rather than the University of Michigan philosophy department should make the moral determinations involved in governing the United States, even if the University of Michigan philosophy department would make better choices.

Although decreasing the possibility of variance and error by the decisionmaker contributes to the ability of addressees of rules to predict the consequences of application of those rules, limited variance can serve other values as well. If decisionmakers are denied jurisdiction to determine whether a particular instance actually justifies its inclusion in a larger generalization or are denied jurisdiction to determine the best result on the basis of all germane factors, the part of the system inhabited by those decisionmakers becomes more stable. Treating a large group of different particulars in the same way—the inevitable byproduct of the generalization of rules—dampens the range of variance in result by suppressing consideration of a wide range of potentially relevant differences. Thus, stability, not as a necessary condition for predictability but as a value in its own right, is fostered by truncating the decisionmaking authority.

Because rule-bound decisionmaking is inherently stabilizing, it is inherently conservative, in the nonpolitical sense of the word.[89] By limiting the ability of decisionmakers to consider every factor relevant to an event, rules make it more difficult to adapt to a changing future. Rules force the future into the categories of the past. Note the important asymmetry here, the way in which rules operate not to enable but only to disable. A decisionmaker can never exceed the optimal result based on all relevant factors. Thus, a rule-bound decisionmaker, precluded from taking into account certain features of the present case, can never do better but can do worse than a decisionmaker seeking the optimal result for a case through a rule-free decision.

Yet this conservatism, suboptimization, and inflexibility in the face of a changing future need not be universally condemned. Rules stabilize by inflating the importance of the classifications of yesterday. We achieve stability, valuable in its place, by relinquishing some part of our ability to improve on yesterday. Again the issue is jurisdiction, for those who have jurisdiction to improve on yesterday also have jurisdiction to make things worse.[90] To stabilize, to operate in an inherently conservative mode, is to give up some of the possibility of improvement in exchange for guarding against some of the possibility of disaster. Whether, when, and where the game is worth the candle, however, cannot be determined acontextually.[91]

89. *See* Horwitz, *The Rule of Law: An Unqualified Human Good?* (Book Review), 86 YALE L.J. 561 (1977). I use the term "conservatism" to refer to the desire to hold onto the past or present in the face of pressures to change. This usage bears only a contingent connection to the range of political views now labeled "conservative." Left-wing conservatism is not oxymoronic, because one can imagine left-wing systems adopting preservational (conservative) strategies or systems to prevent movement away to the right.

90. This is not a logical truth. Grants of jurisdiction can incorporate substantive requirements. Dworkin, *Non-Neutral Principles*, in READING RAWLS: CRITICAL STUDIES OF A THEORY OF JUSTICE 124 (N. Daniels ed. 1975). Insofar as some grants of jurisdiction aim to increase the ability of decisionmakers to adapt to an unknown future, however, they will be comparatively open-ended. It is this open-endedness, whether couched in substantive (do good) or less substantive (determine the purpose) terms, that creates the possibility of unintended and uncontrollable variance.

91. I therefore disagree with Kennedy, *Form and Substance in Private Law Adjudication*, 89 HARV. L. REV. 1685 (1976), insofar as he argues that ruleness is acontextually individualistic and particularization is acontextually altruistic. Even if there is truth in Kennedy's acontextuality, it still is not clear that his analysis of the acontextual tendencies promoted by ruleness is correct. It is quite plausible that the inherently stabilizing tendencies of rule-bound adjudication will dampen individual differences, stifle claims to special treatment as an individual, and encourage decisional modesty rather than decisional arrogance. It could be argued quite sensibly that all these tendencies foster rather than impede altruism.

In sum, it is clearly true that rules get in the way, but this need not always be considered a bad thing. It may be a liability to get in the way of wise decisionmakers who sensitively consider all of the relevant factors as they accurately pursue the good. However, it may be an asset to restrict misguided, incompetent, wicked, power-hungry, or simply mistaken decisionmakers whose own sense of the good might diverge from that of the system they serve. The problem, of course, is the difficulty in determining which characterization will fit decisionmakers; we must therefore decide the extent to which we are willing to disable good decisionmakers in order simultaneously to disable bad ones.

With these considerations in mind, let us approach formalism in a new light. Consider some of the famous marchers in formalism's parade of horribles, examples such as *R. v. Ojibway*, Fuller's statue of the truck in the park, and the poor Bolognese surgeon who, having opened the vein of a patient in the course of performing an emergency operation outdoors, was prosecuted for violating the law prohibiting "drawing blood in the streets."[92] Each of these examples reminds us that cases may arise in which application of the literal meaning of words produces an absurd result. But now we can recast the question, for we must consider not only whether the result was absurd in these cases but also whether a particular decisionmaker should be empowered to determine absurdity. Even in cases as extreme as these, formalism is only superficially about rigidity and absurdity. More fundamentally, it is about power and its allocation.

Formalism is about power, but is also about its converse—modesty. To be formalistic as a decisionmaker is to say that something is not my concern, no matter how compelling it may seem. When this attitude is applied to the budget crisis or to eviction of the starving, it seems objectionable. But when the same attitude of formalism requires judges to ignore the moral squalor of the Nazis or the Ku Klux Klan in First Amendment cases, or the guilt of the defendant in Fourth Amendment cases, or the wealth of the plaintiff who seeks to recover for medical expenses occasioned by the defendant's negligence, it is no longer clear that refusal to take all factors into account is condemnable.

Modesty, of course, has its darker side. To be modest is at times good, but avoiding authority is also avoiding responsibility. In some circumstances we want our decisionmakers to take charge and accept the consequences of their actions.[93] But it is by no means clear that just because it is good for some people to take charge some of the time, that taking charge, even accompanied by acceptance of responsibility, is a universal

92. The last example, from 1 S. Pufendorf, De Jure Naturae et Gentium Libri Octo (1672), comes to us through United States v. Kirby, 74 U.S. (7 Wall.) 482, 487 (1868).

93. For a recent articulation of this view, see Michelman, *Foreword: Traces of Self-Government*, 100 Harv L. Rev. 4 (1986). A useful contrast is Christie, *An Essay on Discretion*, 1986 Duke L.J. 747.

good. "I'm in charge here" has a long but not always distinguished history. Part of what formalism is about is its inculcation of the view that sometimes it is appropriate for decisionmakers to recognize their lack of jurisdiction and to defer even when they are convinced that their own judgment is best. The opposite of modesty is arrogance, not just responsibility. True, modesty itself carries responsibility, because an actor behaving modestly is participating and thus assisting in the legitimacy of the grant of authority to someone else. But this is a responsibility of a different and limited kind. That one accepts partial responsibility for the decisions of others does not entail the obligation to substitute one's judgment for that of others.

The distinctive feature of rules, therefore, lies in their ability to be formal, to exclude from consideration in the particular case factors whose exclusion was determined without reference to the particular case at hand. This formalism of rules is not only conceptually sound and psychologically possible, but it also, as I have tried to show, is on occasion normatively desirable. Insofar as formalism disables some decisionmakers from considering some factors that may appear important to them, it allocates power to some decisionmakers and away from others. Formalism therefore achieves its value when it is thought desirable to narrow the decisional opportunities and the decisional range of a certain class of decisionmakers.

I stress that all of this is compatible with agnosticism about how rule-bound decisionmaking applies to legal systems in general, to particular legal systems, or to particular parts of legal systems. It is far from a necessary truth that legal systems must be exclusively or even largely operated as rule-governed institutions. Judgments about when to employ formalism are contextual and not inexorable, political and not logical, psychological and economic rather than conceptual. It would blunt my point about the simultaneously plausible and contingent nature of decision according to rule to offer in this acontextual setting my recommendations about what if any parts of the American or any other legal system should operate in such a fashion. My goal is only to rescue formalism from conceptual banishment. But having been readmitted to the community of respectable ideas, formalism, or decisionmaking according to rule in any strong sense, still has the burden of showing that it is appropriately used in a particular decisional domain.

## IV. The Degrees of Restriction

I have thus far presented formalism and maximally contextual particularism as mutually exclusive opposites, incapable of coexisting within the same decisional domain. It may therefore appear that the advantages of formalism can be attained only within a system willing to accept some proportion of preposterous results and only within a system willing to have its decisionmakers ignore the novelty of the situations that come before them. Accommodation between these two forms of decisionmaking might be possible, however.

Let us contrast two cases, both arising out of the "No vehicles in the park" rule. The first involves the statue of the truck erected by the veterans' organization. The second involves an electric golf cart, as quiet as a bicycle, incapable of proceeding at greater than ten miles an hour, and emitting no noxious fumes. Can these cases be distinguished? In both cases, exclusion of the object under consideration would not seem to serve any of the purposes behind the rule, regardless of whether the purpose was the suppression of noise, the reduction of noxious odors, the limitation of high speeds, or the restriction of forms of conveyance likely to be dangerous to pedestrians. Yet despite their similarity, there appears to be a difference between the cases. The statue seems to lie *more* outside the purpose behind the rule than the golf cart. If we assume that something like twenty miles per hour is dangerous, a totally immobile vehicle is further away from the danger point than one that can go ten miles per hour. Similarly, a vehicle with a totally inoperative engine makes less noise and emits no more noxious fumes than even an electric motor.

If the difference between the cases is a matter of degree, is there some way of empowering a decisionmaker to draw the distinction without at the same time discarding all of the formalist-inspired virtues from the decisionmaking process? That is, can we empower the decisionmaker to override the rule when its application would be totally preposterous, but not when its application, still outside the purpose of the rule, would fall short of the preposterous?

The question is the same one that arises in discussions regarding higher court scrutiny of lower court decisions, and lower court scrutiny of administrative decisions and state laws. Can a decisionmaker distinguish those state interests that are "compelling" from those that are "important" from those that are merely "rational"? Can a decisionmaker distinguish "proof beyond a reasonable doubt" from "clear and convincing evidence" from "a preponderance of the evidence"? Can decisionmakers distinguish "de novo" review from review only for "abuse of discretion"? The question raised by all of these standards and others is the same: Can we admit the possibility of overriding some judgment while at the same time not opening the door to unconstrained substitution of judgment?

It is debatable whether some form of deferential but genuine review is possible. It might be argued that deferential but not toothless review is an illusion. Once the reviewing decisionmaker has the authority to look at the decision below with at least the possibility of overturning it, deference becomes largely illusory. This hypothesis equates the review process with Pandora's box: Once the record below is opened, the review is in reality de novo, and the language of abuse of discretion—or compelling interest or whatever—is used merely as a tag line when the decisionmaker wishes to reach a conclusion different from that reached below.

An alternative hypothesis posits some ground between no review and unfettered intrusiveness. There might be cases in which the presumption in favor of the result below would cause the decision to stand. Under this hypothesis, we can have rebuttable presumptions—cases in which the presumption might be overcome in particularly exigent circumstances but nevertheless controls in many or even most cases.

If this latter hypothesis is correct, it is correct as a contingent empirical matter and not as a necessary truth. My instincts are that it is *sometimes* correct—that at some times in some domains presumptions can matter without being irrebuttable. This conclusion is based on my also instinctive view that presumptions create attitudes, and that attitudes can matter. I believe, for example, that I am more likely to admire an item of clothing if I discover it myself than if my mother tells me she saw it in a shop and it would look very nice on me. But I might be wrong. Even if I am right about clothing and mothers, those attitudes might not carry over to real decisions by real decisionmakers, and even if it does, it might be empirically false more often than it is empirically true.

Moreover, even if attitudes can be changed, it may be that linguistic instructions are not particularly effective in accomplishing those changes. The observation that linguistic instructions to adopt a certain attitude are in fact potent is not universally proved by the observation that such instructions are sometimes potent, any more than the observation that such instructions are sometimes impotent proves that they are never potent. Given all of this, let me satisfy myself here with the unproved empirical conclusion that linguistic instructions are sometimes potent.

If such instructions sometimes create presumptions, and if those presumptions sometimes work, then what does this say about the possibility of what we might call a *presumptive formalism*? In order to construct such a model, we would want to equate the literal mandate of the most locally applicable written rule with the judgment of the court below. The court below can be taken to have determined, for example, that in one case operable and operating automobiles are excluded from the park, in another case golf carts are excluded from the park, and in a third case immobile statues of trucks are excluded from the park. We can then equate the reviewing court with a determination of the correct result from the perspective of the reasons behind the rule rather than the literal language of the rule itself. We might conclude that in the first case even a de novo application of the reasons would generate the same result as generated by the formalistic reading, and therefore the formal mandate would prevail uncontroversially. In the second, a de novo application of reasons would generate a different result than that generated by the rule, but the result generated by the rule remains "in the ballpark" and therefore is upheld despite its divergence from the result that would be reached by direct application of the reasons. In the third, however, a de novo application of the reasons indicates that the result generated by the rule is so far out of bounds, so absurd, so preposterous that it is analogous to an abuse of discretion and would therefore be reversed—the rule would not be applied in this case.

Under such a theory of presumptive formalism there would be a presumption in favor of the result generated by the literal and largely acontextual interpretation of the most locally applicable rule. Yet that result would be presumptive only, subject to defeasibility when less locally applicable norms, including the purpose behind the particular norm, and including norms both within and without the decisional domain at issue, offered especially exigent reasons for avoiding the result generated by the presumptively applicable norm.

Such a system would bring the advantages of predictability, stability, and constraint of decisionmakers commonly associated with decision according to rule, but would temper the occasional unpleasant consequences of such a system with an escape route that allowed some results to be avoided when their consequences would be especially outrageous. Such a system would not be without cost. First of all, the escape route would necessarily decrease the amount of predictability, stability, and decisionmaker restraint. In short, it would diminish the amount of ruleness by placing more final authority in the decisionmaker than in the rule. Second, the presumptive force attached to the formalist reading of the applicable norms would still result in some odd or suboptimal results. In this sense, such a system would fail to honor all of the goals either of unrestrained particularism or unrestrained formalism. Finally, such a system would risk collapse into one in which the presumptions were for all practical purposes either absolute or nonexistent.

Even on the assumption that such a system might be desirable in some decisional domains, this does not mean that all or part of what we commonly call the legal system might be one of those domains. It might be that formalism, even only presumptively, is a good idea, but that the goals of the legal system, in light of the decisions we ask it to make, are such that it ought not to be designed along such a model. More likely, formalism ought to be seen as a tool to be used in some parts of the legal system and not in others. Determining which parts, if any, would be susceptible to such treatment is not my agenda here, for what I have attempted to offer is only an argument that formal systems are not necessarily to be condemned. That is not to say they are universally or even largely to be applauded, nor that they are to be pervasive or even frequent within that segment of society we call the legal system. To answer this last question we must ask what the legal system, in whole or in part, is supposed to do, for only when we answer that question can we determine what kinds of tools it needs to accomplish that task.

## V. Conclusion

I have concluded this analysis by venturing no more than a prolegomenon to a theory of presumptive formalism, which, to avoid the pejorative (or at least to select a slightly less pejorative pejorative) might be called a theory of *presumptive positivism*. As I have said, to urge the potential advantages of such a view in some domains is to say little if anything about whether the domain of decisions of judges or the domain of decisions of the political state backed by force is amenable to presumptively positivistic decisionmaking. But even if we put aside the question of concrete applications, the presumptiveness that is central to this model may illuminate one final usage of the word "formalistic" in its pejorative guise. It may be that, in practice, to condemn an outlook as formalistic is to condemn neither the rule-based orientation of a decisional structure nor even the inevitable over- and under-inclusiveness of any rule-based system. It may be to condemn such a system only when it is taken to be absolute rather than presumptive, when it contains no escape routes no matter how extreme the circumstances. Such a usage of "formalism" is of course much narrower than is commonly seen these days. But with that narrower usage we see that formalism is no longer something to be roundly condemned, but rather, like the relation of fanaticism to enthusiasm, or bullheadedness to integrity, merely the extreme and therefore unfortunate manifestation of a fundamentally desirable characteristic. If we recognize that, we may ultimately cease to use the epithetical deployment of "formalistic" as a substitute for argument and turn instead to the central questions involved in determining what, if anything, lies at the heart of the idea of law.

# Part IV
# A Panoply of Perspectives

# [18]

# BOOK REVIEW

LEGISLATION. By David R. Miers and Alan C. Page. London, England: Sweet & Maxwell, 1982. Pp. xviii, 266, index. £9.00 cloth.

## THE SEMIOLOGY OF STATUTES

*A Review by Allan C. Hutchinson* and Derek Morgan***

### I. REASSESSING LEGISLATION: THE HISTORICIAL CONTEXT

For the past four centuries, a major feature of English jurisprudence has been the contrast between the stability and continuity of the common law and the volatility and incongruity of legislation.[1] The common law is portrayed as a vast and intricate landscape, carved out with enduring patience over time. Statutes are treated as unsightly man-made structures that disturb the natural beauty and harmony of the common law. The need for legislative intervention is begrudgingly acknowledged, but never fully accepted. Whereas legislation is identified as a temporary structure for accomodating transient economic and political interest groups, the common law is presented as the embodiment of impartial rationality. Its life force is not cold logic, but a living experience that has been forged at the anvil of constitutional history. That history has consisted of a continual, shifting conflict between King and Commons, Parliament and Privy Council, statute and perogative order, and legislature and executive. In short, law is older and more venerable than legislation.[2]

The judicial struggle to enforce or enfeeble statutes is at the heart of the legal process. Throughout English history, differing interpretations have been placed upon the doctrine of the separation of powers. In consequence, the force and nature of the obligations and responsibilities imposed upon the different arms of government have varied considerably. Yet, ever since the days of Sir Edward Coke, the friction between statute and com-

---

* Associate Professor, Osgoode Hall Law School, Toronto. LL.B, London University, 1974; LL.M. Manchester University, 1978.

** Lecturer, Faculty of Law, Newcastle-Upon-Tyne, England. B.A., Kent University, 1976.

[1] *See generally* S. THORNE, A DISCOURSE UPON THE EXPOSICION AND UNDERSTANDING OF STATUTES, WITH SIR THOMAS EGERTON'S ADDITIONS (1942).

[2] I F. HAYEK, LAW, LEGISLATION AND LIBERTY 72 (1973).

mon law has been constant and pivotal. Unfortunately, the sedative rhetoric of the dictates of constitutional liberty has exercised such a powerful hold over the collective legal consciousness that this crucial relationship, and the shifts in legal terrain that it has portended, have been obscured.[3] Time is well past to chart these topographical realignments. Indeed, a thorough inquiry is urgently required. Miers and Page's *Legislation* might have contributed to the necessary reassessment of the relationship between statute and common law. A valuable opportunity seems to have slipped by.

## II. Understanding Legislation: The Crisis in Contemporary Theory

Until very recently, the judiciary perceived legislation as an evil. As late as 1974, Sir Leslie Scarman could suggest that "the modern English judge still sees enacted law as an exception to, a graft upon, or a correction of, the customary [i.e., common] law."[4] His view was not aberrant. In 1979, Patrick Devlin declared that, while they have a responsibility to keep the common law alive, the judges' duty to statute "is *simply* to interpret and apply it and not to obstruct it."[5] This attitude represents the inherited wisdom of contemporary practice. Its modern jurisprudential roots can be traced to the writings of Roscoe Pound.[6] For Pound, the common law was a taught tradition of ideals, methods, doctrines and principles into which legislation and new institutions and adaptations *from without* could be added. It was a tradition in which judging and not administering held the chief place. Sir Frederick Pollock's characterization of this attitude remains pertinent; the rules of statutory interpretation give expression to a judicial belief that "Parliament generally changes the law for the worse and that the business of the judges is to keep the mischief of its interference within the narrowest possible bounds."[7]

The patent difficulty with this attitude is that it begs the foundational question of the appropriate source of adjudicative

---

[3] *See* R. Porter, English Society in the Eighteenth Century 130–31 (1978).

[4] L. Scarman, English Law—The New Dimension 3 (1974).

[5] P. Devlin, The Judge 14 (1979)(emphasis added).

[6] *See, e.g.*, Pound, *Common Law and Legislation*, 21 Harv. L. Rev. 385 (1908); Pound, *The Future of the Common Law*, 7 U. Cin. L. Rev. 483 (1933).

[7] F. Pollock, Essays in Jurisprudence and Ethics 85 (1882).

resources. It assumes that statutory enactments appear as temporary blights on the legal landscape, but never become part of that landscape. It insists that legislative intrusions can be filtered out to leave a full and life-like picture of the common law. Beneath the concrete pathways of legislation, there still thrives the natural countryside of the common law. Yet this picture resides only in the nostalgic mind of the English lawyer. In truth, that picture has not existed for a least a century. In the early twentieth century gathering legislative clouds began to obscure the "brooding omnipresence in the sky"[8] that was the common law.

Although Dicey spotted this increasing legislative trend in the latter decades of the nineteenth century, labelling that time "the period of collectivism,"[9] Maitland recognized the significance of this change. He saw the pervasive impact of regulatory law on our daily life. In response, he demanded that his students lift their gaze from law reports and familiarize themselves with statute books. His demand was as propitious as it was profound: "I have been trying to turn your thoughts away from what I think to be an obsolete and inadequate idea of the province of constitutional history. I have been asking you to set your faces towards the rising sun. And the sun will rise, not a doubt of it."[10] Maitland's radical approach was not the only reaction against the Dicey-inspired apathy to legislation in the legal community. In a popular but highly sophisticated essay, Edmund Robertson argued that the explosion of nineteenth century legislation was a function of deep-seated institutional changes in English society:

> the legislature at the present day undertakes the deliberate alteration of the law to a much greater extent than it has ever done before . . . . Nor is this activity to be accounted for by the theory that the domain of law is more intrusive than in earlier times . . . . The true explanation is that Parliament has effectively secured for itself exclusive authority as the source of legal changes.[11]

There are now some signs of recognition that the legal landscape has undergone a quiet but fundamental revolution. Only eight years after his optimistic eulogies on behalf of the common

[8] Southern Pacific Co. v. Jensen, 244 U.S. 205, 222 (1917) (Holmes, J., dissenting).

[9] A. Dicey, Law and Opinion in England in the Nineteenth Century 64 (1905).

[10] F. Maitland, Constitutional History of England 536–37 (1908).

[11] Robertson, *Law* in 14 Encyclopedia Brittanica 354, 365–66 (9th ed. 1882).

law,[12] legislator Scarman conceded that statutes represent the bulk of English law and that "the common law is delightful, but it is now of marginal importance only."[13] Lord Hailsham has made a similar concession.[14] However, there are still echoes to be heard within the English legal community of Coke's belligerent championing of the medieval legal order.[15] Not surprisingly, the acknowledgement of change has not resulted in a corresponding reorientation of action. Reluctance to change has meant that the judicial struggle with late twentieth century legislation continues to be fought with sixteenth century weapons. This failure to appreciate fully or act upon this statutorification of the law has, regrettably, obscured more pressing and fundamental problems.

Through the mists of institutional myth, a more accurate representation of English constitutional history is emerging.[16] The "matchless constitution" has been pilloried as a "museum of constitutional archaelogy where the relics of past ages accumulate."[17] The common law is becoming a leading candidate for inclusion within such a cultural archive. As Parliament becomes almost exclusively subject to executive control,[18] as law becomes *the* major mode of communicating political ideals,[19] and as senior judges become leading movers in the British legislative process,[20] a deep sense of change and challenge is manifest. The vaunted integrity of the judiciary and its independence from government is in severe jeopardy. The traditional pretence of judges and politicians as distinct creatures is wearing extremely

[12] *See* L. SCARMAN, *supra* note 4.

[13] 437 PARL. DEB. H.L. (5th ser.) 437 (1982).

[14] "[S]tatute law," the Lord Chancellor said, "whether you like it or not, is the fabric upon which the modern state is founded." 437 PARL. DEB. H.L. (5th ser.) 638 (1982). *See also* LORD HAILSHAM, HAMLYN REVISITED—THE BRITISH LEGAL SYSTEM TODAY 66 (1983).

[15] This attitude toward tradition is reflected in the writings of many of the adherents of the new law and economics school. *See, e.g.*, Posner, *Economics, Politics and the Reading of Statutes and the Constitution*, 49 U. CHI. L. REV. 263 (1982).

[16] *See, e.g.*, C. HILL, THE INTELLECTUAL ORIGINS OF THE ENGLISH REVOLUTION 225–65 (1965).

[17] E. HALEVEY, AN HISTORY OF THE ENGLISH PEOPLE IN THE NINETEENTH CENTURY 73 (1961).

[18] This now almost axiomatic point was made early on by, *inter alia*, S.A. Walkland. *See* S. WALKLAND, THE LEGISLATIVE PROCESS IN GREAT BRITAIN 20 (1968); *see also* J. GRIFFITH, PARLIAMENTARY SCRUTINY OF GOVERNMENT BILLS 206–07 (1974); Lord Hailsham, *Obstacles to Law Reform*, 34 CURRENT LEGAL PROBLEMS 279, 286–87 (1981).

[19] Griffiths, *Is Law Important?*, 54 N.Y.U.L. REV. 339, 354 (1979).

[20] R. STEVENS, LAW AND POLITICS 614 (1979); *see also* L. JAFFE, ENGLISH AND AMERICAN JUDGES AS LAWMAKERS 5 (1969).

thin. A crisis is imminent within the modern English constitutional arrangement. Whether this represents a critical Kuhnian revolution from which a novel and more plausible approach will emerge[21] is a matter of speculation. But it is clear that, as the contemporary relationship between executive and judiciary, between enacted law and common law is exposed to keener examination, a legitimation crisis is approaching.[22]

Of course, these problematic relations are an ineradicable feature of political and social discourse. They strike at the heart of the constitutional compact and demand continual reappraisal. The rate and depth of recent change, however, make debate particularly pressing and desirable. In his inaugural Maccabaean lecture almost thirty years ago, Lord Evershed suggested that the volume and character of statutes threatened the very supremacy of the law. Insofar as the principal judicial task had already become statutory interpretation, he pondered over whether the relevant rules and principles accumulated throughout the centuries were adequate and satisfactory in modern society. For him, statute law had so radically changed the structure and dynamics of the judicial process that he felt compelled to pose a critical question: "can there be—ought there to be—some change in the method or character of the judicial function so far as it is concerned with the interpretation of enacted law?"[23]

With Hobbesian echoes, Evershed grasped that the central constitutional question is not simply *how*, but *who* is to interpret the wishes of the senior law-making body in a democracy. Although reluctantly, Evershed confessed that he doubted "whether the practising lawyer, particularly the judiciary, provides the most effective forum."[24] Sadly, this controversial thesis has received scant attention. Yet it lies at the core of the legitimation crisis. There is an urgent need to take a fresh, clear and considered perspective on legislation. Such an assessment would have to embrace a critical stance. Moreover, it would not only have to address Evershed's central question, but also tackle the vexing issue of the new social relations spawned by modern legislation.

---

[21] T. KUHN, THE STRUCTURE OF SCIENTIFIC REVOLUTIONS 77 (2d ed. 1970).

[22] *See generally*, J. HABERMAS, LEGITIMATION CRISIS (1975).

[23] Lord Evershed, *The Impact of Statute on the Law of England*, 42 PROCEEDINGS OF THE BRITISH ACADEMY 247, 261–62 (1956).

[24] *Id.* at 261–62.

## III. Describing Legislation: The Analysis of Page and Miers

Alan Page and especially David Miers[25] seem well placed to meet this challenge. In their recent book, *Legislation*, they set out to redress any previous imbalance and "provide a systematic and comprehensive account of legislation . . . from its inception to its implementation" (p. viii). Sadly, they have completed this task with only mixed success. While they have consolidated and made accessible a vast amount of information, they have been content to accumulate rather than analyse. Despite their contrary ambitions, they rely largely on the same old tired set of legal materials. The reader can be assured of *knowing* more about legislation, but is unlikely to *understand* more. To understand only the rules of the game gives the spectator merely a partial appreciation of the game itself. The legislative process is not simply a static and formal framework; it is a dynamic and vital activity. Unfortunately, Miers and Page concentrate on the former at the expense of the latter, thereby presenting a distortedly simple image of legislation. In short, they have failed to depart from the powerful, traditional vision of legislation. They have painted a legislative still-life when what is demanded is a video of legislation-in-motion.

The first seven chapters of the book focus on the preparation, drafting, enactment and interpretation of legislation. The presentation is informative and incisive. Insofar as they present a full and sequential treatment of the legislative process, the authors eclipse earlier fragmented and unsystematic treatments. In this respect, Miers and Page deserve warm praise. Yet, as they concede at the beginning of the eighth and final chapter, "we have so far adopted a formal approach to the concept of legislation" (p. 211). Indeed, in its stark contrast, their sophisticated and dynamic analysis of the impact and efficacy of legislation merely serves to underline the weakness of the bulk of the book. The strength of this final chapter leaves the reader with a sad glimpse of what might have been. For example, in their very brief review of the pressures that operate to stimulate legislative initiatives (p. 56–59), they gloss over the life-force of the legislative process: the politics and techniques of lobbying. The battle for legislative control is fought and won in the

[25] *See* W. Twining and D. Miers, How to Do Things With Rules (2d ed. 1982).

backrooms and corridors, not in the public chambers and committee rooms. Legislation is a political process and must be studied as such. Miers and Page's treatment is too clean and tidy; they seem reluctant to dirty their hands in the muddy world of political life. Nonetheless, these criticisms do not bring out the main problems with the book. Like so much English scholarship, it is atheoretical and exhibits disciplinal parochialism. Its focus obscures rather than illuminates the background drama.

Miers and Page remain securely within the traditional community of jurisprudential learning, largely ignoring[26] the revealing insights of other relevant disciplines. They do not explicitly relate their account of legal practice to any background theory of law and society.[27] For instance, whereas they emphasise that Hoadly's "true law-givers"[28] comprise many different non-judicial personnel, they do not offer any general account of adjudication. They prefer to describe the practice of statutory interpretation rather than locate it within any broader conception of the judicial role (pp. 178–96). At a time when the jurisprudential scene is marked by a heated and wide-ranging debate over the performance and legitimacy of the judicial function in a liberal democracy, this omission seems difficult to excuse.[29] To write of statutory interpretation without any reference to the work of Dworkin and his detractors is puzzling. Whatever the judges may claim or Miers and Page suggest by their silence, statutory interpretation is a voyage with considerable ideological freight.

## IV. Describing and Understanding Legislation: The Contribution of Modern Language Theory

As Miers and Page neglect the theoretical work of the legal community, it is not surprising that they do not draw on the powerful insights of other relevant disciplines. Within the con-

[26] Again, chapter 8 stands out as the exception.

[27] Of course, this is not to suggest that they do not subscribe to certain jurisprudential assumptions. As F.S.C. Northrop noted, "the only difference between a person without a philosophy and someone with a philosophy is that the latter knows what his philosophy is." F. Northrup, The Complexity of Legal and Ethical Experience 6 (1959). This is not the place to tease out Miers and Page's assumptions.

[28] *Quoted in* J.C. Gray, The Nature and Sources of Law 172 (1948).

[29] For a critical survey of this debate, see Hutchinson & Monahan, *Law, Politics and The Critical Legal Scholars: The Unfolding Drama of American Legal Thought*, 36 Stan. L. Rev. 801 (1984).

fines of a review, we can only refer sketchily and selectively to the potential benefits of such scholarship. A fruitful source of assistance would be the recent developments and controversies in "language theory." Insofar as legislation represents a major form of cultural communication, contemporary research on the significance and complexity of the relationship between language, power and culture seems particularly pertinent. Miers and Page take an elementary and uncritical view of language and interpretation. For them, meaning is an unproblematic concept; "[c]ertainty is a question of degree and can be increased or reduced as a matter of policy" (p. 90). In contrast, those scholars who specialize in the subject recognize the inherently sophisticated and dynamic nature of the meaning-giving enterprise. The difficulty centers on the interaction between the author's intention, the nature of the text, and the reader's knowledge.[30]

Traditionally, the focus was upon the author's intention, but this was rejected by the New Criticism school which maintained that a text possessed a definite meaning within its own four corners. More recently, a deconstructionist movement has sought to demonstrate the self-referential nature of language. They refuse to identify any given set of words with any concept of embodied meaning; "the word carries with it . . . [an] indeterminacy of meaning."[31] Others, while accepting the thrust of this thesis, claim that this does not entail a tailspin into a hopeless nihilism. Although meaning is made and not found, it is not totally subjective. It has a social and conventional existence. Stanley Fish has argued that "meanings are the property neither of fixed and stable texts nor of free and independent readers but of interpretive communities that are responsible both for the shape of a reader's activities and for the texts those activities produce."[32] The central message of contemporary thought is that interpretation is a meta-linguistic exercise. The search for a transcendental truth hidden in the text has been abandoned. Meaning is the product of interpretation and not its determinant. All interpretations are culture-specific. Any theory of meaning

[30] For a survey of the contemporary exchanges, see F. Lentricchia, After The New Criticism (1980) and C. Belsey, Critical Practice (1980).

[31] H. Bloom, J. Derrida, G. Hartman, P. de Man & J. Miller, Deconstruction and Criticism at vii–viii (1979).

[32] S. Fish, Is There A Text In This Class? 322 (1980).

must go beyond words and seek to understand the semiological and ideological dimensions of communication.[33] As Levi-Strauss pithily observes, "the nature of truth is . . . indicated by the care it takes to remain elusive."[34]

Although law is a special category of cultural communication, it shares many of the general characteristics of the more generic form. For instance, while the intention of legislators can claim especial relevance in the democratic context of legal interpretation, the difficulty of isolating that intention in any meaningful way, as Miers and Page point out (pp. 184–90, 204–10), is notorious. Further, after an interval of several years, the relevance of legislative intention becomes suspect. Any attempt to provide a full account of the practice and reform of statutory interpretation must use and integrate legal theory and language theory. The task is formidable, but initial work is already being done.[35] The study of statutory interpretation must become a more sophisticated and embracing enterprise. Words are prisms through which meanings are refracted in many colors and hues. Yet the prism is not natural or static; it is inserted and held in place by a group of cultural actors. The challenge is to analyse the structure and quality of that prism. As Fish might say, the terms and substance of "the interpretive community" must be isolated and evaluated.[36] Accordingly, legal scholars must identify the linguistic and semiological constraints that give meaning and content to the act of statutory interpretation. They must crack the code of legislation. In more familiar terms, a self-conscious ideological element must be incorporated into legal scholarship—the search for the cluster of ideas, beliefs and assumptions that represent a certain way of thinking about legislation and interpretation at any given time.[37] Miers and Page's lack of any ideological reference point troubles their analysis.

---

[33] *See generally* J. CULLER, THE PURSUIT OF SIGNS (1981); G. KRESS & R. HODGE, LANGUAGE AS IDEOLOGY (1980).

[34] C. LEVI-STRAUSS, TRISTES TROPIQUES 44 (J. & D. Weightman trans. 1974).

[35] *See, e.g.*, Fiss, *Objectivity and Interpretation*, 34 STAN. L. REV. 739 (1982). For a more skeptical approach, see Hutchinson & Monahan, *The "Rights" Stuff: Roberto Unger and Beyond*, 62 TEX. L. REV. (forthcoming).

[36] *See* S. FISH, *supra* note 32, at 303–371.

[37] This should not be confused with the Marxist conception of ideology as "false consciousness." It is intended to be used in a more Althusserian sense as a necessary intellectual construct for living. However, that ideology must still be assessed in terms of its potentially distortive effect and political function.

## V. Politicizing Legislation: The Ideology of Statutory Interpretation

In probing the hinterlands of contemporary scholarship, legal scholars will rediscover many familiar common law actors, clothed in different garb. In particular, they will be comforted to find courts as one focal point for the analysis of statutes and semiology. The courts play an important institutional role within the drama of social conflict. This is not to suggest or accept an *instrumental* role for court action. Indeed, quite the opposite is argued. It is sufficient that courts are seen as important by both lawyers and society generally. In one special sense, courts are obviously of significance. It is not the words of the statutes that are law, but the courts' particular exposition of those words. Of course, as Miers and Page reflect (p. 178–80), although courts are not the only code breakers at work, they do help write the code of the statute book.

Law and lawyers are caught in an increasingly self-conscious engagement on the battleground of social and political theory. Insofar as a statute represents the major institutional form of lawgiving in modern society, the courts are engaged in the continual struggle to work out society's positive political commitment. However, if it is conceded that the law's *practical* effect is minimal,[38] any debate over the role of courts must become ideological in nature. As such, the challenge is to identify and bring forward the multi-dimensional ideological backdrop against which the courts must perform. As Edward Thompson has so accurately stated:

> The rhetoric rules of a society are something a great deal more than sham. In the same moment they modify, in profound ways, the behaviour of the powerful and mystify the powerless. They may disguise the true realities of power, but, at the same time, they may curb that power and check its intrusion . . . . The notion of the regulation and reconciliation of conflicts through the rule of law . . . seem to me a cultural achievement of universal significance . . . . The imposing and effective inhibitions upon power and the defence of the citizen from powers or intrusive claims, seems to me to be an unqualified human good. To deny or belittle

[38] And the scant evidence demands this concession. *See, e.g.*, L. Friedman and S. Macaulay, Law and the Behavioural Sciences chs. 2–3 (2d ed. 1977) (the discussions at 141–192 and at 501–575 are particularly significant).

> this good is, in this dangerous century when the resources and tensions of power continue to enlarge, a desperate error of intellectual abstraction.[39]

The orthodox constitutional view that Parliament makes the laws and the judiciary interprets them was recently reiterated by Lord Diplock in *Duport Steels Ltd. v. Sirs*.[40] In performing that task, the role of the courts is to give effect to "the intention of Parliament *as expressed in the words of the statute*."[41] The law-job is to find the meaning of the words that Parliament has used.[42] As most exhaustively elaborated in the recent speeches in *Bromley L.B.C. v. Greater London Council*, the senior judiciary set out on the quest for the "true," "proper," or "correct" meaning of the statutory words under observation.[43] As has been said of Coke's equation of reason with discretion, "rarely can so many questions have been begged in so few words."[44] Indeed, the psychological attitude displayed in the *Bromley* case, which is chosen for its representativeness and not its singularity, is an almost direct descendant of Coke's thinking on the common law.

While there has been a judicial capitulation to the supremacy of Parliament, that surrender is to a command to be obeyed begrudgingly according to its letter. Otherwise, it is of little consequence. For the courts, the triumph of statute over common law is a pyrrhic victory. But this betrays the ideological superstructure of adjudication. Words do not interpret themselves. A sentence will never mean exactly the same thing to any two different people or even the same thing to one person on different occasions. Meaning is shaped by the apperceptive mass of understanding and background that an individual brings to bear on the external fact of a sound or series of marks. As words lack "self-evident reference," purpose and context are ultimately major determinants of meaning.[45] However, as the expression of legislative intent is always more or less incom-

---

[39] E. THOMPSON, WHIGS AND HUNTERS: THE ORIGINS OF THE BLACK ACT 265–66 (1975).

[40] [1980] 1 W.L.R. 142 (Q.B.).

[41] *Id.* at 157.

[42] *Black-Clawson International Ltd. v. Papierwerke Waldhof-Aschaffenburg*, 1975 A.C. 591, 613 (H.L.) (Lord Reid).

[43] 1983 A.C. 801, 829, 836, 839, 842, 850–51 (H.L.).

[44] C. HILL, *supra* note 16, at 252, commenting on E. COKE, A LITTLE TREATISE ON BAILE AND MAINPRIZE 31 (2d. ed. 1635).

[45] Cohen, *Field Theory and Judicial Logic* 59 YALE L.J. 238, 240–41 (1950).

plete, it is doubtful whether any impartial method of adjudication can be fashioned in a liberal society.[46] Indeed, even Ronald Dworkin concedes that legislative intent can never be legitimately characterized as "some complex psychological fact locked in history waiting to be winkled out from old pamphlets and letters and proceedings . . . . There is no such thing as the intention of [the Legislature] waiting to be discovered, even in principle. There is only some such thing waiting to be invented."[47]

The necessity of engaging in such invention requires the courts to make substantive political decisions, the very decisions that semantic, historical or counter-factual approaches *claim* to avoid. No one single "construction" is inevitable or natural. Construction means choice. And choice confers power. Of course, this is not to suggest that judicial creativity breeds constitutional anarchy. Communities of interpretation have their own bonding mechanisms, a mixture of moral values and social customs. Interpretation is inextricably bound up with values and it is nowhere seriously suggested the values do not carry ideological underpinnings. The lesson to be gathered from this realization is quite simple. Courts that shield themselves behind descriptions of law as clear, predetermined and objective norms against which they pitch their neutral decisions are worthy of suspicion. In addition to incorporating, or at least introducing, the insights of contemporary jurisprudential scholarship, a full and proper understanding of legislation must begin by recognizing and addressing the substantive democratic issues that lie behind a formal examination of the legislative process. As it operates today, Parliament is a conduit through which the outcomes of struggles for power between elite interest groups are formally communicated. It is doubtful that it has ever been anything more. The judicial approach to legislation merely confirms and legitimates this veiled relationship.

While courts cast themselves as the dumb-show on the political stage, the inevitably ideological nature of the meaning-giving enterprise ensures that they will be as unrepresentative as the Parliament whose will they purport slavishly to follow. In such

---

[46] R. UNGER, LAW IN MODERN SOCIETY 180 (1976).

[47] Dworkin, *The Forum of Principle*, 56 N.Y.U. L. REV. 467, 475 (1981). *See also* Dworkin, *Political Judges and the Rule of Law*, 64 PROCEEDINGS OF THE BRITISH ACADEMY 259 (1978); Dickerson, *Statutory Interpretation: A Peek into the Mind of a Legislator*, 50 IND. L.J. 206 (1975).

circumstances, those who must abide by their interpretations are entitled to ask the judiciary to recognize and declare that fact. The crisis for the judiciary in our pseudo-pluralistic state is whether, as Evershed suggested,[48] it can still maintain its cloak of neutrality in light of the realities of the struggle for political power. The British legal community has yet to grasp the full force of Ely's pithy remark that "we may grant until we're blue in the face that legislatures aren't wholly democratic, but that isn't going to make courts more democratic than legislatures."[49] In an instrumental sense, courts are an overated past-time. Yet this does not prevent us from remaining alert to Thompson's suggestion about the exhilarating ideological possibilities of the rule of law.[50] In the modern statutory state, law and lawyers have a constitutional obligation to face and to accept this challenge.

Although little mention has been made of it, delegated legislation is perhaps the extreme form of the problem addressed. The statutory instrument has been nicely parodied as the modern form of power fighting against which Hampden died on the battlefield and Sidney on the scaffold.[51] The modern legislative technique of passing acts that confer general powers, leaving the details to the discretion of the executive department, can be seen as both necessary and desirable. But its development needs further and better safeguards. The growth of tribunals is one response to this, but they represent a double-edged sword. Unless and until the courts move from their common law approach to statutes to a fresh and dynamic perspective, the development of any procedural or substantive safeguards is seriously threatened. If the courts are unable so to change, it may be that the citizenry will be left to conclude that the courts are no longer an appropriate or necessary forum for modern dispute-resolution. Then there may well be real ideological crisis, and more.[52]

---

[48] *See generally* LORD EVERSHED, *supra* note 23.

[49] J. ELY, DEMOCRACY AND DISTRUST 67 (1980).

[50] Thompson's evaluation of the Rule of Law as an "*unqualified* human good" is suspect; *see* E. THOMPSON, *supra* note 39 at 235–36. Nonetheless, its potential for good must not be overlooked: *See* Horwitz, Book Review, 86 YALE L.J. 561 (1977).

[51] C. HUGHES, THE BRITISH STATUTE BOOK 45 (1957).

[52] We shall fully elaborate this sketch in a short monograph on statutes which is in preparation.

# [19]

# REVIEW ARTICLE

## Semiotics in the Trial of Jurisprudence

***Peter Rush****

*Bernard S. Jackson,* **Law, Fact and Narrative Coherence,** Merseyside: Deborah Charles Publications, 1988, x and 214 pp, hb £18.00.

In the book under review, the theoretical apparatus of legal semiotics is wielded to give an account of legal adjudication in the common law trial. Looking back at what has been written here, it can be seen that the review takes up three contexts: the machinations of jurisprudence, the detour of legal theory into linguistic meta-*récits* or tall tales, and the genre of legal academic writing. The review argues that what is *not* at stake in *Law, Fact and Narrative Coherence* is the enterprise of jurisprudence. As will become clear, in order to make that argument, it would not be necessary to understand what the *mots clefs* of semiotics *mean*. As Bernard Jackson asks of his own book, 'Is it intended to be taken seriously, or is it play, or even a joke?' (p.5). Jackson's answer is that, apart from a playful remark here and there, the general intention is serious. My own answer would be to ask whether it is necessary to choose.

### A Crisis in Manners: or, how the butler asks the right questions

There are few questions in Jurisprudence. The positivist tradition has been the most succinct, if not the most repetitive and limiting. What is the Law? What is its justification? Or, more narrowly, what is a ver-dict and in what ways can the judicious telling of law's truth be justified? In fact, the separability of these two questions has provided the context of much contemporary jurisprudence: law and facts, description and evaluation, facts and values, law and politics. Just as textbook commentary on law is an extended footnote to legal cases, so too jurisprudence becomes a long and authoritative footnote to the question 'what is it?'. Invariably, this 'what' has been referred and deferred to the institutional context of adjudication, that place where the judge 'reasons'. But such a context is simply a pitstop for jurisprudence in its race towards more inflated issues. For, just as the judge and the magistrate would claim to be acting in the name of something else, so too jurisprudence quickly refers adjudication to Justice, Liberty, Equality, Rationality, Public Policy. One could thus be excused for thinking that jurisprudence conducts its business with all the (im)modesty of a butler. It is modest in its desire to explain the law and nothing but the Law. It is immodest in its abject moralism, which would extend the law to all, which would deploy the law to explain all. The butler is at once guardian and servant of the household. And so the enterprise of jurisprudence takes its place at the door of the law and has repeatedly whispered: will that be all for today, my Honour? Of course, as Dworkin has said, the correct answer is always forthcoming. When and where jurisprudence holds court, there the butler can rest assured, at ease in the knowledge that, having asked the proper questions and asked them with respect, the proper answers will have been given. In short, the butler asks the right questions because he already has the right answers. Up his sleeve.

---

*University of Lancaster

*The Modern Law Review* 53:1 January 1990 0026-7961

The disrespect implicit in such an image of law and its jurisprudence is apposite to a story that has found both favour and disfavour on the academic circuit. Recently, the butler has become disrespectful (some would say critical). 'Trashing' is the order of the day. Meaning, Rationality, Law, Justice, and all those other capital wor(l)ds are now on trial. In one genre of this trial, the robes of linguistics are worn in order to expose the ground rules of the legal system.

Herbert Hart called such ground rules the singular 'rule of recognition'. In a semiotic turn of phrase, Bernard Jackson calls this a 'narrative framework'. A narrative is 'understood, broadly, as actions arranged in a time sequence and forming a meaningful totality' (p.2). And 'laws may be regarded as a particular form of narrative representation of human behaviour, a form peculiar — above all — for the manner in which social approval or disapproval (which attaches to all narrative models of human behaviour) is expressed, and by the institutionalised form in which the "sanction" (in the semiotic sense — the form of recognition, whether approving or disapproving) is conveyed' (p.91). Moreover, the meaning of these legal narratives is a consequence of 'structural features of human rationality in general, the "basic structures of signification"' (p.116). As the language indicates, the method of revelation (special, divine, or expert) has been to take a linguistic turn, if not a semiotic pirouette. As Jackson wryly comments, 'Semiotics starts (and, some would say, ends) with discourse' (pp. 92–3). It would seem that there has crept into the citadel of the jurisprudential exercise a nuisance in the form of a nuance. However, such semiotic nuancing rarely functions to restore a materiality, a fragility to a law which the Law has tried its best to disavow. Rather, against the hysterical and positivist assumption of a unity for Law, there is pitted a plurality of significations. Unity is not countered by a fragmentation of the law's desire for systematicity. Law has nothing to do with law. Unity is countered by a positing of numerous discourses which interlock to form a specific system of Law. The will to coalesce has not been dislodged; fear of collapse drives the legal rap.

For Jackson, a description of 'the pragmatics of the courtroom process' would be a description of 'who speaks, how they speak, and for what purposes' (p.8). A series of interlocking narrative frameworks would make sense of the discontinuous segments by connecting them into an intelligible whole. Hence the central argument of the book: the need to 'narrativise the pragmatics' of the courtroom situation. Of course, a 'structural semiotics' (inspired by Greimas) will provide tools through which to describe the narrative rap. And the importance of the notion of narrative rules is that they 'specify typifications not only of arguments but of enunciations of arguments: who proposes the argument (the authority of the enunciator), how it is proposed (the rhetoric of its presentation), when and where it is proposed (the context of the enunciation).' (p. 153)

In the linguistic turn of jurisprudence, 'What is law' has thus been cross-hatched by other questions. Who speaks and to whom? How is he talking, or to whom is the language destined, and with what effects of power? Such questions may be taken as indicating that law is determined by the positions from which it speaks or from which it is announced. These positions are given in and by language. And, for some, the nuances of language are the nuances of power relations, of subjection. In exposing the ground rules of laws, content is collapsed into form, the 'What is law' into the 'how is law'. In short, the sign of disrespect is not what you say but the ways that you says it.

Of course, Jackson is not the only rapper around that wants his record turning to the tune of language. The linguistic turn has fertile soil in jurisprudence. Yet for this reader of the jurisprudential enterprise (and I come to it with *astonishment* at the course it takes), it seems that it is only possible to continue with jurisprudence on condition that the problematic of language is held in reserve — to be taken up at some later date and displayed as a new jurisprudence. Herbert Hart, deploying the protocols of ordinary language philosophy, accounted for ambiguities in the conceptual rules of law by recourse to the extraordinary notion of its 'open texture'. In so doing, he weighted the linguistic turn with the value of openness. Ronald Dworkin, using the so-called hard case as his lever on rules, claimed that there was even more openness in the Law than the Hartian positivist had dreamt of in his philosophy. With all the *élan* of a new worlder, Dworkin drew an analogy between the Law and the 'chain-novel', and between the jurisprude and the literary critic. While Hart and Dworkin were engaged in a close embrace which set modern jurisprudence alight, others were making similar analogies between law, jurisprudence, and language. James Boyd White imagined law as literature, and jurisprudence as akin to reading poetry rather than the riot act. And while Neil MacCormick puts to work a hermeneutics of narrative in the service of a description of the way law hangs together, William Twining wants to talk of lawyer's stories, if not the stories of academic jurisprudence. At the end of such a long line, there is a place for the work of legal semiotics.

In this latest contribution to the project of legal semiotics, all the above are variously found wanting. And a semiotic understanding of 'narrative coherence' is to satisfy that want. Under the self-proclaimed aegis of a 'meta-discourse', the suggestion is that there is a narrative construction of facts, a narrative construction of laws, and that the two constructions hang together in the courtroom (p. 58). The method of hanging is not logical but analogical entailment. The method of hanging is a 'comparison' (p. 101, 168) of constructions, in order to find a 'resemblance' (p. 169), 'a looser form of analogy' (p. 170), a 'similarity' ( p. 190), a relationship of 'proximity' (p. 89) between the narratives suspended in court. Jackson's rewriting of the normative syllogism, so beloved of jurisprudence, is that legal stories and factual stories are 'coherent' when the narrative 'pattern' of each 'matches' (p. 58), 'fits', the other. Which is also to say that trial by narrative becomes 'plausible' (p. 131) when the stories hang together. As Roland Barthes has noted, 'To rob a man of his language in the name of language: this is the first step in all legal murders' (*Mythologies*, 1973, p. 46).

It would seem that the enterprise of jurisprudence already has a place for a linguistic turn, a niche where the pirouette can be executed. In most of the above writers, the question of law-as-language has been dealt with as a 'special case'. It has been interrogated around situations of undecidability. Analogies with language have been used to explain the 'hard case', the ambiguous, the irrational, and the particular in law. As such, undecidability becomes a question in the guise of a problem — and a problem precisely because it is constructed as a deviation from the norm of legal certainty. In taking up the question of language, jurisprudence has once again assured itself a place as a commentator on the law, has assumed that law is a matter of probability and not possibility, that law is a matter of logic and not rhetoric, that law is a semantic and not pragmatic question. In short, jurisprudence has pathologised the linguistic question of which it writes, held it in reserve, consigned it to the hinterland.

On that reading, the much-vaunted recent turn to language would be a re-turn to the niche given over to language. Of course, there are some differences. One strategy has been to take up the question of language from its delimited and devalued place, in order to elaborate and extend it throughout and within the can(n)ons and protocols of jurisprudence. Such an exegetical practice has been the value of legal semiotics. In *Law, Fact and Narrative Coherence*, Bernard Jackson has left no stone unturned, and not a few thrown, in the pursuit of jurisprudential law's reliance on narrative frameworks. Law is understood as no less and no more than a specific language with its own distinct frameworks of meaning. Legal semiotics would thus take the *analogy* between law and language to its jurisprudential limits, and no further. The ambition of the legal semiotic enterprise would be, in short, to be a text *in and on* jurisprudence. Although one of the stated themes of the book is to take the claims of (linguistic) scepticism seriously (p. 1), it is not sceptical enough: the semiotic re-turn played out here would in its turn re-tain the belief in the enterprise of jurisprudence.

*The Modern Law Review* [Vol. 53

# In Your Own Words or, Nobody Sneezes in the House of Jurisprudence: insider trading and the fragile tissue of quotation

If we cannot judge whether the semantic content of stories ('factual' or 'fictional') is true, we can at least judge who we think is *telling the truth*, in the sense of most adequately persuading us that s/he is fulfilling the sincerity conditions of the act of making a truth-claim. (p.2)

Neither the Common Law of evidence nor the strategies of Anglo-American pleaders necessarily challenge our conventional presuppositions regarding language, truth and reality . . . But these conventional presuppositions have themselves become academically controversial. (p. 12)

This chapter sets the scene by reviewing a number of conceptual frameworks which may assist us in our quest. (p. 12)

'Narrative coherence' currently threatens to become a fashionable slogan within legal philosophy. (p. 18)

each group [legal philosophers, practicing lawyers] is primarily concerned with its own stories (stories about itself). (p. 23)

We know what it takes — who, how, etc., — to persuade, (p. 35)

Descriptive social sciences such as semiotics and social psychology, can certainly provide an account of such justificatory discourse [that found in judicial reasoning]. They cannot, however, step outside it, and pronounce upon whether the arguments of such discourse provide *real* justification. That problem is deferred until the final two chapters. (p. 92)

What resources do we have available to explain the rationality implicit in the examples of law construction and application discussed in this chapter? At one level, no particular explanation is required. . . . The same might be said for the analyses above; they stand or fall, as accounts of underlying legal rationality, in terms of their plausibility[38] or otherwise. However, we would undoubtedly strengthen the case for narrative coherence as a mode of legal rationality were we to be able to relate it to other acceptable models of rationality.

38 Of course, I cannot claim that 'plausibility' here has any greater status than I am willing to accord it in other contexts. See further the argument of the last two chapters. (p. 110)

The fact that the reasons for the decision may be made public, in a judgment[47] which may well be published in the law reports has a special significance, from both semiotic and sociological vantage-points. For here, the judge must not only decide a point of law; s/he must also communicate that decision. That communication of law must also be persuasive . . .

47 Or 'speech', as it is termed, in the House of Lords. (p. 114)

What cognitive apparatus does the lawyer deploy, to render a legal text intelligible? Traditionally, it is said that s/he has been taught to 'think like a lawyer'. This is both true and false. It is true in the sense that lawyers internalise a set of frameworks of understanding which represent the conventions of that particular profession or 'semiotic group' . . . What lawyers internalise is a set of narrative frameworks regarding the legal recognition of typical behaviour patterns — the narrative form of legal rules, as described in section 4.3 above, but here laden not with forms of social approval or disapproval, but rather with those forms of approval and disapproval which legal institutions use in order to confer 'recognition'. (p. 116)

The reader of the legal text cannot understand that text without a pre-existing body of knowledge (a 'legal education', in the wider sense here used), and without an eye to the use to be made of the book in question. (p. 129)

Contemporary legal philosophy has become obsessed with the problem of interpretation. (p. 131)

No one would dream of questioning the idea of 'the Law'. (p. 132)

[the adoption of a positivist methodology and the endorsement of a sceptical ontology by semiotics] allows us to describe our object of study, including the metaphysical claims which that object of study makes about its own nature, without endorsing those metaphysical claims. (p. 132)

The 'audiences' of my communicational model are, in accordance with much continental linguistic theory, to be defined exclusively in terms of those who do receive and use particular messages. (p. 134)

we must find a set of conventions regarding the media of transmission of messages, and the codes in which they are transmitted. (p. 134)

The historian cannot afford to be a mere chronicler (just as the academic lawyer is expected to do more than merely replicate professional discourse), but at the same time must maintain the rigours of meticulous attention to detail, as a purveyor of truth. (p. 159)

The book will be 'reviewed', often by people with a professional interest in its fate . . . S/he may not always write what s/he thinks her audience (especially the institutional audience of her reviewers) wants to hear; but s/he may be constrained from writing that which s/he anticipates will prove unacceptable. Whatever s/he writes, there will inevitably be consequences for her career. (p. 165)

The teller of a story (whether judge, historian, or indeed academic lawyer) has strategic decisions to make in the telling of that story, but even her perception of such strategic decisions is informed by narrative frameworks regarding the telling of stories in *such* an institutional context. (p. 171)

But history, and politics, must necessarily impinge also upon the range of narrative frameworks available to the judge (or the historian, or the academic lawyer) by reference to which s/he may choose to construct the particular facts or events upon which s/he is called to adjudicate. (p. 171)

But how do we arrive at those theories of narrative construction, if not through the plausibility of alternative narrative frameworks? There is, in my view, no escape from this dilemma. (p. 172)

We may affirm these theories as 'sociological truth', a matter of faith not reason. (pp. 172–3)

We must now confront the jurisprudential implications of the argument advanced in this book. (p. 175)

Critical Legal Studies might look at the socio-economic presuppositions and values of semiotic discourse, as well as the conditions of its production. Conversely, semiotics will look at the linguistic and semiotic presuppositions of Critical Legal Studies discourse, and its semiotic contexts. (p. 185)

Demystification of the ground of one's own thought is undoubtedly a necessary condition for demystification of the thought of others. (p. 189)

The effects of demystification should be to produce an individual characterised by 'integrity': having the ability, both in thought and in action, to evaluate not only theories but also policies and strategies with the highest possible degree of self-awareness and criticism. (p. 189)

At the level of theory, I would maintain that semiotics, being purely descriptive, is not of itself either radical or conservative; that depends upon the use to which it is put. (p. 191)

We must have faith in the persuasive powers of demystification itself to generate acceptable forms of justification. (p. 195)

The fact that this project can be simultaneously all of these [trashing, reformatory, legitimatory], indicates that it is located, primarily, at the epistemological level. Above all, the value of 'integrity' requires each subject to indulge in as honest, thorough and critical an introspection upon the basis of his/her own perceptions as he or she is capable. (p.6)

It is the puzzle that counts. (p. 142)

## Before Jurisprudence: on the heels of an enterprise

Let me begin again. For some time now — perhaps since the nineteenth century struggles around hygiene, education, architecture, the family, town planning, and criminal law (an instance would be 'summary jurisdiction') displaced the trial from its place of prominence in the administration of justice — jurisprudes have repeatedly interrogated the common law trial. Of course, despite its pretensions, the enterprise of jurisprudence has not explained, let alone described, everything about the trial. The investment of the jurisprudential enterprise has been in descriptions of legal adjudication. Here it is possible to read the ceaseless — and, according to some, Herculean — formulations of the normative syllogism. The problem that the syllogism would resolve is the application of law to fact. Legal adjudication would be the place where the power of logic is on trial and found to be more than adequate to the task in hand.

Of course, jurisprudes have not been the only ones to hold the keys to the trial (and there is good cause to wonder why there are keys at all). There are sociologists: Pat Carlen's *Magistrates' Justice* is a landmark text, not to mention Harold Garfinkel's work on status-degradation ceremonies. There are novelists: Albert Camus's *L'Etranger* and Franz Kafka's *The Trial* are remembered. There are also literary critics. Psychologists have made laborious and tiresome quests into the conscious operations of witnesses, jurors, judges, police: the work of David Farrington and Sally Lloyd-Bostock would probably rate a footnote here. There is the work of feminists on the organisation of gender in the criminal justice system (for example, see Susan Edwards' *Women on Trial*). There are the criminologists who have concentrated on plea-bargaining and the production of guilty pleas (see Baldwin and McConville's *Negotiated Justice*). Social psychology will have given a place to the trial when it lends prominence to the work of George Herbert Mead on 'the psychology of punitive justice' in the 1930s. Historians, most notably Douglas Hay's work on the eighteenth century criminal trial, have also carved out a niche for themselves. *Law, Fact and Narrative Coherence* would argue that legal semiotics deserves a niche, if not more than a niche, in this repertoire of discourses on the common law trial. Legal semiotics is described as combining a 'positivist' methodology, a 'realist' ontology, and a 'sceptical' epistemology (pp. 11, 175–6). At the intersection of these three domains, the book under review will have read the common law trial as primarily 'legal adjudication'.

The book is a monograph. It is jurisprudential in tone and object. The project of the monograph is to wield the 'resource' (p. 175) of legal semiotics so as to offer up a 'description' of the lore of the courtroom. Such a lore functions in the monograph as an exemplum — an exemplum of what legal semiotics can do with a particular jurisprudential problem. As Jackson makes clear, jurisprudence has repeatedly claimed for itself the ability to explain the working of decision-making and justification in the common law trial. As such, the choice of problem, of 'semiotic object', is a motivated one: it provides the opportunity for a skirmish into the stronghold of jurisprudence. Of course, legal semiotics emerges from the skirmish as the undisputed victor. With surgical precision, Jackson exposes the flaws in the available accounts of the trial lore. Yet whether or not the account offered here by legal semiotics emerges unscathed is another matter.

The description of the common law trial is more or less self-consciously systematic. 'Legal adjudication' is understood as a system of signs. These signs, and their systematicity, are said to obtain and retain their meaning, their form, their intelligibility, from the tain of narrative structures. 'The trial process itself is a complex of pragmatic interactions each one of which individually, and all of which collectively, are themselves discursive constructions, their very intelligibility depending upon their character as such.' (p. 88). Moreover, those discourses have a narrative form. There are 'a plurality of narrative discourses at work in the trial' (p. 85). And although the narratives may be plural and disparate, the trial forms a 'coherent' whole. Legal adjudication is a series of interlocking narratives (p. 66). Which is also to say, and perhaps misleadingly because simply, that legal adjudication is no less and no more than a process of telling stories — stories told in the trial, stories of the trial, told by judges, witnesses, police, experts, lawyers, academics, the media ... Stories in and through which the common law trial obtains its meaning and its plausibility. In short, instead of trial by battle, trial by ordeal, trial by torture, trial by law, Bernard Jackson offers jurisprudence trial by narrative.

Of course, this is a re-view and that is an all-too-brief summary of the semantic orientation of the book. It in no way approximates the way in which Jackson elaborates his position: from chapter to chapter, he turns the argument about, describing it and repeating it in its different inflections, angles, levels, domains, lexicons. Moreover, not only does he turn his own argument about, but he turns traditional argumentative strategies about. Thus, in order to redescribe the project of the book as 'deconstructive' (p. 190), Jackson suggests that a major part of his argument institutes a reversal of the conventional epistemology. Instead of applying a law-based model to the discovery of facts, a fact-based model of narrative coherence is applied to the discovery of law. Of course, while noting that such might be his strategy, one could beg to differ over its effect: 'of course, the very opposition between "fact" and "law" dissolves in the process.' (p. 190). It is possible to imagine other possibilities: that a reversal of the law/fact opposition can only occur in the context of their separation, and thus that a simple reversal does not of itself alter the structure of opposition. In short, something more would be necessary before reversal becomes dissolution. And in vain did I search for that 'something more', unless it was the meta-*récits*, the tall tales of semiotics.

Despite the above appeal for the 'deconstructive' label, the book under review reads as if it is a sustained plea for and a demonstration of the benefits to be conferred by the resourceful faction of legal semiotics. That legal semiotics has much to offer is one of its overwhelming messages: the first sentence of the preface states: 'This book argues that structural semiotics provides crucial insights which may enrich both our theoretical accounts of legal phenomena and our observation and description of the phenomena themselves.' (p. 1). The book reads as if it was a display of riches to those whose robes now appear worn, a votive offering at the altar of the jurisprudential scribes. It is a telling story. Legal semiotics accepts its exclusion from the jurisprudential domain and, from that marginal and subordinated position, advocates that it be let into the enterprise of jurisprudence. The plea for semiotics through a demonstration of its benefits is an address to those who would be jurisprudes. By this I do not mean that it uses a highly specialised language. Jackson does — but in such a way that the book is also a primer for the student of (Greimasian) semiotics. (In fact, a nine point list of semiotic claims relevant to law is provided at pp. 27–33.) Nor am I simply referring to the fact that threaded throughout the book and culminating in the seventh and final chapter is a response to reviewers who were not 'sympathetic' (p. 176) to Jackson's previous work, reviewers who are largely identified here as emanating from and playing in the band of critical legal scholars. In short, the book is a plea that legal semiotics be taken seriously by those whom it would re-cognise as participants in the enterprise of jurisprudence. Legal semiotics will give a better account of the most cherished objets d'art of conventional jurisprudence; and at the same time, it will provide a valuable tool for and complement to the jurisprudence of critical legal scholars.

In so doing, some heterogeneous enterprises are roped into the jurisprudential bag. For example, it is more than arguable that much of 'critical legal studies' has no pretensions to (nor does) share (either as friends or enemies) the agenda of jurisprudence. And with good reason, given that different projects are usually incorporated as additions to a basic jurisprudential grid. What I find astonishing about the book under review is that it claims to be little more than a resourceful addition. The 'humility of lawyers' to which the book is a 'small contribution' (p. 6) would be little more than deference to the enterprise of jurisprudence, an enterprise which would like to tell all for all. In short, I would, and perhaps with the arrogance of the reviewer, read the book as a continuation of the enterprise of jurisprudence.

The problem of course in studying what goes on in the common law trial is not so much the lack but rather the overabundance both of potentially available information and of available frameworks for sorting that information. The problem is exacerbated by the perhaps inevitable way in which frameworks and information constitute each other. Jackson uses several devices to manage these overload problems. One device is the highly formalised semiotic tabulation of the everyday features involved in a *hypothetical* objection during a trial. Of course, the objection is hypothetical, and thus open to the oft-repeated claim that studies of the common law trial are rarely studies of the actual common law court. I want to make a different point. The tabulation is a formalisation which attempts to capture the minutiae of the objection, to provide an essential copy of the transaction. As an essential copy, it claims to describe the full range of possibilities in the trial objection. The description runs for some eight and a half pages (pp. 117–28). Nevertheless, it is difficult to dispel the impression that the tabulation is a quite selective cut *into* the reality it aspires to represent. And it is precisely that impression which is confronted when faced with the claim that the book is concerned with the 'adjudicatory process'. The phrase is deployed to catch a quite delimited field of trial lore: namely, that combination of 'decision-making' and 'justification' which occurs in the common law trial (in the above example, the tabulation of the objection is oriented towards the judge ruling on the objection). The phrase thus has a particular import, and it is this selectivity that gives it an importance. The 'adjudicatory process' is nothing other than the institution of trial by court as inflected in and through the spectacles and monocle of jurisprudence. After briefly stating what a 'complete semiotic account of the trial would be obliged to take account of', Bernard Jackson suggests the task of the book: 'The purpose of this book is, however, less ambitious [than a complete semiotic account]. It is to provide an alternative account of those elements of the adjudicatory process which traditinal doctrine — wrongly perhaps — privileges, through the model of the normative syllogism' (p. 36). A semiotic model, the 'alternative' account, is to *stand in for* the traditional model that constitutes the self-image of the jurisprudential enterprise. Legal semiotics would want to be a semiotic jurisprudence.

In sum, then, my argument is that any account of the trial lore is forced to confront an overload of information-frameworks. Legal semiotics, as with other accounts, employs a variety of selection devices to manage the problem of overloading. Further, those devices are aligned with the selection strategems that constitute the jurisprudential enterprise. The sign of that alignment is the rhetoric of 'adjudication' as 'decision-making' and 'justification'. The effect is that neither the court nor its jurisprudence has been put in its place. The king is yet to be decapitated. Instead, the court and its jurisprudence have been given a significance which is arguably unwarranted — simply remember the struggles over social administration previously mentioned around sanitation or housing. Instead, not only will legal semiotics have followed on the heels of jurisprudence, but it will also have continued the enterprise.

Admittedly, in addressing the problems that jurisprudence would take up and constitute as its own, Jackson skates on theoretically thick ice. A range of disciplines are drawn upon: social psychology, philosophy, and linguistics are the big three, but the whole gamut of the human sciences get a look-in at some point throughout the seven essays that comprise the book. The profit from such a wide range of (re)sources is 'a far richer description of the trial process' (p. 36). It is this thickness, this richness which marks the book as part of the new genre of 'legal theory'. Legal theory is a renovation of the philosophy of law but this time with a multi-disciplinary, and sometimes 'interdisciplinary', bent. Although Jackson describes the project of the book as 'essentially interdisciplinary' (p. 60), it is more like a combination of disciplines: 'In the central chapters of this book, I develop an account of modern trial procedures in Common Law courts inspired by a combination of Greimasian semiotics and the social psychology of Bennett and Feldman' (pp. 17–8). Moreover, it is the 'single theoretical framework', the 'meta-discourse' (p. 24) of semiotics which would overwhelm the other disciplines, which 'transcends the traditional boundaries of the social sciences' (p. 88). In fact, the book is the first in a new series of 'legal semiotics monographs' launched by Deborah Charles Publications (a publisher who has importantly been responsible for making available, in journal formal and to an English audience, a wide range of international writings in legal semiotics).

In the mono-graph, semiotics has medicinal, almost curative, if not corrective, properties, particularly where other 'sciences' are concerned. In chapters 2 and 4, a poultice is applied to the normative syllogism of jurisprudence. In as much as the syllogism relies upon a correspondence theory of truth, jurisprudence is defective and is to be remedied by a thorough-going non-referential or coherence notion of truth as plausible narratives. In chapter 3, it is the social psychology of Bennett and Feldman (*Reconstructing Reality in the Courtroom*, 1981) that is corrected by semiotics: 'the semiotic conception of the narrativisation of pragmatics allows us to remedy some defects in their work — defects which stem from their attempt to reduce the whole trial process to a single, semantic level' (p. 63). In chapter 5, it is jurisprudence in its guise as positivist interpretation that is brought to book: the notion of the unity of the legal system is answered by the plurality of legal significance *within* what is called a legal system, and the notion of legal autonomy is answered by the dependence of legal reasoning on the pressure of both unconscious rationality and narrative frameworks . . . In short, semiotics brings the other disciplines into line, and not only other disciplines but also common-sense: 'For the moment, at least, common-sense, everyday epistemology has not caught up with that of the semiotician!' (p. 167). And that is why legal semiotics must follow on the heels of jurisprudence: because it is too far in advance of the enterprise and is continually looking back down the road beckoning jurisprudence to catch up.

Recently, or so the story goes, that road has been transformed. The road is now the path to language, and there are few clearings along the way. On the road to the sign, to discourse, to language, to text, there are many *jurisprudential* travellers. Bernard Jackson is one of them, and one of the most systematic. And for the reader in search of that jurisprudential road, *Law, Fact and Narrative Coherence* is a good checkpoint. It is one of the most accessible and prominent signposts to the promised land, if that is where you want to go.

*International Journal for the Semiotics of Law* II/6 [1989]

# THE SEMIOTICS OF INTERNATIONAL LAW: INTERPRETATION OF THE ABM TREATY

by

ROBERT W. BENSON*

*Loyola Law School, Los Angeles*

## *The Semiotic Web of Legal Interpretation*

In earlier articles I have advanced a post-structuralist, semiotic theory of legal interpretation and have shown that it explains how statutes, constitutions, and judicial opinions get their meanings.[1] In this paper, I would like to apply the theory to texts of international law, illustrating with the U.S.-Soviet Anti-Ballistic Missile Treaty.

By saying that my theory is post-structuralist I mean that it arises out of that subjectivist thinking that has always been present in twentieth century modernism but which, as we approach century's end, is enjoying a resurgence under the name of post-structuralism or post-modernism in philosophy, in literature, in the arts, in architecture, in science, in the social sciences, and in law.[2] The theory rejects the legal positivism that continues to permeate the law like a grey fog from the nineteenth century. It also rejects the linguistic structuralism with which Saussure's descendants stirred so much excitement in years recently past and which, unfortunately, for a

* Loyola Law School, 1441 West Olympic Blvd, Los Angeles, CA 90015, U.S.A. My thanks to Jacqueline Grunfeld for valuable research assistance.

1 Robert W. Benson, "The Semiotic Web of the Law", in Roberta Kevelson (ed.), *Law and Semiotics, Vol. 1* (New York and London: Plenum Press, 1987), 35-63; *idem*, "How Judges Fool Themselves: The Semiotics of the Easy Case", in Roberta Kevelson (ed.), *Law and Semiotics, Vol. 2* (New York and London: Plenum Press, 1988), 31-60.

2 Benson, *supra* n.1, "Semiotic Web"; *idem*, "Semiotics, Modernism and the Law", *Semiotica* 73/1-2 (1989), 157-173; Joan C. Williams, "Critical Legal Studies: The Death of Transcendence and the Rise of the New Langdells", *New York University Law Review* 62(3), (1987), 429-496.

period was nearly synonymous with semiotics.[3] Structuralist semiotics, in my view, tend to be static, mechanical systems based, at bottom, on claims to universal structures of the human mind which either do not exist at all, or if they exist are so deep and so minimal that they have only feeble influence on the cultural superstructure. Structuralist legal semiotics becomes merely a neo-positivist exercise of analyzing law as an autonomous system of coded norms. It suffers the fatal irrelevance of ignoring historical and social context.[4]

What is needed, instead, is a pragmatic account of legal interpretation which starts with the modernist notion that language and legal meaning are cultural artifacts produced in time and space through specific social institutions. To describe the mode of production of these artifacts is to describe what Wittgenstein[5] called a "form of life" or "language game" and Stanley Fish[6] refers to as the "institutional practices of the interpretive community".[7] Ideally, the effort to describe such a complex phenomenon would involve the kind of "thick description" of cultural practices of which Clifford Geertz is tribal chief,[8] but I think it can at least be outlined by the kind of diagrams that follow below as *Figures 1 and 2* and which comprise what I call the semiotic web of legal interpretation.

In presenting my theory through diagrams, I hope it will not be mistaken for another structuralist model. As I explained recently in another paper,[9] "I find myself in the same quandary as Mr. Palomar

3 John Deely, "Pars pro Toto", in John Deely (ed.), *Frontiers in Semiotics* (Bloomington: Indiana University Press, 1986), vii-xxii.

4 Peter Goodrich, *Legal Discourse* (New York: St. Martin's Press, 1987); Benson, *supra* n.1, *Semiotica*; but see Bernard S. Jackson, *Semiotics and Legal Theory* (London, etc.: Routledge & Kegan Paul, 1985).

5 Ludwig Wittgenstein, *Philosophical Investigations*, trans. by G. E. M. Anscombe (Oxford: Basil Blackwell, 1958, 2nd ed.).

6 Stanley Fish, *Is There a Text in This Class?* (Cambridge, Mass: Harvard University Press, 1980).

7 See Drucilla Cornell, "'Convention' and Critique", *Cardozo Law Review* 7 (1986), 679-691; Williams, *supra* n.2.

8 *The Interpretation of Cultures* (New York: Basic Books, 1973); *idem*, *Local Knowledge* (New York: Basic Books, 1983).

9 *Supra* n.1 (1988).

in Italo Calvino's short stories.[10] Palomar had rejected attempts to tackle 'the most entangled human problems, such as those involving society and the art of government' by means of logical, structural models because the models were never congruent with the 'shapeless and senseless reality of human society, with all its monstrosities and disasters.' He decides that

> what really counts is ... the form that society is assuming slowly, silently, anonymously, in people's habits, their way of thinking and acting, their scale of value. If this is how things stand, the model of models Mr. Palomar dreams of must serve to achieve transparent models, diaphanous, fine as cobwebs, or perhaps even to dissolve models, or indeed to dissolve itself. At this point the only thing Mr. Palomar can do is erase from his mind all models and models of models (1985:111).

But, of course, he finds he can't do that and still have sustained thoughts about human problems, because sustained thoughts always begin to assume the shape of a model, and so he — no doubt an alter ego for Calvino himself in the delicious meditations of his later fiction — lives vacillating between mirages of rational models and the messy, vibrant life world. Models are difficult to escape, then, but if my explanation is a model at all it at least is not a mechanical one: it is not a drawing of the life world, which is impossible, but only a guide through it or a hint of what it is like, in the way a restaurant menu only hints at the meal to come, or a travel guide only hints at the road conditions and culture in the country across the border."

My approach is influenced principally by the post-structuralist semiotics of Umberto Eco[11] and through him the forerunner Charles Peirce ,[12] though it occasionally converges with some parts of the hermeneutics of Heidegger and Gadamer, the literary theory of Stanley Fish, and the work of Derrida, Foucault, Lyotard,

10 Italo Calvino, *Mr. Palomar*, trans. by W. Weaver (San Diego, New York, London: Harcourt Brace Jovanovich, 1985).

11 *A Theory of Semiotics* (Bloomington: Indiana University Press, 1979); *The Role of the Reader* (Bloomington: Indiana University Press, 1979); *Semiotics and the Philosophy of Language* (Bloomington: Indiana University Press, 1984).

12 Robert W. Benson, "Peirce and Critical Legal Studies:", in Roberta Kevelson (ed.), *Peirce and Law* (Dordrecht and Norwell, MA: Kluwer Academic Publishing, 1990), forthcoming.

Volosinov/Bakhtin, and others. I start with Eco's notion of the labyrinth or encyclopedia to describe the network of signs from which meaning is produced. I relabel it, however, with Sebeok's metaphor of "the semiotic web",[13] and describe it as follows:

— It is a metaphor which sees the individual surrounded by a cultural web of signs.

— Any individual who says that something has meaning can simply be called a reader.

— The something that has meaning — it may be words or larger units of discourse in a text, or sounds, or objects, or feelings, or events in nature, anything that stands for something else — can be called a sign.

— A reader looking at a sign explains it in terms of another sign in the web, and that sign in terms of another, and so on in what Charles Peirce called a process of "unlimited semiosis," a process which ends only when the reader loses interest after registering the last sign within the mind, or acting in a certain way.

— The *experience* of the series of signs, ending in some mental or behavioral event, is the *meaning* the original sign has had for that reader on that occasion. (This is not a "behavioral theory of meaning" in the sense of mechanically correlating signs to a catalogue of behaviors they cause. It is phenomenological, calling the experience with the sign its meaning.)

The metaphor of the semiotic web permits us to see that the reader is always embedded in a web of signs (or, as Eco prefers, a multi-level, net-like or rhizome-like labyrinth), which is the entire encyclopedia of signs in a culture. Situated at a node from which every point can be reached from every other point, the reader produces the meaning of a sign by travelling the connections of the web, linking a series of signs until losing interest in the process. At any one node, no reader has global vision of all of possible links because the web grows and contracts over the course of history, and because every reader has limited competence and limiting psy-

13 Thomas A. Sebeok, "The Semiotic Web: A Chronicle of Prejudices", *Bulletin of Literary Semiotics* 2 (1975), 1-63.

chological, ideological, social and other circumstances which affect one's capacity to travel the web.

The experience is the meaning to the individual reader, but if readers wish others to share their meanings, or if others wish them to share their meanings, they must attempt to bring one another to experience the visions from their own nodes in the web. In the end, production of the social meaning of texts is a matter of mutual persuasion, its study is the study of rhetoric, and the legal system is a particular system of rhetoric for cultural persuasion.[14]

Now then, the phenomenological experiences the reader has in the process of producing meaning from the web seem always to be these: one travels virtually simultaneously through portions of the web that consist of signs of *texts*, through portions containing signs of the *sources of texts* which provide additional opportunities for meaning, and through portions consisting of signs given by *other readers* expressing their views of the text. At each step, there are multiple possible selections of signs. Looking at all these signs through lenses of one's own *values*, and limited in vision by personal *psychological*, *historical*, *cultural*, and *sociological circumstances*, the reader selects a number of them to produce the *meaning*.

*Figure 1* (redrawn slightly from my first presentation of it in 1987) attempts to sketch all this together. *Figure 2* (also redrawn) takes two main sections of the web, the *text* and the *source of the text*, and magnifies them in order to reveal some of the routine pathways taken by Anglo-American lawyers and judges in actual practice, showing the multiple possible links that can be combined or ignored among the pathways in producing the legal meaning of any text.

14 Peter Goodrich, *Reading the Law* (Oxford: Basil Blackwell, 1986).

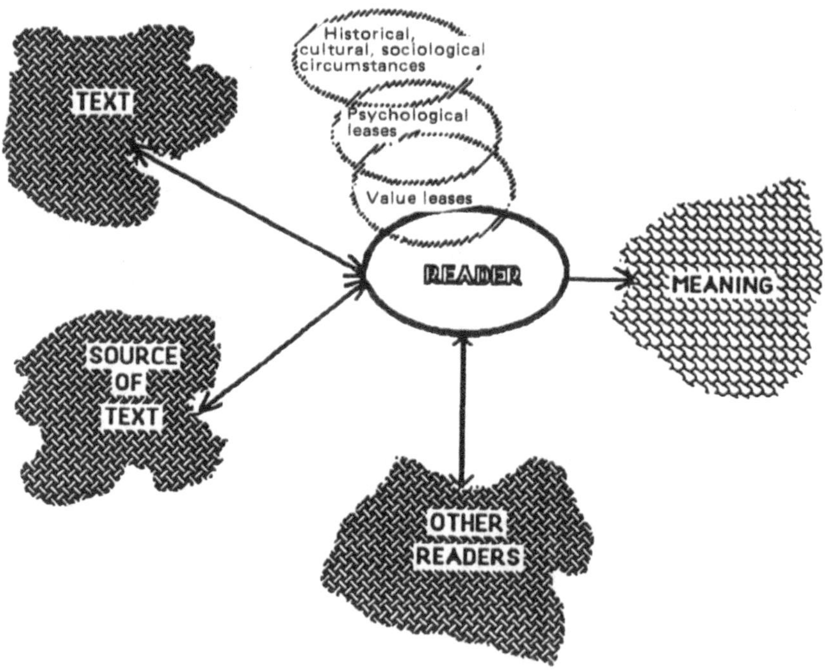


*[Figure 1: Semiotic Web of Legal Interpretation]*

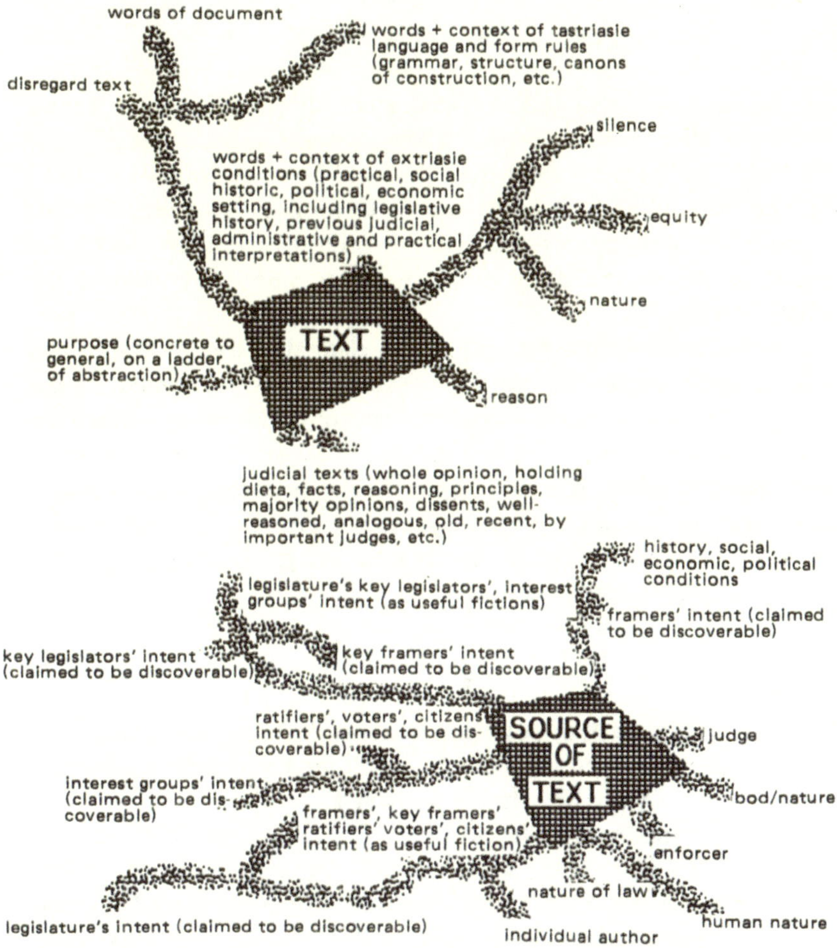


*[Figure 2: Semiotic Web of Legal Interpretation]*

With the aid of these diagrams, I would now like to examine an international legal text, the ABM Treaty.

*The ABM Treaty*

The United States and the Soviet Union signed the Anti-Ballistic Missile Treaty in the spring of 1972 and the U.S. Senate ratified it a few months later. The Treaty limits both countries' missile defense forces and restricts certain development and testing of such weapons. When President Reagan announced his "Star Wars" program in 1983 (he calls it the "Strategic Defense Initiative," but I decline to consent to the Pentagon's Orwellian newspeak for this frightening laser-beams-and-mirrors militarization of space) the question was immediately raised whether Star Wars violates the ABM Treaty.

At first, the Administration made clear that the President was talking about *research* and that research is not prohibited by the Treaty. This was an uncontroversial position. Moreover, everyone seemed to agree that even *testing* is permitted, if it is for a fixed, land-based system. It was thought, however, that mobile or *space-based systems like Star Wars could not be tested.* And no system could actually be deployed. This is what the press commonly refers to as the *narrow interpretation.*

In 1985, the Administration announced a new, *broad interpretation.* It holds that the Treaty's prohibitions on testing apply only to systems which use the physical principles scientifically known in 1972. It is claimed that new-tech systems like Star Wars, based on other physical principles, may be developed and tested in space, though they may not be actually deployed.

The Administration's broad interpretation set off a furor among many citizens, in the U.S. Senate, in allied governments, and in the Soviet government. In American political discourse, the debate over the ABM Treaty nearly overshadowed debate over Star Wars itself. And the Treaty debate, rather than exploring the nefarious motives of Administration officials, the symbolic force of the Treaty, and the strategy of Reagan's reckless adventurism — in other words, the politics, reality and danger of the event — instead quickly became a dry technical exchange between lawyers about the meaning of a document.

Thus, legal discourse moved in once again to assert its hegemony over political and human questions and claimed to resolve them on the basis of its own autonomous techniques. There will be those who welcome this as the very essence of "the rule of law." But if one is convinced, as I am, that "the rule of law" as traditionally practiced is merely the continuation of politics by hypocritical means, one may yearn, when so much is at stake, for a more honest and relevant politics than legal discourse affords.

The ABM debate soon centered around exchanges between the State Department Legal Adviser, who was former federal judge Abraham D. Sofaer, and Senator Sam Nunn, Democrat of Georgia and Chair of the Senate Armed Services Committee, Sofaer issuing official studies supporting the Administration's broad interpretation and Nunn expounding the narrow interpretation on four occasions on the Senate floor. Their statements collect the key documents and articulate the arguments sharply and fully.[15]

In a nutshell, Sofaer's argument was this: The negotiation record reveals that the Soviets never agreed to the narrow interpretation in 1972 even though the U.S. negotiators had pushed for it. The Executive Branch had given the Senate mixed messages on the issue during ratification proceedings, but the matter was a minor part of the Treaty and unimportant to the Senate as a whole which never formed a clear intention about it one way or the other. While Executive Branch practice leaned to the narrow interpretation for fifteen years, the President's review of the negotiating record has now determined that the broad Treaty was the only one actually agreed to, and the Congress owes him great deference on such foreign policy questions.

15 United States Department of State, Office of Legal Adviser (1987): *The ABM Treaty, Part I: Treaty Language and Negotiating History*; *Part II: Ratification Process*; *Part III: Subsequent Practice*; Sam Nunn, "Interpretation of the ABM Treaty", Part One: "The Senate Ratification Proceedings", *Congressional Record*, March 11, 1987, S2967-S2986; Part Two: "Subsequent Practice Under the ABM Treaty", *Congressional Record*, March 12, 1987, S3090-S3095; Part Three: "The ABM Negotiating Record", *Congressional Record*, March 13, 1987, S3171-S3173; Part Four: "An Examination of Judge Sofaer's Analysis of the Negotiating Record", *Congressional Record*, May 20, 1987, S6808-6831.

Senator Nunn countered that the Soviets did indeed agree to the narrow interpretation in 1972, that the Executive had explicitly represented it that way to the Senate, and had adhered to the view for fifteen years, so there was agreement on the issue all around. Moreover, he argued, the Senate has an equal role in approval of treaties. For an administration to argue that new interpretations can emerge from old negotiating records that had been withheld from the Senate would always give rise to the uncertainty that one treaty had been concluded between the parties and a different one approved by the Senate; this would unsettle treaties, denigrate the Senate's role, and provoke a constitutional confrontation between the two branches.

That both men knew their real task was one of rhetorical persuasion can be gleaned from the fact that neither referred merely to the "narrow" and "broad" interpretations. Cleverly, Sofaer called them "restrictive" and "broad," and Nunn the "traditional" view and "the reinterpretation." I am interested at this point, however, in neither the rhetorical flavour nor substantive content of their remarks. I am interested in the form. Like nearly everyone else in the debate, Sofaer and Nunn assumed that the ABM Treaty possesses a legal meaning that is to be discovered. They assumed that the discovery is to be made by applying traditional techniques for exegesis of legal texts.[16] For international texts, those techniques are embodied in custom, in the *Vienna Convention on the Law of Treaties*,[17] in private professional standards like the *Restatement of Foreign Relations Law of the United States*,[18] and in scholars' treatises, but they are little different from the usual techniques employed in both common law and civil law practice for exegesis of other legal texts.

The techniques inquire into the words of the document, its purposes as known from its context and the intentions of its drafters, and the understanding of the document reflected by the practice of those who had to implement it or live under it. These in turn are assumed,

16 *Supra* n.14.

17 Vienna Convention on the Law of Treaties, *done* May 23, 1969, United States Senate Exec. Law 92d Congress, 1st Session (1971).

18 American Law Institute, *Restatement of Foreign Relations Law of the United States (Revised)* (Tentative Final Draft), 1985.

in good positivist fashion, to be organized into a decision-tree like hierarchy of authority, with words being most determinative of meaning, context and intentions weighing somewhat less, and practice less yet. Various canons of interpretation supposedly organize this hierarchy and sort out proper use of the sundry materials within its ranks. If interpreters of a text come up with different meanings, it is thought either that one of them has taken a wrong turn in the decision-tree or that the factual evidence of intentions, practice and the like is too thin or murky to present a clear picture. No one doubts, however, that the meaning resides there in the text and that the job of interpreters is to seek it like hunting dogs after the quarry.

This, of course, is a delusion. No quarry exists, because texts don't possess meanings. Rather, readers use texts (and other signs) to make meanings. The solid hierarchy of organization and rules turns out to be made of putty and to dissolve into the network of signs. I have no space in this paper for a microscopic examination of the ways the ABM adversaries made their meanings. The following macroscopic view, however, should suffice to show that the process was not like following a decision tree, but like shining a flashlight on different portions of a web.

Below are the portions of the web of texts, sources, and other readers, that the State Department and the Senator lit up to make their respective cases. I will presume that the *historical, cultural, and sociological circumstances* of the interpreters are well enough known that they need not be described, and that it is likewise obvious that the State Department was reading through *value lenses* in which Reagan conservatism, bellicosity, and primacy of the Executive Branch were uppermost, while the Senator read through lenses which valued most highly a moderate Democratic conservatism and the primacy of the Congress. (I have no information about the psychology of the two readers.) It is these circumstances and values, of course, that most fully explain the interpretation of legal texts, and if I give them short shrift here it is only because I am anxious to show how the other parts of the interpretive process are open to their influence.

*A. Texts*

In reviewing the astonishingly long list of texts used by the ABM interpreters, one should keep in mind these fundamentals which prevent selection and use of texts from being rule-governed:

— Rules to organize the texts hierarchically (as in the Vienna Convention, etc.) always deconstruct themselves by containing their opposites. The Convention, for example, says the "ordinary meaning" of the terms is to be followed, but "in context" and "in light of its object and purpose." Or, "supplementary" texts such as preparatory work, etc. are not to be used unless (and this can always be so) the ordinary meaning, context and purpose are "ambiguous" or "unreasonable."

— The honesty of many of the texts is questionable (private correspondence, secret memos, paid opinions, etc., even Congressional documents).

— Their accuracy often cannot be ascertained, for either practical or theoretical reasons.

— Their relevance and weight are not ranked; trivial and private fragments of text can be magnified while more obvious, public texts can be ignored.

— Since vague categories like "contexts," "purpose" and "practice" are legitimate, the number of possible texts and combinations is virtually inexhaustible.

| *State Department* | *Senator* |
|---|---|
| [Texts considered and weighted heavily, neutrally, or wholly discounted, differently by each interpreter] | |
| Words of Treaty Articles II, V, Statement D. | Same |
| Intrinsic Treaty structural coherence. | Same |
| Negotiating records of U. S. team, including working papers, draft proposals, public announcements, minutes of meetings, memos of formal and informal conversations, letters, "backchannel" cables, and similar documents, an open-ended collection occasionally revised to | Same |

| | |
|---|---|
| incorporate material "that turned up from time to time" (1987a:13). | |
| Specific original purpose of Soviets/ diffuse purposes of U. S. Executive Branch and Senate. | |
| Silence of Executive Branch letter transmitting Treaty to Senate for ratification. | |
| Inconsistent draft Executive Branch transmittal letter that was never sent. | |
| Silence of Senate ratification resolution. | |
| Silence of other Congressional legislation. | |
| Testimony of Executive Branch officials in Congressional ratification and other hearings, 1972. | Silence of testimony of Executive Branch officials in Congressional ratification and other hearings. |
| Unavailability of negotiating record to Senate. | |
| Paucity of references in Senate floor debates over ratification. | |
| Silence of all but few Senators on the issue, and overwhelming approval (98-2) of Treaty. | |
| Objections of a few Senators who feared the interpretation the Executive Branch now rejects. | Same |
| Soviet officials' public statements Soviet during ratification. | Same |
| Inconsistent Executive Branch internal statements and ambiguous internal written directive, 1972-74. | |
| Executive Branch speeches, reports, 1972. | Same |
| Speech and book of former U.S. negotiator, 1973-74. | |
| Record of U.S.-Soviet discussions monitoring the Treaty, 1974-83. | |
| Negotiating record and agreed language on analogous questions in SALT II discussions, 1974-76. | |

| | |
|---|---|
| Executive Branch annual publication of arms control agreements, 1975-82. | Same |
| Private and public correspondence between several private individuals, some former U.S. negotiators, some at "think tank" institutions, 1974-78. | Same |
| Executive Branch "Arms Control Impact Statements" and other reports to Congress, 1977-85. | Same |
| Executive Branch internal guidance memos 1977-83. | |
| Senators' floor debate during failed effort to fund additional space laser work, 1980. | |
| Executive Branch officials' testimony in Congressional hearings, 1981-85. | |
| Senate Appropriations Committee Report, 1982. | |
| Book by head 1972 U.S. ABM negotiator, 1980. | Same |
| President's and foreign heads of government joint statements, 1984-85. | Book by former Senate staffer based on interviews and classified documents. |
| Technological advances that make laser testing more feasible and desirable than mere research, 1983-present. | |
| Analyses by outside "think tank" lawyer and by others, under Defense Department contracts, 1985. | |
| Records of U.S.-Soviet arms control discussions, 1983-85. | |
| Occasional public statements of Soviet officials and commentators. | Same |
| Lack of evidence of Soviet conduct in technical research and testing. | Same |
| Congressional hearings, committee reports, authorization legislation for Star Wars, 1984-85. | |

| | |
|---|---|
| Limitation of U. S. activity to research, not testing, 1972-85. | Same |
| | Soviet attendance at Senate ratifi-cation hearing and subsequent silence on U.S. interpretation. |

*B. Sources of Texts*

With every text selected, the State Department and the Senator implicitly adopted some philosophy of authorial intent, giving some weight or another to the meaning intended at the source; their weights differed, though both claimed to privilege original 1972 intentions. These choices amount to a philosophy of language and, in this context, a philosophy of government which needs to be articulated and defended but was not. Even if we were to agree on such a philosophy, implementing it is usually impossible except as legal fiction, and then that fiction would have to be defended as legitimate within some philosophy of government. In reviewing the list of sources privileged by the State Department and the Senator, one should keep in mind these problems which normally render the authorial intent of legal texts a mere fiction:

— We have no direct access to most of the minds claimed as sources, and the indirect access is often through textual evidence of dubious reliability (see *Texts* ) or guesswork (as in imputing intent to silence of the speaker).

— When intent is ascribed to an individual, we run into problems of memory lapses, changed views over time, unforeseen contexts, multiple and even conflicting intents, all within a single individual's mind.

— When intent is ascribed to an institutional body like a legislature or a department of government, we run into all the problems of individual intent plus the intractable problem of cumulating many subjective individual intentions together into a single institutional intent, an act of alchemy like that of turning dross to gold.

— There are no rules for weighting and ranking the different sources.

| *State Department* | *Senator* |
|---|---|
| [Sources to which intentions were attributed and weighted differently by each interpreter, with no admission of fictionality nor justification of weight] | |
| Framers (negotiators) | Same |
| Key framers | Same |
| Executive Branch | Same |
| Executive Branch individuals | Same |
| Executive Branch agencies | Same |
| Soviet government | Same |
| Soviet government individuals | Same |
| Senate | Same |
| Key senators | Same |
| Congress | Same |
| Congressional committees | Same |
| Private individuals | Same |

C. *Other readers*

Enlisting the support of other readers for one's interpretation is where the power to make social meaning finally resides. The more powerful the other readers, the greater the chance that the interpretation will become the accepted meaning. Since this is contrary to the positivist myth that meaning awaits in texts to be discovered through legal formalities, the fact that meaning is actually determined by social and political power is hypocritically disguised: other readers' views are said to be sought as expressions of their intention in framing the text or as indirect evidence of the original understanding. Occasionally, we glimpse an admission that other readers' views are used to establish meaning, as when Senator Nunn warned that the Administration's position would provoke a constitutional confrontation between the two branches, and threatened that Congress would refuse to fund Star Wars if the Administration persisted in its broad interpretation. These were simply statements that Congress has considerable power to impose its meaning. On the following list of other readers enlisted by the State Department and the Senator, there is no overt mention of some readers whose views could have been, and perhaps were, sought quietly such as defense industry contractors, peace lobbyists, and the press.

| *State Department* | *Senator* |
|---|---|
| Executive Branch officials today and over fifteen years | Same |
| Senators and Representatives today and over fifteen years | Same |
| Former negotiators | Same |
| Soviets today and over fifteen years | Same |
| Allies | Same |
| Judges | Same |
| Scholars | Same |
| | Six former Secretaries of Defense, three Republican, three Democratic |

### *Conclusion*

As of 1988, the interpretation of the ABM Treaty stands as follows. Congress has shown that it is currently the most powerful reader of the Treaty and has, fortunately, imposed the narrow interpretation by amending the defense appropriations statutes to prohibit spending for Star Wars testing. Senate leaders have also moved to preserve their long range power to control the meaning of treaties by refusing to ratify the recent INF (intermediate-range nuclear forces) Treaty until the Administration submits the negotiating record and promises in writing to be bound by the testimony of its officials in Senate ratification hearings. Meanwhile, the Executive

Branch and the Soviet government have reinterpreted the ABM Treaty in light of each side's new perceptions of its interests. Previously, Star Wars and the dispute over the broad and narrow view of the ABM Treaty had threatened to scuttle the INF Treaty. When the Reagan-Gorbachev summit in December of 1987 produced agreement on INF, the ABM Treaty was not permitted to stand in the way. The two sides papered over their differences, for now at least, by signing a new statement. In it, the sides agree "to observe the ABM Treaty as signed in 1972, while conducting their research, development and testing as required, which are permitted by the ABM Treaty... ".[19] With this studiously ambiguous language the governments imposed the new meaning that each side may read the Treaty as it wishes, once again proving the power of readers to make meaning, even by openly disregarding a text. Disregarding a legal text is a time-honoured technique for interpreting it. (Until recently, I hadn't known of a text that was disregarded even before it was signed. But in the spring, 1988, negotiations between the U.S. and Soviets for withdrawal of Soviet troops from Afghanistan, the press reported[20] that the U.S. agreed to sign a pact and at the same time served notice on the Soviets that the U.S. would violate the agreement by arming the rebels until Moscow halts military aid to the Kabul government. The Soviets, in turn, said they would criticize the U.S. violation but would not seek to stop it.)

### *Practical Consequences*

I hope no one will misunderstand what I have had to say as the language of cynicism, undermining the "rule of law" in general and "international law," which has had such a fragile existence, in particular. I have merely attempted an anthropological description of the reality of legal interpretation, and I have attempted it because I am an idealist, not a cynic. If in fact law is governed by Hobbes

[19] Robert C. Toth, "U.S. Aides Confident SDI Won't Block Treaty", *Los Angeles Times*, March 24, 1988, I, 11; John Marks, "Taiwanization" of SDI Allows the Dialogue to Continue", *Los Angeles Times*, December 20, 1987, V, 5.

[20] Michael Wines, "Tentative Afghan Pact is Reached", *Los Angeles Times*, April 1, 1988, I, 1.

and Machiavelli instead of Aristotle and Austin, then it is we idealists who need to be taught that, because the cynics know it instinctively. If in fact law is a system of cultural persuasion for the powerful, then the powerless need to learn how the persuasion works. If in fact law disguises choices of human values with a hypocritical mask of objectivity, then those who care about the values need to lift the mask with candour. If in fact law does not prevent violence except when it coincides with the interests of the powerful, then those who cherish peaceful resolution of disputes must see how important it is to restructure both law and power.

History shows that none of these idealistic ends will be accomplished by a naive faith in the traditional myth of "the rule of law." Indeed, faith in the myth is dangerous for the innocent. The late Primo Levi illustrated the point, in writing about German Jews before the holocaust:[21]

> Like their "Aryan" quasi-compatriots they loved law and order, and not only did they not foresee but they were organically incapable of conceiving of a terrorism directed by the state, even when it was already all around them. There is a famous . . . verse [by a German poet] . . . which is quite apposite here. . . : Palmström, an extremely law-abiding German citizen, is hit by a car in a street where traffic is forbidden. He gets up bruised and battered and thinks about it. If traffic is forbidden, vehicles may not circulate, that is, they do not circulate. Ergo he cannot have been hit: it is "an impossible reality,". . . . He must have only dreamed it because, indeed, "things whose existence is not morally permissible cannot exist." . . . Many Europeans of that time — and not only Europeans and not only of that time — behaved and still behave like Palmström, denying the existence of things that ought not to exist.

By using the example of the ABM Treaty, I have tried to call attention to an instance of terrorism directed by the state in which I live. We here are for the most part organically incapable of conceiving of the terrorism this scheme involves despite the fact that the evidence is all around us. I think the myth of the "rule of law" has played some part in hiding this terrorism from us, allowing us to deny the existence of things that ought not to exist. It makes it easy for us to willingly suspend moral belief when the official debate

21 Primo Levi, "Beyond Judgment", *The New York Review of Books* 34(20), December 17, 1987, 10-14, at 14.

over militarization of space focuses on technicalities like the legal weight of negotiators' memoranda.

For this reason I'm for abandoning the old "rule of law" and acknowledging the realistic rule of law instead. The realistic rule of law brings into the open those issues of power and of human values that cynics are so anxious to disguise with a mythical "rule of law" that benefits their own power and values. By acknowledging that law is not something objective and fixed which is found in texts, but rather something we are constantly making together out of our own values, idealist lawyers will realize they cannot glide amidst the clouds of the "brooding omnipresence in the sky" as Holmes called the mythical notion of law. They will see that peace, equality, community, liberty, justice and other values are always at stake in the law, and must be openly struggled for in every generation, every day, "like a bird that each second keeps conquering its flight."[22]

22 From João Cabral de Melo Neto, "O Cão Sem Plumas" in *Poesias Completas (1945-1965)*. Rio de Janeiro: Editôra Sabià, 1968.

# Name Index

www.ingramcontent.com/pod-product-compliance
Lightning Source LLC
LaVergne TN
LVHW102106300926
849161LV00014B/3060